CW00767627

Language Asses:
Multilingualism

Proceedings of the ALTE Paris Conference, April 2014

For a complete list of titles please visit: www.cambridge.org/elt/silt

Language Assessment for Multilingualism

Proceedings of the ALTE Paris Conference, April 2014

Edited by

Coreen Docherty
Cambridge English Language Assessment

and

Fiona Barker
Cambridge English Language Assessment

CAMBRIDGE
UNIVERSITY PRESS

University Printing House, Cambridge CB2 8BS, United Kingdom

Cambridge University Press is part of the University of Cambridge.

It furthers the University's mission by disseminating knowledge in the pursuit of education, learning and research at the highest international levels of excellence.

www.cambridge.org
Information on this title: www.cambridge.org/9781316505007

© UCLES 2016

This publication is in copyright. Subject to statutory exception and to the provisions of relevant collective licensing agreements, no reproduction of any part may take place without the written permission of Cambridge University Press.

First published 2016
First paperback edition 2016

A catalogue record for this publication is available from the British Library

Library of Congress Cataloguing in Publication data
Names: ALTE Conference (5th : 2014 : Paris, France) | Docherty, Coreen, editor. | Barker, Fiona, editor.
Title: Language assessment for multilingualism : Proceedings of the ALTE Paris Conference, April 2014 / edited by Coreen Docherty, Cambridge English Language Assessment and Fiona Barker, Cambridge English Language Assessment.
Description: Cambridge ; New York : Cambridge University Press, [2016] | Series: Studies in Language Testing ; 44 | Includes bibliographical references.
Identifiers: LCCN 2015034884 | ISBN 9781316505007
Subjects: LCSH: Language and languages–Ability testing–Europe–Congresses. | Second language acquisition–Ability testing–Europe–Congresses.
Classification: LCC P118.75 A482 2014 | DDC 404/.2–dc23 LC record available at http://lccn.loc.gov/2015034884

ISBN 978-1-316-50500-7 Paperback

Cambridge University Press has no responsibility for the persistence or accuracy of URLs for external or third-party internet websites referred to in this publication, and does not guarantee that any content on such websites is, or will remain, accurate or appropriate.

Contents

Acknowledgements

We would like to express our thanks to everyone who contributed to this volume for developing and writing up their original presentations given at the ALTE Paris Conference in April 2014, and for their willingness to make subsequent revisions in line with our editorial suggestions.

The volume could not have reached publication without the professional, technical and administrative assistance of various colleagues based at Cambridge English including John Savage for his diligent co-ordination of the editorial and production stages of this volume and Evelina Galaczi for her overall management of this volume and expert guidance. We would also like to thank Esther Gutierrez Eugenio and Mariangela Marulli in the ALTE Secretariat, and Elena Louicellier at the Cambridge English Paris office, for their editorial assistance with the articles in French and Italian. We are grateful to all of the above for their support throughout the production process.

Series Editors' note

In April 2014, the Association of Language Testers in Europe (ALTE) celebrated 24 years of achievement in Paris at its 5th International Conference on the theme of 'Language Assessment for Multilingualism: Promoting Linguistic Diversity and Intercultural Communication'.

This conference marked another important stage in ALTE's development since it was originally founded in 1990, primarily to work on common levels of proficiency and common standards for the language testing process. Since the first meeting of its founding members, ALTE has grown to become one of the most important bodies within the language assessment profession and now includes many of the world's leading language assessment bodies among its 33 members and affiliates. Nowadays it represents organisations testing 26 European languages – and so the theme of *multilingualism* is a central interest of the membership and the many stakeholders who participate in ALTE events.

One of ALTE's main aims is to share ideas and know-how, and within the overall context of Language Assessment for Multilingualism, this conference focused on four strands: Mobility; Diversity; Intercultural Communication; Fairness & Quality. It thus provided an opportunity for language teaching and testing professionals from around the world to meet and to pool expertise, and to consider together how best to resolve some of the important challenges posed in these areas which are facing society today.

This volume brings together a selection of original papers that were presented at the conference. It is the fifth volume of its kind in this series, and like its predecessors, provides a vehicle for information on language testing practices that might not otherwise have been published.

Historically, the accessible literature in our field has been written in English – and has consequently been biased towards the assessment of English. We rarely read about what goes on elsewhere in assessing other languages. Thus, in keeping with the theme of multilingualism, the 25 papers in this volume have been selected to cover a spread of languages and interesting topics that will appeal to an international readership who have a professional interest in language testing. All the papers are previously unpublished and have been written with care and rigour, demonstrating analysis and interpretation that is well founded.

Since the first meetings, ALTE members have been aware of the importance of *sustaining diversity* – both cultural and linguistic – and ALTE events and conferences have always been multilingual. In recent years, however, linguistic diversity and intercultural communication have emerged as issues of global relevance, and topics that underpin many debates in language education around the world. For example, there is concern that the growing dominance of English may squeeze out less widely taught national languages, an issue at the heart of the multilingualism debate. There is also the drive to increase multilingual competences, embodied in initiatives such as the Barcelona Agreement – the EU goal that every EU citizen should be able to speak at least two additional languages. ALTE also sees it as part of its mission to promote multilingualism by encouraging language teaching, not only for economic or academic improvement, but also for personal enrichment and lifelong learning.

The ALTE international conferences are now amongst the largest multilingual events for the global language assessment community. The 2014 conference was no exception, with over 100 presenters, and plenary and keynote speakers representing some of the leading voices in the field. The plenary speakers gave their perspectives on the thematic strands of the conference as follows:

- Mobility: Bruno Mègre (in French)
- Diversity: Anne Gallagher (in French)
- Diversity: Lid King
- Intercultural Communication: David Graddol
- Fairness & Quality: Jessica R W Wu

Well over 350 delegates attended from more than 60 countries and regions around the world. It was also a multilingual event, with presentations in five of the many different languages represented at the conference and it provided an opportunity for participants to hear influential voices, discuss key issues and meet colleagues from a variety of backgrounds.

The world thrives on diversity and it is the need to respect and value this diversity while at the same time trying to find common ground that binds us together – this is reflected in ALTE's motto: *setting standards and sustaining diversity*. The event in Paris provided a great opportunity for delegates to participate in a conference that reflected the diversity of Europe and the importance placed on languages, language learning, certification of language competence and the growing significance of the Common European Framework of Reference for Languages (CEFR) in the development of plurilingualism and intercultural competences.

As in the past, this conference had a local host in order to ensure that there was also a focus on issues of local concern in the host country. In this case, Paris is the home of the long-standing ALTE member, the Centre international d'études pédagogiques (CIEP), who was the co-host, as well as the Alliance Française (Paris Île-de-France) and the Chambre de commerce et d'industrie de région (CCI Paris Île-de-France), both active ALTE participants involved in the teaching and assessment of French. In this respect, the Paris conference built upon the success of the four previous ALTE International Conferences which all had strong local support: the first held in Barcelona in July 2001, hosted by the Generalitat de Catalunya, on the theme of 'European Language Testing in a Global Context' to celebrate the European Year of Languages; the second in Berlin in May 2005, hosted by the Goethe-Institut, on the theme of 'Language Assessment in a Multilingual Context' to support the 50th Anniversary of the European Cultural Convention; the third held in Cambridge in April 2008 hosted by Cambridge ESOL, which focused on the theme of 'The Social and Educational Impact of Language Assessment'; and the fourth held in Kraków in July 2011, hosted by the Jagiellonian University on the theme of the 'Impact of Language Frameworks on Assessment, Learning and Teaching, viewed from the Perspectives of Policies, Procedures and Challenges'. Edited proceedings from these events were published as volumes 18, 27, 31 and 36 in the now well-established and highly regarded Studies in Language Testing (SiLT) series.

As will be apparent, the conference papers presented here represent only a selection of the many excellent presentations made in Paris reflecting a wide range of topics and concerns; they provide a flavour of the key themes addressed at the conference.

The introduction to this volume by Coreen Docherty and Fiona Barker helps to highlight and summarise for readers the various strands that resonated throughout the conference, and points to important implications for the language testing community.

Cyril J Weir
Nick Saville
August 2015

Introduction

Coreen Docherty
Fiona Barker
Cambridge English Language Assessment

Multilingualism and language assessment was the theme of the 5th International Conference of the Association of Language Testers in Europe (ALTE) held in Paris in April 2014. The concept of and discussion around multilingualism is ubiquitous, particularly in education, the workplace and society more generally. This is because the notion of multilingualism is multifaceted and linked to issues such as international mobility, migration and social integration, all of which have clear implications for assessment. As increasing numbers of people move from one country to another to work, study or live, there are pressures to manage this flow of people and to develop strategies to address the needs of new migrants in a host country. Assessment often has a significant and complex role in a multilingual world, particularly related to issues of fairness.

ALTE promotes multilingualism in a number of ways: by setting quality standards for language assessment; by supporting its members to deliver language tests; by providing training and expertise; and, most pertinent to this volume, by providing opportunities for discussion and debate of all aspects of creating multilingual societies, including holding an international conference every three years, which this volume is a product of. The 5th ALTE Conference provided an opportunity to discuss issues around multilingualism and assessment, many of which continue the themes of the previous ALTE conference in Krakow on language frameworks. Over 100 papers and plenaries were presented at the Paris Conference and this volume represents a subset of these, selected on the basis of the four core strands addressed during the conference.

This volume supports ALTE's work, its membership and the wider community of language teachers, assessment experts and policy makers by contributing to the ongoing debate on the theory of multilingualism and its impact on the linked areas of language education and migration policy, which are areas of growing concern for Europe and beyond. The ALTE Paris Conference organisers wanted to foreground contemporary research on language policy and practice and through this volume we can highlight the relevance and benefits that research projects undertaken in local contexts have more widely, also making research accessible to a wider audience than attended the Paris event. It is important to note that the majority of ALTE members are multilingual and this diversity is reflected in the contributors to this volume, with most chapters not written in the authors' first language and many of the papers focusing on the teaching, learning and assessment of languages besides English. In total, this volume covers 22 languages, written by contributors based in 16 countries. The aim of this volume is therefore to explore the role of multiculturalism in language learning, teaching and assessment through a collection of 25 edited papers based on presentations given at this event. Although the editors have grouped the papers by theme, the themes and paper topics are not mutually exclusive and alternative groupings would have been possible.

Section 1 addresses the issue of intercultural competence and how pluri-lingualism and pluriculturalism are developed and supported in society. **Neil Jones**' paper begins the section by focusing on the role of intercultural competence in language education. He argues that it should be treated as an integral part of language education because learning a language is not simply about focusing on form and the transmission of knowledge but on helping learners develop new ways of understanding the world and others. Jones points out that the language classroom is an ideal place to discuss both language and culture with the aim being to encourage the development of intercultural understanding. As part of his argument, Jones reminds us of the core values contained within the Common European Framework of Reference for Languages (CEFR) which emphasise plurilingualism and pluricultural-ism and the acceptance of 'otherness'.

Elaine Boyd and **David Donnarumma** build on Jones' overview of inter-cultural communication by providing a practical example of the challenges faced by employees communicating in an international work setting. The authors describe a study which took place in an international hotel group in India. Although employees were highly proficient in English, which was used as a *lingua franca*, there were issues of miscommunication between hotel guests and staff. The paper highlights not only the challenges of successfully communicating in an international setting but the complexity involved in identifying and overcoming the underlying causes of this miscommunication. Using a mixed method research design, the authors explore the interactions of the hotel staff with guests and identify the types of (mis)communication that take place, and then through drama activities explore communication strategies used by staff, encouraging them to reflect on their own interactions and strategy use. The authors found that the loci of miscommunication related to culture and power relationships typical in this workplace context. The expectation of guests, who were also often using English as a *lingua franca*, and their power position in the transactional interactions meant that it became the staff's responsibility to repair miscommunication. Boyd and Donnarumma highlight the difficulties of trying to address intercultural miscommunication within an international workplace but also how important it is to understand these types of interactions as the intercultural workplace is increasingly becoming the norm.

The next two papers move the discussion on to how culture and multilingualism can be conceptualised for assessment purposes. **Maria Stathopoulou** deals with the issue of mediation as a learning outcome that can be assessed. The author describes the Greek national foreign exams which incorporate cross-language written mediation tasks where candidates are given, for example, a text in one language and asked to do something with the content and present it in another language. The author investigates what characterises successful mediation by focusing on strategy use. Stathopoulou's paper not only highlights the importance of mediation as a test feature but also the implications of mediation for teaching. In recent years within language education increasing prominence has been given to making full use of learners' language background, recognising that learners do not use language in a vacuum and that more often than not learners find themselves mediating language for others or for themselves.

Trisevgeni Liontou's paper, which is also related to the Greek context, looks more specifically at the role of culturally familiar reading texts on reading comprehension. Again, focused on testing, Liontou investigates whether texts that are culturally familiar have an effect on test scores and whether they are linguistically comparable to more general texts. The author's premise is that culturally familiar texts may reduce candidate anxiety and provide a fairer test-taking experience for this particular context. Liontou touches on an important issue of fitness for purpose. If the test is being undertaken for local purposes – employment or education in Greece – then would it not be more authentic and appropriate to provide candidates with input texts that are relevant for this context rather than more general educational texts, provided there is no bias? Although this paper taps into the issue of fairness, it highlights the need to consider the purpose of tests in particular contexts and what is fair in an international standardised test may not be fair in a specific context where tests are being used for a particular purpose.

This section ends with a paper which looks more generally at the issue of multilingualism in Europe and whether it is in crisis. **Anne Gallagher** argues that the emergence of English as a *lingua franca* seems to have had a negative effect for the learning of other languages in some European countries, and argues it is in Europe's best interest to ensure the promotion of multilingualism, both at the individual and societal level. Besides merely economic reasons, the author highlights the importance of sustaining the rich cultural and linguistic diversity that has always characterised Europe and that is essential for the maintenance of democracy. In order to ensure a multilingual Europe in the future, the author stresses the importance of adapting language education to the communicative needs of the learners and of implementing valid, reliable and transparent assessment systems. Finally, she emphasises the need for enhanced support from policy makers and governments to encourage stronger collaboration between language testers and teachers, who will be the key contributors towards a Europe more multilingual than ever.

Section 2 builds on the papers from Section 1 but shifts the focus to the implications of international mobility or migration on language learning and how to address the various needs of children and migrants who have very different backgrounds and purposes for emigrating.

Masashi Negishi and **Yukio Tono** begin the section. Although their paper is not directly related to mobility, its focus on the development of the CEFR-J, the adaptation of the CEFR in English language teaching/learning in Japanese contexts, has implications for researchers who are considering modifying the CEFR for migrants and for those who are interested in language learning for school-aged pupils. This project resulted in a range of lower-level descriptors below A1 and the rest of the levels being divided into multiple branching levels. In their paper, Negishi and Tono describe the work that has been done since the introduction of the CEFR-J and then look into its impact by tapping into 'big data'. They find that the CEFR and the CEFR-J still have not made a significant impact in the Japanese context in terms of internet searches. This paper highlights several issues related to the use of the CEFR in educational contexts. That is, it may not be appropriate to simply adopt the CEFR as it is into some educational contexts, but that it is important to have a coherent and integrated solution to ensure the CEFR is appropriate or modified for the specific learning reality and that teachers understand the purpose behind its adoption and its use.

The next paper by **Eli Moe**, **Marita Härmälä** and **Paula Lee Kristmanson** looks more closely at the language of schooling for young learners with an immigrant or minority language background. They investigate the minimum language levels needed for learning mathematics and history in a second language in order to demonstrate that young language learners need to have a certain threshold of language before it becomes possible to learn content in these subjects. The authors then develop a tool to help raise awareness of the challenges faced by language learners when they are learning both content and language. This paper emphasises the need for the primary and secondary educational systems to consider the needs of immigrant learners and the challenges they face in the mainstream classroom. As migration rates in Europe increase, there is a need to develop a clear and flexible approach to addressing the needs of the children who find themselves in the mainstream classroom. This issue is one that faces many European educational systems and is an area of concern in particular with education budgets being cut across the continent.

After having looked at more specific interventions that address language learning, **Enrica Piccardo** deals with the issue of how to promote the development of non-dominant languages in Canada. Even though Canada is home to a linguistically diverse population, Piccardo points out that languages other than French and English are frequently not recognised and undervalued. She describes the development of an e-portfolio that not only supports language learning in general but was designed to encourage the learning of aboriginal languages in particular, which are disappearing at an alarming rate. She hopes that this e-portfolio can act as a catalyst for introducing ideological and pedagogical change in language learning and assessment. This is one of the only papers in this volume that looks specifically at learning languages other than English in an English-dominant environment and the challenges that are faced in supporting multilingualism in these contexts.

The Italian *Progetto Lingue 2000* (*PL2000*) is then discussed, which looks at the impact of a 10-year project to improve the English language levels of Italian school-aged pupils. **Roger Hawkey** and **Sarah Ellis** describe the origins of this project, started in 2000, which aimed to encourage communicative language teaching approaches in schools and to introduce international language certification at all levels. Hawkey and Ellis, who conducted an impact study of this project in 2002, then go on to describe how they retraced their steps 10 years later to investigate longer-term effects of the programme. The iterative Cambridge English impact study of *PL2000* involves language learners, teachers, school heads, parents and exam managers in north, central and southern Italy. Using mixed methods and capturing their data collection processes visually with pictures and images, they identify how the project has developed over the last decade. This paper highlights the need to revisit and monitor large-scale projects to investigate their impact over time, which can be used to provide feedback that can lead to well-intentioned improvements or used by other educational authorities to learn lessons for their own language programmes.

Nowadays a growing number of countries are using formal language testing as a requirement for residency and citizenship. The next two papers address this controversial policy decision. Paola Masillo looks at the situation in Italy while Catarina Gaspar, Maria José Grosso and Heinz-Peter Gerhardt focus on Portugal.

The paper by **Paola Masillo** looks at the fairness, validity and reliability of tests used to test migrants' Italian language ability. Although she finds that the language tests and the criteria for marking written interaction are flawed, the main issue is the language policy which has generated both. The paper deals with a problematic issue of setting language requirements for migrants without considering the reality of their language use in society. In addition, she points out that using the CEFR as the framework to evaluate the language ability of migrants creates further issues as it was not designed for this population. Masillo emphasises the need for language policies and tests which recognise and support the plurilingual context that many migrants find themselves in when they move to a new country.

The next paper deals with migration but from the perspective of the role of non-formal education in supporting immigrants' integration into society. **Catarina Gaspar**, **Maria José Grosso** and **Heinz-Peter Gerhardt** describe a non-formal educational project in Portugal which aimed to address the issue of adult migrants who have had little experience with formal education in their home countries and find it challenging to participate in adult language programmes because of limited literacy and lack of familiarity with the expectations of formal education. If learners are not literate in their L1, the authors wonder how they can be expected to sit a standardised exam which assumes these skills have been developed in the L2. In response to this question, the authors describe the development of a non-formal educational project which aims at attracting learners who traditionally do not enrol in language courses because they lack formal educational experiences and therefore feel uncomfortable in these settings. The paper goes on to investigate whether standardised assessments are appropriate for this population. They conclude, not unlike Masillo's conclusion, that language policies need to take into consideration the reality of migrants and not select a standard that is not achievable for many who have not necessarily had access to formal education. The solution to this issue is not an easy one and the appropriacy of the tests used to test migrants' language ability is a recurring topic at ALTE conferences.

Having looked at the issue of children and migrants who are both groups that are vulnerable in the sense that their language development can easily be affected by the language policies set by governments, the last two papers in this section look at more typical concerns in language assessment, one of which is the identification of standards.

The first paper, by **Beate Zeidler**, focuses on how test developers decide on the characteristics of the minimally competent person (MCP). This is an important question as determining the pass score on a test is often related to this conceptualisation and as Zeidler points out, there is very little agreement about how to best arrive at an understanding of the MCP. This has serious implications for understanding and setting the standard needed to demonstrate competency for a particular purpose. After the author reviews the strengths and weaknesses of different methods to arrive at the MCP, she compares the results of several studies using these methods to try to identify the optimal one. This paper is then followed by **Vivien Berry** and **Barry O'Sullivan** who tackle the same issue of the MCP but for a specific purpose. Their study deals with a topic of current public interest: what English language level should doctors have when seeking to practise medicine in the UK? By leading a standard-setting exercise with healthcare providers, the authors identified the *IELTS* level that would be appropriate for doctors practising in the UK. An important outcome of their research is the insights made by healthcare providers on the language needs of doctors, which were gathered during focus group discussions.

Moving on from the focus on international migration, the next section focuses on teacher competencies and assessment literacy more specifically.

Section 3 deals with aspects of teachers' professional development in relation to assessment in specific contexts. In the opening paper, **Brian North** addresses on profiling teacher competences, describing a study that encompassed multilingual checking of the European Profiling Grid (EPG), which is an online scale containing descriptors of teaching competences across developmental phases. North addresses the questions of whether there is a definable best practice shared between pedagogies for different languages and whether context-free descriptors can be developed for teacher competences in line with the CEFR's generic language learner competences. North describes the validation of the EPG through pilot and main studies, each consisting of a qualitative descriptor sorting and commentary phase together with a quantitative phase. The study's results indicate that the teachers' self-assessments using the EPG helped to produce an effective criterion-referenced measurement scale and that the teachers of the different languages surveyed shared a common view of language instruction, with minor differences by educational sector, as expected. There are, North notes, some disadvantages to using self-assessment data, however the overall impact of the validation study is positive, with the EPG extending its reach and further surveys planned for different contexts. This paper links the EPG with the general aims, design and application of the CEFR, also pertaining to the ALTE conference theme of social mobility for teachers.

Continuing the theme of teacher competences in the broader sense, the following two papers focus on teachers' assessment literacy, which is a combination of all of their competences and a key factor in their ability to engage with assessment both theoretically and in practical ways. The next paper, by **Daniel Xerri** and **Patricia Vella Briffa**, considers teachers' involvement in high-stakes testing in Malta, advocating direct involvement as a route to a better and more equitable testing system for students. The case study reported goes some way towards filling a gap in the assessment literature by showing how teacher involvement in high-stakes test development and delivery can enhance their understanding of assessment and can benefit students by providing a bridge between the local learning context, student cohort and the subject matter, one or more of which, it is argued, may be lacking when teachers are not given the opportunity to be involved in test development activities. This paper affirms the benefits for all stakeholders in direct involvement in assessment and reflects the stages involved in producing test specifications, specimen materials and assessment scales, demonstrating a practical example of assessment literacy happening from grass-roots upwards.

The following paper by **Anthony Manning** reports on a mixed methods study that explored aspects of assessment literacy for English for Academic Purposes (EAP) teachers internationally, based on a desire to enhance EAP teachers' professional assessment practices concerning the admissions of international students into higher education, using theories and principles from language testing and the broader assessment literacy literature. Manning set out to explore whether EAP teachers' views on testing reflect language testing and assessment (LTA) practices around assessment literacy and whether EAP assessment literacy can be sustained or enhanced. Overall, Manning reports a number of examples of good practice in EAP in relation to assessment literacy which reflect theory and research from LTA more widely, adding that there are key areas needing improvement. Manning concludes with a series of actions to be taken including the development of an online framework, bibliography and statistical analysis training for in-service EAP assessment literacy training; provision of collaborative EAP opportunities within and across institutions; and raising awareness of ethics in relation to EAP. This paper shows the way ahead to engaging EAP teachers in higher education which relates to their ongoing training and development and which will enhance their mobility and expertise, and also that of their students who will benefit from their instructors' increased knowledge of assessment for EAP.

The final paper in this section by **Tomoyasu Akiyama** focuses on the concept of test fairness through rater behaviour, looking at prospective English teachers who undertake a microteaching session as part of their teacher employment examinations (TEEs) in Japan. These examinations are high stakes and failing on one occasion means the test taker has to wait another year to retake, which can have negative implications for unsuccessful candidates' employment prospects. Despite this, Akiyama notes the lack of research into 68 regionally produced TEEs, specifically into the microteaching sessions, which are 5–10-minute lessons intended for use in teacher training. Akiyama's paper explores whether the ratings given by employers to prospective candidates of this high-stakes test are fair. Using a mixed methods approach to analyse rating data, Akiyama found that raters, whilst consistent, rated candidates with different degrees of severity and seemed to interpret assessment criteria differently. This study has key implications for rater cognition research and reiterates the importance of piloting rating scales and rater training, as discussed in Xerri and Briffa's earlier paper.

Section 4 of this volume considers the important issues of fairness, quality and validation of assessments across a wide range of contexts in order to ensure that tests are relevant, accessible and fit for purpose. In this section, the first three papers concern language testing in Asia, one of an English test and two of Chinese tests. **Jessica Wu**'s paper provides an overview of the testing of English as a Foreign Language (EFL) in the region, focusing on ensuring that tests of English are designed with quality and fairness in mind and identifying current challenges and opportunities in this area. This paper links to the ALTE conference theme of fairness and quality standards in language test administration. Wu notes that although objective testing started in China, contemporary English language testing in Asia tends to conform to Western testing theories, although EFL tests in Taiwan, Korea, Japan and China are tailored to the educational systems and contexts of test use in these countries. For example, Wu points out that some regionally produced English language tests have up to 18 million test takers per annum. The testing of such large cohorts of test takers provides many challenges to delivering unbiased and high-quality tests, particularly in relation to test design and quality control. The conclusion is that a set of professional standards for test developers and test users is needed for Asia, which take into account context-specific principles along with universal principles of LTA.

The following two papers focus on tests of Chinese, which allows us to explore similarities between testing English and other languages. Firstly, **Xiangdong Gu**, **Yuwen Shen** and **Jian Xu** focus on test takers' mental processes in their reporting of a study that used Think Aloud Protocols (TAPs) to capture Thai test takers' processes when sitting a Chinese vocabulary test, so linking to the ALTE conference theme of language assessment for migration and social integration as well as aiming to better understand test takers' cognitive processes at different proficiency levels. Gu, Shen and Xu focus on the vocabulary component of the reading section of the highest of six levels of the Chinese Proficiency Test (Hanyu Shuiping Kaoshi, HSK), seeking to identify through TAP analysis what level and type of information test takers use to process the reading texts (i.e. text, sentence, extra-textual), their test-taking strategies (i.e. cognitive, metacognitive and test-wiseness) and whether proficiency affects these two aspects of test taking. Their results indicate that clause-level information is the most commonly used by all levels of test taker, with inferring, contextualisation and comprehension monitoring being the most used cognitive and meta-cognitive strategies. Avoidance is the most used test-wiseness strategy, although the study only revealed significant differences in this category amongst higher and lower-scoring groups. This paper suggests implications for teaching and testing reading for Chinese and by extension for other languages, whilst providing an accessible account of aspects of testing reading in a character language.

Next, **Shujiao Wang** considers the broader washback effects of the Chinese Proficiency Test (Hanyu Shuiping Kaoshi, HSK), revised in 2010, on test takers' learning strategies and beliefs, which also links to the ALTE conference theme of language assessment for migration and social integration. This study investigated learner strategies and beliefs using a mixed methods explanatory approach consisting of a survey, interviews and document analysis of related HSK materials. Wang's study reveals that HSK has significant washback on learning Chinese, with both positive (i.e. increased motivation for learning Chinese) and negative impacts (i.e. encouraging memorisation of grammar rules over communicative strategies) on the learners surveyed and differences in learning strategies between regular learning and test preparation being predicted by items including language proficiency, motivation and nationality. An important feature of this paper is the indication of aspects of the validity and reliability of HSK that need improvement, namely more subjective question forms and emphasising the measurement of the productive skills. Further implications involve the teaching and learning of Chinese as a heritage language and using HSK for admissions purposes to Chinese institutions.

The next group of four papers are concerned with assessing speaking, a key communicative skill that presents particular challenges to teachers and language testers. The first pair of papers relate to improving the quality of teaching and assessing speaking in Spain and Italy. The paper by **Jesús García Laborda** and **Mary Frances Litzler** focuses on improving speaking skills through testing in Spanish schools, reporting on the first year of the international OPENPAU Project which applies low-cost technology to the testing of 15–17-year-old Spanish students of English. This project is part of a movement to address the perceived negative washback effects of language assessment in secondary classrooms which do not include listening or speaking components, for example, which means that these skills are not focused on in the classroom. The authors adopt a social-constructivist approach which emphasises test taker interaction and improved teacher training, both of which should be supported by suitable technology. This new approach to testing speaking and listening uses face-to-face group interviews and also delivery via various devices (mobile phones and tablets) and web videoconferencing technologies such as Skype, which were recommended to the relevant Ministry of Education. The OPENPAU project runs until the end of 2015 and further work is envisaged by the authors to design collaborative tasks for all four skills and to find ways of using social networking in testing. Laborda and Litzler's paper has wider implications for test design and delivery, demonstrating the importance of principled test design that is well suited to its context and purpose, adopts technology where appropriate to do so, and has positive impacts on teaching and learning.

In the following paper, **Giuliana Grego Bolli**, **Jane Lloyd** and **Danilo Rini** discuss a project run by Centro per la Valutazione e le Certificazioni linguistiche (CVCL) at the University for Foreigners in Perugia that aimed to improve the quality of rating of high-stakes Italian speaking assessments through examiner monitoring. This paper relates to the quality management of language test administration which is a key a challenge for all language testing professionals; CVCL's project encompasses rater management and training and reports on quantitative data analysis of the speaking component of the Certificates of Italian (CELI). The authors discuss various standards containing guidance on test scoring produced by language testing organisations (i.e. ALTE, EALTA and ILTA) before describing the format and level-specific scoring of the CELI 5-level speaking test which was launched in 1993 and revised in 2004. The monitoring of speaking examining in a large CELI test centre in Athens is reported. The raters' consistency and degree of severity or leniency were calculated using Multi-Faceted Rasch Measurement (MFRM) which revealed aspects of the scoring criteria that raters found more difficult. Outcomes from this project include proposals for sharing the dating analysis with raters, swapping rater pairings and new training focusing on specific criteria that were shown to be problematic in this study.

The following pair of papers focus on important dichotomies in assessing speaking, that of the student versus teacher/examiner dynamic and of the native versus non-native speaker examiner, which have far-reaching implications for the assessment of other skills and into pedagogy. **Pascale Manoïlov** and **Claire Tardieu** report on an experimental study that compared the quality of speaking interactions in teacher-to-student and student-to-student pairings with A2–B1 level secondary students, in order to explore which pairing produces better linguistic and pragmatic outcomes. Given the relatively recent introduction of spoken interaction into the secondary curriculum in France (2005), the authors sought to explore whether the language and interaction patterns between two students would be closer than those between student and teacher, due to the teacher's didactic positioning, and whether talking with peers is the best way of assessing students' English language proficiency. The study uses the the six-yearly Cycle des Evaluations Disciplinaires Réalisées sur Echantillons (CEDRE) evaluations of the knowledge and skills of a sample of secondary-age students across various subjects, including English (this run by the Ministry of Education). The study showed that the student-to-student condition generally favoured students (who tended to achieve higher pragmatic and task achievement ratings when speaking to a peer) whilst in the student-to-teacher condition only three students achieved higher linguistic ratings, with participants' unequal status seeming to affect their linguistic and pragmatic output. Whilst the authors note that replications of this study need to take into account the proficiency levels of learner pairings, this research has implications for classroom practice and assessment since many speaking activities and tests tend to favour one of the conditions explored here.

In the next paper **Rachel L Brooks** contributes to the ongoing debate in applied linguistics concerning the exact definition of a native speaker, with the literature containing two broad definitions which refer to either how they learned a language (the environmental/age dimension) or to their highest level of language attained (the proficiency dimension). Brooks builds on this through her investigation of the relative merits of native and non-native raters, bringing a US perspective to this volume through her study of the role of rater nativeness, speaking proficiency and first language in the assessments of Federal Bureau of Investigation (FBI) examiners from different L1 backgrounds who rated English Speaking Proficiency Tests. Whilst no significant differences were reported between native and non-native raters' performance, the English language proficiency of raters affected their rating performance, with lower English proficiency raters giving lower ratings both overall and for specific linguistic categories, although the study also found that raters could have a lower productive competence than the levels of production being assessed. There are far-reaching implications for language testing in that the English proficiency level of raters is more important than them having being born into an English-speaking community, implying that testing organisations should consider and justify their use of native speakers as this study shows that non-native speakers can display equivalent levels of language acquisition to native raters when rating speaking performances.

The final paper, by **Geraldine Ludbrook**, reports on an often under-represented area in language testing research, the assessment of candidates with special needs and the resulting impact on test validity, especially in the areas of construct relevance and construct representation. Ludbrook focuses on how the use of text-to-speech assistive technology affects the reading process of Italian university students with Specific Learning Difficulties (SpLDs) such as dyslexia. Using a case study approach, Ludbrook reports how three students interact with a reading text when using a voice synthesiser, investigating whether text length, format and language of the texts (English or Italian) influence their use of the assistive technology provided. The participants reported using a range of strategies to ameliorate their SpLDs which were collected using stimulated verbal recall and interviews; their eye movements were also captured via webcam whilst reading three Italian texts followed by five English texts of varying lengths and formats. Whilst the students used the speech synthesiser to help them to a general understanding of longer texts, they preferred to read Italian texts without assistance, due to the perceived slowness of the speech synthesiser. The paper reports that because students tended to read the texts whilst listening to the text-to-speech version, the impact is less than expected on the cognitive processes involved in reading a text. Ludbrook concludes that these students use assistive technology to resolve specific difficulties, such as fluent language comprehension, rather than to help them to read in general and that speech synthesiser use was preferred for longer texts in both L1 and L2. All language testers have to ensure that their tests are fair to all candidates and are a valid means of testing the construct being measured, so this paper has broad relevance and squarely sits within the fairness and quality theme of the ALTE 2014 Conference, and is likely to be an area of interest in future conferences.

We hope that the broad range of topics presented in this volume related to multilingualism and language assessment is useful to academics, teachers and testers who find themselves faced with addressing these issues in their individual contexts.

Section 1
Culture, mediation and interactions

1 Intercultural competence – learning, teaching and assessment

Neil Jones

Consultant, Cambridge English Language Assessment

Abstract

This paper makes the case for treating the development of intercultural competence as an integral aspect of language education, rather than, as the Council of Europe suggests, a separate goal which requires specific training. This begs the question of how we conceive of and implement language education – a current concern for Cambridge English Language Assessment as its exams are increasingly adopted as part of educational reforms at state or institutional level. The paper reviews the socio-cultural theory of learning which is at the heart of the Common European Framework of Reference's action-oriented model of learning, and also of the Cambridge English approach to assessment and learning. Education should not be seen as the transmission of knowledge, but rather as a process of changing the learner, encouraging the development of dispositions and attitudes – perceptions, motivations, feelings of membership and inclusion within the community where learning takes place – which are at the heart of becoming a good learner, at school and through life. Clearly, developing intercultural competence can be seen as an intrinsic part of this process – both an outcome and a mechanism of learning.

Introduction

This paper considers three questions:

- What is intercultural competence?
- How should it be taught?
- How should it be tested?

These prompt a more basic question: what is the relevance of intercultural competence to Cambridge English Language Assessment?

The answer to this question lies in the evolution of our understanding of how assessment should support education. That assessment *should* support education is, of course, a given, in the general context of education in

Europe, and can be traced back to 1858 and the very origins of the University of Cambridge Local Examinations Syndicate (nowadays Cambridge Assessment, the organisation of which Cambridge English Language Assessment is a part). The nature of that support has evolved considerably since then. One significant change came with the recognition that increasingly lower levels of proficiency were worth accrediting. The number of exam levels has grown, particularly in the last 20 years, as exams came to be seen as supports for a student's learning career – a learning ladder of accessible targets. There are now Cambridge exams at every Common European Framework of Reference (CEFR, Council of Europe 2001) level, with the result that the exams are now more involved in the *process* of learning, rather than its simple outcomes.

Another important evolution concerns the increasing proportion of candidates found in contexts where Cambridge English exams have been adopted at state or institutional level, for use in primary or secondary education. This presents new opportunities, but also new issues, challenges and responsibilities – above all, to ensure that the impact of the intervention is a positive one.

Studying the impact of introducing Cambridge English exams into national education systems has become a significant area of work for the Cambridge English Research and Validation Group (now known as Research and Thought Leadership). Impact studies have tended to be understood as *post hoc* endeavours to evaluate the wider effects, intended or unintended, of introducing an educational innovation such as a new exam. However, Cambridge English has argued that an assessment body has an obligation as far as possible to maximise the positive and minimise or eliminate negative impact. Saville (2009) describes this as positive 'impact by design'.

It is clear that the notion of positive impact by design implies closer involvement with teaching, and possibly complex investment in supporting activity. The aim is not to expand the role of large-scale assessment within the classroom, but rather to define fully complementary, coherent roles for the expertise of teachers and assessment professionals, providing a supporting framework for learning, but where essential responsibilities still remain with teachers and students in the classroom. Having said this, coherence and complementarity require a shared theoretical and pragmatic stance on the nature of learning. Recent work on such a stance has led to the construction of a model which Cambridge English is calling Learning Oriented Assessment (LOA) (Jones and Saville forthcoming).

The focus of this paper is not on LOA as a theory of action for supporting language studies, but rather on the model of learning at the heart of LOA, which, I shall claim, has clear relevance to the conceptualisation of intercultural competence; sufficiently so that we can think of the former as, at least, a favourable basis for developing the latter.

This is an important claim because the alternative is to treat intercultural competence as something distinct from language education: an attitude of mind and a set of dispositions which require specific training. This seems to be implied in the Council of Europe's statement that 'attitudes and behaviour, knowledge and skills relevant in intercultural contexts are *not* acquired as a side effect of developing language competences' (Council of Europe 2008, emphasis added). This is a view which I shall challenge in this paper: I would say it all depends on how you treat the development of language competences.

The Council of Europe's position doubtless reflects the fact that developing intercultural competence is an explicit policy, and as such requires modes of implementation. For the Council of Europe Language Policy Division intercultural competence is an important goal of language education, supported through the *Platform of Resources and References for Plurilingual and Intercultural Education* (Council of Europe 2010b) (also referred to as the Languages of Schooling project). Despite the general success of the CEFR in terms of its wide adoption, the Council of Europe has concluded that the goal of intercultural competence has been generally neglected in the way that the CEFR has been interpreted, pointing to an 'obvious imbalance in implementation of the CEFR's provisions' which 'chiefly affects plurilingual and intercultural education, although this is one of the CEFR's main emphases' (Council of Europe 2010a:5).

This same document insists on the interconnectedness of and potential synergies between aspects of language education in schools. Its assertion that 'language teaching in schools must go beyond the communication competences specified on the various levels of the CEFR' (Council of Europe 2010a:29) is one I accept, and this paper explores what this might mean in practice.

What is intercultural competence?

I will define intercultural competence as a very general ability to apprehend and appreciate otherness, with no intrinsic connection to moving between countries, or learning a language.

All learning is built on the learner's previous experience. Thus Ausubel (1968:vi) states this principle of *contingent teaching*: 'The most important single factor influencing learning is what the learner already knows; ascertain this and teach him accordingly'. That is, learning necessarily starts from where we are: we build on experience. The development of intercultural competence can be seen as a process of evaluating new experience in the light of previous experience to date.

Thus with every step that takes you further away from your own family, your own street, your own town, your own social class, or your own country, the more differences from your previous experience are encountered. To appreciate the differences is the essence of intercultural competence. It is about foreignness only in the sense of what is unfamiliar.

In relation to languages, intercultural competence develops in the space between first and second language, or more generally, between the languages you know and the language you are learning; between the worlds you know and the world you are entering.

So intercultural competence is a form of experiential learning. In fact, the CEFR's *action-oriented* model of use and learning aligns strongly with this view. The model is defined in this well-known paragraph, describing:

> ... the actions performed by persons who as individuals and as social agents develop a range of **competences**, both **general** and in particular **communicative language competences**. They draw on the competences at their disposal in various contexts under various **conditions** and **constraints** to engage in **language activities** involving **language processes** to produce and/or receive **texts** in relation to **themes** in specific **domains**, activating those **strategies** which seem most appropriate for carrying out the **tasks** to be accomplished. The monitoring of these actions by the participants leads to the reinforcement or modification of their competences (Council of Europe 2001:9, emphasis in original).

This can be called a socio-cognitive model, because it portrays how a learner's cognition engages in social interaction, and is shaped and developed by it. The above paragraph mentions both general and communicative language competences, and here it is particularly instructive to review how these general competences are defined in the CEFR (Council of Europe 2001:11–12).

- **knowledge, i.e. declarative knowledge (*savoir*)**: all human communication depends on a shared knowledge of the world
- **skills and know-how (*savoir-faire*)**: these depend more on the ability to carry out procedures than on declarative knowledge
- **existential competence (*savoir-être*)**: the individual characteristics, personality traits and attitudes which concern self-image, one's view of others and willingness to engage with other people in social interaction
- **ability to learn (*savoir apprendre*)**: mobilises existential competence, declarative knowledge and skills, and draws on various types of competence.

Ability to learn may also be conceived as 'knowing how, or being disposed, to discover "otherness" – whether the other is another language, another culture, other people or new areas of knowledge' (Council of Europe 2001:11–12).

The CEFR stresses that whilst the notion of ability to learn is of general application, it is particularly relevant to language learning; also ability to learn mobilises a range of other skills, such that 'attitudes and personality factors greatly affect not only the language users'/learners' roles in communicative acts but also their ability to learn' (Council of Europe 2001:11–12).

Clearly, individuals differ in their capacity to appreciate and to learn from otherness; hence the Council of Europe's concern to promote intercultural competence as a matter of policy. The Council of Europe's Languages of Schooling project sees intercultural competence as an essential goal of and condition for achieving harmony and equity in an increasingly multicultural Europe. Ensuring equal access to the benefits of education is a key concern. For the children of migrants this implies, whatever additional support there may be for first-language learning, learning the language of the country quickly and to a high level. It also implies coming to terms with possibly different cultural norms and values, and being ready to step outside one's own community. This is intercultural competence naturally acquired, but certainly benefiting from a supportive school environment.

For the native-language-speaking children in the same classrooms there may be less instrumental motivation to learn intercultural competence, but as envisaged by the Council of Europe's Languages of Schooling project, there is potential benefit from studying in the 'language-friendly' school environment which a multicultural school environment might support.

The Council of Europe also makes reference to the *language awareness* movement, for whom language education implies more than achieving some level of proficiency in a foreign language. It comprises a range of learning skills and objectives that are critical to becoming competent learners not just in one language, but more importantly, of languages generally. It is what Eric Hawkins wrote of as an 'apprenticeship in languages':

> We will no longer measure effectiveness of the apprenticeship in languages by mere ability to 'survive' in a series of situations, but by how the foreign language experience contributes to learning how to learn through language, and to confidence as a (mathetic) language user (Hawkins 1999:138).

By mathetic Hawkins intends: serving discovery, understanding and learning. As Hawkins argued, mother tongue language plays a critical role in learning outcomes, and experience of foreign languages can contribute to learners' awareness of and engagement with languages, including their first language.

This suggests that native speakers and migrants in school have more in common than might be thought: both have to master new competences, and language plays a significant role in this (see too Bernstein's (1971) distinction between *restricted* and *elaborated* codes).

Learning as action in society: Social constructivism

Above I presented the CEFR's action-oriented model and the general competences of *savoir*, *savoir-faire*, *savoir-être* and *savoir apprendre*. These have perhaps not attracted sufficient attention (for example, in a critical review of the CEFR as a basis for school language education Quetz and Vogt (2009) refer to the action-oriented model as 'a vague concept'). But the action-oriented concept in fact presents a quite explicit model of learning, and one which is entirely up to date. The model is recognisably a social-constructivist one.

Two flavours of constructivism are identified. The concept of *cognitive constructivism*, associated with Jean Piaget (Piaget 1976), proposes that learners cannot simply be given information which they immediately understand and use, but rather must construct their own knowledge. Experience enables them to create schemas – mental models of the world which are subsequently enlarged and refined through processes of assimilation and accommodation. The concept of *social constructivism* is associated with Lev Vygotsky (Vygotsky 1986), who stresses the social and collaborative nature of learning. His most well-known construct is the *zone of proximal development*, which denotes the range of what a learner is currently able to assimilate, initially with the assistance of a more knowing interlocutor, such as a teacher.

The two constructivist positions – cognitive and social – are by no means in conflict, but can be seen as different emphases within a general overarching concept of *situated cognition*: the first on an individual's cognition, the second on the larger physical and social context of interactions and culturally constructed tools and meanings within which cognition develops (Wilson and Myers 2000).

Within language learning the importance of interaction has also been stressed: for example, the 'interaction hypothesis' (Gass, Doughty and Long 2007, Long 1996) sees the negotiation of meaning as the means by which learning takes place; and the 'output hypothesis' (Swain 1985) argues that production and practice is necessary for the self-monitoring which enables the learner to test and modify hypotheses about the language. But more recently Swain (2001:281) actually defines learning in terms of interaction: 'learning is understood to be a continuous process of constructing and extending meaning that occurs during learners' involvement in situated joint activities'. This shows how Vygotsky's influence has impacted on second language acquisition (SLA) conceptions of learning.

The zone of proximal development describes not just what a student can do with support, but also the maturing of new psychological functions. A focus in instruction on the maturing psychological functions is most likely to produce a transition to the next developmental level.

Communities of practice

If we accept the above treatment of social constructivism then we may see schools as constituting the necessary social community within which learning can happen. Schools are communities of practice at a number of levels. At the basic level they are institutions which impose certain conventional ways of interacting and promote certain kinds of behaviour. At this level, all children entering the school have to assimilate these conventions, which may be culturally unfamiliar. At a higher level we can see that each subject discipline creates its own community of practice, reflecting the cognitive challenges of the subject, but also the language and the forms of discourse appropriate to it. Learning the subject means tackling both.

Communities of practice have been studied by Lave and Wenger (1991). Strictly speaking, doing science or history at school does not make the child a member of the community of scientists or historians, but Lave and Wenger use the notion of *legitimate peripheral participation* to characterise the nature of discipline-specific study in the classroom. Thus the experience of school is critical to the way individuals come to see themselves and their place in the world.

Our own experience of school is very probably that while there were subjects with which we felt an affinity, there were others that remained alien and unattractive. This does not seem to differ significantly from the way individuals develop their cultural identity.

To provide one last example: the Assessment Reform Group, who were influential in the UK and beyond in promoting the values of formative assessment against or alongside those of summative assessment, proposed the following classification of desirable learning outcomes (James and Brown 2005):

1. **Attainment** – often school curriculum based.
2. **Understanding** – of ideas, concepts, processes.
3. **Cognitive and creative** – imaginative construction of meaning, arts or performance.
4. **Using** – how to practise, manipulate, behave, engage in processes or systems.
5. **Higher-order learning** – advanced thinking, reasoning, metacognition.
6. **Dispositions** – attitudes, perceptions, motivations.
7. **Membership, inclusion, self-worth** – affinity towards the group where learning takes place.

The similarity with the skills identified in the CEFR is striking. Objectives (1) and (2) refer to *savoir*, (3) and (4) refer to *savoir-faire*, (5) refers to *savoir apprendre*, and (6) and (7) refer to *savoir-être*. They seem to include the essential skills, dispositions and attitudes underlying the concept of intercultural competence.

Language classrooms: The cradle of intercultural competence?

The above discussion suggests that the language classroom should be the best possible place to acquire intercultural competence. Learning a language not only gives you access to the community of linguists (and thus to the possibility of learning any number of additional languages): it will also provide some taste of otherness, and an affinity with the culture where the language is spoken. This is generally what happens to those students who achieve real success with a language at school and go on to further language studies in higher education. The fundamental problem is that in many countries in Europe far too few students are achieving success with languages.

As the first European Survey on Language Competences (ESLC) so plainly revealed (European Commission 2012), levels of achievement in languages at the end of lower secondary education vary widely across countries: a few are successful, but many show a disappointing return on the years of study invested. Where there is success it is largely in relation to English, which is acquiring *de facto* the status of an international language.

However, the ESLC questionnaire findings, which show how the context of learning relates to outcomes, could be interpreted to provide a simple recipe for success, summarised in Jones (2013) as follows:

> A language is learned better where motivation is high, where learners perceive it to be useful, and where it is indeed used outside school, for example in communicating over the internet, for watching TV, or travelling on holiday. Also, the more teachers and students use the language in class, the better it is learned.

However, this ideal situation is approximated only in some countries, and mainly for English.

Languages are easy to learn, but we have made them difficult. While nearly all European countries endorse the CEFR as a useful frame of reference, they are clearly not managing to implement the action-oriented model successfully. The social-constructivist perspective on learning which I have presented here, although it might be seen as the current orthodoxy, is probably still unknown in most classrooms.

Content and Language Integrated Learning (CLIL), although widely endorsed, is little practised, according to the data from the ESLC.

What is intended by communicative language teaching is poorly understood even today, with many at tertiary level considering it to equate to 'dumbing down' language education. This is to understand it as the dull drilling of phrasebook texts of no relevance to students, which it doubtless too often is. Of course, communication should not be understood in narrow utilitarian, instrumental or phrasebook terms. Language education should aim higher than that. Communication is at the heart of the human condition, in the here-and-now and over time: Shakespeare continues to communicate with us across four centuries, and the generation of learners growing up in the age of social media is finding new but still language-mediated ways of communicating and sharing their experience of the world. The natural desire to communicate is a powerful force for learning, if it can be harnessed.

In presenting language education from a social constructivist perspective I have made the case that successful language learning requires the individual learner, and the classroom community of learners and teachers, to engage and develop a range of learning skills. *Savoir-faire*, *savoir-être* and *savoir apprendre* must all be mobilised: plain old *savoir* is not going to produce the desired result.

If we can engage and develop all these skills then we have a chance of success. The dispositions and attitudes which underlie intercultural competence are closely linked with these learning skills, and the values of the social-constructivist classroom should favour their development, whether or not we choose to raise the notion of intercultural competence to the level of students' metacognitive awareness – that is, to name it and make it into a subject. In this paper I have attempted to treat intercultural competence, or at least its underlying dispositions and attitudes, as a key mechanism, as well as a key goal, of language learning.

How can intercultural competence be tested?

I have argued in this paper that the important learning outcomes are not about mastery of content, but changing the person and imparting new life skills: becoming a lifelong learner, a member of a learning community, a member of society. We would wish to find forms of assessment which give due weight to these important educational goals.

But can such skills be tested? Can intercultural competence be tested? I have to conclude that they cannot, or at least, not directly.

The metaphor of investment seems appropriate here (and what is education, if not an investment?). Investments are evaluated by the return on them – by the interest they generate. To learn course content is useful, but in itself it pays no interest (and you may easily forget it and lose it). But the skills of learning pay interest in the form of better learning (or greater self-efficacy, more generally), during schooling and then through a lifetime. We are familiar with the magic of compound interest: over time, the benefits accrue faster and faster. That is how we should approach evaluation of the learning skills, within which we can include intercultural competence.

Where we are successful in developing learning skills we will see dramatic changes to learning outcomes, at least in those many contexts where language education is currently so ineffective and inefficient. The results will be evidence of success. Qualitative evaluation of classroom practice, rather than testing, will provide evidence for the source of these profound improvements in learning skills.

By taking this approach we avoid trying to measure and objectify skills and dispositions which cannot really be measured or objectified. Currently governments and other authorities are too concerned with measuring and objectifying, increasingly using *indicators* to drive progress. For example, the UK government uses pupils' exam grades to judge school performance, feeding 'perverse incentives' into the system, encouraging schools and pupils to conspire in beating the system. True learning outcomes are lost sight of, as evidenced by England's last place in the ESLC.

Another example of constructs being shaped by a focus on accountability and measurability is a recent European project to develop an indicator for the skills of *learning to learn* (Fredriksson and Hoskins 2007:251): 'The political imperative to identify indicators . . . has brought about a situation . . . characterised as "the proverbial assessment tail wagging the curriculum dog"'. Turning learning objectives into indicators risks destroying the thing we wished to measure.

Better, perhaps, to avoid treating intercultural competence as a subject to be taught and tested, as it is easy to foresee its trivialisation and subversion.

Rather we should think how to develop the life skills discussed in this paper by implementing social-constructivist concepts and paying due attention to the CEFR's insightful action-oriented approach.

References

Ausubel, D (1968) *Educational Psychology: A Cognitive View*, New York: Holt, Rinehart and Winston.

Bernstein, B (1971) *Class, Codes and Control Volume 1*, London: Routledge and Kegan Paul.

Council of Europe (2001) *Common European Framework of Reference for Languages: Learning, Teaching, Assessment*, Cambridge: Cambridge University Press.

Council of Europe (2008) *White Paper on Intercultural Dialogue*, available online: www.coe.int/t/dg4/intercultural/Publication_WhitePaper_ID_en.asp

Council of Europe (2010a) *Guide for the Development and Implementation of Curricula for Plurilingual and Intercultural Education*, Strasbourg: Council of Europe.

Council of Europe (2010b) *Platform of Resources and References for Plurilingual and Intercultural Education*, Strasbourg: Council of Europe.

European Commission (2012) *First European Survey on Language Competences: Final Report*, Luxembourg: Publications Office of the European Union, available online: ec.europa.eu/languages/eslc/index.html

Fredriksson, U and Hoskins, H (2007) *Indicators of Learning to Learn*, available online: publications.jrc.ec.europa.eu/repository/bitstream/JRC46532/learning%20to%20learn%20what%20is%20it%20and%20can%20it%20be%20measured%20final.pdf

Gass, M, Doughty, C J and Long, M H (2007) *Input and Interaction: The Handbook of Second Language Acquisition*, Malden: Blackwell Publishing.

Hawkins, E W (1999) Foreign language study and language awareness, *Language Awareness* 8, 124–142.

James, M and Brown, S (2005) Grasping the nettle: preliminary analysis and some enduring issues surrounding the improvement of learning outcomes, *The Curriculum Journal* 16 (1), 7–30.

Jones, N (2013) The European Survey on Language Competences and its significance for Cambridge English Language Assessment, *Research Notes* 52, 2–7.

Jones, N and Saville, N (forthcoming) *Learning Oriented Assessment: A Systemic Approach to Language Education*, Studies in Language Testing volume 45, Cambridge: UCLES/Cambridge University Press.

Lave, J and Wenger, E (1991) *Situated Learning: Legitimate Peripheral Participation*, Cambridge: Cambridge University Press.

Long, M H (1996) The role of the linguistic environment in second language acquisition, in Ritchie, W and Bhatiam, T (Eds) *Handbook of Second Language Acquisition*, San Diego: Academic Press, 413–468.

Piaget, J (1976) *The Grasp of Consciousness*, Cambridge: Harvard University Press.

Quetz, J and Vogt, K (2009) Bildungsstandards für die Erste Fremdsprache: Sprachenpolitik auf unsicherer Basis, *Zeitschrift für Fremdsprachenforschung* 20 (1), 63–89.

Saville, N (2009) *Developing a model for investigating the impact of language assessment within educational contexts by a public examination provider*, unpublished thesis, University of Bedfordshire.

Swain, M (1985) Communicative competence: Some roles of comprehensible input and comprehensible output in its development, in Gass, S and Madden, C (Eds) *Input in Second Language Acquisition*, Rowley: Newbury House, 235–253.

Swain, M (2001) Examining dialogue: another approach to content specification and to validating inferences drawn from test scores, *Language Testing* 18 (3), 275–302.

Vygotsky, L (1986) *Thought and Language*, Chicago: MIT Press.

Wilson, B G and Myers, K M (2000) Situated cognition in theoretical and practical context, in Jonassen, D H and Land, S M (Eds) (2012) *Theoretical Foundations of Learning Environments*, London: Routledge, 57–88.

2 Intercultural communication – what's missing?

Elaine Boyd
Trinity College London
David Donnarumma
BPP University, London

Abstract

Intercultural communication has proved an elusive concept embracing the almost indefinable flexibility of English as a *lingua franca* (ELF) and complex notions of what constitutes intercultural awareness (Baker 2011a, 2011b). ELF is the communicative medium of choice for speakers with diverse linguistic and cultural backgrounds in professional settings (Seidlhofer 2011). The focus of this study was one such setting – a large international hotel group in India. The study involved interviews, focus groups and question-naires with hotel employees who reported on the challenges they faced in communication. Drama activities revealed communication strengths, weaknesses and misunderstandings. What emerged was that, although employees demonstrated high levels of competency in English language, miscommunication still occurred, which was exacerbated by very poor repair techniques. Why was this so when it is claimed that ELF communication is more open to negotiation than in typical L1 settings (Watterson 2008:378)? If the context and purpose of communication was clear, and the speakers used error-free language, why was there still so much miscommunication? Is it because the employees lacked 'the capacity to negotiate diverse varieties [of English] to facilitate communication' (Canagarajah 2006:233)? Or does the solution lie in Baker's (2011a) model of Intercultural Awareness? This paper will provide some initial results from the study which suggest different or additional factors may also need to be considered in any effective training programme.

Introduction

A research project to investigate communication issues within a group of customer service staff at a luxury hotel group in India raised key questions about the nature of intercultural communication. This was a stereotypical environment where it was expected that English as a *lingua franca* (ELF) would be used to facilitate communication in a setting of diverse cultural behaviours. The hotel group had identified that this communication was not as effective as it could be and wanted to understand why. The project allowed us to study real-time communications in ELF and explore aspects of intercultural awareness (ICA) in order to understand what difficulties emerged and whether the combination of ELF and ICA would provide the staff with the complete set of tools they needed for effective intercultural communication.

Expectations of intercultural communication

ELF is generally seen as the version of English that non-native speakers utilise to communicate, especially in business settings. ELF communication is widely described as an adaptive, changing, creative, diverse, dynamic, flexible, fluid, heterogeneous, hybrid, indeterminate, shifting, unbounded, unpredictable, unstable, variable but self-regulating system (e.g. Ferguson 2009, Seidlhofer 2009a), whose speakers use different Englishes. Is this slipperiness the problem? In other words does the option for ELF to be so many things result in it meaning nothing? ELF communication is also characterised by its 'community of practice', which is 'mutual engagement, a joint negotiated enterprise, and a shared repertoire of negotiable resources' (Wenger (1998) in House 2003:572). Crucially, it is argued that ELF users are not trying to emulate the idealised competence of a native speaker community, or moving, in a more or less linear progression, towards someone else's target, as in the second language acquisition (SLA) concept of an interlanguage (Selinker 1972).

In Standard English, or other natural languages, agreed strategies for that specific speech community are used to make communication clear and manage any repairs. In ELF, the strategies that are used are not necessarily agreed but each speaker brings his or her own accommodations to the situation, recognising that communicative breakdowns are potentially more likely. 'Lingua franca speakers show considerable awareness of the requirements of the communicative situation in which they find themselves, and are able to regulate their language and interaction accordingly' (Mauranen 2006:147).

In support of this broad notion of accommodation, some findings from *lingua franca* research suggest that misunderstandings are not very frequent (Firth 1990, Meierkord 1998), which may be because 'interlocutors tend to maximize simplicity in their expression, because their command of the vehicular language is far from perfect, and because they can expect the same from their interlocutors' (Mauranen 2006:123). Or it may be that a common feature of ELF is consensus oriented speech and so speakers make extra effort to try and repair communication if a breakdown occurs (Seidlhofer 2004). In fact, the strategies ELF speakers use to negotiate meanings are still under researched, but there seems to be both general agreement that participants are working to a co-operative principle however that might manifest itself.

Firth (1996) argued that a common feature of ELF was consensus oriented speech, and that, in the case of an unclear conversational item, ELF speakers allow any lack of clarity to pass as it is evident that any confusion will either become clear later on or turn out to be irrelevant. Meierkord (1998) investigated turn-taking in ELF speakers' communication, and identified that speakers used back channelling methods to demonstrate the co-operative and consensus oriented nature of ELF speech. House (1999) suggests ELF speakers lack pragmatic fluency in turn-taking, and therefore engage in parallel monologues, although the consensus oriented behaviour could give the impression that subjects were listening to each other.

A feature of consensus oriented speech is to repair if a breakdown occurs (Seidlhofer 2004). One question is whether ELF talk achieves repair through linguistic capability, as is common in native speech, or through avoidance strategies. Firth (1996) made the following observation of ELF speakers: 'faced with the other party's marked lexical selections and unidiomatic phrasings, the hearer behaves in such a way as to divert attention from the linguistically infelicitous form of the other's talk. This commonly precludes doing "other-repair" and "candidate completions"' (Firth 1996:245). In other words, ELF talk is marked by its ability to prevent any misunderstandings occurring, because if they do occur the hearer repairs the conversation by topic change, repetition or rephrasing what the speaker was saying and awaiting approval. This assumes the hearer is capable of doing this. Hence, it appears that ELF talk is repairable, although it seems that this may be through avoidance strategies by the hearer.

Another common issue in ELF is that speakers may be motivated to acquire language skills which are overtly connected to their employment. This can create a focus on lexis and functional language rather than pragmatics and other more subtle aspects of communication. This in turn means that internal training services within organisations pick this up by focusing their training on the wider communication skills relevant to their employees. This was a feature in this study where the hotel group offered such training but was nevertheless frustrated by the ineffective results.

Despite these issues Rogerson-Revell (2010) has highlighted the aim for co-operation for co-operation that *appears* to mark intercultural communication for both native and non-native English speakers. She states:

> What there is evidence of, in all meetings and at both procedural and
> linguistic levels, is interactive accommodation by both native speakers
> of English and non-native speakers of English, indicating an underly
> ing awareness of some of the issues involved in such lingua franca

communication. The analysis has also revealed some of the ways in which participants strive to accommodate different linguistic competences and generic constraints of the large meeting format (Rogerson-Revell 2010:447).

We note 'appears' here as this study raises some challenges for this conclusion.

Baker went further and identified the inherent flexibility of intercultural interactions in ELF that allow speakers to shift from fixed notions of culture and operate in more fluctuating and changeable contexts. 'Crucially, it moves us beyond the national culture and target community associations inherent in previous conceptions of intercultural competence. Instead, while recognising that these concepts may have an influence on intercultural communication, in ELF the connections between language and culture should be viewed primarily as fluid, emergent and liminal with no a priori specified target community' (Baker 2011a:212).

Despite Seidlhofer's (2009b) warning that people learn ELF as a means of communication only and not to 'identify with or accommodate the social cultural values of its native speakers' (Seidlhofer 2009b:199), much current thinking suggests that inherent co-operation can be assumed in these intercultural encounters and that training in or familiarity with ICA would increase the effectiveness in communications in these international settings. Certainly these were our hypotheses as we entered the study.

The research project

Rationale and aims

The hotel group that was the focus of the project has highly trained staff but, in an extremely competitive high-end market, was seeking to develop their team so that they are identifiably better than their counterparts in competitor hotel groups. Their desire is to make more impact internationally and they see their frontline staff in particular (receptionists, butlers, room service, etc.) as essential to the success of this strategy. The hotel Executive felt that this extra edge they wished to achieve sat with their customer service staff in the arena of communicative competence and communication skills, especially how those skills are operationalised for an international clientele.

The purpose of the investigation was to identify gaps and weaknesses in competences or areas which could be improved and thus made more effective. The study aimed to focus on two key areas which were identified by the hotel group as potentially problematic.

a) Communicative competence, which takes account of having a range of grammar and vocabulary to express functions and for that to be expressed reasonably accurately, and with awareness of the target listener or reader. It also includes a good understanding of how this knowledge is 'performed', such as appropriacy, turn-taking, etc.

b) Communication skills, which are a broader set of competencies that include non-verbal communication, an ability to adapt oneself to the needs and language patterns of the listener and a sophisticated understanding of how to manipulate language and other forms of communication to achieve one's end goal. Crucially it involves being able to influence outcomes as well as being able to utilise these skills on behalf of others.

Scope of the project

The research took place over four days in one of the hotels of the luxury group in India. The project followed Baker's model (2011a:206) with the emphasis on an open, qualitative approach to the research so that, while some activities were pre-planned, further investigations were identified in situ from outcomes of the planned research. The focus was on c.250 staff who had a high level of customer interaction, such as guest relations executives, front desk (reception), butlers and associates who work on the business level floors of the hotels. Most of the staff were bilingual or extremely competent second language speakers of English but were generally using English in a *lingua franca* context. Despite their linguistic proficiency in English, the intercultural miscommunications that occurred were sometimes with native English speakers (e.g. British or American English speakers) but more prominently with non-native English-speaking customers, who were communicating through English but who may have very different cultural norms from native speakers of English.

Methodology

Given that the customer service was at an acceptable level, the senior trainers at the hotel group had identified that some of their anticipated needs were around what might be called 'finesse'. Therefore it was decided that the research programme would have to drill down into the deepest layers of staff motivation and interactions in order to understand what might be missing or could be improved. Thus a layered and mixed methods approach to the research was taken following Creswell and Plano-Clark's multi-staged explanatory sequential design (2011:81–86) but with a strong weighting given to qualitative data. This involved a quantitative phase followed by a qualitative phase to explain the initial results in more depth.

The stages were:

a) A questionnaire: This was to gather some exploratory quantitative data to establish staff perceptions on the success of their communications and self-perceptions of the potential causes. Specific questions were informed by input from the hotel staff trainers who had raised concerns. Questions included both open and closed-response formats. Typically a 7-point Likert scale option was used for the closed-response format. The questions reflected practical aspects such as how much of their day was given to spoken communications as well as points raised by their trainers such as their levels of confidence and attitudes. It was intended that the questionnaire would be conducted anonymously on a sample population of 15%. Critically, the purpose of this was to provide guidance for questions/investigations in the following stages.

b) Observation: This consisted of field notes of the researchers' interactions while acting as customers in the hotel as well as observed interactions of other customers and staff, both positive and problematic. In other words, this replicated the guest experience. The observations were noted where customer requests were not resolved quickly and/or where irritation or tension was noted on the part of the customer, including in some cases the observers. A description of the interaction was recorded together with reflective notes on emerging themes or concerns. These observations, which were ongoing, fed into issues to be explored in the discussion and drama groups.

c) Focus group discussions: This was a series of focus groups lasting approximately 45 minutes each with approximately eight participants in each group. Questions were selected from issues emerging from (a) and (b) above. The purpose of these groups was to elicit qualitative data on perceptions and feelings about interactions and to see how much agreement there was across the different customer service teams. Although there were some guided questions there was also free-flowing discussion in order to allow any further points to emerge. This would help establish what might be common to the hotel and what potentially attributable to individuals.

d) Drama roleplay (I): In this stage (and in the later drama activity) it was a deliberate decision to ask staff to participate in a roleplay that was outside their usual context. This was to prevent them simply trying to show how good they were at their job and thus to enable the researchers to observe their behaviours and also to 'free up' issues of status where some staff were very senior. The roleplays were set up as two separate groups of approximately eight participants from the customer service staff. They were asked to engage in a simple roleplay activity designed to see how sensitive they were to a variety of motives or needs of the other participants, how spontaneous and flexible they could be and how well they could manipulate their communicative competences. An example was where the Trinity College researcher (a drama expert) played the role of a shopkeeper and the participants were asked to persuade him individually to give them something for free. In doing this they had to really think about what would resonate with the person they were trying to persuade, how they could obtain this information and then how far they needed to adapt their response to this input. This roleplay forced them to focus on the other participants' needs and motivations and illustrated what communication strategies they could draw on.

e) Group interviews: A series of 30-minute interviews in order to investigate levels of self-reflection. These were set up as separate groups of approximately four participants. They were asked a series of direct questions by one of the researchers. At this stage it was felt the associates were relaxed enough and familiar enough with the project to be fairly open with the researchers. Questions focused on specific examples of incidents that occurred and how associates felt when communication broke down. Senior staff and team leaders were also asked about how their teams coped in these scenarios.

f) Drama roleplay (II): This was set up as a single group of 12. Participants were asked to engage in a series of roleplays designed to both assess their observational skills and status clues following issues identified in (e) above. It was also designed to see how sensitive they were to training in awareness raising.

At each stage different hotel personnel were involved in order to see as wide a cross section as possible with each cohort.

Results and findings

The questionnaire

The group reported good operational language skills and good confidence levels in written and spoken skills. A significant part of their day (80%+) was spent interacting with guests. They dealt with guests across a range of communicative scenarios and generally rated their communication skills and confidence levels as 6 or 7 out of 7 on a Likert scale where 7 represented 'very confident'. This result was interesting in the light of later discussions regarding communication breakdowns which can be found in the 'limitations' section.

Observations

Spoken interactions were noted across a range of contexts. The English in the group generally seemed very good or native like with only very occasional, non-impeding errors. Staff understood overt messages well. However, although unfailingly polite in the linguistic sense, what was noted was a certain 'stiltedness' in their responses; a feeling of them very much following a script rather than a natural or relaxed engagement. The weaker members of this group demonstrated a poor understanding of pragmatics. The most significant finding was that staff were generally poor at reading group dynamics and were sometimes intrusive when dealing directly with customers. The stated hotel requirement to 'anticipate' guest needs sometimes manifested itself as intrusive because these potential needs were not always being interpreted appropriately. Two examples of this were firstly when two of the observers were engaged in deep discussion – very evident from their body language, facial expression and talk ratio – but they were interrupted with a non-critical query as to whether they had everything they needed. This felt highly intrusive and was replicated numerous times. A second, more complex example was when one observer ordered a specific glass of wine. Rather than telling the observer it was not available and a discussion ensuing about what else might be, the waiter returned with three bottles of very expensive wine for the observer to try thus creating a significant interruption to the dinner and with wine which the observer had no intention of buying based on price. This seemed to be driven by a desire to follow hotel policy on offering 'extra' but was at the expense of understanding what might drive a customer's choices and/or their expectations about the dinner.

Focus groups

Issues arising in the questionnaire and the researchers' hypotheses were fed into questions for the focus groups to examine in more detail together with some points noted from the observational activity.

The group reported a very clear understanding of what good communication should look like. Staff listed a sophisticated range of skills including being clear, utilising body language, types of language used, asking questions, having a good knowledge of 'product', using intuition, tone of voice, etc. They claimed to very much enjoy interacting with guests because of what they could learn about other cultures as well as the opportunity to build relationships and job satisfaction. Positive encounters were interpreted as validation from the guests and so gave staff confidence and encouragement. In fact, a significant proportion of the staff seemed to overtly need this positive reinforcement in order to feel comfortable, almost as if they did not have confidence in their skills or abilities without this substantiation. They identified grammar as their weakness though this was un-evidenced and seemed to be a hark back to school (which they laughingly acknowledged). They also said they felt uncomfortable when dealing with areas outside their subject knowledge and asked for more 'cross-training'. They separately identified that communications with colleagues need to be respected as much as with guests. They identified possible improvements such as, for example, learning how to have more positive body language (though they recognised this was cultural), how to express courtesy more effectively and how to improve their tone.

Drama roleplay (I)

The staff varied in their response to the activities included in this session and in how well they approached the communicative challenge, with many focusing on their own needs or desired outcomes. Some proved adept at being flexible and thinking on their feet and demonstrated an acute awareness of the listener's (the other participant's) perspective. Others struggled to adapt to changing situations, were repetitive in their language and tone and became sidetracked from their goal. There was a clear range in levels of 'coping' in this cohort. Even when they could deliver with appropriate pragmatic intent they were less good at spotting sub-texts or illocutionary force in their listener's contributions. What emerged was a dual communicative issue. Despite operating in a culturally diverse community every day, many of the staff were insensitive to the differing cultural expectations they were confronted with to the extent that they were not even aware that there might be cultural differences in communicative interactions. Could we therefore say that the use of a *lingua franca* was feeding assumptions regarding 'likeness'? However, this lack of awareness also appeared to be a sub-issue in a wider problem where it was clear that they lacked the skills in 'perceiving' generally in terms of pragmatic messaging – but especially when this was compounded by cultural differences. We suspect this may be partly due to the fact that their organisational training focused on what they were 'delivering'.

Interviews

This group reported a high level of self-blame when communication went wrong. They had some conventional strategies for dealing with these breakdowns including apologising and showing empathy, as they were trained to do. They correctly identified communication breakdowns through expressions and gestures in the first instance.

The staff did, however, report being very 'scared' both about the prospect of communication breaking down and in the aftermath of when it actually did. They said they were very conscious of what they were saying as a result of this fear and they were very concerned about breaching status. Nevertheless, they were confident they had clear recovery options and cited supportive line managers and peers. In terms of self-reflection they tended to rely more on being told what to do rather than reflecting on their own situations.

Drama roleplay (II)

This was a single activity group with a cohort who appeared to be at the top end of this strata of staff and in their roles most had a high level of interaction with guests. While performance skills were generally limited, they eventually proved good at identifying status clues from observation and identifying intentions based on visual language. They were also effective at extrapolating ideas and situations to imagine other mindsets. Much of their success in this seemed to depend on them developing the confidence to trust their judgements and, as they did, they got better and better at interpreting the notional customers.

Limitations

There were some limitations to the research which will have an impact on any conclusions drawn.

Firstly, it was requested that the questionnaire would be anonymous in order to encourage open responses from respondents. However, staff identified themselves on the questionnaires and this may have had an impact on how they self-reported as they may have felt they were being assessed.

In the observational activity there were a limited number of interactions. However, these did reflect the spectrum of typical hotel interactions with guests, e.g. in restaurant service, queries etc. and seemed to be often replicated.

The senior trainers watched some of the roleplay sessions and this may have had an impact on contributions from the staff, especially the shyer ones, if they felt they were being assessed in their roles. They were reassured this was not the case and we saw no signs that participants did feel intimidated but this is a potential factor to be borne in mind.

Another factor is that, as described by the senior trainers, the customer service staff were naturally trained to manage guests in a certain way and through a certain process to allow standardisation of the hotel chain's customer service. We are unsure if focusing on the need to deliver the messages required ended up in restricting the staff's freedom with their general communication skills.

Summary

The subjects of this study were a group of staff who operated wholly in an ELF context, and not only that but one which was notable for its extreme diversity in terms of other cultures. In addition, the staff were constantly confronted with newness as the variety of guests changed daily. So they were very much in the fluid setting outlined by Baker (2011a, 2011b). However, although the guests and thus interactional participants were hugely varied there were some standardised elements. This was not only the range of their interactions, which was generally prescribed by staff roles, but perhaps more significantly the training they had received from the hotel group. This was designed to be a support for staff and a way of standardising customer service to a high quality across the group with clear expectations set down. Ironically there were signs that the very factor designed to enhance customer service was, with its focus on formulae, actually militating against first class communications.

The conclusions from the study were that although this cohort spoke native, or native-like, English in the sense of their fluency and knowledge and degrees of linguistic competence, they faced various challenges.

Firstly, they appeared to struggle with what seemed to be a kind of dissonance between the use of a first language in an international setting where others were using it very much as a foreign language. In other words, the clash of competencies in a setting where the staff, by the very nature of their roles, were the ones who were expected to drive the co-operation. Their expressed tension around this was exacerbated by what their seniors expected of the staff in the customer service role where comprehension and communication are critical. The staff very much interpreted ELF communications as native like so were perplexed when communication was less than effective. They could deal with breakdowns in linguistic proficiency by guests but they understood illocutionary intent through the filter of of their own native speaker community. This was clearly not always the case as the guests frequently retained their own native meta features of communication which were 'translated' into English. This finding seems to support current intercultural communication theories that proficiency is achieved through awareness training but in the discussion we will consider if this is the whole story.

Certainly, in terms of reporting back to the hotel group, key factors emerging from the study were the need for improved intercultural competence and, critically, the ability to deal with unpredictable communication scenarios, a need for increased flexibility engendered through a variety of communicative strategies and a much greater awareness of the target listener. It may be that the staff struggled to manage scenarios outside of the settings because they had been trained in listening to overt messages and not subtext. This was also worthy of consideration by the hotel group in their aim to seek improvements.

Discussion

Aside from any concerns about the impact of the hotel training system, the issue seemed to come down to which aspects of the problems of ineffective communication or breakdowns in communications were rooted in communication and which in cultural practices – or was it a combination of both? The observation research in many ways seemed the most insightful into what might be going wrong. The other research (questionnaire, interviews, focus groups and roleplays) clarified the participants' feelings and approaches and self-perceptions but the observational study included the other participants in the exchanges, i.e. the guests, and so gave more concrete evidence of when communication was successful or not.

Certainly the matter seemed to go beyond competence, or lack of, in ELF, with its focus on understanding varieties of English. Intercultural studies, as we have outlined above, all refer to the co-operative nature of intercultural exchanges in ELF contexts and the accommodations participants willingly make in order to reach successful outcomes. Contemporary analyses and suggested ways forward for business communities outlined in, for example, Scollon, Scollon and Jones (2012) and Pan, Scollon and Scollon (2002) seem to be built on these assumed principles. It is thus perhaps worth revisiting these earlier theories of interpersonal communication in order not to get sidetracked by this embedded vocabulary of linguistic discussion and any assumptions this entails. Exactly what are the core principles of co-operation and accommodation? Given the nature of these customer service interactions it is also worth touching on theories of politeness and its varieties.

Although clearly much more work has now been done on pragmatics, the basics of Grice's Cooperative Principle (1975) do seem relevant to these exchanges in this international setting. Grice argued that all conversationalists are rational beings who are primarily interested in the efficient conveying of messages. ELF itself focuses on co-operation and 'communities of practice' (Wenger 1998) reiterated in Baker (2011a). It is interesting because Grice's principles apply across participants that have positive expectations about an interaction so one would think that, in a customer service setting, all participants in these exchanges 'know' about the need for co-operation to fuel the service exchange, arguably, according to ELF, even more so in a complex intercultural setting. However, despite significant attempts at co-operation on the part of the staff, communications did sometimes break down. Was this because the staff were not applying the maxims of, for example, quantity and relation appropriately for the particular guest (as in the case of the wine example) thus perhaps allowing the guest to flout the co-operative element? Or did the guests feel that due to the service role of the staff that co-operation was not critical to the communicative endeavour? In some ways what provided further evidence that the staff were not listening to the guests was that if a guest flouted a maxim (e.g. of quality by a short or curt response), the staff did not appear to infer any meaning from this even though Gricean principles would suggest they should. Although they brought a generic worry to all interactions about the guest complaining, they did not try to spot the warning signs nor reflect on the specific communicative intent of an utterance from a guest, and so had no adequate repair strategies beyond apology. As they did not pick up on these warning signs, they could be said to be not competent in the relational aspects of the language. Certainly the co-operative principle seemed to be relevant here as one could relate exemplars of it being flouted to communicative breakdowns (or certainly less than satisfactory encounters).

Another theory which threads into the literature on ELF and is assumed to be in the interests of all participants is based on Giles and Smith's (1979) Accommodation Theory. Again, although this allows for divergence, it would seem to have strong representation in ELF where each party is willing to adjust their input and responses to ensure that communication takes place. Where convergence is desired (and surely we can presuppose, in the context of this study, that guests want their requests fulfilled) we can assume both participants will make every effort at accommodation. Yet again this was not evidenced. Although the staff could often be seen to make allowances for the guests (e.g. excusing abrupt requests), they were perplexed when things went wrong and often guests did not equally co-operate in the accommodation, instantly complaining if staff did not meet their sometimes unclear needs. And this raises a further question of what the staff are accommodating to. The guests' speech? Or their attitude? Or their cultural mores? Or all three? Any of these would be a tough call without adequate or effective training. Of course, we identified above Firth's (1996) point that sometimes this accommodation is achieved through avoidance – this is probably not an option in a setting where one participant has to deliver a service. On the contrary, in order to deliver what is required staff must have a very clear understanding of the request. However, the questioning to establish this may flout some aspects of accommodation potentially making the other participant (in this case the guest) feel incompetent or 'put on the spot'. This latter feeling is probably even more unacceptable in a service setting.

Finally, there seemed to be a real butting of heads on issues around politeness, which builds on Gricean principles. This issue was complex as it was twofold. Firstly, there were clearly issues created by the difference between cultures which see any interruption as an intrusion and thus rude (negative politeness) versus cultures where solicitousness is part of hospitality and general politeness (positive politeness) (Brown and Levinson 1987). This collision can certainly be a crucible for problems with no-one being the winner. In the observations element of the research study and in the role-plays, it becomes clear that cultures which are sensitive to intrusion (e.g. British) saw the staff's solicitousness as an imposition whereas cultures which value positive politeness, including India itself, almost expected more of the staff. The staff seemed unaware of this difference in politeness cultures and any clues which might help them (e.g. body language). They did become sensitive once their awareness was raised, e.g. through the drama exercises which specifically asked them to 'read' people without any words and this supports Baker's (2011a) models of training in ICA to improve intercultural competence. Exacerbating this complication was the issue of politeness and power, which staff appeared to be aware of in their repair work by bending over backwards to help guests achieve their needs. However, what potentially prevented this working effectively every time was the cultural differences and the staff's not unreasonable lack of knowledge of how hierarchical face systems worked across the range of cultures they were encountering. Scollon et al (2012) outline how this can be problematic in intercultural encounters. 'Often at the core of misunderstandings . . . is the fact that politeness strategies are so intimately linked to our ideas about power and our ways of negotiating what kind of conversational rights different people have in different situations' (Scollon et al 2012:57).

In the context of this study even the fairly overt and prescribed power roles delineated by the roles of the participants (i.e. guest vs staff) and the setting (i.e. customer service) suggest there are still subtle variations that throw the effectiveness of the communications.

Each of the above, while not resolving the problem, seemed to confirm that communication was breaking down at the cultural and relationship level and was not to do with pure linguistic competency. ELF in whatever variety would not help here. There seemed to be two real tensions:

a) The staff were speaking in their first or native language and, being so imbued in it and its sociocultural threads, appeared to struggle with seeing how foreign language speakers in an intercultural setting would engage in communication in English. The latter was complicated as the guests communicated according to their own cultural mores with English simply serving as a tool. This problem is one of the *lingua franca*, which has no moorings in any culture and thus becomes a palimpsest or tabula rasa to be overlaid at will. In other words, the so-called 'flexibility' of ELF which allows it to be adapted by its speakers might also create problems when operating with native speaker versions of English. This indicates that studies such as Baker's (2011a), which propose that there is an equal playing field due to the fact there is no agreed standardised version of ELF, might need to explore further the subconscious assumptions that native speakers bring to encounters despite any efforts to accommodate wider versions of their native language.

b) The differing roles of guest and staff, especially in such a high-end service context, appeared to thwart the co-operation needed to successfully communicate across cultures. The difference in power in the roles foregrounded issues of face and meant the co-operation was frequently seen as only working one way. Deviation in this direction of 'travel' often resulted in complaints about staff and damaged the very image the hotel wished to promote. Despite the fact that guests needed to communicate their needs in order to get what they wanted, there was often a real breach of the co-operative principle. The staff were subjugating their own identity in service of the guest and the guests saw no need to co-operate or accommodate because the relationship was one of service not mutual agreement. So the real problem seemed to be caused by the overlay of different roles on a set of cultural differences; a kind of conflict between the requirements of the staff's roles and the communication requirements.

So we were left with the staff in a position where they were performing co-operation assiduously and according to their own culture, which tipped into intrusion for some guests. And guests who, in a position of power and potentially indifference, saw no need to accommodate, either in terms of the interpersonal relationship or via the language or communication aspects. The guests were likely unaware that the *lingua franca* required adjustments by them away from their own cultural expectations. In this environment, suggestions that intercultural competency hinges on understanding and exploiting variety seemed unhelpful. Equally, models which suggest a flexibility in approach and a move away from specifying cultures will deliver the necessary competencies, and make assumptions about co-operation and accommodation which are not evidenced in these settings where not only are the participants far from equal but where there may be an overt expectation that any co-operation or accommodation is one way. There were clearly other competencies beyond language and intercultural awareness that this cohort needed to support successful communicative encounters.

Possible training solutions

Based on the above conclusions, it seems that, in order to enhance the communication skills of the staff, there would need to be a focus on developing:

- **flexibility** in approaches given that the staff could not control the encounters
- **active listening** and improved 'readership' of the audience to help circumvent many of the misunderstandings
- **awareness** of the cultural and linguistic issues raised in (a) and (b) in the 'Rationale and aims' section
- a wider cultural understanding of **participant expectations**.

It was notable that the staff concerned appeared to have the skills and ability to rapidly develop much of the above but confidence was a key factor in how they utilised these skills and abilities to best effect. In other words they have some key resources but need to develop an adaptable or agile stance that required confidence to implement.

The training solution that stood out was not conventional training in the elements of ICA so comprehensively outlined by Baker (2011a, 2011b) but rather it was the use of drama. This has been identified by Fleming (2004) in his keynote speech on Drama and Intercultural Education. He refers to how drama can highlight 'complexity in situations and reveals their cultural dimensions through a process of selection and simplification' (2004:110) and it was noted that the drama activities used in the research phase, although diagnostic, pushed the participants into thinking about alternative approaches and were highly effective during the research study. The participants responded well to the roleplay elements and, critically, gained in the confidence to trust their own instincts and abilities. The ability to 'read' their target audience emerged as crucial but this is very problematic when the audience is so diverse. Drama training, with its facility to act out and thus practise different roles and also to read unpredictable fellow participants through improvisation, positively improved confidence levels and self-assurance. This alone fed the staff's ability to be more adaptable to what they were confronted with and, coupled with their increased assurance in 'reading' guests, had an immediate impact in making communicative encounters more effective. This is partly because the roleplays allowed the staff to go beyond recognising formulae in, for example, body language poses and to read the situation more holistically and according to the specific context. This could be mapped to Baker's (2011b) notions of giving trainees a vocabulary or toolbox to draw on rather than delineating specific 'types'.

A recent study by the Education and Training Foundation (2014) identified that immediate feedback was the single most successful tool in effective learning. Drama training allows for this instant feedback to take place in an unthreatening setting. Negative feedback from guests was delivered in such a frightening context that staff tended to freeze and later dwell on the impact of the complaint rather than how it could be avoided in future or what could be done differently. Drama also allows participants to 're-enact'; in other words having thought about how to manage communication differently they then had an opportunity to practise and see the different outcomes. This was evidenced in the first roleplays in the research activity.

Another critical feature of using drama training to deliver improvements in intercultural competency is that it allows self-reflection. The research study identified that staff were very poor at this and yet it is a recognised key tool in learning (Schon 1983). It forms part of experiential learning together with the feedback element mentioned above. Fleming (2004) argues that drama 'helps people to examine their own practices and assumptions that are so often taken for granted' so this suggests it raises awareness of difference through self-reflection. This in turn can give staff the transferable tools they need without suggesting that there are formulae or fixed points for each situation they encounter.

Conclusions

Leaving aside the training needs for the hotel chain, the study which is the focus of this paper seems to support much of the work now being considered in ELF as it shifts to ICA, such as Baker's notions of training (2011a). However, it does raise some key issues which may need further exploration as we seek to tackle this elusive topic. One suggestion is the need for a more complex consideration of power roles and how they affect intercultural communication and competence training. This would include perhaps more detailed studies of what the other participant is bringing – or not – to the encounter especially when they are in the power position. There is also perhaps a need to untangle differing approaches of non-native and native speakers in English, how far this is bound up with identity (cultural or otherwise) and their expectations of ELF. There then remains the issue of how to support improvements in intercultural competence, for example, by incorporating drama as a more effective training tool rather than solely focusing on communication skills.

References

Baker, W (2011a) Intercultural awareness: Modelling an understanding of cultures in intercultural communication through English as a lingua franca, *Language and Intercultural Communication*, 11 (3), 197–214.

Baker, W (2011b) From cultural awareness to intercultural awareness: Culture in ELT, *ELT Journal* 66 (1), 62–70.

Brown, P and Levinson, S C (1987) *Politeness: Some Universals in Language Usage*, Cambridge: Cambridge University Press.

Canagarajah, S A (2006) Changing communicative needs, revised assessment objectives: Testing English as an international language. *Language Assessment Quarterly* 3 (3), 229–242.

Cresswell, J W and Plano-Clark, V P (2011) *Designing and Conducting Mixed Methods Research*, Thousand Oaks: Sage.

Education and Training Foundation (2014) *Strategic Consultation on Technology in Teaching and Learning*, available online: www.coralesce.com/wp-content/uploads/2014/06/StrategicConsultationOnTechnologyInTeachingAnd LearningReport.pdf

Ferguson, G (2009) Issues in researching English as a lingua franca: A conceptual enquiry, *International Journal of Applied Linguistics* 19 (2), 117–135.

Firth, A (1990) 'Lingua franca' negotiations: Towards an interactional approach, *World Englishes* 9 (3), 269–280.

Firth, A (1996) The discursive accomplishment of normality: On 'lingua franca' English and conversation analysis, *Journal of Pragmatics* 26, 237–259.

Fleming, M (2004) Drama and intercultural education, *gfl-journal* 1, 110–123.

Giles, H and Smith, P (1979) Accommodation Theory: Optimal levels of convergence, in Giles, H and St. Clair, R N (Eds) *Language and Social Psychology*, Baltimore: Basil Blackwell, 45–65.

Grice, H P (1975) Logic and conversation, in Cole, P and Morgan, J (Eds) *Syntax and Semantics volume 3*, New York: Academic Press, 22–40.

House, J (1999) Misunderstanding in intercultural communication: Interactions in English as a lingua franca and the myth of mutual intelligibility, in Gnutzmann, C (Ed) *Teaching and Learning English as a Global Language*, Tuebingen: Stauffenburg, 73–89.

House, J (2003) English as a lingua franca: A threat to multilingualism? *Journal of Sociolinguistics* 7 (4), 556–578.

Mauranen, A (2006) Signalling and preventing misunderstanding in English as lingua franca communication, *International Journal of the Sociology of Language* 177, 123–150.

Meierkord, C (1998) Lingua franca English: Characteristics of successful non- native–non-native speaker discourse, *Erfurt Electronic Studies in English*, available online: webdoc.sub.gwdg.de/edoc/ia/eese/eese.html

Pan, Y, Scollon, S W and Scollon, R (2002) *Professional Communication in International Settings*, Oxford: Wiley-Blackwell.

Rogerson-Revell, P (2010) Can you spell that for us non-native speakers?: Accommodation strategies in international business meetings, *Journal of Business Communication* 47 (2), 432–454.

Schon, D (1983) *The Reflective Practitioner: How Professionals Think in Action*, New York: Basic Books.

Scollon, R, Scollon, S W and Jones, R H (2012) *Intercultural Communication: A Discourse Approach*, Oxford: Wiley-Blackwell.

Seidlhofer, B (2004) Research perspectives on teaching English as a lingua franca, *Annual Review of Applied Linguistics* 24, 209–239.

Seidlhofer, B (2009a) Orientations in ELF research: Form and function, in Mauranen, A and Ranta, E (Eds) *English as a Lingua Franca: Studies and Findings*, Cambridge: Cambridge University Press, 37–59.

Seidlhofer, B (2009b) Accommodation and the idiom principle in English as a lingua franca, *Intercultural Pragmatics* 6 (2), 195–215.

Seidlhofer, B (2011) *Understanding English as a Lingua Franca*, Oxford: Oxford University Press.

Selinker, L (1972) *Rediscovering Interlanguage*, London: Longman.

Watterson, M (2008) Repair of non-understanding in English in international communication, *World Englishes* 27 (3/4), 378–406.

Wenger, E (1998) *Communities of Practice: Learning, Meaning and Identity*, Cambridge: Cambridge University Press.

3 Task dependent translanguaging performance: An empirical study in a testing context

Maria Stathopoulou

National and Kapodistrian University of Athens

Abstract

This work is concerned with the notion of cross-language mediation, which emerged onto the language teaching scene through its inclusion in the Common European Framework of Reference for Languages (CEFR) (Council of Europe 2001) and was introduced in the Greek national foreign language exams, known as KPG, in 2003. This paper discusses results of a large-scale project (Stathopoulou 2013a), the aim of which was to investigate what counts as successful mediation. Understanding that interlingual mediation is a translanguaging and social activity in which any user of two or more languages may become involved (Dendrinos 2006), mediation is investigated with a view to discovering what *written* mediation practices entail and what types of mediation strategies ultimately lead to the achievement of a given communicative purpose. The present paper addresses a specific aspect of the project, that is the extent to which task requirements play a role in mediation strategy use. The results derived from the analysis of candidates' scripts as a result of written mediation have confirmed the inextricable link between mediation task demands and outcome. The paper not only presents the results of such an investigation but it also discusses its implications, especially for the construction of mediation-specific Can Do statements (currently absent from the CEFR), which will consider not only performance but also the task which will trigger performance.

Introduction

This paper deals with the notion of interlingual mediation, a communicative undertaking which entails purposeful selection of information by the mediator from a source text in one language and relaying this information into another language with the intention of bridging the communication gap(s) between interlocutors. Being concerned with the purposeful relaying of information from one language to another, mediation is considered herein to be a translanguaging practice (Stathopoulou 2015), a view which is in accordance with that of García, Makar, Starcevic, and Terry (2011), who define translanguaging as an act of accessing different linguistic features or various modes of what are described as autonomous languages in order to maximise communicative potential (García 2009a, 2009b). Translanguaging, which is also referred to in the literature as 'transcultural repositioning' (Richardson-Bruna 2007:235), is a term coined by Williams (1996) and refers to the alternation of languages (Baker 2001a, 2001b, García 2009a). It has been defined by Baker (2001a:292) as the 'concurrent use of two languages, which may involve random switching to a more justifiable purposeful use of each language, varying the language of input and output in a lesson'.

The notion of mediation in foreign language didactics became widely known with its inclusion in the Common European Framework of Reference for Languages (CEFR; Council of Europe 2001) which considers mediation activity as an important aspect of someone's language ability (along with reception, production and interaction). However, probably because of lack of research in the field, no illustrative descriptors for the mediatory use of language are available therein. In fact, while the CEFR specifies what users of a given language should be able to do with the language at the different levels of competence as regards reading and listening comprehension, written and spoken production/interaction, it does not specify what they should be able to do with the language when mediating.

Given the need for further investigation as to what ensures the success of interlinguistic mediation, a large-scale research project (Stathopoulou 2013a) was undertaken in order to shed light on aspects of this uncharted area. This paper presents part of the results derived from this project (and extensively discussed in Stathopoulou 2015), which has allowed us to understand the mechanisms of mediation as communicative practice in a testing context (Stathopoulou 2013a). The research as a whole has drawn data from the Greek national foreign language exams, known as KPG (acronym standing for Kratiko Pistopiitiko Glossomathias). Specifically, the study has used data from the KPG Task Repository and the KPG English Corpus, both of which have been compiled with information (tasks and scripts respectively) from the particular examination battery (for further information, see the Research Centre for Language Teaching, Testing and Assessment (RCeL) website (rcel.enl.uoa.gr), University of Athens which has responsibility for developing the KPG exams in English). Note that the KPG is to my knowledge the only (foreign language) proficiency testing system in Europe which assesses mediation performance (Dendrinos 2006, 2009, 2014) through both oral and written mediation activities which ask test takers to relay information from a Greek text in order to produce another in the target language. The focus of the study is on written mediation in English, produced by test takers on the basis of messages written in Greek.

The research project has ultimately identified successful mediation strategies in scripts of different proficiency levels from different KPG writing test papers over a period of six years and has led to the development of a model (the so-called Inventory of Written Mediation Strategies (IWMS)) (Stathopoulou 2013a; for a thorough discussion of the Inventory see also Stathopoulou 2015) which focuses on the mediatory use of language, and in what cases it is successful. The success of the mediation outcome is mainly linked to the use of appropriate language following the target generic conventions, the extraction of (task-specific) relevant information and to the effective use of mediation strategies. The particular Inventory can be used in the future for the construction of levelled mediation strategy descriptors, thus complementing the CEFR and other similar documents (Stathopoulou 2012, 2013b, 2014a). These will in turn make reliable assessment of the mediation competence possible. They may also contribute to the development of curricula, based on common objectives and to consistent development of courses, syllabuses and test materials.

This paper focuses on a very specific aspect of the research project which is related to the quantitative analysis of scripts in response to written mediation tasks with the ultimate aim to explore which strategies are linked to what types of tasks, thus foregrounding the importance of task parameters in determining performance in general (Bachman 1990, Bae and Bachman 2010, Foster and Skehan 1996, Iwashita, McNamara and Elder 2001, Koda 1993, Li 2000, Robinson 2001, Skehan 1996, 1998, 2001, Skehan and Foster 1997, Way, Joiner and Seaman 2000) and mediation strategy use, in particular at different levels of proficiency.

Cross-language mediation in foreign language education: Theoretical issues

In recent years, population mobility and the mingling of people with different languages and cultures has led to an inevitable cross-cultural contact between diverse groups from different backgrounds. In this new context, it is likely for language users to assume the role of a mediator, i.e. in a situation in which they have to serve as a linguistic and cultural bridge between individuals who do not share the same language and to relay messages from one language to the other. Having, thus, the ability to translanguage (i.e. flexibly move between languages) and mediate by providing linguistic assistance to a person (or persons) who cannot understand the original message in a given language is considered to be nowadays an important aspect of communication that deserves particular attention in any discussion for appropriate foreign language pedagogies. In the two sections that follow, the notion of mediation is further discussed and it is briefly explained how the term appeared in the field of foreign language teaching and testing.

The European Commission's Civil Society Platform to promote multilingualism (Action Plan for 2014–20), set up in 2009 to help achieve the objectives of Communication 2008/566 on 'Multilingualism: An asset for Europe and a shared commitment', has recognised the need to support 'successful programmes of bilingual and/or multilingual education and use them to build language education pedagogies for the development of plurilingual competences' (European Commission 2011). Actually, the crucial target clearly stated therein is to facilitate a shift from monolingualism to multilingualism by turning monolingual European schools into places where a single language of instruction no longer dominates, but where several languages are used as resources. The goal has been aptly described by Dendrinos (2012), as a non-separatist approach to the use of language(s), codes and semiotic modes, an approach based on a view of languages and cultures not as compartmentalised but as meaning-making, semiotic systems, interrelated to one another. Drawing, thus, upon the semiotic resources they have from a variety of contexts, languages and cultures, it is necessary for people to learn to use translanguaging strategies and resort to interlinguistic mediation, so as to communicate effectively in bi- or multilingual contexts, a view thoroughly discussed by Stathopoulou (2015).

The CEFR has constituted a step in the direction of promoting multilingualism and moving away from monolingual paradigms, by stressing the necessity for language programmes to enhance the development of language users' interlingual strategies and plurilingual competences (Coste, Moore and Zarate 2009). In fact, mediation has been legitimised through its inclusion therein, which demonstrates that there has been a recent development in relation to the exploitation of L1 in the EFL context. According to the CEFR 'the written and/or oral activities of mediation make communication possible between persons who are unable . . . to communicate with each other directly. Translation or interpretation, a paraphrase, summary or record, provides for a third party a (re)formulation of a source text to which this third party does not have direct access' (Council of Europe 2001:14). While the CEFR seems to consider mediation as being synonymous with translation, in this study, the two activities are sharply distinguished. The translator's role as a rewriter is contrasted with the mediator's role as a maker/creator of new meanings. While translation requires unconditional respect of the content of the source text, and the aim of the translator is to render every single message of the original text, mediation entails selection of source information *relevant* to the task at hand and production of a target text which is appropriate for the context of the situation and which respects the constraints that the target environment imposes (Dendrinos and Stathopoulou 2011). Dendrinos (2014:152) also characteristically says that mediators, unlike translators and interpreters, have the prerogative of producing their own text; a text which may not be equivalent in terms of form, while it may be loosely connected in terms of the meanings articulated. Mediators bring into the end product their own 'voice', often expressing their take on an issue.

Following the recommendations of the European Commission and the Council of Europe towards a shift from monolingualism to multilingualism, the KPG examination suite has incorporated interlinguistic mediation tasks as an exam component thus promoting multilingualism and favouring the parallel use of languages. The section below briefly describes the nature, the characteristics and the requirements of written mediation tasks in the KPG exams and defines mediation strategies, which are necessary for the successful execution of such tasks.

From theory to practice: Mediation tasks and strategies

Types and characteristics of mediation tasks

In order to mediate in writing, KPG candidates are expected to assume a specific role and address specific readers conveying specific meanings through a particular type of text (Dendrinos and Mitsikopoulou in press) (see Appendix A for examples of mediation tasks). Test takers are required to *comprehend* a (Greek) text at a higher level than they would from simply reading it and then *produce* their own in English on the basis of information contained in the source text, conforming to different social rules. Source texts serve as 'sources of information' (Dendrinos 2014) and 'reading comprehension serves the following purposes: to access topic knowledge, to understand the task' (Hayes 1996:20), to help the mediators establish new meanings from the reading that they later transfer on paper.

As shown in Appendix A, each written mediation task consists of a) the task instructions which are always written in English and b) the source text(s) written in Greek from which the test takers selectively extract information in order to respond to the task. Task instructions, which are specific and straightforward, always include information about: *what* is to be written by the test taker (type of text, e.g. an email, an article, a leaflet), to *whom* (addressee, e.g. writing to the newspaper editor or to a friend), and *for what purpose* (e.g. to advise, to urge, to inform etc.). The content and linguistic choices of candidates are thus guided by the aforementioned contextual factors, which demand their language awareness, their linguistic and intercultural competence, as well as the literacies they have developed in both languages.

The development of the mediation tasks is always guided by a number of specifications for each proficiency level (find KPG exam specifications at: rcel.enl.uoa.gr/kpg) which are summarised below:

a) The B1 level mediation task requires candidates to assemble pieces of information from one or more short Greek texts from a popular magazine, a travel leaflet, etc., and to produce one single short text in English. The Greek texts, likely to include factual information, contain much more information than what the task demands, so candidates have to select only what is relevant. The production requirement here is informal discourse, and personal, private communication (see, for instance, Appendix A, Tasks 2008B1, 2009B1, 2010B1).

b) The B2 level mediation task requires test takers to extract task-specific information from an authentic Greek text, the ideas in which are somewhat more complex than at B1 level, and to use it in a text in English. Here public discourse is usually required and less flexibility is allowed by the task as to the amount of information to be relayed from the source text (see, for instance, Appendix A, Tasks 2008B2, 2009B2, 2010B2).

c) The C1 level mediation task requires that the candidate be able to produce an even longer text in English than at B2 level on the basis of a rather complex and sophisticated text in Greek. The target text is often of the same genre and register as the source text (see, for instance, Appendix A, Tasks 2008C1, 2009C1, 2010C1).

Test takers' performance is assessed on the basis of how well they have responded to the task at hand, that is, whether they have produced the appropriate text type with the appropriate register and style, whether the text organisation and the language used is conducive to the context of situation and finally whether they have effectively relayed pertinent source information from the Greek text. An example of non-effective relaying is word-for-word translation of the whole (or parts of the) text which usually leads to erroneous lexicogrammatical formations.

According to Stathopoulou (2013a, 2014b, 2015), depending on their mediatory requirements, mediation tasks (either written or oral), are classified into: a) those requiring the production of a *summary* which reflects the gist (central ideas) of the source text (see, for example, Appendix A, 2008B2) and, b) those which require the selection or *picking up of information* found in different parts of the source text. This information is then regrouped into the target text depending on the communicative goal set by the task (see, for example, Appendix A, 2009B2). Tasks can also be described in terms of their linguistic requirements (i.e. type of text to be produced, topic, communicative purpose, role relations between addressor and addressee), which along with their mediatory requirements ultimately determine the final outcome (Stathopoulou 2013c, 2014b).

Types of mediation strategies

Different types of *tasks* are linked to different mediation *strategies*, an issue this paper addresses. Mediation strategies are defined as those techniques used by test takers and manifested through their different linguistic choices at different levels (i.e. discourse, text or sentence level), and ultimately lead to the successful execution of the mediation task. Research distinguishes two general types of strategies (Stathopoulou 2013a, 2015): Type A and Type B mediation strategies, as Table 1 indicates. Note that these seven strategies are further subdivided, all forming the *Inventory of Written Mediation Strategies* which includes 53 strategies in total.

Type A strategies require selecting and integrating the relevant information either by means of summarisation of information or of blending with extra-textual information, of combining information found in different parts of the text, of restructuring (or re-positioning) of source content. By contrast, Type B mediation strategies (i.e. paraphrasing, condensing and expanding) refer to textual borrowing and syntactic transformations. Note that Type A and Type B strategies may occur simultaneously, meaning that they are not mutually exclusive. In other words, a unit of text may be assigned to more than one category only when the two categories (strategies) are of different types. That means that we may find instances of language use in which reorganisation (a Type A strategy) and paraphrasing (a Type B strategy) may occur simultaneously. Similarly, creative blending or combining (both Type A strategies) may be combined with paraphrasing (a Type B strategy). This distinction between Type A and Type B strategies has been empirically derived by looking at a sizeable corpus of texts as a result of mediation and has been creatively exploited for the statistical analysis of the data, as shown in the sections that follow.

Table 1 Mediation strategies as defined by Stathopoulou (2013a, 2015)

Mediation strategies
TYPE A
01. Creative blending between extracted and extra-textual information
02. Combining information
03. Summarising
04. Reorganising extracted information
TYPE B
05. Condensing (at sentence level) by combining two (or more) short sentences into one (sentence fusion)
06. Expanding
07. Paraphrasing

Aim of the study

The examination of mediation performance through the textual analysis of mediation scripts has been attempted to enable an understanding of how task parameters (i.e. the linguistic and the mediatory features of the tasks) affect mediation strategy use. The specific question this study addresses is: which strategies are linked to which tasks?

This paper attempts to show the inextricable link between mediation tasks and mediation performance by drawing upon empirical evidence. The ultimate goal of such an investigation can be the development of illustrative descriptors which would be based on both task and performance analysis thus enabling syllabus designers and test developers to decide through what types of written tasks mediation competence can be developed and measured at each proficiency level. As a matter of fact, any effort undertaken up to now towards the development of mediation-specific descriptors, i.e. the *Profile Deutsch* (Glaboniat, Müller, Rusch, Schmitz and Wertenschlag 2005), and including Can Do objectives at different proficiency levels for reception, production, interaction and mediation, has not taken into consideration the tasks and their demands, thus providing descriptors which are not articulated as task-dependent communicative production. Of course, it is important to note that this particular paper does not focus on the differentiated mediation strategy use across *proficiency levels*, which, in combination with the results presented herein, could be exploited for the construction of Can Do statements relevant to mediation. The degree to which proficiency level affects mediation strategy use has been investigated by Stathopoulou (2013a, 2015) but as already mentioned, is not within the scope of this paper.

Method and corpus

For the purposes of this research, a corpus of 653 mediation scripts produced by KPG candidates sitting for the B1, B2 and C1 level exams over a period of six years (from April 2005 to May 2010) was analysed with a view to identifying the successful written mediation strategies found therein (see Table 2 for the number of words included in the corpus).

Given that no prior model of mediation strategies was available, a necessary step was the development of such a model through a bottom-up

Table 2 Number of words included in the corpus

	B1	B2	C1	Number of words
Phase 1		7,950		7,950
Phase 2	9,000	18,000	18,000	45,000
Total	9,000	25,950	18,000	52,950

approach. The construction of the model was conducted in two phases and it involved multiple stages. The analysis of the data commenced with a sample of 53 fully satisfactory B2 level scripts produced on the basis of four different test tasks. What this pilot stage had to offer was the gradual development of a frame of orientation or a coding scheme which would later be used as a tool for the identification of the mediation strategies in a larger corpus. During the second phase, scripts produced by candidates of different proficiency levels (B1, B2 and C1 level) and competences (fully and moderately satisfactory scripts) were examined with a view to identifying the written mediation strategies found therein. The initially constructed scheme (pilot Phase 1) took its final form and was validated (Phase 2) by looking at a larger number of scripts, as Table 2 also indicates. Each time a new set of scripts from a different examination period was investigated, the scheme was reconsidered, reevaluated, and revised. The revision entailed: adding new categories, leaving out others, merging those which seemed to overlap or rephrasing.

As becomes evident, the model arose inductively and directly from the careful reading and analysis of the raw data with the intent to find out the recurring patterns or dominant and significant themes inherent in raw data (Thomas 2006:239). It has been the final outcome of a long-lasting process involving several steps as summarised above (see Stathopoulou 2013a for a detailed description). Given the interpretative nature of the analysis of data especially at the beginning of the process, a serious attempt was made to ensure the validity and trustworthiness of the model. The validation of the coding scheme, first of all, has been achieved through multiple readings and analyses of the data and interpretations have emerged through careful examination of the meta-data derived from this analysis. The selective sampling conducted at the second phase of the project provided an opportunity not only to enrich the initial category set but also to validate it (Goldkuhl and Cronholm 2010:190) improving my understanding of the characteristics of the mediation product. Actually, for the purposes of the research multiple samples were employed at different stages, providing evidence for the occurrence of the strategies. An attempt was also made to provide justifiable interpretations by means of *transferability* which refers to the use of the coding scheme as a guide for coding a new sample every time the coding of a previous sample had been completed and any relevant reformulations of the scheme had subsequently been done (i.e. continuing revision and refinement of the category system).

The statistical processing of the (meta) data was conducted after strategy location (or identification) in the corpus, and for the purposes of this particular study, it focuses on the variable of task. In fact, the sample of scripts statistically analysed consisted of a total of 540 B1, B2 and C1 level scripts derived from the May 2008, 2009 and 2010 test papers (60 for each task with the number of tasks being nine) (see Appendix A for the tasks).

For the purpose of quantification, tagged instances of the textual data (i.e. stretches of texts coded for particular strategies) were automatically counted by the NVivo 8 software, which was the tool used for strategy location in the corpus. Statistical and data analyses, which involved the investigation of the most and least popular strategies in the corpus, were performed using the Statistical Package for the Social Sciences (SPSS), version 20.0 for Windows. Descriptive statistics were used to compare the incidences of strategies in different scripts and subcorpora. Testing the statistical significance of differences between sets of scores was another crucial part of the statistical processing of the data. Pearson's chi-square test (Fisher 1922, Pearson 1900) was used in order to check whether there is an association between the two categorical variables, i.e. task type in relation to strategy type.

Presentation and discussion of results

Before presenting specific results related to the variable of task (see Stathopoulou 2015, for a thorough discussion for the results linked to additional variables, such as proficiency level or writer's competence), Table 3 gives an overall picture of the types of strategies detected in the corpus. In the vast majority of scripts (72.8%), both Type A and Type B strategies have been detected. Furthermore, Type A strategies appear alone (i.e. without being used together with Type B ones), in only a small number of scripts (5.9%).

Shifting attention to the task variable, the results seem to support the interrelationship between mediation task demands and linguistic outcome and give insights into what strategies are linked to what sort of tasks. One major finding, as shown in Table 4, is that Type A strategies (without being combined with Type B) are mainly found in scripts having resulted from picking-up-information tasks. This means that this sort of task does not seem to trigger the strategies of paraphrasing, expanding and condensing. The combination of Type A and Type B strategies used together is more prominent in scripts produced in response to tasks requiring summarising (80.8% as opposed to 72.3%). The fact that we note more of a certain type in one group of scripts leads us to conclude that the particular requirements

Table 3 Type A and Type B mediation strategies in the corpus: Number of scripts

Strategies (sample)		Count	% of scripts
Types	Type A	32	5.9
	Type B	104	19.3
	Type A & B	393	72.8
	None	11	2.0

Table 4 Type A and Type B mediation strategies: The task type variable

		Task type			
		Picking-up information		Summarising	
		Count	Column N %	Count	Column N %
Strategy type	Only A	14	5.9	1	0.4
	Only B	52	21.8	45	18.8
	Both A & B	172	72.3	193	80.8

Pearson Tests	Chi-Square	SumPick
Strategy type	Chi-square	12.978
	df	2
	Sig.	0.002*

of certain task types seem to play a determining role in the use of particular mediation strategies.

Shifting emphasis to specific tasks of specific exam periods, Figures 1 and 2 demonstrate what tasks with what characteristics are linked to which strategies.

In relation to *creative blending between extracted and extra-textual information*, as is evident in Figure 1 below (see also Appendix B), there is a group of tasks (with certain characteristics) which seem to trigger to a greater or lesser degree the particular strategy (i.e. 2008C1, 2010C1, 2009B2 and 2009C1), and another set of tasks which are related to a low number of scripts exhibiting creative blending (i.e. 2009B1, 2010B1, 2008B1 and 2010B2). Specifically, what seems to lead to the use of this particular strategy is the extent to which the task allows for the insertion of extra-textual (non-stated) information. This has also been confirmed by the qualitative analysis of scripts not actually presented in this paper but discussed by Stathopoulou (2013a, 2015). One such task is from the May 2010 examination period (2010C1) which asks candidates not only to use information from the source text but also to add their own by relating their experience about quitting smoking. Similarly, the mediation task which requires candidates to convince their friend to participate in a summer project on an island (2009B2), even though not explicitly stated, allows for the introduction of information mainly because of its function which is to argue (and argumentation is very likely to be based on extra-textual information as well). The mediation task (2008C1) which requires test takers to produce a letter making suggestions about what can be done to save the planet also provides opportunities for inserting new information even though this is not explicitly stated in the task rubric. What has also been observed and clearly shown in Appendix B

Figure 1 Type A mediation strategies in relation to tasks: Number of scripts

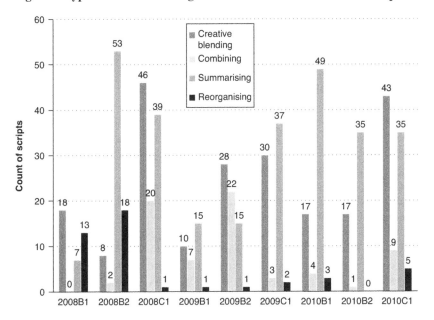

is that a set of tasks (e.g. 2009B2, and 2009C1), which include bulleted texts (as opposed to continuous ones), are linked to high use of the creative blending as they seem to allow for the insertion of information for elaboration or exemplification purposes. By contrast, those tasks which are related to low number of scripts including creative blending:

• are not linked to sophisticated or demanding functions (e.g. candidates are only asked to give tips or explain)
• include short and straightforward source texts (e.g. 2008B1 and 2009B1) (as they target at low levels), or
• include numerical information (e.g. 2010B2).

At this point, it is useful to make a comment relevant to the issue of the insertion of extra-textual information on the part of the test taker and of how this insertion is treated by the rater. What is actually marked is the extent to which the candidates have used information from the source text, whether what they have relayed is *pertinent* to the task information and how effectively they have transferred it into the target environment. If the candidate only includes extra-textual and irrelevant-to-the-task information they are not given a mark for the content criterion because of their inability to selectively extract information from the source text.

As for the *combining* of extracted information, its occurrence seems to be mainly linked to the source text organisation and structure. The source texts of the tasks associated with the highest number of scripts including this particular strategy (e.g. 2008C1, 2009B2), contain information which, though similar, is dispersed in different parts. Naturally, in the successful mediation scripts, similar source information is creatively combined contributing in this way to the overall organisation of the texts. By contrast, the occurrence of the particular strategy is rather limited in scripts produced in response to tasks which contain bulleted source texts (e.g. 2008B1 and 2009C1) or numerical information (e.g. 2010B2). The task requiring the relaying of information from a text presenting the plot of several films in a linear order (e.g. 2008B2), does not seem to trigger combining of extracted information either, due to the way source information is presented (i.e. linearly) and is required to be presented (again linearly) in the target text. In fact, this mediation task mainly triggers the strategy of summarising. Overall, the high percentage of scripts which do not include combining lead us to draw the conclusion that it is not a popular strategy (see Appendix B).

As regards the strategy of *summarising*, it seems that the particular strategy is also linked to source text organisation and the way content is presented therein. Specifically, careful examination of the results shows that continuous source texts (e.g. 2008B2, 2010B1, 2008C1) as opposed to bulleted ones (2008B1, 2009B1 and 2009B2), elicit the use of this particular strategy. It seems that when information is already provided in a condensed form as is the case with bulleted texts, there is no need for summarising. Moreover, in the two C1 level tasks described above (2009C1 and 2010C1), the source texts included information which had to be summarised by the candidates in order to respond to the task and therefore the use of summarising was high. Generally, as both Figure 1 and Appendix B show, the particular strategy is among the most popular ones in the corpus sampled.

The majority of scripts making use of *reorganising* have resulted from the B2 level task (2008B2) requiring the production of a text for a guide recommending films for children and teenagers (see Appendix A). Source text is divided into four parts, the first two corresponding to the two films for teenagers while the other two referring to films for children. The fact that the task rubric clearly states that candidates have to recommend films for children and for teenagers (while the source text starts with the films for the teenagers) may account for the high incidence of reorganising in the scripts for this particular task. Generally, the strategy of reorganising does not seem to be popular in the corpus sampled. Interestingly enough, there is no reorganising at all in the scripts produced as a result of the 2010B2 task which requires transferring of numerical information into verbal.

Moving to Type B strategies and focusing on the degree of their popularity in relation to task characteristics and demands (see Figure 2), the most striking result is associated with the strategy of *paraphrasing* (i.e. syntactic, phrasal and word-level paraphrasing) which seems to occur in almost all scripts under investigation. The lowest number of scripts including paraphrasing (i.e. 34 out of 60) have been produced as a result of the task (2010B2) which asks candidates to present findings of a survey thus transferring numerical information into verbal, a finding which also reinforces the assumption that task characteristics heavily influence mediation strategy use. Needless to say, numerical information depicted in a figure as was the case in this task, cannot be paraphrased.

Figure 2 also shows that the C1 level task asking candidates to write a letter to the readers of a magazine sharing their experience of trying to quit smoking with others (2010C1), seems to trigger the highest use of *expanding* and of *combining two sentences into one* (or condensing). Both strategies are not popular in the scripts of the May 2010 B2 level task which, as already mentioned, requires the relaying of numerical information into verbal.

The findings in relation to the degree to which task types affect mediation strategy use are summarised as follows:

- Type A strategies (without being combined with Type B) are mainly found in scripts produced in response to *picking-up-information* tasks. This sort of task does not seem to trigger strategies of textual borrowing such as paraphrasing, expanding and condensing. Note that while Type A strategies, which are described as information-based strategies, deal with how information is handled by the mediator when transferring it from one text to another, Type B strategies focus more on the language aspects of the relaying process, i.e. on the level of lexis, grammar and syntax.

Figure 2 Type B mediation strategies in relation to tasks: Number of scripts

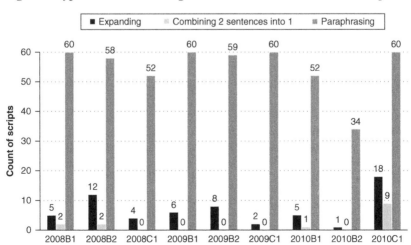

- The combination of Type A and Type B strategies appears more frequently in scripts requiring *summarising*. This sort of task seems to trigger the use of a variety of strategies thus making them more demanding in terms of their mediatory requirements.

A general conclusion, drawn in relation to task features, concerns the crucial role of the source text from which information has been transferred on the basis of task rubrics. For instance, as already shown above, the occurrence of combining of extracted information and reorganising seems to be linked to the structure and organisation of the source text since these strategies were most associated with texts in which the targeted information was spread throughout rather than found in one location. Additionally, continuous Greek texts (as opposed to bulleted ones) seem to favour the strategy of summarising. Finally, despite the fact that paraphrasing is the most popular strategy, it is not very much detected in scripts as a result of tasks requiring the relaying of numerical information.

Based on the evidence presented in this paper, it is also worth raising the issue of *source text regulation*, a term which had initially been used by Stathopoulou (2009) but is also relevant here. What the data has actually shown is that the source text inevitably regulates the target text by exerting control over it. Put differently, because of the dialogic relationship between the source and the target text (Stathopoulou 2015), the structure, the content and the organisation of the former unavoidably affects the content of the latter and the use of mediation strategies. Note, however, that the degree of regulation is dependent upon a variety of factors, such as the mediators' proficiency level or competence, which are not discussed herein but which are equally important.

Apart from the role of the source text, task instructions also seem to affect the use of specific strategies. For instance, it has been found that what seems to trigger the use of the strategy of creative blending between new and old information is the opportunities the task provides for the introduction of extra-textual information. Certain tasks, in other words, may explicitly or implicitly urge the candidates to bring their own experiences and ideas into their texts without solely exploiting or focusing on source information.

Drawing its data from an examination system aligned to the descriptors provided by the CEFR, this study has provided evidence which confirms that mediation performance is task specific, thus stressing the prominent role of tasks in mediation strategy use. The nature and characteristics of tasks seem to determine the type and amount of source information transferred in the target text, the language used in the target environment and of course the type of mediation strategies employed. Interestingly, this finding coincides with relevant findings of studies in writing, which have focused on the impact of tasks on performance (Bae and Bachman 2010, Koda 1993, Li 2000, Skehan 2001).

Conclusions and implications for future research

This study has generally shown that being able to mediate implies (among other things) dealing with task requirements in such a way that the outcome will include – apart from the appropriate language – those mediation strategies conducive to the task at hand, consequently contributing to the success of mediation. Assuming that mediation performance is task specific in the sense that task characteristics unavoidably affect task output and consequently mediation strategy use, this study has attempted to explore which strategies are linked to what types of tasks, while the popularity of certain mediation strategies found in texts in response to different mediation tasks has been thoroughly discussed.

By exploiting not only the findings presented herein but also the results derived from the wider research project (Stathopoulou 2013a, 2015) which discovered what effective mediation entails at different proficiency levels, future research can focus on the development of objective criteria so as to describe levelled language proficiency, which will in turn facilitate the development of standards in language teaching and testing (Alderson, Figueras, Kuijper, Nold, Takala and Tardieu 2004, Green 2010, Krumm 2007). The present paper, which deals with the aspect of task requirements, implicitly addresses the issue of setting standards for the development of learners' ability to function as mediators by taking into account empirical data. The inextricable link between task and mediation strategy use points to the necessity for the development of levelled mediation-specific descriptors, which would take into account *both* task requirements and actual *performance* (rather than solely focusing on performance as is the case of the CEFR or Profile Deutsch). I have elsewhere suggested (Stathopoulou 2013b) that the resulting descriptors should specify: a) what users of specific levels should be able to do, b) through what language to do it and c) in which types of mediation tasks.

Generally, the construction of mediation-specific Can Do statements is a complex endeavour which requires further investigation in the field. It is not only the *what* (and *why*) that matters, however, but also the *how* of the mediation, i.e. through what language mediators relay information from one language to another. Therefore, systematic research into mediation performance when doing certain tasks and employing different strategies across proficiency levels with a view to discovering how *language* is used would actually provide an interesting supplement to the present work. In fact, a lexicogrammatical description of mediators' language production would substantially add to research in linguistic descriptions of the foreign language learner competences (one of which is mediation). The linguistic documentation of the mediation competence across the CEFR levels by systematically analysing the language found in texts produced by mediators of different levels would contribute to the creation of language-specific descriptors relevant to mediation, which 'will add grammatical and lexical details of the target language to CEFR's functional characterisation of the different levels' (Hawkins and Filipović 2012:5). Besides, 'while the CEFR has provided detailed descriptors of language proficiency, it is lacking in linguistic content' (Trim 2010:10), not specifying the lexicogrammatical characteristics of learner language at each proficiency level in various communicative contexts. The resulting descriptors could contribute to the creation of standardised measures and clear benchmarks for reliable assessment of mediation competence and could generally inform mediation task design for teaching and testing purposes in the future. Additionally, such descriptors could generally constitute the basis for the development of multilingual curricula, language exam specifications, and foreign language materials; in Greece especially, they would inform the specifications of the KPG exams and the levelled descriptors for the mediatory use of language included in the newly developed Greek Integrated Foreign Languages Curriculum (IFLC) (see Dendrinos and Stathopoulou 2011/2014).

Acknowledgements

I am deeply grateful to Professor Bessie Dendrinos, for providing me with invaluable help at every step of the research project. I would like to acknowledge the academic and technical support of the Research Centre for Language Teaching, Testing and Assessment (RCeL), University of Athens, where I have been working as a research fellow for seven years. The data provided by the RCeL was a critical part of this study.

References

Alderson, J C, Figueras, N, Kuijper, H, Nold, G, Takala, S, and Tardieu, C (2004) *The Development of Specifications for Item Development and Classification within The Common European Framework of Reference for Languages: Learning, Teaching, Assessment*, available online: eprints.lancs.ac.uk/44/1/final_report.pdf

Bachman, L (1990) *Fundamental Considerations in Language Testing*, Oxford: Oxford University Press.

Bae, J and Bachman, L F (2010) An investigation of four writing traits and two tasks across two languages, *Language Testing* 27, 213–234.

Baker, C (2001a) *Foundations of Bilingual Education and Bilingualism* (3rd edition), Clevedon: Multilingual Matters.

Baker, C (2001b) Education as a site for language contact, *Annual Review of Applied Linguistics* 23, 95–112.

Coste, D, Moore, D and Zarate, G (2009) *Plurilingual and Pluricultural Competence: Studies Towards a Common European Framework of Reference for Language Learning and Teaching*, Strasbourg: Language Policy Division.

Council of Europe (2001) *Common European Framework of Reference for Languages: Learning, Teaching, Assessment*, Cambridge: Cambridge University Press.

Dendrinos, B (2006) Mediation in communication, language teaching and testing, *Journal of Applied Linguistics* 22, 9–35.

Dendrinos, B (2009) Rationale and ideology of the KPG exams, *ELT News*, available online: rcel.enl.uoa.gr/kpg/kpgcorner_sep2009.htm

Dendrinos, B (2012) Multi- and monolingualism in foreign language education in Europe, in Stickel, G and Carrier, M (Eds) *Education in Creating a Multilingual Europe*, Frankfurt: Peter Lang, 47–60.

Dendrinos, B (2014) Testing and teaching mediation, *Directions in English Language Teaching and Testing Volume 1*, available online: http://rcel.enl.uoa.gr/directions/issue1_1f.htm

Dendrinos, B and Mitsikopoulou, B (in press) *The KPG Writing Test in English: A Handbook*, Athens: RCeL Publications.

Dendrinos, B and Stathopoulou, M (2011/2014) *Η Διαμεσολάβηση ως Σημαντική Επικοινωνιακή Δραστηριότητα. Ξενόγλωσση Εκπαίδευση για την Προώθηση της Πολυγλωσσίας στην Ελλάδα Σήμερα: Προσεγγίσεις και Πρακτικές Διδασκαλίας*. Αθήνα: Παιδαγωγικό Ινστιτούτο, Υπουργείο Παιδείας, Δια Βίου Μάθησης και Θρησκευμάτων, available online: rcel.enl.uoa.gr/xenesglosses/guide_kef6.htm

European Commission (2011) *Civil Society Platform on Multilingualism Policy Recommendations for the Promotion of Multilingualism in the European Union, Brussels, 2011*, available online: ec.europa.eu/languages/information/documents/summary-civil-society_en.pdf

Fisher, R A (1922) On the interpretation of chi square from contingency tables and the calculation of P, *Journal of the Royal Statistical Society* 85, 87–94.

Foster, P and Skehan, P (1996) The influence of planning and task type on second language performance, *SSLA* 18, 299–323.

García, O (2009a) Education, multilingualism and translanguaging in the 21st century, in Mohanty, A, Panda, M, Phillipson, R and Skutnabb-Kangas, T (Eds) *Multilingual Education for Social Justice: Globalising the Local*, New Delhi: Orient Blackswan, 128–145.

García, O (2009b) *Reimagining Bilingualism in Education for the 21st Century*, paper presented at the NALDIC Conference 17, University of Reading, UK, 14 November 2009.

García, O, Makar, C, Starcevic, M and Terry, A (2011) The translanguaging of Latino kindergartners, in Rothman, J and Potowski, K (Eds) *Bilingual Youth: Spanish in English Speaking Societies*, Amsterdam: John Benjamins, 33–55.

Glaboniat, M, Müller, M, Rusch, P, Schmitz, H and Wertenschlag, L (2005) *Profile Deutsch. Lernzielbestimmungen, Kannbeschreibungen und kommunikative Mittel für die Niveaustufen A1, A2, B1, B2, C1 und C2 des "Gemeinsamen europäischen Referenzrahmens für Sprachen"*, Berlin: München.

Goldkuhl, G and Cronholm, SA (2010) Theoretical grounding to grounded theory: Toward multi-grounded theory, *International Journal of Qualitative Methods* 9 (2), 187–205.

Green, A (2010) Requirements for reference level descriptors for English, *English Language Profile* 1 (1), 1–19.

Hawkins, J and Filipović, L (2012) *Criterial Features in L2 English*, English Profile Studies volume 1, Cambridge: UCLES/Cambridge University Press.

Hayes, J R (1996) A new framework for understanding cognition and affect in writing, in Levy, C M and Ransdell, S (Eds) *The Science of Writing: Theories,*

Methods, Individual Differences and Applications, Mahwah: Lawrence Erlbaum, 1–27.

Iwashita, N, McNamara, T and Elder, C (2001) Can we predict task difficulty in an oral proficiency test? Exploring the potential of an information-processing approach to task design, *Language Learning* 51 (3), 401–436.

Koda, K (1993) Task-induced variability in FL Composition: Language-specific perspectives, *Foreign Language Annals* 26 (3), 332–346.

Krumm, H-J (2007) Profiles instead of levels: the CEFR and its (ab)uses in the context of migration, *The Modern Language Journal* 91 (iv), 667–669.

Li, Y (2000) Linguistic characteristics of ESL writing in task-based e-mail activities, *System* 28 (2), 229–245.

Pearson, K (1900) On the criterion that a given system of deviations from the probable in the case of a correlated system of variables is such that it can be reasonably supposed to have arisen from random sampling, *Philosophical Magazine* 50 (5), 157–175.

Richardson-Bruna, K (2007) Traveling tags: The informal literacies of Mexican newcomers in and out of the classroom, *Linguistics and Education* 18, 232–257.

Robinson, P (2001) Task complexity, task difficulty and task production: Exploring interactions in a componential framework, *Applied Linguistics* 22 (1), 27–57.

Skehan, P (1996) A framework for the implementation of task-based instruction, *Applied Linguistics* 17, 38–62.

Skehan, P (1998) *A Cognitive Approach to Language Learning*, Oxford: Oxford University Press.

Skehan, P (2001) Tasks and language performance, in Bygate, M, Skehan, P and Swain, M (Eds) *Researching Pedagogic Tasks: Second Language Learning, Teaching and Testing*, 167–187, Harlow: Longman.

Skehan, P and Foster, P (1997) Task type and task processing conditions as influences on foreign language performance, *Language Teaching Research* 1 (3), 185–211.

Stathopoulou, M (2012) *Mediating between languages: A way to promote multilingualism through language testing*, paper presented at the XLVI Congresso Internazionale SLI 2012 Plurilinguismo/Sintassi, Università per Stranieri di Siena, Siena, Italy, 27–29 September 2012.

Stathopoulou, M (2013a) *Task dependent interlinguistic mediation performance as translanguaging practice: The use of KPG data for an empirically based study*, unpublished PhD thesis, University of Athens.

Stathopoulou, M (2013b) Investigating mediation as translanguaging practice in a testing context: Towards the development of levelled mediation descriptors, in Colpaert, J, Simons, M, Aerts, A and Oberhofer, M (Eds) *Proceedings of the International Conference Language Testing in Europe: Time for a New Framework?* Antwerp: University of Antwerp, 209–217.

Stathopoulou, M (2013c) The linguistic characteristics of KPG written mediation tasks across levels, in Lavidas, N, Alexiou, T and Sougari A-M (Eds) *Major Trends in Theoretical and Applied Linguistics: Selected Papers from the 20th ISTAL Volume 3*, London: Versita de Gruyter, 349–366.

Stathopoulou, M (2014a) *Shuttling between languages: Defining interlinguistic mediation as translanguaging practice in the light of research results*, paper presented at LTRC 2014: The 36th Language Testing Research Colloquium Towards a Universal Framework, University of Amsterdam, 4–6 June 2014.

Stathopoulou, M (2014b) Written mediation tasks in the Greek national foreign language exams: Linguistic analysis and description, in Aguilar, J, Brudermann, C and Leclère, M (Eds) *Complexité, diversité et spécificité: Pratiques didactiques en context*, Paris: Université Sorbonne Nouvelle Paris III, 248–271.

Stathopoulou, M (2015) *Cross-Language Mediation in Foreign Language Teaching and Testing*, Bristol: Multilingual Matters.

Thomas, D R (2006) A general inductive approach for analyzing qualitative evaluation data, *American Journal of Evaluation* 27, 237–246.

Trim, J (2010) The Modern Languages Programme of the Council of Europe as a background to the English Profile Programme, *English Profile Journal* 1 (1), 1–12.

Way, D P, Joiner, E G and Seaman, M A (2000) Writing in the secondary foreign language classroom: The effects of prompts and tasks on novice learners of French, *The Modern Language Journal* 84 (3), 171–184.

Williams, C (1996) Secondary education: Teaching in the bilingual situation, in Williams, C, Lewis, G and Baker, C (Eds) *The Language Policy: Taking stock* 12 (2), 193–211.

Appendix A

TASK 2008B1

Imagine you are Toni Alexiou and that your friend Brad is under a lot of stress because of exams, so he doesn't sleep well. Use information from the text below, and write **an email message** (about 100 words), **giving him some tips to help him with his sleeping problem**. Use some of the information below, signing your message as **Toni**. Do **not** use your real name.

Για να απολαμβάνετε τον ύπνο

IMAGE
REMOVED
FOR
COPYRIGHT
REASONS

Ξέρατε ότι η αϋπνία επηρεάζει μέχρι και το 60% του πληθυσμού; Ξέρατε ότι το πρόβλημα γίνεται χρόνιο, όταν για περισσότερο από ένα μήνα δυσκολεύεστε να αποκοιμηθείτε ή να κοιμάστε για ικανοποιητικό χρονικό διάστημα; Ξέρατε ότι μεγάλο ποσοστό του πληθυσμού παίρνει χάπια για να μπορεί να κοιμάται;

Αν κι εσείς έχετε μια κάποια δυσκολία στον ύπνο, να μερικές ιδέες που μπορούν να σας βοηθήσουν:

- Η άσκηση στη διάρκεια της μέρας είναι το καλύτερο «υπνωτικό χάπι»: η ιδανική άσκηση, σύμφωνα με τους ειδικούς, είναι αυτή που γίνεται 4-6 ώρες πριν από τον ύπνο.

- Να διατηρείτε μια σταθερή θερμοκρασία στο υπνοδωμάτιό σας, ούτε πολλή ζέστη ούτε πολύ κρύο.

- Να προσπαθείτε να κοιμάστε σχεδόν την ίδια ώρα κάθε βράδυ. Οι ειδικοί συμφωνούν ότι το μυστικό για έναν μη διαταραγμένο ύπνο είναι να τηρούμε ένα κάποιο σταθερό πρόγραμμα.

- Πίνετε ένα ζεστό ποτήρι γάλα ή χαμομήλι.

- Να φροντίζετε να μην παίρνετε τις έγνοιες στο κρεβάτι μαζί σας.

TASK 2009B1

Last summer, your friend Scott asked you about the "Mediterranean diet" but you had no idea what it was. Now, you've just found the text below. Write an **email** (about 100 words) to Scott, **explaining** what the Mediterranean diet is all about. Sign as Alex.

Μεσογειακή διατροφή

Ο όρος «Μεσογειακή διατροφή» αναφέρεται στον τρόπο που τρέφονται και που ζουν οι λαοί της Μεσογείου. *Είναι συνώνυμος με την υγιεινή διατροφή* και τη μακροζωία. Περιλαμβάνει ψωμί, δημητριακά, φρούτα, λαχανικά, γαλακτοκομικά, όσπρια (φασόλια, φακές, κλπ.), ψάρια, κοτόπουλο, αβγά, ελαιόλαδο και ελάχιστο κρέας. Αποδίδεται σχηματικά με τη μορφή μιας πυραμίδας που δείχνει την καθημερινή, εβδομαδιαία και μηνιαία απαιτούμενη ποσότητα των ειδών διατροφής.

Σύμφωνα με αυτή την πυραμίδα της μεσογειακής διατροφής, συνιστώνται τα εξής:

- Κόκκινο κρέας σε μικρές ποσότητες, λίγες φορές τον μήνα
- Γλυκά, αναψυκτικά και αλάτι, σε μικρές ποσότητες
- Χρήση μελιού αντί ζάχαρης
- Καθημερινά μικρές ποσότητες γαλακτοκομικών προϊόντων, π.χ. τυρί και γιαούρτι
- Κοτόπουλο και ψάρι 1-2 φορές την εβδομάδα
- Αυγά έως 4 την εβδομάδα
- Όσπρια (φασόλια, φακές κλπ.), ξηροί καρποί , 1-2 φορές την εβδομάδα
- Άφθονες τροφές φυτικής προέλευσης όπως φρούτα, λαχανικά, πατάτες και δημητριακά
- Λάδι ελιάς αντί για οποιοδήποτε άλλο λίπος ή έλαιο
- Ψωμί ολικής αλέσεως αντί για λευκό
- Φυσική δραστηριότητα (περπάτημα, κίνηση γενικότερα) για καλή υγεία και ευεξία
- Προαιρετικά: λογική κατανάλωση κρασιού (1-2 ποτηράκια με τα γεύματα)

TASK 2010B1

Imagine your friend Chloe, who has been complaining about feeling down, asks you for help. Using information from the text below, send her an **email** (about 100 words). **Tell her what she can do**, so as to feel better. Sign as Alex (do **not** use your real name).

IMAGE REMOVED FOR COPYRIGHT REASONS

Είναι γνωστό ότι «η καλή μέρα από το πρωί φαίνεται». Γι' αυτό είναι σημαντικό να ξεκινάμε τη μέρα μας όσο πιο ευχάριστα γίνεται. Για παράδειγμα, η μουσική έχει έναν μοναδικό τρόπο να μας φτιάχνει τη διάθεση και είναι εύκολο να τη βάλουμε για τα καλά στη ζωή μας. Τι πιο απλό από το να αντικαταστήσουμε τον βαρετό και πολλές φορές εκνευριστικό ήχο του ξυπνητηριού με το αγαπημένο μας τραγούδι;

ΑΣΚΗΣΗ & ΔΙΑΤΡΟΦΗ

Η άσκηση μας φτιάχνει τη διάθεση. Γυμναστική, γιόγκα, τρέξιμο ή και γρήγορο περπάτημα μας δίνουν την απαραίτητη ενέργεια για να ξεκινήσουμε τη μέρα μας δυναμικά. Ακολουθεί απαραίτητα το πρωινό γεύμα, πλούσιο σε φρούτα και δημητριακά. Οι διατροφολόγοι το θεωρούν ως το πιο σημαντικό γεύμα της ημέρας, γι' αυτό κι εμείς δεν το ξεχνάμε ποτέ.

IMAGE REMOVED FOR COPYRIGHT REASONS

Η ΜΕΛΩΔΙΑ ΤΗΣ ΕΥΤΥΧΙΑΣ

IMAGE REMOVED FOR COPYRIGHT REASONS

Η μουσική καλό είναι να μας συνοδεύει ακόμα κι όταν φεύγουμε από το σπίτι. Ο αγαπημένος μας σταθμός στο αυτοκίνητο, το mp3 ή το iPod με αποθηκευμένα όλα τα αγαπημένα μας κομμάτια μπορούν να κάνουν θαύματα μέσα στο λεωφορείο ή στο μετρό! Φυσικά, αν γνωρίζουμε κάποιο μουσικό όργανο, βρίσκουμε χρόνο να παίξουμε –για τους φίλους μας ή για μας τους ίδιους!

ΕΡΓΑΣΙΑ ΚΑΙ ΧΑΡΑ

Το εργασιακό μας περιβάλλον το φροντίζουμε γιατί είναι σημαντικό για καλή διάθεση. Εδώ, περνάμε αρκετές ώρες της ημέρας και γι' αυτό πρέπει ο χώρος να μας αρέσει και να μας δημιουργεί θετικές σκέψεις. Φυσικά, το τι αρέσει στον καθένα είναι προσωπικό ζήτημα και γι αυτό τον προσωπικό μας χώρο τον φτιάχνουμε όπως αρέσει σ' εμάς – με τα δικά μας αγαπημένα πράγματα.

IMAGE REMOVED FOR COPYRIGHT REASONS

TASK 2008B2

Imagine you are part of a team preparing the **WHAT'S ON guide** for English-speaking visitors to your city. Below is the film section presenting in Greek the films which are now playing. Use the information in Greek to write a text in English (about 150 words) **recommending** two films for children and two for teenagers.

IMAGE REMOVED FOR COPYRIGHT REASONS

IMAGE REMOVED FOR COPYRIGHT REASONS

IMAGE REMOVED FOR COPYRIGHT REASONS

IMAGE REMOVED FOR COPYRIGHT REASONS

Το **HAIRSPRAY** είναι μια κωμωδία που μας μεταφέρει στη δεκαετία του 60, με τα περίεργα χτενίσματα, τα πολύχρωμα ρούχα, τα hits και την τρέλα της εποχής. Σε αυτό το περιβάλλον, μια χοντρούλα προσπαθεί να βρει το δρόμο προς τη διασημότητα...

Στο **SPIDERMAN** 3, ο Σπάιντερμαν χαίρεται την ηρεμία του και κάνει σχέδια να παντρευτεί την αγαπημένη του, η οποία όμως αντιμετωπίζει προβλήματα που θα την κάνουν να απομακρυνθεί – κάτι που επιδρά αρνητικά επάνω του. Ως προς την πραγματική δράση ένας νέος εχθρός ονόματι Sandman εμφανίζεται και μια μαύρη ουσία κυριεύει την ψυχή του Σπάιντερμαν...

Στη θαυμάσια αυτή ταινία, με τίτλο **ΡΑΤΑΤΟΥΗ** ο πρωταγωνιστής είναι ο Ρεμί, ένας αρουραίος που λατρεύει την καλή κουζίνα. Όταν τον διώχνουν από το σπίτι του, για καλή του τύχη καταλήγει στον υπόνομο κάτω από ένα πολυτελέστατο παριζιάνικο εστιατόριο. Η αγάπη του για το καλό φαγητό θα τον οδηγήσουν στο δικό του παράδεισο, που δεν είναι άλλος από την... κουζίνα. Εκεί θα γνωρίσει τον Λιγκουίνι, έναν φιλόδοξο νεαρό σερβιτόρο...

Στο **HAPPY FEET** ο μικρός Mumble είναι ένας πιγκουίνος αλλιώτικος από τους άλλους. Ενώ θα έπρεπε να διαθέτει όμορφη και ρυθμική φωνή, αυτός γεννήθηκε χορεύοντας κλακέτες! Οι γονείς του φοβούνται πως δε θα καταφέρει ποτέ να βρει την αληθινή αγάπη χωρίς να ξέρει το 'Τραγούδι της Καρδιάς', ενώ οι συμμαθητές του τον κοροϊδεύουν λόγω της ιδιαιτερότητάς του.

HAVE A GREEK SUMMER EXPERIENCE: GO TO AN OPEN-AIR CINEMA!

69

TASK 2009B2

You and your friend Martin have decided to spend part of your summer vacation doing volunteer work. Use information from the site below and write an **email** (150 words) to Martin. Try to **convince** him that it's a good idea for the two of you to take part in the Syros project of the Greek Ornithological Society. Sign as Alex.

Helpful hint

Stress those aspects of the project which make it particularly attractive for you. For example:

- location
- flexible dates
- cost
- type of work

IMAGE
REMOVED
FOR
COPYRIGHT
REASONS

TASK 2010B2

Using the information in the text below, write **an article** (150 words) for a European magazine, in which you

- **present** the findings of a survey on how Greek young people spend their free time
- **express your opinion** about the most and least popular leisure activities among young people

The title of your article is: HOW YOUNG PEOPLE SPEND THEIR FREE TIME

IMAGE
REMOVED
FOR
COPYRIGHT
REASONS

TASK 2008C1

Imagine you are Alex Eleftheriou, studying in the UK. Your university newspaper includes a section entitled WHAT *WE* CAN DO TO SAVE THE PLANET. Students often send letters to appear here, with suggestions about what can be done for the planet. Write a letter to the newspaper editor (200 words, in addition to the opening below) with **suggestions** using information from the Greek article below.

> 108 John's Park
> Blackheath
> London SE3 7PJ
>
> Mr Jan Jaworksy
> Editor of University College News
> 45 Gower Street
> London WCIE 6BT
>
> 8 May 2008
>
> Dear Editor,
> I saw your announcement asking us to contribute to the next issue of UCN and I thought that I should give it a try, especially since I read an interesting article in a Greek magazine yesterday and it started me thinking. So here are my suggestions about WHAT WE CAN DO TO SAVE THE PLANET. I hope that some people will agree with me and that all of us WILL **do** something, rather than just talk about what to do!

IMAGE
REMOVED
FOR
COPYRIGHT
REASONS

TASK 2009C1

Imagine that you work for the Greek Tourist Organization. Your department has received a request from the tourist organization of another country for information about the very successful 'Blue Flag' programme. You have been asked to write **a report** (180-200 words) **explaining** how Greece has managed to achieve Blue Flag status for many of its beaches. Use information from the website below to write your report.

IMAGE
REMOVED
FOR
COPYRIGHT
REASONS

TASK 2010C1

Imagine you are an ex-smoker and you want to share your experience of trying to quit smoking with others. Using information from the Greek article below, write a **letter** for the readers' column of the *CARING AND SHARING* magazine (about 200 words), in which you **relate** your experience, and **explain** what you did in order to quit smoking.

IMAGE
REMOVED
FOR
COPYRIGHT
REASONS

Appendix B Degree of popularity of mediation strategies across tasks

Task	Creative blending				Combining				Summarising				Reorganising			
	0[1]		1		0		1		0		1		0		1	
	Count	Row N %	Count	Row N %	Count	Row N %	Count	Row N %	Count	Row N %	Count	Row N %	Count	Row N %	Count	Row N %
2008B1	42	70.0	18	30.0	60	100.0	0	0.0	53	88.3	7	11.7	47	78.3	13	21.7
2008B2	52	86.7	8	13.3	58	96.7	2	3.3	7	11.7	53	88.3	42	70.0	18	30.0
2008C1	14	23.3	46	76.7	40	66.7	20	33.3	21	35.0	39	65.0	59	98.3	1	1.7
2009B1	50	83.3	10	16.7	53	88.3	7	11.7	45	75.0	15	25.0	59	98.3	1	1.7
2009B2	32	53.3	28	46.7	38	63.3	22	36.7	45	75.0	15	25.0	58	96.7	2	3.3
2009C1	30	50.0	30	50.0	57	95.0	3	5.0	23	38.3	37	61.7	57	95.0	3	5.0
2010B1	43	71.7	17	28.3	56	93.3	4	6.7	11	18.3	49	81.7	60	100.0	0	0.0
2010B2	43	71.7	17	28.3	59	98.3	1	1.7	25	41.7	35	58.3	55	91.7	5	8.3
2010C1	17	28.3	43	71.7	51	85.0	9	15.0	25	41.7	35	58.3				

Task	Expanding				Combining 2 sentences into 1				Paraphrasing			
	0		1		0		1		0		1	
	Count	Row N %	Count	Row N %	Count	Row N %	Count	Row N %	Count	Row N %	Count	Row N %
2008B1	55	91.7	5	8.3	58	96.7	2	3.3	0	0.0	60	100.0
2008B2	48	80.0	12	20.0	58	96.7	2	3.3	2	3.3	58	96.7
2008C1	56	93.3	4	6.7	60	100.0	0	0.0	8	13.3	52	86.7
2009B1	54	90.0	6	10.0	60	100.0	0	0.0	0	0.0	60	100.0
2009B2	52	86.7	8	13.3	60	100.0	0	0.0	1	1.7	59	98.3
2009C1	58	96.7	2	3.3	60	100.0	0	0.0	0	0.0	60	100.0
2010B1	55	91.7	5	8.3	59	98.3	1	1.7	8	13.3	52	86.7
2010B2	59	98.3	1	1.7	60	100.0	0	0.0	26	43.3	34	56.7
2010C1	42	70.0	18	30.0	51	85.0	9	15.0	0	0.0	60	100.0

1 In this table, 0 is used when the strategy at hand does not appear in any of the scripts. 1 is used when the strategy appears at least once.

4 A computational and psycholinguistic investigation of cultural familiarity and reading comprehension exam performance in Greece

Trisevgeni Liontou
Greek Ministry of Education

Abstract

The present study aimed at examining whether culturally familiar texts used at the advanced level of the Greek State Certificate of English Language Proficiency Exams (KPG) had a statistically significant impact on a total number of 36,517 KPG test takers' mean reading comprehension exam performance, while, at the same time, exploring their possible impact on test takers' perceptions of text and task difficulty. Twenty-eight advanced KPG reading comprehension exam texts used between April 2005 and November 2011 examination periods were analysed, 13 of which were classified by expert judges as more culturally familiar and 15 as more general ones. The lack of content-specific effect on advanced KPG test takers' mean reading comprehension exam scores provides evidence in favour of the construct validity of the KPG English language exams, since the assessment of reading competence at an advanced level was not found to be affected by culturally related text features. At the same time, the fact that culturally familiar texts were found to have an alleviating effect on advanced KPG test takers' perceived level of test anxiety might indicate that background cultural familiarity was, in fact, a salient factor in their overall performance. Nevertheless, culturally familiar reading texts were found to contain a significantly higher percentage of less frequent words belonging to the third BNC frequency band, were assigned higher grade levels by the Flesch Reading Ease Index, the Dale-Chall Grade Level Index and the Fry Readability Graph and were characterised by a significantly higher proportion of longer words in terms of average number of syllables and characters per word, all of which could have contributed to their increased complexity. The present study could be best viewed as a springboard for a wider number of EFL test designers and curricula developers to consider promoting in practice cultural awareness through the implementation of culture-specific elements in pertinent reading comprehension texts.

Introduction

Over the last 20 years there has been an increasing interest in exploring and better defining the interaction between the reader and the text, rather than text features alone, acknowledging that reading is a multifaceted phenomenon, reflecting properties of both the texts and the readers and the interaction between them. Research in foreign language reading has highlighted the significant effect of reader factors on comprehension and further supported the view that a satisfactory understanding of the reading process depends not only on an accurate identification of the various text elements and the connections among them, but also on that of readers' prior knowledge of and interest in the topic as well as the strategies used to actively construct meaning (Alderson 2000, Drucker 2003, Farhady 1982, Freebody and Anderson 1983, Keshavarz, Atai and Ahmadi 2007, Rupp, Ferne and Choi 2006, Yin 1985). Especially in relation to language testing, Sullivan stressed (2000:373) the importance of better defining those reader variables that may affect overall test performance in order to be able to detect and eliminate any test features that can be sources of measurement error and thus distort testers' attempts to achieve an accurate assessment of learners' language proficiency. At the same time, a fundamental issue in validating reading comprehension test scores is the effect of the topic on test takers' performance. Jennings, Fox, Graves and Shohamy (1999:426) termed this threat a 'topic effect' and argued that 'it may constitute a source of construct-irrelevant variance because aspects of the task that are extraneous to the construct of interest, that is, language proficiency, make the test easier or more difficult for some individuals'. They further contended that investigating the possibility of any culture-specific topic effect is a critical step in establishing the construct validity of all language tests (Jennings et al 1999:426). In accord with their view, Alderson (2000:63) emphasised the need for test developers to ensure that test takers are neither advantaged nor disadvantaged when presented with a specific topic.

Background to the study

Although a lot of research has focused on the effect background knowledge or schemata can have on foreign language reading comprehension (Bügel and Buunk (1996:15), Floyd and Carrell (1987:103), Hudson (1982:20), Krekeler (2006:121), Langer (1984:469)), less information is available regarding the influence of specific cultural knowledge, maybe due to the difficulty of distinguishing between cultural knowledge and general background knowledge (Alptekin (2006:494), Carrell and Eisterhold (1983:73), Pritchard (1990:273)). Ketchum (2006:23) proposed a definition of cultural schemata as a culture-specific extension of content schemata because they refer to the role of cultural membership that is needed to fully comprehend the meaning intended by the writer. In this sense, cultural schemata can help readers reconstruct the story line through referring to more personally and culturally relevant scripts (Oller 1995:299). Thus, one effect of this process is a lessened workload when making personal interpretations, because such texts entail involvement with 'real persons, events, places and sociocultural relations with which [readers] can identify and find some common ground' (Oller 1995:299).

In a seminal study exploring cultural differences in background knowledge, Steffensen, Joag-Dev and Anderson (1979:18) demonstrated that implicit cultural knowledge presupposed by a text and the reader's own cultural background knowledge interact to make texts based on one's own culture easier to read and understand than syntactically equivalent texts based on more distant cultures. More specifically, Steffensen et al asked subjects from two different cultural heritages, i.e. 19 Asian Indians living in the USA but whose English was a second language, and 20 native English-speaking Americans, to read and recall two personal letters about an American and an Indian wedding (1979:15). According to the researchers, syntactic complexity of each letter, which was written by a member of that culture, was controlled (Steffensen et al 1979:15). Since the wedding is a ceremony of great social significance, it was assumed by the researchers that all adult members of a society would have a well-developed system of background knowledge about the marital customs of their own culture and a comparative lack of knowledge about the customs of less familiar cultures (Steffensen et al 1979:14). Data analysis showed that both groups of subjects read the passage dealing with their own culture more rapidly, recalled a larger amount of information and produced more culturally appropriate elaborations (Steffensen et al 1979:17–19). On the other hand, when the subjects read the foreign passage, more culturally inappropriate distortions surfaced (Steffensen et al 1979:17). The authors concluded that the implicit cultural knowledge underlying a text exerts a profound influence on how well the text will be understood and recalled (Steffensen et al 1979:19).

Similar findings were reported by Johnson (1981:169), who demonstrated that the cultural origin of a text can have a greater effect on foreign language reading comprehension than linguistic complexity. In Johnson's study, Iranian intermediate-to-advanced-level English as a Foreign Language (EFL) students along with native English-speaking American ones read American and Iranian folk-tales. Subjects were tested on their reading comprehension competence via multiple-choice questions on textually explicit and implicit information, as well as free written recalls (Johnson 1981:173).

Statistical analyses of the data indicated that the cultural origin of the story had greater effect on their comprehension than did the level of syntactic and semantic complexity of the text. In another study on the cultural specificity of content schemata and their effects on foreign language reading, Johnson (1982:503) examined the effect of prior cultural experience on students' comprehension of information in a text linked to familiar aspects of an American custom, i.e. Halloween, as opposed to information linked to unknown aspects of the custom. Prior to the experiment, some of the subjects had experienced a typical American Halloween celebration. So the text each student read contained both familiar and unfamiliar information. Statistical analysis of the recalls of the passage and a sentence recognition task showed that prior cultural experience prepared readers for better comprehension of the unfamiliar information in the passage and facilitated their overall comprehension. However, Johnson does not provide more detailed information regarding the rhetorical structure of each text and the extent of their equivalence.

In a later study, Carrell (1987:461) investigated the simultaneous effects on foreign language reading comprehension of both culture-specific content schemata and formal schemata, as well as the potential interaction between them. To be more specific, high-intermediate EFL students of Catholic or Muslim religions were asked to read, recall and answer comprehension questions on two texts of both culturally familiar and unfamiliar content in terms of religion and rhetorical organisation (ibid:465). According to the researcher, various formal aspects of the texts were controlled, i.e. both versions of both texts were of approximately equal length, consisted of approximately the same number of clauses and the same reading level on the Dale-Chall readability formula (Carrell 1987:467). Data analysis confirmed the effect of both rhetorical organisation and cultural familiarity on comprehension, but further revealed that content schemata affected reading comprehension to a greater extent than formal ones, i.e. unfamiliar content posed more difficulties to the readers than unfamiliar structure (Carrell 1987:476). It is worth mentioning that participants in Carrell's study were also asked to assess on a 5-point scale the degree of difficulty of each text in terms of grammar, vocabulary, content and overall organisation and their ratings were found to significantly correlate with their familiarity with the topic and structure of the text (Carrell 1987:471).

In a more recent study on the effect of cultural schemata on cloze test performance, Sasaki (2000:89) administered two cloze-test versions, one with culturally familiar references and one with unfamiliar ones, to two groups of 60 Japanese university students with equivalent English reading proficiency. After completing the whole test, participants were also asked to recall, either in Japanese or in English, anything they could remember from the given text (Sasaki 2000:91). The test results demonstrated that changing culturally unfamiliar words to more familiar ones in a cloze test had some impact on participants' test-taking processes, supporting the speculation that the culturally familiar text could have activated appropriate schemata more efficiently than its unfamiliar counterpart (Sasaki 2000:103). Sasaki concluded that test developers should take such potential obstacles into consideration when selecting reading texts, since text unfamiliarity can be too overwhelming for some readers and may lead to their poor performance (Sasaki 2000:107). For Sasaki, text selection becomes even more important if the purpose of a test includes measuring examinees' linguistic ability, in which case culturally unfamiliar texts may present a serious threat to adequate test score interpretation (Sasaki 2000:107).

More recently, the influence of cultural familiarity on the comprehension of short stories read by 44 advanced-level students of English at a state university in Turkey was the focus of Erten and Razi's study (2009:60). Applying a 2×2 experimental research design they investigated whether adding culturally familiar elements to the stories could compensate for the lack of prior knowledge and found a powerful impact of cultural schemata on overall comprehension, i.e. students seemed to find it easier to allocate attentional resources to more linguistic elements and construct more mental representations of the familiar context (Erten and Razi 2009:70). To sum up, although there has been an increasing interest in exploring and better defining the interaction between foreign language learners' background cultural knowledge and their reading comprehension performance, it is worth mentioning at this point that the majority of past research was based on case studies or small-scale surveys with foreign language users taking part in specially designed experiments in laboratory settings. Such a practice, although informative to a certain extent, has *per se* produced results of limited generalisability and practicability in relation to real high-stakes exam conditions. The present study has, thus, been designed to fill this void and add to our present state of knowledge on foreign language reading performance by examining the effect culturally familiar texts might have on actual test takers' reading comprehension performance in the Greek State Certificate of English Language Proficiency (KPG) exams while exploring text complexity from test takers' points of view.

Aim of the study

The aim of the present study was threefold: a) to examine whether culturally familiar texts have a statistically significant impact on KPG advanced test takers' reading comprehension performance, b) to examine whether culturally familiar texts were related to KPG advanced test takers' perceptions of reading difficulty, and c) to examine whether culturally familiar texts were lexicogrammatically different from more general ones. Although it is beyond the scope of the present paper to provide a detailed description of the KPG

English Language exams, it is worth mentioning that it is a relatively new multi-level multilingual suite of national language examinations developed by teams of experts from the foreign language departments of the National and Kapodistrian University of Athens and the Aristotle University of Thessaloniki and administered by the Greek Ministry of Education (more information available online at rcel.enl.uoa.gr/kpg/en_index.htm). Despite being in its infancy, KPG is rapidly gaining acceptance as a high-stakes exam in Greece and, because of its official recognition by the state, it can influence one's future prospects for employment and education. Exams are administered twice a year and, since November 2003, more than 500,000 test takers have taken the English language exams. According to the KPG specifications, at the C1 level of the reading comprehension exam paper, candidates are expected to skim through or read carefully longer (mean text length: 500 words) and more linguistically demanding texts of varied discourse, register and style, which they are likely to encounter in their social, professional or academic environment, and respond to a total of 60 items of various types designed to assess their ability to understand the overall meaning or partial meanings of these texts, to make reasoned inferences and draw conclusions as well as understand the relationships between different parts of a single text or among various texts (KPG C1 specifications, 2005). At the same time, the KPG exams, according to the rationale and ideology underlying their creation, focus on the Greek user of the target language and aspire to cover local needs by responding to the demands of education and the labour market in Greece (Dendrinos (2009:1–2, in press:7). Given such an intention, the present study was stimulated by the need to explore whether the inclusion of culturally familiar texts in the KPG reading comprehension exam paper might have introduced construct irrelevant variance into test scores or might have resulted in particular KPG test takers been affected in an unexpected way by the complexity of the texts or their own background knowledge. In order to explore these issues, the following research questions were formed:

1. Is there a significant difference in advanced KPG test takers' exam performance between culturally familiar and general reading comprehension exam texts?
2. Are there any significant differences in advanced KPG test takers' perceptions of text and task difficulty between culturally familiar and general reading comprehension exam texts?
3. Are there any significant lexicogrammatical differences between culturally familiar and general KPG reading comprehension exam texts?

Methodology

Text classification by judges

For advanced KPG reading comprehension texts to be classified into culturally familiar or general ones, two expert judges were recruited to take part in the research. Twenty-eight authentic advanced KPG reading comprehension exam texts used between April 2005 and November 2011 examination periods were analysed. To avoid contamination of human ratings due to text source effects no information was provided regarding the origin of the texts. Both judges were considered highly qualified for the task at hand since they were both EFL teachers with a Master's degree in Teaching English as a Foreign Language (TEFL) and years of experience in foreign language teaching and testing. Both judges were brought up in Greece and had first-hand experience of cultural beliefs and practices in the specific context. During the training session, judges were informed about the aims of the research and the importance of their contribution to the overall validity of the study. They were also provided with a specially designed leaflet that included Ketchum's definition of cultural schemata as 'a culture-specific extension of content schemata because they refer to the role of cultural membership that is needed to fully comprehend the meaning intended by the writer' (2006:23) along with a list of culture-specific topics Greek learners of English might have been exposed to through their national school textbooks, produced by the Greek Ministry of Education and approved to be used as the standard textbooks throughout the country. Judges confirmed their lack of familiarity with the selected texts and, working independently, classified them according to the predefined set of criteria. To avoid contamination of results, there was no personal communication between the two judges. Once the text classification process was completed, individual ratings were compared and analysis of inter-rater reliability showed that consensus between the two judges reached 89% with 25 out of the 28 texts been classified to the same categories by both raters. To solve the rating discrepancy in the remaining three texts, a third judge with a PhD in English Language and years of experience as an EFL teacher and KPG researcher was kindly requested to assess their cultural specificity and provide her own rating. This way, ratings for all 28 texts were collected and each text was classified as either culturally familiar or a general one based on inter-rater agreement. For example, texts related to Greek history, customs and traditions ('Zorba the Greek', 'Cretan tradition', 'Alexander the Great', etc.) were classified as culturally familiar, whereas more general ones referred to environmental issues, modern educational practices and scientific developments ('Climate crisis', 'Soya', 'Teaching History', etc.).

Mean task scores

The relationship between reading comprehension exam performance and culturally familiar or general KPG advanced texts was explored by estimating the mean task scores per text and per examination period of a total number of 36,517 test takers who had participated in advanced KPG English language exams over a period of seven years (2005–2011). For texts to be appropriate for comparisons and avoid any test-method effects a specific set of criteria was followed during their selection. To be more specific, only those reading passages that contained multiple-choice reading comprehension questions with three options (A, B or C) per item were considered appropriate for further analysis. The testing focus of the analysed items was reading for detail. Thus, mean task scores used in the present study related to the specific multiple-choice reading comprehension questions included in each set of analysed texts.

Automated text analysis tools

Advances in computational linguistics and machine learning systems have made it possible to go beyond surface text components and adopt more theoretically sound approaches to text complexity, focusing on a wider range of 'deep' text features that take into account semantic interpretation and the construction of mental models and can, thus, offer a principled means for test providers and test takers alike to assess this aspect of test construct validity (Graesser, McNamara, Louwerse and Cai 2004:193). In the present study Coh-Metrix 2.1 (cohmetrix.memphis.edu), Linguistic Inquiry and Word Count 2007 (www.liwc.net), VocabProfile 3.0 (www.lextutor.ca/vp), the Computerized Language Analysis (CLAN) suite of programs (childes.psy.cmu.edu), Computerized Propositional Idea Density Rater (www.ai.uga.edu) and Gramulator (umdrive.memphis.edu) were used to estimate a range of lexicogrammatical features pertinent in culturally familiar and general KPG advanced reading comprehension texts. More specifically, the presence of cohesive ties created by referencing, conjunction and lexical cohesion as well as that of nominal group structure, grammatical intricacy and lexical density was explored. Moreover, the occurrence of surface text features, such as number of words, sentences and paragraphs per text, word frequency, lexical diversity, propositional density, proportion of passive sentences, negations, phrasal verbs and idioms per text along with estimates from four well-known readability formulas, namely the Flesch Reading Ease Index (Flesch 1948:222), the Dale-Chall Grade Level (Chall and Dale 1995:13), the Fry Readability Index (Fry 1968:514) and the Gunning Fog Index (McAdams 1993:51), was determined. The 135 text variables analysed in the present research were chosen for both practical and theoretical reasons. First, from the practical standpoint of comparability, it was important to establish whether particular features existed, whose presence in the KPG English language reading comprehension exam texts might have introduced construct irrelevant variance into test scores. If this turned out to be the case, then steps could be taken to incorporate such factors into subsequent revisions of the text selection guidelines. In addition, given that previous research had failed to produce a definite set of text variables, no *a priori* decision was made in terms of their expected impact. To avoid contamination of results due to text length effect, the first 300 words from each reading passage (mean text length: 500, SD: 112.65) were analysed.

The KPG national survey

In order to collect valuable information on KPG test takers' background knowledge, topic preference and cultural familiarity as well as their perceptions of text and task difficulty, a longitudinal paper-and-pencil survey was conducted by the KPG English team at the Research Centre for Language, Teaching, Testing and Assessment on a national scale in the form of a self-completion questionnaire administered to all KPG test takers sitting for the B2 and C1 English language exams in the May and November 2006 and 2007 and May 2008 examination periods. The KPG team's decision to use a survey instrument (rather than another instrument such as interviews/ focus group protocols, etc.) was mainly based on the following two aims: a) the purpose of the survey was to investigate test takers' general views on various aspects of the KPG language exams in English by obtaining relatively standardised information from a large number of people, and b) the geographical distribution of the target population that included all KPG test takers sitting for the B2 and C1 English language exams around Greece, both of which in practice left us no choice but to use a questionnaire. The questionnaire was administered on a group basis, along with the test papers, to all KPG exam centres around Greece. Test takers wishing to take part in the survey were requested to fill it in right after completing their reading comprehension exam paper. Thus, feedback was received straight after the KPG test administration. All KPG test takers were explicitly informed that participation in the KPG English Candidate Survey was voluntary and anonymous. To facilitate understanding and make respondents feel comfortable when answering the questions and, thus, minimise reliability and validity problems caused by the language factor, the instrument was written in the respondents' native language, i.e. Greek, and participants were asked to rate on a 5-point scale their level of agreement/disagreement with 20 statements regarding text and task difficulty, text lexical complexity, feelings of anxiety, topic familiarity and preference. For the KPG survey sample to be appropriate for statistical analysis and as representative as possible of the target population, a decision was made for its size to be at least 10% of the total number of test takers sitting each exam, with a minimum of 500 participants per examination period. In order to ensure a balanced geographical distribution and avoid any variation in response rates due to urbanisation, 50% of the participants were randomly drawn from the five most densely populated cities in Greece (according to the most recent official records of the Hellenic Statistical Authority), 25% from rural areas and the remaining 25% from the Greek islands. For the purposes of the present study a total of 2,500 questionnaires from five examination periods were analysed (Table 1).

Results

Once the classification of KPG advanced reading comprehension texts into two categories, i.e. culturally familiar and general ones, by the two judges was completed, an independent samples t-test was carried out in order to explore the existence of any significant differences in advanced KPG test takers' mean reading comprehension scores regarding culturally familiar and general texts and thus answer the first research question ('Is there a significant difference in advanced KPG test takers' exam performance between culture-specific and general reading comprehension exam texts?'). The homogeneity of group variances per score variable was assessed using Levene's Test for Equality of Variances (p > .05). No significant difference in advanced test takers' mean multiple-choice reading comprehension exam scores was found in relation to culturally familiar (Mean=67.88) and general KPG reading comprehension texts (Mean=64.61) (F=2.120, t=.566, df=26, Adj. sig. (2-tailed)=.255).

In order to answer the second research question ('Are there any significant differences in advanced KPG test takers' perceptions of text and task difficulty between culturally familiar and general reading comprehension exam texts?') a set of independent samples t-tests was carried out. Homogeneity of group variances per question variable was assessed using Levene's Test for Equality of Variances (p > .05). The alpha level of 0.05 was corrected to 0.005 for multiple tests using the Holm-Bonferroni adjustment. In addition to t, df and p values, the effect size was estimated as $r = \sqrt{\frac{t^2}{t^2 + df}}$. The magnitude of the effect was considered 'small' for values lower than 0.3, 'medium' for

Table 1 KPG national survey advanced-level questionnaires

	Number	Percentage of exam population	Cronbach's Alpha
May 2006	500	13%	0.771
November 2006	500	31%	0.822
May 2007	500	16%	0.801
November 2007	500	47%	0.774
May 2008	500	20%	0.773

values ranging from 0.3 to 0.5 and 'large' for values above 0.5. Significant differences in advanced KPG test takers' average perceptions between culturally familiar and general KPG reading comprehension texts were found with regard to perceived reading text complexity, task and exam difficulty. To be more specific, test takers on average reported finding the general texts significantly more difficult than the culturally familiar ones (t=−1.719, df=26, r=0.3, p < 0.001), and their pertinent tasks more difficult than expected (t=−2.224, df=26, r=0.4, p < 0.001), whereas culturally familiar texts were perceived as significantly easier to process. In addition, a statistically significant increase in advanced KPG readers' mean self-reports on their feelings of test anxiety was concomitant with general reading exam texts (t=−3.621, df=26, r=0.6, p < 0.005).

Regarding the third research question ('Are there any significant lexico-grammatical differences between culture-specific and general KPG reading comprehension exam texts?') a new set of independent samples t-tests was carried out. Homogeneity of group variances per question variable was assessed using Levene's Test for Equality of Variances (p > .05). Significant differences between culturally familiar and general KPG advanced reading comprehension exam texts were found for 10 text variables, that is, syllables per word, characters per word, Flesch Reading Ease Index, Dale-Chall Grade Level Index, Fry Readability Graph, BNC-K1 Words (1–1,000), BNC-K3 Words (2,001–3,000), negations, verb density and present tenses. More specifically, culturally familiar reading texts included a significantly higher percentage of less frequent words belonging to the third BNC frequency band (t=2.711, df=26, r=0.47, p=0.012), and were assigned higher grade levels by the Flesch Reading Ease Index (t=−2.157, df=26, r=0.39, p=0.016), the Dale-Chall Grade Level Index (t=2.908, df=26, r=0.49, p=0.004) and the Fry Readability Graph (t=2.719, df=26, r=0.47, p=0.007). Texts classified as culturally familiar were also characterised by their significantly higher proportion of longer words in terms of average number of syllables (t=2.988, df=26, r=0.5, p=0.004) and characters per word (t=2.373, df=26, r=0.4, p=0.003), all of which could have contributed to their increased complexity. On the other hand, advanced KPG reading comprehension exam texts that were classified as general ones by the two judges contained a significantly higher percentage of more frequent words belonging to the first BNC frequency band (t=−3.087, df=26, r=0.52, p=0.005) and were characterised by the significantly higher presence of negations (t=−2.695, df=26, r=0.47, p=0.012), verbs (t=−2.794, df=26, r=0.48, p=0.005) and present tenses (t=−2.792, df=26, r=0.48, p=0.010), all of which could have facilitated comprehension by clarifying the relationships among ideas and providing a clear structural pathway for advanced KPG readers to follow.

Discussion

The present study aimed at examining whether culturally familiar texts used in the advanced KPG English language reading comprehension exam paper had a statistically significant impact on a total number of 36,517 KPG test takers' mean reading comprehension scores, while, at the same time, exploring their possible impact on 2,500 test takers' perceptions of reading text and task difficulty and the extent to which such texts were lexicogrammatically different from more general ones. Twenty-eight authentic advanced KPG reading comprehension exam texts used between April 2005 and November 2011 examination periods were analysed, 13 of which were classified by expert judges as culturally familiar and 15 as more general ones. The lack of content-specific effect on advanced KPG test takers' mean reading comprehension exam scores provides evidence in favour of the construct validity of the KPG English language exams, since the assessment of reading competence at an advanced level was not found to be affected by culturally familiar text elements. Such a lack might also be taken to demonstrate the absence of significant test bias attributed to the nature of the input, given that no culture-specific text features were found to contaminate advanced KPG test takers' reading comprehension exam scores. Therefore, it could be argued that the inclusion of culturally familiar reading comprehension texts in this study did not constitute a source of measurement error as they were in accordance with the ideology of the specific exam. This approach could be viewed as a springboard for a wider number of EFL test designers and curricula developers to consider promoting cultural awareness through the implementation of culture-specific elements in pertinent reading comprehension texts.

At the same time, the fact that the specific set of culturally familiar exam texts was found to have an alleviating effect on advanced KPG test takers' perceived level of test anxiety might indicate that background cultural familiarity was, in fact, a salient factor in their overall performance. Acknowledging the lack of a significant effect of culturally familiar texts on KPG test takers' exam scores, it might, nevertheless, be worth pointing out the more subtle emotional and psychological effects of such an inclusion and suggest that, since testing is more than just scores, offering test takers a range of culturally familiar topics to choose from may be a means of alleviating some of their test-taking concerns. Finally, the existence of statistically significant lexicogrammatical differences between culturally familiar and general KPG advanced reading comprehension exam texts is worth test designers' attention for texts used at the same level of the KPG English language exams to be equivalent in their lexicogrammatical complexity. On the other hand, one might argue that it is due to their increased lexicogrammatical complexity that culturally familiar texts were not found to have a positive impact on mean reading comprehension exam scores. Having said that, the findings of the present study could serve as a yardstick for item writers to select future reading texts by taking into account the average linguistic profile of advanced reading comprehension exam texts used so far in real KPG English language exams.

To conclude, the present study aspired to provide useful insights into the reading comprehension process of Greek learners of English while shedding light on the effect that culturally familiar text elements have on the reading outcome and the extent to which these interfere with perceived text and task difficulty under real high-stakes exam conditions. Until now, these issues have been mainly explored through case studies or small-scale surveys, whose results were of limited generalisability since they were carried out in laboratory settings. Nevertheless, acknowledging that advanced KPG test takers made their own interpretations to questionnaire items and reported perceived cultural familiarity and topic preference along with text, task and exam difficulty to the best of their conscious knowledge, we must be wary of the limitations of the obtained data. As in other studies, at best, this data indicated personal attitudes to specific exam texts. On the other hand, the fact that a large number of responses (2,500 questionnaires) were collected over a period of time (2.5 years) could have added to the reliability of the reported findings. In this sense, echoing Jennings et al (1999: 451), it is strongly believed that factors that test takers identify as important in the testing experience should not be overlooked, but rather more broadly surveyed and seriously considered during the test construction and validation process. Along with research-based adjustments to exam specifications, test developers could also consider providing test takers with more content-specific information about each reading text in the rubrics section of the exam paper.

Finally, the present study attempted to make a methodological contribution in that, instead of exploring text complexity through traditional readability formulae, it made use of advanced computational linguistics and machine learning systems to estimate a range or in-depth lexicogrammatical features and trace finer differences between advanced KPG culturally familiar and general reading comprehension exam texts. At the same time it investigated advanced KPG test takers' perspectives on various aspects of text comprehensibility but, instead of examining text variables in isolation, it explored and cross-related the simultaneous effect of a range of text variables for their interaction to be better defined within the context of the KPG exams. On the other hand, as with all studies, the implementation of the present one presented a number of challenges and limitations that we hope will be overcome in future research. For instance, due to the fact that the KPG English language exam battery is still in its infancy, the number of available texts was inevitably constrained to a total of 28; should the number of exam texts increase, the generalisability of present results might be further strengthened. It would also be useful to extend the present analysis to texts at both lower and higher levels of a range of English language exams following a comparative corpus-based approach for evidence-based conclusions to be drawn from a more extensive reading dataset. Without doubt, given the complexity of the reading comprehension process and the limitations of the present study, more research is needed to better define text difficulty in terms of actual reader performance and further explore the effect of culturally familiar text features on task-based performance across a variety of text types and tasks. By following such an approach, EFL test designers will be able to provide more empirical evidence that the methods they employ to elicit data are appropriate for the intended purposes, that the procedures used provide stable and consistent data and, consequently, that the interpretations they make of the results are justified, since they are based on a valid and reliable exam system.

Acknowledgments

Special thanks are due to Prof. Dendrinos, President of the KPG Central Examination Committee and Director of the Research Centre for Language Testing and Assessment, for granting me access to KPG test takers' exam scores. Statements expressed in this paper do not reflect the official policy of the Research Centre for Language Testing and Assessment and responsibility for all expressed views relies entirely on the author.

References

Alderson, C (2000) *Assessing Reading*, Cambridge: Cambridge University Press.

Alptekin, C (2006) Cultural familiarity in inferential and literal comprehension in L2 reading, *System* 34 (4), 494–508.

Bügel, K and Buunk, B (1996) Sex differences in foreign language text comprehension: the role of interests and prior knowledge, *The Modern Language Journal* 80 (1), 15–31.

Carrell, P (1987) Content and formal schemata in ESL reading, *TESOL Quarterly* 21 (3), 461–481.

Carrell, P and Eisterhold, J (1983) Schema theory and ESL reading pedagogy, *TESOL Quarterly* 17 (4), 553–573.

Chall, J and Dale, E (1995) *Readability Revisited: The New Dale-Chall Readability Formula*, Cambridge: Brookline Books Inc.

Dendrinos, B (2009) *Rationale and Ideology of the KPG Exams*, available online: rcel.enl.uoa.gr/rcel/texts/Rationale_and_Ideology_of_the_KPG_Exams

Dendrinos, B (in press) Social meanings in global-glocal language proficiency exams, in Tsagari, C, Papadima-Sophocleous, S and Ioannou-Georgiou, S (Eds) *Language Testing and Assessment around the Globe: Achievements and Experiences*, Bern: Peter Lang Publishing Group.

Drucker, M (2003) What reading teachers should know about ESL learners, *The Reading Teacher* 57 (1), 22–29.

Erten, I and Razi, S (2009) The effects of cultural familiarity on reading comprehension, *Reading in a Foreign Language* 21 (1), 60–77.

Farhady, H (1982) Measures of language proficiency from the learner's perspective, *TESOL Quarterly* 16 (1), 43–59.

Flesch, R (1948) A new readability yardstick, *Journal of Applied Psychology* 32 (3), 221–233.

Floyd, P and Carrell, P (1987) Effects on ESL reading of teaching cultural content schemata, *Language Learning* 37 (1), 89–108.

Freebody, P and Anderson, R (1983) Effects of vocabulary difficulty, text cohesion and schema availability on reading comprehension, *Reading Research Quarterly* 18 (3), 277–294.

Fry, E (1968) A readability formula that saves time, *Journal of Reading* 11 (7), 513–516.

Graesser, A, McNamara, D, Louwerse, M and Cai, Z (2004) Coh-Metrix: Analysis of text on cohesion and language, *Behavior Research Methods, Instruments & Computers* 36 (2), 193–202.

Hudson, T (1982) The effects of induced schemata on the 'short-circuit' in L2 reading: non decoding factors in L2 reading performance, *Language Learning* 32 (1), 1–25.

Jennings, M, Fox, J, Graves, B and Shohamy, E (1999) The test takers' choice: an investigation of the effect of topic on language-test performance, *Language Testing* 16 (4), 426–456.

Johnson, P (1981) Effects of reading comprehension on language complexity and cultural background of a text, *TESOL Quarterly* 15 (2), 169–181.

Johnson, P (1982) Effects on reading comprehension of building background knowledge, *TESOL Quarterly* 16 (4), 503–516.

Keshavarz, M, Atai, M and Ahmadi, H (2007) Content schemata, linguistic simplification and EFL readers' comprehension and recall, *Reading in a Foreign Language* 19 (1), 19–33.

Ketchum, E (2006) The cultural baggage of second language reading: An approach to understanding, *Foreign Language Annals* 39 (1), 22–42.

Krekeler, C (2006) Language for special academic purposes (LSAP) testing: the effect of background knowledge revisited, *Language Testing* 23 (1), 99–130.

Langer, J (1984) Examining background knowledge and text comprehension, *Reading Research Quarterly* 19 (4), 468–481.

McAdams, K (1993) Readability reconsidered: A study of reader reactions to Fog indexes, *Newspaper Research Journal* 13 and 14 (4), 50–59.

Oller, J (1995) Adding abstract to formal and content schema: Results of recent work in Peircean semiotics, *Applied Linguistics* 16 (3), 273–306.

Pritchard, R (1990) The effects of cultural schemata on reading processing strategies, *Reading Research Quarterly* 25 (4), 273–295.

Rupp, A, Ferne, T and Choi, H (2006) How assessing reading comprehension with multiple choice questions shapes the construct: a cognitive processing perspective, *Language Testing* 23 (4), 441–474.

Sasaki, M (2000) Effects of cultural schemata on students' test-taking processes for cloze tests: a multiple data source approach, *Language Testing* 17 (1), 85–114.

Steffensen, M, Joag-Dev, C and Anderson, R (1979) A cross-cultural perspective on reading comprehension, *Reading Research Quarterly* 15 (1), 10–29.

Sullivan, B (2000) Exploring gender and oral proficiency interview performance, *System* 28 (3), 373–386.

Yin, K (1985) The role of prior knowledge in reading comprehension, *Reading in a Foreign Language* 3 (1), 375–380.

5 Le plurilinguisme et la lingua franca: un rôle pour l'évaluation dans le redressement du déséquilibre linguistique en Europe[1]

Anne Gallagher
Language Centre, National University of Ireland
Maynooth

Introduction

Le premier janvier 1973, l'Irlande entra dans le Marché Commun. Même les opposants de cet événement historique estimaient qu'elle n'avait pas vraiment le choix, puisqu'elle suivait le Royaume-Uni dont son économie dépendait fortement pour ses marchés. Toutefois, la majorité s'en réjouissait, anticipant un nouvel avenir, au-delà des frontières du Royaume-Uni et de son passé de colonisée, un avenir qui l'enrichirait, la rendrait plus sophistiquée et plus européenne.

Afin de participer au projet européen, il fallait tout de suite commencer à apprendre des langues étrangères, principalement le français et l'allemand. Cela a pris un certain temps, mais finalement Maupassant, que l'on étudiait au lycée de la même manière que Tite Live, a cédé la place à un programme qui privilégiait la communication. Toutefois, la vision nationale d'une Europe multilingue à capacité plurilingue, et le rôle éventuel de l'Irlande dans ce processus, s'est estompée au fil des années. En dépit de nombreux colloques et réunions ayant pour thème « l'anglais seul ne suffit pas », l'aspiration du plurilinguisme a plus ou moins été consignée à un univers parallèle, et ceci dans un pays qui reconnaît deux langues officielles.

La langue maternelle plus deux autres langues

L'Union européenne a été fondée sur le principe de « l'unité dans la diversité ». Dès ses origines, sa politique linguistique avait comme ambition d'encourager les citoyens des Etats membres à apprendre deux ou trois des autres langues du Marché / de la Communauté / de l'Union, en partie pour des raisons économiques, en partie pour une meilleure cohésion sociale et aussi pour permettre une plus grande participation au projet européen. Dans tous les cas, l'objectif à long terme déclaré par la Commission européenne (2003) est « d'accroître le multilinguisme individuel (plurilinguisme) jusqu'à ce que chaque citoyen ait des compétences pratiques dans au moins deux autres langues que sa langue maternelle ». La définition précise de cet objectif échappe à beaucoup de nos concitoyens européens. Le terme « langue maternelle » est chargé de connotations: les anglophones irlandais, pour ne citer qu'un exemple, parlent souvent de leur désir « d'apprendre leur langue maternelle », en parlant de la langue irlandaise (le gaélique) que beaucoup d'entre eux maîtrisent mal.

Par ailleurs, le fait que ce terme (langue maternelle) est employé au singulier implique une communauté de nations monolingues. Dans le rapport final du projet VALEUR (Lo Bianco 2007) qui a été financé par le Conseil de l'Europe, Joanna McPake (2007:8) résume très bien cette question:

> On peut caractériser les politiques élaborées vers la fin du 20ᵉ siècle comme *monolingues* – ou *monolinguistes* – dans la mesure où elles tendent à supposer que tout le monde a une seule « première langue » ou « langue maternelle » et que tous vont donc acquérir une langue seconde (et leurs langues suivantes) de manières similaires (par un moyen formel quelconque), et ayant des objectifs comparables.

On estime généralement que « les deux autres langues » signifient deux autres langues de l'Union européenne. Mais que faire dans le cas de pays tels que l'Irlande, et nombre d'autres pays européens, qui ont plus d'une langue officielle, ou de ceux qui sont locuteurs de langues minoritaires qui ne sont pas reconnues comme langues officielles ou de travail de l'UE? En effet, d'après le dernier rapport Eurydice (2012:17) sur l'enseignement des langues à l'école en Europe, plus de la moitié de tous les pays européens reconnaît officiellement des langues régionales ou minoritaires à l'intérieur de leurs frontières.

L'Europe officielle: « Gauck möchte, dass Europa Englisch spricht » (Krauel 2013)

La Commission européenne traite ses affaires internes dans trois langues « procédurales », à savoir l'allemand, l'anglais et le français. Depuis l'élargissement oriental de 2004, l'emploi du français lors des colloques et des réunions a baissé, et nombreux sont ceux qui pensent que le rôle de l'allemand en tant que langue procédurale n'existe plus que sur le papier. L'Union européenne reconnaît actuellement 24 langues officielles et de travail, ce qui suscite de plus en plus de commentaires négatifs à propos du coût de la traduction, qui est de l'ordre d'un milliard d'euros par an, ou l'équivalent d'une tasse de café par citoyen par an. On comprend la tentation de réduire les dépenses, surtout dans le climat économique actuel. Chose inquiétante toutefois, il semblerait que les événements soient en train de nous dépasser. L'année dernière, peu avant de célébrer la fin de sa première année à la tête de son pays, le président allemand, Joachim Gauck, a signalé que l'Europe devrait avoir une langue véhiculaire et que cette langue devrait être l'anglais (European Commission 2013):

> Plus d'Europe ne signifie pas seulement plus de multilinguisme pour une élite, mais pour de plus en plus de groupes de populations, pour de plus en plus de gens, enfin pour tous ! Je suis persuadé que peuvent coexister en Europe une manière d'être imprégné de sa langue maternelle et de sa poésie, et l'usage pratique de l'anglais dans toutes les situations et pour tous les âges.
>
> Une langue commune permettrait une réalisation plus facile de mon rêve pour l'Europe de l'avenir: c'est-à-dire une agora européenne, un espace commun pour la discussion d'une coopération démocratique. (trad. A.G.)

Comme nous l'avons indiqué plus haut, il se peut que la vision du Président Gauck soit déjà en cours de réalisation, bien que, paradoxalement, le nombre de Britanniques qui travaillent à la Commission européenne ait considérablement diminué. D'après un rapport de *The House of Commons Foreign Affairs Committee* (2013), ces derniers constitueraient aujourd'hui seulement 4,6% du personnel exécutif, bien inférieur aux 12,5% qui est la proportion de la population de l'Union européenne que représentent les habitants de ce pays. La situation n'est guère mieux en ce qui concerne la proportion d'Irlandais employés à la Commission, ce qui a été confirmé récemment par un haut fonctionnaire européen à Dublin, qui ironisait sur le déclin des effectifs anglophones dans un contexte de consolidation de la langue anglaise dans les institutions européennes. Le président Gauck est certainement bien intentionné. Cependant, force est de constater que sa vision pour l'anglais (et pour les autres langues) au sein des institutions européennes correspond tout à fait à la diglossie, telle que l'a redéfinie Fishman (1987), c'est-à-dire la coexistence de deux langues (ou variétés de langue) côte à côte, où l'on emploie la langue plus prestigieuse, en l'occurrence, l'anglais, dans des contextes formels ou officiels, et où la deuxième langue, moins prestigieuse (ici toutes les autres langues), se cantonne au cadre privé ou personnel.

Bien que l'on cite souvent l'élargissement oriental de 2004 comme étant le moteur de l'hégémonie anglophone dans l'administration européenne, il nous semble raisonnable de demander si cette évolution en faveur de l'anglais a réellement sa source dans les politiques linguistiques de l'Union, autrement dit, celles qui cherchent à influencer l'apprentissage et l'acquisition des langues étrangères. Dans une analyse très intéressante du discours concernant les stratégies politiques et linguistiques de l'UE, Krzyzanowski et

(2011) parlent d'une « instrumentalisation linguistique croissante » (2011: 123) ayant pour toile de fond *L'économie fondée sur le savoir*, où l'on traite des langues simplement en termes de compétences. Malgré un éloignement de cette politique pendant deux ans, de 2005 à 2007, du moins au niveau du langage, où il était question également de motifs démocratiques et sociaux, depuis 2008 on constate un retour aux arguments économiques. Pour citer Krzyzanowski et Wodak (2011:131):

> [. . .] La politique linguistique et multilinguistique de l'Union européenne fait preuve d'une meilleure compréhension du rôle social, politique et économique des langues et du multilinguisme. Malheureusement, suite à la crise financière de 2008 et à cause du transfert du Portefeuille de multilinguisme de la Commission européenne à Education, Culture et Jeunesse en 2010, la plupart des dispositions clefs des politiques élaborées en 2008 n'ont toujours pas été exécutées. Par conséquent, les politiques provenant de (du traité de) Lisbonne restent en place [. . .] (trad. A.G.)

En septembre 2013, la Commission européenne publie un communiqué de presse intitulé *Foire aux questions concernant les langues en Europe* sous forme de questions réponses. L'une des questions posées est celle de l'introduction d'une langue unique. Voici la réponse: « Il est trop simpliste de penser qu'une langue unique pourrait répondre à tous les besoins linguistiques. C'est la raison pour laquelle l'engagement de la Commission en faveur du multilinguisme met l'accent sur la diversité plutôt que sur l'uniformité. » (European Commission 2013)

Cette déclaration est rassurante. Toutefois, la réalité semble la contredire, la conjoncture économique ayant l'air de l'emporter sur l'objectif très désirable mais coûteux de la diversité linguistique, aussi bien au sein des institutions mêmes qu'au niveau des politiques linguistiques.

L'Europe multilingue

La réalité sur le terrain en Europe est bien différente. A vrai dire, l'Europe n'a jamais été aussi multilingue. Le rapport Eurobaromètre de 2012 compte au total 23 langues reconnues officiellement (il y en a désormais 24), plus de 60 langues autochtones minoritaires ou régionales et, enfin, un grand nombre de langues non autochtones parlées par les communautés de migrants. En 2007, le projet VALEUR, déjà cité, a fait état d'au moins 440 langues parlées et au moins 18 langues des signes dans les 21 pays participants. Nos propres recherches (Gallagher 2006) ont révélé l'existence d'environ 200 langues parlées/employées tous les jours en Irlande, un pays de seulement un peu plus de 4 millions d'habitants. Un premier total avéré de 167 langues ne prenait pas en compte un certain nombre de langues minoritaires, telles que le kachoube, par exemple, qui ne s'affichent pas toujours dans les documents administratifs ou dans les demandes de traduction lorsque le locuteur parle une langue majoritaire de son pays, comme le polonais dans l'exemple cité.

En dépit d'une récession économique foudroyante, l'Irlande reste un pays fortement multilingue. D'après Lorna Carson (2014), on a cité 182 langues différentes lors du recensement de 2011 et 26% des locuteurs de ces langues étrangères étaient nés en Irlande:

> En ce qui concerne les ressortissants européens, le polonais est de loin la langue la plus courante, suivi par le lituanien, le russe, le roumain et le letton. Ceux d'origine asiatique parlent surtout le tagalog, ensuite le chinois (le mandarin et le cantonais), le malayalam, l'ourdou et le hindi. Le yoruba prédomine chez les Africains, suivi par le français, l'arabe, l'igbo et l'afrikaans. Le portugais a été fortement représenté parmi les ressortissants d'Amérique du Nord et du Sud; viennent ensuite l'espagnol, le français, le polonais et l'allemand. (trad. A.G.)

Dans cet exemple également, il est très probable que les 182 langues citées constituent une sous-estimation, car, d'après notre expérience, les immigrants tendent à minimiser le nombre de langues qu'ils possèdent. Ceci est particulièrement vrai en ce qui concerne les Africains, qui négligent souvent de mentionner leurs langues qui ne sont pas écrites. De plus, la question sur les langues pratiquées à la maison a été posée au singulier: « Parlez-vous une langue autre que l'anglais ou l'irlandais à la maison? » (trad. A.G.) Les personnes interrogées auraient très bien pu interpréter littéralement la question, en ne citant qu'une langue là où en réalité elles en parlaient plusieurs. Finalement, nous avons rencontré des migrants en Irlande pour qui l'appartenance à une communauté à capacité multilingue est gênante, étant convaincus que la tradition monolingue est plus prestigieuse. Un vestige, sans doute, d'un vécu colonial.

Les minorités et l'état d'esprit monolinguiste

Le linguiste français Alexandre François (2013:144) résume très bien ce qui est la réalité quotidienne pour beaucoup de locuteurs de langues minoritaires:

> Une minorité linguistique est une communauté qui subit des pressions constantes pour renoncer à l'emploi de sa langue et adopter celle d'un groupe majoritaire. La pression prend parfois la forme d'une loi, mais le plus souvent s'exerce dans les esprits, par une incitation économique, sociale, scolaire, vers l'uniformisation linguistique.
>
> C'est que nos sociétés modernes se construisent autour d'une idéologie étroitement monolingue, selon laquelle la cohésion d'une nation impliquerait nécessairement l'allégeance de tous à une langue unique.

> Dans ce modèle jacobin, très prégnant en France, en Chine et ailleurs, les minorités linguistiques sont perçues par la majorité comme une survivance, voire un facteur de division. On oublie un peu trop vite que les hommes sont capables de parler plusieurs langues.

Le monde de l'anglophone monolingue est assez limité dans la mesure où il admet difficilement la production culturelle provenant d'autres langues. La production romanesque issue de traductions, par exemple, peine à se tailler une place sur le marché, donc les anglophones ne s'exposent que peu à la littérature et aux idées émanant des pays non anglophones. A titre d'illustration, d'après Laurence Marie (2014), écrivant dans le *Nouvel Observateur*, seulement 1% des romans publiés tous les ans aux Etats-Unis sont traduits du français, qui est, par ailleurs, la langue la plus traduite du monde après l'anglais. En revanche, 33% des romans lus en France sont des traductions. Dans un article paru l'année dernière sur un site d'association d'éditeurs Publishers' Perspectives, les auteurs nous apprennent que « les traductions représentent seulement 4,5% de la totalité de la production littéraire publiée au Royaume-Uni et incroyablement en Pologne 46% de tous les livres publiés sont issus de traductions; en Allemagne le chiffre dépasse les 12%, en Espagne il se situe autour des 24% et en France il est d'environ 15%. » (trad. A.G.)

Sur le plan de l'enseignement, l'anglophonie prédomine aussi. Seulement six universités sur « les cinquante meilleures universités du monde » se trouvent dans des pays non anglophones selon le Times Higher Education World University Rankings 2013–2014 (Classement mondial des universités par le *Times Higher Education Supplement*, journal consacré à l'enseignement supérieur). De plus, aucune université allemande et aucune université française n'y figurent. On peut également noter l'absence d'universités non-anglophones dans le classement de Shanghai où il n'y en a que huit parmi « les cinquante meilleures du monde »; deux françaises et une allemande selon leurs indicateurs. Dans de nombreux pays anglophones, les universités établissent des comités afin d'assurer des progrès dans ce genre de classement, qui joue un rôle important dans le marché lucratif des étudiants internationaux, c'est-à-dire non-ressortissants de l'Union européenne. Nous connaissons au moins un établissement qui décourage les publications, même celles sur les langues étrangères, en langues autres que l'anglais, de peur que cela compromette leurs chances de figurer dans les citations internationales de publications, un des indicateurs utilisés dans la création des classements.

Cependant, aux limites imposées par la perception du monde à travers une seule langue s'ajoutent d'autres coûts. Deux pays anglophones, l'Irlande et l'Ecosse sont les seuls pays d'Europe où l'apprentissage d'une langue étrangère n'est pas obligatoire. En Angleterre, au Pays de Galles et en Irlande du Nord, l'apprentissage des langues est obligatoire, mais seulement jusqu'à l'âge de 14 ans. Au niveau de l'enseignement supérieur, la situation n'est guère meilleure. On enseigne de plus en plus de programmes de langue, y compris des cours pour spécialistes, à travers l'anglais. Autrement dit, la langue cible s'apprend en cours de langue mais tous les autres aspects du cursus (littérature, civilisation, etc.) ne sont accessibles qu'en anglais. L'évaluation de ces modules se fait généralement en anglais aussi.

Il en résulte que les étudiants anglophones qui passent leurs années Erasmus sur le continent sont souvent dépourvus des compétences nécessaires à une participation active aux programmes d'études ou, pire encore, on leur propose des cursus entièrement en anglais. Comme l'a noté Elizabeth Murphy-Lejeune (2002) la lingua franca des étudiants Erasmus est presque exclusivement l'anglais. Bien entendu, nous ne remettons pas en question la valeur de l'année à l'étranger. Il faut néanmoins avouer que les résultats en ce qui concerne les compétences linguistiques acquises sont souvent décevants, et bien en deçà de ce qu'ils pourraient ou devraient être. Les implications quant à la vie sociale et culturelle dans la langue cible sont évidentes.

Le coût économique

Que savons-nous sur les compétences linguistiques d'un diplômé en langues? A vrai dire, très peu. Dans tous les cas, dans les pays anglophones, nos universités, pour la plupart, ne produisent pas de diplômés en langues avec les compétences requises par le monde du travail. Leur niveau de compétences linguistiques est un des facteurs (mais pas le seul) qui empêche les candidats anglophones d'accéder aux postes dans les institutions européennes.

Ce déficit linguistique des pays anglophones leur est onéreux. Deirdre Hunt (2009), professeur de management à l'université de Cork, nous rappelle que 75% de la population du monde ne parlent pas l'anglais et 94% ne le parlent pas comme langue maternelle. Un communiqué de presse sur les langues en Europe, émis par la Commission européenne en septembre 2013 et déjà cité, confirme les propos de professeur Hunt: « L'anglais est la deuxième langue la plus répandue dans l'Union européenne. Toutefois, des études récentes montrent qu'aujourd'hui encore, la part de la population de l'Union qui maîtrise suffisamment cette langue pour pouvoir communiquer n'atteint pas les 50 %. »

La professeur Hunt cite une étude réalisée par Frankel et Rose (2002) qui ont quantifié l'impact du manque de compétences en langues sur les performances des entreprises: « En mesurant les différences de langues comme barrières commerciales, ils calculent que les coûts de ces barrières linguistiques sont entre 15% et 22% en termes de tarifs équivalents. Ils évaluent de 75% à 170% la croissance de commerce bilatéral possible grâce à une langue commune. » (trad. A.G.)

La Commission (2013) affirme autrement l'importance des langues pour les entreprises:

En 2006, une étude a été menée pour la Commission européenne afin d'évaluer le coût du déficit linguistique pour les entreprises européennes. Il en est ressorti que, chaque année, des milliers de ces entreprises ratent ou perdent des contrats, faute de compétences linguistiques. D'après les estimations de l'étude, 11% des PME européennes travaillant à l'exportation (au nombre de 945 000) sont susceptibles de se retrouver dans ce cas de figure à cause d'obstacles à la communication.

En Irlande, les demandes répétées de la part des industriels, y compris du secteur de la technologie et de l'information, de meilleures compétences en langues n'ont jusqu'ici mené à rien. Nous ne savons pas pourquoi. Comme tout le monde le sait, l'enseignement des langues est coûteux. Il se peut que son gouvernement ait décidé que l'investissement que demanderait une approche sérieuse est trop important, ou bien qu'il croie vraiment que l'anglais suffit.

L'apprentissage des langues sur le continent

Force est de constater cependant que sur le continent européen, l'apprentissage des langues signifie de plus en plus seul l'apprentissage de l'anglais. L'anglais est la langue la plus enseignée dans presque tous les pays d'Europe. D'après le rapport Agence Executive Education, Audiovisuel et Culture (2012:75), « Dans la très grande majorité des pays, 90% des élèves au moins apprennent l'anglais au niveau CITE 2 et au niveau CITE 3 (enseignement général). Il est néanmoins important de noter qu'en moyenne, en 2009–2010, 60,8 % des élèves de l'enseignement secondaire inférieur en Europe apprenaient au moins deux langues étrangères. Cela représente une augmentation de 14,1 points en comparaison à l'année 2004–2005 ». Toutefois, il y a de quoi se préoccuper en considérant les niveaux de compétences atteints dans la deuxième langue étrangère, c'est-à-dire les langues autres que l'anglais.

SurveyLang

L'Etude SurveyLang (European Commission 2012a), qui a évalué les compétences des élèves en compréhension orale, compréhension écrite et production écrite en langues étrangères, fut établie pour fournir aux pays participants des données comparables sur les compétences en langues étrangères et les bonnes pratiques dans le domaine de l'enseignement des langues afin de mettre au point des indicateurs de compétences linguistiques. Les participants étaient des élèves ayant accompli le premier degré de l'enseignement secondaire ou qui étaient au début du deuxième degré. Ils ont passé les tests dans les deux langues étrangères les plus fréquemment étudiées parmi les langues proposées (allemand, anglais, espagnol, français et italien) et étaient issus de quatorze pays européens. Les participants étaient: Angleterre, Belgique, Bulgarie, Croatie, Espagne, Estonie, France, Grèce, Malte, Pays-Bas, Pologne,

Table 1 Pourcentage d'élèves de chaque pays atteignant le niveau B dans chaque compétence (première langue étrangère)

Première langue étrangère	Pays	Comp. écrite (lecture)	Comp. orale (écoute)	Production écrite (écriture)
anglais	Estonie	60 %	63 %	60 %
anglais	Malte	79 %	86 %	83 %
anglais	Pays-Bas	60 %	77 %	60 %
anglais	Suède	81 %	91 %	75 %

Portugal, Slovénie et Suède. L'anglais était la première langue étrangère de chaque pays sauf la Belgique où c'était le français. Les résultats des tests ont été reliés au Cadre européen commun de référence pour les langues (CECR).

Quelques résultats

Considérons d'abord les pays où les élèves ont le mieux réussi dans la première langue étrangère, c'est-à-dire avec les pourcentages les plus élevés atteignant le niveau B (utilisateur indépendant) du CECR et qui figurent dans la Table 1.

Il est peut-être peu étonnant que les élèves aient obtenu des scores plus élevés en anglais que dans la deuxième langue étrangère. On parle des langues germaniques dans deux des pays qui figurent dans la table (l'Allemagne n'y a d'ailleurs pas participé). Historiquement, Malte a été très liée au Royaume-Uni. Toutefois, l'Estonie, où le russe a été une langue seconde obligatoire pendant de nombreuses années, n'a jamais connu de telles affiliations, bien que l'estonien ait beaucoup emprunté à l'allemand à travers les siècles. Il se peut, bien entendu, que certains pays bénéficient d'un professorat plus compétent et que certains élèves soient plus motivés ou plus assidus. Considérons ensuite les résultats de ces memes pays pour la deuxième langue étrangère dans la Table 2. On peut déduire assez naturellement à partir des résultats de SurveyLang que les élèves dans beaucoup de pays européens apprennent mieux l'anglais que les autres langues. L'équipe de SurveyLang (European Commission 2012a:6) en tire ses propres conclusions:

> En effet, même dans les systèmes éducatifs où l'on enseigne l'anglais en tant que deuxième langue étrangère, les performances en anglais ont tendance à être meilleures que dans les autres langues testées. Il en ressort davantage de preuves sur le statut particulier de l'anglais, à partir des réponses des élèves aux questionnaires, de leur perception quant à son utilité, du degré d'exposition à la langue et de son usage dans les médias traditionnels ou nouveaux. (trad. A.G.)

Table 2 Pourcentage d'élèves de chaque pays atteignant le niveau B dans chaque compétence (deuxième langue étrangère)

Deuxième langue étrangère	Pays	Comp. écrite (lecture)	Comp. orale (écoute)	Production écrite (écriture)
allemand	Estonie	27%	24%	22%
italien	Malte	34%	46%	23%
allemand	Pays-Bas	54%	60%	31%
espagnol	Suède	7%	3%	2%

La lingua franca

Nous avons donc un problème. Le prestige de l'anglais s'accroît de même que son usage. Par conséquent, le statut des langues autres que l'anglais fait l'objet d'une mise en question presque quotidienne. Même des langues avec des centaines de millions de locuteurs à travers le monde commencent à exhiber en Europe des caractéristiques plus habituelles chez les langues minoritaires. Un statut mitigé entraîne des compétences mitigées. En outre, la position de l'anglais comme langue véhiculaire décourage l'apprentissage des langues étrangères chez les anglophones créant ainsi une relation de dépendance entre ces derniers et les locuteurs d'autres langues. Par conséquent, les questions pour les linguistes professionnels européens doivent être les suivantes:

(1) Comment fait-on pour renforcer le statut des langues autres que l'anglais sur le plan national aussi bien qu'européen?

(2) Etant donné la situation que nous venons de décrire, que faut-il faire pour améliorer les compétences en langues étrangères des anglophones?

Il n'y a malheureusement pas de solution-miracle. Ceci étant, nous sommes persuadés que l'évaluation joue un rôle clef dans le redressement du déséquilibre entre l'anglais et les autres idiomes de l'Europe.

Valoriser toutes les langues: Un rôle pour l'évaluation

Le linguiste américain Joshua Fishman a défini la planification linguistique comme « L'attribution de ressources de la part d'un organisme faisant autorité afin de réaliser des objectifs quant au statut d'une langue et le développement du corpus, que cela concerne de nouvelles fonctions ambitionnées ou des fonctions plus anciennes qui doivent s'effectuer de manière plus adéquate. » Baker et Prys Jones (1998:204) citant Cooper la décrit comme « [. . .] des efforts délibérés pour influencer le comportement des autres quant à l'acquisition, la structure ou la répartition fonctionnelle de leurs codes linguistiques ». (trad. A.G.) Il propose qu' « [. . .] une telle planification linguistique implique une planification de statut (changement de statut de la langue dans la société en augmentant ou réduisant ses fonctions), une planification du corpus (concernant le remaniement de la standardisation d'une langue afin d'accomplir de nouvelles fonctions), et la planification de l'acquisition (propagation de la langue en augmentant le nombre de locuteurs et d'usages, au moyen de l'enseignement de la langue, par exemple) ». (trad. A.G.)

La planification du statut constitue donc un aspect important de la planification et de la normalisation de la langue minoritaire (ou étrangère). Une mesure d'appui au plurilinguisme, qui contribue au renforcement du statut d'une langue, qu'il s'agisse d'une langue minoritaire ou étrangère, est la reconnaissance formelle des compétences du locuteur / de l'utilisateur par le biais de l'évaluation. Nombre de langues minoritaires ou régionales ont connu un passé difficile, associé souvent à un manque général d'instruction et d'assurance. Le fait de reconnaître ces compétences tend à rendre plus positives les attitudes des locuteurs mêmes vis-à-vis de leur langue et à leur donner du courage et une certaine confiance en soi en tant que locuteurs minoritaires. Le CECR peut jouer un rôle clé dans la reconnaissance de ces compétences. Par exemple, la manière dont les niveaux du CECR se définissent permet l'affirmation de compétences partielles, ce qui représente la réalité linguistique pour beaucoup de locuteurs de langues minoritaires. En Irlande, les maternelles de langue irlandaise demandent désormais un certificat de compétence orale, niveau B2, pour ceux qui souhaitent y travailler, n'ayant nul besoin des autres compétences linguistiques dans le cadre de leur travail. Les tests de gallois privilégient les compétences orales, encore une réponse à la réalité et aux enjeux sociolinguistiques de certaines régions du Pays de Galles.

Il va de soi que l'évaluation liée au CECR constitue une partie intégrante de la planification de l'acquisition des langues minoritaires et étrangères. En plus des nombreux avantages conférés par l'usage du cadre de référence, l'existence d'un parcours cohérent, associé à un système d'évaluation entraînant un effet de *washback* (impact) positif, sert à motiver les apprenants à progresser jusqu'au niveau suivant et à se concentrer sur les compétences linguistiques les plus adaptées à leurs besoins. En outre, les apprenants adultes apprécient le fait qu'ils appartiennent à une communauté européenne plus large, et qu'ils suivent un chemin d'acquisition linguistique semblable à celui de leurs homologues à travers l'Europe.

Que signifie un diplôme en langues?

A notre avis, le CECR pourrait jouer un rôle clé dans la description des programmes de diplômes en langues dans l'enseignement supérieur. Comme nous l'avons démontré, il n'y a actuellement aucun moyen d'établir de façon formelle les compétences linguistiques d'un diplômé en langues. Aux Etats-Unis, la plupart des universités relient le contenu linguistique de leurs programmes de langues aux niveaux de compétences de *l'American Council on the Teaching of Foreign Languages*, qui sont comparables aux niveaux du CECR en Europe. Ce dispositif paraît logique, puisqu'il sert à communiquer au public, aux étudiants tant qu'aux employeurs, les niveaux et les domaines de compétences auxquels ils peuvent s'attendre de la part des diplômés de ces établissements, étant donné que les compétences acquises se situent par rapport à des points de référence extérieurs. C'est également un moyen d'aborder la question de la baisse de niveau d'exigence, dont s'alarment un bon nombre de professionnels de l'éducation et d'employeurs, du moins en Grande Bretagne et en Irlande.

Dans son intervention au Forum politique intergouvernemental de 2007 intitulé « Le Cadre européen commun de référence pour les langues et l'élaboration de politiques linguistiques: défis et responsabilités », organisé par la Division des politiques linguistiques du Conseil de l'Europe à Strasbourg du 6 au 8 février 2007, Brian North (2007:19), un des auteurs du CECR, résume les trois objectifs principaux de départ du cadre de référence:

- Définir un métalangage commun à tous les secteurs de l'éducation, par-delà les frontières nationales et linguistiques, qui puisse être utilisé pour parler des objectifs et des niveaux de maîtrise des langues. Aider ainsi les praticiens à dire à leurs collègues et à leur clientèle ce qu'ils attendent de leurs apprenants et comment ils envisagent de les aider à y parvenir.
- Encourager les professionnels à réfléchir sur leur pratique, en particulier s'agissant des besoins concrets des apprenants, de la fixation d'objectifs appropriés et du suivi des progrès des apprenants.
- Adopter des points de référence communs fondés sur les travaux réalisés dans le cadre du projet « Langues vivantes du Conseil de l'Europe depuis les années 1970 ».

A l'origine, l'élaboration du CECR ne visait pas l'évaluation formelle, bien que cet emploi fût anticipé. North précise qu'« on espérait qu'à la longue l'existence de ce cadre de référence faciliterait la comparaison de cursus et d'examens, atteignant ainsi « la transparence et la cohérence » qui avaient été le thème du Symposium de Rüschlikon. » Il souligne aussi la notion d'un usage adapté au contexte local. A vrai dire, l'un des grands atouts du CECR est sa flexibilité. Toutefois, il ne faut pas confondre flexibilité et absence de rigueur. On peut constater que le CECR s'est développé bien au-delà de ce qui a été prévu au départ, entre autres pour assurer qu'il constitue un outil approprié à l'évaluation linguistique. Ceci étant, il reste encore un élément essentiel à compléter: celui de la responsabilité.

On pourrait dire que le CECR est l'innovation la plus importante en matière d'éducation linguistique de ces cinquante dernières années. Mais, chose incroyable, il n'y a toujours pas, à notre connaissance, de suivi formel de son usage, ni sur le plan national ni sur le plan international. En effet, cela veut dire que tout un chacun peut déclarer que ses cursus/méthodes de langue/examens/certificats ou diplômes correspondent à un niveau particulier du CECR. Ceux dont le travail fait référence au CECR sont, sans doute, pour la plupart bien informés et bien intentionnés. Mais North lui-même affirme que le principal danger en ce qui concerne les cadres de référence communs en est une interprétation simpliste. L'utilisation naïve du CECR est certainement un problème, mais il y a inévitablement des établissements qui ne prennent pas la peine de s'informer ou qui sont mal informés, sans parler de ceux qui apposent de manière cynique voire malhonnête à leurs cursus, ressources ou diplômes l'étiquette du CECR.

Dans le rapport sur le Forum intergouvernemental (Goullier 2007a:15) sur les politiques linguistiques, on souligne la question de responsabilité quant à l'usage approprié du CECR. On propose qu'il faut être particulièrement attentif en utilisant les niveaux de compétence pour l'évaluation en langues:

- Chaque Etat membre doit se sentir responsable, dès lors que son système éducatif ou des organismes qui dépendent de lui utilisent la référence aux niveaux du Cadre pour l'évaluation en langues des apprenants, de réunir toutes les conditions pour que cette référence soit valide.
- Toutes les mesures doivent être prises pour garantir l'application de bonnes pratiques reconnues au niveau international dans l'élaboration d'examens équitables, transparents, valides et fiables. Des dispositions doivent être prises au niveau national ou local pour assurer l'établissement de liens entre les niveaux de compétences certifiés par leurs examens de langue et les niveaux de référence du CECR, de manière transparente et fiable. Ces dispositions peuvent être très différentes, même si l'idée d'une agence nationale a été citée à plusieurs reprises pendant le Forum.

Les conclusions du Forum intergouvernemental furent adoptées par le Comité des Ministres[2] qui recommande aux gouvernements des Etats membres d'assurer que tous les dispositifs d'évaluation donnant lieu à des certifications de compétences en langues officiellement reconnues prennent en considération tous les aspects d'utilisation et de compétences en langues tels qu'énoncés dans le CECR, qu'ils soient utilisés avec une gestion de qualité et que ces tests et examens soient reliés au CECR de façon fiable et transparente, suivant la bonne pratique internationale en la matière.

Des associations comme ALTE mettent en place des dispositifs afin d'assurer une application rigoureuse du CECR. Les agences d'évaluation, membres d'ALTE, y adhèrent volontairement. Mais il y a d'autres organismes responsables de l'évaluation, y compris dans les universités et les établissements scolaires, qui utilisent les niveaux du CECR de manière désinvolte sans avoir à rendre compte à qui que ce soit. Si cette pratique continue, elle pourrait mener à une diminution de l'influence et de l'intégrité du cadre de référence, et, à la fin, à son abandon. A notre avis, on y a investi trop d'efforts et il a trop de valeur pour envisager ou permettre une telle éventualité. Dans l'intervention qu'il a faite lors du Forum intergouvernemental, Francis Goullier (2007:36) soulève de façon très succincte cette question de responsabilité et les implications d'une continuation du statu quo:

> Il semble être admis que chaque Etat et chaque institution étaient responsables de la qualité de ses procédures concernant l'évaluation des niveaux de compétences. Mais devant qui? Devant le Conseil de l'Europe? Pas seulement ! La nature même des enjeux de cette question d'un lien correct des épreuves de certification avec les niveaux de compétences montre que cette question a des conséquences sur le profit que les différents Etats et institutions peuvent espérer de la référence à ces niveaux de compétences. Si un Etat laisse se développer une utilisation abusive des niveaux de compétences, il met en cause la construction entreprise dans d'autres Etats, dans la mesure où il fragilise la valeur paneuropéenne de la référence à ces niveaux. Il prive également les apprenants des avantages que leur procure une fiabilité des certifications de compétences, en rendant plus aléatoire leur reconnaissance internationale et en réduisant la valeur de ce qui représente un atout important dans le contexte de la mobilité en Europe.

Il faut agir maintenant, car une fois le CECR discrédité, ce sera trop tard. Une solution possible serait l'établissement de comités nationaux qui serviraient à la fois à surveiller et à donner des conseils sur son utilisation, en bref, à assurer la gestion de qualité. La Division des politiques linguistiques du Conseil de l'Europe pourrait coordonner des réunions de représentants de ces comités en vue d'organiser des stages de formation et la participation d'experts en la matière.

Le CECR a servi à structurer l'apprentissage et l'évaluation d'une vingtaine de langues à travers l'Europe depuis maintenant plus de dix ans. C'est un travail encore à ses débuts qui a un potentiel encore inexploité surtout en ce qui concerne la comparabilité des certifications et les langues moins répandues, mais à condition d'en éviter l'usage abusif.

L'avenir du plurilinguisme?

Il paraît évident que le rôle de l'anglais en Europe officielle va en grandissant. Il est inutile d'essayer d'arrêter le raz-de-marée anglophone. Il faut néanmoins faire de notre mieux pour assurer que les autres langues d'Europe en sortent indemnes et qu'elles continuent à prendre part au projet européen. La prédominance de l'anglais n'est pas sans implications pour la démocratie européenne. Il ne s'agit pas de freiner le développement d'une langue véhiculaire, il s'agit tout simplement d'en connaître et reconnaître les limites. Il faut à l'Europe une politique linguistique qui mette en valeur toutes les langues présentes sur ses territoires, qui exploite son potentiel linguistique dans l'intérêt social, économique et culturel de tous les citoyens de l'Union. En même temps, il faut réduire la relation de dépendance entre les anglophones et les autres. Comme l'a exprimé un chroniqueur du journal anglais, *The Economist* (RLG 2014), l'année dernière:

> Aucun pays n'a rejoint l'Union afin d'être écrasé sous une roue homogénéisante. On promulgue des lois importantes au niveau de l'UE et les Européens ont le droit d'être capables de les comprendre, c'est-à-dire non seulement les versions finales des lois, mais également les débats au Parlement européen. L'UE fait déjà de grands gestes envers les petits pays (en donnant par exemple le même vote à Malte qu'à l'Allemagne à la Banque centrale européenne). Encourager le multilinguisme (plurilinguisme) pas seulement une aisance en anglais, me semble plus logique si l'on veut démontrer que tous les pays sont importants. (trad. A.G.)

A ce propos, nous voudrions saluer le fait qu'ALTE, qui est en tout premier lieu une association d'évaluateurs, considère que la promotion du multilinguisme et du plurilinguisme fait partie de sa mission.

Dans un entretien avec le Goethe-Institut en 2006, on a demandé à Gerhard Stickel (2006), directeur de *l'Institut für Deutsche Sprache* de prédire l'avenir des langues en Europe. Les suivants sont les cas de figure qu'il propose, non sans humour:

> Le scénario pessimiste: dans les années à venir, l'apprentissage des langues se limitera de plus en plus à l'anglais. L'intérêt porté aux autres langues diminuera même chez ceux qui les parlent en tant que langues maternelles. On parlera toujours l'italien, l'allemand, le néerlandais et les autres langues européennes, mais seulement au sein de la famille, en jouant aux cartes et dans les kermesses. D'un autre côté, on traitera de plus en plus les affaires importantes dans le monde du travail, des sciences et de la politique dans un anglais créolisé (un anglais américain saupoudré de français, d'allemand et d'italien). Dans les Iles Britanniques, la variété britannique de l'anglais sera un dialecte qui se fera de plus en plus rare.
>
> Le scénario optimiste: presque tous les Européens, à savoir nous les Allemands, les Italiens, les Néerlandais, les Polonais, etc. avons réussi à bien faire apprendre à nos enfants deux langues autres que leur langues maternelles et peut-être d'autres langues également. Les Anglais sont la seule exception. Ils sont habitués au fait que presque tout le monde parle leur langue. Par conséquent, ils ont arrêté d'apprendre d'autres langues il y a longtemps. Toutefois, étant un peuple sensé, ils vont s'apercevoir

à la longue que leur pensée et leur perception vont en diminuant. Leur monolinguisme acharné fait qu'ils n'ont qu'une vision très étroite sur un monde qui est devenu de plus en plus complexe. Et puisqu'ils ne veulent plus de ces limites, ils commencent à apprendre de façon rapide et intensive au moins deux autres langues et ils insistent que leurs enfants le fassent aussi. Par conséquent, à travers toute l'Europe dans 50 ou 100 ans, la société sera à nouveau (ou toujours) multilingue et multiculturelle, riche et créative. (trad. A.G.)

Comme nous l'avons démontré plus haut, les scénarios proposés par le professeur Stickel ne sont pas tout à fait irréalistes. L'anglais prédomine au sein de la Commission européenne, les anglophones maîtrisent de moins en moins bien les langues étrangères, sur le continent européen l'anglais est la première langue étrangère dans la plupart des pays et l'intérêt porté aux autres langues semble diminuer; les anglophones ne s'exposent que peu aux idées émanant d'autres pays. Il reste à savoir si ces derniers s'adonneront à l'apprentissage des langues étrangères dans les années à venir !

Ce qui compte ne peut pas toujours être compté, et ce qui peut être compté ne compte pas forcément

L'Europe a de bonnes raisons de continuer à encourager le multilinguisme, la présence d'un grand nombre de langues sur nos territoires, et à promouvoir le plurilinguisme, la capacité de communiquer dans la langue de l'autre: certaines sont économiques, d'autres sont dans l'intérêt d'une démocratie plus puissante et d'une diversité culturelle enrichissante. Un enseignement bien adapté aux besoins communicatifs des apprenants et une évaluation valide, fiable et transparente des acquis de l'apprentissage joueront un rôle clé dans la formation de citoyens plurilingues et ainsi dans la promotion et la préservation des langues en Europe. L'évaluation ferait également partie intégrante de la mise en œuvre des indicateurs de compétences linguistiques, proposés en 2002, si cette initiative importante se réalise un jour. Il est évident que l'ambition d'un ensemble de citoyens plurilingues ne se réalisera qu'avec le concours des enseignants et des évaluateurs.

Le poète irlandais, Séamus Heaney[3] (2015), lauréat du prix Nobel de la littérature en 1995, dont la langue maternelle était l'anglais et qui a disparu en 2013, a parlé de l'importance pour lui d'avoir appris l'irlandais.

Ses arguments s'appliquent pour toutes les langues et contre l'homogénéisation linguistique. Nous lui laissons le dernier mot:

Ne pas apprendre l'irlandais, c'est perdre l'occasion de comprendre ce qu'a signifié la vie dans ce pays et ce qu'elle signifierait dans un avenir meilleur. C'est se couper de manières à être chez soi. Si nous considérons la compréhension de soi, la compréhension réciproque, un imaginaire plus dynamique, la diversité culturelle et un climat politique de tolérance comme des acquis désirables, alors nous devrions nous rappeler que la connaissance de l'irlandais constitue un élément essentiel dans leur réalisation. (trad. A.G.)

Not to learn Irish is to miss the opportunity of understanding what life in this country has meant and could mean in a better future. It is to cut oneself off from ways of being at home. If we regard self-understanding, mutual understanding, imaginative enhancement, cultural diversity and a tolerant political atmosphere as desirable attainments, we should remember that a knowledge of the Irish language is an essential element in their realisation.

Notes

1   Dans le cadre de cet article, nous suivons les définitions du Conseil de l'Europe (Council of Europe 2001) en ce qui concerne le plurilinguisme et le multilinguisme: le «multilinguisme» étant un phénomène de société et indiquant la présence d'un certain nombre de langues et le «plurilinguisme» ayant trait au répertoire langagier de l'individu. Le terme «lingua franca» est employé au sens de « langue véhiculaire». La « langue maternelle» (ou «les langues maternelles ») se réfère à la première langue apprise par l'enfant, en général avant l'âge de cinq ans.

2   Recommandation CM/Rec (2008)7 du Comité des Ministres aux Etats membres sur l'utilisation du Cadre européen commun de référence pour les langues (CECR) du Conseil de l'Europe et la promotion du plurilinguisme 1 *(adoptée par le Comité des Ministres le 2 juillet 2008, lors de la 1031e réunion des Délégués des Ministres)*.
Le Comité des Ministres, selon les termes de l'article 15.*b* du Statut du Conseil de l'Europe,
[…] recommande aux gouvernements des Etats membres :
— d'utiliser tous les moyens à leur disposition pour mettre en œuvre les mesures énoncées dans l'Annexe 1 à cette recommandation concernant l'élaboration de leurs politiques linguistiques éducatives, conformément à leur constitution, à leur contexte national, régional ou local et à leur système éducatif;
Annexe I à la Recommandation CM/Rec (2008)7
Les autorités éducatives nationales, régionales et locales sont invitées à :
4.5. à assurer que tous les tests, examens et dispositifs d'évaluation donnant lieu à des certifications de compétences en langues officiellement reconnues prennent pleinement en considération tous les aspects d'utilisation et de compétences en langues tels qu'énoncés dans le CECR, qu'ils soient appliqués conformément à des principes de bonne pratique internationalement reconnus et avec une gestion de qualité, et

que les procédures pour relier ces tests et examens aux niveaux communs de référence (A1–C2) du CECR soient suivies de façon fiable et transparente ;

4.6. à assurer que toute information concernant les procédures utilisées dans l'ensemble des tests, examens et systèmes d'évaluation donnant lieu à des certifications officiellement reconnues, en particulier celles utilisées pour les relier aux niveaux communs de référence (A1–C2) du CECR, soit publiée de façon très accessible et mise à la disposition gratuitement de toutes les parties intéressées ;

4.7. à encourager toutes les autres entités responsables de l'évaluation et de certifications en langues étrangères/secondes à adopter des mesures garantissant la production de tests et examens équitables, transparents, valides et fiables répondant aux principes énoncés au paragraphe 4.5 et de publier les procédures utilisées, en particulier celles utilisées pour relier les tests et examens aux niveaux communs de référence du CECRL (A1–C2), tel qu'énoncé au paragraphe 4.6.

Recommandation CM/Rec(2008)7 du Comité des Ministres aux Etats membres sur l'utilisation du Cadre européen commun de référence pour les langues (CECR) du Conseil de l'Europe et la promotion du plurilinguisme: https://wcd.coe.int/ViewDoc.jsp?Ref=CM/Rec(2008)7&Language=lanFrench&Ver=original&Site=COE&BackColorInternet=DBDCF2&BackColorIntranet=FDC864&BackColorLogged=FDC864

3   L'auteur tient à remercier Gael-Linn pour l'autorisation de reproduire cette citation de Séamus Heaney.

Références

Agence Exécutive Éducation, Audiovisuel et Culture (2012) *Chiffres clés de l'enseignement des langues à l'école en Europe – 2012*, available online: eacea. ec.europa.eu/education/eurydice

Baker, C and Prys Jones, S (1998) *Encyclopedia of Bilingualism and Bilingual Education*, Multilingual Matters: Clevedon.

Carson, L (2014) *Understanding and developing plurilingual resources in the multilingual classroom*, ELSTA conference, English Language Support Teachers' Association, St Patrick's College, Drumcondra, Dublin, 13 February 2014.

Council of Europe (2001) *Common European Framework of Reference for Languages: Learning, Teaching, Assessment*, Cambridge: Cambridge University Press.

Council of Europe (2008) *Recommandation CM/Rec(2008)7 du Comité des Ministres aux Etats membres sur l'utilisation du Cadre européen commun de reference pour les langues (CECR) du Conseil de l'Europe et la promotion du plurilinguisme*, available online: wcd.coe.int/ViewDoc.jsp?Ref=CM/Rec%282008%297&Language=lanFrench&Ver=original&Site=COE&BackColorInternet=DBDCF2&BackColorIntranet=FDC864&BackColorLogged=FDC864

European Commission (2003) *Promouvoir l'apprentissage des langues et la diversité linguistique: un plan d'action 2004–2006*, Strasbourg: European Commission.

European Commission (2012a) *First European Survey on Language Competences: Executive Summary*, available online: ec.europa.eu/languages/library/studies/executive-summary-eslc_en.pdf

European Commission (2012b) *Foire aux questions sur le multilinguisme et l'apprentissage des langues*, available online: europa.eu/rapid/press-release_MEMO-12-703_fr.htm

European Commission (2012c) *Les Européens et leurs langues*, available online: ec.europa.eu/public_opinion/archives/ebs/ebs_386_fr.pdf

European Commission (2013) *Foire aux questions concernant les langues en Europe*, available online: europa.eu/rapid/press-release_MEMO-13-825_fr.htm

Fishman, J A (1987) Conference comments: Reflections on the current state of language planning, in Laforge, L (Ed) *Proceedings of the International Colloquium on Language Planning*, Quebec: University of Laval Press, 405–428.

Fox, B (2013) *EU Observer*, available online: euobserver.com/opinion

François, A (2013) Les minorités selon le linguiste, in Le Monde (Ed) *L'atlas du monde de demain*, Paris: Le Monde, 144.

Frankel, J and Rose, A K (2002) An estimate of the effect of common currencies on trade and income, *Quarterly Journal of Economics*, 117 (2), 437–466.

Gallagher, A (2006) Speaking in tongues, who we are: The Irish in 2006, *Irish Times Supplement*.

Goullier, F (2007a) *Rapport sur le Forum intergouvernemental sur les politiques linguistiques: Le Cadre européen commun de référence pour les langues (CECR) et l'élaboration de politiques linguistiques: défis et responsabilités*, available online: www.coe.int/t/dg4/. . ./CEFR_SupportingDocs_fr.docx

Gouillier, F (2007b) *L'impact du Cadre européen commun de référence pour les langues et des travaux du Conseil de l'Europe sur le nouvel espace éducatif européen*, available online: www.coe.int/t/dg4/. . ./CEFR_SupportingDocs_fr.docx

Heaney, S (2015) Preface, in *Aspects of a Shared Heritage: Essays on Linguistic and Cultural Crossover in Ulster*, Dublin: Gael Linn, ii.

House of Commons Foreign Affairs Committee (2013) *The UK Staff Presence in the EU Institutions Second Report of Session 2013–14*, available online: www.publications.parliament.uk/pa/cm201314/cmselect/cmfaff/219/219.pdf

Hunt, D (2009) *Talking World Class: Language and Business in an Open Economy*, paper presented at the Ministry of Education, Dublin, 11 February 2009.

Krauel, T (2013) Gauck möchte, dass Europa Englisch spricht, *Die Welt*, available online: www.welt.de/politik/deutschland/article113840698/Gauck- moechte-dass-Europa-Englisch-spricht.html

Krzyzanowski, M and Wodak R, (2011) *Political strategies and language policies: The European Union Lisbon strategy and its implications for the EU's language and multilingualism policy*, available online: www.academia.edu/1563358/Political_Strategies_and_Language_Policies_The_European_Union_Lisbon_Strategy_and_its_Implications_for_the_EUs_Language_and_Multilingualism_Policy

Lo Bianco, J (2007) *VALEUR project*, available online: archive.ecml.at/mtp2/valeur/html/Valeur_E_pdesc.htm

Marie, L (2014) Mais bien sûr que si, les livres français se vendent à l'étranger! *Le Nouvel Observateur*, available online: bibliobs.nouvelobs.com/

actualites/20131231.OBS0992/mais-bien-sur-que-si-les-livres-francais-se-vendent-a-l-etranger.html

Murphy-Lejeune, E (2002) *Student Mobility and Narrative in Europe: The New Strangers*, London: Routledge.

McPake, J (2007) *VALEUR Final Report*, Graz: ECML.

North, B (2007) Les Niveaux communs de référence du CECR: points de référence validés et stratégies locales, in Gouillier, F (Ed) *Rapport sur le Forum intergouvernemental sur les politiques linguistiques: Le Cadre européen commun de référence pour les langues (CECR) et l'élaboration de politiques linguistiques: défis et responsabilités*, Unité des Politiques Linguistiques, Conseil de l'Europe: Strasbourg, février 2007, 21–22.

RLG (2014) Johnson: Just speak English? *The Economist*, available online: www.economist.com/blogs/prospero/2013/09/language-diversity

Stickel, G (2006) Europas Reichtum beruht ganz wesentlich auf seiner sprachlichen Vielfalt, *Mehrsprachigkeit ohne Grenzen*, available online: www.goethe.de/ges/spa/prj/sog/mup/de1399909.htm

Zgadzaj, J et Roberts, N (2013) Books in translation: It's time for others to join the fight, *Publishing Perspectives*, available online: publishingperspectives.com/2013/02/books-in-translation-its-time-for-others-to-join-the-fight/

Section 2
Language learning and assessment for education and migration

6 An update on the CEFR-J project and its impact on English language education in Japan

Masashi Negishi
Tokyo University of Foreign Studies
Yukio Tono
Tokyo University of Foreign Studies

Abstract

In this paper we report on our project of the CEFR-J, the adaptation of the Common European Framework of Reference (CEFR) (Council of Europe 2001) in English language teaching/learning in Japanese contexts. We discuss the process of adaptation of the CEFR for this context and the rationale behind the branching of the lower levels.

After completion of the CEFR-J Version 1, its related resources, such as the CEFR-J Wordlists, the Can Do Descriptor Database and the *CEFR-J Handbook* were made available for use.

Our search for Reference Level Descriptions or criterial features for the CEFR and/or CEFR-J is still in progress. The goal is similar to that of the English Profile Programme and the Core Inventory, in that our project is based on spoken and written corpora of Japanese learners of English and textbooks, although different methodologies are being adopted depending on the nature of the analyses.

In order to investigate how people discuss and respond to these frameworks, we investigated so-called 'big data'. According to the analyses of big data regarding the 'CEFR' and the 'CEFR-J', however, the impact of the CEFR-J as well as that of the CEFR seems to have been limited. Discussion regarding the CEFR-J centres around 'levels' and 'branching', rather than 'language policy'; a pattern also observed in research on the CEFR. Possible implications of the survey as well as the CEFR-J project and its future directions are discussed.

The development of the CEFR-J

This paper presents an overview of the development of the CEFR-J, an adaptation of the Common European Framework of Reference for Languages (CEFR, Council of Europe 2001) to English language teaching in Japan. A more detailed description of the process can be found in Negishi, Takada, and Tono (2013). Figure 1 shows the major research activities from April 2008 to March 2012, when the first version of the CEFR-J was released.

The original impetus for developing the CEFR-J came out of attempts to determine the CEFR's applicability to Japanese learners of English. A number of studies have assessed the applicability of the CEFR; for example, Negishi (2006) collected self-assessment data from upper secondary school learners of English through CEFR Can Do questionnaires, whereas Nakajima and Nagata (2006) collected data from university students. The results of the surveys indicated that the order of difficulty of these European-born CEFR descriptors is more or less the same for Japanese English as a Foreign Language (EFL) learners. However, the tasks which learners had little experience of in real life or in the classroom were judged to be more difficult than the levels they were originally assigned to, whereas the tasks they had experience with tended to be judged easier. For example, a Reading A2 descriptor 'I can understand simple instructions on equipment encountered in everyday life – such as a public telephone' was placed at B1 level, and a Writing A2 descriptor 'I can explain what I like or dislike about something' was placed at A1

Figure 1 Overview of the CEFR-J Project from 2008 to the release of Version 1 in 2012

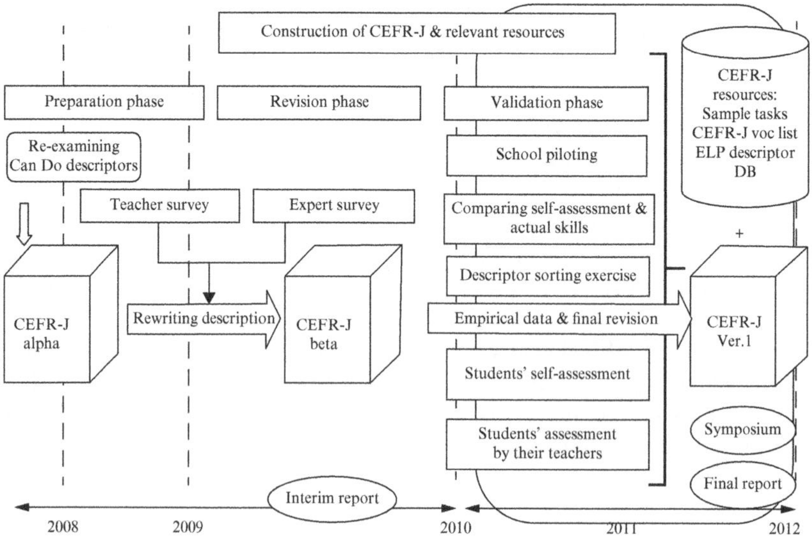

level. Few Japanese students seem to have experience in the above reading task, whereas it is highly probable that many Japanese students have experience in the above writing task. Cultural differences regarding linguistic communication, such as the style of a postcard, might have been the cause of the misplacement of the levels of some of the CEFR Can Do descriptors. Negishi (2006) showed that it was possible to adjust most of the outlier CEFR Can Do descriptors in the aforementioned survey by providing examples. This demonstrates the need for real examples for unfamiliar Can Do descriptors.

Having determined that the CEFR is applicable to the Japanese educational context, provided some culturally specific examples are included, the next stage of the project focused on identifying Japanese EFL learners' CEFR levels in order to investigate what kind of branching is necessary for them. However, we found it extremely difficult to get 'a representative sample' of an entire nation, based on exam results, and to align them to the CEFR levels. What limited data was collected by the author from surveys conducted seemed to indicate that more than 80% of Japanese EFL learners are Non/Basic Users (pre-A1 to A2 level), less than 20% Independent Users (B1 and B2), and that Proficient Users (C1 and C2) are almost nil. It would be fair to say that the EFL learner population in Japan is heavily skewed towards the lower levels.

This situation led us to the decision to subdivide the lower CEFR levels (A1–B2 levels) and also to add a lower stage below A1 so that the progress of learning could be made more tangible to learners and teachers. The inclusion of pre-A1 was necessary because L1 Japanese speakers do not share the Roman alphabet, the knowledge of which most European learners of English possess, and also because a great number of Japanese learners do not reach A1 as defined by some test alignment tables.

All of these relevant surveys suggested that we need to develop a modified version of the original CEFR for English language learning and teaching in Japan, which we later referred to as the CEFR-J. The principles of the development of the CEFR-J are summarised as follows:

- add a pre-A1 level
- divide A1 into three levels: A1.1, A1.2, A1.3
- divide A2 into two levels: A2.1, A2.2
- divide B1 into two levels: B1.1, B1.2
- divide B2 into two levels: B2.1, B2.2
- no change for C1, C2
- adapt Can Do descriptors to a Japanese context.

Subsequently, we built a database of descriptors from the CEFR and the European Language Portfolio (ELP) (available from www.coe.int/t/dg4/education/elp/), which was later supplemented by those descriptors available in Japan. Based on this database, we developed the initial version of the CEFR-J, both in Japanese and English, which took a so-called 'learner-oriented' 'I can . . .' format. However, some inconsistencies in the wording of the descriptors were found. One such example is 'I can understand words in a picture book that are already familiar through oral activities, and point to the objects in the picture'. Pointing to the objects in the picture is a type of physical action, and such an action is not a typical element in other reading Can Do descriptors. In order to eradicate the inconsistencies, the descriptors for productive skills were broken down into (1) performance, (2) criteria/quality, and (3) condition, whereas those for receptive skills were broken down into (1) task, (2) text, and (3) condition. Later, Green (2012) proposed five component elements which include activity, theme/topic, input text, output text, qualities, and restrictions. Activity corresponds to performance, input text to text (in receptive skills), qualities to criteria/quality, and restrictions to condition, while there were no corresponding categories to theme/topic and output text. This, however, does not necessarily mean that Can Do descriptors in the CEFR-J do not include those elements.

In 2011, we began validating the Beta version of the CEFR-J. The validation studies of the CEFR-J are based on the following data:

- learners' self-assessment
- learners' assessment by their teachers
- descriptor sorting exercise
- comparing self-assessment and actual performance.

The main data, on which we carried out item response theory (IRT), comes from learners' self-assessment. The descriptors in the CEFR were developed on the basis of an empirical research project that used teachers as informants (North 2000, North and Schneider 1998). However, we used learners as informants, because it was almost impossible for Japanese teachers to assess all the students in their large classes in terms of five skills.

Based on the results of the IRT analyses, we checked if the descriptors were in order of difficulty (see Figure 2), and revised the Beta version.

Overall, most of the items were ordered as expected, although there were some items which behaved unusually in each skill. Lower level items which had been created for the newly branched levels did not match the original order, e.g. Listening A1.3 through B1.1 (see Figure 2) and Spoken Production A1.2 through A2.2. Most of the Writing items matched the original order except for an A1.2 item, which was a little too difficult. Spoken Interaction had a number of unusual items, and there was little difference among A1.2 and A1.3 items. Reading also had several unusual items across the levels. The problems found in the analyses and the corresponding solutions are summarised in Table 1. After this revision process, we finalised the CEFR-J Version 1, released it on the web in 2012, and published *The CEFR-J Guidebook* (Tono 2013).

Table 1 Problems and solutions for CEFR-J Can Do descriptors

	Problems	Solutions
1	The perceived difficulties were not necessarily ordered as we had expected.	Reordering the descriptors according to the item difficulties.
2	The same condition, such as 'provided they are delivered in slow and clear speech involving rephrasing and repetition', was repeated for different items, which gave the participants an impression that they were at the same level regardless of the following statements, especially because the condition comes at the beginning of the descriptors in the Japanese version.	Putting the condition part in the middle in the Japanese version, unless moving it made the Japanese descriptor unnatural.
3	Can Do descriptors which the participants had never experienced seemed to be judged to be more difficult. **Writing: A1.2 Beta version** I can write simple postcards, messages, short memos about events of personal relevance, using simple words and basic expressions. **Reading: A1.2 Beta version** I can understand very short reports of recent events such as simple letters, postcards or e-mails from friends or relatives describing travel memories, etc.	Eliminating the unfamiliar elements for Japanese learners. **Writing: A1.2 Version 1** I can write message cards (e.g. birthday cards) and short memos about events of personal relevance, using simple words and basic expressions. **Reading: A1.2 Version 1** I can understand very short reports of recent events such as text messages from friends or relatives, describing travel memories, etc.
4	Can Do descriptors consisting of technical 'CEFR wordings' seemed to be judged to be more difficult. **Spoken Interaction: Pre-A1 Beta version** I can express my wishes and make requests in areas of immediate need, using basic phrases. I can express what I want by pointing at it, if necessary. **Spoken Production: Pre-A1 Beta version** I can carry out a simple 'show and tell' using basic formulaic expressions, provided I can prepare my speech in advance.	Revising or avoiding technical 'CEFR wordings'. **Spoken Interaction: Pre-A1 Version 1** I can express my wishes and make requests in areas of immediate need such as 'Help!' and 'I want . . .', using basic phrases. I can express what I want by pointing at it, if necessary. **Spoken Production: Pre-A1 Version 1** I can give a simple explanation about an object while showing it to others using basic words, phrases and formulaic expressions, provided I can prepare my speech in advance.
5	A Can Do descriptor might include a wide range of tasks, and tasks imagined by the participants might be more or less difficult than those implied by the writers of those descriptors. **Spoken Interaction: A2.1 Beta version** I can give directions including simple sequencers such as 'first', 'then', and 'next'.	Narrowing down the range of interpretation by inserting examples; the insertion of concrete examples in English was only possible for lower level descriptors. **Spoken Interaction: A2.1 Version 1** I can give directions such as 'turn right' and 'go straight' including simple sequencers such as first, then, and next.

Table 1 (continued)

Problems	Solutions
Spoken Interaction: B2.1 Beta version I can discuss the main points of what I have read and listened to, provided the topic is familiar to me.	**Spoken Interaction: B2.1 Version 1** I can discuss the main points of news stories I have read about in the newspapers, on the Internet or watched on TV, provided the topic is reasonably familiar to me.
6 Because of some performance conditions in the Can Do descriptors, the participants had an impression that they could cope with the specified tasks.	Deleting conditions as necessary.
Reading: B1.2 Beta version I can follow the plot of narratives written in plain English, provided I can consult the glossary or a dictionary.	**Reading: B1.2 Version 1** I can understand the plot of longer narratives written in plain English.
Spoken Production: A2.1 Beta version I can give a brief speech, introducing myself, using a series of simple phrases and sentences, provided I can prepare my speech in advance and refer to my notes.	**Spoken Production: A2.1 Version1** I can introduce myself including my hobbies and abilities, using a series of simple phrases and sentences.

Figure 2 An example of item difficulty line graphs: CEFR-J Listening Can Do descriptors*

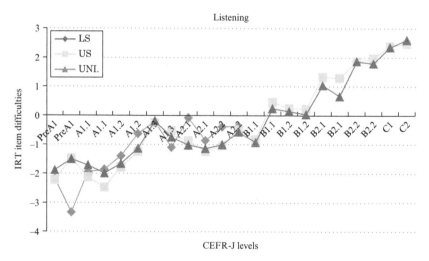

LS – Lower Secondary students, US – Upper Secondary students, UNI – University students

Accompanying resources for the CEFR-J

Since the public release of the CEFR-J in March 2012, we have been working on the following two areas of research. One is to develop resources accompanying the CEFR-J for preparing syllabuses, teaching materials and classroom tasks. To do this, we have developed resources for each level, such as a wordlist, a database of available ELP descriptors, and a handbook for the CEFR-J.

We are also working on the reference level descriptions (RLDs) for the CEFR-J, the work similar to the English Profile Programme (www. englishprofile.org). To this end, we have compiled several different corpora to explore the most valid and efficient ways to select criterial features which differentiate CEFR or CEFR-J levels. We will explain each of these research areas briefly below.

So far, in order to promote the use of the CEFR-J, three kinds of companion resources have been developed.

The CEFR-J Wordlist

The CEFR-J Wordlist was developed based on the analysis of common vocabulary used in the EFL textbooks at primary and secondary schools in China, Korea, and Taiwan. These countries are similar to Japan in terms of school settings, EFL environment, and the introduction of English as a school subject at Grade 3 or 4 of primary school.

The analysis revealed that approximately 1,000 words are covered in pre-A1 and A1 levels, with another 1,000 words at A2, 1,900 words at B1, and 1,700 words at B2. Altogether, 5,639 words were identified. This figure is, however, relatively conservative since it only shows the words which commonly appear across the three countries. The vocabulary covered in Chinese textbooks *per se* is much larger. Thus, we decided to supplement the list by incorporating the words which uniquely appear in the English Vocabulary Profile (Capel 2012), prepared by the English Profile Programme. As a result, we ended up with the list of 7,570 items in total (see Figure 3).

The unique feature of this wordlist is that it not only consists of the list of lemmas with part-of-speech information, but the noun entries also contain the information about notional properties specified in the T-series, such as general and specific notions.

For instance, if one wants to use one of the A1-level descriptors, 'I can exchange simple opinions about very familiar topics such as likes and dislikes for sports, foods, etc., using a limited repertoire of expressions, provided that people speak clearly', then you can identify the key expressions such as 'I like . . .', 'I don't like . . .', or 'Do you like . . .?' As you create some language activities, you might want to choose topics like sports or foods.

Figure 3 The breakdown of the CEFR-J Wordlist

CEFR – level	Pre-A1	A1	A2	B1	B2	Total
Text analysis	976	1,057	1,884	1,722	5,639
Our target	1,000	1,000	2,000	2,000	6,000
+ EVP integrated → Final version	**1,068**	**1,358**	**2,359**	**2,785**	**7,570**

Then the CEFR-J Wordlist can provide the list of pre-A1 (or A0 in this table) or A1 level words with notion categories 'Food and drink' or 'Hobbies and pastimes', which are the same categories specified in the T-series. This will facilitate the process of implementing descriptors into specific tasks (see Figure 4).

The Can Do Descriptor Database

The Can Do Descriptor Database is a collection of descriptors collected from the European Language Portfolio in various countries. Altogether, 2,800 descriptors were gathered and analysed according to their content, and then similar descriptors were combined. In total, 647 descriptors remained and are in the final database (see Figure 5).

For each descriptor, you can identify CEFR levels and specific skill categories, and both original English descriptors and Japanese translations are available. For A level descriptors, versions for younger children were also prepared (see Figure 6).

The CEFR-J Handbook

Fifteen members of the CEFR-J project team published a handbook on using the CEFR-J in 2013 (Tono 2013). The MEXT (Ministry of Education, Culture, Sports, Science and Technology) started promoting the development of Can Do descriptors as the attainment target of foreign language education. Many secondary school teachers need to develop their own Can

Figure 4 Extract of vocabulary related to a Can Do descriptor from the CEFR-J Wordlist

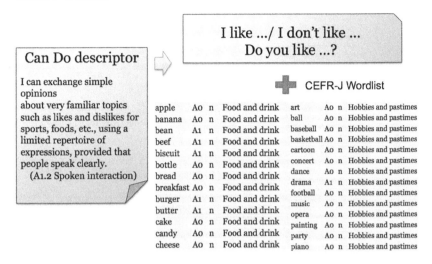

Figure 5 The Can Do Descriptor Database

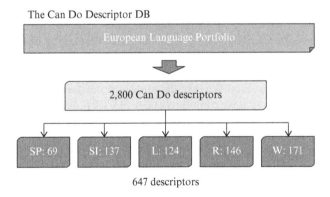

Do descriptors but they find it very difficult. The handbook is designed to help those who lack the basic understanding of the concepts related to the CEFR and the reason for using Can Do descriptors. It also helps to utilise the CEFR-J as a reference point as they prepare their own Can Do descriptors.

Figure 6 Format of the Can Do Descriptor Database

Lev.	Category/Code	ELP descriptor(s)	General descriptors (Japanese)	Descriptors for children (Japanese)
A1	IS1-A1	I can say who I am, ask someone's name and introduce someone.	自分が誰であるか言うことができ、相手の名前を尋ねたり、相手のことを紹介することができる	自分の名前を言ったり、相手の名前を聞いたり、相手の紹介ができる
A1	IS1-A1-1	I can ask and answer simple questions, initiate and respond to simple statements in areas of immediate need or on very familiar topics[1.2000-CH].	簡単な質問をしたり、簡単な質問に答えることができる。また必要性の高いことや身近な話題について発言したり、反応することができる	簡単な質問をしたり、簡単な質問に答えることができる。また身近なことについて話したり、質問に答えることができる
A1	IS1-A1-1	I can make myself understood in a simple way but I am dependent on my partner being prepared to repeat more slowly and rephrase what I say and to help me to say what I want.	簡易な方法であれば通じるが、ゆっくり繰り返してくれたり、自分が言った事を言い直してくれたり、自分が言いたいことが言えるよう助けてくれるような相手に依存している	相手がゆっくり話したり、自分が言ったことを確認してくれるなど、やさしい人だったら自分の簡単な英語は通じる
A1	IS2-A1	I can understand simple questions about myself and my family when people speak slowly and clearly (e.g. "What's your name?" "How old are you?" "How are you?" etc.).	相手がゆっくりはっきり話してくれれば、「名前は？」「歳は？」「調子はどう？」などの自分や家族についての簡単な質問を理解することができる	相手がゆっくりはっきり話してくれれば、自分や家族についての簡単な質問が分かる
A1	IS2-A1	I can understand simple words and phrases, like "excuse me", "sorry", "thank you", etc.	「すみません」「ごめんなさい」「ありがとう」といった簡単な語句を理解することができる	「すみません」「ごめんなさい」「ありがとう」といった簡単な語句が分かる
A1	IS2-A1	I can understand simple greetings, like "hello", "good bye", "good morning", etc.	「やあ」「さようなら」「おはよう」といった簡単な挨拶を理解することができる	「やあ」「さようなら」「おはよう」といった簡単な挨拶が分かる

Reference Level Descriptions for the CEFR-J

We are also working on a new project which started in 2012, right after the release of the CEFR-J. The goal is similar to that of the English Profile Programme and the Core Inventory (North, Ortega and Sheehan 2010), to identify linguistic properties which serve as criteria for distinguishing one CEFR level from another. We take the same approach as the English Profile Programme team in that we compile corpora of CEFR-based coursebooks as input and corpora of learner production data as output. Between 2012–2013, we focused on the compilation of various corpora. Over 2014 and 2015, we worked on various methods of criterial feature extraction and preparation of the inventory for the CEFR-J. We hope to contribute to both L2 profiling research and a standard procedure for criterial feature extraction from CEFR-based corpora.

Table 2 shows the list of learner corpora and textbook corpora we have been compiling.

In order to identify criterial features, various approaches are possible. We aim to seek the answer to a methodological question: Which method is the best to find criterial features for the CEFR levels? We will take a few different approaches. One is a data-driven approach, in which we search and extract all the grammar points taught at secondary school across the texts classified according to the CEFR levels. Then we use machine learning techniques to find out which features best classify texts according to the CEFR levels.

Table 2 The list of learner corpora and textbook corpora

Learner corpora	Mode	Participants	Sample size	Corpus size
JEFLL Corpus	WR	Junior and senior high (all grades)	c. 10,000	c. 670,000
NICT JLE Corpus	SP	Adult	1,281	c. 2,000,000
MEXT Data	WR/SP	Junior High 3rd	1,600 (random)	
GTEC for STUDENTS Writing Corpus	WR	Senior High 1–3	30,000	c. 2,500,000

Textbook corpora	CEFR level	Skills	Number of titles	Corpus size
ELT Textbook Corpus	A1 to C2	All skills	95	c. 2,800,000

Different algorithms will be tested; for example, decision tree, support vector machine, random forest, among others (for these algorithms, see Alpaydin 2004).

The same procedures will be applied to learner errors. For extracting errors, we are working on semi-automatic error tagging using the edit distance, which is a method of quantifying how dissimilar two strings of texts are to one another using the minimum-weight series of edit operations (insertion, deletion, substitution), between the original learner data and the proofread version in parallel texts (Jurafsky and Martin 2008). Also some members in our group are working on automatic error identification and annotation using n-gram data from the web. After identifying errors across CEFR levels, we can employ the same machine learning techniques to see if any error category will serve as criteria to classify CEFR-level texts. A similar approach has been used by the English Profile team (Hawkins and Buttery 2010, Hawkins and Filipović 2012), thus we hope to compare the results.

There is the possibility of employing particular lexis or grammar as potential criterial feature candidates based on theories postulated by Second Language Acquisition (SLA) researchers so that we can test the related hypotheses against our corpus evidence. This is especially suitable for those grammatical constructions which are known to have developmental stages, such as relative clause construction, post-nominal modification, verb subcategorisation, article system, tense and aspect, among others.

Finally, in order to better understand textual characteristics, some metrics for lexical profiling like the following would be strong candidates for criteriality; lexical measures such as Guiraud Index (Guiraud 1954), Yule's K (Yule 1944); complexity measures such as T-unit length (Hunt 1965), VP per T-unit, clause per sentence, complex nominal per clause or T-unit, among others (Lu 2009).

We will work on these different areas and systematically identify criterial features. First, we will make a list of criterial features useful for classifying the CEFR levels. Then we will make more fine-grained inventory of language features for each of the different CEFR levels. Finally, we need to examine how far we can go in identifying criterial features for further-branched sublevels of the CEFR, like A1.1, A1.2, etc., which is the central issue of Reference Level Descriptions for the CEFR-J.

We hope to prepare an inventory of lexis and grammar for each CEFR-J level with some evidence regarding how well a particular criterial feature can classify texts based on the CEFR-J levels.

The impact of the CEFR-J

Background

The CEFR-J Version 1 was released in 2011. As three years have passed, at the time of writing, since its release, it is an opportune time to investigate the current impact of the CEFR-J on English language teaching in Japan.

The washback of language tests has been investigated mainly by using questionnaires, interviews to teachers and learners, and classroom observations (e.g. Alderson and Hamp-Lyons 1996, Muñoz and Álvarez 2010, Watanabe 1996). The impact of such comprehensive frameworks as the CEFR or the CEFR-J, however, is far-reaching, and therefore should be explored not only at the classroom level, but also in a much wider context. With regard to impact analysis, Chalhoub-Deville (2009:119) states as follows:

> Somewhat simply, impact analysis calls for documentation of the influence of test content, results, and practices on learning, instruction, and the curriculum. Impact could be examined at the micro or macro level. Investigations could be set up to study impact in terms of direct or indirect influences on test takers, the educational community, or society at large.

What has been missing in impact analyses seems to be research into indirect influences of language tests at the macro level. This is especially the case when the tests are large-scale high-stakes tests. Though the CEFR and the CEFR-J are not language tests themselves, they are tools for language assessment as well as those for language learning and teaching, and therefore we need to investigate the influence of those frameworks at the macro level.

The recent trend in coping with large-scale data is to analyse so-called 'big data' on the web. This method is being used for a variety of purposes such as spotting business trends, preventing diseases, etc. The authors examined this 'big data' in order to investigate how people respond to such frameworks as the CEFR and the CEFR-J and discuss them.

Samples

In order to see the impact of these frameworks, we analysed 15,579,018 texts, which were available on the web, from August 2012 to September 2013. The texts analysed were those written in the Japanese language. The engine automatically surfed the web, with no text selection made in advance, which is the very nature of big data analysis. Then the engine searched the texts for the specified words. The data gave us a picture of current beliefs and attitudes regarding a specified topic such as the CEFR. This approach to the analysis of the impact of assessment, we believe, is not something which takes over the conventional one, such as classroom observation and questionnaires to teachers and learners; both approaches reinforce each other.

Methods of analyses

The analyses were carried out by Jetrun Technology Inc., a company specialising in analysing big data. The results of the analyses include 'Positive/ Negative Graphs' and 'Word Maps'. The 'Positive/Negative Graphs' were created by analysing the comments in terms of the attitude of the writer, based on the semantic database. If a text includes such positive phrases as 'It is useful' or 'I find this interesting', it is classified as a positive text.

The 'Word Maps' indicate the relationship of the key words in the writing. The words were automatically analysed based on the tailored database of Jetrun Technology Inc. The connections shown in the 'Word Maps' are those of the key words in the same sentence. It is necessary to interpret the relationships between the key words by looking not only at the main webs but also at the extended webs. The computer program was customised for this particular research so that such everyday words as 'Can Do' 'level(s)', 'A1', 'A2', etc. could be categorised as key words. Otherwise, these words would have been excluded from the analyses. Since these are *the* crucial terms for this analysis, however, we made a special request to include them as key words.

Results

Figure 7 shows the numbers of websites per month in which the words 'TOEIC', 'TOEFL', 'Juken eigo' (English for entrance exams), 'CEFR', and 'CEFR-J' appeared; the first three words were included for comparison. The number of websites which included a mention of 'CEFR' and 'CEFR-J' were very limited compared with those of the other words. So the impact has not been as big as we expected (see Figure 7).

However, the graphs shown in Figure 8 show that the CEFR-J has been received very positively, with 75% of the texts showing that people are expressing positive attitudes towards it (see Figure 8).

Figure 7 The numbers of websites per month

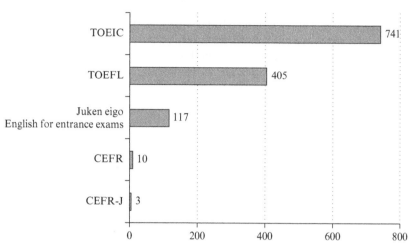

Figure 8 The positive/negative graphs

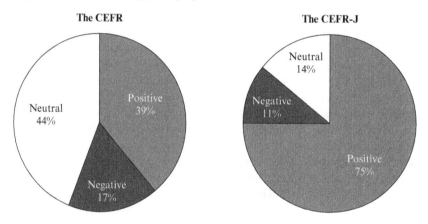

The word map for the 'CEFR' (see Figure 9) shows that the CEFR has strong connections with 'Europe', 'level(s)', 'B1', 'B2', and 'Can Do'. People seem to relate the CEFR to three aspects: 'Europe', 'Can Do', and 'level(s)' including specific CEFR levels. The connection with the word 'Europe', along with the words in the extended web in the map, i.e. 'plural', 'language', and 'policy', seems to demonstrate the interest of the researchers, especially in the field of language policy, because the CEFR is quite often mentioned in the context of language teaching policy. On the other hand, there are a number of references to school at different stages in the extended webs of 'level(s)', 'B1', and 'B2', which indicates that people are attempting to specify their attainment

Figure 9 The word map for the 'CEFR'

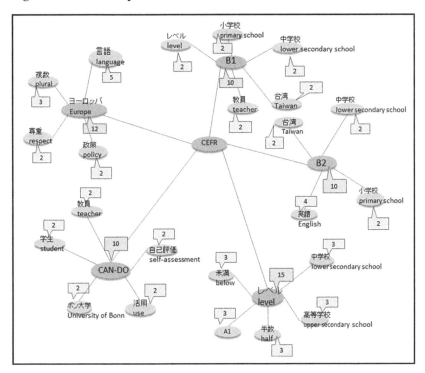

targets at each school stage in terms of the CEFR levels. The connections of the word 'CEFR' with the words 'Can Do' and 'level(s)' seem to have been generated by the MEXT reform plans on English Language Education, since MEXT stipulated that each school specify their attainment targets in the form of a Can Do list by referring to the CEFR.

The next word map for the 'CEFR-J' (see Figure 10) shows that the word 'CEFR-J' has strong connections with 'level(s)', 'Can Do', 'CEFR', 'learner(s)', and 'research'. The strong connections with the words 'Can Do' and 'level(s)' are the same with the 'CEFR'. Great interest in the levels or self-assessment grid was confirmed by these analyses. In addition, the co-occurrence of the word 'research' and the 'CEFR-J' also seems to indicate interest in the CEFR-J from a research perspective, though this interest, as the words in the extended web shows, is more concrete and towards levels and branching, rather than language policy. The fact that the word 'learner(s)' include such words as 'goal' and 'degree of achievement' in the extended web suggests that the CEFR-J provides Japanese learners, and possibly Japanese teachers, with concrete attainment targets.

Figure 10 The word map for the 'CEFR-J'

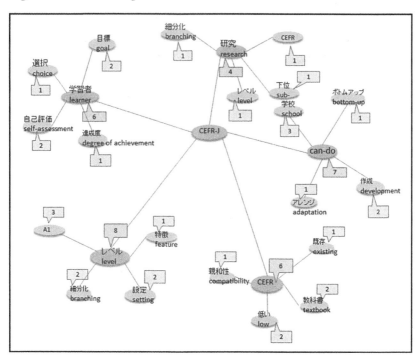

Discussion

North (2009:370) argues that '. . . the impact of the descriptive scheme or other aspects of the CEFR on curriculum or teaching have as yet been very limited', and he quotes Little (2007) as follows:

> "To date (*the CEFR's*) impact on language testing far outweighs its impact on curriculum design and pedagogy . . . (Little 2007: 648)" *and* "On the whole the CEFR has no more occasioned a revolution in curriculum development than it has promoted the radical redesign of language tests (Little 2007: 649)" (Italics added by North).

As the word maps of the 'CEFR' and the 'CEFR-J' show, people are mainly concerned with the 'levels' and possibly with assessment, which might be an indication of the initial stage of the dissemination of such a framework as the CEFR. It might be certain that the CEFR-J has made a significant impact on high-stakes tests in Japan, although achievement tests we have collected so far seem to indicate that the CEFR-J has not yet made a noticeable impact on classroom testing.

However, the first reference to the CEFR in a MEXT official document may well have an impact on all levels of language policy in Japan from now on. The document was released by MEXT in December 2013, and it was entitled *English Education Reform Plan Corresponding to Globalization* (Ministry of Education, Culture, Sports, Science and Technology 2013). The Japanese version included a specific reference to the CEFR levels. The plan specifies the attainment targets of Japanese students' English proficiency in terms of the CEFR levels. For example, under the current course of study, they expect Japanese upper secondary school graduates to attain A2 or B1, whereas they propose these levels should be raised to B1 or B2 in their new scheme. This is, as far as we can see, the very first time that MEXT has defined the attainment target of Japanese learners of English in terms of the CEFR in their official documents.

The reform plan also proposes that Japanese teachers of English should assess four skills with the use of Can Do descriptors. Prior to the abovementioned document, MEXT issued another document entitled *Five Proposals and Specific Measures for Developing Proficiency in English for International Communication* (Ministry of Education, Culture, Sports, Science and Technology 2011), which stipulated that each secondary school set the attainment target in the form of a Can Do list, and publish it. Since the concept of Can Do descriptors was completely new to most teachers, they did not know where to start. The authors' experience with Japanese English teachers tells us that not many teachers have experience using the English language for real communication, and therefore find it difficult to come up with their own Can Do descriptors. Another fundamental problem might be that teachers do not have a long-term perspective of English language teaching; they tend to focus on everyday teaching. In this kind of situation, they gradually started to search for reference materials such as the CEFR and the CEFR-J, instead of developing their own Can Do list from scratch.

In contrast with the CEFR, the CEFR-J descriptors are adjusted to the Japanese context, while retaining the reference to the CEFR levels. This nature seems to make the CEFR-J look more attractive to Japanese teachers. Furthermore, the additional branching of lower levels applied to the CEFR-J provides Japanese teachers and students with clear attainment targets. Perhaps for this reason, the CEFR-J is beginning to be used to specify tangible short-term goals for the learning and teaching of English. It should be noted that, because of these characteristics, the framework is beginning to be used for other languages, e.g. French, Japanese, etc. For example, Tokyo University of Foreign Studies has, with the support of the Super Global University Project (tufs-sgu.com/cefr-jx27/), started a project called CEFR-J x 27, in which they are planning to apply the CEFR-J to 27 languages they teach.

While the CEFR-J was welcomed by many teachers, some of them find it difficult to connect the targets and their own everyday teaching, and others claim that some of the Can Do descriptors in the CEFR and the CEFR-J are too narrowly focused. This may originate in the fact that some of the CEFR-J descriptors are more like CEFR illustrative descriptors than those in the self-assessment grid.

Efforts were made to maximise item discrimination by making the CEFR-J descriptors as specific as possible, which was good for assessment purposes. However, there might have been a price to pay for this. Consider the following example:

CEFR-J Version 1: A2.1 Spoken Interaction
I can give simple directions from place to place, using basic expressions such as 'turn right' and 'go straight' along with sequencers such as first, then, and next.

This is one of two Can Do descriptors for A2.1 Spoken Interaction. Japanese teachers may well be wondering if this is one of the attainment targets for their students with years of experience of English language learning. In their school syllabus, they are supposed to get their students engaged in many other language activities and to expect them to be able to perform them. Part of their dissatisfaction with the CEFR-J appears to derive from our inclination to make the Can Do descriptors as specific as possible in order to enhance their discriminatory power. In this respect, we should encourage them to refer to the bank of descriptors and other language resources we have published in *The CEFR-J Guidebook*, although, unfortunately, they have not been classified according to the CEFR-J levels yet.

Conclusion

After the completion of the CEFR-J Version 1, *The CEFR-J Guidebook*, and its related resources have been available for use. Our search for criterial features for the CEFR and CEFR-J is still in progress. According to the analyses of big data regarding the CEFR and the CEFR-J, however, the impact of the CEFR-J as well as that of the CEFR seems to have been limited. Discussions regarding the CEFR-J centre around levels and branching, rather than language policy as found for the CEFR.

It should be noted that there might be some limitations of this big data approach, since it is an innovative one in this field. This approach enabled us to capture the impact of the topic we were interested in, on a larger scale, but it should be noted that it was, by its nature, based only on the data available on the web. As North (2014) shows in his presentation, younger teachers exceed the older generations in the use of digital media, which might suggest that big data mostly reflects the interests of and the impact of the younger generation. Also there is a possibility that this approach underestimates the impact of those frameworks, because, as the Organisation for Economic Co-operation and Development (2011) shows, Japanese secondary school teachers are the busiest in the world, and they may not have time to tweet or write a blog.

It might be true that some teachers find it hard to see the link between the narrowly focused Can Do descriptors and their teaching. In this respect, it is our duty to continue our research and provide them with more empirically validated Can Do descriptors along with a database of language resources related to the CEFR-J. With these, the CEFR-J will help teachers and policy makers set attainment targets for Japanese learners of English, and eventually improve English language teaching in Japan. It is our sincere hope that our research and experience demonstrate how the CEFR might be adapted to a specific context and, furthermore, that it contributes to the advancement of language learning, teaching, and assessment worldwide.

References

Alderson, J C and Hamp-Lyons, L (1996) TOEFL preparation courses: A study of washback, *Language Testing* 13 (3), 280–297.

Alpaydin, I (2004) *Introduction to Machine Learning*, Cambridge: MIT Press.

Capel, A (2012) Completing the English Vocabulary Profile: C1 and C2 vocabulary, *English Profile Journal* 3, available online: journals.cambridge. org/action/displayJournal?jid=EPJ

Chalhoub-Deville, M (2009) The intersection of test impact, validation, and educational reform policy, *Annual Review of Applied Linguistics* 29, 118–131.

Council of Europe (2001) *Common European Framework of Reference for Languages: Learning, Teaching, Assessment*, Cambridge: Cambridge University Press.

Green, A (2012) *Language Functions Revisited: Theoretical and Empirical Bases for Language Construct Definition Across the Ability Range*, English Profile Studies volume 2, Cambridge: UCLES/Cambridge University Press.

Guiraud, P (1954) *Les Charactères Statistiques du Vocabulaire. Essai de méthodologie*, Paris: Presses Universitaires de France.

Hawkins, J and Buttery, P (2010) Criterial features in learner corpora: Theory and illustrations, *English Profile Journal* 1, available online: journals. cambridge.org/action/displayJournal?jid=EPJ

Hawkins, J and Filipović, L (2012) *Criterial Features in L2 English: Specifying the Reference Levels of the Common European Framework*, English Profile Studies volume 1, Cambridge: UCLES/Cambridge University Press.

Hunt, K W (1965) *Grammatical Structures Written at Three Grade Levels*, NCTE Research Report No 3, Champaign: National Council of Teachers of English.

Jurafsky, D and Martin, J H (2008) *Speech and Language Processing*, New Jersey: Prentice Hall, 2nd edition.

Little, D (2007) The Common European Framework of Reference for Languages: Perspectives on the making of supranational language education policy, *The Modern Language Journal* 91 (4), 645–655.

Lu, X (2009) Automatic measurement of syntactic complexity in child language acquisition, *International Journal of Corpus Linguistics* 14 (1), 3–28.

Ministry of Education, Culture, Sports, Science and Technology (2011) *Five Proposals and Specific Measures for Developing Proficiency in English for International Communication*, available online: www.mext.go.jp/component/english/__icsFiles/afieldfile/2012/07/09/1319707_1.pdf

Ministry of Education, Culture, Sports, Science and Technology (2013) *English Education Reform Plan Corresponding to Globalization*, available online: www.mext.go.jp/english/topics/__icsFiles/afieldfile/2014/01/23/1343591_1.pdf

Muñoz, A P and Álvarez, M E (2010) Washback of an oral assessment system in the EFL classroom, *Language Testing* 27 (1), 33–49.

Nakajima, M and Nagata, M (2006) CEFR no nihonjin gaikokugo gakusyusya heno tekioukanousei [The applicability of the CEFR to Japanese learners of foreign languages], *JAFLE Bulletin* 9, 5–24.

Negishi, M (2006) CEFR no nihonjin gaikokugo gakushusha heno tekiyoukanousei no koujouni mukete [Towards the improvement of the applicability of the CEFR to Japanese learners of foreign languages], in Negishi, M, Umino, T and Yoshitomi, A (Eds) *Gengo Johogaku Kenkyu Houkoku 14: Dainigengo Syutokuriron ni Motoduku Gengokyoiku to Hyoka Moderu [The Report on Linguistic Informatics Research 14: Language Pedagogy and Assessment Model Based on Second Language Acquisition Theory]*, Tokyo: Tokyo University of Foreign Studies, 79–101.

Negishi, M, Takada, T and Tono, Y (2013) A progress report on the development of the CEFR-J, in Galaczi, E D and Weir C J (Eds) *Exploring Language Frameworks: Proceedings of the ALTE Kraków Conference, July 2011*, Studies in Language Testing volume 36, Cambridge: UCLES/Cambridge University Press, 135–163.

North, B (2000) *The Development of A Common Framework Scale of Language Proficiency*, New York: Peter Lang.

North, B (2009) The educational and social impact of the CEFR in Europe and beyond: A preliminary overview, in Taylor, L and Weir, C J (Eds) *Language Testing Matters: Investigating the Wider Social and Educational Impact of Assessment, Proceedings of the ALTE Cambridge Conference April 2008*, Studies in Language Testing volume 31, Cambridge: UCLES/Cambridge University Press, 357–378.

North, B (2014) *Profiling teacher competences: The multilingual validation of the European Profiling Grid (EPG)*, paper presented at the ALTE 5th International Conference, Paris, France, 10–11 April 2014.

North, B and Schneider, G (1998) Scaling descriptors for language proficiency scales, *Language Testing* 15, 217–262.

North, B, Ortega, A and Sheehan, S (2010) *British Council–EAQUALS Core Inventory for General English*, available online: englishagenda.britishcouncil.org/sites/ec/files/books-british-council-eaquals-core-inventory.pdf

Organisation for Economic Co-operation and Development (2011) *Education at a Glance 2011: OECD Indicators*, Paris: OECD Publishing.

Tono, Y (2013) *CEFR-J gaidobukku [The CEFR-J Guidebook]*, Tokyo: Taishukanshoten.

Watanabe, Y (1996) Does grammar translation come from the entrance examination? Preliminary findings from classroom-based research, *Language Testing* 13 (3), 318–333.

Yule, G U (1944) *The Statistical Study of Literary Vocabulary*, Cambridge: Cambridge University Press.

7 Learning subject matter in a second language: A CEFR-based tool to support immigrant and migrant students

Eli Moe
University of Bergen
Marita Härmälä
University of Jyväskylä
Paula Lee Kristmanson
University of New Brunswick

Abstract

This article focuses on the importance of language proficiency when acquiring content knowledge in particular academic subjects. The study had a twofold aim: 1) to indicate minimum language standards, in terms of CEFR levels, which students at the age of 12/13 and 15/16 need to have to experience success in history or civics and mathematics in compulsory education; and 2) to develop a tool to support teachers and students which will make them aware of the language challenges students are faced with when learning subject matter in a second language. The tool itself is a set of language descriptors linked to the CEFR and tailored to history and mathematics. The study was conducted in 2012 and 2013. CEFR-linked language descriptors relevant for the two subjects and age groups were developed and collated. Then 78 CEFR experts from different countries validated the descriptors by assigning them to CEFR levels. Using the mode of the expert level assignments, each descriptor could be labelled with a CEFR level. Finally, 229 teachers of history and mathematics gave feedback on which language descriptors were relevant for the two subjects and age groups. Results of the study indicated that the minimum language standard for students at the age of 12/13 is B1 in all skills in history and mathematics. The standard for 15/16 year old students is B2. Teachers and students can use the descriptors to raise awareness of the language-related aspects of various school subjects, to determine language objectives for lessons, and to use as formative assessment criteria.

Introduction

One of the aims of primary and secondary education is to prepare students for their future lives by empowering them with the relevant skills and knowledge to enable them to live and work as social and independent human beings. In order to reach this goal, students need to be able to understand and communicate in the language of schooling in order to acquire knowledge and master different contexts in and outside school. Language plays an important role in all subject areas, and the lack of language skills may hinder students' access to knowledge and therefore impede success in life. In particular, some young immigrant or minority students may not be able to reach their full potential because they are still learning the language of schooling (Christensen 2014a, 2014b, Gudbrandsen 2014). Not having adequate language skills does not simply mean that these learners will encounter obstacles in language classes; this gap may also manifest itself in content areas like history and mathematics (the term 'history' refers to history and civics throughout the whole paper).

The project *Language descriptors for young migrant and minority learners' success in compulsory education* set out to develop a tool which could guide non-language teachers in their teaching of migrant and minority students. This was done to increase awareness among teachers, parents and school authorities of the language challenges faced by young migrant and minority students. The project, hosted by the European Centre for Modern Languages (ECML) in Graz, Austria, had four European project members and one Canadian associated member: Eli Moe (Norway), Marita Härmälä (Finland), Meilute Ramoniene (Lithuania), José Pascoal (Portugal) and Paula Lee Kristmanson (Canada).

The tool itself, a set of descriptors linked to levels of the Common European Framework of Reference for Languages (CEFR, Council of Europe 2001), is tailored to reflect the language competence migrant and minority students at the ages of 12/13 and 15/16 need have in order to do well in history and mathematics. The aim of the project was to determine minimum standards in terms of specific CEFR level(s) that students in the two age groups needed in order to succeed.

Aim

The aim of this paper is to describe how a set of language descriptors can be linked to the CEFR and tailored to history and mathematics and migrant or minority students at the age of 12/13 and 15/16. The set of descriptors is a tool meant to support teachers and students in compulsory education and make them aware of the language challenges second language students are faced with when acquiring knowledge. The article will give an outline of the theoretical background for the tool, describe the development process and also give ideas for how it can be used by teachers and students. The full version of the project report and the descriptors are available in the project report on the ECML website (www.ecml.at).

Background

In this section, we give a short summary of the previous research done on language of schooling to contextualise our study. Much of this research is based on Cummins (1979) who was the first to bring to light the important role that language skills play in acquiring content knowledge.

Language of schooling

In educational settings, language has the dual function of being both an area of study and also a means of instruction and acquisition of other subject areas. Consequently the term *language of schooling* includes both foreign language education and the language used when teaching and studying subjects other than languages. According to this definition, all school subjects are involved in teaching and developing language, and consequently, all teachers are language teachers. Although the embedded nature of language in content area teaching and learning is recognised today (Fleming 2009), focus on *language* in teaching content is still less emphasised than *content* in language teaching (italics in original, Schleppegrell 2006).

The educational system has an important role in developing language competencies for all students. At school, language is used in different situations and for different purposes. In order to succeed, students need to have two types of language skills (Cummins 1979). First, when communicating with peers and interacting in various kinds of social, everyday situations, students need basic interpersonal communication skills (BICS) (Cummins 1979). BICS are necessary in context-dependent, cognitively undemanding situations, which do not usually require specialised language. For new immigrants, for instance, these are the primary language skills developed in a new language.

In order to cope with more demanding, academic language use situations, another kind of language proficiency is required. Cummins (1979) refers to these skills as cognitive academic language proficiency (CALP). It takes time to develop CALP skills both in a first and especially in a subsequent language. Language functions related to CALP include being able to describe, interpret, compare, etc. while listening, reading, speaking and writing. Since such situations have, to a large extent, a reduced context, many students struggle if they are not familiar with these kinds of contexts.

Subject-specific language

Each school subject, task and topic has its own ways of using language, which clearly contrast with the way language is used in typical informal interaction outside of school (Schleppegrell 2006). According to Schleppegrell (2001, 2006), 'schooling' is a particular kind of situational context where the typical kinds of meaning can be described following Halliday's categories of ideational ('content'), interpersonal ('voice'), and textual meaning ('structure') (Halliday 1994). The 'content' of schooling is displaying knowledge of some kind, the 'voice' expected in schooling is typically an authoritative one, and there are expected ways that each text type will be organised ('structure'). To construct these three kinds of meaning, Schleppegrell (2001, 2006) summarised linguistic features that characterise the language of schooling, namely *density of information, high level of abstraction, technical lexis*, use of *multiple semiotic systems* (e.g. maths symbols), *conventional structuring of the texts*, and *authoritative voice*.

The registers and text types for schooling, which are displayed, for example, in lexical and grammatical choices of the texts, relate to the functional purposes of the texts. Failure to understand and conform to these academic expectations is reflected in the texts produced by linguistically inexperienced students. In sum, linguistic competence is not enough; students also need sociolinguistic competence related to the language of schooling (Schleppegrell 2001).

Discourse genres are, however, not universal but differ from one community of practice to another (e.g. Beacco, Coste, van de Ven and Vollmer 2010). For example, mathematical discourse genres may differ between languages. It is the school's role to widen the range of the genres to which learners have access (Beacco et al 2010:16).

Beacco (2010), Vollmer (2010), Pieper (2011) and Linneweber-Lammerskitten (2012) have studied the language learners aged 15/16 need in order to do well in history, science, literature, and mathematics respectively. In all these studies, very similar discourse functions were identified as being necessary for educational success in the subjects mentioned. These functions are summarised in Table 1.

At the bottom of each column, the discourse functions in italics are examples of functions, which do not directly overlap between the four subjects. The discourse functions in each list are presented alphabetically to underline the similarities between the four lists. This ordering is done by the authors of this article.

137

Table 1 Relevant discourse functions/cognitive operations in history, science, literature and mathematics

History	Science	Literature	Mathematics
Beacco (2010:20–21)	Vollmer (2010:21)	Pieper (2011:20)	Linneweber-Lammerskitten (2012:27)
analyse	analyse	analyse	analyse
argue	argue	argue	argue
classify	classify	classify	classify
compare	compare	compare	compare
correlate/contrast/match	correlate/contrast/match	correlate/contrast/match	correlate/contrast/match
deduce	deduce	deduce	deduce
define	define	define	define
describe/represent	describe/represent	describe/represent	describe/represent
discriminate	distinguish	distinguish	distinguish
enumerate	enumerate	enumerate	enumerate
explain	explain	explain	explain
illustrate/exemplify	illustrate/exemplify	illustrate/exemplify	illustrate/exemplify
infer	infer	infer	infer
interpret	interpret	interpret	interpret
judge/evaluate/assess	judge/evaluate/assess	judge/evaluate/assess	judge/evaluate/assess
name	name	name	name
prove	prove	prove	prove
recount	recount	recount/narrate	recount
report (on) a discourse	report (on) a discourse	report (on) a discourse	report (on) a discourse
specify	specify	specify	specify
summarise	summarise	summarise	summarise
calculate	*assess (also mentioned above)*	*assess (also mentioned above)*	*assess (also mentioned above)*
quote	*calculate*	*outline/sketch*	*calculate*
	outline/sketch		*outline/sketch*

Linking discourse functions in history and mathematics to the CEFR

The CEFR was initially designed to function as a framework for describing the development of an adult foreign language learner's language proficiency. It includes 56 scales of language descriptors covering several language functions and five different language skills (listening, reading, spoken production, spoken interaction and writing). Its 6-grade scale describes the development of language competence all the way from a Basic User (Levels A1 and A2) via Independent User (B1 and B2) to an Advanced User (C1 and C2). The levels A1, A2, and to some extent also Level B1 focus on basic interpersonal skills (BICS), and the Levels B2, C1, C2 on cognitive academic language proficiency (CALP).

In the current project, an attempt was made to link the different discourse functions described in Table 1 to the CEFR descriptors by complementing them with subject matter contents. The Levels A2, B1 and B2 were considered to best match the age groups studied. At Levels B1 and B2, the learner's language proficiency is also considered to be sufficient to cope independently in educational settings. A further motivation for taking the CEFR as a starting point was that in previous studies (Hasselgreen 2003, 2010), the CEFR descriptors are shown to be adaptable to second language contexts and also for younger learners in primary school.

Even though cognitive functions are not explicitly mentioned in the CEFR, many descriptors in the area B2–C2 address cognitive dimensions inherently. This view is seconded by Little (2010:22): 'Although the CEFR does not explicitly address the challenges of academic language, the more advanced levels (B2–C2) are defined in terms that imply advanced levels of educational achievement and/or professional development.'

Developing language descriptors for history and mathematics – process and results

In order to develop language descriptors tailored to history and mathematics for two age groups (12/13 and 15/16) that were linked to CEFR levels and reflected the discourse functions pointed to by Beacco (2010) and Linneweber-Lammerskitten (2012), a process involving three stages was implemented. Figure 1 illustrates this step-by-step process.

The first stage was to decide on which language functions to include within each skill, and to design descriptors mirroring different CEFR levels for each of these functions. Then in stage 2, the level assignment of the descriptors was validated by an external group of CEFR experts from several countries through Questionnaire 1. Finally, it was important to collect perceptions from teachers of history and mathematics related to what students in the different age groups needed to be able to do language wise within their content area. This was done in stage 3 through Questionnaire 2. While Questionnaire 1 was in English, Questionnaire 2 was presented in six languages: English, French,

Figure 1 Overview of stages in the development of language descriptors tailored to history and mathematics and students at the age of 12/13 and 15/16

Finnish, Lithuanian, Norwegian and Portuguese. The reason for having six language versions of Questionnaire 2 was twofold: 1) English and French were the two mandatory project languages and versions of the questionnaire in these languages enabled us to approach teachers across Europe; 2) since one part of the final project output was versions of the language descriptors in the project members' native languages (Finnish, Lithuanian, Norwegian and Portuguese) we included these versions of Questionnaire 2 to make the content more accessible to subject teachers in Finland, Lithuania, Norway and Portugal.

Development

Several educators and researchers contributed to developing language descriptors for history and mathematics. While the project members were responsible for collecting, designing and revising the descriptors, language and subject experts provided relevant feedback on the descriptors at different stages in the process. Figure 2 gives an overview of this process.

The project focuses on history and mathematics; therefore it was important to include language functions relevant to these subject areas. Initially relevant functions were accessed through a number of functions mentioned by Beacco (2010) and Linneweber-Lammerskitten (2012) as well as the Finnish and Norwegian curricula for history and mathematics for the relevant age groups. In Finland and Norway (and some other countries) basic skills such as listening, reading, writing and speaking are inherent in curriculum goals for all subjects. In addition to providing information on relevant language functions, the Finnish and Norwegian curriculum goals provided input on relevant tasks students in the different age groups were expected to be able to do. This information was useful when designing the descriptors.

Figure 2 The process of developing language descriptors for history and mathematics

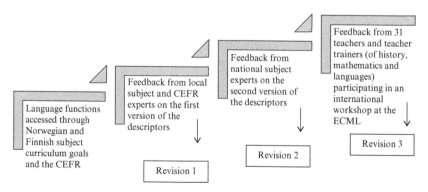

In addition, the CEFR provided a solid base from which descriptors and functions could be 'borrowed' and/or adapted to the two subjects, as well as detailed information on the different levels that was a useful guide through the development process.

The descriptors were targeted to CEFR Levels A2 to C1 for the receptive skills (listening and reading), and A2 to B2 for the productive skills (speaking and writing). The project members disagreed on whether to include descriptors for C1 or not. The main argument for including C1 descriptors was that some felt that the 15/16 year old student may have listening and reading competencies mirroring C1. Therefore, it would be useful to include C1 descriptors for listening and reading. The counter-argument was that since this project focused on minimum standards, several project members doubted that C1 competence could be the minimum requirement for 15/16 year old students in listening and reading.

Feedback collected at the different stages resulted in several revisions of the descriptors. A major revision took place after a workshop in Graz with 31 teachers and teacher trainers of history, mathematics and second languages. The participants worked with the descriptors for two full days, and suggested a number of revisions. As to whether to include C1 descriptors, the workshop participants, as was the case for the project team, were not all in agreement. Therefore, the project team decided to include the C1 descriptors in the two questionnaires and make a final decision when the results of Questionnaire 2 became available.

As a result of the feedback the team collected at the different stages, the set of descriptors increased from 20 language functions (listening, reading, speaking and writing) and 85 descriptors in the first version to 39 language functions and 166 descriptors in the version included in the two online questionnaires at a later stage. The final set of descriptors contains six listening and reading functions, 15 speaking functions and 11 writing functions with 150 descriptors in total.

Validation

In order to validate the initial CEFR level assignments done by the project members, an online questionnaire, Questionnaire 1, was set up. External CEFR experts were asked to assign individual language descriptors to CEFR levels. All the 166 descriptors were included in the questionnaire. Within each skill the sequence of the descriptors was randomised.

A link to the questionnaire was sent out to approximately 400 CEFR experts from Europe. Seventy-eight experts from 16 countries completed the questionnaire with one of these participants only completing the task for reading descriptors.

Using the *mode* to determine the final level assignment, the data showed a surprisingly high agreement between the project team's initial assignment of descriptors to CEFR levels and that done by the language experts. Only six out of the 166 descriptors were assigned to a different level by the experts. Regarding the final level assignment, the team decided to follow the experts' assignment for four of these descriptors, while the initial level assignment was kept for two of them.

Table 2 shows the correlation between the individual CEFR experts' assignments and the final level assignment of the descriptors.

Table 2 shows that the correlation is above 0.70 for 75 of the 78 experts, and above 0.80 for 46 of them. The mean correlation for the experts is 0.83. One of the experts must be considered an outlier with a correlation of −0.159. This person's responses were removed from the analysis to avoid the responses impacting the mean.

In order to check the reliability of the final level assignment, a classical reliability analysis and a bootstrap analysis were conducted. Table 3 shows the results of the analyses.

Table 3 shows that the experts have assigned descriptors to CEFR levels in a reliable way. The reliability estimates vary from 0.819 for listening to 0.936 for writing. The estimates for speaking and writing are higher than those for listening and reading. The main reason for the difference is that there are more speaking (64) and writing (48) descriptors than listening (25)

Table 2 Correlation between individual CEFR experts' level assignment of descriptors and final level assignment

Correlation	Number of experts
−0.159	1
0.5–0.59	1
0.6–0.69	1
0.7–0.79	29
0.8–0.89	24
Above 0.9	22

Table 3 Reliability estimates of the level assignments

Skill		Bootstrap ($n = 1,000$)		
	Reliability	Mean reliability	Confidence interval	
			2.5%	97.5%
Listening	0.819	0.803	0.668	0.883
Reading	0.845	0.840	0.775	0.887
Speaking	0.926	0.923	0.882	0.949
Writing	0.936	0.933	0.898	0.958

and reading (26) descriptors. The bootstrap analysis confirms the original reliability analysis.

At this point the team had validated CEFR descriptors tailored to history and mathematics. Still lacking was an indication of what minimum level of competence teachers thought was necessary for students at the ages of 12/13 and 15/16 in order to reach competence goals in the two subjects.

Required CEFR levels

When the data collection of Questionnaire 1 was finished, a second online questionnaire was set up to collect feedback from history and mathematics teachers on the minimum level of language competence students in the different age groups would need in order to reach curriculum goals in the two subjects. Questionnaire 2 was set up with six parallel language versions: English, French, Finnish, Lithuanian, Norwegian and Portuguese. The teachers had to tick the subject and age group they represented, and all their answers would relate to these two variables.

The teachers were presented with the descriptors skill by skill and language function by language function. Within each function the descriptors were presented in randomised sequence. The teachers had to tick 'Yes' or 'No' for each descriptor (see example in Table 4).

The reason for presenting the experts with descriptors in a mixed order of difficulty was to encourage them to carefully consider whether the competence presented in each descriptor was actually necessary for a particular subject and age group. It is possible that if they knew which descriptors were considered most easy/difficult, it could affect their responses.

On the basis of the teachers' answers, one single CEFR level, for instance B2, was decided upon for most language functions. This was done when two thirds of the teachers (67%) or more indicated one level. In a few cases, however, a level requirement was marked as a transition phase from one level to another, for instance B1–B2. This was done when:

Table 4 Read and analyse graphically represented information in tables, graphs, maps, charts, as well as photographs, paintings and drawings

In order to do well in the subject, should the student be able to:	
1 Understand specific information and identify facts from tables, graphs, maps and charts? (B1)	Yes/No
2 Analyse tables, graphs, maps and charts and make inferences about the data? (B2)	Yes/No
3 Identify basic information communicated in simple tables, graphs, maps and charts? (A2)	Yes/No
4 Analyse and interpret complex tables, graphs, maps and charts and use them to make inferences and calculations? (C1)	Yes/No

- more than two thirds of the teachers agreed on one level (for instance B1), and more than 60% agreed on the next (B2)
- there were two or more descriptors describing a function and level, and the teachers (at least two thirds) said that the students needed the competence expressed by some of the descriptors but not all.

Two hundred and twenty-nine teachers answered the online Questionnaire 2, 127 history teachers and 102 mathematics teachers. Their answers indicated that the minimum language standard for students at the age of 12/13 is B1 in all skills in history and mathematics, while the standard for 15/16 year old students is B2. The general picture is that these 'main levels' are required for between 80% and 100% of the language functions within the different skills. The required level for the writing, however, differs slightly from this main rule. Apart from writing in history for 12/13 year old students, there seems to be fewer writing functions for which teachers indicated the main levels of B1 or B2. In addition, there are also fewer speaking functions in mathematics for 15/16 year old students where B2 is required. See the Appendices A to D at the end of the article for more detailed results.

Initially descriptors were developed for Levels A2 to C1 for the receptive skills and A2 to B2 for the productive skills. In the final stage the project team decided to drop the C1 descriptors for listening and reading. This decision was made on the basis of history and mathematics teachers' feedback related to the minimum level of language competence required in the different subjects and age groups.

The project team believes that the detailed set of descriptors that resulted from this research could be a practical pedagogical tool for content teachers. The next section will describe the ways that this tool could be used to support immigrant and migrant students learning mathematics and history in the language of schooling of the country in which they reside.

The tool: Language descriptors for mathematics and history

As is the case with the general descriptors of the CEFR, the more specific content-related descriptors such as the ones developed in this project can be used by teachers for a variety of purposes:

- to raise awareness of the language-related aspects of various school subjects
- to determine language objectives for lessons
- to use as formative assessment criteria
- to use as self-assessment criteria for students.

First of all, these descriptors remind content-area educators of the fact that all teachers are teachers of language. Without language, students are not able to access any particular topic or content area. Being able to read, write, listen and speak in the language of schooling is essential for engagement and success. For example, success in mathematics cannot simply be equated to a mastery of computational skills that focus on numbers and operations. It is also necessary that students understand oral and written instructions, are able to read graphs and tables, communicate their thinking related to problem solving, and so on. In history classes, teachers not only ask students to listen to lectures and read textbooks, but also to engage in discussions and debates about topics related to historical thinking, civic engagement and cultural awareness. In addition, students are asked to compose various genres of written texts: informative, persuasive, biographical, and narrative. All of these tasks take into consideration descriptors related to the five language skills (i.e. spoken interaction, spoken production, writing, reading, and listening) as described in the CEFR and as further specified by the tool created in this project. Appendices A–D outline the minimum CEFR levels required for each skill in mathematics and history.

Raising awareness of language in content classes

Language descriptors for content areas focus an educator's attention on the linguistic aspects of learning school subjects. By emphasising the language required to participate in content classes, teachers are able to set objectives that relate not only to the acquisition of content-related information, but also to the language functions necessary to negotiate meaning in that content area. According to Sherris (2008), establishing specific content and language objectives is a necessary prerequisite for lesson planning in content classes where language learners are present.

Language and mathematics

To illustrate the potential role of language in mathematics, consider an example from the mathematics classroom. If students are expected to read a graph and communicate the key information included in this graph, teachers need to equip their learners with the linguistic tools necessary to perform this function, e.g. 'This graph tells me that 60% of boys prefer basketball'; 'I can see in this graph that 10% of boys prefer hockey'. Being cognisant of the language required to express certain ideas reminds content teachers to provide language models for learners to follow. Whether or not they need to rely on these models depends on the language proficiency of the learner, but providing the models can be beneficial both from a mathematical and linguistic perspective. In addition, the provision of linguistic scaffolding through modelling is not only useful for the speakers of other languages, but also for learners who speak the language of schooling but may need instructional support. It is important to keep in mind that the language models provided in mathematics will be influenced by teaching styles and priorities as well as the curriculum of the country which reflects both cultural aspects and content priorities (Beacco et al 2010).

Language and history

To illustrate a history example, teachers may want students to read primary source documents in order to extract differing points of view of the same historical event. If teachers keep in mind that this is not simply a history-related task, but also a linguistic one, they would be sure to present examples of ways to express points of view. In addition, they would also provide students reading strategies to facilitate the extraction of main ideas from a text. Moreover, knowing in advance that language functions related to comparing and contrasting would facilitate the achievement of this task would remind teachers to provide examples of ways to communicate comparisons, e.g. 'From the point of view of the women working in munitions factories, the war provided a meaningful purpose. However, from the perspective of men in the trenches, the reasons for war were less clear.' One can see from this example that certain content vocabulary (e.g. munitions, trenches), expressions for expressing opinion (e.g. from the point of view of . . .), and transitional terms (e.g. however) would be useful to learners in order to be able to achieve the curricular outcomes. Being mindful of such linguistic scaffolding gives teachers a way to see themselves not simply as content area teachers, but also as contributors to their language development.

Language descriptors as an instructional tool

The descriptors included in this study can be used not only to develop language objectives for content lessons, but they can also be used to monitor individual students' language development. Teachers might choose to develop general checklists for all students or more specific checklists for an individual student who may not be a proficient user of the language of schooling. These descriptors may also prompt teachers to differentiate their instruction and provide small group scaffolding if it is evident that some learners are in need of specific support in order to achieve a language objective that would allow better access to the course content.

In the development of these descriptors, mathematics and history teachers were asked to identify the language functions that they considered essential to function well in these subject areas. During this development process, it became clear that there is indeed a language component to content classes. In order to illustrate how these descriptors might be used as an instructional tool for teachers, consider an example from both the mathematics and the history classrooms.

Mathematics example

The following descriptors for listening were deemed important to teachers of mathematics.

Language function: Understand factual information, and explanations
Descriptors:

- can grasp the main point of short, clear, simple presentations or explanations by teachers and peers, if people speak slowly and clearly and time is allowed for repetition (A2)
- can follow straightforward presentations and explanations by teachers and peers on subject related issues (B1)
- can follow elaborated presentations and explanations by teachers and peers on subject related issues (B2).

When a mathematics teacher of 12/13 year olds examines this listening function and these descriptors, he/she might decide that students can function well in his/her mathematics classroom by being able to follow straightforward presentations and explanations by both teachers and peers (A2). In this way, a teacher will be reminded to keep presentations and explanations concise and clear. Also, if many of the students in the class are still not able to function at this level and are still needing very slowly articulated and repetitive explanations, the teacher will modify and scaffold instructions by giving them both in writing and orally and by giving the opportunity for small group and individual support. Also, keeping language proficiency in mind, teachers may wish to highlight key words in the instructions and make readily available visual and text-based definitions to support the listening function (understanding factual information and explanations).

History example

To examine another example, this time from a history perspective at the 15/16 year old level, a teacher might want to consider the language necessary to successfully complete the particular writing task (e.g. summary).

Language function: Summarise
Descriptors:

- can pick out and reproduce key words and phrases or short sentences from a short text (A2)
- can collate short pieces of information from several sources and summarise them in writing (B1)

- can paraphrase short written passages in a simple fashion, using the original text wording and ordering (B1)
- can summarise a wide range of information and arguments from a number of sources (B2).

In this case, a teacher may determine that for students to be successful in their history classes, they should be able to summarise a wide range of information and arguments from a number of sources. However, if there are students in the class who are still only able to 'paraphrase short written passages in a simple fashion', they will need to scaffold this much more difficult task by providing examples, templates and models that students can use as a guide. In addition, they may need to differentiate the task by providing levelled texts that accommodate the reading-related needs of different learners. Although the teacher may have set the higher linguistic level goal, they may need to keep in mind that it is still possible to complete this language function (i.e. summarise) at a more basic level. In this way, students will be able to participate in the history class to the best of their linguistic ability without feeling that they are not able to participate at all. Being aware of the varying levels possible for a specific function will help teachers plan lessons that meet various learner needs.

Language descriptors as assessment tools in the content classroom

Although the priority of content teachers is often perceived to be the achievement of content-related goals, it is clear that language goals play a key role in the content classroom. Success in content areas requires a certain level of language proficiency. We have discussed briefly how these descriptors can be used as an instructional tool. It is also important to consider how language descriptors could complement content outcomes in order to create comprehensive assessment criteria. Content teachers who have language learners in their classrooms may want to create formative and summative assessment tools that consider language. For example, in a mathematics classroom, a concept such as probability is not simply a computational concept, but also one with linguistic dimensions. For this reason, a mathematics teacher might want to develop assessment criteria that reflect the mathematical and linguistic aspects.

In addition to teacher-directed assessments, self-assessment might also be a tool that content teachers wish to consider. As is evidenced in much of the documentation related to the CEFR and the European Language Portfolio (ELP), self-assessment and goal-setting should be a priority for language teachers (e.g. Council of Europe 2004). Self-assessment helps learners take ownership of their learning and requires teachers to carefully and clearly articulate the objectives of a unit of study. In content classes where there are learners of varying proficiency levels, making both content and language goals accessible to the learners can be one way to help learners understand expectations. In order to create a self-assessment scheme, teachers are required to thoughtfully break down the components of the content-related tasks. By doing so, content teachers will likely discover that some of these components are linguistic in nature. The language descriptors developed in this project, in combination with curriculum outcomes from content areas such as mathematics and history, can be a starting point for developing assessment criteria that can form the foundation of both teacher-led assessment tools and self-assessment tools.

Self-assessment

This tool, the language descriptors, can also be used as an instructional tool to help encourage students to set goals and to raise awareness related to the language skills necessary in the history or mathematics classroom. The teacher and the students can discuss which skills it makes sense to focus on, and the teacher can provide them with relevant language descriptors and CEFR levels. It is probably wise to not focus on too many descriptors at a time.

Students need to know what they are aiming towards; therefore the teacher has to 'show' them what the relevant descriptors mean and provide them with concrete examples. If students are asked to describe something, what will be expected of them? What does a description sound or look like? What are the elements of a good description? When language descriptors are used with young students or beginner language learners, it may be a good idea to rephrase some of them in a way that makes them easy to understand, as in the following examples.

Student .... Age: 15/16   Subject: History
My goals for speaking

		I can do this			
My objectives What I can do What I will work on	I have not managed this yet	with help from classmates or the teacher	quite well	very well	I have evidence
	Date	Date	Date	Date	Date
Express opinions, discuss					
B2: I can talk about historical topics and share in formation, ideas and my attitudes about the topic.					
B2: I can give my opinion and give details to explain it.					

B1: I can explain why I am for or against something.					
Give a presentation or talk in class					
B2: I can give a detailed presentation that includes different points of view and emphasises the most important points related to the topic.					
B1: I can give a prepared talk about a topic and answer clear questions from the teacher and classmates.					

Student .... **Age: 12/13**   **Subject: Mathematics**
My goals for writing

My objectives What I can do What I will work on		I can do this				
		I have not managed this yet	with help from classmates or the teacher	quite well	very well	I have evidence
		Date	Date	Date	Date	Date
Describe						
B1: I can describe how I am thinking when solving a task in a simple and clear way.						
B1: I can briefly describe a graph, a figure or a table and point out important things.						
A2: I can write very short, basic descriptions of something I have worked on in class.						
Explain						
B1: I can explain and give reasons for why something related to mathematics is the way it is, and why something is a problem in a simple and clear way.						
A2: I can explain how to do something or what I have done in simple sentences.						

Conclusion

Language proficiency is a necessary requisite to experience success in schooling and success in life. For immigrant and migrant students required to learn cognitively demanding academic subjects such as mathematics and history while simultaneously acquiring language skills, the task can be daunting. Success may seem like an unattainable goal when, from a linguistic perspective, students are in survival and coping mode. It is hoped that the tool developed in this project will help raise awareness of the linguistic dimensions of content area learning and prompt content teachers to consider their role in the overall language development of their students. Taking time to reflect on the language necessary for success in subjects such as mathematics and history may remind teachers of the scaffolding needed to achieve some success in school. By using the language descriptors included in this tool as lesson objectives and assessment criteria, teachers can be more intentional in their instruction in order to better support the immigrant and migrant students in their classes.

References

Beacco, J C (2010) *Items for a Description of Linguistic Competence in the Language of Schooling Necessary for Learning/teaching History (End of Compulsory Education): An Approach with Reference Points*, available online: www.coe.int/t/dg4/linguistic/Source/Source2010_ForumGeneva/1_LIS-History2010_en.pdf

Beacco, J C, Coste, D, van de Ven, P H and Vollmer, H (2010) *Language and School subjects. Linguistic Dimensions of Knowledge Building in School Curricula*, Strasbourg: Council of Europe, available online: www.coe.int/t/dg4/linguistic/ListDocs_Geneva2010.asp

Christensen, R (2014a) Mange av elevene forstår ikke norsk [Many students do not understand Norwegian], *Bergens Tidende*, available online: www.vg.no/nyheter/innenriks/skole-og-utdanning/mange-norske-elever-gir-opp-for-lett/a/10139877/

Christensen, R (2014b) Det er hyklersk å droppe språkkrav [The hypocrisy of dropping language requirements], *Bergens Tidende*, available online: www.bt.no/nyheter/lokalt/-Det-er-hyklersk-a-droppe-sprakkrav-3130917.html

Council of Europe (2001) *Common European Framework of Reference for Languages: Learning, Teaching, Assessment*, Cambridge: Cambridge University Press.

Council of Europe (2004) *European Language Portfolio (ELP): Principles and Guidelines*, Strasbourg: Council of Europe, Language Policy Division.

Cummins, J (1979) Cognitive/academic language proficiency, linguistic interdependence, the optimum age question and some other matters, *Working Papers on Bilingualism* 19, 121–129.

Fleming, M (2009) *Languages of schooling and the right to plurilingual and intercultural education*, paper presented at the Intergovernmental Conference, Strasbourg, 8–10 June 2009, available online: www.coe.int/t/dg4/linguistic/Source/ReportConf_09LangScol_en.doc

Gudbrandsen, F (2014) Norsk først [Norwegian first] *Bergens Tidende*, available online: www.bt.no/meninger/kommentar/Norsk-forst-3127879.html

Halliday, M A K (1994) *Introduction to Functional Grammar* (2nd edition), London: Edward Arnold.

Hasselgreen, A (2003) *The Bergen Can-do Project*, Graz: European Centre for Modern Languages.

Hasselgreen, A (2010) *The Ayllit Project*, Graz: European Centre for Modern Languages.

Linneweber-Lammerskitten, H (2012) *Items for a Description of Linguistic Competence in the Language of Schooling Necessary for Learning/Teaching Mathematics (At the End of Compulsory Education). An Approach with Reference Points*, available online: www.coe.int/t/dg4/linguistic/Source/ Source2010_ForumGeneva/4_LIS-Mathematics2012_EN.pdf

Little, D (2010) *The Linguistic and Educational Integration of Children and Adolescents from Migrant Backgrounds*, Strasbourg: Language Policy Division, Council of Europe, available online: www.coe.int/t/dg4/linguistic/ Source/Source2010_ForumGeneva/MigrantChildrenConceptPaper_EN.pdf

Pieper, I (2011) *Items for a Description of Linguistic Competence in the Language of Schooling Necessary for Learning/Teaching Literature (End of Compulsory Education). An Approach with Reference Points*, Strasbourg: Council of Europe, Language Policy Division, available online: www.coe.int/t/dg4/ linguistic/Source/Source2010_ForumGeneva/1_LIS-Literature2011_EN.pdf

Schleppegrell, M (2001) Linguistic features of the language of schooling, *Linguistics and Education* 12 (4), 431–459.

Schleppegrell, M (2006) The challenges of academic language in school subjects, in Lindberg, I and Sandwall, K (Eds) *Språket och kunskapen: att lära på sitt andraspråk i skola och högskola*, Göteborg: Göteborgs universitet institutet för svenska som andraspråk, 47–69.

Sherris, A (2008) *Integrated Content and Language Instruction*, Washington, DC: Centre for Applied Linguistics, available online: www.cal.org/resources/digest/ integratedcontent.html

Vollmer, H J (2010) *Items for a Description of Linguistic Competence in the Language of Schooling Necessary for Learning/Teaching Mathematics (At the End of Compulsory Education). An Approach with Reference Points*, available online: www.coe.int/t/dg4/linguistic/Source/Source2010_ForumGeneva/1-LIS-sciences2010_EN.pdf

Appendix A

Minimum CEFR levels required for listening in history or civics and mathematics

Listening CEFR levels indicated by teachers	History/civics		Mathematics	
Age groups	12/13	15/16	12/13	15/16
Understand factual information and explanations	B1	B2	B1	B2
Understand instructions and directions	B1	B2	B1	B2
Understand opinions	B1	B2	A2–B1	B1–B2
Understand arguments and reasoning	B1	B1–B2	B1	B2
Follow subject related conversations	B1	B2	B1	B2
Understand audio recorded materials (including videos)	B1	B2	B1	B2

Appendix B

Minimum CEFR levels required for reading in history or civics and mathematics

Reading CEFR levels indicated by teachers	History/civics		Mathematics	
Age groups	12/13	15/16	12/13	15/16
Understand factual information and explanations	B1	B1	B1	B1
Understand instructions and directions	B1	B2	B1	B2
Understand opinions	B1	B2	N/A	N/A
Understand arguments and reasoning	B1	B2	B1	B2
Find and localise information	B1	B2	A2–B1	B2
Read and analyse graphically represented information in tables, graphs, maps, charts, symbols, as well as photographs, paintings and drawings	B1	B2	B1	C1

Appendix C

Minimum CEFR levels required for speaking in history or civics and mathematics

Speaking CEFR levels indicated by teachers	History/civics		Mathematics	
Age groups	12/13	15/16	12/13	15/16
Describe	B1	B2	B1	B2
Explain	B1	B2	B1	B2
State facts, outline, give an account of something	B1	B2	B1	B2
Express opinions, discuss	B1	B2	B1	B2
Express arguments, prove	B1	B–B2	B1	B2
	Relevant?*	Relevant?*		
Summarise	B1	B2	B1	B2
Define	B1	B2	B1	B2
Evaluate, interpret	B1	B2	B1	B1–B2
Compare and contrast	B1	B1	B1	B1–B1
Make oneself understood and clear up misunderstandings/misconceptions	A2–B1	B2	A2–B1	B2
Talk to teachers and classmates	B1	B1–B2	B1	B1–B2
Ask for clarification	A2–B1	B2	A2–B1	B2
Respond to what people say	B1	B2	B1	B2
Interact in teamwork	B1	B2	B1	B1–B2
Give a presentation or talk about subject matter issues in class	B1	B1–B2	B1	B1–B2

* The comments regarding whether a language function is relevant are based on the data and/or responses from teachers and experts.

Appendix D

Minimum CEFR levels required for writing in history or civics and mathematics

Writing CEFR levels indicated by teachers	History/civics		Mathematics	
Age groups	12/13	15/16	12/13	15/16
Describe	B1	B2	B1	B2
Explain	B1	B2	B1	B2
State facts, outline, give an account of something	B1	B2	B1	B2
Express opinions, discuss	B1	B2	Below A2? Relevant?*	Below A2? Relevant?*
Express arguments, prove	B1 Relevant?*	B1 Relevant?*	B1	B2
Summarise	B1	B1	Below A2? Relevant?*	Below A2? Relevant?*
Define	B1	B2	B1	B2
Organise	B1	B1	A2	A2
Evaluate, interpret	A2	B1–B2	A2	A2–B1
Compare and contrast	B1	B2	B1	B2
Work with forms, tables, charts, graphs etc.	B1	B2	B1–B2	B2

* *The comments regarding whether a language function is relevant are based on the data and/or responses from teachers and experts.*

8 Assessment as recognition: An e-portfolio for valuing North America's linguistic diversity

Enrica Piccardo

OISE – University of Toronto

Abstract

Even though Canada is home to linguistically diverse populations, 'non-dominant' languages are frequently not recognised and undervalued in both mainstream society and education. In contrast with policy and curricula documents from provincial Ministries of Education supporting the use of multiple languages in classrooms and first language maintenance for minority language students, recent analyses of Canadian educators' discourse reveal a distinct lack of support for linguistic diversity in schools. This discrepancy, coupled with the reality of rapidly disappearing aboriginal languages, suggest a dire need for ideological and pedagogical change in relation to language learning and assessment. The creation and introduction of an e-portfolio (Language Integration Through E-portfolio, LITE) inspired by the European Language Portfolio (ELP) but designed specifically for the diversity of the Canadian linguistic landscape could function as a catalyst for introducing such change. LITE encompasses and goes beyond Canada's two official languages and includes (in the pilot version) two of the country's many 'heritage' languages, and one of the three of Canada's aboriginal languages that are secured from the threat of long-term extinction.

This paper presents a project, involving researchers and practitioners from Canadian and American universities and educational institutions, in collaboration with a European university, encompassing a multi-stage research process that comprises cycles of collaborative design and development of LITE, classroom trials, and collaborative revision of the drafts.

Introduction: Context and background of the project

Canada is home to a linguistically diverse population. Around 7 million Canadians (20.1% of the population) speak a language other than English and French at home; nearly 8 million (22.1%) people speak

French, and just above 20 million (57.8%) speak English (Statistics Canada 2012).

The diversity of the Canadian context results from the wealth of immigration languages on one side and of native and aboriginal languages on the other. The immigration movements dominated for centuries by the languages and cultures of the historic colonial powers, English and French, have relatively recently witnessed an exponential growth of linguistically and culturally diverse populations. This diversity represents a new layer that added up to the wealth of aboriginal languages of the First Nations, Métis and Inuit communities. The result of this phenomenon is that, in addition to the official national languages, numerous aboriginal languages and a multitude of heritage languages are spoken in Canada. If we look deeper into these non-official languages, we see that they belong to very diverse linguistic families, of which the most represented are, in decreasing order, Indo-Iranian, Chinese, Romance, Germanic, Slavic and Aboriginal, which altogether cover 5 million speakers, followed by other smaller communities speaking languages of other families for the remaining 2 million speakers.

In spite of this extreme diversity though, Canada's linguistic and cultural diversity is still not widely known or as much of a commonly accepted reality as it could – and should – be. The dominant position of English and French, which are not only the country's official languages, but also internationally dominant languages, is a factor that needs to be taken into consideration when trying to understand why the value of linguistic diversity is still underestimated. As a matter of fact, linguistic diversity is *de facto* still seen as an issue rather than a potential resource. The problem is particularly serious and extensive for aboriginal languages, whose social and political recognition is a recent phenomenon, in spite of their ancient origin.

Canada is considered a linguistic 'hotspot' (Anderson 2010, 2011, Harrison 2007), as languages are vanishing more rapidly than in other parts of the world. Statistics from the past 25 years show that many aboriginal languages in Canada have undergone long-term declines in intergenerational transmission and mother tongue (first-language) populations, most suffering a steady erosion (Crystal 2000, Norris 2007, 2011) with their use being systematically discouraged (MacMillan 1998). In the world, it is estimated that between 50 and 90% of the languages spoken today will have become extinct by the end of the century (Evans 2010:212). Knowing that 'each language is a semiotic system of understanding the world, immeasurably rich in diversity of ideas expressed' (Crystal 2000:36), the disappearance of any aboriginal language would represent a great cultural loss not only for that community, but also for the culture of the country and of the world (Fishman 1996, Harrison 2007, 2010, Henze and Davis 2008).

The problem of lack of real recognition of language diversity is a complex and somehow tricky one, which spans from language policies to the everyday language education practices.

Both mainstream society and education fail to recognise and value *non-dominant* languages (Hornberger 2002, Wiley and Lukes 1996). Homogenising and assimilationist language policies still prevail (Cantoni 1997, Connelly 2008, Hornberger 2002) in spite of the active voice of educators and academics who advocate for multilingual language policies that support cultural and linguistic diversity (Cummins 2001, García, Skutnabb-Kangas and Torres-Guzmán (Eds) 2006, Lo Bianco 2010). These policies contribute to the decline of home languages (Cantoni 1997, Crawford 2000) by perpetuating *de facto* a negative perception of bilingualism among many educators (unless bilingualism concerns the official languages).

Things are not improving at the tertiary level of education. In fact, while many institutions have made it part of their strategic plans to increase internationalisation through the recruitment of foreign students, resulting in a growingly multicultural and multilingual student population at Canadian universities, strategies to educate local Canadian students to become global citizens able to cope with the multicultural/multilingual environments and globalising experiences are strikingly underdeveloped. As it is already the case for secondary education, the focus is on proficiency in the language of instruction. Beyond paying lip service to the importance of linguistic and cultural diversity, no action is undertaken for valuing linguistic diversity. Any deviation to the norm is seen from a deficiency perspective, and there is no requirement, nor encouragement, for students to preserve or expand their linguistic and cultural capital.

In sum, despite there being a discourse in the public in Canada that multiculturalism is a good thing or valued, there is actually no mechanism for supporting it within the educational system. Above all, there is no support for helping practitioners overcome the current monolingual vision of education and accept and implement a plurilingual paradigm shift (Kramsch, Levy and Zarate 2008), something which implies ideological and pedagogical change (Piccardo 2014), where languages would cease to be considered in isolation and become elements acting concurrently and collectively to shape individuals' cognition, socialisation and identity.

Looking for possible ways to raise awareness of these issues, to help educators deal effectively with linguistic and cultural diversity, and to foster innovation in language education, colleagues and I focused on the pedagogical dimension and conceived of a project (LINguistic and Cultural DIversity REinvented, LINCDIRE) whose goal is to develop a tool (Language Integration Through E-portfolio, LITE) aiming at facilitating first language maintenance, supporting language diversity as well as encouraging plurilingualism among students in secondary and post-secondary institutions, through an explicit focus on the presence of multiple languages and cultures in the classroom. The acronym LINCDIRE was introduced to mark the fact that our project broadened its initial scope and developed its conceptual apparatus. The initially envisaged tool was called Personal Language Portfolio (PLP). This tool has been replaced by LITE. As LITE encompasses and goes beyond the PLP, I will use LITE throughout the paper in order to avoid confusing readers, mentioning the PLP only when I am referring to development of the first part of the project.

The remainder of this paper will provide the rationale of this project, its underpinning theoretical framework as well as its methodology. I will start by defining the issues LINCDIRE intends to address; I will then describe the tool (LITE) and explain its conceptualisation and the methodology used to conceive of it. After a brief description of the state of the project, I will conclude discussing the implications and potential of such a tool for the Canadian, and in general the North American, context.

Linguistic and cultural diversity: Issue or resource?

In the Canadian context, at various levels, we are often faced with a double discourse: there is a great disparity between the extensive rhetorical support for multiple language use in the classroom expressed in official documents and the everyday teaching reality and practice.

At the national level a recent document issued by the Council of Ministers of Education of Canada (CMEC) (2010) underlines the importance and value of linguistic and cultural diversity and itemises it into several aspects such as recognition of pluriliterate competencies, a new vision of teaching to reflect language alternation among immigrant learners, transfer of discursive competencies from one language to another, acquisition of metacognitive strategies as a condition for ensuring development of academic skills and the promotion of socialisation and autonomy, or the use of integrated learning approaches. Needless to say, this document limits itself at suggesting principles and guidelines rather than reaching the operational level as education is under the purview of the provincial governments.

Various policy and curriculum documents from provincial ministries of education also appear to support the use of multiple languages in classrooms and first language maintenance for minority language students (Alberta Education 2010, British Columbia Ministry of Education 2009, Ontario Ministry of Education 2005, 2006). These documents advise teachers to encourage first language use in certain situations, providing theoretical justification for multiple language use by citing research that has illustrated the social and academic benefits of first-language maintenance and bilingualism (Cook 2001, Cummins 2007a, Cummins, Bismilla, Chow, Cohen, Giampapa, Leoni, Sandhu and Sastri 2005, Taylor, Bernhard, Garg and Cummins

2008). Nevertheless, teachers are not provided with the tools, resources, and support that they need to achieve these aims.

Still, all these proclamations and statements of intent could give the impression that Canada is moving towards more recognition and integration of language plurality in education. Unfortunately this is not the case: in contrast to this rhetorical support for multiple language use, recent analyses of Canadian educators' discourse reveal a distinct lack of support for linguistic diversity in schools. Schools typically mirror Canadian society, which sees homogeneity as a gauge of success (Connelly 2008). This also translates at the school level: homogenous schools are in fact 'considered apt to success, while a school with a high proportion of "underperforming" recent immigrants is seen as having a handicap' (Connelly 2008:166–167). Linguistic minority students frequently cease to use their first language in the classroom and even outside of it as they soon realise that others may perceive their linguistic status as failure and difference may be seen as inadequate performance (Connelly 2008, Flecha 1999). This trend is a contributing factor to widespread language attrition which affects students, families, linguistic or cultural communities, and the entire Canadian society.

In general, in spite of a solid scholarly research body that shows how bilingual and first language maintenance provides social, cognitive and academic benefits (Bialystok 2001, Cook 2001, Cummins 2007a, Fishman 1996, Taylor et al 2008), and even though Canada adopted an official policy of multiculturalism in 1988, approaches to multicultural education are viewed as *folkloric* (Gérin-Lajoie 2011, Haque 2012, Nieto 2004), and barriers include the stipulation that Heritage language instruction is only extra-curricular in provinces such as Ontario (Carlino 2009). In general teaching remains strictly monolingual, one language at a time, even in the case of immersion programmes, where each subject is taught in a specific language. The underlying assumption is that using more than one language in a course either through a comparative approach or any form of code switching, mixing or meshing, is detrimental to the learning process. Such vision does not make space for any non-curricular language and cuts students from their linguistic roots and identities. This is particularly serious for aboriginal learners as not only are aboriginal languages at risk but also 'many of the social dysfunctions plaguing aboriginal peoples and communities can be traced to the loss of language' (Little Bear 2009:22).

To sum up, the main obstacles towards a move from seeing linguistic and cultural diversity as an issue rather than as a resource are: (1) a mismatch between rhetorical, institutional discourse and educational reality when it comes to linguistic and cultural diversity; (2) a lack of recognition of the cognitive and academic value of linguistic diversity in everyday classroom reality; and (3) a lack of targeted pedagogical tools and support for practitioners. We are hoping to challenge the status quo and contribute to the reduction of some of these obstacles by developing a flexible and effective tool for teachers, learners and communities, able to bring about new linguistic and pedagogical thoughts and processes.

LITE: Underlying theoretical framework

The theoretical framework underpinning LITE draws upon the notions of plurilingualism, critical thinking and indigenous epistemology and pedagogies. Each of these will be presented and explained in turn, starting with plurilingualism.

The notion of plurilingualism is quite distinct from that of bi- and even multilingualism. A plurilingual framework considers that linguistic competencies do not refer to several compartmentalised language competencies but to a dynamic and composite competence from which the social actor may draw (Coste, Moore and Zarate 1997), which includes partial competences rather than a balance of skills. Ultimately, it recognises the holistic and interconnected nature of language, identity and culture, and therefore treats proficiency as highly individualised, dependent on life paths, and subject to evolution and change (Coste, Moore and Zarate 2009, Council of Europe 2001).

Plurilingualism is a fundamental trait of a world characterised by mobility and change (Piccardo 2013), but we are often unaware of plurilingual competences in ourselves and others due to our monolingual social conditioning, or *monolingual disposition* (Gogolin 1994). Even bilingual and multilingual educational approaches (while better than *English only* environments) are still 'a pluralization of monolingualism' (Makoni and Pennycook 2005:147). Bi- and multilingual approaches often perpetuate the notion that language can be reduced to a linguistic system that is capable of existing independently from the social world (Makoni and Pennycook 2007). This ideology often corresponds with the valorisation of a *symmetric* version of bilingualism that positions equal competency in the first and target language as the primary goal for learners (Piccardo 2013). Unfortunately, this rather unrealistic goal often creates feelings of inadequacy in learners and diminishes their self-esteem. In fact, as students dwell on their *imperfect* competence in the target language, they may begin to perceive their language competency as a burden (Puozzo Capron 2009), which can create feelings of uneasiness and over time, insecurity and even hatred towards the second language (Piccardo 2013).

Rather than compartmentalising language competencies, plurilingualism grants significance to the relationships between lived experience and language use, and the relationships between all of the languages spoken by an individual (Piccardo 2013). It is a holistic approach that recognises that all languages are in an ongoing process of creation and modification (Wandruszka 1979), and therefore cannot be contained and positioned as a stationary target for learners.

At a global level, institutions are still struggling with integrating a plurilingual vision due to a rooted monolingual attitude, which sees each language as a discrete entity with definite boundaries and established rules. The paradigm shift from multilingualism to plurilingualism appears very challenging. The multilingual vision where languages are considered and taught separately and separately tested is deeply entrenched in the western, North American education system and school culture, something that, as we will explain later, makes opening to indigenous pedagogies even more challenging. Drawing upon the plurilingualism theoretical framework, LITE aims at facilitating this paradigm shift.

Adopting a plurilingual paradigm implies fostering linguistic and cultural/ intercultural awareness, which in turn are strictly linked to the development of critical thinking, another focal point of LITE.

Let us consider the second notion we mentioned, precisely critical thinking. Following Benesch, who in turns refers to other researchers in the field, we define critical thinking as 'a search for the social, historical, and political roots of conventional knowledge and orientation to transform learning and society . . . in this view [Benesch argues] those who think critically focus on social inequities and probe the disparities between democratic principles and undemocratic realities' (1993:546). Critical thinking encompasses and goes beyond a pure cognitive view. A broader perspective embedded in the socio-cultural-historical dimension favours high-order skills such as analysis, synthesis or inference. 'We can adopt a cognitive orientation, inviting ESL [English as a Second Language] students to analyze, synthesise, and evaluate topics divorced from the social origins of these themes. Or, we can ask them to investigate their experience and its relationship to the language, politics, and history of the new culture. According to the view presented here, the latter approach is critical, the former is not' (Benesch 1993:547). This view of critical thinking encompasses and extends the classical view of critical thinking (Glaser 1941), which implies the attitude and disposition to consider problems and experiences in a thoughtful way and to examine any belief or supposed form of knowledge in the light of evidence, as well as the knowledge of methods of logical enquiry and reasoning and the capacity of applying these methods. It proposes a more holistic view of critical thinking, which sees individuals within the social and cultural context. The approach adopted by LITE embraces Benesch's version of critical thinking.

This vision of critical thinking is not only fundamental in the conceptualisation of LITE's theoretical framework but also helps to make the transition towards the third component of this framework: indigenous knowledge, epistemologies and pedagogies. As such it will act as leverage for connecting western and aboriginal pedagogies.

Indigenous knowledge refers to the wisdom, skills and experience accumulated by communities and nations living in different parts of the

Americas, Oceania, Africa and Asia covering over 5,000 languages and 70 nation-states (Battiste and Youngblood Henderson 2000). As stated by the United Nations[1] 'the heritage of an indigenous people is a complete knowledge system with its own concepts of epistemology, and its own scientific and logical validity' (Battiste 2002:7–8). Drawing from studies of several other scholars (Aluli-Meyer 2001, Deloria 1999, Ermine 1995, Friesen and Friesen 2002, Lane, Bopp and Bopp 1984), Leik explains that 'indigenous epistemology understands the world from a holistic perspective where all things, material and spiritual, are interconnected and interdependent . . . understanding the interdependence of all things requires attention to individual identity, relationships, and responsibility to the whole' (1992:19). Leik adds that 'indigenous epistemologies understand that all things are in a constant state of motion and change' (1992:20).

Indigenous epistemology is about acknowledging and honouring diversity rather than searching 'the truth', thus recognising that people have different perceptions of events is key. Indigenous epistemological perspectives are often expressed through the teaching of culture often in the form of stories and are the basis of indigenous pedagogy. According to Battiste, aboriginal epistemology is found in theories, philosophies, histories, ceremonies, and stories as a way of knowing. Aboriginal pedagogy is found in talking or sharing circles and dialogues, participant observations, experiential learning, modelling, meditation, prayer, ceremonies, or storytelling as ways of knowing and learning.

While we want to avoid essentialising either a western or aboriginal epistemological frameworks, i.e. considering them as having fixed traits and neglecting the wealth of variations they present, there are some salient similarities between the two that are apparent even in the early stages of this research. According to Battiste, 'focusing on the similarities between the two systems of knowledge rather than on their differences may be a more useful place to start when considering how best to introduce educational reform'(2002:11). In fact, she continues, 'Canadian administrators and educators need to respectfully blend indigenous epistemology and pedagogy with Euro-Canadian epistemology and pedagogy to create an innovative Canadian educational system' (2002:21).

In the same vein a model has been developed in the Australian context, which synthesises aboriginal pedagogies, but also aims at engaging educators in a dialogue between indigenous and mainstream pedagogies. This framework, called the Eight Ways Aboriginal Pedagogy Framework (Yunkaporta 2009), is organised around the following eight key concepts: 1) Story Sharing; 2) Learning Maps; 3) Non-verbal Learning; 4) Symbols and Images; 5) Land Links; 6) Non-linear Concepts; 7) Deconstruct/Reconstruct; 8) Community Links. This is how Yunkaporta unpacks them (2009:35–38): *Story Sharing* is about teaching and learning through narrative; *Learning Maps* is about making learning pathways and processes explicit visually; *Non-verbal Learning* is about hands-on learning, critical reflection and least-intrusive management strategies; *Symbols and Images* is about exploring content through imagery and using visual cues and signals; *Land Links* is about place-based pedagogy, linking content to local land and environment; *Non-linear Concepts* is about indirect management strategies, lateral thinking, comparing and synthesising diverse cultural viewpoints, innovating, adapting, working with cycles and working with holistic knowledge; *Deconstruct/Reconstruct* is about modelling and scaffolding, balancing teacher instruction with independent learning and working from wholes to parts; *Community Links* is about grounding learning content and values in community knowledge, working on community projects and using or displaying knowledge products publicly for local benefit.

National borders as we said do not limit aboriginal knowledge insofar as they are a product of the western culture and they have been imposed on societies which pre-existed European settlers. Thus, even if the framework was developed outside of the North American context the model appears very appropriate for linking western and indigenous pedagogies and it was taken into consideration for the conceptualisation of LITE.

Battiste argues for education that 'moves beyond rule-based learning and considers life-long learning, learning how to learn in diverse contexts, and ability to apply knowledge to unfamiliar circumstances' (2002:16). Similarly, LITE will facilitate critical thinking such as using metacognitive strategies to reflect on learning processes and to learn how to learn. LITE, in the vein of the European Language Portfolio (ELP), will also support learner autonomy and life-long learning.

Above all, LITE will reflect the concept expressed by Battiste that knowledge is a 'living process to be absorbed and understood [rather than] a commodity that can be possessed or controlled by educational institutions' (2002:15), as it will provide the space for reflection on lived experiences (linguistic, intercultural, or otherwise), thus transforming the subjective experiences of all students into potential sources of knowledge. The aboriginal vision is reflected in aboriginal languages, for instance the focus on verbs of most indigenous languages instead of nouns as it is the case with western languages, namely English, conveys the understanding that life is a process (Ross 2006), thus the preservation of indigenous languages is fundamental to support indigenous views of education. With its focus on plurilingualism, LITE will not only serve this goal but also help create bridges between different languages, epistemologies and education visions.

Towards LITE: The LINguistic and Cultural DIversity REinvented (LINCDIRE) project

The discrepancy between Canada's linguistic diversity and educational environments that recognise and reward only majority language speakers, coupled with the reality of rapidly disappearing aboriginal languages, suggest a dire need for ideological and pedagogical change in relation to language learning and use. We may posit that the introduction of LITE, a language portfolio designed specifically for such a diverse linguistic landscape will function as a catalyst for introducing the necessary change. LITE will be a fully online tool, consisting of different parts (including more or less linguistic content), flexible, customisable and expandable.

The initial project started at the end of 2012 under the name of the Personal Language Portfolio Project (PLP) and gathered a team of four researchers from different Canadian provinces (Ontario, New Brunswick and Alberta) respectively and one from a US educational institution based in Vermont. One year later, one researcher expert in aboriginal studies joined the team to assure greater consistency between the western and indigenous pedagogies inspiring the PLP. Graduate students and practitioners assist this core group. The geographical main focus of the project is the Canadian context. The presence of the US institution was justified mainly by two reasons: the US institution represents an ideal terrain for trialling LITE due to its specific international character; and it allows for the exportability of the tool beyond Canada to be tested, stressing similarities rather than differences between the two contexts as far as linguistic and cultural diversity are concerned. At the end of 2014 the project was expanded to include two more institutions (one more from the US and one from France) which have expertise in dealing with language diversity. This will provide extra support in the domain of plurilingualism and will allow a broader experimentation of LITE thus strengthening its exportability. It also allowed for the inclusion in LITE of a second heritage language, Italian, which is the language of one of the largest communities not only in Canada but also in the two areas where the US and French institutions are located.

All the members of the project team are active in applied linguistics and language education and/or teacher development. They are all familiar with the notion of portfolio assessment in general and some of them with the ELP.

The first phase of the project has focused on three fundamental aspects of the research:

1. Analysis of the linguistic situation of the different Canadian provinces and of related official documents in education. A study of the US linguistic characteristics has also been conducted, albeit in less depth.

2. Study of existing language portfolios and of their characteristics, in particular the ELP and its underlying philosophy.
3. Study of the characteristics of aboriginal educational visions and of the compatibility (or lack thereof) of the PLP (later of LITE) with indigenous pedagogies.

In relation to these three main domains of investigations, a series of practical/operational decisions has been made, in particular concerning the format and the structure of the tool, and the languages to be used for the first phase of the project.

The second phase of the project, in progress, has expanded the conceptualisation of the tool, moving from the PLP to LITE, pursues the developmental research and seeks to create a finalised draft of LITE. The first part of this draft, consisting of the master template beta version, is expected to be ready for trialling by mid-2016.

A third phase is foreseen, starting at the end of the project, once both the master template and the portfolio content have been finalised, aiming at validating the tool and at studying its assets and limitations in the educational practice.

First phase: Conceptualisation

Linguistic diversity and the institutional reaction

The first phase started with a documentary research aiming at providing a thorough overview of the linguistic situation of both Canada and the US. The data published by the official statistics bodies (Statistics Canada and US Census Bureau) and their evolution since 2000 were studied. The results showed a very dynamic linguistic and cultural panorama, with a growing number of languages and of people speaking a language other than the official one(s) at home, due mainly to the high immigration rate. It also showed a geographically vast and numerically important presence of aboriginal languages, albeit without a growing trend.

Subsequently, a thorough analysis of the institutional documents in the domain of language education in Canada has been conducted both at the national and at the provincial level with the goal of checking if such growing linguistic and cultural diversity had been integrated in the educational practice. As I mentioned earlier in the article, we discovered a clear discrepancy between discourse and practice when it comes to integration of language diversity and plurilingualism. In fact, while many overarching policy and curriculum documents advocate for teachers to encourage and support multiple language use in their classrooms, there is an absence of official documents that actually provide practitioners with the tools and support that they need to do so. For instance, although the subject curriculum documents published by the Ontario Ministry of Education do include information regarding multiple language use and first language maintenance, these are always relegated to the margins of these documents. Additionally, there are no activities outlined within the core content of the curriculum documents for implementing a plurilingual approach, nor grading schemata that would allow teachers the opportunity to value or grade the additional language resources that their students possess. Ontario curricula in general do not include an explicit focus on the multiple languages that are likely to be represented in a diverse classroom, a practice that would probably increase cross-cultural understanding of the students in a much broader and more representational way than a linguistic focus that is limited to Canada's two official languages. All this renders implementation of multiple language use in the classroom implicitly *optional, ad hoc,* or *idiosyncratic.* And this scenario, which applies to Ontario, the most populated Canadian province, is replicated with little variation in other provinces.

This documentary research confirmed how critical it is to move from theory to practice, and to develop a tool able to facilitate the adoption of a plurilingual approach in the classroom.

Study of existing documents and supporting experimentation

Once we had a clear view of the *status quo*, we turned to existing experiences and tools for inspiration. It was natural then to look at the Council of Europe experience and documents in the domain of language education, in particular the Common European Framework of Reference for Languages (CEFR) (Council of Europe 2001), the Autobiography of Cultural Encounters (Council of Europe nd) and, above all, the ELP.

While we recognise the vast political, economic, and linguistic differences between the European context and the North American one, we ultimately believe that the latter can greatly benefit from the fundamental aims of the ELP. The ELP is a document that allows learners to engage in self-assessment of their language competencies (in multiple languages) based on the CEFR. Essentially, the ELP aims at fostering the Council of Europe's commitment to education for democratic citizenship and lifelong learning by promoting plurilingualism, respect for cultural and linguistic diversity, increased learner autonomy and life-long learning (Little 2009, 2011). In the European context, the ELP has been utilised in many different language-learning contexts with excellent results (Schärer 2007, Stoicheva, Hughes and Speitz 2009). Furthermore, conceiving of a tool that shows some coherence with these European documents will support the vision articulated in the 2010 document published by the CMEC (2010), which advocates for the official adoption of the CEFR in Canada to improve language education and value cultural diversity.

In this phase, we proceeded with a second documentary research on the existing ELP models and literature on the ELP use and impact, and listed all the features and underpinning principles we considered relevant to our own prospective tool. On top of learner autonomy that we already mentioned above, reflective skills, learner responsibility and CEFR-based self-assessment of language competences were the main aspects underlined by different studies on the impact of the ELP (Bompolou 2012, Egel 2009, Kühn and Cavana 2012, Stoicheva et al 2009, Yilmaz and Akcan 2012). Furthermore, the analysis of the ELP models showed that the reflective dimension of the documents, particularly the metalinguistic/metacultural and the metacognitive ones took more and more space and played an ever-growing role with the time, from the first models to the most recent ones.

To get a more complete picture, we also researched existing North American portfolios and their use. There have been some North American adaptations of the ELP model, such as LinguaFolio® developed by the US National Council of States Supervisors of Foreign Languages (Cummins 2007b, National Council of State Supervisors for Languages 2011) and LinguaFolio Online developed by the University of Oregon's Center for Applied Second Language Teaching and Learning (Center for Applied Second Language Teaching and Learning 2008). But language portfolios have not yet been widely implemented. In particular, no language portfolio exists that is rooted in the specific Canadian linguistic landscape, and that aims at overcoming the *monolingual disposition* of North American education and at valuing existing linguistic diversity. Generally, Canadian language portfolios, such as the Collaborative Language Portfolio Assessment (Manitoba Labour and Immigration 2009) and the Second Language Research Institute of Canada School-Based Language Portfolio (nd), have limited themselves to focusing on linguistic competences (providing learners with the self-assessment checklists that are based upon the CEFR levels scales) rather than explicitly fostering cultural and linguistic diversity and a plurilingual dimension.

While the pedagogical function of self-assessment is important to promote learner autonomy and motivation (Little 2009), other aspects of the ELP, particularly those aiming at developing metacognition in all forms as well as intercultural awareness, were more relevant for the scope of our project and potentially able to help students develop life-long learning skills and to embrace a plurilingual vision.

This documentary research was complemented by a related local research and development project conducted by the US partner within their 4-week language immersion programme for students from 8th through 12th grade in the US, offered in Arabic, Chinese, French, German and Spanish.

A Student Learning Portfolio was developed to capture student learning and transformation across a broad spectrum of outcomes in the areas of language proficiency, cultural knowledge, intercultural communication and competency, and 21st century learning strategies. The design of the portfolio drew upon different documents developed both in Europe and in the US[2]. The portfolio was tested during the summer of 2013 with 800 students learning all the languages offered. Even though this Portfolio was different from LITE, the positive experimentation of such a tool provided extra solid ground for the development of LITE and reinforced the idea of the feasibility of (and value in) drawing inspiration from the European documents and projects to produce a specific tool tailored to the needs and reality of the North American context.

A new ideological and pedagogical perspective: The aboriginal point of view

The main new feature of LITE and a crucial one for introducing real change in the North American context is its role of bridge linking western and indigenous epistemologies in education.

In order to seek secure ground in this domain of knowledge and research, we conducted first an extensive documentary research and literature review, with the aim of seeking compatibility between the LINCDIRE project, and its resulting tool LITE, and the ongoing discussion about aboriginal revitalisation in the educational culture in Canada. We then integrated this with an exploratory study after receiving ethics clearance from the University of Toronto ethics board. The study consisted of a series of interviews of aboriginal educators. Two of the aboriginal educators interviewed were working in a reservation school and one was working at the university level and teaching an internationally acclaimed open online course on Aboriginal Worldviews and Education.

The findings from these interviews were highly encouraging as they stressed the importance of the language to the revitalisation of indigenous cultures: 'almost **every education movement** in indigenous communities **is about language**' (author's emphasis) . . . 'just to talk about how language and worldview are so intimately connected . . . So, it's very valuable . . . the value of different languages giving you different insights into the way things are related or the way things work'. Certainly different voices also exist, but the awareness of the importance of the language comes out clearly when one participant reported some of these different discourses in their community and commented: '. . . *like "oh, that's the past, we gotta get on with what's new and our current reality", and* **I think they're missing out on, on a big part of what makes them unique, is the language**' (author's emphasis).

One of the interviewees stressed how teaching aboriginal languages requires a different approach, where context and community play a crucial role: 'The classroom is such a strange space to be learning these languages that evolved in certain activities and relationships with land, and with community . . . some say the language is from the land . . .' and also 'Unless . . . they're being taught in a way that's engaging to them too, it's not going to be passed on'.

Aboriginal languages occur intergenerationally and within the family unit. Learner autonomy, intrinsic motivation, and connecting young learners with family and community are emphasised as essential components to the successful study of any of these languages. One important point stressed was how the community members need to be seen as *allies* rather than someone who put extra stress on the youth, generating feelings like 'if I don't pick this up, I'll be the last person who ever spoke this language in my family, or something like that'. This same point was reinforced by approaching it from a different angle: 'if those ones who have facility and fluency aren't helping them [the younger generation], instead they're teasing them, making fun of them, in way that feels . . . I mean, there's for teasing, but my understanding that this is like this real putting down that happens. That makes it, makes you just not want to try at all'. The exchange ended with a concluding remark, which showed both awareness of the issue and hope: 'I think that's something that's important for the communities to, for speakers to understand too that this is hard for those learners, and they need your help'.

Those core values expressed in the interviews, among others, thoroughly align with the LITE's aims to increase autonomy and foster linguistic and cultural pride by providing a forum to reflect on life experiences and develop intergenerational connections. By allowing learners to showcase their linguistic competency and personal experiences, LITE could also assist in revealing untapped resources of speakers of aboriginal languages seeking teacher accreditation. By offering a holistic alternative to standards-based assessment and by providing space for plurilingualism, LITE could contribute to overturning the vision of languages as discrete entities and foster openness and translanguaging. Also, the technological focus of LITE could assist in linking learners of common languages living in geographically disparate locations, thus overcoming the limitation represented by the many individuals who, when seeking to connect with their indigenous identity through language, often end up by studying one offered locally. This removal of geographical barriers could indeed contribute to language reclamation efforts.

To sum up, the conceptualisation of LITE has followed three parallel threads: 1) analysis of the present situation concerning language diversity and of the institutional response; 2) analysis of existing tools and resources developed in a different geographical context following a partially related philosophy together with a related experimentation testing transferability and adequacy to the North American context; and 3) study of the guiding principles of the indigenous pedagogies and epistemologies related to education supported by empirical data collection.

All these threads have confirmed the need for a tool able to act as a catalyser for valuing linguistic and cultural diversity and as a bridge towards integration of western and indigenous visions. It has also confirmed the need for a tool able to raise the status of heritage and aboriginal languages by integrating formal and informal/non-formal learning (Piccardo and Ortiz 2013)[3].

Developing LITE: A work in progress

Rationale for methodological and linguistic choices

The type of work carried out during the first phase of the project responds to the criteria of developmental research. This methodology is also guiding the second phase of the project, which is in progress.

Developmental research 'is a way to establish new procedures, techniques and tools based upon a methodical analysis of specific cases. As such, developmental research can have a function of either creating generalisable conclusions or statements of law, or producing context-specific knowledge that serves a problem solving function' (Richey and Klein 2005:24).

The methodology chosen for the LINCDIRE project aiming at developing LITE can best be described by what Richey and Klein term 'Type 1 developmental research [which has a] focus upon a given instrumental product, program, process, or tool [and often addresses] not only product design and development, but evaluation as well' (2005:24–25).

van den Akker characterises developmental research as a 'balance between development and research' (1999:6). Fundamental to our project is such a balanced process by which we are developing a portfolio based on a blend of extensive theoretical research (on portfolio use, plurilingualism and the cultural and linguistic needs of Canadian and US students, as well as indigenous pedagogies and epistemologies), and of local, on-site practical research with students and educators. Furthermore, our decision to engage in developmental research to create, pilot and evaluate LITE responds to van den Akker's call for 'more evolutionary (interactive, cyclic, spiral) approaches' (1999:2) in the development of complex educational reform policies.

An important element of developmental research is its potential to 'meet . . . the pressing needs of practitioners' and to address a problem that 'is currently critical to the profession' (Richey and Klein 2005:25). The increasing linguistic and cultural diversity of the classes represents a challenge for teachers who are demanding support and tools. This paired with a growing interest in aboriginal languages and cultures calls for a context-specific research, a blend of research and practice, leading to practical results (looked at through various theoretical lenses), which will allow broader implications to be made. 'Developmental studies are often structured in phases. For example . . . a Type 1 study would include phases directed toward first analysis, then prototype development and testing, and finally prototype revision and retesting' (Richey and Klein 2005:26). LITE follows precisely this type of organisation.

Our second phase started in late 2014 with the development of the prototype. Initially, under the inspiration of the ELP and other European documents, we had envisaged the creation of one single document, which would have then been made available in different languages and both online and on paper. This initial idea of the team has been submitted to selected practitioners for feedback and then discussed again in the team. The second version of the prototype was then designed. This version, which is presently being technically developed, consists of:

- a master template relying on iconic representation with virtually no use of words
- a range of categories conceived for facilitating the creation of personalised and multimodal portfolio content in different languages.

Both the master template and the portfolio content will be made available (along with related resources) on a website designed for students and educators.

In the pilot version of LITE, in addition to English and French, the two official languages, two heritage languages, German and Italian, and one aboriginal language, Ojibwe (from the Anishinaabe language family) will be included.

The rationale for choosing Italian and German is twofold: 1) they are heritage languages with a significant population of immigrants in Canada (the country's fourth and fifth largest language group respectively according to the 2011 Census (Statistics Canada 2012) and well present among the heritage languages of the US); 2) there is an interest in studying these two languages for reasons linked to family origin and/or interest in arts, music and culture. For German there is also an increase in study and research exchanges as well as internships in Germany (Deutscher Akademischer Austauschdienst 2012). Besides, we have had a strong interest in the project coming from German and Italian instructors.

Ojibwe was chosen for two reasons: 1) it is one of Canada's aboriginal languages that has a sufficiently large population of fluent speakers to be secure from long-term extinction (Crystal 2000, Fettes 1998, Norris 1998, Sarkar and Metallic 2009), making it a priority choice for language maintenance or revitalisation (Royal Commission on Aboriginal Peoples 1996); besides, it is the sole language with provincial funding for cultural centres strategising language maintenance and pedagogy (Hill 2004); 2) the base of Ojibwe speakers is geographically well situated for our research, distributed across central Canada, and well into the US and an explicit focus on Ojibwe exists within the University of Toronto community, including language classes, ceremonies, linguistic and documentary research, workshops, and community events.

The main evolution between the initial concept and the present design was linked to the need for consistency between the rationale of LITE and its actual shape and configuration. The feedback given suggested it was important not to privilege any particular language but to rely upon visual/iconic representation of concepts as much as possible, something that is also very consistent with indigenous epistemologies. The idea of a *language-neutral* master template able to flexibly accommodate language-specific portfolio content also underlines the needs for securing space for culture-specific sections. It also helped us understand that users need to be granted the freedom to mix languages if we really want to be coherent with the plurilingualism framework adopted. The rationale for going completely paperless includes free access, ease in overcoming geographical barriers, increased possibility of customising and of filing and eventually to create a record. Finally, after common refection following the feedback, we decided to focus on late teens and young adults at first in order to span from secondary to post-secondary education and to include community centres. Furthermore, a focus on younger learners would need an extra phase of linguistic adaptation of the portfolio content, so this can be a longer-term project.

In general, gathering feedback from potential users will play a crucial role in the conceptualisation of LITE which has been, and will continue to be, informed by teacher and student input and therefore strongly shaped by their articulated needs. Rather than a top-down prescriptive, pedagogical approach, the design of LITE will be highly dependent on the research site and the opinions and experiences of site-based participants (teachers, students and elders). Research participants' involvement in shaping the portfolio will also provide opportunities for their own professional development. As Richey and Klein (2005) argue, the developmental approach allows for research that is intertwined with 'real world practice', creating a 'loop with practice informing research and research, in turn, informing practice' (Richey and Klein 2005:35).

Conclusion: Where we are now, next development and potential impact of LITE

As we said at the beginning, LITE is a work in progress and the first phase of the research confirmed that there is space and need for such a tool so that students can: 1) acquire a new attitude towards language and cultural diversity; 2) be more motivated to learn languages; and 3) become more reflexive and autonomous in their language learning processes. Specifically, LITE can target several areas by helping learners:

- record their experience learning languages and show what they can do in different languages (metacognition)
- think about how they learn languages best and strategies used (cognitive strategies)
- organise language learning as a way to show how much they have already learned (language learning assessment)
- set future goals to help them learn more about the languages they are studying and other languages (linguistic goals)
- record stories and traditions about their culture and share them with friends, family, and the school community (cultural awareness)
- record intercultural experiences they have had with other people so they can learn more about other cultures (intercultural awareness).

At a broader level, LITE has the potential to:

- support the maintenance and appreciation of a plurality of languages and cultures at both individual and social levels
- allow students to develop awareness of their language learning process
- provide recognition for all of their linguistic and cultural resources from their first language(s) to languages with which they have had contact
- promote an explicit focus on language diversity and provide a place for students to record and monitor their abilities in any language
- foster autonomy in language learning through a synchronous and asynchronous collaborative online tool
- foster creativity through artwork developed by learners using several types of media (audio, video, drawings, photographs, storytelling, among others).

LITE will facilitate a process of increased language awareness, as students will be provided with a medium to engage with and reflect upon home or community languages that may not be included in the ordinary school curriculum. In the long term, educators will be provided with portfolio content in multiple languages together with resources and guidance to help students create and upload a personalised version of LITE that best suits their linguistic and cultural needs. Thus, students who do not speak the dominant languages of the school will have access to a resource in their first (or one of their first) languages. This process will likely begin to increase attention to minoritised languages in the community, and to foster interaction with speakers of non-dominant languages. The process of recording and reflecting upon contacts with languages and cultures, even very brief ones, that LITE enables and supports, will help students realise that their linguistic experiences are important sources of linguistic, cultural and self-knowledge. Over time, this will foster students' interest in learning languages that they had previously dismissed or been unaware of and engage them in self-directed language learning.

Through a tool that emphasises reflection on the learning process – of any language – and of intercultural encounters rather than solely on learning outcomes in one – or more – specific language, we intend to enhance awareness of individual learning preferences, practices and strategies, as well as to identify factors that foster or that hinder students' learning and motivation.

For universities to better educate future plurilingual global citizens ready for the professional world, LITE supports broader pedagogical and practical objectives: 1) it assists students to gain a better understanding of their learning progress, and skill development; 2) it cultivates the recognition of transferable skills trained in language learning, such as creativity, flexibility, adaptability and problem-solving; and 3) it develops the meta-communicative tools to utilise and describe their competences to prospective employers. The positive approach of LITE can facilitate intrinsic motivation, a crucial factor in student success, countering possible reluctance in learning languages, particularly when mandated.

Finally the increased language awareness and desire to further one's own linguistic and cultural competencies can support current aboriginal language revitalisation efforts. In fact, despite the lack of official language policy for aboriginal languages in Canada (the US passed the US Native American Languages Act in 1990 and 1992) (De Korne 2010:116), speakers of aboriginal languages in Canada are increasingly demanding status from communities and governing bodies (Corbiere 2000, Pheasant-Williams 2003, Royal Commission on Aboriginal Peoples 1996). Aboriginal communities in Canada are deeply committed to revitalising their ancestral languages, and we seek to act as allies to these communities by engaging collaboratively, developing a tool that can support these language revitalisation processes.

As 'indigenous languages . . . structure indigenous knowledge' (Battiste 2002:17), creating legitimate space for minoritised languages in the classroom will result in balancing hegemonic *Euro-American* pedagogies that characterise North American educational institutions with indigenous epistemologies and in supporting non-dominant knowledge as well.

Introducing LITE in the Canadian context has the potential to shift entrenched language hierarchies that privilege the country's two official languages and to empower linguistic minorities by changing attitudes towards all languages and cultures, even those marginalised or neglected. A tool can facilitate a plurilingual paradigm shift (Kramsch et al 2008) by recognising the diverse linguistic and cultural competencies that are possessed by all individuals, and acknowledging the interconnectedness of language, culture, lived experiences and identity negotiation.

Notes

1. Principles and Guidelines for the Protection of the Heritage of Indigenous Peoples Elaborated by the Special Rapporteur, Mrs. Erica-Irene Daes, in conformity with resolution 1993/44 and decision 1994/105 of the Sub-Commission on Prevention of Discrimination and Protection of Minorities of the Commission on Human Rights, Economic and Social Council, United Nations (E/CN.4/Sub.2/1995/26, GE. 95-12808 (E), 21 June 1995).
2. In particular different models of the ELP (www.coe.int/t/dg4/education/elp/, the ACTFL/NCSSFL) LinguaFolio Project (www.ncssfl.org/LinguaFolio/index.php?linguafolio_index), and the Framework of Reference for Pluralistic Approaches to languages and cultures (FREPA-CARAP) (2012) (carap.ecml.at/).
3. *Formal learning* is something happening in an organised and structured context, for instance in an educational institution or training/working place), is specifically identified as learning (in terms of objectives, time and resources), it is intentionally done by the learner, and finally it results in validation and certification. *Informal learning* is a consequence of everyday life activities linked to work, family or leisure. It is neither organised nor structured and is done non-intentionally by the learner. Finally, *non-formal learning* is integrated in planned activities that are not explicitly identified as learning activities but imply some form of learning. Non-formal learning is done intentionally by the learner (CEDEFOP 2009).

References

Alberta Education (2010) *Making a Difference: Meeting Diverse Learning Needs with Differentiated Instruction* available online: education.alberta.ca/teachers/resources/cross/making-a-difference.aspx

Aluli-Meyer, M (2001) Acultural assumptions of empiricism: A native Hawaiian critique, *Canadian Journal of Native Education* 25 (2), 188–198.

Anderson, G (2010) Perspectives on the global language extinction crisis: The Oklahoma and eastern Siberia language hotspots, *Revue Roumaine de Linguistique* LV(2), 128–142.

Anderson, G (2011) Language hotspots: What (applied) linguistics and education should do about language endangerment in the twenty-first century, *Language and Education* 25 (4), 273–289.

Battiste, M (2002) *Indigenous Knowledge and Pedagogy in First Nations Education: A Literature Review with Recommendations*, paper prepared for the National Working Group on Education and the Minister of Indian Affairs, available online: www.afn.ca/uploads/files/education/24._2002_oct_marie_battiste_indigenousknowledgeandpedagogy_lit_review_for_min_working_group.pdf

Battiste, M and Youngblood Henderson, J (2000) *Protecting Indigenous Knowledge and Heritage: A Global Challenge*, Saskatoon: Purich.

Benesch, S (1993) Critical thinking: A learning process for democracy, *TESOL Quarterly* 27 (3), 545–548.

Bialystok, E (2001) *Bilingualism in Development: Language, Literacy, and Cognition*, Cambridge: Cambridge University Press.

Bompolou, E (2012) Prospects of using the European language Portfolio as pedagogical and assessment tool in Greek schools, *Research Papers in Language Teaching and Learning* 3 (1), 189–199.

British Columbia Ministry of Education (2009) *English as a Second Language and Francisation: Langue seconde in the Conseil scolaire: Policy and Guidelines*, available online: www.bced.gov.bc.ca/esl/policy/guidelines.pdf

Cantoni, G (1997) Keeping minority languages alive: The school's responsibility, in Reyhner, J (Ed) *Teaching Indigenous Languages*, Arizona: Northern Arizona University Press, 1–9.

Carlino, F (2009) The history and current status of the instruction of Spanish as a heritage language in Canada, *International Journal of Canadian Studies* 38, 263–277.

Center for Applied Second Language Teaching and Learning (2008) *LinguaFolio Online*, available online: linguafolio.uoregon.edu/

Connelly, C (2008) Marking bodies: Inhabiting the discursive production of outstanding 'Canadian education' within globalization, in Gérin-Lajoie, D (Ed) *Educators' Discourses on Student Diversity in Canada: Context, Policy and Practice*, Toronto: Canadian Scholar's Press Inc, 163–182.

Cook, V (2001) Using the first language in the classroom, *Canadian Modern Language Review/La Revue canadienne des langues vivantes* 57 (3), 402–423.

Corbiere, A (2000) Reconciling epistemological orientations: Toward a wholistic nish[n]aabe (Ojibwe/Odawa/Potowatomi) education, *Canadian Journal of Native Education* 24 (2), 113–119.

Coste, D, Moore, D and Zarate, G (1997) *Competence Plurilingue et Pluriculturelle*, Strasbourg: Council of Europe.

Coste, D, Moore, D and Zarate, G (2009) *Plurilingual and Pluricultural Competence: Studies Towards a Common European Framework of Reference for Language Learning and Teaching*, Strasbourg: Council of Europe, available online: www.coe.int/lang

Council of Europe (nd) Autobiography of Intercultural Encounters, www.coe.int/t/dg4/autobiography/default_en.asp

Council of Europe (2001) *Common European Framework of Reference for Languages*, Cambridge: Cambridge University Press.

Council of Ministers of Education Canada (2010) *Working with the Common European Framework of Reference for Languages (CEFR) in the Canadian Context: Guide for Policy Makers and Curriculum Designers*, available online: www.cmec.ca/docs/assessment/CEFR-canadian-context.pdf

Crawford, J (2000) *At War With Diversity: US Language Policy in an Age of Anxiety*, Clevedon: Multilingual Matters.

Crystal, D (2000) *Language Death*, Cambridge: Cambridge University Press.

Cummins, J (2001) *Negotiating identities: Education for empowerment in a diverse society*, Los Angeles: California Association for Bilingual Education, 2nd Edition.

Cummins, J (2007a) Rethinking monolingual instructional strategies in multilingual classrooms, *Canadian Journal of Applied Linguistics (CJAL)/Revue canadienne de linguistique appliquée (RCLA)* 10 (2), 221–240.

Cummins, P (2007b) LinguaFolio: American model for the European Language Portfolio, *Modern Language Journal* 91, 117–121.

Cummins, J, Bismilla, V, Chow, P, Cohen, S, Giampapa, F, Leoni, L, Sandhu, P and Sastri, P (2005) Affirming identity in multilingual classrooms, *Educational Leadership* 63 (1), 38–43.

De Korne, H (2010) Indigenous language education policy: supporting community-controlled immersion in Canada and the US, *Language Policy* 9 (2), 115–141.

Deloria, V (1999) *Spirit and Reason*, Golden: Fulcrum Publishing.

Deutscher Akademischer Austauschdienst (2012) *Jahresbericht*, available online: www.daad.de/imperia/md/content/presse/daad_jahresbericht-12-de_130528.pdf

Egel, I P (2009) The yesterday and today of the European Language Portfolio in Turkey, *GEMA Online Journal of Language Studies* 9 (1), 1–16.

Ermine, W (1995) Aboriginal epistemology, in Battiste, M and Barman, J (Eds) *First Nations Education in Canada: The Circle Unfolds*, Vancouver: UBC Press, 101–112.

Evans, N (2010) *Dying Words: Endangered Languages and What They Have to Tell Us*, Oxford: Wiley-Blackwell.

Fettes, M (1998) Life on the edge: Canada's aboriginal languages under official bilingualism, in Ricento, T and Burnaby B (Eds) *Language and Politics in the United States and Canada: Myths and Realities*, Mahwah: Erlbaum and Associates, 117–147.

Fishman, J (1996) What do you lose when you lose your language? in Cantoni, G (Ed) *Stabilizing Indigenous Languages*, Flagstaff: Northern Arizona University Press, 186–196.

Flecha, R (1999) New educational inequalities, in Castells, M, Hecha, R, Freire, P, Giroux, H A, Macedo, D and Willis P (Eds) *Critical Education in the New Information Age*, Lanham: Rowman and Littlefield, 65–82.

Friesen, J W and Friesen, V L (2002) *Aboriginal Education in Canada: A plea for integration*, Calgary: Detselig Entrerprises Ltd.

García, O, Skutnabb-Kangas, T and Torres-Guzmán, M (Eds) (2006) *Imagining Multilingual Schools: Languages in Education and Glocalization*, Clevedon: Multilingual Matters.

Gérin-Lajoie, D (2011) Multicultural education: Nothing more than folklore? *Canadian Issues*, 24–27.

Glaser, E (1941) *An Experiment in the Development of Critical Thinking*, New York: Teacher's College, Columbia University.

Gogolin, I (1994) *Der monolinguale Habitus der multilingualen Schule*, Münster: Waxmann.

Haque, E (2012) *Multiculturalism Within a Bilingual Framework: Language, Race, and Belonging in Canada*, Toronto: University of Toronto Press.

Harrison, D (2007) *When Languages Die: The Extinction of the World's Languages and the Erosion of Human Knowledge*, Oxford: Oxford University Press.

Harrison, D (2010) *The Last Speakers: The Quest to Save the World's Most Endangered Languages*, Washington, DC: National Geographic.

Henze, R and Davis, K A (2008) Authenticity and identity: Lessons from indigenous language education, *Anthropology and Education Quarterly* 30 (1), 3–21.

Hill, K (2004) First nations languages and education in Ontario, *All Ontario Chiefs*, available online: www.chiefs-of-ontario.org

Hornberger, N (2002) Multilingual language policies and the continua of biliteracy: An ecological approach, *Language Policy* 1, 27–51.

Kramsch, C Levy, D and Zarate, G (2008) Introduction générale, in Zarate, G, Levy, D and Kramsch C (Eds) *Précis du plurilinguisme et du pluriculturalisme*, Paris: Édition des archives contemporaines, 15–23.

Kühn, B and Cavana, M L P (2012) *Perspectives from the European Language Portfolio: Learner Autonomy and Self-assessment*, New York: Routledge.

Lane, P, Bopp, J and Bopp, M (1984) *The Sacred Tree*, Lethbridge: Four Worlds Development Press.

Le Centre européen pour le développement de la formation professionnelle (2009) *Lignes directrices européennes pour la validation des acquis non formels et informels*, Luxembourg: Office des publications de l'Union européenne, 81–82, available online: www.cedefop.europa.eu/EN/Files/4054_fr.pdf

Leik, V (1992) *Bringing Indigenous Perspectives into Education: A Case Study of 'Thunderbird/Whale Protection and Welcoming Pole: Learning and Teaching in an Indigenous World'*, unpublished MA Thesis, University of Victoria, available online: dspace.library.uvic.ca/bitstream/handle/1828/1584/VivianLeikFinalThesispdf..pdf?sequence=1&isAllowed=y

Little, D (2009) Language learner autonomy and the European language portfolio: Two L2 English examples, *Language Teaching* 42 (2), 222–233.

Little, D (2011) The Common European Framework of Reference for Languages: A research agenda, *Language Teaching*, 44 (3), 381–393.

Little Bear, L (2009) *Naturalizing Indigenous Knowledge, Synthesis Paper*, University of Saskatchewan, Aboriginal Education Research Centre, Saskatoon, Sask. and First Nations and Adult Higher Education Consortium, Calgary, Alta, available online: www.afn.ca/uploads/files/education/21._2009_july_ccl-alkc_leroy_littlebear_naturalizing_indigenous_knowledge-report.pdf

Lo Bianco, J (2010) The importance of language policies and multilingualism for cultural diversity, *International Social Science Journal* 61 (199), 37–67.

MacMillan, C M (1998) *The Practice of Language Rights in Canada*, Toronto: University of Toronto Press.

Makoni, S and Pennycook, A (2005) Disinventing and (Re)constituting languages, *Critical Inquiry in Language Studies: An International Journal* 2 (3), 137–156.

Makoni, S and Pennycook, A (2007) *Disinventing and reconstituting languages*. Clevedon: Multilingual Matters.

Manitoba Labour and Immigration (2009) *Collaborative Language Portfolio Assessment Manitoba Best Practices Guide: A Resource for Integrating the CLPA into the Teaching-learning Cycle of Adult EAL Instruction*, available online: www.winklerchamber.com/pdf/eaw/foundations_mb09.pdf

National Council of State Supervisors for Languages (2011) *LinguaFolio*, available online: www.ncssfl.org

Nieto, S (2004) *Affirming Diversity. The Sociopolitical Context of Multicultural Education*, New York: Allyn and Bacon.

Norris, M J (1998) Canada's Aboriginal languages: Canadian social trends, *Statistics Canada* 11, 8–16.

Norris, M J (2007) Aboriginal languages in Canada: Emerging trends and perspectives on second language acquisition, *Canadian Social Trends* 83, 19–27.

Norris, M J (2011) Aboriginal languages in urban Canada: A decade in review, 1996 to 2006, *Aboriginal Policy Studies* 1 (2), 4–67, available online: ejournals.library.ualberta.ca/index.php/aps/article/view/8965

Ontario Ministry of Education (2005) *Many Roots, Many Voices: Supporting English Language Learners in Every Classroom*, available online: www.edu.gov.on.ca/eng/document/manyroots/manyroots.pdf

Ontario Ministry of Education (2006) *The Ontario Curriculum, The Kindergarten Program*, available online: www.edu.gov.on.ca/eng/curriculum/elementary/kindercurrb.pdf

Pheasant-Williams, S (2003) The development of Ojibway language materials, *Canadian Journal of Native Education* 27 (1), 79–83.

Piccardo, E (2013) Plurilingualism and curriculum design: Towards a synergic vision, *TESOL Quarterly* 47 (3), 600–614.

Piccardo, E (2014) The impact of the CEFR on Canada's linguistic plurality: a space for heritage languages? in Trifonas, P and Aravossitas, T (Eds) *Rethinking Heritage Language Education*, Cambridge: Cambridge University Press, 183–212.

Piccardo, E and Ortiz, I (2013) Le plurilinguisme dans les entreprises: un atout cache. Le projet LINCQ du Centre européen pour les langues vivantes, *Repères DoRif* 3, available online: www.dorif.it/ezine/ezine_articles.php?id=105

Puozzo Capron, I (2009) Le sentiment d'efficacité personnelle. Pour un nouvel enseignement/apprentissage des langues, *Revue Sciences Croisées* 6, 1–29, available online: sciences-croisees.com/N6/PuozzoCapron.pdf

Richey, R and Klein, J (2005) Developmental research methods: Creating knowledge from instructional design and development practice, *Journal of Computing in Higher Education* 16 (2), 23–38.

Richey, R C (1997) Research on instructional development, *Educational Technology Research and Development*, 45 (3), 91–100.

Ross, R (2006) *Returning to the Teachings: Exploring Aboriginal Justice*, Toronto: Penguin Canada.

Royal Commission on Aboriginal Peoples (1996) *Report of the Royal Commission on Aboriginal Peoples*, Ottawa: Libraxus.

Sarkar, M and Metallic, M A (2009) Indigenizing the structural syllabus: The challenge of revitalizing Mi'gmaq in Listuguj, *The Canadian Modern Language Review* 66 (1), 49–71.

Schärer, R (2007) *European Language Portfolio. From Piloting to Implementation 2001–2007. Interim report November 2007*, Strasbourg: Council of Europe.

Second Language Research Institute of Canada (nd) *School-Based Language Portfolio*, available online: www.unb.ca/fredericton/second-language/research-publications/current-projects/schoolbasedlanguageportfolio.html

Statistics Canada (2012) *Linguistic Characteristics of Canadians*, available online: www12.statcan.gc.ca/census-recensement/2011/as-sa/98-314-x/98-314-x2011001-eng.cfm

Stoicheva, M, Hughes, G and Speitz, H (2009) *The European Language Portfolio: An Impact Study*, Strasbourg: Council of Europe.

Taylor, L K, Bernhard, J K, Garg, S and Cummins, J (2008) Affirming plural belonging: Building on students' family-based cultural and linguistic capital through multiliteracies pedagogy, *Journal of Early Childhood Literacy* 8 (3), 269–294.

van den Akker, J (1999) Principles and methods of development research, in van den Akker, J, Branch, R M, Gustafson, K, Nieveen N, and Plomp T (Eds) *Design Approaches and Tools in Education and Training*, Dordrecth: Kluwer Academic, 1–14.

Wandruszka, M (1979) *Die Mehrsprachigkeit des Menschen*, Stuttgart: Kohlhammer.

Wiley, T G and Lukes, M (1996) English-only and standard English ideologies in the US, *TESOL Quarterly* 30 (3), 511–535.

Yilmaz, S and Akcan, S (2012) Implementing the European Language Portfolio in a Turkish context, *ELT Journal* 66 (2), 166–174.

Yunkaporta, T (2009) *Aboriginal pedagogies at the cultural interface*, unpublished PhD thesis, James Cook University, available online: researchonline.jcu.edu.au/10974/

9 Impacts of international language assessments on multilingualism: Evidence from an iterative impact study of Progetto Lingue 2000

Roger Hawkey
Consultant, Cambridge English Language Assessment
Sarah Ellis
Cambridge English Language Assessment, Southern Europe

Abstract

In its *Progetto Lingue 2000* (Ministero della Pubblica Istruzione 1999), the Italian Ministero dell'Istruzione, dell'Università e della Ricerca (MIUR) introduced innovation in key aspects of language teaching and assessment in schools. In the interest of multilingualism, the changes included certification in four foreign languages: English, French, German and Spanish, through a funding agreement with foreign exam boards, including Cambridge English Language Assessment. Cambridge English is carrying out an iterative impact study of the *Progetto Lingue 2000 (PL2000)* project to analyse its effects on key stakeholders, and to identify potential areas of support from exam providers. The first phase of this impact study of the *PL2000* project is described in Hawkey (2006). This chapter describes the latest period of the iterative Cambridge English impact study of the *PL2000*, from 2012 to 2014.

The chapter begins with an analysis of the nature of 'impact', especially in its language assessment validation context. The research design of the study is then established, in pursuit of answers to research questions on the impacts of the *PL2000* on: language; on student and teacher performance; on heads of schools, and on teacher support.

The impact study data from video- or audio-recorded interviews of school heads, teachers, (ex-) students, parents and officials, and from videoed classroom observation analyses in schools in northern, central and southern Italy are described. The impact categories emerging from the research include the changing sociolinguistic context in Italy. Most of the students concerned apparently use more English now, in its growing role as the language of international communication. The increasing momentum of the Content and Language Integrated Learning (CLIL) initiative is further evidence of MIUR encouragement of this trend.

Other areas of the *PL2000* impact include: communicative language teaching (CLT) approaches; computer-based approaches; teacher:student relations; teacher training and support; parental attitudes and influences, and Cambridge English assessment services.

Introduction

In its significant educational reform project, *Progetto Lingue 2000*, first published in 1999, the Italian Ministero dell'Istruzione, dell'Università e della Ricerca (MIUR), sought to introduce innovation in key aspects of language teaching and assessment for schools.

The main aims of the *Progetto Lingue 2000* (*PL2000*), covering foreign language teaching from nursery to high school, included:

- the establishment of small learning groups
- specific numbers of annual language learning hours in short learning modules
- the strengthened use of new technologies, and
- in significant support of multilingualism, certification in four foreign languages through a funding agreement between MIUR and foreign exam boards, including Association of Language Testers in Europe (ALTE) members: Alliance Française, Goethe-Institut, Instituto Cervantes, and Cambridge English Language Assessment (then 'University of Cambridge ESOL Examinations')
- access for schools to extra language tuition, training and materials.

With the agreement of MIUR, the Research and Validation Group of Cambridge English Language Assessment, supported by the Cambridge English Bologna Office, is carrying out a long-term impact study of the *PL2000* to record and analyse evidence of the effects of the implementation of the recommendations of the *PL2000* on learners, parents, teachers, school heads and other education officials.

Given the intended long-term nature of the effects of measures promoted by the *PL2000*, the impact study is iterative. Its key data collection activities were carried out between 2001 and 2002 (Hawkey 2006), and again, through the *PL2000 Impact Study Revisit* (PLISR), between 2012 and 2014 (Hawkey 2014). It was the intention of the impact study team and the Research and Validation Group of Cambridge English to trace how the language teaching and assessment measures implemented under the *PL2000* were faring over more than 10 years in changing language developmental and socio-economic times.

As would be expected, some of the research areas and findings of the *PL2000* impact studies discussed in this chapter are directly relevant to the April 2014 ALTE Paris Conference theme of 'Language assessment for multilingualism: Promoting linguistic diversity and intercultural communication'. The *PL2000* impact study also raises issues concerning some of the named ALTE Paris Conference strands, for example: assessing language for specific purposes, living with a *lingua franca*, fairness and quality standards in language test administration, and language assessment for migration and social integration. This chapter also presents impact study evidence related to 'the ways in which effective testing can encourage learning across the whole range of languages, and . . . how the huge body of research on the assessment of English language skills can be applied more widely' (Association of Language Testers in Europe 2014).

Multilingualism and linguistic diversity, in Europe and in Italy

At the Fifth Annual European Day of Languages meeting at the European Parliament in October 2012, for example, the theme 'Is English enough?' was addressed. ALTE's then European Projects Manager, Martin Nuttall, replied: 'When we asked this question we already knew that the answer would be: 'No, of course not'. What we're trying to do is encourage discussion of the importance of teaching languages and using a wide range of languages at a time when English is becoming more and more widely used' (Nuttall 2012).

The researchers and practitioners at the 2014 ALTE Paris Conference were invited explicitly 'to contribute to a major international conference on *how language testing can support the learning of a wide range of languages*' (Association of Language Testers in Europe 2014, italics added). The gathering of members of '33 organisations assessing 26 languages', as Martin Nuttall explained, had the following strongly multilingual purpose:

> This conference addresses a pressing issue for education systems in Europe and beyond. As demand for English and other major languages grows, there is a real danger that other national, regional and minority languages will be squeezed out of the picture. Our conference will be looking at the ways in which effective testing can encourage learning across the whole range of languages, and at how the huge body of research on the assessment of English language skills can be applied more widely (Association of Language Testers in Europe 2014).

Multilingualism includes *linguistic diversity*, taking account of issues such as the assessment of less widely-taught languages, language for specific purposes and sign language. Barni (2012:146) cites Italian as used 'as the main language by around 90% of the Italian population' and quotes the Italian National Institute of Statistics (ISTAT) figure of 6.4% of the population as 'now speaking only dialect inside and outside the home'.

A new factor in recent years is the growing number of foreign nationals resident in Italy. In January 2013 there were around 4,400,000 foreign nationals, 7.4% of the population, which means, of course, that a range of languages are being spoken in the home (Baldwin-Edwards and Zampagni 2014:3). This has also led to the introduction of tests of Italian (at A2 level) for immigrants following an agreement between the Ministries of the Interior and Education and the Centri Teritoriali Permanenti (CPTs), a network of continuing education centres (Bolli 2013:56). This is an example of a national language test in response to and accepting of, a multilingual situation.

The nature and context of impact

For Cambridge English, positive impact belongs with validity, reliability, practicality and quality management as a requirement of a high-stakes language assessment. The latest version of this set of target values is shown in Figure 1 here, taken from the Cambridge English *Principles of Good Practice* (Cambridge English 2013:10).

Figure 1 Cambridge English Language Assessment key test validation criteria

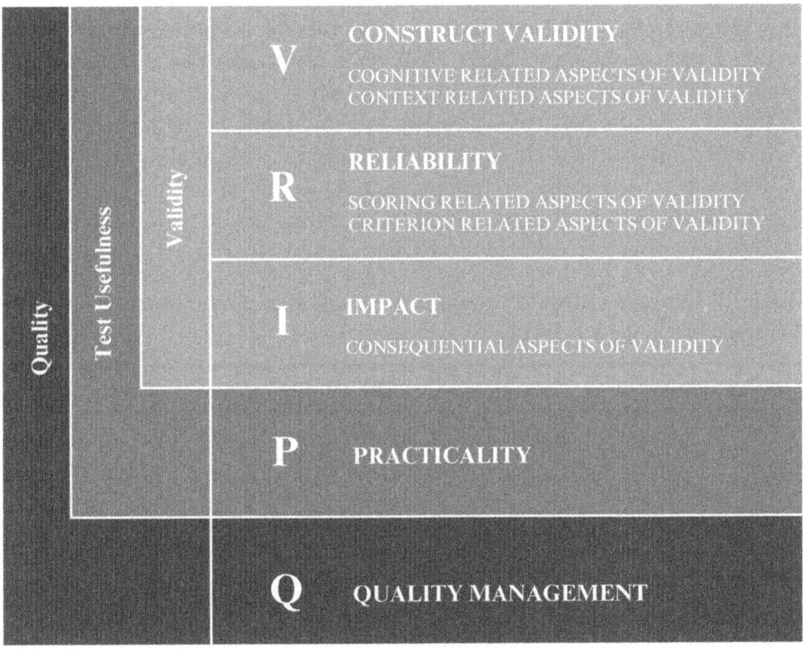

Saville (2012:5) refers relatedly to *impact by design*, by which he means that 'assessment systems should be designed *from the outset* with the potential to achieve positive impacts'.

When we search for impacts from a key educational reform programme such as the *PL2000*, we may identify some which the *PL2000* can actually be said to *cause*, for example students taking Cambridge English exams subsidised, as they were originally, by the MIUR. Or, the *PL2000* may have impacts *in a less direct way*, as in teachers' use of language teaching approaches to which they had been introduced on the *PL2000* in-service courses they have attended.

Mixed methods research design

The choice of methodology such as an impact study for educational research normally involves consideration of the advantages and feasibility of *quantitative* and *qualitative research* methods. Weiss (1998:335) helpfully defines two broad approaches to research, as follows:

- quantitative research *examines phenomena that can be expressed numerically and analysed statistically*
- qualitative research *examines phenomena primarily through words, and tends to focus on dynamics, meaning and context; qualitative research usually uses observation, interviewing and document reviews to collect data.*

But Weiss (1998:263) also reminds us that there is no necessary opposition between the two kinds of data: 'Many evaluators combine qualitative and quantitative methods in their studies . . . to corroborate information [the evaluator] obtains [it] from different sources, [and] triangulates the data. Triangulation is a cross-check through different modes of inquiry'.

Referring specifically to language test development and validation, Lazaraton (2004:52) discusses further the characteristics of qualitative and quantitative research from Larsen-Freeman and Long (1991:12) as in Table 1.

Table 1 Characteristics of quantitative and qualitative research (Larsen-Freeman and Long 1991:12)

Quantitative research	Qualitative research
Controlled	Naturalistic
Experimental	Observational
Objective	Subjective
Inferential	Descriptive
Outcome-oriented	Process-oriented
Reliable	Valid
Particularistic	Holistic
Hard, replicable data	'Real', 'rich', 'deep' data
Generalisable aggregate analysis	Ungeneralisable single case analyses

Figure 2 Cambridge English exploratory mixed methods research design (Cresswell and Plano Clark 2011:69)

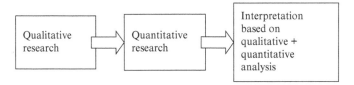

Hawkey (2006:30) notes 'the non-monolithic and iterative nature of impact studies' as likely to 'require a range of approaches'. Watanabe (2004:20) suggests that since impact is 'conceptualised on several dimensions, the methodology that attempts to disentangle the complexity has inevitably to be multifarious'. Thus an impact study such as the *PL2000* or the PLISR will show influences from both ends of the *continua* in Lazaraton's Table 1, but perhaps with an inclination towards the qualitative end. Watanabe (2004:22) notes that 'qualitative or enthnographic research has been increasingly widely used among researchers in the field of language teaching and learning'.

In its quest for research approaches that can take account of the complexities of the impacts of language educational developments such as the *PL2000*, the current Cambridge English 'impact toolkit' includes a two-stage sequential, exploratory mixed methods design (Creswell and Plano Clark 2011:69). In this design, interview or classroom observational data, for example, may be collected and analysed qualitatively as part of a first stage, to be followed, in a second stage, by the design and analysis of questionnaires informed by the interview data (see Figure 2).

We see this sequence of impact research events below in the case of the PLISR.

Research Notes 50 (Cambridge English 2012) refers to Cambridge English impact studies in China, Spain and Vietnam, all of which employ mixed methods designs. The PLISR follows a similar design in recording and analysing, as ever with the agreement of the MIUR, evidence relevant to measures taken as a result of the *PL2000* on learners, teachers, school heads, parents and exam officials.

Research questions, data collection approaches and topic areas

So, as in the original 2001–2002 *PL2000* impact study, recorded interviews and classroom observations made at selected schools were analysed in a systematic search for potentially generalisable information in response to three research questions on the *longer-term* impacts of the *PL2000*, namely:

- What are the longer-term impacts of the *PL2000* on language teaching pedagogy, materials, media and assessment?
- What is the longer-term impact of changes in language teaching pedagogy, materials, media and assessment on student and teacher performance and attitudes?
- What is the longer-term impact of the *PL2000* on heads of schools and on professional support for teachers?

Like many researchers, Gill, Stewart, Treasure and Chadwick (2008:291–292) distinguish three fundamental types of research interviews:

- *structured* interviews 'in which a list of predetermined questions are asked, with little or no variation and with no scope for follow-up questions to responses . . .'
- '*semi-structured* interviews, with several key questions . . . to define the areas to be explored' but with the interviewer or interviewee able to pursue 'an idea or response in more detail . . .'
- '*unstructured* interviews', which 'may simply start with an opening question such as "Can you tell me about your . . .?"'

A key element of the semi-structured interviews is the *interview guide*, described by Hoepfl (1997:6) as 'a list of questions or generated topics that the interviewer wants to explore during each interview'. Although the target is information and opinion on a similar range of topics from each participant, 'there are no predetermined responses, and in semi-structured interviews the interviewer is free to probe and explore within these predetermined inquiry areas' (Hoepfl 1997:6). The advantage of interview guides is that they help 'keep interactions focused' (Hoepfl 1997:6) while yet being amenable to modification to take account of emerging key areas, or even to exclude unproductive questions. It was also noted that, according to Gall, Gall and Borg (2003), the open-ended interview tends to reduce researcher biases.

The relative freedom for participants to go beyond tightly controlled topics was intended to produce more varied and, possibly, deeper insights into the PLISR's areas of interest (see Table 2). It was the unanimous opinion of the PLISR team that this aim was achieved, as we see further below.

The interview procedures

To collect and retrieve information, opinions and actions taken from the range of stakeholders involved, the PLISR used one-to-one, pair or small group interviews. The option on which language was used for the interviews, English or Italian, put interviewees at their ease and almost certainly facilitated the collection of richer qualitative data. Some parents, too, were very willing to be interviewed, usually giving up their time specifically to be available for the study.

Table 2 PLISR interview plan

1	OPENING: Thanks for participation; exchange of introductions; interviewer(s), role with Cambridge English; timing.
2	CONTEXT: Explain recording and use of interview: Reference to student permission letters, already signed; use for Cambridge English enquiry re the *PL2000* longer-term effects, to help with EL learning and assessment in Italy.
3	ORIENTATION: Recap the PL2000 key points, e.g.: Learning of foreign languages from kindergarten to end secondary; small homogeneous learning groups; focus on *communicative* competence, oral–aural, learner autonomy, modern technology, school self-access centres; provincial resource centres; support and in-service for teachers; subsidised internal or external exams, including from Cambridge English. Inform of the Cambridge English 2001–2003 PL2000 impact study: finding out from school heads, teachers, students, parents, officials, how the *PL2000* was going, using interviews, classroom observations, and questionnaires with schools in Novara/Oleggio, Rome and Taranto. Explain the Cambridge English 2012–2013 PLISR: Now a Cambridge English *follow-up* impact study to trace longer-term effects of the *PL2000*, from same kinds of participants at the same or similar schools.
4	QUESTION AREAS: Your view of the PL2000 legacy? o Own experience of the *PL2000*? o Views on its effects, success? Your experience/views of English teaching/learning in Italy now? o Changes? o Attitudes and actions of schools in relation to English? o Communicative language teaching approaches? o Learning groups? o Materials, curriculum and lesson planning? o Learner autonomy? o Self-access; modern technologies? o Resource centres? o Support and in-service for teachers? o Content and Language Integrated Learning (CLIL)? o Related matters? EL assessment o External and internal exams, including Cambridge English? o Changes in exams over the 10 years? o Changes in the *levels* of external exams taken? o Impact of external exams and support e.g. on: motivation/attitudes, proficiency; perceptions, teacher actions? Initiatives from the PL2000 not able to be pursued? Other views, related topics?
5	NEXT STEPS: What they may hear, get from us in the future?
6	ROUND UP AND THANKS.

True to the conventions of the semi-structured interview (above), the PLISR used open-ended questions on the topics specified in the interview guide (e.g. 'What do you think about *group work* in your primary English classes?'), with other related questions arising naturally during the interview ('. . . you said a moment ago that some of the textbooks you use don't seem to be the right level for your pupils. Can you tell me more?'). In many ways, the interview is like a conversation, though keeping to the impact study theme and topics. The researcher tries to build a rapport with the respondents and allows time and scope to talk about their opinions on particular subjects. The objective really is to understand the respondent's point of view. Given these kinds of criteria, the wording of questions was, of course, not likely to be the same for all respondents.

Throughout the study the impact team found a great willingness among key stakeholders to participate. Sarah Ellis, the main Cambridge English Italy member of the PLISR team, notes a key change, as each visit progressed from the formal introductions at the beginning (only Roger Hawkey would have met the individuals involved in the previous study) through to the data collection interviews. As rapport with the impact study team grew, so people at the impact study schools seemed more willing to be recorded and to give up their time to be interviewed.

By the end of each school visit it was clear, from their comments, that for many of those involved, the opportunity offered by the PLISR to discuss and share information with the research team about their school and their teaching, was a positive impact of the study in itself.

The recorded classroom observations

As in the original *PL2000*, classroom lessons in the PLISR schools were observed and video-recorded by three PLISR team members, each manning a camera from a different strategic position in the classroom, as noted in Figure 3.

Figure 3 Typical PLISR video camera stations for classroom observation recordings

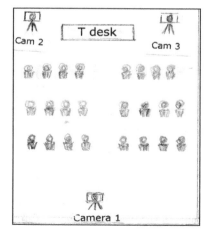

The video-recorded classroom observation data collected for the PLISR was analysed using the grid developed for the *PL2000* (e.g. Hawkey 2006:152) in a slightly updated form. The example of part of the analysis of an observed PLISR lesson shown in Table 3 indicates how the observation grid was completed after the event using the recording(s) from one or more of the ideo cameras used by the team to film the lessons concerned. In the anonymised excerpt exemplified here, from the classroom observation form for an observed class of 7-year-olds at a PLISR primary school, different fonts are used to indicate different themes in the impact study evidence: *italics* for evidence related to technology use; **bold** for more communicative teaching actions, and grey for possible evidence on teacher:student relations. In the original classroom observation forms completed from the video-recordings for the PLISR, nine different impact topics were colour-coded by the lesson analyst if they occurred in an observed lesson, as shown in Table 3.

The completed classroom observation grids were found capable of producing enough relevant information on the events, activities, teaching and learning methods, materials and psycho-social resonance occurring in the classrooms to prove informative on the data areas targeted by the PLISR.

Lesson observation by externals is not common practice in Italian schools and many teachers will not have been observed in their classrooms for a very

Table 3 Excerpt from a completed PLISR classroom observation form*

School/class	Date	Participants	
Primary school x	Xx xx 2012	Teacher and 24 7 year-olds	1 class of 3 hours per week
Episode	**Timing (mins)**	**Activity, participation, materials**	**Comment**
1. T greets pupils and receives loud choral response		Disabled child *receives nice individual attention from T.* T recalls song 'Goodbye Summer'. Asks about the next line and about the word 'fall', inviting US vs UK words. Checks pronunciation, too.	Hugely decorated 'English' room, **desks in U shape**; *plenty of hitech equipt, including cassette players.* *Sts very responsive.*
2. Singing		Class choral singing (with cassette) of 'It's the first hour, of the first day . . . of school'.	*T leads and conducts.* *Sts thoroughly enjoying*
	2'36	Cassette leads on p.58 to 'Goodbye Summer, Hello Fall' with gestures.	*the singing and gestures.*
Remainder of lesson also described continuing to use the PLISR classroom observation grid . . .			

*T = Teacher, Sts = Students

long time, if at all. Once it was clear that the real purpose of the visits was indeed to collect data rather than to inspect or check on what was happening, the teachers and heads were very helpful in facilitating this part of the PLISR data collection.

Permissions

In accordance with data protection laws, formal documented permission was obtained for all the impact study data collection activities and in particular for the video recording and photography in schools. Ahead of the PLISR visits, the teachers arranged for the parents of their students to be asked whether they were willing or not to give their consent to allow them to participate in the data collection activities. Students without parental consent would leave their class for the duration of the impact study data collection.

Much of the administration for these formal permissions was, as for other key impact study functions, facilitated by the local Cambridge English Centre Exam Managers who are in closer, more regular contact with the schools in the PLISR through their candidate Preparation Centres for the Cambridge English exams. For the younger children, in the rare instances where it had either not been possible to obtain parental consent or where additional classes or students were included, the team was given permission to observe lessons without video recording. Audio recording was still possible.

All other impact study participants also gave their written consent.

PLISR data collection topic areas

The data for the PLISR was collected at schools in the same northern, central and southern cities (Novara/Oleggio; Rome; Taranto) as for the original *PL2000* study. The schools chosen were all users of Cambridge English exams, and, in the case of four of the 14, had actually been visited for data collection for the original impact study. This meant that some of the teachers participating in the PLISR had also been interviewed and/or observed in the earlier study.

Summary key aspects of the PLISR data collection were as follows:

- Dates and venues: Educational institutions in:

  Novara/Oleggio, 27–30 May 2012 (three schools)

  Rome 16–20 October 2012 (five schools)

  Taranto 14–20 January 2013 (six schools).

- Data collection for evidence in response to the three PLISR research questions (see above) and reconnecting with the research questions of the original *PL2000* (2001–2002).

- Interviewees: 9 school heads; 34 teachers; 8 students/ex-students; 10 parents (not including the c.80 parents attending two Cambridge English evening presentations).
- Episodes: The 65 PLISR recorded episodes for data analysis included:
  - 18 English classroom lessons, lasting a total of 7 hours 40 minutes, four lessons at primary, seven at middle school and seven at secondary schools, involving 382 students and 23 teachers.
  - 47 interviews involving 65 interviewees, total interview time 822 minutes (13 hrs 42 minutes).
- Recording modes and languages for the PLISR data collected episodes were as in Table 4 (see below).

In addition to 12 state schools visited, the PLISR carried out stakeholder interviews at two private language institutes, for additional insights on key issues and because some of the participating PLISR students attended both their state school and, for extra English classes, a private school.

The PLISR audio- and video-recorded episodes were supplemented by a photographic record of the range of contexts within which the research took place – classrooms, offices, computer labs, and corridors. For those wishing to understand the implications of the physical contexts involved, this is a helpful supplement to the data collection.

The photographic documentation of the research episodes includes each part of the visits to the schools involved in the study, from the arrival of the team at the venues, the school grounds, initial courtesy and administration meetings with school authorities, the classroom observations, the locations for the interviews with different stakeholders: school heads, teachers, (ex-) students, parents, as well as the small group discussions and the presentations given to larger groups of parents and teachers.

The images show the different realities found in the various schools, the physical contexts of the schools and classrooms and the resources available, whether chalkboard or an interactive whiteboard or a multimedia classroom, for example. They record the different class sizes as well as illustrating the range of lesson types which took place, in terms of teacher and student activity as well as the use of digital and traditional

Table 4 PLISR impact episode record

Impact episodes	Recording modes			
	Total	Video	Audio	Notes
Total Impact data, collections	65	55	6	4
in English	55	49	3	3
in Italian	10	6	3	1

resources, all this in the real contexts within which the impact study took place.

Most fundamentally, the PLISR photos provide a visual record of the people under study and those involved in the carrying out the study. The record includes interesting non-linguistic clues, which show not only the relationships between the teachers and their students but also the rapport with the impact study team and the willingness of the stakeholders to be recorded in both formal and less formal parts of the study.

The photographic images provide a supplement to the information from the other research tools in the PLISR's range. They would also appear to suggest evidence of positive impacts of the study on stakeholders, both those contributing to the evidence it was collecting and those doing the collecting.

Analysing qualitative data

The PLISR team, like their predecessors in the *PL2000*, were aware of the difficulties of analysing qualitative data from interviews with key participants. Miles (1979:591) had put it this way:

> The most serious and central difficulty in the use of qualitative data is that methods of analysis are not well formulated. For quantitative data, there are clear conventions the researcher can use. But the analyst faced with a bank of qualitative data has very few guidelines for protection against self-delusion, let alone the presentation of unreliable or invalid conclusions to scientific or policy-making audiences. How can we be sure that an "earthy", "undeniable", "serendipitous" finding is not, in fact, *wrong*?

As noted above, however, there is a strong tradition of the more naturalistic interview paradigm producing the qualitative and potentially valuable data of monologue, verbal responses and dialogue, though with attention to input control measures such as:

- interviewers following the *interview guide* (see above)
- a focus on 'What . . .?' questions
- efforts to avoid the researcher/interviewer affecting or influencing the data
- marking quotations as such.

Folkestad (2008:5) sees the first steps in sorting qualitative interview data as 'unitizing and categorizing' using 'a step-by-step procedure':

1. Read the first unit of data.
2. Read the second unit.
3. Proceed in this fashion until all units have been assigned to categories.

4. Develop category titles or descriptive sentences or both that distinguish each category from the others.

As we see below, the analysis of the PLISR data followed a similar approach, the final two steps being crucial in the description and discussion of main tendencies in the impacts of developments from the *PL2000* on the key participants, individuals and groups, in our study.

Establishing the PLISR categories

The development of themes or categories to be used for the analysis of the considerable quantity of PLISR interview and classroom observation data was carried out taking the following steps:

1. Watching the *classroom video-recordings* carefully and summarising them using the PLISR forms designed for the purpose, viewing recordings of the same actions from more than one of the classroom cameras if it could be helpful in clarifying or enhancing points of particular relevance to the research questions.
2. At all times during the data viewing and listening process, remaining aware that the aim in the *written interview summaries* was to note down points relevant as evidence on developments since the beginning of PLIS concerning:
   - language teacher and learner performance and attitudes
   - language learning materials and media
   - teacher support
   - foreign language assessment.

   These were the themes, of course, on which the PLISR interview *guide* (see above) was based.
3. As already noted, summarising the *classroom observation episodes* using the instrument developed at the time of the original *PL2000* (see Table 3 above).
4. Undertaking the analysis of the 68 episodes of the PLISR data, a major undertaking, eventually producing a 104-page, 44,000-word narrative document of key points from the interviews and the classroom observations (Hawkey 2014). This analysis included English translations by Mariangela Marulli of the ALTE Secretariat at Cambridge English, of episodes that had been recorded in Italian, and a translation from Italian by Sarah Ellis of a school head interview.

Once the episode summary was completed, the next task was to search the points identified and assign each of them to one of the key themes or data categories for the impact study. The categories or themes as initially identified (for example language teacher and learner performance and attitudes;

language learning materials and media; teacher support; foreign language assessment) were being modified as the data analysis proceeded, a process described as follows by Ryen (2002:157):

> After one has inductively identified a theme, one goes on to try verifying or confirming the finding (deductive), which again gives an inductive loop. Miles and Huberman (1994) see it as legitimate and useful to both start with conceptual analytical categories, that is deductive, or to gradually develop them, that is inductive.

In presenting and underlining key points, the PLISR Report makes use of quotations from interviews and classroom observation recordings. But Ryen's (2002:169) caution is noted: 'While using quotes to describe the data is not a problem in itself, it becomes a problem when this is the only way of analysing the data'.

The categories derived from the analysis were now labelled and colour-coded in the 104-page document. The numbers of references in parentheses after the emerging PLISR main topics or categories in the list of key PLISR categories or impact topics in Table 5 below, indicate their prominence in the summary of the PLISR episodes. Given that the PLISR interviews were very much a shared communicative experience, interviewees being encouraged, and, as the PLISR team interviewers frequently noted, proving very willing to play a major role in the interactions, the high-mention numbers of some of the topics did tend to indicate the prominence given to them. The high score for 'communicative and less communicative approaches to English language teaching', for example (304 positive mentions though also 95 examples of less communicative practices), seemed to suggest that communicative language teaching (CLT), which certainly reflected some of the principles and recommended practices of the *PL2000*, remained one of its key impacts.

Table 5 Data analysis categories in order of numbers of mentions by the PLISR interviewees

Data analysis categories: numbers of mentions by the PLISR interviewees
1. Communicative and less communicative approaches to English language teaching (304 + 95)
2. Cambridge English exam approaches, services and influences (245)
3. Computer-based and other technological approaches to ELT (119)
4. Teacher training and support (81)
5. Language textbooks (74)
6. Changing sociolinguistic context in Italy (60)
7. Student:teacher relations (55)
8. Attitudes and influences of parents (53)
9. Content and Language Integrated Learning (CLIL) (31)

Note topics 6 and 9 as particularly relevant to the themes of the ALTE Paris conference. But note also the relevance of all the other themes in the list to the areas of potential language education development covered by the *PL2000*.

Inferences from the PL2000 impact areas

So, the PLISR had produced rich qualitative data, which had been summarised and ordered in terms of frequency of occurrence as shown in the previous section. The next issue was to present a valid analysis of the data. In this section some inferences are thus drawn which are relevant to the current topic of the impacts of international language assessments on multilingualism, citing the qualitative results of the impact study and some subsequent quantitative validation measures applied according to the mixed methods model introduced in Figure 2.

The topics under which the impacts related to the *PL2000* were categorised are discussed here in their approximate order of frequency in Table 5 above. However, 'student:teacher relations' are considered alongside 'communicative and less communicative approaches to English language teaching'; and 'language textbooks' alongside 'computer-based and other technological approaches to ELT'. The topic 'Cambridge English exam approaches, services and influences' is presented *after* the other eight topics as its prominence may well have been influenced by the fact that the PLISR research team was known to have connections with Cambridge English, their visits to schools thus seen as convenient opportunities to raise exam-related matters.

Communicative and less communicative approaches to language teaching and teacher:student relations

The PLISR sees impacts from the *PL2000* on both 'communicative and less communicative approaches to language teaching' and good 'student:teacher relations' (1 and 7 in the list of key impact areas above). It is worth mentioning at the outset of the analysis and as an impact point in itself, that the *PL2000*, first published in 1999, still appeared remarkably fresh in our 2012–2013 participants' minds. School Heads, teachers and parents appeared to need no reminder of what this particular government educational plan had intended or how it had worked.

The fact that communicative and less communicative approaches to language teaching were actually the most commonly occurring topic in all the PLISR data indicates that CLT was indeed seen as a major area of interest for participants. At primary level the emphasis was on pupils' activity in and for the target language in class; at secondary level, CLT tended to involve task-based approaches and activities to develop particular language micro-skills. In both cases CLT was often sufficiently explicitly linked to the *PL2000* to be seen as an impact of it.

Not that the classroom teaching we observed in the course of the PLISR could be generalised under a 'communicative' label. This is rarely, of course, likely to be the case as the language teaching:learning process will always remain a complex matter to analyse, especially when it is taking place in groups of learners with one, or perhaps two, teachers (as seen in some PLISR classrooms).

During the classroom observations for the PLISR, the impact study team noted frequent comfortable teacher:student classroom lesson collaboration and friendly relations at primary and secondary levels, whether with teachers working with groups of primary learners sitting round small tables, or older students collaborating in a topical presentations, with the teacher also playing a part. The many PLISR conversations with English teachers at the Italian schools sampled reinforced the view, expressed by some of the teachers themselves, that learner:teacher relationships were tending to become closer, actually helped, as one teacher suggested, by greater ability and willingness on the part of students to use more English in their interactions outside school. The impression of generally good teacher:student relationships was reinforced by what we heard at our interviews, individual and group, with the language teachers, sometimes held in rooms where students were also around and relaxed, for at least part of the time.

Using questionnaires to validate qualitative data

In a *trial* teacher questionnaire for the PLISR, designed by the team as part of the PLISR's mixed methods approach (see the previous section on mixed methods research design), whereby the more quantitative data from questionnaires may be used to check and validate qualitative interview and classroom observational data, 155 Italian teachers of English were asked to rate the frequencies, in their own English classes, of a range of possible classroom activities. Certain of the items were subsequently deselected once the trial teachers had indicated their unlikelihood and a PLISR teacher questionnaire was developed to be completed by a larger sample of teachers from across the Italian regions and teaching mainly at secondary schools (see excerpt in Table 6).

To help validate the qualitative and more quantitative PLISR data collection modes, tendencies analysed from the questionnaire responses would be compared with the findings from the interviews and lesson observations already carried out.

The first of the following two excerpts here from the PLISR teacher questionnaire responses (N=355), shows a selection of potentially communicative teaching:learning activities noted as quite prominent in the classes of the teachers completing the PLISR questionnaire (numbers and percentages of teachers selecting both given).

Apparently *non*-CLT English lesson activities were also reported by teachers in the questionnaire (expressed, in column six of Table 7 in terms of teachers' combined 'frequently' and 'quite often' percentage ratings).

Although Table 7 here and some of the PLISR *lesson observation* reports also cite examples of non-communicative classroom teaching, the communicative language teaching message from the *PL2000* and indeed from the current language teaching context in general, seems to have impacted quite strongly on Italian foreign language teaching classrooms.

Table 6 Questionnaire responses (percentage and numbers of teachers) showing potentially communicative classroom activities*

Activity in class	Frequently	Quite often	Sometimes	Never	1+2 %
Discussions or conversations in small groups	29.1% 100	32.6% 112	34.0% 117	4.7% 16	62%
Discussions or conversations with a partner	31.9% 109	37.7% 129	29.0% 99	2.1% 7	70%
Discussions for the whole class	49.3% 168	31.7% 108	16.7% 57	2.6% 9	81%
Students doing role plays (giochi di ruolo)	14.9% 51	35.9% 123	41.1% 141	8.8% 30	51%
Students writing notes	29.2% 100	44.9% 154	23.6% 81	2.9% 10	74%
Students writing letters or compositions	25.6% 88	44.2% 152	29.9% 103	1.2% 4	70%

Some percentages do not sum to 100 due to rounding.

Table 7 Prominence of teachers' English lesson activities which would *not* normally be seen as 'communicative'*

Activity in class	Frequently	Quite often	Sometimes	Never	1 + 2 %
Students doing grammar exercises	46.1%	39.4%	14.3%	0.9%	86%
Students explaining the meaning of words in Italian	15.8%	32.5%	40.9%	11.3%	48%
Students reading aloud in English	42.0%	39.4%	17.5%	1.5%	81%
Teacher talking to the whole class	67.2%	27.2%	5.8%	0.3%	94%

Some percentages do not sum to 100 due to rounding.

ELT textbooks, computer-based and other technological approaches

The potential *PL2000* impact areas of ELT textbooks and computer- and other technology-based approaches in ELT, were also shown as significant, at third and fifth positions out of nine in the PLISR category list in Table 5. The 'strengthened use of new technologies' was, it will be recalled, an explicit aim of the *PL2000*, thus a target area for the impact study. The head of a comprehensive school describes the changes in the status of English in Italy as follows (translated from the Italian):

> There is more interest from students, who are more flexible; they have greater interest in English, realising that knowing English will help them a lot in their use of tablets, iPads, the internet. When they buy a gadget, more often than not, the instructions are in English . . . students are more eclectic than us, and students have greater mental agility.

The excerpt from the PLISR teacher questionnaire in Table 8 shows quite high estimates (expressed as combined 'frequently' plus 'quite often' percentage estimates in the final column) of most of their technology-related teaching activities. Notice here the combination of internet and other computer-based technology involved.

Teachers participating in the PLISR tended also, however, to support the continued use of textbooks alongside fast-developing higher technological approaches to language education, and to emphasise how the textbooks themselves were being modernised.

As the PLISR accounts of the lessons observed in the participating schools suggest, it is unlikely that the textbook or the communication-technology input to a lesson will ultimately determine its effectiveness, but rather the way

Table 8 Technology-related EL activities reported in the PLISR teacher questionnaires*

Activity	Frequently	Quite often	Sometimes	Never	1+2 %
Watching English videos in class	14.7%	35.8%	44.9%	5.3%	51%
Using the internet in class or for homework	13.2%	30.3%	48.5%	8.2%	44%
Using emails in English	9.1%	20.4%	46.0%	24.8%	30%
Using an interactive whiteboard	17.6%	26.4%	34.3%	22.0%	44%
Using the computer lab in your English studies	12.4%	26.3%	38.2%	23.4%	39%
Using exercises from the digital version of English textbook(s)	14.8%	27.6%	38.6%	19.3%	42%

Some percentages do not sum to 100 due to rounding.

these inputs are handled by the teacher and the learners. The many other factors involved and often the focus of this study, make significant differences to the motivation and skills of the teachers and the learners concerned. What does seem to be the case from PLISR evidence is that influences from the priorities set by the *PL2000* continue to help motivate language teachers in Italy, and through them their students, to make better use of the improving paper-based *and* computer-based digital and web-based language learning resources available.

The changing sociolinguistic context in Italy

A common view expressed in the PLISR interview evidence is that it is because of the increasing importance of the English language in the world that changes in the learning, teaching and assessment of the language are taking place in Italy. In the words of the mother with a son wishing to enter university: 'Today without English language, you can't find a job. It's the first language in the world for all people to study for work'. Another parent, who himself uses English for technical purposes in his work and with his foreign contacts, considers that the prevalence of English nowadays means that his daughter at primary school is already 'very interested in the internationality of the world'. This may be a reflection of what a teacher at the same school says at her interview: 'Yes, parents and students hear more English, have higher expectations, and know how important it is for jobs, the future. And exams!'

Not that the increasing prevalence of English or even the awareness of its importance can guarantee motivation to learn it. As two teachers of 11 and 12 year-olds put it at their interview, the students know English is more important now, and they have more opportunity to use it, for example, watching TV programmes and using the internet. But, although some want to use the language in their practical lives, some are not so motivated, which means that teachers have to 'work at different levels'.

The importance of the English language as a means of international communication is both a sociolinguistic feature of the period of influence and an indirect impact in Italy of the *PL2000* itself. The *PL2000* gives its clear recognition to the changing status of English and seeks a role in developing ways of dealing with this and with changes in the status of other foreign languages in Italy. Evidence collected by the revisit impact study from key participants, teachers, learners, school heads and parents, suggests that English is even more a priority now, as the language of international face-to-face and online communication, professional and social. Not that this fact by any means guarantees motivation or success for all learners of English.

Teacher training and support

Gisella Langé, Foreign Languages Inspector and Special Advisor at the MIUR, reminded us at a MUIR presentation entitled *Implementing language policies: The Italian experience* (Langé 2014) of the importance of teachers' qualification and recruitment procedures; special initial and in-service training and qualifications in both non-language and language subjects; and incentives for teachers. In the original *PL2000*, communicative approaches to teaching English had been quite strongly in evidence. In the 2012–2013 PLISR, communicative and less communicative approaches to language teaching were the most recurrent theme in the PLISR data.

Although recent financial difficulties in Italy have led to reduced spending on education, teacher in-service matters were prominent in discussions and findings at almost all the PLISR schools. Eighty-one references to various forms of teacher in-service training and other support were recorded in the PLISR data and the English language teachers tended to set up their own ELT meetings, some also attending available school groups or other institutional in-service meetings. Support offered by EL teaching or assessment organisations, such as Cambridge English or the British Council, appeared to be in demand.

Attitudes and influences of parents

The PLISR data indicates strength of parental support for their children's learning of English, with 53 cases analysed in the data, from parents who do not speak English themselves, as well as from those who do. Acknowledging perhaps the changing sociolinguistic role of English in Italy, two parents with children at a *liceo* (high school) emphasised how the language was helping to give their children 'the opportunity to choose the job they like', this an apparent impact development across the period covered by the two studies, the *PL2000* and the PLISR, and noted that their children attend extra English classes.

The impact study interviews with parents also indicated how highly valued *certain PL2000* ideas often were, for example, the initiative towards external language assessments. The PLISR team itself also benefited from extra insights gained from attending two of the after-hour school meetings on their children's foreign language learning and assessment that the parents had requested at the impact study schools.

Content and Language Integrated Learning (CLIL)

Bilingual education, defined by the European Commission as 'teaching in two languages; the country's native language and a secondary language'

(*Bilingual Education* (2012) available online: http://ec.europa.eu/languages/ policy/language-policy/bilingual_education_en.htm), involves Content and Language Integrated Learning (CLIL). CLIL, one of the data categories in the PLISR analysis (see above) is described in the same article, as the 'teaching of a subject in a non-native language'. Following education reforms in Italy in 2010, CLIL has been compulsory for the first foreign language since 2012–2013 in the final year of *licei linguistici* (high schools specialising in modern languages) and, from 2013–2014, for the second language in year 4 of *licei linguistici*. Implementation of CLIL in year 5s of all *licei* and *istituti tecnici* (technical schools) is now being achieved.

Though there is no direct reference to CLIL in the original *PL2000* document, the construct may be inferred in the *PL2000* stated commitment to 'the design of courses for specific purposes, including literary and professional language'. CLIL is also evidenced in the first *PL2000* internal report (Hawkey 2002:59) in the conclusion from a *scuola media* parent focus group in October 2001 that 'English also opens horizons for the study of languages and other subjects in English'.

At the time of the PLISR (in 2012–2013) there was some uncertainty among the English teachers interviewed about the form that CLIL training would or should take, with the need expressed for it to ensure that the English language teaching professionals, like the subject teachers also involved, should share key responsibilities and acknowledgement.

The PL2000, Cambridge English Language Assessment and impact

The delegation to international exam bodies of formal foreign language assessments previously carried out nationally, was a major impact of the *PL2000*, as noted above. Given the four foreign languages involved, French, German, Spanish and English, this represented a significant step in support of multilingualism, and indeed, of internationalism. It was thus no surprise that the whole *PL2000*:Cambridge English relationship, would figure large in the PLISR (as the high 245 occurrence figure in Table 5 of data analysis categories shows).

The clearest impact of the *PL2000* on Cambridge English exams is shown by the significant increase in enrolments since the beginning of the *Progetto*, even with Italian government financial support for exam entries now reduced. Enrolments for Cambridge English exams in Italy almost trebled between 2001–2002 and 2013–2014, with many more students taking the higher level (B2–C2) exams.

The clear and well-documented relationship between the explicit and target-oriented A1 to C2 levels of the Common European Framework of Reference (CEFR) and the Cambridge English exams is seen by many stakeholders as further strengthening the impact of the exams as a *PL2000* initiative, alongside, of course, the appeal of the multilingualism of encouraging exams in four different foreign languages (French, German, Spanish and English) as in the original *PL2000*.

Important, sometimes overlapping, issues were raised by impact study participants concerning the Cambridge English exams as shown in Figure 4 below.

Other Cambridge English exam matters discussed during the PLISR included:

- the positively perceived validity, reliability and practicality of the exams
- their coverage of reading, writing, listening and speaking and their component skills
- their strict management and delivery systems
- their support materials and services.

The advantages of international certificates such as those awarded for successfully passing Cambridge English exams were seen by PLISR participants as significant in their 'added value', international certification representing *recognised* proof of achievement in broader international contexts.

There was evidence from the PLISR data of positive stakeholder perceptions that the skills assessed and the grades assigned by the Cambridge English exams are valid and accurate. The head of an elementary and a middle school spoke interestingly at an interview of her perceptions and

Figure 4 Cambridge English examinations, from pre- CEFR Level A1 to C2

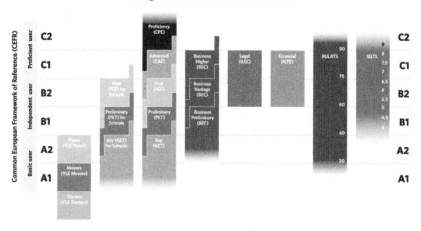

Source: www.cambridgeenglish.org/images/126130-cefr-diagram.pdf

experience of the quality of the exams across all four skills. She sees this in combination with the 'way the teachers have prepared the students' so enthusiastically and 'the passion of the students themselves' as motivating the students on their route from *Cambridge English: Starters* in their fourth year, to *Cambridge English: Movers* in their fifth, and so on.

A long-serving English teacher at a *liceo*, with experience working with Cambridge English in their continuing field studies to validate their exams (i.e. pretesting), noted at her PLISR interview that Cambridge English has a whole department doing research on the exams all year round, meaning, she feels, that 'nothing in the exam is by chance'. As part of her professional support to her school colleagues, she is able to show precisely what each item is designed and validated to test. 'So,' she adds, 'if it's a B1, it's a B1.' The perceived quality of the Cambridge English exams (characterised as Validity, Reliability, Impact and Practicality, as shown in Figure 1) was quite a frequent reason for their endorsement among the PLISR interviewees. So was the belief that 'every aspect of the language is being tested' (said a student who has taken *Cambridge English: First*, *Cambridge English: Advanced* and *Cambridge English: Proficiency*); 'the exam organisation ... test rooms with the candidate names on the desks, spacing between candidates according to strict regulations and so on' (the manager of a language school); 'the freedom from politics of having exams from outside the school' (a *liceo* head of English).

The PLISR interviews revealed that the participating schools now had broader and stronger requirements and expectations of a language assessment organisation such as Cambridge English Language Assessment. In response, Cambridge English, as 'experts in language assessment: delivering excellence and innovation' and 'positive impact' (taken from www.cambridgeenglish.org/about) depends on the work of '40,000 registered preparation centres' in addition to its tens of thousands of examiners, teachers and publishers. There is evidence from the PLISR interviews that teachers do indeed seek and benefit from Cambridge English support activities. Mentioned in the data are activities such as 'Cambridge Days' and Webinars (online seminars for teachers, live, downloadable and offering certificates of attendance).

Conclusion

Given that the objectives of the *PL2000* were significant and long term, the idea of a *revisit* impact study 10 years after the original is considered a logical step in keeping track of change and progress in relevant areas of language learning and assessment. The PLISR is considered to have obtained rich and relevant data in response to its research questions on the current impacts of the *PL2000* on students, teachers, school heads and parents. In the analysis of the *PL2000* impacts which have relevance to *multilingualism*, examples have been presented and discussed which support a claim that international language exams such as those of Cambridge English play a role in strengthening levels of proficiency in English and other foreign languages in a country like Italy which supports multilingualism.

Following a mainly similar method and scale of enquiry as the original *PL2000*, though of course with parameters updated to take account of changed circumstances and with a focus on the same or similar schools and participants, the PLISR's potential for measuring and evaluating *change* is good. The revisit idea has proved helpful in updating information for the extension, expansion, deepening and further validation of evidence of the *PL2000* impact.

The relatively small scale of the qualitative impact study may be seen as a limitation of the PLISR, even though data obtained may be claimed to be in depth (see the 68 episodes of video- and audio-recorded data and the 40,000-word/113-page analysis). The amount of *quantitative* questionnaire data collected, to help validate the qualitative interview and observation data and to extend the depth and breadth of the impact study, could still be increased. The PLISR teacher and student questionnaires are already being found useful beyond the PLISR, for example, to better understand the professional development needs of English teachers in Italy.

Though the *PL2000* and the PLISR were carried out by Cambridge English, as part of its research in the interests of the validity, reliability, positive impact and practicality of its exams, the approaches and findings of the studies may be expected to have broader relevance than solely in the field of language assessment. Not least, perhaps, as we have seen above, is the relevance of the studies to the ways in which languages are learned and taught in this era of growing multilingualism.

References

Association of Language Testers in Europe (2014) *Language Assessment for Multilingualism*, available online: www.cambridgeenglish.org/news/view/paris-conference-language-assessment-for-multilingualism

Baldwin-Edwards, M and Zampagni, F (2014) *Regularisations and Employment in Italy*, REGANE Assessment Report, Munich Personal RePEc Archive, available online: mpra.ub.uni-muenchen.de/59754/

Barni, M (2012) 'Italy', in Extra, G and Yağmur, K (Eds), *Language Rich Europe. Trends in Policies and Practices for Multilingualism in Europe*, Cambridge: Cambridge University Press, 146–153.

Bolli, G (2013) Migration policies in Italy in relation to language requirements. The project Italiano, lingua nostra: impact and limitations, in Galaczi, E D and Weir, C J (Eds) *Exploring Language Frameworks. Proceedings of the ALTE Kraków Conference, July 2011*, Studies in Language Testing volume 36, Cambridge: UCLES/Cambridge University Press, 45–61.

Cambridge English (2012) *'Is English enough?' ask experts at the European Parliament*, available online: www.cambridgeenglish.org/news/view/is-english-enough/

Cambridge English (2013) *Principles of Good Practice Quality Management and Validation in Language Assessment*, available online www.cambridgeenglish.org/images/22695-principles-of-good-practice.pdf

Carless, D (2009) Trust, distrust and their impact on assessment reform, *Assessment and Evaluation in Higher Education* 34 (1), 79–89.

Creswell, J and Plano Clark, V (2011) *Designing and Conducting Mixed Methods Research*, Thousand Oaks: Sage.

European Commission (2012) *Bilingual Education*, available online: ec.europa.eu/languages/policy/language-policy/bilingual_education_en.htm

Extra, G and Yağmur, K (Eds) (2012) *Language Rich Europe: Trends in policies and practices for multilingualism in Europe*, Cambridge: Cambridge University Press.

Folkestad, B (2008) Analysing interview data: possibilities and challenges, *Online Working Paper No. 13*, Eurosphere Working Paper Series, available online: eurospheres.org/files/. . ./Eurosphere_Working_Paper_13_Folkestad.pdf

Gall, M, Gall, J and Borg, W (2003) *Educational Research: An Introduction*, Boston: Allyn and Bacon.

Gill, P, Stewart, K, Treasure, E, and Chadwick, B (2008) Methods of data collection in qualitative research: interviews and focus groups, *British Dental Journal* 204, 291–295.

Hawkey, R (2002) *The Cambridge ESOL Progetto Lingue 2000 Impact Study*, Cambridge: Cambridge ESOL internal report.

Hawkey, R (2006) *Impact Theory and Practice: Studies of the IELTS test and the Progetto Lingue 2000*, Studies in Language Testing volume 24, Cambridge: UCLES/Cambridge University Press.

Hawkey, R (2014) The *Progetto Lingue 2000 Impact Study Revisit: a study of the Progetto Lingue 2000 carried out in 2012–14 following the original study of 2001–2: Main Report*, Cambridge: Cambridge English internal report.

Hoepfl, M (1997) Choosing qualitative research: A primer for technology education researchers, *Journal of Technology Education* 9 (1), available online: scholar.lib.vt.edu/ejournals/JTE/v9n1/hoepfl.html

Langé, G (2014) *Implementing language policies: The Italian experience*, paper presented at Ministero dell'Istruzione, dell'Università e della Ricerca, Palma de Mallorca, 4 April, 2014, available online: cercleeducatiu.org/wp-cercleeducatiu.org/wp-content/uploads/2014/04/lange_Palma_Ap_4_2014.pdf

Larsen-Freeman, D and Long, M (1991) *An Introduction to Second Language Acquisition Research*, London: Longman

Lazaraton, A (2004) Qualitative research methods in language test development and validation, in Milanovic, M and Weir, C J (Eds) *European Language Testing in a Global Context, proceedings of the ALTE Barcelona Conference, July 2001*, Studies in Language Testing volume 18, Cambridge: UCLES/Cambridge University Press.

Miles, M (1979) Qualitative data as an attractive nuisance problem of analysis, *Administrative Science Quarterly* 24, 590–601.

Miles, M and Huberman, A (1994) *Qualitative Data Analysis: an Expanded Sourcebook*, Thousand Oaks: Sage.

Ministero della Pubblica Istruzione (1999) *Progetto Lingue 2000* available online: archivio.pubblica.istruzione.it/argomenti/autonomia/progetti/lingue.htm

Nuttall, M (2012) *'Is English enough?' ask experts at the European Parliament*, available online at: www.cambridgeenglish.org/news/view/is-english-enough/

Ryen, A (2002) *Det Kvalitative Intervjuet: fra Vitenskapsteori til Feltarbeid*, Bergen: Fagbokforl.

Saville, N (2012) Applying a model for investigating the impact of language assessment within educational contexts: The Cambridge ESOL approach, *Research Notes* 50, 4–8.

Watanabe, Y (2004) Methodology in Washback Studies, in Cheng, L and Watanabe, Y with Curtis, A (Eds) *Washback in Language Testing: Research Contexts and Methods*, Mahwah: Lawrence Erlbaum Associates.

Weiss, C (1998) *Evaluation*, New Jersey: Prentice Hall.

10 Language assessment for migration and social integration: A case study

Paola Masillo
University for Foreigners of Siena, Italy

Abstract

Increasing attention has been given to investigate the language policy currently used in many European countries for migration. A growing number of European countries nowadays are requiring immigrants to pass language tests in national and/or official languages as a condition for obtaining residency rights and citizenship. The ability to use the host country language is considered concrete evidence of a migrant's willingness to adhere to a shared national identity. Success in language tests is associated with the willingness to integrate and, as a consequence, succeed in the workplace and in society as a whole.

These language policies reflect a static, mono-normative and artefactualised concept of language and the language tests designed for migrants seem to be underpinned by that theoretical model. As a consequence policy makers are ignoring the plurilingual and superdiverse repertoire of the test takers and the use they make of languages in real life. A consequence of this is the misrecognition or under-recognition of 'competence' in actual communication in a rapidly changing communication and language landscape.

The aim of this paper is to show how this unitary concept of language underpins the language tests developed in Italy for obtaining a long-term residence permit and, taking participants' performances as a key point of reference, reflect on how the assessment criteria in use cannot fit in the emergent nature of social interaction in a multi/plurilingual society.

Overview of the study

Introduction

The aim of this paper is to show the partial results of a three-year PhD research project which deals with a comparability study of two Italian language tests for non-European Union migrants in Italy.

In 2009, an ideological link between the Italian language and residence rights was established. For the first time, Italian language ability was considered when making decisions about whether a person would be granted the right to stay in the country. In accordance with the provisions of current immigration legislation, the following changes were introduced (Law no. 94/2009, *Provisions relating to public safety*): 'the issuance of the EU [European Union] long-term residence permit is subordinated to the passing of a test of knowledge of the Italian language, whose procedures are established by decree of the Ministry for Internal Affairs, in consultation with the Ministry of Education, University and Research' (article 1, paragraph 22, letter i).

According to the Ministerial Decree of 4 June 2010, which defines the procedures of the Italian language test, 'for the issuance of a permit for EU long-term residents, the foreigner must possess a level of knowledge of the Italian language that allows him/her to understand sentences and frequently used expressions in current areas, at Level A2 of the Common European Framework of Reference' (article 2, paragraph 1, and see Table 1).

Table 1 Common European Framework of Reference Level A2: Global scale

Can understand sentences and frequently used expressions related to areas of most immediate relevance (e.g. very basic personal and family information, shopping, local geography, employment). Can communicate in simple and routine tasks requiring a simple and direct exchange of information on familiar and routine matters. Can describe in simple terms aspects of his/her background, immediate environment and matters in areas of immediate need.

Source: (Council of Europe 2001:24)

The use of the Common European Framework of Reference (CEFR, Council of Europe 2001) as a standard of reference for the definition of language proficiency required for non-EU migrants includes Italy in the language policy trends in which the CEFR is improperly used in the development and diffusion of language programmes for adults in the context of migration (Little 2008).

According to the agreement signed in November 2010 between the Italian Ministry for Internal Affairs and the Ministry of Education, University and Research, the latter developed official guidelines for test design and the assessment of performances of migrants[1]. As explained in these guidelines, which contain basic test specifications and the required competence level (i.e. CEFR Level A2), the test must consist of three sections: Listening, Reading and Written Interaction. The Ministry of Education provided only these test specifications and guidelines which each educational centre, located all across Italy, was to use to design their own test and administer it. The decision of the Italian government not to use a centralised and national test, but to leave test development and administration in the hands of each educational centre for adults (Ministerial Decree 4 June 2010, *Procedures of the Italian language test*; *Framework Agreement* 16 November 2010 between the Ministry of Interior and Ministry of Education, University and Research) was divisive and raised the issue of *fairness, validity* and *reliability* of the exam(s). As Shohamy (1997:340) states, 'language tests employing methods which are not fair to all test-takers are unethical. Equally, uses of language tests which aim to exercise control and manipulate stakeholders rather than provide information regarding proficiency levels are also unethical'. Shohamy's words seem to capture the situation in the Italian context perfectly, where language tests are being used to determine whether a specific group of immigrants, the non-European ones, will be granted a regular permit to stay which can be described as a type of control over this group's social inclusion.

Research has shown that the pass rates vary greatly and this variation seems to reflect a geographical distribution, as shown in Figure 1.

Figure 1 Pass rates by location from January to June 2011

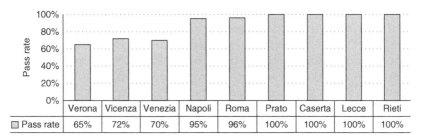

	Verona	Vicenza	Venezia	Napoli	Roma	Prato	Caserta	Lecce	Rieti
☐ Pass rate	65%	72%	70%	95%	96%	100%	100%	100%	100%

Source: Ministry of the Interior – Department for Civil Liberties and Immigration

The review of pass rates provided me with the starting point for developing the main hypothesis of my PhD research project, which is a comparability study of two selected tests, in order to investigate their degree of validity and reliability in terms of being *equivalent forms*. However, the main focus of the paper is about one stage of the whole PhD project, which deals with the appropriacy of the assessment criteria used which were provided by the Italian Ministry.

Research context

The research context takes into account three major factors influencing language use and policies in Europe (Barni 2014).

The first factor arises from increasing migration and easier international and intra-national communication (Extra, Spotti and Van Avermaet 2009b, Saville 2009, Vertovec 2006). Linguistic and cultural diversity are key features of EU policy because this reflects the realities of social interactions among and between European citizens. According to Van Avermaet (2009:21), 'integration is only possible if we start to accept the idea of a multicultural and multilingual society, and consequently the concept of multicultural citizenship'.

However, managing this policy presents a challenge for European institutions and citizens, since it generates widespread concern about social cohesion and integration (Barni 2014). Although in most EU documents, multilingualism is considered an asset to be promoted and defended (Extra et al 2009b, Van Avermaet 2009), most often it is treated as a problem, particularly in the case of migrants. As Blommaert, Leppänen and Spotti (2012:1) argue, 'not all forms of multilingualism are productive, empowering and nice to contemplate. Some – many – are still unwanted, disqualified or actively endangering to people'.

The second factor arises from the long tradition of using language assessment as a strategy and an instrument of social policy or practices. Nowadays language tests are increasingly seen as tools with a divisive linguistic gatekeeping role (McNamara 1998, 2005, Pochon-Berger and Lenz 2014, Spolsky 1997). This has been observed especially in reference to migration and integration, where tests have become a *source of power* used against groups in society (Shohamy 2001, 2006, 2009). As Hogan-Brun, Mar-Molinero and Stevenson (Eds) (2009:3) claim, 'linguistic proficiency has now emerged as one of the key conditions for the granting of permission to stay and for naturalisation in an increasing number of European states, and where it is the case more formal mechanisms for testing have generally been introduced'. Consequently, the purpose of testing in Europe has undergone a change in that tests are increasingly being used as a form of *modernist linguistic border control*, which can lead to discrimination and social exclusion (Blommaert et al 2012).

Furthermore the use of language tests for purposes of social inclusion or integration hides a political ideology, dominant in some countries, based on the so-called principle *one nation, one language* (Horner 2009, Mar-Molinero and Stevenson 2006, Shohamy 2009). It is an interpretation of the relationship between language and nationhood as *unique* and *static* (Extra and Spotti 2009, Mar-Molinero and Stevenson 2006) in which, as highlighted by Spotti (2011:40), 'the nation is therefore imagined as a homogeneous entity, with one language that covers the role of official/national language and with one of its varieties – a standardized register – presented as a neutral medium of communication between and among fellow-citizens'.

The third factor arises from the publication of the CEFR and its impact upon language policies in Europe. Since 2001 the CEFR has become – both in Europe, and beyond – the main reference document in the field of language learning, teaching and assessment. It has even become an operational tool used to justify language policy, both at the educational and, more generally, at the social level (Barni 2014, Blommaert et al 2012, Thalgott 2010,

Van Avermaet 2009). In recent years, an increase in the use of language tests based on the CEFR has been found across the whole of Europe (Extra, Spotti and Van Avermaet (Eds) 2009a, Mar-Molinero and Stevenson 2006, Van Avermaet 2010). The language descriptors of the CEFR are used more and more as benchmarks to describe the minimum competence needed for migrants, even though they were not designed for this purpose (Extra et al (Eds) 2009a, McNamara 2011, Shohamy 2007a). Krumm (2007), who draws attention to the fact that the CEFR levels initially were not developed as a basis for assessing the language skills of migrants, but of 'classic foreign language learners'. Van Avermaet (2010:21) further develops this idea:

> . . . the CEFR descriptors at the lower levels clearly imply an already existing basic knowledge and literacy. This is problematic when they are used for integration and citizenship programmes and for tests where a large part of the target group are either functionally illiterate or have low literacy skills. The CEFR descriptors at higher levels presuppose higher levels of education. Lower- and semi-skilled people that have no higher education background or do not study at a higher level are not part of the target group.

The theoretical model that underlies language test policy in testing regimes reflects a conception of linguistic competence defined as *static* and *mono-normative* (Blommaert et al 2012, Extra and Spotti 2009, Extra et al 2009b, Hogan-Brun et al 2009, Shohamy, 2009). Similar ideological and linguistic bases underlie, as Van Avermaet (2009) and Barni (2014) state, the theoretical approach of the CEFR scale and descriptors. This implies a lack of consideration of the profile and language needs of the potential target test takers. As Barni states (2014:41), 'for migrants, in most cases the official language of the host country is an L2, while one, two, or more language(s) and also mixtures of languages are used in their daily linguistic exchanges'. Furthermore, this implies a need for a new validity framework in language tests, which considers the multilingual competence, the linguistic repertoire and cultural background of immigrants (Van Avermaet 2009).

The (mis)use of the CEFR as a standard of reference in migratory contexts is also confirmed by Extra et al (Eds) (2009a) who highlight how the CEFR has become a tool for prescriptive purposes concerning immigration and integration, as opposed to the initial descriptive and illustrative purpose for which the scales were developed.

The CEFR, and the tests which are derived from it, become even more powerful when it affects language policy and is used to make decisions about people's future. Van Avermaet (2010:21) explains that:

> . . . policy makers determine a level of language proficiency required for admission, residence or citizenship of immigrants by using the CEFR

six-level system . . . often without any rationale or validation, a particular CEFR level of language proficiency is chosen when developing a language policy for integration of immigrants. This is clearly illustrated by the variation in CEFR levels chosen for admission, residence or citizenship across Europe.

The Italian case represents an example of a controversial language policy which has resulted in the development of tests which lack a clear rationale and calls into question their validity and reliability.

Case study

The recent introduction of language tests for long-term residency permits in Italy has officially confirmed the Italian government's adherence to the 'one language, one nation and one territory' ideal (Blackledge and Wright 2001).

The Italian immigration and integration legislation identified the skills of oral and written comprehension and written interaction as the main language features to be used to determine the language competence required for non-EU citizens who intend to stay in the country.

Section 3: Written Interaction test

The remainder of this paper focuses on the third section of the Italian language test – *Written Interaction* – and on the assessment procedures and criteria in use. It analyses whether they fit the emergent nature of social interaction in a *plurilingual* society. According to the ministerial guidelines, the Written Interaction test should consist of one task, which is related to one of the language sub-skills shown in Table 2.

The Written Interaction test takes 10 minutes and test takers are requested to reply to emails, postcards, invitations or to fill in a form (e.g. enrolment in

Table 2 CEFR Level A2 – Written Interaction

A2	
Correspondence notes, messages and forms	Can write very simple personal letters expressing thanks and apology. Can take a short, simple message provided he/she can ask for repetition and reformulation. Can write short, simple notes and messages relating to matters in areas of immediate need.

Source: VADEMECUM (ai sensi della nota n. 8571 del 16 Dicembre 2010 del Ministero dell'Interno). Indicazioni tecnico-operative per la definizione dei contenuti delle prove che compongono il test, criteri di assegnazione del punteggio e durata del test. Direzione Generale dell'Istruzione e Formazione Tecnica Superiore e per i rapporti con i sistemi formativi delle Regioni-Ufficio IV.

courses or schools, personal data, permit requests, bank accounts, etc.) in accordance with the CEFR descriptors of Level A2. In addition, the ministerial handbook gives an holistic assessment scale, which is reported in Table 3, in order to guarantee a standardised, reliable, and consistent assessment of written production.

Table 3 Written Interaction test – Assessment scale

Test is performed in a complete and correct way	Answers are provided consistently and appropriately to the information required or the form is filled in all its parts	29–35 points
Test is performed in a partial way	Answers are not always provided consistently and appropriately to the information required or the form is filled in partially	1–28 points
Test cannot be evaluated	Answers are not provided or the form is not completed	0 point

Source: VADEMECUM (ai sensi della nota n. 8571 del 16 Dicembre 2010 del Ministero dell'Interno). Indicazioni tecnico-operative per la definizione dei contenuti delle prove che compongono il test, criteri di assegnazione del punteggio e durata del test. Direzione Generale dell'Istruzione e Formazione Tecnica Superiore e per i rapporti con i sistemi formativi delle Regioni-Ufficio IV.

As we can see, the assessment scale provided by the Italian Ministry of Education implies a scoring system based on three bands, where the descriptors focus on two formal aspects of language competence: *consistency* and *appropriateness*.

According to the CEFR (Council of Europe 2001:88), 'evaluation takes place at a communicative level (checking *congruence*) and at a linguistic level (checking *consistency* of usage)'.

The above-mentioned assessment criteria are mainly based on a criterion of *consistency*, which measures and assesses formal linguistic aspects and minimises the communicative aspects of a language performance. CEFR descriptors which contain the expressions *consistently*, *consistent* and the like, can only be found in the linguistic scales, such as *vocabulary control*, *grammatical accuracy* and *orthographic control*, and only at C levels (i.e. Proficient Users). On the contrary, at the A levels (i.e. the Basic Users), we can generally find expressions related to the ability to control or use *simple structures*, the chance *to make basic mistakes*, and to write with reasonable phonetic accuracy (*but not necessarily fully standard spelling*).

The second criterion, *appropriateness*, is concerned with sociolinguistic aspects of communication, but it still seems inadequate to the CEFR level that the test intends to measure. As for the CEFR descriptors which contain the expressions *appropriateness*, *appropriate* and the like, one finds them once again corresponding to levels which are higher than the target test level A2, for example at the B2 level for 'Sociolinguistic appropriateness': a language user 'can express him or herself confidently, clearly and politely in a formal or informal register, appropriate to the situation and person(s) concerned' (Council of Europe 2001:122). On the contrary, the equivalent A2 descriptor says: 'can perform and respond to basic language functions ... in a simple way; can socialise simply but effectively using the simplest common expressions and following basic routines . . .' (Council of Europe 2001:122). Moreover, the CEFR descriptors which contain such elements of appropriateness are located in the following tables: 'General linguistic range' of the level C1; 'Vocabulary control' of the level C2; and 'Coherence and cohesion', again at Level C2. Therefore, it would seem that the assessment criteria provided is not in accordance with the CEFR level it is meant to be measuring.

Research questions

In light of these observations, the main research hypothesis deals with the lack of conformity between the assessment criteria and the *test criterion*, based on a *communicative language competence of Level A2*.

The main research question is the following: in light of the distribution of scores (see Figure 1) and the selection of the assessment criteria for the above-mentioned written interaction skill, can we say that the test in question is a valid and reliable measure to assess language-related communicative competence?

The focus of this paper lies on the two assessment parameters – *consistency* and *appropriateness* – and their suitability to describe a language-related communicative competence of CEFR Level A2.

Study procedures and sample characteristics

My research project was divided into three years. In the first year, a database of the tests developed for migrants, using the ministerial guidelines, was created. The tests collected were developed by different centres and previously administered in Italy. I gathered 83 examples of these tests. Following a review of the test scores, I selected two examples of tests by the two most representative areas according to the pass rates: Piemonte (the highest ones) and Veneto (the lowest ones).

During the second year, I administered the two selected tests to a representative sample of test takers. In the third year, I focused on the data analysis.

The aim of this paper is to show the main results reached during the last stage, which focused on the third section of the test: *written interaction*.

Test instruments

In the first Written Interaction test (see Figure 2), test takers are required to fill in a form (job request) and then to explain what kind of job they

Figure 2 Test 1 – Written Interaction task

INTERAZIONE SCRITTA

QUESTO È IL MODULO PER LA RICHIESTA DI LAVORO.
DEVI COMPILARE IL MODULO

M.IT

logo di m0rula www.flickr.com

ALL'AGENZIA DI LAVORO
IL SOTTOSCRITTO-LA SOTTOSCRITTA:

(NOME) ....

(COGNOME)..

NATO A (CITTÀ DI NASCITA) ....(STATO) ....

INDIRIZZO: VIA... NUMERO ....

CITTÀ..

NUMERO DI TELEFONO ....

PATENTE ITALIANA SÌ [ ]   NO [ ]

CHIEDE DI LAVORARE COME: _____

SPIEGA PERCHÉ

....

....

....

....

....

....

....

FIRMA_____

DATA____/_____/ 2013

are asking for (*chiedere di lavorare come*) and the reason why (*spiega perché*).

In the second Written Interaction test (see Figure 3), test takers are required to send a message (e.g. note, email or text message) to a friend and write about one of the three given bullet points: job (*lavoro*), market (*mercato*), study (*studiare*).

Figure 3 Test 2 – Written Interaction task

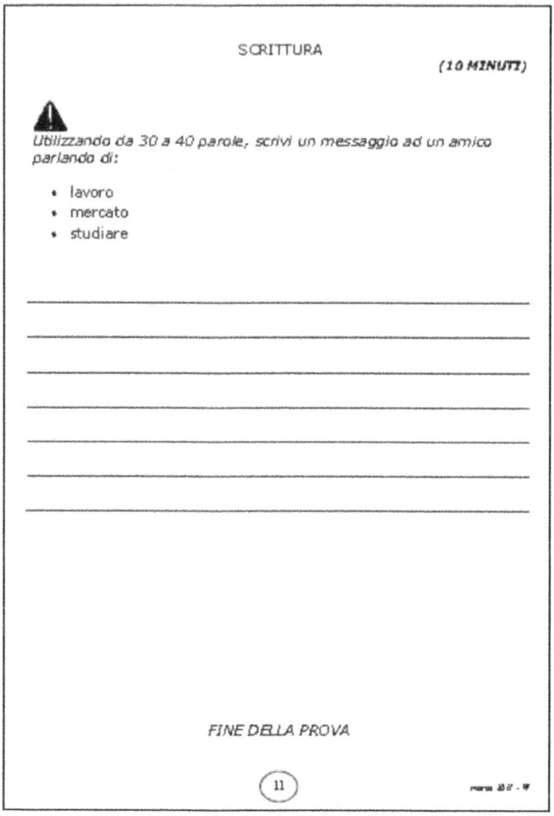

SCRITTURA

(10 MINUTI)

Utilizzando da 30 a 40 parole, scrivi un messaggio ad un amico parlando di:

* lavoro
* mercato
* studiare

FINE DELLA PROVA

11

The sample

As for the administration, in order to compare the two tests, I gave them to an appropriate single group of 157 test takers within a short period between the two administrations (Weir and Wu 2006).

Then, a random sample of 40 scripts was selected from a collection of 314 written productions by 157 migrants who had a range of language abilities between CEFR Levels A1 and B1. The random sample is made up of: 20 scripts for Written Interaction Test 1 and 20 scripts for Written Interaction Test 2.

Those 40 scripts were scored by 11 raters, using the above-mentioned ministerial 35-point scale. The pool of raters consisted of: six test developers and teacher trainers; four teachers and raters of Italian as a second language and one rater of Italian as a second language. As reported in Table 4, six out of 11 raters have more than 10 years' experience in the field of language testing and assessment of Italian as a second language. All the raters involved in the research have experience with CEFR Level A2.

Table 4 The rater pool

Rater no.	Profile	Experience in the field of language testing and assessment (number of years)	CEFR levels of competence assessed so far
1	Test developer and teacher trainer	11	A1, A2, B1, B2, C1, C2
2	Teacher and rater	4	A1, A2, B1
3	Test developer and teacher trainer	20	A1, A2, B1, B2, C1, C2
4	Teacher and rater	7	A1, A2, B1, B2, C1
5	Rater	1	A2
6	Teacher and rater	3	A2, B1
7	Test developer and teacher trainer	18	A1, A2, B1, B2, C1, C2
8	Teacher and rater	4	A1, A2, B1
9	Test developer and teacher trainer	19	A1, A2, B1, B2, C1, C2
10	Test developer and teacher trainer	20	A1, A2, B1, B2, C1, C2
11	Test developer and teacher trainer	18	A1, A2, B1, B2, C1, C2

The method

This study was divided into three main phases: phase one consisted of a qualitative analysis and is related to the content analysis of the two Italian language tests in question; the second phase was based on an item analysis in order to check the two Italian language tests' reliability and comparability.

This paper reports on the third phase of the project in which the main objective was to investigate the extent to which the written interaction tasks of the two selected Italian language tests and the ministerial assessment criteria could be considered valid and reliable.

This section discusses the four stages of the method used for the third phase. The organisation and development of each stage was guided by the following research: Bacha 2001, Fulcher and Reiter 2003, Huot 1990, Kroll 1998, Lumley 2002, Lumley and McNamara 1995, Sawaki 2007, Shohamy, Gordon and Kraemer 1992, Wang 2010, Weigle 2002, Wu and Ma 2013.

Stage 1: Familiarisation

This stage is focused on *Familiarisation* through reading the CEFR descriptors (Council of Europe 2001:83–84) of *Overall Written Interaction* and the *ministerial guidelines*, particularly in reference to the section containing the Written Interaction test specifications.

During the familiarisation session, raters were introduced to the potential test takers' profile and language needs, to the test design and to the ministerial assessment criteria.

Stage 2: Task analysis

This stage involved the analysis of the two selected tasks. The raters were asked to indicate for each task:

- *Level of clarity* (i.e. how clear or unambiguous each task is)
    0. Totally unclear
    1. Slightly unclear
    2. Clear
    3. Absolutely clear
- *Level of appropriateness* (i.e. how appropriate the task is to the CEFR Level A2)
    0. Absolutely inappropriate
    1. Slightly inappropriate
    2. Appropriate
    3. Absolutely appropriate
- *Level of relevance to the test taker*
    0. Not at all relevant
    1. Slightly relevant
    2. Relevant
    3. Very relevant

Table 5 shows an example of a rater sheet for Written Interaction Test 1.

Table 5 Stage 2 – Rater sheet Test 1

Test 1			
Clarity	0	1	2	3
Appropriateness	0	1	2	3
Relevance to the test taker	0	1	2	3

Stage 3: Rating process

The third stage focused on the rating process based on the assessment grids provided by the Ministry of Education. Raters were asked to insert their comments and explanations, in order to help the researcher detect which factors (i.e. grammatical correctness, lexical richness, interference, punctuation, effective communication) had an impact on the assignment of their marks (in a positive or negative way).

Stage 4: Validity of scoring procedures

In this final stage, raters were asked to indicate the appropriacy of the assessment criteria in reference to the criterion and the construct of the test. At this point, the aim was to have the raters reflect, after their rating activity, on the assessment tool they used, taking into consideration the difficulties or the choices they made when faced with the Ministry's holistic assessment scale (see Table 6).

Table 6 Stage 4 – Rater sheet

Do the assessment criteria proposed by the Ministerial Handbook accurately reflect the test criterion and test construct?	0	1	2	3

Findings and discussion

Results from Stage 2 and 3 are presented, followed by a discussion and final considerations.

Stage 2: Task analysis

In order to analyse the two tasks, Table 7 reports the *mode* of the rater responses.

Table 7 Stage 2 – Frequencies (mode)

Mode	Clarity	Appropriateness	Relevance
Task – Test 1	2	2	3
Task – Test 2	0	2	2

The outcome of this analysis shows a slight difference between the two tasks, which can be summarised as follows:

- Task 1: clear, appropriate and very relevant to the test takers
- Task 2: totally unclear, but appropriate and slightly relevant to the test takers.

The criteria selected (i.e. *clarity, appropriateness, relevance*) allow us to investigate the adequacy and compliance of the two selected Written Interaction tests for their specific purpose (Weigle 2002:40).The outcome of the task analysis gave first partial confirmation of the different level of complexity of the two selected tests, in terms of alignment with the intended CEFR level of the test and to the main purpose of the assessment itself.

Stage 3: Rating process

Table 8 shows some examples of test takers' performances on the Written Interaction tests. Data was gathered within eight months of administration from April to November 2013 in 12 classes of Italian as a second language.

Table 8 Examples of written interaction performances

Written Interaction Test 1 – Candidate 07	
Chiede di lavorare come	*Commesa*
You ask to work as a	Saleswoman
Spiega perché	*perché ho già lavorado in passato como commesa in un negozio di abbigliamento. Per tanto tempo credo di aver la speriencia per il posto.*
Please explain why	because I previously worked as a saleswoman in a clothing store for so long. I think I have the experience for this job.

Written Interaction Test 2 – Candidate 09	
Mercato	*Celine te scrivo questo messaggio x andare il mercoledì al mercato per comprare abigliamenti de questa temporada, anche puoi dire a tua sorella Vilma. Te saluto y aspetto tu messaggio. Civediamo verso le 9.00 am. Baci. Maribel*
Market	Celine I am writing this message to ask you to go to the market on Wednesday to buy clothing for this season. Tell also your sister Vilma. Bye. I wait for your message. See you at about 9.00 am. Kisses. Maribel

To have an overall idea of the judgements the raters gave, the *mean, mode, standard deviation, range, minimum* and *maximum value* were calculated and reported in Table 9.

Table 9 Stage 3 – Rating process (Statistics)

	Written Interaction Test 1	Written Interaction Test 2
Valid	20	20
Missing	0	0
Mean	29.80	29.25
Mode	27	29
Std. deviation	2.707	3.810
Range	10	16
Minimum	24	18
Maximum	34	34

The following measures of central tendencies are important:

- *Mean*: the mean value is around 29 out of 35 points for both of the tasks.
- *Standard deviation*: the standard deviation in the ratings of Test 1 show more similar scores and more clustered scores around the mean (29.80). On the contrary, for Test 2, the standard deviation shows the test scores are more widely spread both above and below the mean (Green 2013).

- *Range*: for both tasks the range is very low, particularly for Test 1 (10). This means that the assignment of marks covers only the highest third of the ministerial scale (Weir, Chan and Nakatsuhara 2013). This observation is further underlined by the *minimum and maximum values*, i. e. that only the upper third of the 35-point scale was applied, but no rater awarded the maximum score.

In order to analyse the consistency of the scores given by different raters, inter-rater reliability was calculated. It shows that one-third of the correlations (16 out of 55) is .7 or higher, i.e. good in both assessment cases (Green 2013).

Stage 4: Validity of scoring procedures

All 11 raters considered the assessment scales to be *slightly acceptable*. This is highlighted by three of the most meaningful comments that were collected:

- 'The main difficulty I found in a scale of this kind (0–35 marks) was the choice of the appropriate score. It seems ambiguous and at the end there is the risk of choosing a score by chance' (Rater 7).
- 'The assessment criteria of the Ministry of Education seem to me very little detailed and lend themselves to multiple interpretations. An assessment scale from 0 to 28 is very vague' (Rater 9).
- 'The assessment criteria of the Ministry of Education are not adequate; the margins are very wide and leave room for subjective judgements. It lacks a valid grid to be followed' (Rater 10).

The group of experts involved includes raters with a familiarity and experience with assessment grids of a different type, i.e. namely *analytical*, in which the reflection, being drawn from judgements, focuses on individual aspects of competence and not on global observations of the performance (Shohamy et al 1992:27). The analyses run so far suggest that the raters' *professional background* may be impacting their attitudes towards the scale and their rating behaviour (Shohamy et al 1992:28).

The lack of consistency in the rating process can be attributed to the holistic nature of the Ministry scale, particularly to the brevity and vagueness of the descriptors that are a challenge for the raters to interpret because they give ample space for subjectivity and variability in judgements (Brown 2000, 2006). Our observations are in line with other studies (Bauer 1981, Cast 1939), which focused on the reliability of assessment grids, where analytical frameworks are likely to be more reliable than holistic frameworks, regardless of any initial training. The results indicate that raters may be applying the rating scale in slightly different ways. That is the application of the assessment criteria is ultimately dependent on how raters interpret them, in spite of the preliminary training process of familiarisation.

Final considerations

As we have seen, the study adopted both qualitative and quantitative methods. Results obtained by both analyses show that the vagueness and the brevity of the performance descriptors included in the official assessment grids are problematic for making consistent judgements and may have pushed raters to go beyond the grids and rely on their expertise and previous experience in order to reach their judgements (Shohamy et al 1992, Wu et al 2013). Secondly, the inappropriacy of the ministerial assessment criteria is confirmed, on the one hand, by the trend of the raters to interpret and apply the assessment criteria differently; as well as by the use of other criteria, supplementary to the ministerial ones (Wang 2010, Wu et al 2013). The noticed lack of reliability refers mainly to those aspects concerning the rating consistency, therefore, there is, firstly, a differentiated interpretation of the criteria and, secondly, the inclusion of 'alternative' criteria to those specified in the ministerial grids (Brown 2006, Weigle 2002).

Moreover, this suggests that the rating scale does not address all the factors that influence raters' decisions (Wu et al 2013) and does not reflect the criterion and the construct that the test intends to measure.

The research hypotheses are confirmed in the last part of the rater sheet, where raters were asked to indicate the appropriacy of the assessment criteria (Stage 4). The findings can be summarised in the following comments, which suggest the need for a revision of the procedures, particularly with regard to the assessment criteria, in order to improve *scoring validity* (Wu et al 2013):

- 'the message is not completely effective'
- 'I find it very difficult to attribute a score with those parameters, since it does not refer to . . . efficacy, but only to the completeness of the information'
- 'I choose this mark because the effectiveness is not good due to a wrong grammar'
- 'the message is clear'
- 'lack of effective communication'
- 'the production is not very effective'.

As demonstrated by the alignment to the CEFR descriptors (see Section 3: Written Interaction test), the assessment criteria in use in the Italian context tend to impose homogeneous criteria of *consistency* and *correctness*. As Shohamy (2007b:124) highlighted, tests which are used as part of language policy 'deliver a message that languages are uniform, standard and follow the same written norms', and this hardly fits in the emergent nature of social interaction in a multi/plurilingual society.

Consequently, as Barni stated (2014:44), 'this implies a potential mis-recognition or under-recognition of 'competence' in actual communication in a rapidly changing communication and language landscape, and a consequent call for a new validity framework in language tests'.

In conclusion, the Italian case study, which at the time of writing was still being analysed, confirms that once competence standards are established, they can constitute an instrument of power that can easily be incorporated into laws and have inevitable impact on language and social policies (Shohamy 2001). This has happened with the CEFR and its descriptors of language competence, which have become the most important standard for assessing the language proficiency of migrants, despite the fact that they were never intended for this specific purpose.

As suggested by Barni (2014:51), 'a deeper reflection on the concept of plurilingual competence and on individual patterns of language acquisition and learning is now needed, and the approach which is only sketched out in the CEFR itself should be a starting point for further development'.

Notes

1. *VADEMECUM (ai sensi della nota n. 8571 del 16 Dicembre 2010 del Ministero dell'Interno). Indicazioni tecnico-operative per la definizione dei contenuti delle prove che compongono il test, criteri di assegnazione del punteggio e durata del test.* Direzione Generale dell'Istruzione e Formazione Tecnica Superiore e per i rapporti con i sistemi formativi delle Regioni-Ufficio IV.

References

Bacha, N (2001) Writing evaluation: what can analytic versus holistic essay scoring tell us? *System* 29, 371–83.

Barni, M (2014) In the name of the CEFR: individuals and standards, in Spolsky, B, Inbar-Lourie, O and Tannenbaum, M (Ed) *Challenges for Language Education and Policies*, New York: Routledge, 41–51.

Bauer, B A (1981) *A study of the reliabilities and cost-efficiencies of three methods of assessment for writing ability*, ERIC Document Reproduction Service No. Ed. 216 357, Champaign: University of Illinois.

Bettoni, C (2001) *Imparare un'altra lingua. Lezioni di linguistica applicata*, Roma-Bari: Laterza.

Blackledge, A and Wright, S (2001) *Testing for citizenship: why tests and why not?* paper presented at Communicating European Citizenship, London, Lancaster House, 22 March 2010.

Blommaert, J, Leppänen, S and Spotti, M (2012) Endangering Multilingualism, in Blommaert, J, Leppänen, S, Pahta, P and Räisänen, T (Eds) *Dangerous Multilingualism: Northern Perspectives on Order, Purity and Normality*, Basingstoke: Palgrave Macmillan, 1–21.

Brown, A (2000) An investigation of the rating process in the IELTS Oral interview, in Tulloh, R (Ed) *IELTS Research Reports Volume 3*, Canberra: IELTS Australia, 49–85.

Brown, A (2006) An examination of the rating process in the revised IELTS Speaking test, in McGovern, P and Walsh, S (Eds) *IELTS Research Reports Volume 6*, Canberra: IELTS Australia, 1–30.

Cast, B M J (1939) The efficiency of different methods of marking English composition, *British Journal of Educational Psychology* 9 (1), 257–269.

Council of Europe (2001) *Common European Framework of Reference for Languages: Learning, Teaching, Assessment*, Cambridge: Cambridge University Press.

Extra, G and Spotti, M (2009) Language, migration and citizenship: A case study on testing regimes in the Netherlands, in Hogan-Brun, G, Mar-Molinero, C and Stevenson, P (Eds) *Discourses on language and integration: Critical perspectives on language testing regimes in Europe*, Amsterdam: John Benjamins, 61–82.

Extra, G, Spotti, M and Van Avermaet, P (Eds) (2009a) *Language Testing, Migration and Citizenship: Cross-national Perspectives on Integration Regimes*, London/New York: Continuum Press.

Extra, G, Spotti, M and Van Avermaet, P (2009b) Testing regimes for newcomers, in Extra, G, Spotti, M and Van Avermaet, P (Eds) *Language Testing, Migration and Citizenship: Cross-national Perspectives on Integration Regimes*, London/New York: Continuum Press, 3–33.

Fulcher, G and Reiter, M R (2003) Task difficulty in speaking tests, *Language Testing* 20 (3), 321–44.

Green, R (2013) *Statistical Analyses for Language Testers*, London: Palgrave Macmillan.

Hogan-Brun, G, Mar-Molinero, C and Stevenson, P (Eds) (2009) *Discourse on language and integration*, Amsterdam: John Benjamins Publishing Company.

Horner, K (2009) Language, citizenship and Europeanization, in Hogan-Brun, G, Mar-Molinero, C and Stevenson, P (Eds) *Discourse on language and integration*, Amsterdam: John Benjamins Publishing Company, 109–128.

Huot, B (1990) Reliability, validity, and holistic scoring: What we know and what we need to know, *College Composition and Communication* 4 (2), 201–213.

Kroll, B (1998) Assessing writing abilities, *Annual Review of Applied Linguistics* 18, 219–40.

Krumm, H-J (2007) Profiles instead of levels: the CEFR and its (ab)uses in the context of migration, *The Modern Language Journal* 91 (4), 667–669.

Little, D (2008) *The Linguistic Integration of Adult Migrants, Intergovernmental Seminar 2008*, Strasbourg: Council of Europe.

Lumley, T (2002) Assessment criteria in a large-scale writing test: What do they really mean to the raters? *Language Testing* 19 (3), 246–76.

Lumley, T and McNamara, T (1995) Rater characteristics and rater bias: Implications for training, *Language Testing* 12 (1), 54–71.

Mar-Molinero, C and Stevenson, P (2006) *Language Ideologies, Policies and Practices: the Future of Language in Europe*, Basingstoke: Palgrave Macmillan.

McNamara, T (1998) Policy and social consideration in language assessment, *Annual Review of Applied Linguistics* 18, 304–319.

McNamara, T (2005) 21st century shibboleth: language tests, identity and intergroup conflict, *Language Policy* 4, 1–20.

McNamara, T (2011) Managing learning: authority and language assessment, *Language Teaching* 44 (4), 500–515.

Pochon-Berger, E and Lenz, P (2014) *Language Requirements and Language Testing for Immigration and Integration Purposes. A Synthesis of Academic Literature*, Fribourg: Institute of Multilingualism.

Saville, N (2009) Language Assessment in the management of international migration: a framework for considering the issue, *Language Assessment Quarterly* 6, 17–29.

Sawaki, Y (2007) Construct validation of analytic rating scales in a speaking assessment: Reporting a score profile and a composite, *Language Testing* 24, 355–390.

Shohamy, E (1997) Testing methods, testing consequences: are they ethical? Are they fair? *Language Testing* 14 (3), 340–349.

Shohamy, E (2001) *The Power of Tests: A Critical Perspective on the Uses of Language Tests*, London: Longman.

Shohamy, E (2006) *Language Policy: Hidden Agendas and New Approaches*, New York: Routledge.

Shohamy, E (2007a) Tests as power tools: Looking back, looking forward, in Fox, J, Wesche, M and Bayliss, D (Eds), *Language Testing Reconsidered*, Ottawa: University of Ottawa, 141–152.

Shohamy, E (2007b) Language tests as language policy tools, *Assessment in Education* 14 (1), 117–130.

Shohamy, E (2009) Language tests for immigrants: Why language? Why tests? Why citizenship? in Hogan-Brun, G, Mar-Molinero, C and Stevenson, P (Eds) *Discourse on language and integration*, Amsterdam: John Benjamins Publishing Company.

Shohamy, E, Gordon, C M and Kraemer, R (1992) The effect of raters' background and training on the reliability of direct writing tests, *Modern Language Journal* 76 (1), 27–33.

Spolsky, B (1997) The ethics of gatekeeping tests: What have we learned in a hundred years? *Language Testing* 14 (3), 242–247.

Spotti, M (2011) Ideologies of success for superdiverse citizens: The Dutch testing regime for integration and the online private sector, in Blommaert, J, Rampton, B and Spotti, M (Eds) *Language and Superdiversity – Special issue, "Diversities"* 13 (2), 39–52.

Thalgott, P (2010) Council of Europe: The linguistic integration of adult migrants, in ALTE and Centro Valutazione Certificazioni Linguistiche – CVCL – Università per Stranieri di Perugia (Ed) *Valutazione Linguistica ed Integrazione nel contesto italiano: Atti del Convegno LAMI. Language assessment for integration in the Italian contexts: Proceedings*, Roma, 10–15.

Van Avermaet, P (2009) Fortress in Europe? in Hogan-Brun, G, Mar-Molinero, C and Stevenson, P (Eds) (2009) *Discourse on Language and Integration*, Amsterdam: John Benjamins Publishing Company, 15–44.

Van Avermaet, P (2010) Language assessment and access. A climate change, in ALTE and Centro Valutazione Certificazioni Linguistiche Università per Stranieri di Perugia (Ed) *Valutazione Linguistica ed Integrazione nel contesto italiano: Atti del Convegno LAMI. Language assessment for integration in the Italian contexts: Proceedings*, Centro Valutazione Certificazioni Linguistiche Università per Stranieri di Perugia: Rome, 16–24.

Vertovec, S (2006) *The Emergence of Super-diversity in Britain*, Working Paper 25, Oxford: University of Oxford.

Wang, B (2010) On rater agreement and rater training, *English Language Teaching* 3 (1), 108–113.

Weigle, S C (2002) *Assessing Writing*, Cambridge: Cambridge University Press.

Weir, C J and Wu, J (2006) Establishing test form and individual task comparability: A case study of a semi-direct speaking test, *Language Testing* 23 (2), 167–197.

Weir, C J, Chan, S H C and Nakatsuhara, F (2013) *Examining the criterion-related validity of the GEPT advanced reading and writing tests: Comparing GEPT with IELTS and real-life academic performance*, LTTC-GEPT Research Report RG-01.

Wu, J and Ma, M (2013) *Investigating rating processes in an EAP Writing Test: Insights into scoring validity*, paper presented at the 35th Annual Language Testing Research Colloquium, Seoul, Korea.

11 Migrant associations get involved: Non-formal education and learning Portuguese as a host language

Catarina Gaspar
University of Lisbon

Maria José Grosso
University of Macau

Heinz-Peter Gerhardt
Technical Federal University of Public Administration

Abstract

Portugal is traditionally a country of massive emigration, but during the past 40 years it has become a prime destination for migrants from other countries. Recently, the migration policy of this small southern European country, particularly its educational efforts, has been recognised as an award-winning standard for receiving migrants (MIPEX III 2011).

We report on a non-formal education (NFE) project administered by the state-run High Commission for Intercultural Dialogue and Immigration (*Alto Comissariado para a Imigração e Diálogo Intercultural*, ACIDI) in collaboration with researchers from the Post-Graduate Programme in Portuguese as a Foreign Language/Second Language at the University of Lisbon (FLUL, Faculty of Arts). In this project, migrant associations were given the financial and logistical support needed to provide their members with Portuguese language courses that led to the A2 level examination. Our analysis focuses on the courses for adults offered by four migrant associations. We discuss how the self-organised nature of this NFE educational enterprise, the relatively homogeneous language background of the participants and the relatively non-hierarchical supervisory style of the funding agency contributed to the project's outcome. We conclude that standardised formal examinations may not be the most appropriate method for determining the success of learning and teaching Portuguese as a host language to this audience.

Introduction

Since its return to democratic rule in 1974, Portugal has become a country of immigration. In 2013, there were 894,000 immigrants living in Portugal (8.1% of the total population, see UN Population Division 2014), only half of them with resident status (see Figure 1). These changes have generated a change in immigration policies, which aim for an appropriate response to the ever-changing Portuguese human and social landscape.

According to the Migrant Integration Index III[1] (MIPEX III 2011), Portugal is one of the countries 'that [has] made the biggest effort in assuring the right to long term residency [for migrants] (2007 Immigration Law) and in responding specifically to the immigrant labour situation' (MIPEX III 2011:26). In the same report, Portugal is also identified as one of the countries with the 'best educational policies towards migrants, political participation opportunities and anti-discrimination laws', along with school admittance and intercultural education (MIPEX III 2011:27). The educational policies mentioned here are associated with the work done to recognise and validate competences through the *Programa Novas Oportunidades* and with the *Português para Todos* (PPT) programme, which is under the auspices and co-ordination of the High Commission for Intercultural Dialogue and

Figure 1 Total foreign population with legal residency status: All nationalities (PORDATA 2014)

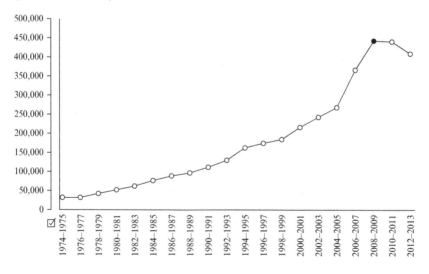

Immigration (*Alto Comissariado para a Imigração e Diálogo Intercultural*, ACIDI), now *Alto Comissariado para as Migrações* (ACM).

ACIDI's pioneering PPT programme focuses on teaching Portuguese as a host language and as a language for integration (Grosso, Tavares and Tavares 2008, Grosso 2010). The courses in the PPT programme are offered in formal educational settings in Portugal, such as schools and professional education centres. Enrolment in these courses is free and students who complete the course earn a qualification certificate that is equivalent to the *Certificado Inicial de Língua Portuguesa* (CIPLE), which is a Portuguese qualification at the A2 level of the Common European Framework of Reference for Languages (CEFR, Council of Europe 2001). This A2 level certificate can be used instead of the CIPLE certificate as proof of knowledge of the Portuguese language when applying for Portuguese nationality (Portaria nº 1262/2009 de 15 de Outubro, alterada pela Portaria nº 216-B/2012, de 18 de Julho). Although the PPT programme courses are easily accessed, some groups have nevertheless stayed away, usually due to a lack of time or anxiety associated with formal educational settings (Malheiros and Esteves 2013:168–170).

Within the framework of the ACIDI Programme supporting the forming of immigrant associations (*Programa de Apoio ao Associativismo Imigrante*, PAAI), we designed an experimental programme to reach this 'non-captive public'. The experiment provided this group with a more flexible, attractive programme for learning Portuguese that had non-formal education (NFE) features. The involvement of the immigrant associations added value, as they work closely with the immigrant communities. The following five immigrant associations[2], primarily from the Lisbon area, Setúbal or from the Algarve in the south, were chosen to participate in the project:

- AITMMM: *Associação 'A comunidade islâmica da Tapada das Mercês e Mem Martins'* (Tapada das Mercês, Mem-Martins, Sintra) – mostly sub-Saharan African clients
- AMRT: *Associação de Melhoramentos e Recreativo do Talude* (Bairro do Catujal, Unhos, Loures) – mostly sub-Saharan African clients
- AUCQM: *Associação Unida e Cultural da Quinta do Mocho* (Quinta do Mocho, Sacavém) – mostly Cape-Verdian and sub-Saharan African clients
- DOINA: *Associação dos Imigrantes Romenos e Moldavos do Algarve* (Almancil, Loulé) – mostly Romanian and Moldavian clients
- FRATIA: *Associação dos Imigrantes Romenos e Moldavos* (Setúbal) – mostly Romanian and Moldavian clients.

These associations provide legal advice, social services and educational support to their communities. Their work fosters immigrants' integration into the relevant geographical group of origin and into Portuguese society.

Non-formal education

Since the 1970s, UNESCO has played a key role in shaping and disseminating policies for adult education and the idea of lifelong learning. This organisation within the UN System has been instrumental in promoting adult learning and education, which has been, and still is, a chronically neglected and under-prioritised policy area.

The concept of NFE was developed in the 1960s and 1970s, mainly in Latin America, to describe educational developments outside the formal school system. It had become clear by then that education and schooling are not synonymous.

By 1963, Paulo Freire was already pointing out that everyone has attended the 'school of life' (Gerhardt 2013:655) and that everyone is learned or schooled. Thus, educators 'only' have to observe the would-be participants and 'tune in' to the universe of the participants' vocabulary and life situations. The first step in teaching adult literacy, therefore, is an arduous search for participants' generative words and themes – topics that 'generate' others – that takes place at two levels: syllabic richness and a high degree of experiential involvement of this unit of a given language. These key words, e.g. well, bicycle, work (Freire 1974/2013:79), are codified into visual images, which stimulate people 'submerged' in the culture of silence to 'emerge' as conscious makers of their own culture and history. This approach, referred to as the 'anthropological concept of culture', regards men and women as 'producers of culture and therefore, producers of history' (Freire 1974/2013:45), and gives the illiterate pride in what they have learned in the 'school of life'. The next step is the decoding – the process of discussing and assimilating creatively – of the generative words and themes within a 'culture circle' – the classroom – under the self-effacing stimuli of a co-ordinator who is no longer a 'teacher' in the conventional sense, i.e. not a formal system educator who treats students as passive recipients of knowledge. This co-ordinator has become an educator–educatee in dialogue with his students – in the conceptualisation of Freire, the educatee–educators (Goulet 2013:8). The latter contribute their worldview and competencies to the decoding task. A mutual learning–teaching process begins. New codifications may arise, which are often critical of the participants' former circumstances and views. These might encourage actions that use the newly learned competencies, such as reading and writing the host country's language, agricultural skills and IT skills. People who were formerly 'illiterate' in some spheres of their life begin to reject their role as mere 'objects' in history and society. They undertake to become 'subjects' of their own destiny. Proud of their new competencies, they take their place in the labour market and potentially participate more in society (Gerhardt 1993/2000:6).

The global Freirean legacy and the need to educate and train wider segments of modern societies stimulated discussions within UNESCO about Lifelong or Permanent Education and the limits of educational conceptualisations that are based solely on formal schooling at the primary, secondary or tertiary level. In 1974, Coombs and Ahmed defined non-formal education (NFE) as any educational activity organised outside the established formal educational system, with a defined learning clientele in mind and certain mutually agreed upon objectives. The distinction is a mere administrative one: formal education occurs in schools and training institutions; non-formal education involves community groups and other organisations. Very often, there are more developmental objectives in non-formal projects (e.g. agriculture, health, energy, population growth, nutrition), but at the same time many issues are akin to the 'normal' school curricula. Educational goals have been an explicit part of NFE projects from their very beginning, especially educational goals that the formal system has difficulty addressing (e.g. literacy, educating women, an ever-increasing drop-out population, school–labour market transition, integration of migrants and refugees). Any organised structured educational enterprise directed at a predefined target group with certain learning ambitions is considered an NFE project. These projects address a student population that is no longer regularly registered in, or has never managed to enter, a formal education system (Hamadache 1993).

Non-formal education today

Today the demarcations between formal and non-formal education are fading. NFE is still seen as an alternative or supplement to formal education, although in some countries it has already been institutionalised (Thailand's NFE and Informal Education Act of 2008; South Korea's Lifelong Learning Account System of 2011). UNESCO (2006) points to the fact that NFE is usually more flexible and innovative in its approach to education, and therefore better able to serve the needs of disadvantaged students. It may allow individuals to take more control and ownership of their education and is frequently better able to help individuals connect learning with their lives and previous knowledge, their informal learning history. The purpose of our research project is to investigate whether this is the case for non-formal education programmes run by migrant associations. We illustrate the wide variation in the use and significance of key terms in adult education, such as functional literacy, non-formal and informal education and lifelong learning.

We offer our definitions of these debated terms (see Figure 2) and discuss their theoretical underpinnings. We then use these terms and draw upon our particular fields of expertise to investigate an NFE project for migrants in Portugal.

NFE today provides educational services to a wide variety of people and

Figure 2 Interactions between formal, non-formal and informal education and learning

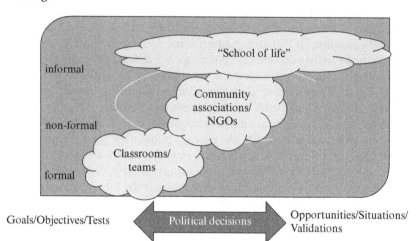

groups who seek a greater degree of autonomy in their learning endeavours and/or shun formal settings due to the former or current inadequate responses of the system to their learning needs. NFE is not necessarily associated with poverty or 'latecomers' to formal schooling. The internet, blended learning and Web 2.0 are some of the learning venues into which NFE is moving. NFE is a home for innovation and an experimental testing ground that the formal system typically shuns, yet benefits from.

When an NFE project ends, the participants usually do not receive a title or certificate, and the organisations involved usually do not receive a reward. Instead, the learners decide for themselves whether a certain goal has been reached. The educators involved can only be sure that they have had the desired 'developmental impact' (Ahmed 1990) if the funding body involved continues the project or invests in a similar one.

NFE projects derive much of their legitimacy from their voluntary nature. Participation in NFE is never meant to be compulsory and the instructional methods, content and evaluation schemes work because they are neither formalised nor standardised, but are instead adapted to individual learners' needs within particular target groups. If funding bodies and/or ministries start to emphasise the formalisation and standardisation of NFE and align it strictly with educational and economic demands, then the very advantages of NFE disappear (UNESCO 2006:93). The same body (2006:94) thus argues that NFE should be clearly separated from the formal sector when it comes to qualifications and validation schemes. Other frameworks should be developed and welcomed. As NFE settings are participatory and instructional methods are highly individualised, the validation procedures need to reflect these principles and procedures.

Evaluation of NFE

Due to the often highly political and social character of NFE projects, particularly in the field of migrant workers and refugee education, some form of evaluation is required. The formal system is full of examples for the assessment of learning outcomes. As the criteria for designing evaluations are typically set by the organising educational authority, or even by political bodies, there is a clear preference for the established formal schemes. Academic work on the formal sector is often used to streamline the internal processes and content criteria of the non-formal sector. NFE stakeholders are consulted and included in the formative and summative assessment procedures. Thus, the varied objectives of NFE projects make it difficult to implement a one-size-fits-all approach to learning outcome assessment and programme evaluation.

As Rogers (2005:164–165) pointed out, the appropriate evaluation of an NFE project depends on the balance between the educational and developmental goals that the project set out to affect. An evaluation can be conducted through formalised learning tests (by measuring an individual's achievement in learning retention) and/or through an impact assessment (e.g. by evaluating the trained group's use of the learned material to deal with health, agricultural or administrative problems). In the field of migrant worker and refugee education, it is time to move on from the still-dominant preoccupation with integrating people into the formal schooling system, with its focus on continuing education and constant testing, towards integration into a more informal system. Such informal integration would allow confirmation and use of migrants' existing skills and knowledge that are needed for them to actively participate in the community of the host country. The reprocessing and repackaging of culturally and locally relevant knowledge into examination questions can be a first step in this direction (Rogers 2005:164–165). Validation schemes and equivalence tests are the necessary second and third.

The literature shows that NFE in general demands a qualitative approach to assessment and evaluation. However, money or time constraints and a lack of know-how make developing qualitative frameworks challenging for educators and organisers. Hamadache's (1993:29) urgent plea for the training of polyvalent teachers, who are able to teach children and adults in and out of school settings, has not yet been answered. Furthermore, we still do not have a code of conduct for educators and organisers of NFE projects that differs from the code for educators in the formal system. We are a long way from developing polyvalent teachers or providing teacher training specifically for non-formal educators. Yet those involved in non-formal education have significantly different needs in areas such as the development of the curriculum and the integration of adults' and out-of-school adolescents' former life experiences – their informal learning history – into the 'classroom' (Hamadache 1993:31).

This brief review of the NFE literature points to two research questions that we aimed to address in our NFE project. To what extent is the world of the target group and its viewpoints present in classroom interactions? To what extent do the learners and teachers participate in these interactions?

Teaching Portuguese as a host language and for integration

The learning of a host language is a right that is consecrated in the European Social Charter (Council of Europe 1996). All members of the European Council are obliged to foster and facilitate immigrants in learning the national language of the host country. However, the way in which host countries welcome their immigrants is complex and depends on many factors, including the interactions between groups. Knowledge of the host language is one of the most important factors, which affects immigrants' level of integration and has consequences for finding employment, confirming residency and acquiring nationality. Those arriving need to be able to communicate and act autonomously in all social spheres, and in unfamiliar contexts.

The concepts of 'immigrant' and 'foreigner' are often used as synonyms, although they are two distinct concepts. The distinction between the immigrant and the foreigner is significant when teaching Portuguese as a foreign language or as a host language. Although foreigners and immigrants are both non-native speakers, their goals and motivations, and consequently the texts and study materials they need, are different. For example, the frameworks *O Utilizador Elementar no país de acolhimento (A2)* and *O Utilizador Independente no país de acolhimento (B1)* (Grosso et al 2008, 2009) are designed for the immigrant audience. They present themes, task suggestions, texts and grammar resources that are considered suitable for promoting immigrant integration into the Portuguese host context where these immigrants are now living and working.

The immigrant audience is highly heterogeneous in age, mother tongue, profession and education (Grosso 2010:67–68, Kluzer, Ferrari and Centeno 2010:7, Little 2012:6). Understanding the types of professional and linguistic know-how present within this heterogeneity is key to successfully teaching Portuguese as a host language. The motivation to take the A2 examination is also important because it encourages immigrants to enrol on a language course and to persevere with language learning. Identifying the target audience's communication needs in terms of written or oral comprehension/production is also relevant for deciding the instructional content of a course.

Effect of assessment

In the particular case of immigrant groups, the Association of Language Testers in Europe's special interest group, 'Language Assessment of Migration and Integration' (ALTE LAMI) (ALTE LAMI Authoring Group/Council of Europe 2008) stated that the issue of equity is of major importance, as it can result in citizenship rights being denied (Saville 2006:3). Being familiar with the specificities of immigrant groups, the authors were open to the possibility of other sorts of assessment, acknowledging that a test may not always be the best way to evaluate competence in a host language. Among the suggested alternatives is formative evaluation throughout the course.

The same ALTE LAMI Authoring Group/Council of Europe (2008:3) document discusses the advantages of using a more formative evaluation system. Separating assessment from the context in which real evaluations take place inhibits the candidates and does not allow them to show their real competence in the use of the language. Evaluations using tasks that mimic the true use of the language narrow the distance between what is asked for in the test and what is actually demanded in the immigrant's daily life in the host country. These more holistic assessments can focus on the student's ability to perform tasks and put less weight on the assessment of skills such as reading comprehension that may not be relevant to their daily lives.

The organising bodies in action: The ACIDI and the immigrant associations

This NFE experiment was supported by the ACIDI. Involving the immigrant associations allowed researchers to take advantage of their knowledge of the local social contexts in which they were based, their outreach work and their praxis concerning NFE and informal education projects. At least three of the five associations, among them AMRT and FRATIA, were involved in other educational projects supported by the ACIDI.

The associations implemented the NFE sessions themselves, including providing the classroom and materials, recruiting the teacher, publicising the course and selecting the participants. From the start of the project, the associations were informed that the ACIDI's goal was that at least 10 learners should successfully complete the A2 level examination provided by the Centre for the Evaluation of Portuguese as a Foreign Language. The A2 level examination was seen as an instrument to verify the effectiveness of the language teaching and learning and to evaluate the advantages and disadvantages of the NFE course.

The assessment at the end of the process aimed to answer some of the questions raised by the funding authorities. The authorities required concrete, reliable data, such as that obtained through examination results and the consequent certification of the learners. They also wanted to know how the NFE sessions could be turned into something useful for the participants. The sessions were useful, as the participants had the possibility of obtaining an official Level A2 certificate of their knowledge in the host language; immigrants are required by law to acquire the A2 level certificate or equivalent in the Portuguese language (Decreto-Lei n° 237-A/2016, de 14 de Dezembro, Decreto-Lei n.° 43/2013, de 1 de Abril). They also had the chance to develop their language knowledge and competence, allowing them to progress professionally, personally and socially in Portuguese society. As the sessions took place in the immigrant associations, outside the scope of formal education institutions, it was important to assure the quality of the training and to demand maximum commitment from the association leaders enrolled in the project.

Research questions

These issues give rise to our research questions on the teaching and learning of Portuguese as a host language. Were participants in the NFE sessions given enactment opportunities allied to their social practices (public, professional and private)? Was an effort made to predict the (daily) communication tasks of the target audience, as recommended by the CEFR (Council of Europe 2001:87)? Did the immigrant associations contribute to that goal? Was it possible, in these sessions, to identify the characteristics of the non-formal teaching and learning process, such as interaction, co-operative learning, differentiated methodology, and activities and tasks related to the experiences of the target audience? These questions were answered using data gathered during in-class observations of five NFE sessions in Associação de Melhoramentos e Recreativo do Talude (AMRT).

Methods

The qualitative field study approach (Erickson 1986, Geertz 1973) was the most appropriate method for organising the data. We used an ethnographic toolkit consisting of participant observations, in-depth interviews with learners, teachers and association leaders, document analysis and global project analysis.

We were also drawn to this procedure and transdisciplinary approach by our professional backgrounds. Two of the researchers have a background in administering and supervising language tests for citizenship and/or other reasons. One has been prominently involved in adapting the CEFR for Portuguese linguistic studies in general and to migrant populations in particular. One of the researchers is familiar with the international discussion of NFE, especially the Freirean contributions. This project was developed to involve post-graduate students of the MA course in Portuguese as a Foreign or Second Language in the Faculty of Arts, University of Lisbon. The project gave the students the opportunity to apply research methods in a real context. As can be seen below, the researchers co-operated with each other, discussed the materials used and collected data during different phases of the project.

Discussing the professional backgrounds of the acting research personnel is appropriate in a qualitative research project, as they are the primary instruments for data collection and analysis. Our data was mediated through us as human research instruments. We used continuous and repeated rounds of data collection, analysis, reflection and verification to counterbalance the human factor and to improve the reliability and validity of our data. The combination of the researchers' backgrounds and this qualitative research approach resulted in new insights into the practice and process of language acquisition and learning by migrants in their natural setting within a host language environment. This approach also allowed us to develop and analyse questionnaires under multiple realities and perspectives. Fieldwork was undertaken whenever possible to observe some of the NFE project sessions and activities, and to make contact with the participants, the educators and those in charge of the associations.

Triangulation

Triangulation was used to validate the data collected and to answer the research questions about the advantages and disadvantages of NFE in teaching and learning a host language to adult immigrants. As Lessard-Hébert, Goyette and Boutin (1994:75) pointed out, researchers often have a strong theoretical background but little realistic knowledge about what occurs in the field. Our research team thus visited the immigrant associations, and compared their previous ideas and theories with the reality of the NFE sessions. We ensured objectivity and overcame the problem of complicity between observer and observed by applying different methodological procedures and cross-analysing them. This ensured that the study had enough detachment and critical distance from the field to produce objective scientific data.

Assessment data was collected from four of the five immigrant associations, AMRT, FRATIA, DOINA and AUCQM. Due to time constraints, the research team could not visit all of the associations to observe classes, so it was decided to choose one as a case study. Therefore, in-class observations were collected only from AMRT, although visits were made to all of the associations.

Our toolkit

The research instruments consisted of a questionnaire and in-depth interviews. The questionnaire was adapted from the ALTE LAMI Questionnaire (www.lami-q.org) and the in-depth interview script was created by the research team members. The questionnaire was administered to all of the AMRT and FRATIA participants to determine their schooling and professional profiles, their reasons for attending the NFE course, their opinions about the course and their reasons for wishing to sit the A2 level examination. In-depth interviews were held with the teacher and seven AMRT participants to learn more about their life stories and their relationships outside the classroom. Participant observation was conducted in five classroom sessions at AMRT using an in-class observation sheet. This data was used to produce observation reports about the teaching and learning process and the relationships inside the classroom. Finally, we analysed the test results of a November 2013 A2 level examination session and compared them with the observed learning processes.

Findings: AMRT case study

The NFE sessions at AMRT took place in a small room in the association's main building. The classroom equipment was basic, consisting of a board and conference chairs with writing tables for all of the learners. The recruited teacher held a bachelor's degree and a post-graduate degree in Modern Languages and Literature (Portuguese Studies). She also had special training as a Portuguese as a Foreign Language teacher, through the national Recognition, Validation and Certification of Competences Programme. The NFE course was publicised by AMRT and its members in the borough of Bairro do Catujal and neighbouring boroughs.

The learners

The AMRT group mostly consisted of individuals from sub-Saharan Africa, some from the Portuguese-speaking African countries – PALOP (Angola, Guiné-Bissau and São Tomé e Príncipe) – and some from countries such as Senegal. One of the participants was from India. The AMRT group was linguistically and culturally diverse. Forty people initially applied to the course. Many of them left the course because they found employment or because they were accepted onto other kinds of courses that offered financial support. Eighteen learners completed the full course.

The teacher administered some diagnostic tasks at the beginning of the course to determine the learners' previous knowledge of the host language. The group was heterogeneous in terms of age, language, cultural and professional profiles. It was a low literacy group, as four of the learners were illiterate and the majority of them had attended school in their home country for four to nine years. The learners had difficulties in oral comprehension and in writing. In the first session the teacher realised that most of the learners could not understand what she was saying. To adjust to the learners' needs, she began with the A1 level course, rather than the A2 level.

The in-depth interviews with the teacher and the survey answers collected from the learners clearly showed that although the group was heterogeneous, it had enough common features for us to classify it as a homogeneous group for the purposes of this study. All of the learners had little schooling experience and their life stories in Portugal were similar, with many of them unemployed. Nine of the learners had arrived in the country one to three years previously, but some had just arrived (six months previously) and others had lived in Portugal for more than 10 years. Even those who had lived in Portugal for 10 years or more had a low communicative competence in the host language.

Inside the classroom, the researchers observed that the teacher was able to address different learning needs. Those who had learned French in their home country applied this knowledge to help them learn Portuguese. Although they were less proficient in reading and writing than in listening and speaking, the learners' language levels and skill profiles were similar. The majority of the class preferred listening and speaking tasks. This was closely related to the good interpersonal relationships and co-operation that developed between the learners and the teacher. These tasks (discussions, storytelling, reading aloud, enacting daily life scenes and formative evaluations) also brought their everyday life experiences into the classroom. The observed differences between reading/writing skills and listening/speaking skills were confirmed by the results reached in the A2 level test that will be discussed further.

Classroom interactions

In the six observed sessions, the subjects and themes raised were directly connected to the participants' life stories. This was confirmed in interviews with seven participants. During the sessions, the connection between the teacher and learners was relevant and perhaps had a direct influence on their comments about Portugal, its culture and language. We were able to identify concerns about learning and teaching Portuguese as a host language in the NFE sessions. A description of the sessions written by the researchers stated that the teacher made an effort to give the learners chances to improve their reading, writing, listening and speaking, although they were better at speaking and listening. Reading and writing tasks were performed, but with some difficulty. Although this group could be seen as an example of a homogeneous learning group, the test results showed that the variation in the immigrants' schooling experience in their home countries had an effect on individual learning outcomes.

Assessment practices in the project

The effect of assessment ('washback') on the teaching/learning of languages has been studied extensively, for example by Bailey (1999), Messick (1996), Alderson and Wall (1993) and others. We were particularly interested in observing whether the assessment in our NFE experimental project had a negative effect (as defined by Messick 1996:252), or whether it was positive in this context.

In the ACIDI project, the organisers largely borrowed evaluation features from the formal system, but included some evaluation features that acknowledged the unique features of NFE, such as learning outside a formal school setting and including content close to the everyday life of the target groups. The inclusion of the CEFR Level A2 certification test affected the process in three discrete ways: the teaching/learning process, the ACIDI's evaluation of the immigrant associations enrolled in this project and the test takers.

Most NFE courses do not include a foreign language test at the end of the programme. Instead, formative evaluations associated with competence validation are usually used in NFE courses. The test's existence in this programme was justified, in part, by the responsible authorities' requirements and by the wish of the associations' representatives. At an April 2013 ACIDI-sponsored workshop with educators and association representatives, it was observed that getting the candidates ready for the test was a major concern shared by all of the associations.

In the last two AMRT NFE sessions that the researchers attended, which were near the exam session date, the teacher gave more exercises and tasks that were similar to test tasks. There were also detailed explanations of the examination itself and the formal procedures that would be followed during the examination. Similarly, when the research team made its last visit to FRATIA, the A2 level examination session was the main topic. However, the members of this group had more schooling experience in their home countries. The learners and those in charge of the association discussed types of tasks and their previous examination experiences. Here, the learners' life stories gave them more confidence.

In the questionnaires, the participants at AMRT and FRATIA positively evaluated the NFE sessions. They recognised the courses as very useful in improving their knowledge of the Portuguese language and their social and cultural competences, although the last sessions were more focused on the examination, particularly on its difficulties and rules.

As stated previously, the main goal of the ACIDI was for 10 learners in this NFE project to pass the A2 level exam. Therefore, ACIDI decided to use the exam results to evaluate the effectiveness of the associations' programmes and to justify their funding and participation in future similar initiatives. Those in charge of the immigrant associations were affected by this decision in two ways. It affected their relationships with the teachers that they recruited, by creating expectations and by pressuring the teachers to produce good test results. It also affected their relationships with the participants, who relied on them for help to fulfil the administrative procedures associated with the exam.

As previously mentioned, the target group for Portuguese as a host language is, in general, heterogeneous. However, in this particular project, because the NFE sessions were organised by immigrant associations, the learning groups were more culturally and socially homogenous.

The FRATIA and DOINA groups were particularly homogenous, with most of the participants coming from a Moldavian or Romanian background. Most of the participants knew each other before the course and were part of the same local social networks. Most of the AMRT group were from sub-Saharan Africa, with one participant from India. Although the AMRT group was more diverse than some of the groups, the common African background meant that we could still consider this a homogenous group. The NFE sessions fostered closer relationships and social interactions that did not exist outside the classroom, except in the case of a few participants who were members of the same family. These cases known in AMRT, FRATIA and DOINA proved that the involvement of the immigrant associations produced more homogenous learning groups.

The test results

Only the November 2013 CIPLE test results of the participants in the NFE courses at FRATIA, DOINA, AMRT and AUCQM were considered in this analysis. The number of candidates from each association varied: 26 FRATIA participants, 19 DOINA participants, 14 AMRT participants and six AUCQM participants took the test. We therefore did not consider the number of candidates from each association who passed the test, as the result would be necessarily asymmetric. Instead, we considered the distribution of the participants along the 0–100 scale to find and compare the common trends and differences between the four groups. We first considered the most common scores (Figure 3).

In Figure 3a there is an evident concentration in the 41–55 range for the FRATIA group, corresponding to the lower limit for passing the test and obtaining the certificate. It is interesting to see that in the Moldavian and Romanian immigrants' association, DOINA, the results concentrated in the 71–90 range (Figure 3b). The differences in the results of the two associations were probably due to the number of participants in each session. The original demand for the FRATIA course was very high, leading to the organisation of two groups of more than 10–15 participants. A more stable, smaller group was organised at DOINA, which contributed to a more homogeneous collective evolution and learning environment, with better results.

In spite of the differences, a similarity can be found in the results of these two associations, showing that the teaching–learning process resulted in very positive progress in mastering the Portuguese language. These groups included Romanian speakers, which is a Romance language like Portuguese. Furthermore, most of the participants had completed a high level of schooling in their countries of origin, in clear contrast with the AMRT group.

Most of the AMRT candidates scored in the 21–40 range and the second largest group scored in the 41–55 range (Figure 3c). In AUCQM (Figure 3d), we observed similar results. This differentiates these groups from FRATIA and DOINA. The mother tongue of these candidates belonged to a different family of languages than Portuguese (African and Creole languages); those from countries where Portuguese is the official language whose first language was Creole with a Portuguese lexical base revealed little initial knowledge of the Portuguese language. We thus concluded that the distribution of results showed some progress in mastering the host language. The AMRT participants also had a few years of schooling in their countries of origin. This factor is of high relevance in explaining the results and the reactions to the test, as most of the AMRT participants had never been confronted with this

Figure 3 The distribution of test scores for participants from (a) FRATIA, (b) DOINA, (c) AMRT and (d) AUCQM

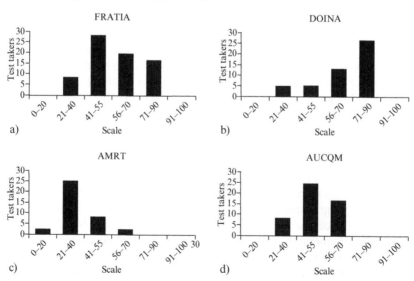

sort of evaluation before. Furthermore, their current professional activities or unemployment situations meant they had few opportunities to practise Portuguese in their daily lives. This was particularly reflected in some areas of the evaluation, as their partial results showed. Figure 4 shows the results of the individual CIPLE test components, reading, writing, listening and speaking.

It is interesting to observe that the reading and speaking scores show a contrasting pattern in Figures 4a, b and d, (the FRATIA, DOINA and AUCQM groups, respectively). Listening is the most stable component and has a central position. It is also interesting to note the patterns in speaking scores. Speaking reflects not only what is learned in the classroom but also the daily, immersive and informal use of the language, whereas written expression is generally used less outside the classroom. In all four associations, the writing results were mostly in the 41–60 range, but with a significant number in the 0–20 and 21–40 ranges. It is interesting that better mastery of writing was evident in DOINA, with corresponding reading scores in the 61–80 range. In contrast, the AMRT group, as shown in Figure 4c, struggled the most with writing. These results were consistent with the prior school attendance and socio-professional profiles of most of the participants in this group.

In general, speaking and reading scores were higher than writing scores.

Figure 4 The distribution of the test scores, broken down into the test components, for the participants from (a) FRATIA, (b) DOINA, (c) AMRT and (d) AUCQM

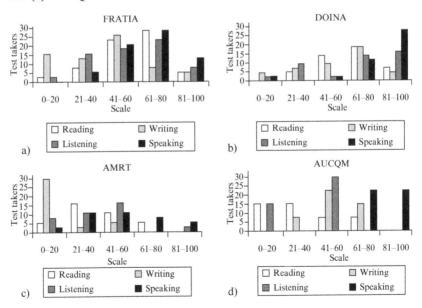

Although they live in a context of linguistic immersion in a welcoming country, immigrants make their living in a very restricted social environment, where the use of Portuguese language is not frequent and a certain level of isolation from Portuguese society is common. These facts are important in understanding the speaking results. Participants in the FRATIA, DOINA and AUCQM groups had overall high speaking scores, whereas the AMRT speaking scores were evenly distributed along the scale. Learning Portuguese in these non-NFE environments may have also helped the reading and listening scores (the 41–60 range), which was no doubt a very positive result.

Conclusions

NFE

We began by asking whether the 'world' of the target group was present in the five observed AMRT classroom interactions; the answer is 'very much so'. The migrants' home countries were less frequently discussed, ranging from 5% of the class time to a peak of 60% on 31 October 2013. The student observers noted that the current world of the target group, Portugal, and their view of it appeared in nearly 100% of the first three observed sessions. However, this dropped to 0% during the final sessions on 18 and 19 November, due to examination preparations. In these sessions neither the country of origin nor the host country was discussed.

We were also interested in the overall rate of class participation as measured by the protocols and internal discussions within the NFE groups. We found that learners' participation in classroom activities (discussions, storytelling, reading aloud, enacting daily life scenes and formative evaluations) were always somewhat higher than the teacher's participation.

Host language teaching and learning

Learning the host language on the premises of immigrant associations was an attractive, positive experience for this audience, which until then had stayed away from formal educational institutions offering language courses like the PPT. Learning the host language in a well-known place linked this educational experience to their socialising and fellowship in other activities. Thus, learning Portuguese also gave the participants an opportunity to share their experiences – fun, dutiful and difficult – related to their life in Portugal. Involving the immigrant associations brought a varying degree of commitment from the immigrant communities and their leaders to this learning project. A closer examination of this variation would help the broader success of this innovative NFE endeavour in host language courses for migrants in Portugal.

The results suggest that the language learning programme should include more sounds and images and more new technologies, and should include content related to the sociocultural aspects of the host country such as shopping, using public services or social and administrative interactions. Real-life materials can be used to generate tasks and exercises that are closer to real-life experiences. In-class observations showed that good interpersonal interactions between teachers and learners allowed the teacher to focus on the communicative needs of the learners. We also suggest a holistic survey of the socio-professional needs of immigrants to facilitate their integration into the host country, especially into the labour market.

We uncovered differences between reading, writing, listening and speaking competencies in this population. Future studies should rank these skills to determine what order they should be worked on and how they should be assessed. This may avoid the negative effect that tests have in this target group and lead to research on different ways of assessing host language knowledge.

General conclusions and suggestions

This NFE project was successful in attracting an immigrant audience that is not represented in formal educational courses. Despite a heterogeneous public and partial data set of only four immigrant associations, our qualitative research produced some important conclusions. The more complete teaching and learning data collected in the AMRT classes allowed us to understand that although the teachers avoided using more formal education procedures and integrated their clientele's former and actual 'school of life' experiences into the classroom, the pressure and need to obtain good results in the A2 level examination directly affected their teaching and the selection of activities undertaken in class. The teachers' work and the examination results were also affected by the formal and informal schooling experiences of the learners. We found that the immigrants' profiles often resulted in classrooms that were simultaneously homogeneous and heterogeneous depending on which criteria – age, sex, schooling level and cultural background – were used. This NFE experiment run by migrant associations allowed more homogeneous groups, especially with regard to their social and cultural backgrounds. Nonetheless, the teachers and learners required active, flexible attitudes to deal with the problems that arose from the remaining diversity.

The results achieved in the A2 level test allowed for a global evaluation of the candidates' Portuguese language knowledge. The use of this formal test in an NFE experiment, and the data associated with its evaluation, may be useful for a more complete and accurate understanding of the knowledge and skills acquired in the classroom.

Presenting the results along a numerical scale helped to build a clearer image of the audiences' profile and their progress in learning Portuguese.

Oral expression scores were higher than writing scores, which was consistent with what was demanded by the learners, some of whom could barely write, in the NFE classrooms that we observed. To avoid excluding anyone in the group, oral exercises and reading short texts aloud were used to allow all of them to progress in their learning.

Although lower results than expected were achieved in the A2 level CIPLE type test, the analysis of the observed NFE sessions showed that the majority of the AMRT learners reached the A2 level, according to the CEFR descriptions. The learners' actions, co-operation and interaction in tasks and exercises in the classroom suggested that they did acquire A2 level competence in the host language. Most of them could successfully speak, understand and, with some more difficulty, read and write. We conclude that there are differences between the formative assessment held during the NFE sessions and the results achieved in the examination, which we will expand on in a future publication.

It is important to highlight that many of the participants wished to take the test to be able to apply for Portuguese nationality and/or to improve their employability and working conditions. However, the opportunity to take the course and improve their Portuguese language competences was a strong motivation for this audience, regardless of the result achieved in the test.

Alternative assessment methods for this NFE project might have been helpful, and perhaps fairer, due to the heterogeneity in the immigrant groups, particularly in relation to their formal schooling experiences. For this NFE target audience, it would have been beneficial to have greater coherence between the test features and the learners' concrete language needs.

The use of the final test and the need for certification of a sufficient number of candidates is a good example of a multitasking evaluation in an educational project that attempts a one-size-fits-all approach. The choice of evaluation method affected the process, as the results of the evaluation were very important for the analysis of the project and for its stakeholders. It may also be an important element for overcoming negative public opinions of more qualitative and formative evaluation methods.

Notes

1. MIPEX measures integration policies in all European Union Member States plus Norway, Switzerland, Canada and the USA up to 31 May 2010. Using 148 policy indicators, MIPEX creates a rich, multi-dimensional picture of migrants' opportunities to participate in society by assessing governments' commitment to integration. By measuring policies and their implementation it reveals whether all residents are guaranteed equal rights, responsibilities and opportunities.
2. More information on the five associations is available at: AITMMM – acitm. wordpress.com; AMRT – www.amrtalude.org; AUCQM – redeuniva. acidi.gov.pt/index.php?option=com_contact&task=view&contact_

id=15&Itemid=47; DOINA - doinalgarve.com/?lang=pt; FRATIA - www.
fratia2004.blogspot.pt.

References

Ahmed, R (1990) *Developmental Impact of Rural Infrastructure*, Dhaka: Institute
of Developmental Studies.

Alderson, J C and Wall, D (1993) Does washback exist? *Applied Linguistics* 14
(2), 115–129.

ALTE LAMI Authoring Group/Council of Europe (2008) *Language Tests for
Social Cohesion and Citizenship – An Outline for Policymakers*, Strasbourg:
Council of Europe.

Bailey, K M (1999) *Washback in Language Testing*, Princeton: TOEFL
Monograph No. MS-15.

Council of Europe (2001) *Common European Framework of Reference for
Languages: Learning, Teaching, Assessment*, Cambridge: Cambridge
University Press.

Council of Europe (1996) *European Social Charter*, available online: www.coe.
int/en/web/conventions/full-list/-/conventions/treaty/163

Coombs, P and Ahmed, M (1974) *Attacking Rural Poverty. How Non-formal
Education Can Help*, Baltimore: John Hopkins University Press.

Erickson, F (1986) Qualitative methods in research on teaching, in Wittrock,
M C (Ed) *Handbook of Research on Teaching* (3rd edition), New York:
Macmillan, 119–161.

Freire, P (1974/2013) *Education for Critical Consciousness*, London: Bloomsbury
Academic.

Geertz, C (1973) Thick description: Toward an interpretive theory of culture, *The
Interpretation of Cultures: Selected Essays*, New York: Basic Books, 3–30.

Gerhardt, H P (1993/2000) Paulo Freire 1921–1979, *Prospects, the Quarterly
Review of Comparative Education* 22 (3/4), 439–458, available online: www.ibe.
unesco.org/publications/ThinkersPdf/freires.pdf

Gerhardt, H P (2013) Thematic reduction: A useful instrument for teaching as a
craft, *E-Curriculum* (11) 3, 651–683.

Goulet, D (2013) Introduction, in Freire, P (1974/2013) *Education for Critical
Consciousness*, London: Bloomsbury Academic, vii–xiii.

Grosso, M J (2010) Língua de acolhimento, língua de integração, *Horizontes de
Linguística Aplicada* 9 (2), 61–77.

Grosso, M J, Tavares, A and Tavares, M (2008) *O Português para falantes de
outras línguas. O Utilizador Elementar no país de acolhimento*, available online:
www.oi.acidi.gov.pt/docs/Seminario_LPIntegracao/3_Maria_Jose_Grosso.pdf

Grosso, M J, Tavares, A and Tavares, M (2009) *O Português para falantes de
outras línguas. O Utilizador Independente no país de acolhimento*, available
online: www.dge.mec.pt/sites/default/files/Basico/Documentos/referencial_
independente.pdf

Hamadache, A (1993) *Articulation de l'education formelle et non formelle.
Implications pour les enseignants*, available online: unesdoc.unesco.org/
images/0010/001001/100125f.pdf

Kluzer, S, Ferrari, A and Centeno, C (2010) *ICT for Learning the Host Country's
Language by Adult Migrants in the EU. Workshop Conclusions, Seville, 1–2
October 2009*, Luxembourg: Office for Official Publications of the European
Communities.

Lessard-Hébert, M, Goyette, G and Boutin, G (1994) *Investigação qualitativa. Fundamentos e práticas*, Lisboa: Instituto Piaget.

Little, D (2012) *The Linguistic Integration of Adult Migrants and the Common European Framework of Reference for Languages*, available online: www.coe. int/t/dg4/linguistic/Source/Little_CEFRmigrants_EN.doc

Malheiros, J M and Esteves, A (2013) *Diagnóstico da população imigrante em Portugal: desafios e potencialidades*, available online: www.oi.acidi.gov.pt/ docs/Col%20Portugal%20Imigrante/EstudoNacional_Web.pdf

Messick, S (1996) Validity and washback in language testing, *Language Testing* 13 (3), 241–256.

MIPEX III – Migrant Integration Policy. Index III Portugal (2011) Bruxelas: British Council – Migration Policy Group, available online: www.mipex.eu/ portugal

PORDATA (2014) *www.pordata.pt*, available online: www.pordata.pt/Portugal/ Ambiente+de+Consulta/Gráfico

Rogers, A (2005) *Non Formal Education. Flexible Schooling or Participatory Education*, Hong Kong: Comparative Education Research Centre University of Hong Kong/Springer Science and Business Media, Inc.

Saville, N (2006) Language testing for migration and citizenship, *Research Notes* 25, 2–4.

UN Population Division (2014) *International Migration Statistics*, available online: www.migrationpolicy.org/programs/data-hub/international-migration-statistics

UNESCO Section for Literacy and Non Formal Education (2006) *Synergies between Formal and Non Formal Education. An Overview of Good Practices*, Paris: UNESCO.

12 Getting to know the minimally competent person

Beate Zeidler
telc gGmbH

Abstract

Standard setting requires a common understanding of the standard, or minimum passing requirement of a test, that is shared between all members of a standard setting panel. Awareness of the difficulties involved in reaching a common understanding has developed gradually, in step with the progress of standard setting research. However, even though different stages of standard setting have been explored in numerous studies, comparatively little attention has been given to how a common notion of the target ability is reached. In this paper, a classification of methods is proposed to define target ability. Two perspectives used to define target ability are identified, and exemplified: 1) the descriptor-centred and 2) the candidate-centred perspective. A description of a method that can be classified as candidate centred, namely, the test-centred method is given, followed by a rationale for choosing this method. Methods from the two perspectives are then compared, using rater consensus as an indicator of success. It was found that the test-centred method does not necessarily produce more consensus than a candidate-centred method, but that a purely descriptor-centred method may produce less consensus. This may be due to the greater mental effort required to keep a number of separate target level characteristics in mind, as compared to a unitary picture of one hypothetical person.

Another interesting finding is that the panellists' definitions of borderline ability for different levels are similar, a result that echoes the study conducted by Giraud, Impara and Plake (2005). Panellists not only look to a candidate's ability, but also to his or her confidence and ease in demonstrating it, as an important characteristic. This may have consequences for construct definition, where the factor of 'ease' may have to be taken into account.

Introduction

As Buckendahl (2005:219) put it, 'The challenge for all standard-setting methodologies is to effectively translate a participant's mental model of the target examinee (e.g. barely proficient student) into judgments that communicate the participant's recommendation of a value that characterizes the point of separation between one or more categories'. Standard setting thus deals with judgements that are based on a foundation which is difficult to grasp, namely, each judge's individual idea of the 'minimally competent person' (MCP), also known as the 'minimally qualified' (Cizek, Bunch and Koons 2004:31), the 'just qualified' (Tannenbaum and Baron 2011:4, Tannenbaum and Wylie 2008:17), or 'borderline' candidate (Eckes 2012:259, Livingston and Zieky 1983:1, Papageorgiou 2010b:2) to name just a few. It stands to reason that the more varied these ideas are, the less valid the result of a standard setting will be. Therefore, it seems advisable to think carefully about the methods applied to engender a uniform understanding of the MCP's abilities. This is an important consideration whenever a standard setting event has to be planned, as the choice of method will influence the result.

This paper will outline difficulties that are encountered when conceptualising the MCP. It will then give an overview of some methods for MCP conceptualisation that have been described, and attempt to categorise them into the descriptor-centred and the candidate-centred perspectives. It will then go on to give a rationale for a method that can be classified as candidate-centred, namely, the test-oriented method. This method, which was used in a standard setting conducted by the author, will be described, and the outcome compared to those found in some other studies using different approaches.

Difficulties in conceptualising the MCP

The aim of standard setting is to define the level of ability which is just good enough to obtain a pass grade. There are many different ways in which this can be done (see Cizek and Bunch 2007, Kaftandjieva 2004), several of which involve a personalised concept of the target level ability which is in these cases conceptualised as the ability of a fictitious 'minimally competent person' (MCP).

Where this is the case, there are then two steps that judges have to perform in order to fulfil their task of answering questions like: 'would the MCP be able to solve this item?' or 'is this work attributable to the MCP?'

In step 1, the MCP model is constructed. The basis for this is the judge's expertise, plus additional knowledge or expertise which he or she acquires in the course of the standard setting workshop, e.g. training with standard descriptors, or insights gained in the process of defining the standard in the first place, when this is part of the standard setting. The second step is to apply the MCP model to a number of items or samples of candidates' work. The judgement process, step 2 (involving feedback about rating behaviour, use of empirical data, conducting group discussions) has received an increasing amount of attention. However, step 1, the focus of this article, remains a problem, even though it is central to standard setting. Hambleton (2001:111) identifies the clarity of the performance categories to the panellists as one validity criterion to be met in a standard setting study, pointing out that it has moved to the focus of attention as 'one of the major challenges in standard setting practices over the last 10 years', while previously it 'may not have even been included in the process'. But 10 years later, in a study on the decision-making process of standard setting participants which applied verbal protocol analysis, Papageorgiou (2010a:270) noted that '"examinee performance" and "target examinee definition" were the most frequent codes in the data', indicating that these are topics that panellists feel a strong need to discuss. 'Difficulty in grasping the notion of the borderline examinee' (Papageorgiou (2010a:275) is identified in this study as one of the problems that could potentially endanger the validity of cut scores.

The elusiveness of the MCP may be due to several reasons, one of these being that it cannot be taken for granted that the competence in question is clearly defined. Where standard setting is performed in relation to existing level descriptors, such as the Common European Framework of Reference (CEFR, Council of Europe 2001) scales, step 1 also involves the conceptualisation of these descriptors in each panellist's mind, before they can make use of their individual conception of the descriptors to build a model of the MCP. This is an issue explored by Papageorgiou (2009) in his research on judges' interpretations of the CEFR descriptors. In this study, he found that judges interpreted the wording of the level descriptors differently in some cases (Papageorgiou 2009:53) which led to inconsistencies that affected particularly the higher levels (B2 to C2), and the writing competence.

Hein and Skaggs (2010) identify another issue, which is related to the idea of the MCP as a person. In their study which was focused on the thought processes of participants in a mock standard setting session, the conceptualisation of the level definition did not play a role, as participants were instructed to think of the cut score of an actual test that they were familiar with. Their task was to imagine a classroom full of students who would just pass this test. This very concrete task revealed the following difficulty: the competence in question may have several facets, and MCPs may vary in their pattern of strengths and weaknesses, and also in their level of attention or motivation over time, so that an abstract MCP must be conceived not as one, albeit fictitious, person, but as the average of a number of possible competence profiles. The notion of a hypothetical person, instead of being helpful, may thus confront panellists with an additional problem. Hein and Skaggs' panellists solved this problem by imagining one or two concrete students whom they knew, thus working not with a unified, abstract or typical MCP but with different individual ones. Hein and Skaggs (2010:42) observe that 'the standard setting literature . . . does not address the issue of what "typical" means in this regard. That is, conceiving of the typical borderline examinee becomes problematic when there is variability in the ways in which examinees can be borderline.'

Hein and Skaggs' results reveal a problem that has hitherto not received much attention: namely, that there is a difference between defining borderline ability in an abstract sense and defining the ability found in a 'borderline person'. This difference is mirrored in the two prevailing perspectives on target level definition, which focus on descriptors (i.e. *abstract definitions* of target level competence) on the one hand, and borderline candidates (i.e. *concrete manifestations* of borderline ability) on the other hand.

Descriptor-centred and candidate-centred methods of target level definition

The development of a standard setting methodology has been described as a transition from the ages of innocence (up to the mid-1950s), to the awakening (to the late seventies), and to disillusionment (to the early eighties), to finally reach a stage of realistic acceptance which has lasted for the last 30 years (Kaftandjieva 2004:4, following Zieky 1994). In this historic model, the age of innocence is deemed to end when the first standard setting method was described by Nedelsky in 1954, that is, when the setting of a pass score was identified as an issue to be addressed through a rational explanation of procedures, rather than as a matter of course justified by a general appearance of plausibility. Ever since, an increasing number of standard setting features have been scrutinised and called into question. In order to illustrate this, Kaftandjieva (2004) compares the 1985 and 1999 editions of the American Psychological Association (APA) Standards for Educational and Psychological Testing, and demonstrates how these become more fine-grained with regard to statistical matters, the adequacy of the actual procedures (procedural validity), standards for documentation, the use of empirical data, and the training of judges. As the conceptualisation of the MCP fits best into the 'training of judges' category, I shall look closer at standard setting features usually described under this heading, to see how and if it is addressed.

In 1985, the APA Standards demand that 'a clear explanation should be given of any technical basis for any cut score used to make personnel decisions' (Standard 10.9, quoted from Kaftandjieva 2004:7). Fourteen years later, 'the judgmental process should be designed so that judges can bring their knowledge and experience to bear in a reasonable way' (Standard 4.21), and Standard 1.7 specifies 'When a validation rests in part on the opinion or decisions of expert judges, observers or raters, procedures for selecting such experts and for eliciting judgments or ratings should be fully described. The description of procedures should include any training and instruction provided, should indicate whether participants reached their decisions independently, and should report the level of agreement reached.' While these requirements are much more detailed, addressing the selection of experts as well as the methods for eliciting judgements, and here specifically the training of judges, the independence of judgements, and their level of agreement, there are no further specifications as to the purpose, nature or content of the training.

Training content will depend on its purpose. Kaftandjieva (2004:29) describes the aim of training to:

(a) ensure a unified interpretation of proficiency levels by all judges
(b) guarantee that every judge understands completely the judgement task
(c) get information about rating behaviour and the degree of competence of every rater.

The MCP model is a way of operationalising the judges' understanding of the target proficiency level, and would thus fall under point (a). There is, however, little documentation on how this is actually done. Reckase (2000:46) notes that 'most reports of standard-setting procedures provide little detail about training'. In the end, even though the APA standards show a development towards greater detail in their demands on the standard setting process, the construction of an MCP model remains under their radar.

As the target proficiency level is the starting point of test construction, and judges are chosen because of their expertise regarding the competence that the test is supposed to tap into, a common understanding of it may well be taken for granted. However, even though each judge may be quite confident of their individual understanding of the target level, the assumption that these understandings overlap should be tested. In a study, Skorupski and Hambleton (2005:240) found that prior to training, participants in a standard setting showed 'relatively little agreement with respect to the definitions of the four performance levels' they were to deal with.

There are several conceivable ways to address the issue of the target level:

1. Working from level descriptors without reference to concrete candidates.
2. Working from level descriptors and deriving a notion of the MCP from group discussion.
3. Working from a description of 'good' vs. 'weak' proficiency (i.e. constructing own level descriptors).
4. Trying to describe the MCP themselves (e.g. writing down MCP characteristics for reference during standard setting).

To illustrate these methods, I shall quote some examples from published standard setting studies where details about the definition of the MCP model are given.

Papageorgiou (2010b) shows the application of method 1. In his description of the standard setting for the Michigan English Test, he reports that 'fifty-six reading, 71 listening, 17 grammar and 25 vocabulary sentence-level statements from the CEFR descriptors ... were presented to the judges asking them to choose the CEFR level they belong to (A1–C2). No indication of the level was presented to the judges.' The descriptors were 'atomized' into short statements, based on Kaftandjieva and Takala (2002), in order to familiarise the judges with all constituent statements of the descriptors. In this study, the target level was described in wholly abstract terms.

This is also the case in a study by Figueras, Kaftandjieva and Takala (2013). They conducted a standard setting study with a focus not on the test (a reading test which was created for the purpose of the study), but on the process of standard setting. Prior to the workshop, in addition to working with the Dutch Grid training website (a tool for analysing item content, see www.lancaster.ac.uk/fss/projects/grid/), participants were asked to rate 56 reading comprehension descriptors from the CEFR as to their level, without consulting the CEFR. At the workshop, the results were discussed in detail with a focus on those descriptors where the raters had displayed the highest disagreement. Again, target level definition relied only on work with the descriptors, exemplifying method 1.

Tannenbaum and Wylie (2004:4) applied a similar method: 'Prior to the meeting, each panellist was given a homework assignment to review the CEF and selected tables of level descriptors and to write down key indicators' (i.e. characteristics of the level, not of the minimal competence at that level), and at the meeting participants were asked to work in small groups and record on chart paper the main points that defined each of the relevant CEFR levels. The papers thus produced were not discussed in plenary, but remained posted on the wall for reference during the standard setting. MCP characteristics were not specifically recorded. The definition of the minimally acceptable ability was left to the discussion in plenary. Before making their judgements, they were however instructed to think of 'the skill set of a B1-level candidate (as previously defined)' (Tannenbaum and Wylie 2004:5), so that their approach can be seen as exemplifying method 2.

Wylie and Tannenbaum (2006) pursued a different approach, which may illustrate method 3. Prior to the standard setting of a test for academic speaking, panellists were asked to 'think about critical tasks and skills for speaking, and to write down key indicators that distinguished someone with weak skills from someone with strong skills. They were asked to bring these responses to the study, since they would be helpful for some of the group discussions' (Wylie and Tannenbaum 2006:4). In the actual workshop, participants then noted down the minimally acceptable skills for the test in question. So in this case, the attention of the panellists was directed towards the actual candidates and the descriptors were derived from the performance that panellists thought they were likely to produce. In a second step, the test in question was to be mapped onto another test, using the notion of a candidate with a specific score on the second test as a link. While in the first step descriptors could not be used because none existed, in the second step this could have been done by, for example, using the rating scale from the existing test, but it was preferred to work with a description of a hypothetical candidate's abilities because this would provide the link to the first exam. The abilities were described in terms like 'Reasonable speed, well paced – Appropriate register – On-target word choice' etc. (Wylie and Tannenbaum 2006:28).

Finally, Tannenbaum and Wylie (2008:7) integrated this approach into their work with the CEFR by asking their participants to 'review selected tables from the CEFR . . . for each language modality and to write down key characteristics or indicators from the tables that described an English-language learner (candidate) with just enough skills to be performing at each CEFR level. . . . As they completed this pre-study assignment, they were asked to consider what distinguishes a candidate with just enough skills to be considered performing at a specific CEFR level from a candidate with not enough skills to be performing at that level'. At the standard setting workshop, panellists worked in small groups to produce agreed-upon descriptions of minimally acceptable candidate abilities, directing their attention to the fact that the CEFR descriptors do not relate to minimally acceptable, but to typical performance in an ability band. This study focuses on the MCP as a person, and is quoted here to illustrate method 4.

Just as there are candidate-centred and item-centred methods in standard setting, there appear to be candidate-centred and descriptor-centred methods in the definition of the minimally acceptable skill.

Introducing a test-centred target level definition method

The aim of standard setting is to define a score in a test above which the candidate shall be judged to be 'at target level'. From his or her performance in the test a generalisation will be made to that candidate's probable real-life performance. It is therefore interesting to ask which of these two spheres should inspire the MCP model. Is it test performance or real-life performance? One common way of constructing an MCP model in standard setters' minds is to draw on Can Do statements, in many cases the level descriptors of the CEFR. These are clearly constructed not with test performance but with real-life performance in mind. This fact sometimes presents problems for test constructors, as many CEFR descriptors relate to features of language competence that are not easily, or not at all observable in tests:

- language competence relative to the familiarity of the topic; common CEFR terms include: 'own field of interest/specialization' (CEFR, Council of Europe 2001:24, 58, 59, 61, 62, 66, 69, 96)

- language production in a non-neutral or even emotional context: 'Can handle difficult and even hostile questioning', 'emotional, allusive and joking usage' (CEFR, Council of Europe 2001:60, 76, 83, 122)
- language activities that require a certain scope of language material, which it would be impractical to provide in a test context: 'wide range', 'summarise information from different spoken and written sources' (CEFR, Council of Europe 2001:24, 58, 59, 66, 68, 69, 70, 74, 96, 110, 122, 124, 125, 129).

But even features that can more easily be put in a test will have to undergo a transformation. Thus, if the target performance is described as: 'Can read straightforward factual texts on subjects related to his/her field and interest with a satisfactory level of comprehension' (CEFR, Overall Reading Comprehension, B1; Council of Europe 2001:69), performance in the test will actually mirror something like: 'Can read straightforward factual texts on subjects of general interest and answer multiple choice questions targeted at salient points.'

If we look at the receptive skills, from a real-life perspective the determining factor for a candidate's comprehension of a text (in any depth, be it gist or details of the text) should be text difficulty. It has however been shown (Freedle and Kostin 1993, Kostin 2004) that (at least for some tests) text-item-interaction, especially vocabulary overlap between text and item, is among the best predictors of an item's difficulty. Difficulty is thus partly determined by features that are only present because the candidate is taking a test.

Language use in a test is different from language use in real life in several ways. A test, however authentic, does not capture real life. In addition, it may contain tasks that are *more* or *less* difficult than real-life tasks for a variety of reasons, outlined below.

The proof of comprehension (in the receptive skills) is not success in an action, but the answer to an item. The item thus functions as a filter through which we only perceive an impression of the candidate's comprehension – not comprehension itself. The answer to the item may be influenced by the item's (not the text's) linguistic difficulty, or by test-taking skills.

Test takers may not choose texts according to their need or interest. Their motivation to read or listen may be higher or lower, but it will be different from real life (the 'artificiality of educational assessments' (Hambleton 2001:100)).

Test takers may not resort to 'real-life' problem-solving strategies, such as asking somebody else, looking something up, or giving up altogether. Their propensity for guessing will be higher than in real life.

Test takers have to understand an artificial context in which their communication is supposed to take place. In some cases they have to imagine themselves in a role, which they have to understand before the task makes sense. This requires an extra effort which makes the task more difficult.

Comprehension can be looked at as a process of understanding words, constructing propositions and then making sense of them by integrating them into a situational model that is made up of the new information and already existing information (Kintsch 1988, 1998). Knowledge of, and familiarity with, artificial test contexts is at best restricted, at worst not available to candidates. Test contexts do not have a history which helps to interpret them. Hence any information the candidate receives can only be embedded in general situational knowledge where this knowledge is very general indeed. Situations in the public domain (e.g. taking part in elections, shopping) will be more accessible than situations in the private, work, or educational domain, where there is typically more shared knowledge or common history among the participants in communication. Where items are set in the private, work or educational domains, texts will have to make up for less shared knowledge by more explicitness.

However, the test taker cannot even be sure that the situational knowledge he or she has can be relied on in a test context, because guided by the effort to cleanse the test from any influence of non-linguistic knowledge, item writers will in my experience be inclined to make the right answer counter-intuitive more often than not. Comprehension tasks in a test thus typically require closer reading or listening than in real life. This is legitimate, but it makes test comprehension different from real-world comprehension.

It is a truism that in a test we see (at most) a subset of the test takers' real-life performance. For the reasons stated, their test performance will also be different from their real-life performance. Perhaps this should be reflected in the way we think about an MCP's abilities, as all we shall ever see of a test taker is his or her test performance and not his or her functioning in real life. It may make sense to pay attention to test-specific language behaviour when constructing the MCP model.

Building on the above considerations, a two-day standard setting workshop was set up in order to identify the MCP for a specific exam. Seventeen experts with long-standing experience in teaching and item writing took part. The examination in question, telc English B1–B2 (http://www.telc.net/prue-fungsteilnehmende/sprachpruefungen/pruefungen/detail/telc-english-b1-b2. html), consists of three papers (receptive skills, writing and speaking), for which results are reported separately. The aim of the standard setting was to set the cut score for the receptive skills, linking the examination in question with existing B1 and B2 examinations which had been linked to the CEFR. An approach was chosen that would integrate the candidate-centred and the test-oriented perspective, the latter being introduced on the basis of the considerations described above. One day was dedicated to the training, where the conceptualisation of the MCP played a central role.

In a first phase, participants were provided with the CEFR scales for overall listening comprehension and overall reading comprehension, and were instructed to underline the key competence features for each level. Results were compared and discussed in plenary. Although all experts were known to be familiar with the CEFR and using it in their daily work, this preliminary activity was conducted in order to focus participants on the CEFR levels. Their attention was drawn to the fact that these were descriptions of *'typical'* abilities, while the next phase would focus on *'borderline'* ability.

In this second phase, participants were invited to work with the descriptions of borderline ability from Tannenbaum and Wylie (2008), to discuss whether they agreed with them and to supplement them, where needed.

Participants were asked, in the third phase, to take a closer look at the B1 level for reading and listening, and the B2 level for reading and listening, consecutively. They were provided with statistics from the existing examinations, in order to help them form a picture of the ability of a just-passing candidate, who would be regarded as a B1 (or, in the case of the B2 exam, a B2) MCP. Both existing examinations report a compound result, i.e. there is no cut score for each individual skill. It may thus be questioned whether the MCPs identified with the help of this compound score, are true MCPs as far as the single skills are concerned that were under scrutiny in the standards setting event described here. They could not be regarded as such if their results in the reading part were very different from their results in the listening part. The candidates in question however showed no great differences in their performance in the reading and listening sections of the examination. Of the 609 candidates in the B1 examination, 78% differed by no more than three (of 20) items answered correctly; of the 435 candidates in the B2 examination, 93% differed by no more than three (of 20) items. The reading and listening parts carry equal weight in both examinations.

The method applied for B1 reading and listening, and B2 reading and listening, was the same and is described here for the B1 reading part.

Participants were provided with a reading paper from the existing B1 examination that was to be used for comparison purposes, and some statistics on the performance of test takers in this examination. For every item, two figures were communicated: the proportion of correct answers from candidates who had obtained scores just above the cut score in the already existing examination as a whole, who were to be regarded as the target MCPs, and the proportion of correct answers from candidates who had obtained scores at the border between grades 2 and 3 (a middling performance). These were communicated in the form of lists, but the performance of the MCPs was also printed directly beneath each of the items. As a further visual signal, MCPs' p-values were highlighted in bold if higher than 0.5 (i.e. the MCP candidates had done well on those items). Item numbers were circled where there was a difference of 20 percentage points or more between MCP candidates and middling candidates (i.e. items that differentiated strongly between MCPs and middling candidates), this particular value being chosen because of its plausibility and because it yielded a reasonable number of items that the participants could work with. The panellists were oriented as to the meaning of these figures, and were then asked to look at the items and derive an idea of what a B1 MCP could and could not do, also drawing on their experience as teachers and consulting the borderline competence descriptors from Tannenbaum and Wylie (2008), if they wished. Their task was then to write characteristics of MCP ability on cards and arrange them on pinboards, sorted under the following four headings: things that a B1 MCP *can* do (in concrete and abstract terms), things that a B1 MCP *cannot* do (in concrete and abstract terms). To illustrate this, some observations that were found were:

Table 1 Characteristics of B1 MCP reading

B1 reading	Abstract	Concrete
Can understand/use	Using vocabulary 'matching' but missing the concepts behind them. Relies on strategies (vocab overlap etc.). Straightforward and concrete successful completion of the item.	'To reduce' leads to 'is less'. Make the connection waste → save 'I would like to' + verb.
Cannot understand/use	Increased difficulty when unnecessary difficult words are in the text. Difficulty with unusual sentence structure. The closer the distractor is to the native language or the correct answer, the more likely it is to be chosen. Distracted by vocab, picks up wrong key words. Cannot 'juggle' three different key words at the same time. Reading between the lines/implied meaning is not possible at this level. Can't identify word families easily or quickly (sometimes not at all). Lack of selective strategy. Scanning is difficult.	'Take hold' could be confusing. 'Bother' – too advanced? 'don't mind' – expression has positive meaning. 'Long' 'time' together create a phrase, which may have misled the weaker candidate. Didn't understand that an adverb was necessary. Couldn't distinguish 'this' and 'these'. Confuse 'all'/'everything'. Vocab: 'cause' (n). Mixed up 'last' with 'at last'. Verbal phrases (deal with). Difficulty to separate this, that, these, those.

The cards remained on the wall during the workshop for reference in the actual judgement phase.

After all cards had been put up, the most interesting findings were collected in a plenary discussion. The following characteristics of B1 and B2 MCPs were identified – B1 MCPs have problems with:

- difficult words, especially at the beginning of a text
- unusual sentence structure

- correct answer demands that more than two information items are processed
- gapped text
- counter-intuitive items (correct answer is not the expected one)
- vocabulary overlap between text and wrong answer
- more easily misled by the distractor being close to the correct answer.

Criteria for identifying a word as 'difficult' or a structure as 'unusual' were the participants' teaching experience at the respective levels, as well as whether that word or structure was defined as being accessible at that level in the vocabulary and grammar inventory of the respective examination.

B1 MCPs can deal with:

- straightforward text in a logical, linear order
- everyday situations
- vocabulary suited to everyday situations.

B2 MCPs have problems with:
- idiomatic language
- phrasal verbs
- less frequent collocations
- complex structures ('she was never offered . . .')
- time management (they run out of time)
- vocabulary overlap between text and wrong answer
- items where one option is 'none of the options is correct'
- being misled by their expectations of the tests' design characteristics in terms of difficulty, or how distraction is embedded into the test ('this cannot be right, it is too easy').

B2 MCPs can deal with:
- guessing meaning from context
- understanding new structures that consist of familiar elements
- following text logic
- a more natural rate of speaking.

As the panellists' attention was focused on language use in a testing context, it is not surprising that a number of the features identified are due to the testing situation. For example, vocabulary overlap seems to play a role for both MCPs, in that it can provide guidance if the overlap is between text and correct answer, but can be misleading if it occurs between text and distractor. Participants considered the closeness of the correct answer and distractors, and the degree to which the correct answer can be anticipated, as crucial for item difficulty. Taken together, this describes the MCP as a candidate who is lacking in self-monitoring skills – he or she is not a confident language user, and is easily misled, even though he or she possesses the required language competence if the language use context is supportive and non-challenging.

This supports one of the findings of Giraud et al (2005:231) who compared standard setting events across different content domains (L1 reading and mathematics) and grade levels. In these workshops each participant was asked to describe the MCP in their own words. It emerged that the panellists' descriptions of the MCP were similar even though the competences tapped in the two tests were quite different. The MCP was described as lacking in attention to detail, and unable to process items requiring abstraction. Giraud et al (2005:231) hypothesise that this may result from 'some idea of competence that is common across teachers who serve as judges. That is, the target examinee . . . may have similar characteristics under almost any circumstances.' A borderline target examinee could thus be characterised as a candidate possessing the target ability but hindered in applying it fully by carelessness, lack of the ability to concentrate (perhaps attributable to the required language processing not being sufficiently automated), or lack of confidence.

Checking success

The second day of the workshop was dedicated to the judgement process, and was conducted according to a modified Angoff procedure (Cizek and Bunch 2007:81). In the first round, panellists were asked to answer, for each item, the question 'how many of 100 MCPs would answer this item correctly?' A mean cut score for B1 and B2 respectively was calculated from the answers and presented to the panellists. In round 2, they were asked not to look at individual items any more, but to give a holistic B1 and B2 cut score that seemed plausible. These were again collected and presented to the panellists, who then had the opportunity, in round 3, to modify their individual cut scores once again. There was a convergence of cut scores between rounds from a range of 18 points (of 59) in round 1, to 6 points in round 3, for B1, and from a range of 12 points to 5 points for B2. In round 3, panellists were also asked to indicate their confidence in the cut scores they had decided on. A satisfactory level of confidence was reached with a mean of 4.31 on a scale ranging from 1 (not at all confident) to 5 (very confident) for the B1 cut score, and a mean of 4.06 for the B2 cut score. No panellist rated his or her confidence lower than 3 (two panellists rated it as 3 for the B1 cut score, five panellists did so for the B2 cut score).

This is perhaps not an unusual result in a standard setting session. If the time spent on target level definition made a difference, one would now expect the result to be different from comparable standard setting events. The question was therefore explored how it would be possible to quantify the success of target level definition methods.

Target candidate definition activities have two purposes:

- validity: getting closer to defining a *meaningful* cut score
- reliability: helping the group towards a more *unified* idea of a cut score.

Standard setting has been described by Cizek and Bunch (2007:18) as 'functioning to evoke and synthesize reasoned human judgement in a rational and defensible way so as to *create* those categories and partition the score scale on which a real trait is measured into meaningful and useful intervals'. Following this approach, there is no empirically 'true' cut score, and validity in a cut score is an issue of the plausibility of the resulting classification of candidates. But it seems reasonable that more extensive thinking about the MCP, and integrating all features that play a role in the actual examination situation, leads to a better understanding of the threshold ability – as it emerges in a test.

As there is no 'true' cut score, reliability in a cut score cannot not be conceived as the closeness of the judges' estimates to any 'true' value. However, the more unanimousness there is in a competent group of judges, the more faith can be put in a cut score, as obviously a reasonably large group of experts could agree on this cut score quite readily. The more disagreement there is, i.e. the farther apart the judges' individual cut scores are, the less convincing it will be. Therefore any measure of the dispersion of judgements can serve as a means of comparison.

Some of the studies cited in the section on 'Descriptor-centred and candidate-centred methods of target level definition' to illustrate different ways of building an MCP model provide the individual cut scores given by the judges. It is thus possible to compare the amount of agreement among judges in these studies. Tannenbaum and Wylie (2004) and Papageorgiou (2010b) were selected in addition to telc English B1–B2, because they are also comparable in some other ways:

- they concern multi-level examinations (in most cases two levels, in one case three)
- they were conducted with a comparable number of panellists (12 and 21, with 17 for telc English B1–B2)
- the method applied was an Angoff-type method
- the level descriptors used were from the CEFR.

In short, they can be characterised as shown in Table 2.

They are however different in test content and in the maximum number of points. In order to equalise the latter difference, cut scores were divided by the maximum possible number of points in the respective examination, thus making ranges (maximum cut score minus minimum cut score) comparable. In addition, standard errors of the mean of judgements (SE_j) were calculated. Ranges were calculated although they are much affected by outliers, because the question to be investigated was: are there indications that the method of MCP definition has an impact on the spread found in panellists' judgements?

Table 2 Standard setting studies in comparison

Source	Test	Method	Target candidate definition method	Can be characterised as
Tannenbaum and Wylie (2004)	TOEFL Structures TOEFL Reading TOEFL Listening TOEIC Listening TOEIC Reading	Angoff probabilities (0.1, 0.2, . . . 0.9)	Homework: read global scale, write down key characteristics of level (not MCP). At workshop: Summarise key descriptors and produce panel-agreed version for reference during workshop.	Descriptor/candidate-centred
Papageorgiou (2010b)	Michigan English Test, Listening Michigan English Test, Grammar+Reading	Modified Angoff (100 borderline candidates)	'Atomised' descriptors, choose right level.	Descriptor-centred
telc (2012)	English B1–B2 (receptive skills)	Modified Angoff (100 MCPs)	Mark key characteristics in scale, discuss. Consider target candidate definitions from Tannenbaum and Wylie (2008). Look at MCPs' work and describe their ability.	Candidate/test-centred

If so, outliers might be prevented by the choice of method. However, ranges may also be affected by the number of panellists in the study, as fewer panellists have fewer opportunities for disagreement.

Judgements for the first of the levels addressed, and made in the first round, were chosen as the parameters for comparison, because any effects of the method of MCP definition are most likely to be found there (in later rounds, panellists will also have been influenced by general discussion in the group, and the knowledge of the cut scores of their fellow panellists).

It should be noted that no criticism of the cut scores found in these studies is implied. The figures looked at here are in a way taken out of context, as they deliberately tune out the effects of group discussion and adjustment in later rounds that were used to establish robust cut scores. The focus is exclusively on any effects of MCP model building.

The examinations listed in Table 2, then, compare as shown in Table 3.

Table 3 Comparison of range and standard errors of the mean of judgements

Column	A	B	C	D	E	F	G	H
Target candidate definition method		Descriptor/ candidate-centred				Descriptor-centred		Candidate/test--centred
Test	TOEFL Structures	TOEFL Reading	TOEFL Listening	TOEIC Listening	TOEIC Reading	Michigan English Test, Listening	Michigan English Test, Grammar + Reading	English B1–B2
Number of panellists	21	21	21	21	21	12	13	18
Range	0.425	0.500	0.440	0.300	0.230	0.271	0.652	0.306
SE$_j$	0.0248	0.0295	0.0206	0.019	0.0158	0.0262	0.0468	0.0241

As the cut scores were converted into percentages of the maximum possible score for the purposes of this comparison, ranges can vary between 0 (all panellists agreed on the same cut score) and 1 (at least one panellist put the cut score at 0, saying that everybody will pass, and one panellist put it at the maximum of possible points, saying that nobody should pass). Thus 0.652 in column G is quite a high value. However, in the same study, but for another skill, one of the lowest ranges was reached (column F). This may partly be explained by the lower number of panellists. Low values are however to be found for any target candidate definition method (columns D, E, F and H).

Looking at the SE_j values, the lowest values are in columns C, D and E, followed by H. It appears that the purely descriptor-centred method made for quite a lot of initial disagreement, while the candidate/test-centred method can at least hold its own. One can, however, think of many more factors that could influence the initial agreement of panellists, and that can hardly be controlled, such as their previous experience with standard setting, or their working together in the same institution, or in different ones. For conclusive results, more research would be needed.

Conclusion

Many standard setting methods, most notably the Angoff method with its derivatives, require the conceptualisation of the MCP, which has been shown to be a demanding task because it comprises:

1. Understanding and internalising the target competence as defined in level descriptors.
2. Weighting different aspects of the target competence, so that theoretically any competence profile could be sorted into a unified rank order.
3. Bridging the gap between real-life skills and skills as observable in a test.

Methods to help panellists build a mental image of the MCP were scrutinised and classified into 'descriptor-centred', 'candidate-centred' and 'test-centred' methods. It was hypothesised that a combined candidate and test-centred method would facilitate this task, because it would at least minimise the third challenge. The test-centred method however has its own challenges, in that it directs panellists' attention towards features of competence in the wider sense of intellectual capacity, and towards level-independent test-taking skills, and away from the concrete skills tapped in the examination. It could not be proven that the candidate/test-centred method yielded more unified panel-list ratings. There is however an indication that a purely descriptor-oriented method may produce less unified ratings. This may be because it requires a greater mental effort to keep a number of separate target level characteristics in mind, as compared to a unitary picture of one hypothetical person. If this holds true, candidate-centred methods should be given preference. However, even though it may be cognitively easier to operate holistically on the basis of a hypothetical candidate, this presents other difficulties, as different hypo-thetical candidates (i.e. different skill profiles) may be conceivable on the basis of the same set of target level descriptors, which means that not only the target level characteristics as such but also their weighting must be discussed by the panel.

The test-centred method appears plausible, especially where a new test is to be linked to an existing test, although – as has been shown – it is not necessarily more exact than a purely candidate-centred method. It may produce results that are different from a candidate-centred standard setting, as it looks at target level characteristics from a different perspective. This is not to be wondered at, as it is a well-documented fact that different methods of standard setting will likely result in different cut scores (see Cizek and Bunch 2007:41). The decision on which method to apply will have to be informed by considering which method is likely to yield the most valuable information in the context of the examination at stake. The proposed classification of target level definition methods may be a helpful tool for decision-making.

References

Buckendahl, C W (2005) Qualitative Inquiries of Participants' Experiences with Standard Setting, *Applied Measurement in Education* 18 (3), 219–221.

Cizek, G J and Bunch, M B (2007) *Standard Setting. A Guide to Establishing and Evaluating Performance Standards on Tests*, Thousand Oaks: Sage Publications.

Cizek, G J, Bunch, M B and Koons, H (2004) Setting Performance Standards: Contemporary Methods, *Educational Measurement: Issues and Practice* 23 (4), 31–50.

Council of Europe (2001) *Common European Framework of Reference for Languages: Learning, Teaching, Assessment*, Cambridge: Cambridge University Press.

Eckes, T (2012) Examinee-centred standard setting for large-scale assessments: The prototype group method, *Psychological Test and Assessment Modeling* 54 (3), 257–283.

Figueras, N, Kaftandjieva, F and Takala, S (2013) Relating a reading comprehension test to the CEFR levels: A case of standard setting in practice with focus on judges and items, *The Canadian Modern Language* 69 (4), 359–385.

Freedle, R and Kostin, I (1993) *The Prediction of TOEFL Reading Comprehension Items Difficulty for Expository Prose Passages for Three Item Types: Main Idea, Inference, and Supporting Idea Items*, ETS Report RR-93-13, TOEFL-RR-44, Princeton: Educational Testing Service.

Giraud, G, Impara, J C and Plake, B S (2005) Teachers' conceptions of the target examinee in Angoff standard setting, *Applied Measurement in Education* 18 (3), 223–232.

Glass, G V (1977) *Standards and Criteria*, available online: www.globalhivmeinfo. org/CapacityBuilding/Occasional%20Papers/10%20Standards%20and%20 Criteria.pdf

Hambleton, R K (2001) Setting performance standards on educational assessments and criteria for evaluating the process, in Cizek, G J (Ed) *Setting Performance Standards. Concepts, Methods, and Perspectives*, Mahwah: Lawrence Erlbaum Associates, 89–116.

Hein, S F and Skaggs, G (2010) Conceptualizing the classroom of target students: A qualitative investigation of panellists' experiences during standard setting, *Educational Measurement: Issues and Practice* 29 (2), 36–44.

Kaftandjieva, F (2004) Standard setting, in Council of Europe (Ed), *Reference Supplement to the Preliminary Pilot Version of the Manual for Relating Language Examinations to the Common European Framework of Reference for Languages: Learning, Teaching, Assessment*, Strasbourg: Language Policy Division, 1–43.

Kaftandjieva, F and Takala, S (2002) Council of Europe scales of language proficiency: A validation study, in Alderson, J C (Ed) *Common European Framework of Reference for Languages: Learning, Teaching, Assessment. Case Studies*, Strasbourg: Council of Europe, 106–129.

Kintsch, W (1988) The role of knowledge in discourse comprehension: A construction-integration model, *Psychological Review* 95 (2), 163–182.

Kintsch, W (1998) *Comprehension: A Paradigm for Cognition*, Cambridge: Cambridge University Press.

Kostin, I (2004) *Exploring Item Characteristics That Are Related to the Difficulty of TOEFL Dialogue Items*, ETS Report RR-04-11.

Livingston, S A and Zieky, M J (1983) *A Comparative Study of Standard Setting Methods*, Princeton: Educational Testing Service.

Papageorgiou (2009) *Setting Performance Standards in Europe. The Judges' Contribution to Relating Language Examinations to the Common European Framework of Reference*, Language Testing and Evaluation vol. 16, Frankfurt am Main etc: Peter Lang.

Papageorgiou, S (2010a) Investigating the decision-making process of standard setting participants, *Language Testing* 27 (2), 261–282.

Papageorgiou, S (2010b) *Setting Cut Scores on the Common European Framework of Reference for the Michigan English Test*, Ann Arbor: Testing and Certification Division, English Language Institute, University of Michigan.

Reckase, M D (2000) A survey and evaluation of recently developed procedures for setting standards on educational tests, in Bourquey, M L and Byrd, S (Eds) *Student Performance Standards on the National Assessment of Educational Progress: Affirmations and Improvement*, Washington: NAEP, 44–70.

Skorupski, W P and Hambleton, R K (2005) What are panellists thinking when they participate in standard-setting studies? *Applied Measurement in Education* 18 (3), 233–256.

Tannenbaum, R J and Baron, P A (2011) *Mapping TOEFL ITP Scores Onto the Common European Framework of Reference. Research Memorandum ETS RM-11-33*, Princeton: Educational Testing Service.

Tannenbaum, R J and Wylie, E C (2004) *Mapping Test Scores onto the Common European Framework: Setting Standards of Language Proficiency on the Test of English as a Foreign Language (TOEFL), the Test of Spoken English (TSE), the Test of Written English (TWE), and the Test of English for International Communication (TOEIC)*, Princeton: Educational Testing Service.

Tannenbaum, R J and Wylie, E C (2008) *Linking English-Language Test Scores Onto the Common European Framework of Reference: An Application of Standard-Setting Methodology*, TOEFL iBT Research Report, TOEFLiBT-06, Princeton: Educational Testing Service.

Wylie, E C and Tannenbaum, R J (2006) *TOEFL Academic Speaking Test: Setting a Cut Score for International Teaching Assistants*, ETS Research Memorandum RM-06-01, Princeton: Educational Testing Service.

Zieky, M (1994) A historical perspective on setting standards, in Crocker, L and Zieky, M (Eds) *Joint Conference on Standard Setting for Large-Scale Assessments. Proceedings Volume 2*, Washington, DC: US Government Printing Office, 1–38.

13 Language standards for medical practice in the UK: Issues of fairness and quality for all

Vivien Berry
British Council
Barry O'Sullivan
British Council

Abstract

This study was undertaken in order to refresh and extend a previous investigation into *IELTS* band score levels and International Medical Graduates (Banerjee 2004) and to develop a stronger evidence base for the UK General Medical Council's requirements when setting minimum language standards for overseas applicants to their register. Current required *IELTS* levels were considered in order to determine if they are adequate in light of issues of patient safety; the matter of requiring evidence of English language ability from all non-native English-speaking medical practitioners seeking admission to the General Medical Council register was also investigated; finally, the question of whether *IELTS* is an appropriate instrument to assess the language proficiency of prospective doctors was considered. Data was gathered from panels of participants geographically located throughout the UK and Northern Ireland; probability-based statistical analysis, many-faceted Rasch analysis and detailed qualitative analysis of the data gave rise to recommendations that can be shown to be valid and robust.

Introduction

Appropriate language skills are absolutely fundamental to medical trainees' performance in face-to-face interactions with patients (Elder, Pill, Woodward-Kron, McNamara, Manias, McColl and Webb 2012). However, the question of how to determine which language skills are appropriate and how to assess them is problematic. An early published study into the development of a test designed to evaluate both the professional and the language abilities of overseas doctors was that of Rea-Dickens (1987), who describes the development of the Temporary Registration Assessment Board (TRAB), the forerunner to the Professional and Linguistics Assessment Board (PLAB) test. The development of TRAB was innovative at the time as linguists and medical experts worked collaboratively to analyse the language used by health professionals in British hospitals and used this knowledge to inform decisions on test content. Another study published at around the same time, also emphasising the importance of close collaboration between linguists and health professionals, was that of Alderson, Candlin, Clapham, Martin and Weir (1986), in relation to the revision of the Occupational English Test (OET).

Criticisms of how the assessment of language for health professionals is carried out in the USA and the UK originally came from researchers working in the health professions but one of the major criticisms, namely that of the use of international language proficiency examinations such as the Test of English as a Foreign Language (TOEFL) or the *International English Language Testing System (IELTS)* spread to include researchers in the field of applied linguistics. In the early 1990s, Friedman, Sutnick, Stillman, Norcini, Anderson, Williams, Henning and Reeves (1991) examined both the spoken proficiency and clinical competence of overseas medical graduates and found that the language examination used (TOEFL) offered an insufficiently complete estimate of the English ability of candidates in specific medical contexts. This criticism was echoed by both Chur-Hansen (1997) and Whelan, McKinley, Boulet, Macrae and Kamholz (2001), who acknowledged that although what they see as international general purpose proficiency examinations may function well as predictors of general language proficiency, they are of little value in predicting ability in medical communication. Similarly, the use of the *IELTS* test for the purpose of high-stakes decision-making in the medical language domain has been criticised in the language testing literature by McNamara (2000), McNamara and Roever (2006), Read and Wette (2009) and Wette (2011), *inter alia*. The main criticism lies in the fact that the *IELTS* was originally designed for use in the academic domain and is not considered appropriate for use in other domains without substantial empirically derived evidence in support of this usage.

Watt, Lake, Cabrnoch and Leonard (2003), researching in the Canadian context, suggest that the tasks included in tests for medical professionals should reflect the physical setting and performance parameters (e.g. location, audience and other characteristics of task performance) of tasks performed in the real world of medical practice, referred to in the literature as 'situational authenticity'. They also comment that such test tasks should mirror the communication or interaction type found in these medical communication settings and that the procedures for assessing performance (who should perform the assessing, what aspects of language the rating scale/ rubric should focus on) should also reflect the real world of medical practice.

Lear (2005) also implies that this need for situational authenticity should be reflected in medical language assessment. However, if language tests are developed according to the idealised criteria of situational authenticity, as seems to be the consensus of recent research, a problem then arises with assessment and with the fact that assessors may need to be both language aware and highly content familiar (Harding, Pill and Ryan 2011, Pill 2013, Pill and Woodward-Kron 2012).

In addition, when exploring the self-expressed language needs of trainee medical professionals, Lepetit and Cichocki (2002) report that oral skills are considered to be the most relevant to medical professionals, a finding also reflected in the work of Lear (2005). This finding highlights the need to move away from a conception of overall level (e.g. Band 7 on *IELTS*; C1, a level of the Common European Framework of Reference for Languages (CEFR, Council of Europe 2001); or 237, a TOEFL score) to the realisation that different language sub-skills may prove to be important for individuals engaged in different professional roles. A forthcoming paper comparing methods of assessing the English language proficiency of health professionals, mainly doctors, seeking to practice in the UK, North America and Australia, concludes that the inter-relationship between language proficiency, communicative competence and clinical communication skills is an extremely complex problem which requires much further study (Taylor and Pill in press).

In the United Kingdom, existing registration requirements for non-native speakers of English who hold medical qualifications obtained in countries other than the UK or those of the European Economic Area (EEA) and Switzerland, known as International Medical Graduates (IMGs), are first of all that they provide evidence of English language ability by achieving a minimum overall score, until 2014 set at Band 7 with no separate skill (listening, reading, writing and speaking) score lower than Band 7[1], on the Academic module of the *IELTS* test in a single sitting. Having achieved this, they are then eligible to register to take Part 1 of the PLAB test (a 200-item multiple-choice test) which must be passed in order for them to be eligible to take Part 2 of the PLAB test (an Objective Structured Clinical Examination (OSCE) consisting of 14 clinical scenarios or stations), success in which makes them eligible for registration with the General Medical Council (GMC) and thus able to practice medicine in the UK. When the PLAB test was initially introduced in 1979, it was jointly assessed by medical practitioners and language experts; however this is no longer the case. Since the main purpose of the PLAB test is to assess medical knowledge, the test is now only assessed by medical practitioners, which is why separate evidence of language ability is required. Until recently, in accordance with European law and the Medical Act, 1983, graduates with acceptable, recognised medical qualifications from within the EEA and Switzerland were exempt from providing evidence of English language ability when applying for registration in the UK. This was revised in the summer of 2014 (General Medical Council 2014) and all non-native English-speaking doctors must now provide evidence of English language proficiency before being allowed to practise medicine in the UK.

Aims and objectives of the study

The aims of the study are twofold:

1. To address concerns relating to the language competence of non-native English-speaking medical practitioners in the UK and to confirm, strengthen and extend the findings of a previous study (Banerjee 2004, Banerjee and Taylor 2005), by investigating the current required *IELTS* levels to determine if they are adequate in light of issues of patient safety.
2. To investigate the issue of requiring evidence of English language ability from all non-English native speaker medical practitioners seeking admission to the GMC register.

The study had three main objectives, namely:

1. To determine if the current overall *IELTS* score of Band 7, with no separate skill score lower than Band 7, is adequate as a preliminary language screening device for IMGs.
2. To determine if EEA graduates should provide the same evidence as IMGs if evidence of English language competence should ever be required in order for them to be admitted to the GMC register.
3. To determine if the *IELTS* test, by and of itself, provides an adequate measure of English language ability for overseas medical practitioners seeking admission to the GMC register.

When we consider how medical professionals are assessed using international proficiency tests, the following quote highlights both the concerns of some members of the language assessment community and their failure to date to respond to them: 'There has been a disquieting lack of empirical evidence to validate the decision to use these tests for uses other than those for which they have been designed (in the case of IELTS, academic English)' (O'Sullivan 2012:75). The formal report to the GMC (Berry, O'Sullivan and Rugea 2013) presented the full range of evidence gathered in order to support their recommendations. This paper, on the other hand, presents the views of the participants in order to both respond to the first two of the above objectives and to begin the process of building a substantive validity argument (Messick 1989) in order to either support or reject the use of the *IELTS* test in this particular context.

Research design

Approach

In order to arrive at appropriate cut-scores enabling us to determine what would constitute an appropriate level of achievement on the *IELTS* test for prospective doctors in the UK, a methodology called standard setting was used; qualitative data relating to the decisions was also collected from the participants in the study.

The detailed approach to the standard setting aspect of this study was designed to make the entire process both transparent and theoretically sound. The use of quantitative probability-based statistical analysis in tandem with a detailed qualitative analysis of the data gives rise to recommendations that can be shown to be valid and robust. In addition to the innovative use of many-faceted Rasch (MFR) statistical analysis to support the decisions of the stakeholder focus groups (SFGs), the approach included an additional validation process, whereby the recommendations were debated by an expert focus group (EFG) who made the final recommendations offered to the GMC. Figure 1 shows the basic design of the approach.

Standard setting

Standard setting, which is essentially what this study can be described as doing, has been defined by Cizek (1993:100) as 'the proper following of a

Figure 1 Approach

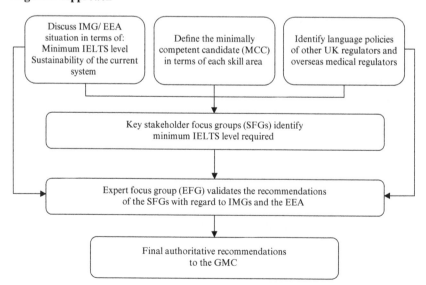

prescribed, rational system of rules or procedures resulting in the assignment of a number to differentiate between two or more states or degrees of performance'. In other words, standard setting is the process by which we establish the critical boundary point or points which will be used to interpret test performance, in this case, the criterion level on the *IELTS* test above which medical doctors must perform in order to be allowed to practise medicine in the UK.

There are two approaches to standard setting: test centred and examinee centred (see Kaftandjieva (2004) for an exhaustive overview of the area). In the first approach the focus is on the test as opposed to the test takers. It involves a number of judges who are asked to review a test or a section of a test and to estimate the likely difficulty of each item (or question). The second approach is examinee centred. As the name implies, this approach uses as its basis examples of actual examinee/candidate behaviour, and in the case of the productive skills, this would include either audio recordings of spoken language or copies of responses to writing tasks. Because the *IELTS* test comprises two receptive skills papers (listening and reading) and two productive skills papers (speaking and writing), both approaches to standard setting are required for this research.

Test-centred approach

The first of these approaches is the one applied to the receptive papers. The most commonly used approaches include the modified Angoff method (Hambleton and Plake 1995) and the Yes/No method (Impara and Plake 1998), which is a variant of the Angoff and modified Angoff methods. Since neither of these methods result in exact cut-scores (i.e. they are not integers), the results need to be rounded to the nearest integer. Cizek and Bunch (2007) suggest two ways of doing this: the first involves rounding to the nearest score (up or down), while the second one means rounding up to the next integer. The latter approach represents the more conservative option and is likely to be more appropriate to this project, where it is important to be certain that only really suitable candidates are deemed acceptable. It would certainly be consistent with the current scoring of Part 2 of the PLAB test where one standard error of measurement (SEM) is added to the cut score to reduce false positives in the interests of patient safety and which a recent GMC-commissioned report recommends as appropriate (McLachlan, Illing, Rothwell, Margetts, Archer and Shrewsbury 2012:56–57).

Examinee-centred approach

When it comes to standard setting for performance-based language tests (i.e. writing and speaking), the most appropriate method is an examinee-centred approach. With regard to the requirements of this project, the most appropriate of these appears to be the 'Examinee Paper Selection' method

(Hambleton, Brennan, Brown, Dodd, Forsyth, Mehrens, Nellhaus, Reckase, Rindone, van der Linden and Zwick 2000), also known as the Benchmark method (Faggen 1994). In this approach, judges are asked to make decisions based on test task performance (i.e. recordings of speech or copies of written work) rather than by reviewing the task input material from the test paper. Typically, the group of panel members will first operationally define the person who just meets the required standard (referred to in the educational measurement literature as the 'minimally acceptable person' and in the language assessment literature as the 'minimally competent candidate'). Panel members typically make judgements on a set of test performances and then discuss their decisions before progressing to another round of judgements.

Initial stakeholder panels

Eleven initial stakeholder focus group panels were convened comprising doctors x 3 (15 participants); nurses x 3 (15 participants); public/patients x 3 (20 participants); allied health professionals x 1 (5 participants); responsible officers/medical directors x 1 (7 participants). A total of 62 people, 30 males and 32 females, 53 white and 9 ethnic minorities, ranging in age from early 20s to late 60s, from various regions of the UK and Northern Ireland, participated. Sessions were conducted over two days; the procedures followed are illustrated in Figure 2.

The lead moderator introduced the project and explained the background, aims and objectives. Questions from panel participants relating to the project were responded to as appropriate and essential administrative procedures were completed. The IMG/EEA distinction was explained to participants and the following scenario (originally provided by the GMC – see Berry

Figure 2 Procedures followed by initial SFGs

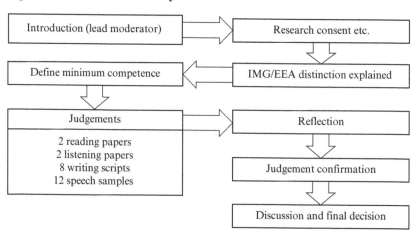

et al 2013) was outlined to further explain the intricacies and subtleties of the IMG/EEA distinction:

> EEA doctors would include EEA nationals, Swiss nationals and those entitled to be treated as such (by virtue of a European Community right). A European Community right can be demonstrated in a number of ways. One example would be a Chinese doctor married to a French national who is working in Belgium. This doctor would then be treated in the same way as an EEA national.

The panel then discussed the IMG/EEA distinction issue to decide if both should be treated as a single population with the same language requirements or as separate populations with different language requirements. Discussions, both of this issue and of all further SFG panel deliberations, were recorded, transcribed and analysed qualitatively using NVivo 10 (QSR International 2012).

Immediately prior to considering each skill individually, participants were asked to brainstorm the language characteristics that they believe a minimally competent candidate (MCC) should possess for each skill. These characteristics were summarised as Can Do statements and supplemented by *IELTS* descriptors and CEFR Can Do statements (see Berry et al 2013 for the full list of Can Do statements produced for each skill). Participants were then asked to judge a series of oral performances/writing samples/reading and listening task responses and make individual initial decisions as to the acceptability of the performance in relation to the Can Do statements/agreed characteristics of an MCC. Judgements of individual skills were made as described below.

Judgements of productive skills

Eight writing scripts were studied and 12 speech samples were listened to. Participants were asked to state which script/speech sample represented the minimum acceptable level of writing/speaking ability acceptable for a doctor. Each script/speech sample was then ranked on a 5-point scale where:

1 = not acceptable writing/speaking for a doctor
2 = borderline not acceptable
3 = borderline acceptable
4 = acceptable writing/speaking for a doctor
5 = very good writing/speaking, better than acceptable

Initial individual decisions for the writing and speaking tests were analysed by averaging the score given to each writing and speech sample. Those in the 4 or over range were definitely acceptable. Those in the 3–4 range were almost, but not definitely acceptable, so the panel members were asked to discuss their decisions and come to a collective agreement as to the acceptability of each writing and speech sample and the definition of the writing/ speaking competence of a minimally competent candidate. Speech samples for some candidates were replayed, as requested.

Participants were then told what band each script/speech sample represented according to the score to band conversion tables supplied by Cambridge English Language Assessment and were again asked to consider the minimum band they would accept from an MCC.

Judgements of receptive skills

Participants first defined the minimally competent reader/listener. They then took two reading and two listening tests (40 questions for each test) and estimated the probability of an MCC answering each item correctly. The totals were averaged for each test and converted to a band score according to the raw score to band conversion tables supplied by Cambridge English Language Assessment. Participants then discussed their estimates and re-judged if necessary.

Final panel

Representatives from each category of SFG panel were invited to participate in a final confirmatory panel which comprised two patients, two doctors, two nurses, one allied health professional and one responsible officer/medical director. The convener reminded the panel of the basic aims and objectives of the research and reviewed the methodology of the study. Participants were presented with summarised comments from initial SFGs on each of the *IELTS* skills tests plus summaries of qualitative judgements for each skill; these were discussed and this discussion, and all subsequent ones, were recorded for later transcription and review.

Descriptive statistics for reading and listening, converted to band scores, plus means of scores ranging from 1–5 which had been allocated to speech samples and writing exemplars, were presented and discussed. Decisions were made regarding appropriate levels to recommend for each skill and overall.

The appropriacy of *IELTS* as a screening test for overseas doctors prior to registration for PLAB Part 1 was discussed and decisions on recommendations were made. The IMG/EEA distinction was discussed and decisions on recommendations were made bearing in mind evidence relating to the testing systems in place for other UK professionals, other UK regulators and overseas medical regulators.

Overall recommendations to be offered to the GMC were further discussed and confirmed. On completion of the first draft of the report, the executive summary and recommendations therein were circulated to the final panel for confirmation that the recommendations reflected the panel's decisions.

Summary of overall findings from initial SFG and final panels

Following completion of the initial SFG panels, all judgements and data were analysed and comments on each of the skills discretely and overall were collated. A full presentation of all quantitative findings, including ANOVA (SPSS) and MFR (Facets) analyses and all comments from both the initial SFG panels and the final panel, can be found in Berry et al (2013). However, since this paper is particularly concerned with comments made by panels regarding the fairness of requiring evidence of English language ability from non-native speakers, overall findings relating to *IELTS* will simply be summarised here and the focus will then turn to the actual comments made during the data-gathering process.

- Some variation was found between the individual panels although the judgement of appropriate overall band scores required was quite consistent across groups.

- Perhaps unsurprisingly considering the amount of contact they have with overseas-trained doctors, nurses tended to be the most demanding of all participant categories in requirements for aural and oral skills.

- There was very little difference overall between the qualitative and quantitative data across groups. Patients, doctors and allied health professionals had higher band score equivalents for their quantitative judgements than their subjective judgements, whereas the reverse was true for nurses and responsible officers/medical directors.

- Most panels criticised some aspects of the *IELTS* test, notably the Listening paper, but all stated that it is a very good test of English language ability; all panels thought that the level demanded could be increased, particularly for the aural/oral skills.

- Of the four skills judged, listening was considered to be the most important and a higher level was demanded for this skill than for any other, closely followed by speaking (supporting the research findings of Lepetit and Cichocki 2002 and Lear 2005); the demands for reading and writing were given more leeway.

- All panels found it very difficult to arrive at an overall band score to recommend, many preferring to specify a profile (supporting the research findings of Chalhoub-Deville and Turner 2000). However, it was agreed that since an overall band score is an essential component of *IELTS* reporting, an average of the profile scores would be recommended as an overall band score.

Comments from all panels on IMG/EEA distinction

As mentioned previously, the current situation regarding IMGs and those from the EEA or holding EC rights was explained to each panel. Each panel then discussed the IMG/EEA distinction issue to decide if both should be treated as a single population with the same language requirements or as separate populations with different language requirements. Each panel was asked the following question: If evidence of English language competence should ever be required of EEAs in order for them to be admitted to the GMC register, should they provide the same evidence as IMGs?

In response to this question, every panel gave the following response or a very close variant of it: 'Yes, they should all provide the same evidence.' This is perhaps unsurprising given the media's collective and persistent focus on an earlier tragic accident where a British man died after being treated by a European doctor. However, although regulations have now been introduced requiring EEA doctors to provide evidence of English language ability, they are not required to provide the same evidence as IMGs, i.e. they are not required to provide *IELTS* scores.

Specific comments can be divided into three main themes: comments relating directly to the IMG/EEA distinction question; comments relating to the main purpose of testing English language skills, namely, that of ensuring patients' safety; and comments relating to broader issues arising from it including the testing of UK graduates' language and communication skills.

Selected comments addressing the IMG/EEA distinction and patient safety

Doctors:

> 'I think anyone whose first language is not the language they are going to be conducting their job in should have to exhibit a proficiency in that second language.'

> 'It's only reasonable that both IMG and EEA, rest of the world and Europeans should all provide the same evidence of ability to speak English.'

> 'Just because employment law in the EEA means that people can move freely and work freely doesn't lessen the language barriers they are going to face so I think I agree there should be the same requirements.'

> 'The bottom line is patients' safety and we can't ensure patients' safety unless we ensure communication.'

'The fact that you have a medical degree doesn't mean to say that you are a safe doctor, part of being a safe doctor is being able to communicate.'

Nurses:

'I think they should all be the same.'

'Anybody who is not a native speaker of English should provide the same standard of evidence of language ability.'

'We should ask EEA doctors for the same evidence of language ability that we ask of IMG doctors.'

Patients:

'Everybody should provide the same evidence of language ability, it's ridiculous not to.'

'It's only fair if they come to work in this country that people should be able to communicate in the language of the country.'

'It's a very serious issue, it's life or death.'

Allied health professionals:

'I think everybody should be made to provide evidence, I don't see how you can differentiate in any way.'

'If you have a test for everyone to prove they can speak English, that test should be for everyone for whom English is a second language.'

Responsible officers/medical directors:

'If there is a sort of escape route for IMGs to become EEA then that is an issue so all IMG and EEA graduates should provide the same evidence of language ability.'

'Our first duty has to be to the patients.'

'Consequences are much greater than going to the supermarket and ending up with the wrong vegetables.'

'If reception of what the patients are saying is misinterpreted it can go in all sorts of directions that aren't appropriate.'

Selected comments relating to the issue of assessing the English language ability of UK graduates

Doctors and responsible officers/medical directors:

'There should be no difference between a graduate from the UK or an IMG or an EEA doctor.'

'There is a separate argument about whether UK graduates should be subjected to the same test.'

'If there is a principle of fairness then the argument to test everyone is the right one to take.'

'They should decide to put English or language testing into medical school curriculum; that would mean you couldn't graduate without achieving a standard of communication.'

'This is fundamentally about patient safety so despite the extra cost it might incur really everyone should undergo a test and they should go through the same rigorous test.'

As can be seen from the above comments, all participants in all the SFG panels and final panel were strongly of the opinion that in the interests of patient safety all overseas applicants to the GMC register should provide the same evidence of English language ability, regardless of where they originally qualified or which country they came from. There was also a substantial body of opinion, primarily on the part of doctors and responsible officers/ medical directors (who are, of course, also doctors), that the issue of requiring evidence of English language ability from graduates of British medical schools should also be addressed by means of the inclusion of courses on communication in the curriculum and the testing of language and communication skills as part of a primary undergraduate medical qualification. This last point is, however, outside the scope of this study since the GMC were not in agreement that we should include it in our recommendations.

Discussion and recommendations

This study was undertaken in order to refresh and extend a previous investigation into *IELTS* band score levels and IMGs (Banerjee 2004) and to develop a stronger evidence base for the GMC's requirements when setting minimum language standards for overseas applicants to their register. Current required *IELTS* levels were investigated to determine if they are adequate in light of issues of patient safety; the issue of requiring evidence of English language ability from all non-native English-speaking medical practitioners seeking admission to the GMC register was also investigated.

Objective 1:

To determine if the current overall *IELTS* score of Band 7, with no separate skill score lower than Band 7, is adequate as a preliminary language screening device for IMGs.

There are a number of alternative pathways available for fulfilling GMC requirements for registration to practise medicine in the UK, the current most popular way being for IMGs to provide initial evidence of English language competence by achieving a minimum overall score of Band 7 on the Academic module of the *IELTS* test in a single sitting, with no separate skill score lower than Band 7. The final panel, in keeping with several of the initial SFG panels, found it very difficult to arrive at an overall band score to recommend, many participants preferring to specify a profile. This is congruent with other research findings such as the study by Chalhoub-Deville and Turner (2000) who reviewed all the major tests used around the world for undergraduate and postgraduate admissions to university. They suggest that good selection practice should take into account not only an overall band score, but also scores in the different skills areas, as different academic programmes may require different profiles of language ability. Although this present study is not concerned with university admissions, it could be argued that there may be more demands made on doctors' oral/aural skills than on their receptive reading and productive written ability and this is something the GMC may wish to take into consideration when determining the English language requirements for overseas applicants to their register. We therefore made the following recommendation with respect to Objective 1.

Recommendation 1:

The band score level requirements for *IELTS* should be revised and the GMC should consider adopting a profile which reflects the importance of oral skills, with listening being of paramount importance, but allowing for some flexibility in assessing reading and writing ability.

Objective 2:

To determine if EEA graduates should provide the same evidence as IMGs if evidence of English language competence should ever be required in order for them to be admitted to the GMC register.

Despite an EU directive which currently exempts graduates with acceptable medical qualifications from within the EEA and Switzerland from providing evidence of English language ability when applying for registration in the UK, this is not considered an acceptable situation with regard to patient safety. As can be seen from the comments presented earlier, it has been forcefully argued that both IMGs and EEA graduates should all provide evidence of English language ability in order to register with the GMC. We therefore made the following recommendation with respect to Objective 2.

Recommendation 2:

> The GMC should attempt to find a way of requiring all non-native speakers of English to provide evidence of English language competence before being allowed to practise medicine in the UK and that if ever it becomes possible to require evidence of language ability from EEA graduates, they should provide the same evidence as IMGs.

Objective 3:

As shown in the introduction, assessing language ability in professional contexts is a highly complex and somewhat daunting task. In a medical context, with the exception of the OET, no other medically oriented language proficiency test of English for doctors exists. However, a recent empirical study by Elder et al (2012) has highlighted the critical importance of doctors having a good command of lay language, in addition to medical terminology. Wette (2011) and Pill and Woodward-Kron's (2012) response to Wette, have also highlighted the tensions that exist between the assessment of general language proficiency and medical communication skills. It appears, then, that in addition to having acceptable medical qualifications, prospective doctors should be able to demonstrate a high level of general English language proficiency.

Despite the criticisms made of the *IELTS* test, which were mainly concerned with the appropriacy of using a test designed for use in the academic domain in other domains (McNamara 2000, McNamara and Roever 2006), *IELTS* has been shown to be a robust general language proficiency test. This is reinforced by comments from the initial SFG panels and from the final panel, most of whom criticised certain aspects of the test but also considered it to be a very good test of general English ability (see Berry et al 2013). It is clear, therefore, that although *IELTS* obviously cannot be used as a test of medical competence, it is certainly an appropriate instrument to use to assess the language ability of prospective medical doctors to the GMC register. We therefore made the following recommendation with respect to Objective 3.

Recommendation 3:

> The *IELTS* test should be retained as an appropriate test of the English language competence of overseas trained doctors.

Conclusion

This research was conducted in isolation from any organised medical contexts. Given the well-documented, highly interactive nature of communication in medical settings and the fact that there already exists a test of medical communication skills for overseas-trained doctors as well as numerous specialist communication skills tests, such as that for GPs, it would have perhaps been useful to co-operate with medical professionals to see if we could contribute to each other's understanding of necessary language competence and communication in a medical context. In terms of overseas-trained candidates applying for admission to the GMC register, it may be that language is not the only issue and perhaps there should be a closer look at the relationship between language ability as assessed by *IELTS* and medical knowledge as assessed by PLAB. Nevertheless, by thoroughly investigating the use of *IELTS* as a screening tool for overseas applicants to the GMC register, we believe that the research presented in this paper goes some considerable way towards building a substantive validity argument for the use of *IELTS* in the context of the UK medical domain, at least for the foreseeable future.

Acknowledgements

The research reported in this paper was funded by the UK General Medical Council.

Examination materials used in the study were provided by Cambridge English Language Assessment (formerly Cambridge ESOL); we acknowledge the support of the *IELTS* partners.

Our Research Administrator at the University of Roehampton, Sandra Rugea, provided invaluable assistance at all stages of the study.

We extend our thanks to all panel members who participated in the study, especially those who set up, or helped to organise, the panels.

Notes

1. The required overall band score level was increased to Band 7.5 with no skill score lower than Band 7 in summer 2014. See http://www.gmc-uk.org/news/23792.asp

References

Alderson, J C, Candlin, C N, Clapham, C M, Martin, D J and Weir, C J (1986) *Language Proficiency Testing for Migrant Professionals: New Directions for the Occupational English Test*, report submitted to the Council on Overseas Professional Qualifications.

Banerjee, J (2004) *Study of the Minimum English Language Writing and Speaking Abilities Needed by Overseas Trained Doctors*, report to the General Medical Council, July 2004.

Banerjee, J and Taylor, L (2005) *Setting the Standard: What English Language Abilities do Overseas Trained Doctors Need?* paper presented at the Language Testing Research Colloquium, Ottawa, Canada, July 2005.

Berry, V, O'Sullivan, B and Rugea, S (2013) *Identifying the Appropriate* IELTS *Score Levels for IMG Applicants to the GMC Register*, report submitted to the General Medical Council, February 2013, available online: www.gmc-uk.org/ Identifying_the_appropriate_IELTS_score_levels_for_IMG_applicants_to_ the. . ..pdf_55207825.pdf

Chalhoub-Deville, M and Turner, C (2000) What to look for in ESL admissions tests: Cambridge certificate exams. *IELTS* and TOEFL, *System* 28, 523–539.

Chur-Hansen, A (1997) Language background, English language proficiency and selection for language development, *Medical Education* 31, 312–319.

Cizek, G J (1993) Reconsidering standards and criteria, *Journal of Educational Measurement* 30 (2), 93–106.

Cizek, G J and Bunch, M B (2007) *Standard Setting*, Thousand Oaks: Sage.

Council of Europe (2001) *Common European Framework of Reference for Languages: Learning, Teaching, Assessment*, Cambridge: Cambridge University Press.

Elder, C, Pill, J, Woodward-Kron, R, McNamara, T, Manias, E, McColl, G and Webb, G (2012) Health professionals' views of communication: Implications for assessing performance on a health-specific English language test, *TESOL Quarterly* 46 (2), 409–419.

Faggen, J (1994) *Setting Standards for Constructed Response Tests: An Overview*, Princeton: Educational Testing Service.

Friedman, M, Sutnick, A I, Stillman, P L, Norcini, J J, Anderson, S M, Williams, R G, Henning, G and Reeves, M J (1991) The use of standardized patients to evaluate the spoken-English proficiency of foreign medical graduates, *Academic Medicine* 66, 61–63.

General Medical Council (2014) *GMC welcomes support to check language skills of European doctors*, press release issued 25 February 2014, available online: www.gmc-uk.org/news/23792.asp

Hambleton, R K and Plake, B S (1995) Using an extended Angoff procedure to set standards on complex performance assessments, *Applied Measurement in Education* 8 (1), 41–55.

Hambleton, R K, Brennan, R L, Brown, W, Dodd, B, Forsyth, R A, Mehrens, W A, Nellhaus, J, Reckase, M D, Rindone, D, van der Linden, W J and Zwick, R (2000) A response to 'Setting Reasonable and Useful Performance Standards' in the National Academy of Sciences' grading the nation's report card, *Educational Measurement: Issues and Practice* 19 (2), 5–14.

Harding, L, Pill, J and Ryan, K (2011) Assessor decision making while marking a note-taking listening test: The case of the OET, *Language Assessment Quarterly* 8 (2), 108–126.

Impara, J C and Plake, B S (1998) Teachers' ability to estimate item difficulty: A test of the assumptions in the Angoff standard setting method, *Journal of Educational Measurement* 35 (1), 69–81.

Kaftandjieva, F (2004) *Reference Supplement to the Preliminary Pilot version of the Manual for Relating Language Examinations to the Common European Framework of Reference for Languages: Learning, Teaching, Assessment. Section B: Standard Setting*, Strasbourg: Council of Europe.

Lear, D W (2005) Spanish for working medical professionals: Linguistic needs, *Foreign Language Annals* 38, 223–232.

Lepetit, D and Cichocki, W (2002) Teaching languages to future health professionals: a needs assessment study, *The Modern Language Journal* 86, 384–396.

McLachlan, J, Illing, J, Rothwell, C Margetts, J K, Archer, J and Shrewsbury, D (2012) *Developing an evidence base for the Professional and Linguistics Assessments Board (PLAB) Test*, unpublished literature review submitted to GMC.

McNamara, T (2000) *Language Testing*, Oxford: Oxford University Press.

McNamara, T and Roever, C (2006) *Language Testing: The Social Dimension*, Malden and Oxford: Blackwell.

Messick, S (1989) Validity, in Linn, R L (Ed) *Educational Measurement* (3rd edition), New York: Macmillan, 13–103.

O'Sullivan, B (2012) Assessment issues in languages for specific purposes, *Modern Language Journal* 96, 71–88.

Pill, J (2013) *What doctors value in consultations and the implications for specific purpose language testing*, unpublished PhD dissertation, University of Melbourne.

Pill, J and Woodward-Kron, R (2012) How professionally relevant can language tests be? A Response to Wette (2011), *Language Assessment Quarterly* 9, 105–108.

QSR International (2012) *NVivo 10*, available online: www.qsrinternational.com/products_nvivo.aspx

Rea-Dickins, P (1987) Testing doctors' written communicative competence: An experimental technique in English for specialist purposes, *Quantitative Linguistics* 34, 185–218.

Read, J and Wette, R (2009) Achieving English proficiency for professional registration: The experience of overseas-qualified health professionals in the New Zealand context, IELTS *Research Reports* 10, 181–222.

Taylor, L and Pill, J (in press) Assessing Health Professionals, in Kunnan, A J (Ed) *The Companion to Language Assessment*, Malden: Wiley Blackwell, 497–512.

Watt, D, Lake, D, Cabrnoch, T and Leonard, K (2003) *Assessing the English Language Proficiency of International Medical Graduates in their Integration into Canada's Physician Supply*, report commissioned by the Canadian Task Force on Licensure of International Medical Graduates, Ottawa, Ontario, Canada, available online: www.mcap.ca/pdf/Assessing%20ELP%20of%20 IMGs_Final_2003.pdf

Wette, R (2011) English proficiency tests and communication skills training for overseas-qualified health professionals in Australia and New Zealand, *Language Assessment Quarterly* 8 (2), 200–210.

Whelan, G, McKinley, D, Boulet, J, Macrae, J and Kamholz, S (2001) Validation of the doctor–patient communication component of the Educational Commission for Foreign Medical Graduates Clinical Skills Assessment, *Medical Education* 34 (8), 757–761.

Section 3
Teachers' professional development and assessment

14 Profiling teacher competences: The multilingual validation of the European Profiling Grid (EPG)

Brian North

Eaquals

Abstract

Two interesting, related questions in language education are (a) whether languages have radically different pedagogic cultures and (b) the extent to which there is such a thing as 'best practice' that can be defined and shared between teaching cultures. Can one develop 'context-free' descriptors not just for learner competences (e.g. the Common European Framework of Reference for Languages (CEFR)) or for institutional competences (e.g. the standards for test providers produced by the Association of Language Testers in Europe (ALTE), the standards for programme providers produced by Evaluation and Accreditation of Quality Language Services (Eaquals)) but also for teacher competences? Can one develop descriptors for the main stages of a teacher's career? Teacher training and qualifications related to the teaching of English in England, French in France differ greatly; is there any communality? Is there any clear relationship between qualifications and experience on the one hand and competences on the other? Do teachers, trainers and academic managers relate to such descriptors in a similar way? These are some of the questions that the European Profiling Grid (EPG) project, initiated by Eaquals and co-ordinated by the Centre internationale d'études pédagogiques (CIEP), sought to address. The EPG emulates the CEFR self-assessment grid for learners, which also appears in the Language Passport of the European Language Portfolio (ELP) with three broad developmental phases each divided into two to make six bands for a number of categories. An electronic version that prints a profile is online. In the piloting and field testing, qualitative and quantitative validation were carried out in English, French, German, Spanish and Italian in a variety of teaching contexts from secondary school to adult education and the university sector. In the main data collection for a Rasch analysis, 2,100 teachers from 86 countries self-assessed with descriptors from the grid.

Introduction

The European Profiling Grid (EPG) is an analytic rating scale that provides descriptors for different aspects of teacher competences at different stages of their training and career. It is available on the website www.epg-project.eu in an interactive, electronic form in English, French, German and Spanish, with downloadable pdf files of the EPG itself plus a User Guide in those languages, plus certain others including Italian and Polish. The EPG has three broad development phases, each themselves divided into a lower and upper band to give a total of six bands. The 13 categories are grouped under four headings: *Training and Qualifications*; *Key Teaching Competences*; *Enabling Competences*, and *Professionalism*, as shown below:

- Training and Qualifications: Language proficiency; Education and training; Assessed teaching; Teaching experience.
- Key Teaching Competences: Methodology, knowledge and skills; Lesson and course planning; Interaction management and monitoring; Assessment.
- Enabling Competences: Intercultural competence; Language awareness; Digital media.
- Professionalism: Professional conduct; Administration.

Each subcategory at each band is a cell on the grid that contains between two and five bullet-pointed descriptors. For example, the entries for bands 2.1, 2.2 and 3.1 for the subcategory 'Lesson and course planning' looks as shown in Table 1.

It would be highly unusual for any teacher to be in exactly the same phase for each of all the 13 categories; indeed the EPG is rather intended to enable teachers to profile their strengths and weaknesses. A second major exploitation of the EPG is to provide a group profile of a staffroom or faculty, by aggregating the profiles of individual teachers, in order to identify priorities for training and/or recruitment. The EPG is used in this second way, to provide an institutional profile, in the Eaquals inspection scheme[1].

The origins of the EPG

The EPG uses a style of descriptors reminiscent of the Common European Framework of Reference (CEFR, Council of Europe 2001) and was indeed inspired by the CEFR's self-assessment grid, CEFR Table 2, which appears in the European Language Portfolio (ELP). The methodology used to validate the descriptors is also reminiscent of that used for the CEFR descriptors

Table 1 EPG extract: Lesson and course planning (Phases 2.1–3.1)

Phase 2.1	Phase 2.2	Phase 3.1
• Can use a syllabus and specified materials to prepare lesson plans that are balanced and meet the needs of the group. • Can plan phases and timing of lessons with different objectives. • Can compare learners' needs and refer to these in planning main and supplementary objectives for lessons.	• Can plan a course or part of a course taking account of the syllabus, the needs of different students and the available materials. • Can design tasks to exploit the linguistic and communicative potential of materials. • Can design tasks to meet individual needs as well as course objectives.	• Can conduct a thorough needs analysis and use it to develop a detailed and balanced course plan that includes recycling and revision. • Can design different tasks based on the same source material for use with learners at different levels. • Can use analysis of learner difficulties in order to decide on action points for upcoming lessons.

(North 2000, North and Schneider 1998), as explained later in this paper. The EPG is one of a series of three European projects that, in the wake of the CEFR, have concerned themselves with the definition of teacher competences in Can Do CEFR style. The other two projects were the following: the *European Profile for Language Teacher Education – A Frame of Reference* (Kelly and Grenfell 2004), which provides a definition of the needs of teachers in initial training, organised under Knowledge and understanding, Strategies and skills, and Values, and the European Portfolio for Student Teachers of Languages (EPOSTL, Newby, Allan, Fenner, Jones, Komorowska and Soghikyan 2006), covering a similar area with 190 'Can Do' style descriptors grouped in seven areas: Context; Methodology; Resources; Lesson planning; Conducting a lesson; Independent learning, and Assessment of learning. However, both these projects define desirable characteristics of future language teachers that may be orientation tools for initial teacher training courses. There is no attempt to define levels of competences or to provide a metalanguage to highlight strengths and weaknesses in relation to the requirements of a particular teaching context.

The EPG has its origin in such a practical need to profile teacher competence and diagnose training and recruitment needs. The context was a private primary and secondary school in Brazil in which Eurocentres[2] was carrying through a curriculum reform for English language teaching in 1997–1999. The main aspects of the reform were to regroup paired school years into sets by proficiency, to introduce CEFR-based syllabus aims and international course books for more precise levels, and to create a focus on pair work and interaction in small groups. Two grids were developed in order to gather information about the teachers already employed in the programme:

one a performance assessment grid, the other a professional profiling grid. The former considered key aspects of a teacher's performance such as their rapport with the class, their projection of their personality to inspire students, plus more 'objective' factors like their ability to answer student queries adequately, called 'Language awareness', and their classroom management skills. This performance grid was used to evaluate a teacher after observation of a lesson, in addition to a more conventional observation sheet that followed the phases of the lesson, the setting and the achievement of objectives, etc. The companion profile grid was completed beforehand by the teacher; it recorded their view of their experience and broader professional issues, using the following categories: Experience, Qualifications, Computer literacy, Professionalism, and Mentoring and teamwork. At an Eaquals conference in Athens in 2005 in which Special Interest Projects were set up, these two grids were presented to a small group with the question: should we in Eaquals develop a self-assessment grid for teachers based on this? The response was great interest in the general concept, with a reservation about the subjectivity of judgements on projection, rapport and sensitivity used in the first grid, since these were considered personality factors. Over the next year Galya Mateva and the current author developed the Eaquals Teacher Profiling Grid, which was presented at an Eaquals conference in San Sebastian in 2006 and at an international seminar in Siena in 2009 (North 2012, Rossner 2012). The style of the grid was very much influenced by CEFR Table 2 (self-assessment grid).

The aims of the EPG project

The EPG project (2011–2013), funded by the European Union's Leonardo Programme, set out to validate the Eaquals grid and provide equivalent versions in different languages. The EPG is intended for three groups of users:

- for teachers, as a self-assessment tool offering a stimulus for reflection about development needs
- for academic managers, giving them an overview of the make-up of a teaching team, a means to identify development needs, and a set of 'objective', external criteria that could be a neutral reference point in yearly appraisals, in which teacher and manager could compare their respective profiles for the teacher and discuss personal development, and last but not least
- for teacher trainers, to orient the content of continuous professional development, as a source for observation criteria, and above all as a means of raising awareness about specific competences that the team would profit from working on.

The key issue in these exploitations is that, like the CEFR descriptors, the EPG descriptors offer a common, context-neutral metalanguage to facilitate discussion and networking.

The EPG Validation Project

In the same way that the style and format of the grid was influenced by the CEFR (CEFR Table 2), the validation methodology was based on that adopted for the CEFR illustrative descriptors (North 2000, North and Schneider 1998). This involved a qualitative phase in which informants sort descriptors and comment on them, plus a quantitative phase in which data from a large-scale survey is used to calibrate the descriptors using the Rasch model from Item Response Theory (IRT).

Qualitative analysis

The informants for this phase were academic managers and teacher trainers. The main task, undertaken by both groups, was to place the contents of each cell of one part of the grid into the correct cells on a blank grid and to mark any reversal for further discussion with the animator, as shown in Figure 1. This sorting task was carried out at the level of the cell rather than at the level of the descriptor, because the role of the informants was to give feedback on the grid holistically – in contrast to the discrete data on separate descriptors from the survey described below.

Figure 1 Descriptor sorting task

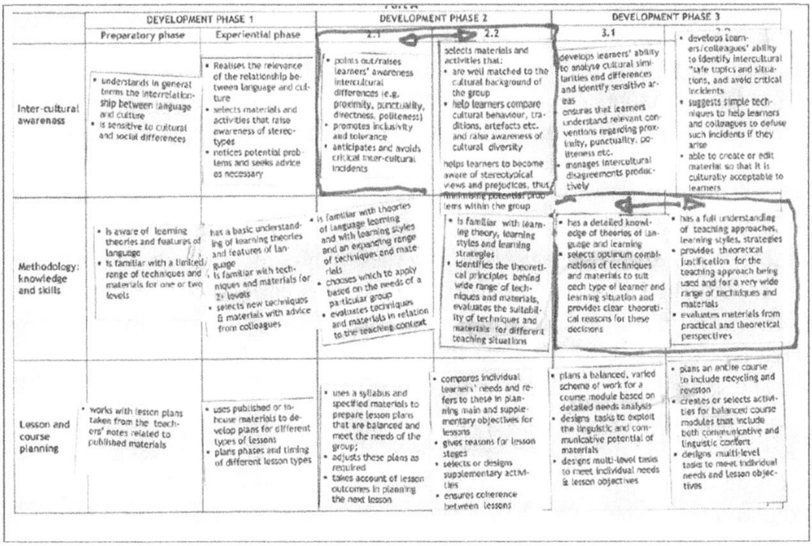

The second task, undertaken only by the academic managers, was to select four teachers from their staff and to assess those four teachers in order to produce a profile, to get the same four teachers to assess themselves producing their own profile, and then to have an individual meeting with each of the four teachers in order to compare and discuss the viewpoints expressed by the two profiles (self-assessment, external assessment). The final task, undertaken by both academic managers and teacher trainers, was a structured interview with the animator about the experience as a whole.

Quantitative analysis

In creating a set of level descriptors for language proficiency (as in the CEFR) or for professional proficiency (as with the EPG) a decision must be taken as to what content goes at which levels. A methodology has existed to mathematically *scale* descriptors for almost as long as scales of professional proficiency have existed. Smith and Kendall (1963) used analysis of the way in which senior nurses used descriptors to rate the performance of trainee nurses to scale the descriptors to the continuum of nursing ability – required for criterion-referenced assessment. An adaptation of this approach was developed in order to calibrate illustrative descriptors for the CEFR (North 2000, North and Schneider 1998). Despite the existence of such methods, it is, however, still generally the case that content on frameworks of levels in the language world is placed at the different levels concerned on the basis of intuition alone, with editorial support from a working group, but no data analysis. The danger of this approach is that conventions and clichés are copied from instrument to instrument without ever being properly validated. Another issue is that committee authoring of profiling or assessment grids often produces description that is relative, the description at one level only making sense in relation to the description at other levels. As has long been pointed out, this is not criterion-referenced assessment; in order for a descriptor to qualify as a criterion statement, it must be possible to answer 'yes' or 'no' to it in isolation, irrespective of any other descriptor (Skehan 1984). A profiling grid needs to contain independent criterion statements; thus the question was: will the answers that teachers give when self-assessing their competences by answering 'Yes' or 'No' to the EPG descriptors presented in isolation actually create such a criterion-referenced measurement scale (or set of measurement scales)? That is to say, will the EPG 'work'?

The second issue that the analysis was to address was, as with the CEFR descriptor research, to investigate the extent to which the EPG offers a 'common meta-language'. Do teachers of French and teachers of German think in a sufficiently similar way about aspects of their competence for a common grid to be justifiable?

To put this another way the purpose of the analysis was twofold:

1. To scale the criterion descriptors (i.e. the bullet points in the cells of the pilot grid) and to set provisional cut-points between the six development phases, and, in so doing:
   a. recommend which descriptors should be removed or amended
   b. investigate the relationship between aspects of 'Qualifications and Training' on the one hand and the descriptors of aspects of language teacher competence on the other hand.

2. To determine whether there are any statistically significant differences in the interpretation of the difficulty of the descriptors by teachers of different languages, from different educational sectors, at different stages in their career, i.e. to carry out studies on Differential Item Functioning (DIF).

These two aims suggested the use of an IRT methodology rather than a Classical Test Theory (CTT) methodology. IRT produces an objective scaling of the items (here, the descriptors) that is independent of personal opinion. Secondly, whereas the results of any CTT analysis are only valid in relation to the particular group of individuals who completed the instruments that provided the data, IRT results can be generalised to other members of the same population. That is to say, scale values for descriptors should remain stable, i.e. show no statistically significant variation, for the different sub-populations of the group of persons who completed the instruments – if those groups really are sub-groups of the same population. In other words, the scale values for the descriptors produced by using only the data from native-speaker teachers compared to those values produced by using only the data from non-native-speaker teachers should be almost the same. Similarly the scale values for the descriptors produced by using only the data from teachers of German should be substantially the same as those produced with only the data from teachers of French.

The Rasch Model (IRT) analysis programme Winsteps (Linacre 2012) was therefore used for the analysis. The data came from self-assessment by teachers on SurveyMonkey online questionnaires. The 144 descriptors for the major categories Key Teaching Competences and Enabling Competences plus for Professionalism were presented by categories, with the order of the descriptors randomised within each category, on four overlapping questionnaires, each made available in English, French, German, Spanish and Italian. In order to ensure a solid scale, the questionnaires were linked by 50% anchoring, each sharing the descriptors for two categories as shown in Table 2. Thus every descriptor was used on two of the four questionnaires. In addition, all respondents were asked to provide demographic data and were presented with the descriptors for Training and Qualifications (Language proficiency; Education and training; Assessed teaching; Teaching

Table 2 Linking between questionnaires

A	Intercultural Competence	Language Awareness	Methodology	Planning					
B			Methodology	Planning	Interaction management	Assessment			
C					Interaction management	Assessment	Digital media	Professionalism
D	Intercultural competence	Language awareness					Digital media	Professionalism

experience). The data on these descriptors was, however, not included in the initial analyses that built the scale. It was added in a final stage in order to inform the process of setting cut-offs.

Since the analysis method is inspired by that used to validate the CEFR descriptors, it is interesting to compare the methodologies used in the two projects, as in Table 3. The most significant differences are that the Swiss CEFR project used teacher assessment of their learners to calibrate the descriptors, whereas the EPG project used self-assessment by teachers of their own competences. Secondly, whilst in the Swiss CEFR project the quantitative analysis followed the qualitative analysis in a logical manner, the restrictions of a Leonardo project led to these two steps happening in parallel for the EPG. Therefore the formulation of the descriptors in the final version of the EPG is informed by both analyses (qualitative and quantitative) simultaneously. In practice, this turned out to be no disadvantage as is discussed in the conclusion.

Table 3 CEFR and EPG descriptor research methodology compared

Swiss CEFR project	EPG project
Assessment of learners by their teachers at the end of school year	Self-assessment by teachers of own competences
250 teachers, 2,500 learners	2,100 teachers
Paper questionnaires	Online questionnaires
50 items + demographic information	c.60 items + demographic information
After qualitative validation: • sorting descriptors • highlighting problematic elements of descriptors • identifying good descriptors.	*Parallel to* qualitative validation: • sorting cells of existing grid (teacher trainers and academic managers) • highlighting problematic elements of descriptors (teacher trainers and academic managers) • using existing grid to assess staff (academic managers).

Project phases

The EPG project had six sequential steps that are summarised below:

Pre-pilot: Qualitative only, English only

This was a consultation phase in order to get feedback on the existing Eaquals grid and to trial on a small scale the qualitative methodology later used in the pilot and main field-testing. As a result of comments made, it was decided to extend the original grid to include Intercultural competences, Digital media and Professionalism, two of which, interestingly, had been in the original Eurocentres grid.

Translation into French, German, Spanish and Italian

The translation process was far from straightforward because those responsible for the translation work package were not initially aware of the technical issues involved. It required a principled intervention in order to raise awareness and establish common procedures, guidelines and tools. In translating descriptors, the following issues are central:

- The different language versions of descriptors are intended to be exact equivalents. Therefore, it should be possible to compare them directly during the translation process. This is best done by creating a master file of all the translations as an Excel or Word table in which descriptors are rows and languages are columns.

- Descriptors employ technical terminology that needs to be translated systematically. This has two implications. Firstly, the expression 'progress test' should be translated the same way in each descriptor in which it appears. Secondly, the project concerned is probably not the first occasion on which the technical expression concerned (e.g. 'progress test') has been translated. There should be a search for relevant glossaries. In this case both the ALTE glossary, published in the Studies in Language Testing (SiLT) series (Association of Language Testers in Europe 1999) and the Eaquals glossary, available from the Eaquals office, proved helpful. The ALTE glossary is set up like a dictionary with separate alphabetical sections for each language, in which each entry has a definition and cross-references to the equivalent entries in the other languages. The Eaquals glossary is simpler, set up as a table of expressions (rows) and languages (columns).

- The translation process is a cyclical, interactive one: a translation into, for example French may give the translator into, for example Italian, an idea on how to improve their initial version. Furthermore, translations or translation difficulties may impact back onto the formulation of the original, which may have knock-on effects on some of the translations. A master file such as that described above assures transparency during this cyclical development.

- Finally, there needs to be systematic quality control of the adequacy of the translations. This evaluation can take various forms. The simplest is that a plurilingual person or group of persons with the necessary technical expertise undertakes a formal review. An alternative, particularly when no one understands all the languages involved, is back translation, in which the translated descriptors are translated back into the source language, with these retranslations being compared to the original formulation to see if there are significant differences. In addition, systematic differences in the interpretation of the descriptors when used in different languages for assessment can be investigated statistically. In the EPG project, the first and last methods were used: the current author became quality controller and then any remaining translation problems were identified through the DIF analyses with the Rasch model that were mentioned above and that are described later in the paper.

Pilot: Qualitative and quantitative (5 languages)

The idea of the pilot was to trial the instruments for both the qualitative and the quantitative analyses in all languages. For the qualitative part, participants were asked to place the contents of the different cells of the draft grid into the correct spaces on a blank version of the grid. Here no changes were necessary, except for more explicit instructions. For the quantitative part, data for the calibration of the descriptors with the Rasch model was to be collected through self-assessments in relation to descriptors from the draft grid presented in a series of overlapping questionnaires in a SurveyMonkey online survey. Here, piloting of the online survey indicated several problems. First and foremost, animators reported that respondents had great difficulty using a 6-point rating scale for each descriptor. About a quarter of the respondents dropped out during questionnaire completion, leaving only 150 for the pilot analysis, and this was attributed to the complexity of the rating scale. Secondly, an 'I can' formulation had not been used for all categories and some counter-intuitive calibrations suggested that this had caused problems. A glaring example was the item: 'I work with lesson plans taken from the teachers' notes related to published materials'. Many people said 'No' to this because they don't need this support and therefore do not do this, although they could if they wanted to. However, because so many said 'No', this item came out as the most difficult descriptor in the category Lesson and course planning. As a result almost all the descriptors for Key Teaching Competences and Enabling Competences were given 'I can' formulation, except those for Intercultural competence, where actually doing it seemed the issue rather than a theoretical capability to do so. Finally, the formulation of some original descriptors and of some translations was improved as a result of feedback or the analysis.

Main field testing: Qualitative and quantitative (5 languages)

The main data collection was relatively problem free as a result of the thorough piloting. The qualitative feedback from the academic managers and teacher trainers was overwhelmingly positive, with certain suggestions for improved formulations of descriptors. In general, however, the informants restricted their comments to possible uses – and abuses – of the grid. This section therefore concentrates on the quantitative data. A total of 1,817 usable questionnaires were completed by teachers in 76 countries, with 12 main European countries (Austria, Bulgaria, France, Germany, Greece,

Italy, Netherlands, Poland, Romania, Spain, Turkey, United Kingdom) accounting for 1,414 of these. English (748) was the main target language followed by German (409), French (269), Spanish (249) and finally Italian (139). Three respondents reported another target language. The number of respondents teaching their mother tongue (912) was almost identical to the number not teaching their mother tongue (905). Over 1,100 of the respondents taught mainly in either the Higher Education (622) or in the Adult and Vocational training sectors (488). Three hundred and six taught in Lower secondary (13–16) whilst 205 taught in Upper Secondary (17–18). Finally, 163 taught in Primary and 13 taught children under 6. The majority of the respondents were very experienced teachers: 1,038 had more than 10 years' experience, 496 had 4–9 years' experience and there were very few inexperienced teachers. Of the respondents, 729 had a Master's degree.

This weighting of the sample of respondents towards teachers with a lot of experience had an effect on the analysis. Because the Rasch model was used, it does not prevent scaling of all the descriptors. However it meant that because very few respondents said 'No' to the descriptors in the lower part of the scale, the descriptors calibrated to this range have much higher Standard Error. This means that the precision of the calibrations is more restricted and led to differences in the rank ordering of the descriptors in this range when different types of analyses were undertaken (a Global Analysis with all the descriptors as opposed to separate Category Analyses for each category).

The analysis followed the following steps:

1. Global Analysis of all the descriptors together, including (a) checking the stability of the values for the descriptors on the two questionnaires they appeared on, and (b) identifying removing any misfitting items, or items with strange calibrations.
2. DIF analyses, investigating the extent to which the descriptors provided teachers with a common metalanguage, focusing on the native speaker/ non-native speaker divide, target languages, educational sectors, and experience.
3. Separate analyses for each category (= Category Analyses), building separate scales for each of the main categories, which are listed in Table 2.
4. Setting cut-points between phases, by comparing the results from the Global Analysis and the Category Analyses, guided by placement on the scale of the descriptors for Qualifications and Training.

Results

Global Analysis

With the data collection design shown in Table 2, each competence descriptor appeared on two questionnaires. The value on the scale produced by an independent analysis of each of the two questionnaires on which the items occur should produce a very similar result – a result without a statistically significant difference. Wright and Stone (1979:92–96) offer a quality control technique to check this. Any item occurring on a scatter plot outside the lines representing a test of significance at the 95% level (or 0.05 level) should be rejected as unstable. Such scatter plots are known as *Standard Error Plots* because the Standard Error of Measurement (SEM) is used with the scale value to calculate where the dots representing items appear in the plot. Such plots were created for each pair of questionnaires, with the one for Questionnaires B and C, shown in Figure 2, showing significant differences. As can be seen in Figure 2, all four descriptors mentioning the CEFR plus one saying 'I can write progress tests for any level' are outside the quality control lines and so highlighted with a circle. The five items concerned are the following:

Figure 2 Standard Error Plot (Questionnaires B and C)

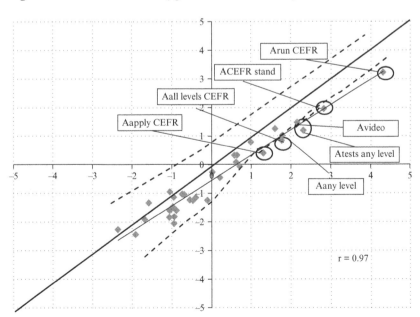

- ACEFRstand: I have taken part in standardisation training for assessing learner performance in terms of the levels of the CEFR
- ArunCEFR: I can run CEFR standardisation sessions
- AapplyCEFR: I can apply CEFR criteria when assessing proficiency in speaking and writing
- AalllevelsCEFR: I can assess spoken and written proficiency reliably at all levels according to CEFR criteria
- Atestsanylevel: I can write progress tests for any level.

Another two assessment descriptors were also very close to a significantly significant difference:

- Avideo: I can use video recordings to help learners recognise their strengths and weaknesses
- Aanylevel: I can develop assessment tasks for any level.

These items are all noticeably easier for respondents on Questionnaire C, five of them significantly so. Yet it is not as if the respondents to Questionnaire C had more qualifications or years of experience. 40.1% have a Master's degree – exactly as for the total 1,817 respondents. The proportions of responses in the other answer categories for qualifications or years of experience are astonishingly similar to the overall proportions. There is no concentration of responses from one single country or target language that might explain a greater familiarity with assessment in general or with the CEFR. There are perhaps three possible interpretations. Maybe the CEFR levels are just not (yet?) really a stable part of teachers' key core competences. On the other hand, maybe the problem reflects the way many teachers may not feel confident of their interpretation of all the levels, especially when they tend to teach one particular level. Yet again, perhaps people who are more expert at assessing levels become more aware of their limitations in doing so as they gain experience and attend standardisation sessions in which they experience differences of opinion. Perhaps less experienced teachers are less aware of the pitfalls; perhaps teacher self-assessment of ability to assess level is a bit like learner self-assessment of grammatical ability, which tends to be less reliable than self-assessment of functional ability: you are less aware of what you do not know.

How should one respond to this? In defining descriptors for assessment for a European grid to profile teacher competences, we could hardly exclude the CEFR. Therefore, these items were deleted temporarily for the series of final analyses that determined the calibrations. Then, however, because the EPG is to some extent aspirational, they were added back in on the basis of their rank ordering in the earlier analyses.

The Global Analysis produced a scaling of the descriptors that seemed intuitively sensible, with only one item that was clearly 'misfitting' (i.e. was interpreted inconsistently): 'I am familiar with teaching techniques and learning materials suitable for one or two levels'. It never became clear why this is such a bad descriptor, but it also produced the most DIF, so it clearly invited variability in the way people interpreted it. In addition to the misfitting item, however, there were another nine descriptors calibrated to a point on the rank ordered scale that appeared strange. Misfit in a Rasch analysis often suggests random answering, but may also signal the presence of a different construct that does not 'fit' in the main construct, hence the name. The low misfit (one item) but relatively large number of oddities (10 items) contrasted with the CEFR descriptor research (North 2000), in which a number of descriptors were 'misfitting' (e.g. all descriptors for socio-cultural competence, for telephoning) but after their removal from the data there had been no strange calculations in the descriptor scale, as shown in North (2000:274–279) and CEFR Section 3.6 (Council of Europe 2001:33–36). In this project, the nine descriptors with suspicious calibrations were removed in addition to the single misfitting item.

In the discussion that follows, reference is made to the six bands of the grid (Phases 1.1 and 1.2; Phases 2.1 and 2.2; Phases 3.1 and 3.2) in order to describe calibration. One example of a strangely calibrated item was: 'I have taken part in standardisation training for assessing learner performance in terms of the levels of the Common European Framework of Reference (CEFR)' which was calibrated (in the borderline area between Phase 3.1 and Phase 3.2) as being more difficult than 'I can assess spoken and written proficiency reliably at all levels according to CEFR criteria' (placed at Phase 3.1). This is a logical impossibility, yet perhaps it reflects the fact that teachers do not always appreciate that they need to have attended standardisation in order to assess reliably in relation to CEFR criteria. If they have not attended standardisation sessions in which they become aware that people have different interpretations, they may radically underestimate the difficulty of accurately assessing the CEFR levels of a piece of speaking or writing. The reversal also may reflect the lack of availability of any CEFR standardisation training. Some very experienced teachers said 'No' to this item, placing it higher up the scale and making it 'more difficult.' Interestingly, teachers of French found this item significantly easier than teachers of other languages, perhaps reflecting the fact that for a considerable period the DVD of illustrative samples (Centre international d'études pédagogiques/Eurocentres 2005) was supplied with the CEFR book in French.

Other examples of this type, where items appeared to be calibrated too high as a probable result on non-availability, were:

- 'I can prepare basic lesson plans using the teachers' notes related to published materials' placed at the very top of Phase 1.2, just below the bottom Phase 2.1 item 'I can use a syllabus and specified materials to prepare lesson plans that are balanced and meet the needs of the group' rather than in Phase 1.1 as intended

- 'I can use published or in-house materials to prepare plans for different types of lessons' placed near the top of Phase 2.1 and above the considerably more sophisticated 'I compare individual learners' needs and refer to these in planning main and supplementary objectives for lessons'
- 'I take part in teacher training sessions when these are available', again placed at the very top of Phase 1.2.

The other five items that were removed seemed to have been calibrated too low, certainly far lower than had originally been intended. They were:

- 'I create an atmosphere of inclusiveness and mutual understanding in both staffroom and classroom', which was placed near the bottom of Phase 1.2 instead of in the intended Phase 3.1, which in retrospect does appear to have been clearly mistaken
- 'I use learning materials that contain information about cultural behaviour, traditions, artefacts etc.' placed at Phase 2.2 instead of Phase 1.2, perhaps reflecting the lack of an 'I can' formulation ('I don't do this even though I can') or maybe because the teacher would have to find or produce the materials
- 'I can notice what is really confusing learners and offer guidance so they can resolve their queries themselves', which was placed at Phase 1.2 rather than the intended Phase 3.1, perhaps reflecting the fact the teachers do not notice what they do not notice
- 'I can evaluate materials from both practical and theoretical perspectives' placed at Phase 1.2 instead of the intended Phase 3.1, which in retrospect does seem to have been exaggerated
- 'I can evaluate the suitability of techniques and materials for different teaching situations' placed at Phase 1.2 instead of the intended Phase 2.2, which again may have been exaggerated.

Because of the doubts about these nine descriptors, they were deleted from the analysis.

Differential Item Functioning

Standard Error Plots are also a convenient way of diagnosing DIF in a Rasch analysis. Figures 3 and 4 give examples, for the native speaker/non-native speaker divide and for years of experience. The number of respondents teaching their mother tongue (912) was almost identical to the number not teaching their mother tongue (905) and this balance was very useful for

Figure 3 DIF: Native-speaker and non-native-speaker teachers

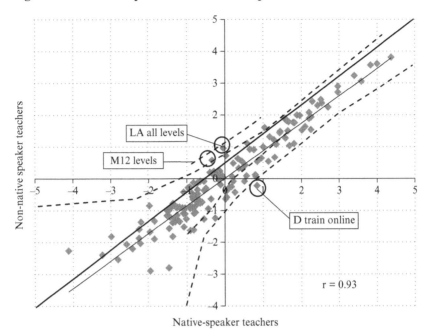

Native-speaker teachers

investigating whether non-native teachers would interpret the descriptors differently from native speakers (i.e. produce DIF). In the event only three items showed a statistically significant difference of interpretation and one of these was the sole misfitting item. The other two were: 'I can teach usage and register at all levels', and 'I can train students to select and use on-line exercises'.

It is not difficult to understand why non-native teachers might be more reluctant to say that they can teach usage and register at all levels. They may be being more modest, or it may reflect the fact that a higher proportion of the non-native teachers will be working in the school sector, where they do not teach the full range of levels. The *Digital* item also shows DIF in relation to educational sectors: school teachers (primary, lower and upper secondary) finding it an easier item than teachers in the adult and vocational training sector. The DIF shown in relation to non-native teachers and native-speaker teachers probably reflects the same point: more school teachers are non-natives and online work may be more widespread in mainstream education.

Qualifications and experience

Here, contrasts were made between teachers with and without a Master's degree, with and without a degree, between those with 10 years' experience and less than 10 years and between those with 2,400 hours' experience and those with less than 2,400 hours. The correlations between the sets of values for the contrasted analyses were as follows: Master's/non-Master's: 0.92; degree/no degree: 0.92; 2,400 hours or more/under 2,400 hours: 0.91; 10 years or more/under 10 years: 0.93. There was no DIF in relation to whether teachers had a Master's degree or not and DIF on only one item in relation to degrees: 'I observe colleagues and provide useful feedback'. Teachers with a degree interpreted this descriptor as more difficult than those without a degree. However, the item is right on the borderline of statistical significance. For 'Hours of Experience' there was DIF on two items. The teachers with less than 2,400 hours' experience found it more difficult to 'develop assessment tasks for any level', which seems logical enough. However they considered it significantly easier to 'answer all language queries accurately'. This seems counter-intuitive. However, the more experienced teachers calibrated this item to almost exactly the same value as 'I can give full, accurate answers to language queries on all occasions'; they were clearly thinking of 'all possible' questions, whereas the less experienced teachers seem to have interpreted it as 'all the questions I get asked (at the level I teach)'.

With 'Years of Experience' there was a far greater amount of DIF, as shown in Figure 4. The younger teachers, with less than 10 years' experience, interpreted seven items concerning Digital Media as being significantly easier. These seven items showing DIF were the following: Dsoundvideo: 'I can edit and adapt sound and video files'; Dnewmedia: 'I can show colleagues how to exploit teaching potential of new media (e.g. mobiles, interactive whiteboards)'; Dnewsofthardware: 'I can show colleagues how to use new soft/hardware'; Dtroubleshoot: 'I can troubleshoot problems with classroom digital equipment'; DWindowsMac: 'I can use any standard web or Windows/Mac software, including media players'; DIWBs: 'I can use interactive whiteboards (IWBs)'; Dimagesound: 'I can use software for handling images, DVDs, and sound files'.

Figure 4 DIF: Years of experience

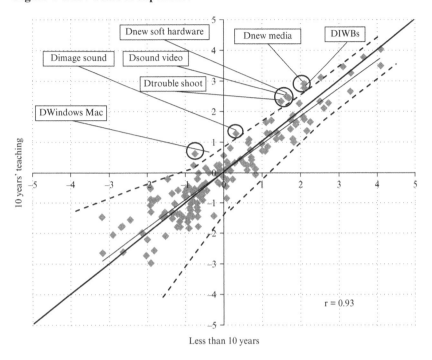

Less than 10 years

Rather than being surprised at this, one might ask oneself what it is about the other Digital Media items which makes for less significant differences of interpretation. Two are right at the top of the scale; everybody finds them difficult: 'I can design blended learning modules using a "Learning Management System" (LMS) e.g. Moodle'; 'I can train students to participate in IWB (interactive whiteboard) use and the use of mobiles, tablets etc. profitably for language learning'. The other Digital Media items were what might be described as routine activities for an experienced teacher who is not a complete novice with media: 'I can co-ordinate project work with digital media (camera, internet, social media)'; 'I can create lessons with downloaded texts, pictures, graphics, etc'; 'I can download resources from websites'; 'I can use menus to operate software'; 'I can organise materials in logically ordered folders'; 'I can recommend appropriate online materials'; 'I can search for potential teaching material on the internet'; 'I can set and supervise individual online work'; 'I can train students to select and use online exercises'; 'I can use data projectors for lessons involving the internet, DVD etc.'; 'I can write a worksheet in Word or similar following standard conventions'; 'I can use PowerPoint creatively'. By contrast, the seven items with DIF, with the exception of the item about using any standard software, all involved quite sophisticated media activity one associates with younger people. On DWindowsMac, the words 'any' and 'media players' probably suggest a difficulty that younger teachers do not share. All in all, it is not difficult to understand that older people find some digital activities significantly more difficult than younger people.

Educational sectors

There were no significant differences at all between the interpretations of primary and lower secondary; primary and upper secondary; lower second-ary and upper secondary; lower secondary and the adult and vocational training sector; upper secondary and the adult and vocational training sector; upper secondary and higher education, or between the adult and vocational training sector and higher education. There was DIF, however, in the follow-ing contrasts: in contrasting the mainstream school sector (primary, lower and upper secondary) to the adult/vocational and higher education sectors, the adult/higher education teachers found the following two items easier: 'I can teach usage and register at all levels' and 'I give correct models of usage on almost all occasions at all levels'. This seems entirely logical, reflecting the reality of their respective teaching situations. On the other hand mainstream school teachers found easier the item concerning online training – discussed when considering native and non-native teachers – and the (misfitting) item 'I am familiar with teaching techniques and learning materials suitable for one or two levels'. There are also two interesting cases in the contrast between lower secondary and higher education. The lower secondary teachers – perhaps more likely to be all-rounders – found troubleshooting with equip-ment easier than their HE colleagues. The latter found planning specialised courses – which they may need to do sometimes – significantly easier.

Summary on DIF

Most of the occurrences of DIF that occurred could be simply explained:

- one was the misfitting item already mentioned in the previous section
- two were anchor items that were significantly less difficult for the teachers who completed Questionnaire C, but which came out at 3.2, in whatever way they were calibrated, and so were left alone
- seven were clearly and only translation issues (e.g. 'I act as mentor to less experienced colleagues' translated as 'Je suis disponible pour conseiller des collègues moins expérimentés'); these items were temporarily removed from the analysis, with the translation issue addressed before publication
- another three showed translation problems but also DIF for other reasons; they were also temporarily removed

- seven were the descriptors concerning Digital Media as shown in Figure 4, which (younger) teachers with less experience not surprisingly found significantly easier
- one concerned teaching all levels, which is unsurprisingly easier for native speakers of the target language and those in adult and higher education, whilst being more difficult for primary school teachers
- one concerned giving correct models of usage on almost all occasions – easier for those in adult and higher education, which seems logical since they are more used to teaching all levels
- one concerned planning specialised courses – again unsurprisingly easier for those in adult and higher education whilst being more difficult for school teachers, particularly at lower secondary
- two concerned Digital Media again and three concerned Professionalism, areas which are not part of Key Teaching Competences anyway.

With the remaining cases, there is, however, a significant difference of some kind in the interpretation of difficulty by teachers of the different target languages concerned:

- four were CEFR items already mentioned in the previous section, which were easier for teachers of French, a fact that is easy to explain because the standardisation DVD comes with the book, as previously mentioned
- two were items on homework marking codes and training learners to code errors – considered significantly more difficult by teachers of French, a curriculum effect, since unlike for the other target languages, this attitude to error is not yet common in Français langue etrangère (FLE)
- two were considered easier by teachers of English: 'I can use published or in-house materials to prepare plans for different types of lessons, and I can monitor individual and group performances accurately and thoroughly' reflecting the more widespread use of course books and perhaps group work in the teaching of English
- 'I can give clear explanations on all occasions' was considered easier by teachers of French
- 'I can identify the theoretical principles behind techniques and materials' was considered easier by teachers of German.

The question is whether one should keep these items showing DIF in the EPG. In reporting on the DIF studies during the research project to create the CEFR scale of levels with descriptors for speaking, North (2000) reported:

> Many items which showed variability across regions or across sectors appeared nonetheless to be good items, well calibrated, well fitting, sensible, saying something . . .
>
> Failing 95% stability across sectors/regions draws attention to an item, but is *not* in itself necessarily an argument for dropping the descriptor concerned. Twenty-five items which showed significant variation across sectors or regions, but no other signs indicating that they were problematic were retained in the descriptor bank. However, such items which show significant variation across sectors or regions should only be included in profiling grids which are meant to be used to plot such variation, and should *not* be subsumed into a holistic descriptor on a global scale purporting to report achievement independent of context. Putting this result more positively, 183 of the 209 descriptors finally calibrated (87.5%) show no significant (0.05) variation across sectors or regions (2000:259–60).

In this EPG study 34 of the 144 items showed significant variation across sectors, target languages and degrees of experience. Expressed in positive terms, 76.3% did not show DIF. The worst DIF concerned the sole misfitting item which had been dropped. Apart from that item and the 10 translation cases, which can be addressed, there are 24 items showing DIF – that is to say 83.2% do not show significant variation. This is similar to the 87.5% with the CEFR illustrative descriptors.

Separate analyses for each category

After investigating DIF, the next step was to undertake separate analyses for each category. The scale values produced correlated 0.98 with those from the Global Analysis, however there were certain categories that had no descriptors at the top or at the bottom or in the middle, when these descriptors were merged with those from the other categories in the Global Analysis. In addition, 31 descriptors showed a significant difference in the scale values produced by the two types of analysis, including nine for Professionalism and eight for Interaction Management – but none from Methodology or Assessment. The fact that these items have significantly different difficulty values in the two types of analysis is not a comment on their quality. It is an indication that a global analysis alone is inappropriate. Bejar (1980) proposed that, whenever possible, content strands should each be analysed on their own to see if there is any significant difference in the difficulty estimates for the items in the content strand when they are calibrated alone or in the context of the rest of the items. He considered that when such a significant difference occurs, the values from the separate analysis should take precedence. A comparison of the scale values between the two analyses (Global/Category) for each category showed the following:

Intercultural Competence

The rank order from the two analyses was identical with the exception of two items reversing inside Phase 1.2. However, there was no Phase 3.2 in the Global Analysis – Intercultural Competence is one of the 'easier' categories. The descriptors at 3.2 are at 3.1 in the Global Analysis, but from 2.1 downwards the two scales are the same.

Language Awareness

This is the only category for which the two analyses put all descriptors at the same phases. The rank order is also identical – except at Phase 1.1 for which in the Category Analysis all the items had maximum scores (100%). However, this is also the only category for which a separate analysis did not work satisfactorily. As 'misfitting persons' (people giving inconsistent responses) were progressively removed, there was then more, rather than less, misfit and the analysis collapsed completely. This indicates that although the order and so calibration were solid, there is a degree of inconsistency in the way in which teachers responded to these descriptors.

Methodology

There was no Phase 3.2 in the Global Analysis – Methodology is also one of the 'easier' categories. The descriptors intended for Phase 3.2 came out at Phase 3.1 in the Global Analysis, but those written for Phase 2.2 came out calibrated as intended. From Phase 2.1 downwards there is a considerable difference in the rank order, even though the allocation to phases is not contradictory.

Planning

The global scale had no Phase 3.2 or Phase 1.1, but rank ordering was identical with one reversal at the very bottom. Descriptors at Phase 1 are concerned with planning lesson to lesson. Those at Phase 2.1 were concerned with what one expects from teachers in terms of planning modules (e.g. weeks) using a syllabus. New descriptors to describe planning at more advanced level, focusing on aiding colleagues, which seemed to be a strong feature of Phase 3.2, were therefore produced for the final grid: 'can guide colleagues in assessing and taking account of differing individual needs in planning courses and preparing lessons'; 'can take responsibility for reviewing the curriculum and syllabuses'.

Interaction Management and Monitoring

Again there was no Phase 3.2 in the Global Analysis – Interaction Management is also one of the 'easier' categories. In this case, the second 3.2 item in the Category Analysis is at Phase 2.2 on the Global Analysis. This category showed differences in the rank order around Phases 1.2/2.1. One noticeable feature was that many of the descriptors on monitoring clustered at Phase 3.1. These were therefore edited substantially for the final grid.

Assessment

The rank order was identical at Phases 2.1 to 3.2, but different in the lower part of the scale. The most noticeable feature, however, was the hole in the middle of the scale: on the global scale there was *nothing* at 2.1. Phase 1 was concerned with assessment of learning, whereas Phases 2.2 to 3.1 were concerned with learner training and the assessment of level. The approach taken here was to use the calibration from the separate analysis.

Digital Media

This is the most solid scale that best reflects the original intention, with calibration to phases identical from the two forms of analysis. The only weak point in the scale was that the item 'I can use IWB or/and PowerPoint creatively' which comes out calibrated below DIWBs 'I can use interactive whiteboards', which came calibrated at the bottom of Phase 3.2, perhaps because of the distraction of PowerPoint. This IWB/PowerPoint item was dropped.

Professionalism

Here the rank orders between the two analyses were identical, with items at the same phase on both scales, except inside Phase 1.2. Organising peer assessment came out right at the top of the Phase 3.2 in the Global Analysis, even above running teacher development programmes. This may reflect the fact that it is a politically sensitive task.

Setting cut-points between phases

The approach taken was to set cut-points between phases separately on the two types of analysis (Global/Category) and then – following the advice of Bejar (1980) mentioned above – to compare them in order to make a final decision, preferring the calibration in separate analysis in cases of conflict.

Global Scale

The procedure followed to set cut-points between phases on the Global Scale was as follows:

1. Identify the descriptors for Qualifications and Experience (Hours, Years, Assessed Teaching, Qualifications) and colour-code these. They clustered well on the scale.
2. Identify, by the same colour coding, the main range on the scale of clusters of descriptors that were originally authored for the same level, Mark the 'Core Range' for each phase in this way.

3. Identify the borderline area at the top and bottom of each range by comparing the results of the two above methods of determining the range on the scale for each phase.

After setting the cut-offs and borderline areas for each phase, subscales were created for each of the categories, each marked with the start and end of each phase, plus of the borderline areas. These subscales from the Global Analysis were later compared to the scales produced from separate Category Analyses (below) in order to inform the final decision as discussed at the beginning of this section.

Category Scales

The procedure followed to set cut-points between phases on the Category Scales was as follows:

1. Identify big gaps between clusters of descriptors on the scale and set these as provisional cut-points.
2. Identify concentrations of descriptors originally authored for the same phase and mark these as that phase.
3. Count the number of bands (= provisional phases) on the scale, reducing to six.
4. Count the space on the scale taken by each band, including any gap without descriptors in the border between phases.
5. Juggle the cut-points up or down – moving a descriptor up/down to the adjacent phase – until the distances covered by the phases is roughly symmetrical, with larger distances at top and bottom reflecting the distortion caused by very high and very low scores.

The process of determining the final cut-scores on the basis of the results from the two analyses (Global/Category) was not entirely straightforward. Some large gaps on the Category Scales, plus values towards infinity at the two ends of the logit scale, made interpretation difficult. In addition, the Category Scales sometimes had as few as 13 items on them. By contrast with the scale of CEFR illustrative descriptors, over 200 descriptors had been all on the same scale, making the process of identifying content clusters and gaps between them far easier. As a result the strict approach taken for the CEFR descriptors did not seem appropriate for the EPG. In the CEFR scale analysis, an absolutely strict measuring out of equidistant spaces on the scale (allowing for symmetrical distortion towards the top and bottom) was juggled with content clusters associated with particular levels in order to fix the final cut-offs. Afterwards there were no adjustments: items calibrated as the lowest B2 item or highest B1+ item stayed where they were.

In this case of the EPG, the process of producing the final grid on the basis of both the feedback from academic managers and teacher trainers plus the need to provide balance led to further checking of some borderline cases, which in turn led to a couple of items being promoted/demoted from one phase to another.

Conclusions

Two fundamental questions that a grid like the EPG poses are, as stated earlier:

- Will the answers that teachers give when self-assessing their competences by answering 'Yes' or 'No' to the descriptors presented in isolation actually create such a criterion-referenced measurement scale (or set of measurement scales)? Will the EPG 'work'?
- Do teachers of French and teachers of German think in a sufficiently similar way about aspects of their competence for a common grid to be justifiable?

In relation to the first question, the small amount of misfit in the data and the high correlation between and consistency of the scaling from the two analysis methods (Global Analysis and separate Category Analyses), suggests a positive answer. It is true that the Assessment items showed some lack of stability in the values produced from the two questionnaires, particularly the four descriptors relating to the CEFR, but otherwise the scale appears to be solid.

As regards the second question, teachers of English, French, German, Spanish and Italian do appear to share a common way of thinking about language teaching, as do teachers teaching their mother tongue and teachers teaching a language that they themselves have learned. Those few differences visible between educational sectors appear entirely logical, e.g. that primary and secondary teachers do not teach all levels. Of the 144 competence descriptors in the analysis, only 10 showed a significantly different interpretation of difficulty by teachers of different target languages that could not be immediately explained as a translation issue. In other words, some 93% of the descriptors showed a similar interpretation in the context of the pedagogic cultures associated with the different languages. There were no significant effects at all for Spanish and Italian. Of the 10 items showing DIF for Target Language that were not just translation problems, four were the CEFR-related items that had proved to be unstable anchors and to be interpreted as easier by teachers of French, two were items on error coding, interpreted as more difficult by teachers of French, two concerned curriculum-related issues considered easier by teachers of English (course books and group activities), one reflected French teachers' apparent confidence in giving grammatical explanations and one reflected German teachers' apparent confidence in understanding the theoretical principles behind what they were doing.

There do therefore still appear to be some distinctions between some of the pedagogic cultures, but in relation to Methodology, knowledge and skills; Lesson and course planning; Interaction management and monitoring; Assessment; Intercultural competence; Language awareness; Digital media, and Professional conduct these differences appear dwarfed by the amount of communality shown.

One aspect of the result that this researcher found surprising was the extent to which the more demographic factors on Training and Qualifications: (Language proficiency; Education and training; Assessed teaching; Teaching experience) fitted into the scale. These factors did not build the scale. The data from these items was only added in for the final, Global Analysis and did not substantially affect either the length of the scale nor the calibrations on it. The intention was to use the more numerical and 'objective' pointers in this scale to ensure the link to the six phases envisaged for the EPG. There was no misfit, and the items bunched pretty much where they would be expected to – the only complication being that some of the items for Phase 1.1 landed below the rest of the scale, marking a kind of zero point.

One final reflection concerns the use of data from self-assessment for scaling descriptors, or the use of self-assessment with descriptors for setting cut-offs between performance levels on tests. Space does not allow a repeat of the debates on this issue. The ALTE Can Dos were successfully scaled with self-assessments from learners taking Cambridge English exams (Jones 2002), but this was not done in isolation; examination data on these learners was also available. There have also been spectacular failures, the most noticeable of which was in the European Survey on Language Competences on school leavers, in which teenage students tended to tick all of the descriptors for all six CEFR levels, whilst being below A1 (Jones 2013, personal communication).

In the EPG project, the use of self-assessment data produced from an online survey 'worked'. However, there were nine oddly calibrated yet not misfitting items. This contrasts with the rock solid consistency of the descriptor scale produced for the CEFR, which had only one single contradiction without any corrections to the data (North 2000:289): at B1+ 'does not make mistakes which lead to misunderstanding', while at B2 one is said to be able to 'correct mistakes which have led to misunderstanding' (which should not have happened, should they?). In the CEFR descriptor calibration, with data from teachers assessing their classes at an official assessment point at the end of the school year, one had 'real' assessment data. There were things that the teachers could not give consistent judgements about because they just didn't know (e.g. Telephoning); there were types of formulation that confused them (e.g. CAN do X but CANNOT do Y). But these questionable items misfitted and could be excluded from the scale with objective reasoning. Where the teachers *could* give judgements, although of course some individual teachers gave inconsistent judgements (i.e. misfitted), the data from the judgements of those who did not misfit produced a solid item scale requiring no subjective correction. In this project, the nine identified 'odd' calibrations indicate that this was not the case with the EPG scale. One of the descriptors sums up the problem: 'I can notice what is really confusing learners and offer guidance so they can resolve their queries themselves' was placed at Phase 1.2 rather than the Phase 3.1 intended, perhaps reflecting the fact that people unfortunately do not notice what they do not notice. This type of problem can be expected to be present in any self-assessment data, suggesting that it should be exploited with care for scaling descriptors or for standard setting.

To return to the EPG itself, as mentioned at the beginning of the paper, the e-Grid website provides an electronic version with which teachers can create and print a professional profile. It is also possible for teacher trainers to create a profile of teachers they are training and for academic managers to profile a whole staffroom. It is the latter use that is most common in Eaquals-accredited institutions, since they are asked to provide such a profile before an Eaquals inspection. Exploitation of the grid is spreading – even to China, where it featured at the 13th Congress of the International Association for Germanic Studies in August 2015 in Shanghai. Surveys planned for 2015 should throw light on the ways in which it is being used in practice in different contexts and highlight areas for further development. One such development already being worked on is the extension of the grid to cover the specialised competences required for teaching languages for study purposes. An Eaquals working group is currently considering what new categories may need to be defined and the extent to which such categories might apply across the different possible contexts of language teaching for academic purposes (e.g. Content and Language Integrated Learning (CLIL), international schools with a foreign language as the medium of instruction, foundation courses for students going on to university, university language service departments). More information can be found via www.epg-project.eu/grid/ and on the Eaquals, Goethe-Institut and Instituto Cervantes websites.

Notes

1   Eaquals (www.eaquals.org) is an international association of providers of language education that operates an inspection scheme for its 100+ Accredited Members. Some 27 other institutions are Associate Members, including cultural institutes like the British Council, the CIEP, Goethe-Institut, Instituto Cervantes, a number of national quality associations, language test providers, government agencies and other providers of language learning services. Like ALTE, Eaquals was founded in 1991 and

like ALTE has been a non-governmental organisation (NGO) to the Council of Europe's Language Policy Unit since 2005. Eaquals produced the first European Language Portfolio (ELP) for adults and the first electronic ELP that enabled learners to print a Language Passport.

2   Eurocentres (Foundation for Language and Cultural Centres) was founded in 1960, on the basis of a school group existing since 1948, as the first organisation to offer language stays abroad to adults for English, French, German and Italian. Eurocentres has been an NGO consultant to the Council of Europe's Language Policy Unit since 1968, organised the 1971 intergovernmental symposium that recommended the Modern Languages Project and the 1991 intergovernmental symposium that recommended the CEFR. The ELP at that conference was a Eurocentres proposal, and Eurocentres produced the illustrative descriptors included in the CEFR, on the basis of the research in a Swiss National Science Research Council project (North 2000, North and Schneider 1998, Schneider and North 2000), plus the first video clips with CEFR Illustrative performance samples for English (2004 with Migros Club Schools) and French (2005 with the CIEP).

References

Association of Language Testers in Europe (1999) *Multilingual Glossary of Language Testing Terms*, Studies in Language Testing volume 6, Cambridge: UCLES/Cambridge University Press.

Bejar, I I (1980) A procedure for investigating the unidimensionality of achievement tests based on item parameter estimates, *Journal of Educational Measurement* 17 (4), 283–296.

Centre international d'études pédagogiques and Eurocentres (2005) *DVD de productions orales illustrant pour le français, les niveaux du Cadre européen commun de référence pour les langues du Conseil de l'Europe*, Paris: Centre international d'études pédagogiques/Didier.

Council of Europe (2001) *Common European Framework of Reference for Languages: Learning, Teaching, Assessment*, Cambridge: Cambridge University Press.

Jones, N (2002) Relating the ALTE framework to the Common European Framework of Reference, in Alderson, J C A (Ed) (2002) *Case Studies in the Use of the Common European Framework*, Strasbourg, Council of Europe, 167–183.

Kelly, M and Grenfell, M (2004) *European Profile for Language Teacher Education – A Frame of Reference*, available online: www.lang.soton.ac.uk/profile/report/MainReport.pdf

Linacre, J M (2012) *Winsteps: Rasch-model Computer Program*, Chicago: MESA Press.

Newby, D, Allan, R, Fenner, A, Jones, B, Komorowska, H and Soghikyan, K (2006) *The European Portfolio for Student Teachers of Languages, EPOSTL*, available online: www.ecml.at/mtp2/FTE/pdf/STPExtract.pdf

North, B (2000) *The Development of a Common Framework Scale of Language Proficiency*, New York: Peter Lang.

North, B (2012) A profiling grid for language teachers, in Diadori, P (Ed) *How to Train Language Teachers*, Newcastle upon Tyne: Cambridge Scholars Publishing, 190–217.

North, B and Schneider, G (1998) Scaling descriptors for language proficiency scales, *Language Testing* 15 (2), 217–262.

Rossner, R (2012) Methods of assessment and the Eaquals Profiling Grid for language Teachers, in Diadori, P (Ed) *How to Train Language Teachers*, Newcastle upon Tyne: Cambridge Scholars Publishing, 218–239.

Schneider, G and North, B (2000) *Fremdsprachen können: was heisst das? Skalen zur Beschreibung, Beurteilung und Selbsteinschätzung der fremdsprachlichen Kommunikationsfähigkeit*, Nationales Forschungsprogramm 33, Chur/Zürich: Wirksamkeit unserer Bildungssysteme, Verlag Rüegger.

Skehan, P (1984) Issues in the testing of English for specific purposes, *Language Testing* 1, 202–220.

Smith, P C and Kendall, J M (1963) Retranslation of expectations: An approach to the construction of unambiguous anchors for rating scales, *Journal of Applied Psychology* 47, 2.

Wright, B D and Stone, M H (1979) *Best Test Design*, Chicago: MESA Press.

15 Teacher involvement in high-stakes testing

Daniel Xerri
Patricia Vella Briffa
University of Malta

Abstract

This paper explores the premise that teachers' involvement in high-stakes testing is desirable because the resulting test is a product of their knowledge of the learning context, the student cohort, and the subject content. Such involvement is indicative of an increased sense of trust in teachers' judgements. By means of a case study approach, this paper discusses the process of developing a public examination from the authors' combined perspectives as researchers and teachers whose assessment literacy was enhanced because they were privileged to be involved at every stage. This paper outlines the challenges faced and elaborates on the lessons learned from their prolonged involvement. It evaluates the implications of teachers' involvement in high-stakes testing and seeks to contribute to a better understanding of the benefits that may arise when teachers are invited to play an instrumental role in the design and implementation of such examinations.

Introduction

Teachers' involvement in high-stakes test development can enhance their assessment literacy and result in examinations that are informed by their knowledge of the learning context, the student cohort, and the subject content. There is a dearth of research on how teachers' involvement in public examinations translates into such potential benefits. The idea that teachers should be encouraged to don the examiner's hat has not been given sufficient attention in the assessment literature. In fact, Sasanguie, Elen, Clarebout, Van den Noortgate, Vandenabeele and De Fraine (2011:908) point out that 'Despite [high-stakes tests'] great impact, discussions on the separation versus combination of teaching and assessment roles are rare and empirical research is nearly absent'. This paper therefore sheds light on the benefits that may be derived when teachers actively contribute to high-stakes examinations.

In this paper we present a case study of our involvement in high-stakes testing by evaluating our role as teachers in the design and implementation of a newly introduced English speaking component forming part of a popular public examination at Advanced level in Malta used for university admissions. Our experience as teachers allowed us to identify and address the gaps present in the syllabus in order for our students and other candidates to be provided with a reliable and valid form of assessment of their speaking skills at this advanced stage of language learning. This paper analyses our contribution to this speaking examination from its inception up to the first sitting by a national cohort of candidates. By demonstrating what we learned from a three-year process made up of a number of test development stages, this paper illustrates how teachers' involvement in public examinations could help develop their assessment literacy and lead to a more equitable form of high-stakes testing.

Concerns with high-stakes testing

The impact of language tests can be far-reaching, especially if these tests are of a high-stakes nature. Taylor (2005:2) affirms that 'the use of tests and test scores can impact significantly on the career or life chances of individual test takers'. Over the past few years a number of countries seem to have placed a stronger emphasis on high-stakes testing. A case in point is the USA where high-stakes testing is becoming the chief means of assessing students and gauging teacher and school accountability. However, high-stakes testing receives a fair amount of criticism, especially because it is accused of reproducing social and educational inequality (Au 2008) and for being mechanistic and reductive (Allen 2012). It does so by binding academic success to performance on tests that might be based on a limited set of measurable outcomes to the exclusion of other significant areas of learning. Grant (2004:6) labels high-stakes tests 'oppressive' because they impair quality teaching and learning, subject students to a restricted curriculum, and push teachers to teach to the test. In their research on the impact of a school-leaving English examination in Poland, Lewkowicz and Zawadowska-Kittel (2008:30) found that teachers focus on task types that feature in examinations and teach students strategies that enable them to do well on a test. Similarly, a study focusing on the Nigerian context found that a preoccupation with attainting certification has promoted teaching and learning oriented primarily towards passing the test rather than enhancing language use (Christopher 2009:12). Nichols's (2007:57) review of the literature on the impact on student achievement of high-stakes tests leads her to posit that 'the findings from the most rigorous studies on high-stakes testing do not provide convincing evidence that high-stakes testing has the intended effect of increasing student learning'. In fact, the unintended outcomes of high-stakes testing are largely negative, especially on instruction and on teacher and student motivation (Jones 2007).

However, high-stakes tests have become an intrinsic part of the contemporary educational milieu and they can have a positive washback effect on teaching and learning. Hence, it might be better for teachers to use them to their advantage rather than seeking to debunk them at every turn. In our case, we argued that it would be more profitable for us to be involved in a high-stakes examination rather than distancing ourselves from it and complaining about its effects.

High-stakes testing can affect teachers in a number of ways, especially if they are made to feel that they have no sense of ownership over the test or that it is exclusively determining the nature of teaching and learning. Currently, the driving force behind the curriculum that teachers focus on in class seems to be constituted by 'the pressures of assessment systems that pay little heed to consistency or coherence between teachers' visions of desirable education and those articulated in high-stakes examinations' (Atkin 2007:57). These pressures can impinge on classroom practice, stifle teachers' views and make them feel disenfranchised (Nichols and Berliner 2007). This is especially so when teachers are not given the opportunity to be involved in the development of high-stakes tests. High-stakes testing can lead teachers to 'increasingly feel that they are at the mercy of forces beyond their control' (Reich and Bally 2010:181). For example, Costigan (2002:32) reports that the amount of high-stakes testing that a small group of primary school teachers were faced with when they entered the profession not only affected the quality and type of instruction they delivered but also made them feel disempowered. Focusing on public school teachers in New York City, Crocco and Costigan (2006:1) contend that 'high-stakes testing has produced high-stakes teaching in many schools, raising the risk of aggravating the already high level of teacher attrition'. Such assessment-driven teaching burdens teachers with undue pressure. A study by Assaf (2008:249) shows how an English Language Learner (ELL) reading teacher struggled to act autonomously due to testing pressures and felt forced to reinvent her professional identity so as to be in synch with the testing culture in her context. This is in line with studies indicating that the pressure of high-stakes testing might lead teachers to change their instructional practices (Hoffman, Assaf and Paris 2001) and affects the way they respond to students' learning needs (Flores and Clark 2003, Pennington 2004). Rubin (2011) explains that the present emphasis on standardised testing in the USA as embodied by the No Child Left Behind Act is generating low levels of morale, an increase in stress and anxiety, a sense of deprofessionalisation of teaching, and teacher attrition. Such unintended outcomes have an impact on teachers' attitudes towards assessment.

Negative attitudes towards high-stakes testing might lead teachers to demonise it and disregard the fact that it can be beneficial. In fact, Taras (2005:469) argues that 'the terrors evoked by the term "assessment" have distorted its necessity, centrality and its potentially neutral position'.

Pishghadam, Adamson, Sadafian and Kan (2014:46) found that 'teachers who do not esteem assessment as a sign of school quality or an improvement tool for learning, and deem assessment negative, bad and unfair, may become exhausted, indifferent, and finally experience burnout to a higher degree'. However, when teachers are convinced that a high-stakes test is rigorously designed and has the potential to aid teaching and learning then their attitudes towards it may be positive. In her study on perceptions of English language testing in Taiwan, Wu (2008:8) found that despite some teachers' concern that external exams are the driving force behind teaching and learning, they also concede that good exams might have a positive washback effect. Teachers are more likely to perceive the introduction of external standardised assessment as motivating for students and supportive of learner autonomy if tests are deemed to be a well-designed measure of an appropriate range of knowledge and skills (Docherty, Casacuberta, Rodriguez Pazos and Canosa 2014). It seems as if the negative attitudes engendered by high-stakes testing are a result of teachers being deprived of a sense of ownership over high-stakes tests and being unconvinced of their potential to lead to quality teaching and learning. Providing teachers with ownership over high-stakes testing by encouraging them to be involved in test development might be one way of changing their attitudes towards high-stakes tests.

Teacher as examiner, examiner as teacher

Mostly characterised as negative due to the uses of high-stakes tests and the attitudes towards them, the washback effect of such tests on classroom practice is potentially strong. Nonetheless, some researchers argue that 'high-stakes tests, powerful as they are, might not be efficient agents for profound changes in an educational context' (Tsagari 2009:8). Irrespective of the level of strength, the washback effect of such tests need not always be negative and stultifying. While acknowledging that there is scant empirical evidence on the formative use of summative assessment data, Hoover and Abrams (2013) found that the majority of teachers of English and other subjects in their study used such data to change their instruction. Moreover, positive washback is more likely to ensue if tests are produced with an awareness of the learning context. According to Whitehead (2007:449), the validity of tests can be enhanced if they possess ecological validity, i.e. if they reflect teaching and learning, and students' use of the assessed content. Providing teachers with a sense of ownership by encouraging them to play an active role in high-stakes testing is likely to increase its formative potential.

Teachers' involvement in high-stakes testing can help in reducing the alienation that they sometimes experience in relation to tests that are implemented without their consultation. Gregory and Clarke (2003:72) argue that teachers must be able to engage with any assessment systems that are about to be implemented and evaluate their strengths and weaknesses. This is crucial if they are to contribute to policy-making in relation to assessment and thus prevent the kind of centralisation of power that can damage students (Gregory and Clarke 2003:73). Teachers who are not involved in language testing may 'feel that a gap between teaching and testing is in evidence. They often feel that those who write the tests are not in touch with the realities of the classroom' (Coombe, Al-Hamly and Troudi 2009:15). Marshall (2011) discusses how the London Association for the Teaching of English acted as a platform from which teachers could take a more active role in high-stakes examinations and thus reform the assessment system by encouraging examination boards to adopt a bottom-up approach. This case study epitomises 'the growing role of the teacher as examiner, and the examiner as teacher' (Norman 2011:1,055). By being encouraged to position themselves in this way teachers are likely to feel that their judgement matters. Klenowski and Wyatt-Smith (2012:75) point out that in order for national testing programmes to improve outcomes there needs to be agreement on the idea that teachers, rather than tests, are the primary change agents. This entails foregrounding teacher judgement. The latter can serve to heighten the formative potential of high-stakes tests and it is for this reason that there should be more opportunities for teachers to play the role of examiners. Sloane and Kelly (2003:12) highlight the need for teachers to contribute to test design so that the resulting test is aligned with the curriculum and has the potential to heighten student motivation. Harlen (2005a:221) is in favour of involving teachers in public tests because through such 'involvement they develop ownership of the procedures and criteria and understand the process of assessment, including such matters as what makes an adequate sample of behaviour, as well as the goals and processes of learning'. The implication is that the knowledge and skills they develop by being involved in such high-stakes tests will feed into their own classroom practices. However, such involvement might first require bolstering their confidence in their own judgement. One way of doing this is by developing an assessment community within a school so as to increase confidence in teacher judgement amongst teachers and test users (Harlen 2005b:266). Teachers' confidence in preparing their students for high-stakes tests 'is less likely to come from pep rallies or inspirational speakers than it is from the slow, steady work of teachers working together to understand the tasks their students will face on high-stakes exams' (Reich and Bally 2010:182). Enabling teachers to position themselves as examiners empowers them to play a role in reforming high-stakes testing so that it is more equitable and more likely to enhance classroom practices.

Most probably one of the reasons for which teachers are not encouraged to be more actively involved in high-stakes testing is the perception that their assessment practices in other non-high-stakes situations are insufficiently reliable (Brookhart 2013, Harlen 2005b). It is due to this that teacher assessment is most often pushed out of national assessment. However, there is a danger in such exclusion, particularly in relation to the validity of the assessment system. Talking about the UK context, Stobart (2001:37) argues that the validity of national curriculum assessment can only be safeguarded if there is a balance between teacher assessment and external tests. The two forms of assessment are mutually beneficial and both teachers and the assessment system stand to gain by maintaining the balance. For example, Chisholm and Wildeman (2013:98) report how in South Africa 'other forms of assessment continue to exist alongside tests and the focus is on the teacher development, infrastructural and textual resource interventions necessary to address the weaknesses revealed by tests'. An assessment system that aims to safeguard its validity while improving outcomes will seek to harness teachers' knowledge of the learning context. According to Johnson (2013:93), 'there can be little doubt that teachers represent a wealth of knowledge about students' achievements and capabilities that is indispensable in the assessment of learning progress and achievement, and which, in principle, could usefully be exploited in high-stakes examination and certification systems'. Tapping teachers' knowledge of the learning context might be carried out not only by allowing teacher assessment to complement high-stakes testing but also by providing teachers with the necessary training in order for them to contribute to the latter. For example, in the case of GCSEs, secondary school leaving examinations for 16-year-olds in the UK, the fact that teachers will still be able to receive face-to-face training focusing on the knowledge and skills they need to conduct controlled assessment is for Crisp (2013:142) an acknowledgement of the valuable role that teachers play in such assessments and the significance of providing them with adequate support. This is in line with the idea that 'teachers in general are capable of internalizing a standard accurately . . . provided they are trained in that standard' (North and Jarosz 2013:122). The solution to a lack of reliability in teachers' assessment practices is best addressed by means of training and not by barring them from participating in high-stakes testing.

Developing teachers' assessment literacy

Developing teachers' assessment literacy seems to be necessary for them to operate more effectively in an educational culture dominated by high-stakes testing. This is defined as 'the ability to design, select, interpret, and use assessment results appropriately for educational decisions' (Quilter and Gallini 2000:116). According to Gulek (2003:49), teachers 'need to be assessment literate in order to respond to the demands of the avalanche of high-stakes testing. Being assessment literate broadens one's perspective to view assessment as a dynamic process'. However, it seems as if many education systems globally face the problem of a lack of assessment literacy among educators (Koh 2011:256). Research seems to show that teachers' assessment literacy is rather poor (Chisholm and Wildeman 2013, Earl 2003, Guskey 2004, Quilter and Gallini 2000) and this leads them to assess students in the largely ineffective way they themselves were assessed (Guskey 2004). According to Coombe et al (2009:15), 'without a higher level of teacher assessment literacy, we will be unable to help students attain higher levels of academic achievement'. Moreover, teachers' failure to understand the purpose of high-stakes testing affects their classroom practices and attitudes towards assessment (Bracey 2005, Burger and Krueger 2003, Earl 2003, Lewis 2007). Developing teachers' assessment literacy might be a means of addressing some of these problems.

Providing teachers with adequate training is crucial, especially since professional development opportunities that target teachers' assessment literacy have been associated with an improvement in student outcomes (Timperley, Wilson, Barrar and Fung 2007). Klenowski and Wyatt-Smith (2012:75) point out that high-stakes testing should serve to nurture, rather than minimise, teachers' professional abilities if tests are to contribute to student learning. Developing teachers' assessment literacy might entail having 'to divert some of the funding for test development and trialling into professional development opportunities to build teacher assessment capabilities, especially in task design and the use of achievement standards' (Klenowski and Wyatt-Smith 2012:75). According to Costigan (2002:33), teacher education programmes need to evaluate whether teacher candidates are adequately prepared for the high-stakes testing culture that is currently in existence. Teacher education programmes 'must provide opportunities for candidates to consider and discuss issues associated with high-stakes testing of their future students' (Martin, Chase, Cahill and Gregory 2011:367). This is fundamental because 'pre-service teacher education has a critical role to play in promoting assessment literacy in beginning teachers and in providing a foundation for teachers' continued learning about assessment throughout their careers' (DeLuca, Chavez and Cao 2013:123). According to Brookhart (2013:86), unless the quality of teacher judgement is addressed by means of research and practice, teachers will continue being excluded from high-stakes testing. It seems clear that training programmes targeting teachers' assessment literacy are essential, especially because they enhance teacher judgement and recognise teachers' professionalism and ability to contribute to high-stakes testing.

Training programmes would be even more effective if they consisted of teacher involvement in high-stakes testing. This would help address a problem identified by Watanabe (2011:33), who acknowledges that while promoting assessment literacy among teachers is significant, it has not yet been determined what kind of knowledge and skills need to be developed and to what extent. When teachers are involved in high-stakes testing, their own assessment literacy is higher than when they are excluded from the process (Runté 1998). This kind of involvement serves as a valid form of professional development that has a positive impact on classroom assessment as well as on high-stakes testing. According to Tang (2010:676), 'opportunities of and support in reflection, conscious deliberation, and theorization of practice are important to bring about a more sophisticated form of professional knowledge integration'. Black, Harrison, Hodgen, Marshall and Serret (2011) show that with the right kind of strategic support, teachers' competence in summative assessment results in a positive effect on teaching and learning. However, this can only be achieved by means of extensive professional development involving hands-on work rather than just through reading material and a brief training session (Black et al 2011:463). In fact, in line with the relevant literature (McMunn, McColskey and Butler 2004, Wiliam and Thompson 2008), Koh's (2011:272) study underscores the fact that 'ongoing, sustained professional development is more powerful than short-term, one-shot professional development workshops'. Focusing on educators in Germany and Sweden, Forsberg and Wermke (2012) found that teachers' assessment literacy was mostly a product of their professional experiences and collaboration with colleagues rather than formal training. This shows that the latter needs to provide opportunities for hands-on, non-formal learning by teachers. Formal training, especially when it is theoretically oriented, needs to operate in tandem with practice-based activities.

A crucial part of any training programme is the one highlighting teachers' beliefs and attitudes in relation to assessment. Quilter and Gallini (2000:128) show that 'personal experiences with testing play an important role in understanding teachers' current attitudes toward assessment, whereas their professional training in educational measurement may play a negligible role'. This seems to imply that training needs to target not only teachers' assessment literacy but primarily their perception of assessment. In describing how two teachers implemented new assessment practices in their respective contexts, Sato, Coffey and Moorthy (2005:190) feel 'convinced that for the sustained and powerful spread of ideas, new programmes or approaches need to honour the individual teacher's priorities, visions and contexts'. This implies that in order for training to be truly effective it needs to take into account teachers' attitudes and beliefs, and draw upon their experiences and classrooms. Helping teachers to identify their beliefs about assessment is essential if they 'are to differentiate their initial ideas about assessment from the ideas they are being asked to accept, to challenge them and to integrate aspects of these new ideas into a new set of beliefs' (Vandeyar and Killen 2006:44). This is in line with the idea that a training programme needs to first identify teachers' theories, assumptions and practices and then work to improve these by encouraging participants to reflect amongst themselves (Black, Harrison, Hodgen, Marshall and Serret 2010).

Context

In 2010, MATSEC, Malta's national examination body, published a new syllabus for the Advanced English Examination that students typically sit for at the end of a two-year course at a post-16 institution like the one where we teach. This examination forms part of second language education and caters for the needs of around 600 candidates, who typically sit for the examination at the age of 18. If taken as part of a Matriculation Certificate, candidates would usually aspire to further their studies at the country's sole university. Most undergraduate courses that consider Advanced English to be one of their entry requirements specify that applicants need to have a pass at grade C or better. Even though it has not been officially aligned to the CEFR, this would be equivalent to at least C1.2 level, i.e. the upper end of effective operational proficiency. The 2010 syllabus contained a brief outline of a speaking component that had not featured in previous syllabuses. It also specified that the first sitting of this speaking examination would take place in May 2013, allowing adequate time for post-16 institutions to start developing their students' speaking skills.

The introduction of this speaking component served to address a lacuna in relation to the testing of candidates' speaking skills, a lacuna that was allowing candidates to be awarded a qualification testifying to their high level of proficiency in English without ever needing to demonstrate evidence of spoken fluency. The revised syllabus meant that suddenly it was considered 'desirable that candidates studying English at Advanced level demonstrate an evolved proficiency in speaking and listening skills' (MATSEC 2010:6). The speaking component was intended to act 'as a measure of the candidates' ability to speak and converse in English' (MATSEC 2010:6). The Advanced English Examination was finally catering for the assessment of oracy.

Together with our colleagues within the English department of Malta's largest post-16 school, we welcomed the inclusion of a speaking component in the Advanced English Examination, however, we were somewhat disappointed by the lack of detail in the syllabus's description of this component. We felt that as teachers we were not sufficiently confident as to what was expected of our students in each part of the speaking examination and that more detailed specifications were required in order for us to know what they were going to be assessed on. The speaking examination was meant to be developed by MATSEC to serve the needs of the national cohort but it was immediately clear to us that there would not be any further elaboration beyond the syllabus description unless we took the lead to develop the examination by first of all writing a manual for the benefit of all stakeholders. For a number of years we had worked as examiners for the *International English Language Testing System* (*IELTS*), *Cambridge English: Advanced*, also known as *Certificate in Advanced English* (*CAE*), and *Cambridge*

English: Proficiency, also known as *Certificate of Proficiency in English* (*CPE*). This familiarity with international examinations made us realise that what both teachers and candidates truly needed was a comprehensive test manual that elaborated on each part of the new speaking component and provided detailed information on content, structure, timing, techniques, criterial levels of performance, and scoring procedures. MATSEC had never produced thorough examination manuals in accompaniment to syllabuses. Hence, together with a small group of colleagues, we took the initiative to create such a manual. Our decision was supported by the Head of Department, who also formed part of the team. We reasoned that by doing so we would be able to set a standard for the examination that would be extremely hard to reject. Moreover, such a manual would improve our ability to fulfil our roles more effectively and be of benefit to our students and other examination candidates. Despite the fact that we had not been commissioned by MATSEC to do this work, it had been informally told that it was being carried out.

After reviewing a number of manuals for a range of international speaking examinations as well as assessment textbooks by Hughes (2003), Fulcher (2003) and Luoma (2004) amongst others, we realised that there were many elements we wanted to incorporate into the Advanced English Speaking Examination in order for it to be a more reliable, valid, and equitable example of a high-stakes test. We wanted to produce a speaking examination that the relevant stakeholders could value. In the process of discussing the different decisions that needed to be taken in order to improve the syllabus description of this examination, we became aware that our own assessment literacy, attitudes and beliefs were being developed by the very act of reflecting on what suited the needs of the colleagues we worked with and the hundreds of students we taught.

The following sections describe the stages we followed in developing the speaking examination, starting with the writing of the specifications and their eventual incorporation into a manual, moving on to the writing of items, moderation and trialling, followed by the development of a rating scale, and finally ending with examiner training.

Examination specifications

Our first challenge was to write a comprehensive set of specifications for this speaking component while keeping in mind the syllabus outline. Given the official nature of the syllabus we could not avoid working within the parameters set by its description of the component. The syllabus specified that the speaking examination was to carry 6% of the global mark and to last a total of 15 minutes. Moreover, the syllabus described this component as being made up of three parts:

Part 1 is a guided examiner-to-candidate conversation.
Part 2 is a guided examiner-to-candidate conversation.
Part 3 is a candidate-to-examiner 'long turn' (MATSEC 2010:6–7).

An appendix to the syllabus gave an example of the kind of task/s that the candidate would have to complete in each part. It also indicated the approximate amount of time that each part should take as well as the number of marks allotted to each one.

In deciding to write this examination's specifications we were subscribing to the idea that 'the greater the detail in the specification of content, the more valid the test is likely to be' (Hughes 2003:116). We decided to write a thorough explication of each part by first presenting its aims and content, and then carefully listing the procedures to be used by examiners. We knew that this information would serve as the backbone of the examination manual we wanted to present to MATSEC at the end of the process.

Aims and content

Our description of the aims and content not only specified what kind of tasks candidates would have to complete in each part but also explained what they were expected to achieve in doing so. For example, the syllabus specified that Part 1 was 'an informal interview intended as a conversation starter, where the examiner will ask basic questions about topics such as work, study, leisure and career plans' (MATSEC 2010:6). In our gloss we thought that it would be more helpful to inform stakeholders that the purpose behind Part 1 was to assess candidates' ability to give basic information about themselves and express general views as well as specific details on familiar topics. This was based on our familiarity with international speaking examinations and with recommendations made by the literature on assessing speaking. We also considered it expedient to indicate that the examiner's questions could focus on past, present and future situations, and that they were not meant to be specifically challenging in terms of language and content. In this way we sought to underscore the fact that Part 1 was intended to enable candidates to talk about what was highly familiar to them before being expected to engage in more demanding tasks in the following two parts of the examination.

Examination procedures

Our elaboration on the procedures was meant to be as exhaustive as possible so that examiners would behave in a standardised fashion when conducting the examination. In this way we sought to enhance the examination's reliability. This entailed scripting most of what the examiners were required to say in conducting the examination and providing them with information about what they were expected to do in case candidates were unable to sustain a particular turn or gave overlong responses. It also necessitated being highly specific about the structure and timing of each part of the examination. The syllabus used the word 'about' to describe how long each part should take and this provided us with some crucial leeway when specifying the exact amount of time that each part was meant to take. For example, according to the syllabus, Part 2 was meant to take 'about four minutes' and to involve 'a conversation initiated by the interlocutor, based on a prompt such as a photograph or other image that is presented to the candidate at this point in the interview' (MATSEC 2010:6). After the candidate 'briefly' describes the picture, 'The examiner will then follow one set of questions from a number of options available' (MATSEC 2010:9). In writing the procedures for Part 2 we wanted to confirm for examiners and candidates how long each one of these two stages should actually take. Based on our experience, we also considered it fair that candidates should have some time in which to study the visual prompt before describing it. Hence we agreed that the examiner should first present the candidate with the prompt and then provide them with 30 seconds in which to look at it before asking them to describe it. We specified that the description should not last longer than 1 minute and that this was to be followed by a two-way exchange between the examiner and the candidate lasting no longer than 3 minutes. By being so attentive to timing we felt that candidates preparing for this examination would know exactly what was expected of them in each part. We considered this important given our aim to achieve accountability by means of the examination manual (McNamara 2000).

Examination manual

The examination manual we wrote was not conceived to be a monolithic document. Fulcher (2003:116) claims that 'specifications are dynamic, evolving, documents that should be related to the process of test design, piloting and revision'. The specifications we wrote for the Advanced English Speaking Examination are a product of reflection and discussion, trialling, and research data. Moreover, we always intended them to be open to regular reevaluation. This resonates with Luoma's (2004:116) idea that the act of writing specifications is educational for novice test developers given that it facilitates the process of 'making concrete connections between the theory and practice of oral assessment in their own context, through their own data'. We realised that the more we would learn about the examination, the more adept we would become at improving its specifications.

Two versions of the examination manual were written, one for the needs of teachers and candidates and another one for the needs of examiners. The former version sought to reassure candidates that they would not experience any surprises upon sitting for the examination. We considered this to be fundamental given that 'the degree of a test taker's familiarity with the demands of a particular test may affect the way the task is dealt with' (Weir 2005:54). The examiners' version of the manual guided them as to what they should do in each part and when they should do it. This involved instructing examiners of the exact time when they should provide candidates with printed prompts and when to collect them as well as outlining what kind of assistance should be provided to candidates. For example, the syllabus specified that Part 3 should last 'about 3 minutes' and in it a candidate should engage in a 'presentation expressed as a long turn . . . based on a question selected by the candidate from a list of five presented to her/him some minutes before entering the interview room' (MATSEC 2010:6–7). We decided that if candidates were to be given 10 minutes before the beginning of the examination to prepare a 3-minute presentation they would need some time during the actual examination to go over the main points of the presentation and make notes. Hence we agreed that it was only reasonable to provide candidates with a maximum of 2 minutes at the start of Part 3 in which they could gather their thoughts and jot down any important points on a sheet of blank paper given to them by the examiner. Candidates were to be allowed to refer to these notes when delivering their presentation but they were to be handed to the examiner at the end of the examination in order to avoid cheating. On the basis of our experience and the trialling of sample test materials we felt that our students would most likely consider Part 3 to be the toughest, so by introducing these procedures we were providing candidates with an opportunity to be fairly assessed on their speaking skills.

Writing items, moderation and trialling

After having constructed a comprehensive set of specifications for the Advanced English Speaking Examination, we considered it worthwhile to write specimen test materials in line with these specifications (Hughes 2003:63). This was particularly important given that for inexperienced test developers 'writing specifications together with the first versions of the tasks and scales will help them avoid some problems with test use' (Luoma 2004:115). We formed three groups and each one focused on creating materials for a specific part of the examination. In writing these materials we sought to imagine how our students would interpret the wording of the different tasks in each part of the examination. In this way we attempted to preempt any misinterpretations and ascertain that the tasks were truly testing what we intended them to test, hence ensuring validity. Subsequently, we exchanged materials so that we could moderate each other's work. In addition, a colleague who was external to the whole process contributed to this end.

In line with its purpose (Hughes 2003:63), moderation allowed us to identify a number of flaws in the tasks we had created and make the necessary adjustments.

We trialled the specimen examination materials with a group of students who were very similar in terms of age and educational level to the examination's eventual candidates. We each conducted five to eight mock sessions and we also observed one another on several occasions. Before every session we provided the student with as much information about the content and structure of each part so as to approximate the level of familiarity that a typical candidate would have after adequate preparation for the examination. Whilst conducting these sessions we made a note of any problems we encountered and if colleagues were acting as observers they did the same. At the end of every session we asked for detailed feedback from the student so that we could factor in the students' point of view of the examination we had designed. Moreover, a number of colleagues working at other post-16 schools were asked to trial the materials we had developed with a sample of their own students. Trialling allowed us to make further changes to the examination materials as well as to tweak the procedures we had devised. It is for this reason that trialling is described as a 'critical phase of the work' (Fulcher 2003:118) involved in test development. Trialling 'ensures that there is sufficient time available for candidates to produce a situationally and interactionally authentic spoken contribution' (Galaczi and ffrench 2011:137). For example, it was only after the materials had been trialled in four different schools that we took the decision to extend the preparation time in Part 3 to 2 minutes. Initially, we had specified that this should not be longer than 1 minute, but after trialling it became clear that this was insufficient for most students. This kind of trialling was highly useful as it enabled us to improve the design of the examination. However, we realised that further trialling would be necessary once we had developed a rating scale and calibrated it. The latter process was significant given that MATSEC had not specified any criteria in terms of the level of proficiency expected of candidates.

Rating scale calibration

Given that there was no indication on the part of MATSEC of what kind of instrument was going to be used in order to assess candidates' speaking skills we agreed that the best way of doing this was via an analytic rating scale. The four assessment criteria we opted to base our rating scale on were: fluency and coherence; pronunciation; vocabulary; and grammar. Like Weir (2005:191), we considered it 'useful if the criteria employed in the assessment of language production on tasks could be related in a principled way to the criteria for the teaching of a skill'. We wanted the examination to have a positive washback effect on certain aspects of speaking deemed as a priority in the classroom context.

The main hurdle we faced was that the syllabus did not only specify a global mark (i.e. 18 marks) for the speaking component but also prescribed the total number of marks for each part (i.e. Part 1: 4 marks; Part 2: 6 marks; Part 3: 8 marks). This meant that we could not easily use a system of bands as in the *IELTS* test. Hence, as shown in Table 1, we decided to subdivide each set of marks into three groups and create a separate descriptor for each group in terms of each one of the four assessment criteria. This meant that we had to write a total of 36 descriptors. However, some of the descriptors for certain criteria could be used for more than one part of the examination.

Table 1 Rating scale example

Part 1			
Marks	1–2	3	4
Fluency & Coherence	Descriptor	Descriptor	Descriptor

The writing of the descriptors was a lengthy process that underwent many redrafts by different members of the team. We were only satisfied with the rating scale once trialling and our professional experience led us to feel convinced that the three descriptor levels for each assessment criterion would enable examiners to discriminate amongst different candidates depending on their level of speaking proficiency in a particular area.

In order to calibrate the scale we decided to video record a series of 50 mock examinations with students who had a very similar profile to the candidates who would eventually be sitting for the Advanced English Speaking Examination. In order to do this we trained a group of three colleagues in terms of the content and procedures we had devised; for the sake of standardisation we used the same set of specimen examination materials we had developed for the manual. Before we started filming the sessions we needed for calibration purposes, we ensured that these three 'examiners' had mastered the procedures and materials through a number of non-recorded sessions. The 50 videos provided us with samples of performance covering the entire range of the scale (Hughes 2003). Subsequently, we assigned each one of these samples to a relevant point on the scale in terms of each criterion and for each part. However, we chose to focus on calibrating the descriptors of each part in turn so as to facilitate our understanding and effective use of these descriptors. For example, we would watch Part 1 of a session and then each one of us would assign marks for every criterion. After assigning marks individually we would discuss amongst ourselves the reasons why a student was assigned that mark for that particular criterion in that specific part of the examination. The initial challenge was to reach a consensus but once we grew familiar with how to interpret the descriptors in a uniform manner, our scoring became highly standardised. The videos we used to calibrate the rating scale eventually became a crucial part of the training of examiners given that they constituted reference points for the different descriptors.

Examiner training

Once we had finalised the rating scale and the elucidation of the examination's content and procedures, we contacted MATSEC to let it know of our work. Despite the fact that we were not commissioned by MATSEC to do this work, we felt confident that it would appreciate our efforts and seek to implement them. This, in fact, happened and we were invited to present the draft of our manual to all the English teachers working in post-16 institutions in Malta. These teachers were encouraged to test the specimen materials with their students and to provide us with feedback; on the basis of this feedback we made some slight changes to the manual.

Subsequently, MATSEC agreed with our suggestion to organise a training course for prospective speaking examiners and we were asked to run this course. According to Luoma (2004:177–178), 'the use of rater training . . . means that the developers recognise the impossibility of giving comparable ratings without training, and they take steps to ensure comparability because they consider it important'. A group of 18 trainee examiners made up mostly of teachers working in post-16 schools attended the 9-hour training course and by means of it we sought to consolidate their understanding of the different parts of the speaking examination, the assessment criteria, and the examination procedures. We also aimed to provide them with plenty of practice in conducting the examination and in using the rating scale to assess a candidate's performance. For the purposes of the training course we created a list of FAQs that future examiners could refer to when they had any queries about a number of common issues that we had encountered whilst carrying out the mock examinations. Our intention was to add to these FAQs after each sitting of the examination.

After adequate numbers of hands-on activities intended to familiarise the trainee examiners with structure, rubrics and timing, they practised using the rating scale by means of the samples of performance we had recorded. This was in line with Hughes's (2003) suggestion to use calibrated videos when training speaking examiners. Each time the trainees were shown a video clip, they were asked to write down the marks they had assigned to the 'candidate' according to the rating scale descriptors; then a discussion followed. The rating forms used for this purpose were kept as a record of the trainees' performance. Fulcher (2003:145) points out that 'the process of rater training is designed to "socialize" raters into a common understanding of the scale descriptors, and train them to apply these consistently in operational speaking tests'. Achieving a satisfactory level of standardisation in scoring was a lengthy and challenging process but eventually we were pleased that a fair number of trainees were using the rating scale appropriately, leading to a high degree of intra-rater and inter-rater reliability. By the end of the course around half of the trainees were certified as examiners. Given our awareness of training attrition, we envisaged the course to be part of 'a cyclical, iterative process which goes beyond the initial standardization phase' (Taylor and Galaczi 2011:213). Hence we specified that these examiners needed to be recertified every year. As test developers and trainers, we joined this group of examiners in conducting the sessions forming part of the first sitting of the Advanced English Speaking Examination. Our participation in assessing actual candidates was the culmination of three years' involvement in different stages of this examination.

Conclusion

When a high-stakes test is introduced at a national level it is important that the teachers who are going to be affected by this test are provided with the right kind of support so that they may understand the purposes and procedures governing the test. Yip and Cheung (2005:161) affirm that 'to empower teachers, they should be given more opportunities to develop the knowledge and skills necessary for implementing the innovations, through the provision of supporting materials and the organisation of training workshops and courses or experience-sharing sessions'. Involving teachers in the design and implementation of the test is a highly effective way of ensuring such empowerment. It can be argued that developing educators' professional judgement through such involvement is crucial given that the ideal of scientific measurement is impossible to attain (Yorke 2011). Our experience has shown us that the involvement of teachers in high-stakes testing leads to an increased level of assessment literacy, the cultivation of positive beliefs and attitudes in relation to assessment, the bolstering of confidence in teachers' judgement, and more equitable examinations. Further research might indicate whether such implications resonate with the experiences of educators in other contexts.

Acknowledgements

The design and implementation of the Advanced English Speaking Examination described in this paper was conducted together with our colleagues Clyde Borg, Andrew Farrugia, Joseph Gerardi, and Odette Vassallo. We would like to thank the British Council for having recognised the merits of our project by awarding us the 2014 Innovation in Assessment Prize.

References

Allen, A (2012) Cultivating the myopic learner: the shared project of high-stakes and low-stakes assessment, *British Journal of Sociology of Education* 33 (5), 641–659.

Assaf, L C (2008) Professional identity of a reading teacher: responding to high-stakes testing pressures, *Teachers and Teaching: Theory and Practice* 14 (3), 239–252.

Atkin, J M (2007) Swimming upstream: relying on teachers' summative assessments, *Measurement: Interdisciplinary Research and Perspectives* 5 (1), 54–57.

Au, W W (2008) Devising inequality: a Bernsteinian analysis of high-stakes testing and social reproduction in education, *British Journal of Sociology of Education* 29 (6), 639–651.

Black, P, Harrison C, Hodgen J, Marshall, B and Serret, N (2010) Validity in teachers' summative assessments, *Assessment in Education: Principles, Policy & Practice* 17 (2), 215–232.

Black, P, Harrison, C, Hodgen, J, Marshall, B and Serret, N (2011) Can teachers' summative assessments produce dependable results and also enhance classroom learning? *Assessment in Education: Principles, Policy & Practice* 18 (4), 451–469.

Bracey, G W (2005) The 15th Bracey report on the condition of public education, *Phi Delta Kappan* 87 (2), 138–153.

Brookhart, S M (2013) The use of teacher judgement for summative assessment in the USA, *Assessment in Education: Principles, Policy & Practice* 20 (1), 69–90.

Burger, J M and Krueger, M (2003) A balanced approach to high-stakes achievement testing: an analysis of the literature with policy implications, *International Electronic Journal for Leadership in Learning* 7 (4), available online: www.ucalgary.ca/iejll/burger_krueger

Chisholm, L and Wildeman, R (2013) The politics of testing in South Africa, *Journal of Curriculum Studies* 45 (1), 89–100.

Christopher, N M (2009) Interrelation between environmental factors and language assessment in Nigeria, *Research Notes* 35, 10–15.

Coombe, C, Al-Hamly, M and Troudi, S (2009) Foreign and second language teacher assessment literacy: issues, challenges and recommendations, *Research Notes* 38, 14–18.

Costigan, A T (2002) Teaching the culture of high stakes testing: listening to new teachers, *Action in Teacher Education* 23 (4), 28–34.

Crisp, V (2013) Criteria, comparison and past experiences: how do teachers make judgements when marking coursework? *Assessment in Education: Principles, Policy & Practice* 20 (1), 127–144.

Crocco, M S and Costigan, A T (2006) High-stakes teaching: what's at stake for teachers (and students) in the age of accountability, *The New Educator* 2 (1), 1–13.

DeLuca, C, Chavez, T and Cao, C (2013) Establishing a foundation for valid teacher judgement on student learning: the role of pre-service assessment education, *Assessment in Education: Principles, Policy & Practice* 20 (1), 107–126.

Docherty, C, Casacuberta, G G, Rodriguez Pazos, G and Canosa, P (2014) Investigating the impact of assessment in a single-sex educational setting in Spain, *Research Notes* 58, 3–15.

Earl, L M (2003) *Assessment as Learning: Using Classroom Assessment to Maximize Student Learning*, Thousand Oaks: Corwin.

Flores, B B and Clark, E R (2003) Texas voices speak out about high-stakes testing: preservice teachers, teachers, and students, *Current Issues in Education* 6 (3), available online: cie.asu.edu/volume6/number3/

Forsberg, E and Wermke, W (2012) Knowledge sources and autonomy: German and Swedish teachers' continuing professional development of assessment knowledge, *Professional Development in Education* 38 (5), 741–758.

Fulcher, G (2003) *Testing Second Language Speaking*, Harlow: Pearson Education.

Galaczi, E and ffrench, A (2011) Context validity, in Taylor, L (Ed) *Examining Speaking: Research and Practice in Assessing Second Language Speaking*, Studies in Language Testing volume 30, Cambridge: UCLES/Cambridge University Press, 112–170.

Grant, C A (2004) Oppression, privilege, and high-stakes testing, *Multicultural Perspectives* 6 (1), 3–11.

Gregory, K and Clarke, M (2003) High-stakes assessment in England and Singapore, *Theory Into Practice* 42 (1), 66–74.

Gulek, C (2003) Preparing for high-stakes testing, *Theory Into Practice* 42 (1), 42–50.

Guskey, T (2004) Zero alternatives, *Principal Leadership* 5 (2), 49–53.

Harlen, W (2005a) Teachers' summative practices and assessment for learning: tensions and synergies, *Curriculum Journal* 16 (2), 207–223.

Harlen, W (2005b) Trusting teachers' judgement: research evidence of the reliability and validity of teachers' assessment used for summative purposes, *Research Papers in Education* 20 (3), 245–270.

Hoffman, J, Assaf, L C and Paris, S (2001) High stakes testing in reading: today in Texas, tomorrow? *The Reading Teacher* 54, 482–499.

Hoover, N R and Abrams, L M (2013) Teachers' instructional use of summative student assessment data, *Applied Measurement in Education* 26 (3), 219–231.

Hughes, A (2003) *Testing for Language Teachers* (2nd edition), Cambridge: Cambridge University Press.

Johnson, S (2013) On the reliability of high-stakes teacher assessment, *Research Papers in Education* 28 (1), 91–105.

Jones, B D (2007) The unintended outcomes of high-stakes testing, *Journal of Applied School Psychology* 23 (2), 65–86.

Klenowski, V and Wyatt-Smith, C (2012) The impact of high stakes testing: the Australian story, *Assessment in Education: Principles, Policy & Practice* 19 (1), 65–79.

Koh, K H (2011) Improving teachers' assessment literacy through professional development, *Teaching Education* 22 (3), 255–276.

Lewis, A C (2007) How well has NCLB worked? How do we get the revisions we want? *Phi Delta Kappan* 88 (5), 353–358.

Lewkowicz, J and Zawadowska-Kittel, E (2008) Impact of the new school-leaving exam of English in Poland, *Research Notes* 34, 27–31.

Luoma, S (2004) *Assessing Speaking*, Cambridge: Cambridge University Press.

Marshall, B (2011) *Testing English: Formative and Summative Approaches to English Assessment*, London: Continuum.

Martin, S D, Chase, M, Cahill, M A and Gregory, A E (2011) Minding the gate: challenges of high-stakes assessment and literacy teacher education, *The New Educator* 7 (4), 352–370.

MATSEC Examinations Board (2010) *Advanced Matriculation Syllabus English 2013*, available online: www.um.edu.mt/__data/assets/pdf_file/0015/108024/AM10.pdf

McMunn, N, McColskey, W and Butler, S (2004) Building teacher capacity in classroom assessment to improve student learning, *International Journal of Educational Policy, Research, & Practice* 4 (4), 25–48.

McNamara, T (2000) *Language Testing*, Oxford: Oxford University Press.

Nichols, S L (2007) High-stakes testing, *Journal of Applied School Psychology* 23 (2), 47–64.

Nichols, S L and Berliner, D C (2007) *Collateral Damage: How High-stakes Testing Undermines Education*, Cambridge: Harvard Education Press.

Norman, P (2011) Testing English: formative and summative approaches to English assessment, *British Educational Research Journal* 37 (6), 1,055–1,057.

North, B and Jarosz, E (2013) Implementing the CEFR in teacher-based assessment: approaches and challenges, in Galaczi, E D and Weir, C J (Eds) *Exploring Language Frameworks, Proceedings of the ALTE Kraków Conference, July 2011*, Studies in Language Testing volume 36, Cambridge: UCLES/Cambridge University Press, 118–134.

Pennington, J L (2004) Teaching interrupted: the effect of high-stakes testing on literacy instruction in a Texas elementary school, in Boyd, F B and Brock, C H (Eds) *Multicultural and Multilingual Literacy and Language*, New York: Guilford Press, 241–261.

Pishghadam, R, Adamson, B, Sadafian, S S and Kan, F L F (2014) Conceptions of assessment and teacher burnout, *Assessment in Education: Principles, Policy & Practice* 21 (1), 34–51.

Quilter, S M and Gallini, J K (2000) Teachers' assessment literacy and attitudes, *The Teacher Educator* 36 (2), 115–131.

Reich, G A and Bally, D (2010) Get smart: facing high-stakes testing together, *The Social Studies* 101 (4), 179–184.

Rubin, D I (2011) The disheartened teacher: living in the age of standardisation, high-stakes assessments, and No Child Left Behind (NCLB), *Changing English: Studies in Culture and Education* 18 (4), 407–416.

Runté, R (1998) The impact of centralized examinations on teacher professionalism, *Canadian Journal of Education* 23 (2), 166–181.

Sasanguie, D, Elen, J, Clarebout, G, Van den Noortgate, W, Vandenabeele, J and De Fraine, B (2011) Disentangling instructional roles: the case of teaching and summative assessment, *Studies in Higher Education* 36 (8), 897–910.

Sato, M, Coffey, J and Moorthy, S (2005) Two teachers making assessment for learning their own, *Curriculum Journal* 16 (2), 177–191.

Sloane, F C and Kelly, A E (2003) Issues in high-stakes testing programs, *Theory Into Practice* 42 (1), 12–17.

Stobart, G (2001) The validity of National Curriculum assessment, *British Journal of Educational Studies* 49 (1), 26–39.

Tang, S Y F (2010) Teachers' professional knowledge construction in Assessment for Learning, *Teachers and Teaching: Theory and Practice* 16 (6), 665–678.

Taras, M (2005) Assessment: summative and formative: some theoretical reflections, *British Journal of Educational Studies* 53 (4), 466–478.

Taylor, L (2005) Washback and impact: the view from Cambridge ESOL, *Research Notes* 20, 2–3.

Taylor, L and Galaczi, E (2011) Scoring validity, in Taylor, L (Ed) *Examining Speaking: Research and Practice in Assessing Second Language Speaking*,

Studies in Language Testing volume 30, Cambridge: UCLES/Cambridge University Press, 171–233.

Timperley, H, Wilson, A, Barrar, H and Fung, I (2007) *Teacher Professional Learning and Development: Best Evidence Synthesis*, Wellington: Ministry of Education, available online: www.educationcounts.govt.nz/publications/series/2515/15341

Tsagari, D (2009) Revisiting the concept of test washback: investigating FCE in Greek language schools, *Research Notes* 35, 5–10.

Vandeyar, S and Killen, R (2006) Beliefs and attitudes about assessment of a sample of student teachers in South Africa, *Africa Education Review* 3 (1–2), 3–47.

Watanabe, Y (2011) Teaching a course in assessment literacy to test takers: its rationale, procedure, content and effectiveness, *Research Notes* 46, 29–34.

Weir, C J (2005) *Language Testing and Validation: An Evidence-Based Approach*, Basingstoke: Palgrave Macmillan.

Whitehead, D (2007) Literacy assessment practices: moving from standardised to ecologically valid assessments in secondary schools, *Language and Education* 21 (5), 434–452.

Wiliam, D and Thompson, M (2008) Integrating assessment with learning: what will it take to make it work? in Dwyer, C A (Ed) *The Future of Assessment: Shaping Teaching and Learning*, New York: Lawrence Erlbaum Associates, 53–82.

Wu, J (2008) Views of Taiwanese students and teachers on English language testing, *Research Notes* 34, 6–9.

Yip, D Y and Cheung, D (2005) Teachers' concerns on school-based assessment of practical work, *Journal of Biological Education* 39 (4), 156–162.

Yorke, M (2011) Summative assessment: dealing with the 'measurement fallacy', *Studies in Higher Education* 36 (3), 251–273.

16 Investigating aspects of Assessment Literacy for teachers of English for Academic Purposes

Anthony Manning
University of Kent

Abstract

This paper investigates key aspects of Assessment Literacy amongst teachers of English for Academic Purposes (EAP). The enquiry which underpins the paper is driven by an objective to explore and enhance the professional practice of EAP teachers involved in the testing and assessment of EAP in the context of international admissions for institutions of higher education. The research conducted used a mixed methods approach with questionnaire and interview tools. The observations and associated recommendations highlight key areas where the assessment practices of EAP teachers can be improved or enhanced significantly, with closer reference to theories emerging from language testing research and principles associated with Assessment Literacy. These areas include the need to:

- provide accessible in-service or pre-service training associated with EAP assessment
- design mechanisms which encourage practitioners to access and consult research into assessment associated with EAP
- encourage practitioners to use principled approaches to EAP test design
- maximise the potential benefits to validity for EAP testing when collaboration takes place between EAP and with subject teachers across the institution
- familiarise EAP assessors with descriptive statistics and inferential statistics in the process of analysing tests and test scores
- continue to raise awareness related to ethics of EAP testing and assessment.

Introduction and background

The research conducted during this project was inspired by the aim to evaluate English for Academic Purposes (EAP) teacher Assessment Literacy, along with an interest in the identification of recommendations and mechanisms for its maintenance and/or enhancement. It was hoped that the research findings would yield a number of potential applications which could be disseminated to practitioners involved in the teaching and assessment of EAP. The terms 'testing' and 'assessment' will be used interchangeably as umbrella terms for both formal and informal procedures associated with gathering language data for the purpose of evaluation (Davies, Brown, Elder, Hill, Lumley and McNamara 1999:11).

Despite the growing global importance of EAP for international student success in higher education (Hyland and Hamp-Lyons 2002:2–3), until relatively recently there has been very little practical guidance for test and assessment development associated with EAP and indeed teachers have been left with the challenge of converting teaching materials into mechanisms for assessment (Douglas 2000:ix). In addition, the importance of EAP assessment arguably needs to be given more emphasis. As noted by Schmitt (2012), 'High stakes is happening in classrooms – we need to work together more to support EAP practitioners developing greater Assessment Literacy and practical skills.'

Stiggins (1995) is generally accredited with introducing the term Assessment Literacy to describe the need for educators to acquire the necessary skills in order to enable them to produce high-quality tests and assessments and to evaluate critically the data which such assessments produce. Since the introduction of this concept, there appears to have been a growing consensus in the field of language teaching and general pedagogy that there is a need to describe what language teachers need to know about assessment matters (Inbar-Lourie 2008, Malone 2011, Stiggins 1991, Taylor 2009). Connections have also been made between the social impact of EAP assessment practice (Benesch 2001, McNamara and Roever 2006, Shohamy 2001) and the need for Assessment Literacy in order to assess EAP in a principled and meaningful manner.

The research questions which have driven this particular investigation into EAP Assessment Literacy are described below:

- To what extent do EAP teacher views on EAP testing and assessment practices reflect language testing research and practices which comprise Assessment Literacy?
- How can EAP Assessment Literacy be sustained or enhanced?

The hypothesis which was formulated for the purpose of this research was:

> *EAP teachers who are involved in EAP testing and assessment have certain identifiable development requirements with regard to their knowledge and ability to implement assessment good practice and recommendations stemming from research.*

In order to explore the above theory, the research agenda has sought to test the 'null' version of this hypothesis to see if it can be rejected and therefore if support is available for the original hypothesis itself. This was achieved through the collection of a range of qualitative and quantitative data in order to identify patterns in the views and practices of EAP tutors who are involved in assessment.

Supporting literature

This section will now explore research material which is relevant to the research questions identified. The areas in focus include:

- Proponents of Assessment Literacy
- Features of Assessment Literacy and examples of supporting research in Education, Applied Linguistics and EAP.

Proponents of Assessment Literacy

Over the last two decades, a number of experts in the field of education have drawn more explicit attention to the need for educationalists and other stakeholders to develop Assessment Literacy. Given the high-stakes nature of EAP testing and assessment the key considerations raised by experts from the broader field of education are referenced here given their perceived relevance to EAP practitioners. A number of key protagonists in this field are discussed below.

Stiggins and Popham

Stiggins (1991, 1995) is generally accredited with introducing the term Assessment Literacy, the different aspects of which are summarised as:

1. Approaching assessment with the full knowledge of what is being assessed.
2. Understanding the purpose of assessment.
3. Familiarity with the available means of assessing the achievement in focus.
4. The expertise to generate sound samples of performance.
5. An awareness of what can go wrong and how problems can be prevented before they arise.

Given the important role played by EAP study and assessment in universities which use English as a medium of instruction, it is clear to see how the components of Assessment Literacy, as identified by Stiggins (1995), are relevant to the EAP context as well as that of the broader field of education. The key aspects of Assessment Literacy, as described by Stiggins, provide a practical framework for assessment in educational contexts which can assist in establishing a more scientific approach to undertaking and maintain standards. Using the framework provided by Stiggins in this way is particularly useful in EAP, given the high-stakes nature of EAP assessment and the effect that poor assessment-related decisions can have on people's lives.

In his various reports on Assessment Literacy, Popham (2001, 2006, 2009) challenges the quality of high-stakes testing, the outcomes of which can have key implications for test takers' lives, and the negative impact which this is having on students in education. Popham (2001:29) seeks to encourage educational practitioners to reconsider the ways in which they use tests and their results in the classroom. Popham promotes proactivity amongst educationalists in developing Assessment Literacy skills and supports action in response to poor-quality assessment processes.

ASKe and empowerment of test takers through Assessment Literacy

Members of the Assessment Knowledge Standards Exchange (ASKe 2012), a Centre for Excellence in Teaching and Learning (CETL) based at Oxford Brookes University, have been investigating assessment practices in Higher Education over the last two decades with a view to promoting the importance of Assessment Literacy, with a particular emphasis on student involvement. Although the research undertaken by this group extends beyond the context of EAP, it is notable that some of the organisation's members have a background linked to EAP teaching and teaching and learning in the international context.

Inbar-Lourie's constructivist approach to fostering Assessment Literacy

With a specific focus on language testing, Inbar-Lourie (2008) considers the core skills required in order to undertake assessment in the contemporary educational context. Emphasis is placed on the importance of multiple forms of assessment and the contextual evaluation of language skills is recognised. An environment is promoted which seeks to replicate the true roles of language users and which adopts a social reconstructivist paradigm. Inbar-Lourie (2008) notes that, whilst some language testing courses maintain a focus on test design and proficiency assessment, others go as far as to include coverage of the social implications of language testing such as those highlighted by McNamara (2001), McNamara and Roever (2006) and Shohamy (1998, 2001).

The BALEAP Working Party on Testing

With particular linkage to EAP, a number of key developments have emerged in recent years from the BALEAP Working Party on Testing (BWPT) (BALEAP 2012) which has investigated assessment practices at various stages associated with EAP in university education in the UK (Schmitt 2012). These include:

- pre-entry screening
- end-of-course assessment
- in-sessional screening.

In addition to the contribution which BWPT makes to the enhancement of EAP Assessment Literacy, the need for an ongoing collaborative approach through assessment communities is also highlighted by Schmitt (2012), the current president of BALEAP.

Features of Assessment Literacy and examples of supporting research in education, applied linguistics and EAP

The research questions which have steered this research project have led to an investigation of EAP testing and assessment practices which are considered to comprise Assessment Literacy. With this objective in mind, the key aspects of Assessment Literacy, as described by Stiggins (1995) have been used as a means of organising a series of relevant examples from available literature.

Aspect 1: Approaching assessment with the full knowledge of what is being assessed

Understanding what is being assessed – the role of construct validity

Understanding what is being assessed in EAP, through the process of defining EAP skills and abilities which need to be measured, is a key part of assessment in educational contexts, including EAP. If the EAP test items do not accurately represent or collect data linked to the knowledge or attributes which the assessor has in mind, then this can challenge construct validity. Chapelle (1998:34) defines a construct as 'a meaningful interpretation of observed behaviour' and acknowledges that the difficulty in defining constructs lies in 'hypothesizing the source of performance consistency'. In Stiggins' terms (1995), evidence of construct validity can be seen to assist as it provides users of tests and their results with fuller knowledge of what is actually being assessed.

The connection between EAP assessment and construct validity is further strengthened by Blue, Milton and Saville (2000:26–27) who share the belief that construct validity is an overarching form of validity which is crucial to EAP assessment and testing. If construct validity is weak, then the inferences drawn from EAP tests may be flawed and important decisions which affect the lives of students and the operation of institutions can be affected.

Understanding what is being assessed – the outcomes-based model

With the aim of understanding what is being assessed, research associated with the outcomes-based approach to education and assessment can also be considered to offer an important resource to those seeking to cultivate or encourage Assessment Literacy in the field of EAP. In the view supported by Driscoll and Wood (2007:5), by identifying learning outcomes, or stated expectations of what someone will have learned and how they will be assessed, student-centred learning can be promoted along with the improvement of curriculum and pedagogy. Such good practice forms a key feature of many contemporary EAP courses which now commonly seek to specify learning outcomes in order to provide transparent assessment goals for students and to adhere to requirements for accreditation as set by professional bodies such as BALEAP (Alexander, Argent and Spencer 2008:309). The establishment and monitoring of such outcomes can also be linked to construct validity, as mentioned earlier. Some of the promising practices of good assessment which exemplify the outcomes-based approach are also cited by Driscoll and Wood (2007:4):

- assessment information should be provided to students in advance of instruction
- students should be able to direct their learning efforts to clear expectations
- student progress and completion of learning outcomes are determined by achievement of learning outcomes.

The practices described above are of key relevance to Assessment Literacy in English for Academic Purposes. This is due to challenges faced by international students who, when studying EAP, are usually studying in a second language, and therefore need clear guidance and criteria related to their curriculum and its measurement. EAP courses also often have challenging proficiency development aims over short time spans in high-stakes situations. This means that working towards clearly defined achievements and understanding what is required is particularly important for students to understand.

Aspect 2: Understanding the function and purpose of assessment and how this relates to EAP

Given that EAP assessments can take different forms and be used for a variety of purposes, it is important that assessors understand what type of

EAP test is being used and why it has been selected. As clarified by Berry (2008:13), assessment is used for a range of different functions which can be categorised in a series of differing ways. In broad terms, these can be divided into two areas, namely for drawing inferences related to the performance of individuals or the effectiveness of the system, perhaps linked most closely to summative assessment and secondly for the improvement of learning and the provision of feedback, also described as formative assessment (Biggs and Tang 2011:141).

Alexander et al (2008:307) describe the complexities of trying to separate the functions of tests into formative and summative categories, as some summative EAP tests may also have a formative function whilst a test designed for EAP proficiency measurement may also yield diagnostic information. Through explanations of this type, it becomes clear that the task of understanding test purpose is a complex and multi-faceted aspect of Assessment Literacy. Crucially, however, it is identified that it is important to be clear about test uses so that measures can be taken to ensure that tests are appropriate for the selected purposes. If the wrong type of EAP test is employed in the wrong context then the results will not yield information which is relevant to the assessment purpose and this may lead to poor decision making, if the mistake is not identified.

Aspect 3: Familiarity with the available means of assessing the achievement in focus

The test design process and using test specifications

Understanding different stages and processes which are commonly involved in principled EAP test design is important when developing EAP tests, so that the activity can be approached in an informed manner from the outset. The Test Design Framework (Fulcher 2010:94), see Figure 1, provides a useful guidance tool for EAP teachers in the process of navigating the various stages of test design (Davidson and Lynch 2002, Fulcher and Davidson 2007).

According to Davidson and Lynch (2002:3) the test specification is the primary tool for language test development. In the view of these researchers, by using a specification, even less experienced language testers can enhance their assessment practice and consequently their Assessment Literacy.

Marking, grading and giving feedback

Providing feedback, and in many cases the award of marks, represents the means of communicating performance to test takers and other users of test scores. As a result, undertaking this activity appropriately is very important so that EAP students and others consulting EAP test results can accurately

Figure 1 The test design framework (Fulcher 2010:94)

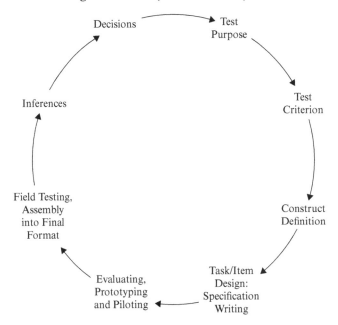

interpret strengths and weaknesses and consider ongoing learning objectives. Fulcher and Davidson (2007:91) explain the importance of scoring by explaining that the test score is the link between the evidence we elicit from the task on the one hand and the construct and domain on the other.

Bachman and Palmer (1996:51–52) describe two key processes which should be undertaken in order to attribute scores to students' performance in tests or assessments; the first of these includes identifying the number of items which have been successfully answered or completed. This approach involves:

- specifying criteria in order to determine what constitutes successful completion
- deciding whether responses will be scored as either correct or incorrect or with varying levels of correctness.

Alternatively, scoring can be undertaken according to levels of language ability. This criterion-based approach involves:

- identifying rating scales in order to assess the language
- considering how many stages of ability are to be incorporated into the different scales.

This criterion-based approach links back to outcomes-based planning, as outlined by Fry, Ketteridge and Marshall (2003:26–41).

Statistical analysis

Given the close association of high-stakes testing with measurement and aspirations of precision, it is necessary for EAP language Assessment Literacy to involve development of at least some skills in using statistics. Through using statistics in the analysis of EAP test results, the creators of EAP tests can look beyond trends which have been initially observed and provide additional evidence linked to a test's reliability and validity.

Benefits of the use of statistics are described in terms of the manner in which they facilitate analysis of complex numerical data and the identification of trends (Woods, Fletcher and Hughes 1986:1), in addition, in line with a multidimensional view of validity (Messick 1989:20).

Aspect 4: The expertise to generate sound samples of performance

Reference to the ability to gather sound samples of performance relates to reliability in the assessment process. Whilst reliability is a condition of construct validity and therefore test usefulness, reliability alone is not indicative of construct validity (Bachman and Palmer 1996:23). Given this distinction and Stiggins' (1995) identification of this area as an aspect of Assessment Literacy, it is useful to describe further this facet of assessment in relation to EAP Assessment Literacy.

Reliability, also described as consistency of measurement, is an essential quality of any test (Blue et al 2000:35). In other words, a test score which is reliable will be consistent across different characteristics of the testing situation (Bachman and Palmer 1996:19–20). Reliability also provides a major justification for using scores for the basis of making decisions. The need for EAP tests, which are often high stakes and used for gate-keeping purposes, to be open to scrutiny and criticism of such factors, which would include reliability is identified by Blue et al (2000:35). Whilst many Higher Education professionals are aware of the admissions function to which results for tests such as *IELTS* and TOEFL are applied, in-house testing systems developed and used within universities also play a key gate-keeping role. This therefore suggests a critical need for EAP practitioner competence in identifying features of a reliable or unreliable measure.

Aspect 5: An awareness of what can go wrong and how problems can be prevented before they arise

EAP tests and their results can have an important impact on the lives of test takers and the courses of study which they are eligible to pursue. As a result, EAP tests and the results derived from them can raise ethical concerns if unreliability or inaccuracy is noted. Enquiry into the ethics of language testing draws on the methodology of critical social theorists (Bachman 2000, Lynch 2001, McNamara 2001, McNamara and Roever 2006, Shohamy 1998, 2001) and is grounded in Messick's holistic view of validity (Messick 1989:20). Spolsky (1981) may be considered to be one of the first researchers to refer to the ethicality of test use and to discuss the political purposes for which language testing is sometimes used. In Spolsky's view (1981:20) language tests should be given a health warning similar to those given to dangerous drugs or chemicals. This is particularly significant in the context of EAP, given the important gate-keeping function which it performs, institutionally, nationally and internationally (Flowerdew and Peacock 2001:192) and the effect that poor assessment or assessment-related decisions can have on people's lives.

Research undertaken by Shohamy (1998:331–332) shows that there is growing interest in the role played by language testing in society. Consequently, topics such as test ethicality and bias are now being discussed in research, publications and conferences. Shohamy (1998:332) advocates a critical approach to language testing which acknowledges that the act of testing is not neutral.

As many EAP testing contexts fall into the high-stakes category (Alexander et al 2008:307) the need for an appropriate amount of piloting and trialling seems evident in order to avoid any problems which might influence the lives of test takers, should their results on EAP tests not reflect their true abilities.

The research paradigm and methodological approach

This section of the paper provides an overview of the research paradigm which has been selected and the methodology which has been used by the researcher.

As Duff (2002:22) and Dörnyei (2007:44) acknowledge, in Applied Linguistics, a greater understanding and appreciation of different research methods and complementary realities can assist in developing the scope of research. For the purposes of this research project, where the views of EAP teachers need to be collected, an approach which enables the identification of complementary realities is seen as positive for the validity and reliability of interpretations.

After considering the range of research philosophies available and the most suitable approach for this project, pragmatism has been identified as an appropriate paradigm, given a perceived need for a programme of mixed methods inquiry (Denscombe 2003a:116).

For mainly quantitative data-collection purposes, a questionnaire tool was identified as an appropriate method, as it provides a self-report research instrument which members of the target population can be asked to complete (Tashakkori and Teddlie 2003:303–304). Efforts were made to construct the questionnaire in a manner which complies with its formal research context and avoids the inclusion of faulty or leading questions.

The constructs, as listed below, which were operationalised within both the questionnaire and interviews were linked to the research questions and the key areas of Assessment Literacy as identified by Stiggins (1995):

- training, skills, strengths and weaknesses in EAP testing and assessment
- approaches to EAP testing and assessment design
- views on/experience of validity and reliability in EAP testing and assessment
- practices involving analysis and interpretation of the results and scores of EAP tests and assessments
- consideration of ethics in EAP testing and assessment
- influence of research and other resources for the purpose of EAP testing and assessment on EAP teacher assessment practices.

In order to ensure, as far as possible, that the questions which were designed for use in the questionnaire were fit for purpose the following steps were implemented (Bryman 2008:241–244):

- The research questions were kept in view in order to ensure that the questionnaire items accurately reflected the research objectives.
- Questions were written with the solicitation of specific types of information in mind and questions were revised in order to attempt to ensure that they were not too general or obtuse in nature.
- Where possible ambiguous and technical terminology was avoided and where applicable complex concepts were explained.
- Overly lengthy questions were avoided so that respondents are able to follow the key points without losing track or motivation.
- Individual questions with double-barrelled elements were avoided as these are complex, if not impossible to answer in situations where only one response is made possible.
- Where possible, all questions which were initially formatted to include negative structures such as 'not' were rephrased in a positive form. This was undertaken as in some cases respondents can misread questions which are negatively phrased thus risking a misinterpretation.
- A considerable amount of attention was paid to the nature of each question and the scale or answer format which was provided, in order to ensure the request symmetry and balance of response options available.

This was particularly important for the purpose of the items which collectively formed a Likert scale.

- Question choice and phraseology was also reviewed by another colleague before being operationalised.

Figure 2 provides an overview of the questionnaire structure and objectives of each element and question item. Further linkage of the questionnaire to the research questions is demonstrated through Table 1.

Figure 2 Questionnaire structure and item features

(Page 1) Welcome page	- Welcome message - Topic background overview - Definition of assessment - Details of incentives - Context of study at the University of Leicester - Instruction for survey page navigation - Survey duration indication - Overview of survey organisation - Remainder of opportunity to opt in survey participation - Thank you message

Save & Continue to Next Page

(Page 2) Data protection & ethics	- Confirmation of adherence to data protection protocols - **(AQ1) FACTUAL** MCQ single answer(yes/no) – Participants agreement for the use of data - Hyperlink to download *Research Information Sheet* providing full details of the research project - **(AQ2) FACTUAL** MCQ single answer (yes/no) – Participant confirmation of access to *Research Information Sheet* - Invitation to email researcher with additional queries - **(AQ3) FACTUAL** MCQ single answer (yes/no) – Respondent's acknowledgement of voluntary participation and facility to withdraw - **(AQ4) FACTUAL** MCQ single answer (yes/no) – Agreement request for respondent participation in the survey - **(AQ5) FACTUAL** MCQ single answer (yes/no) – Permission request for the researcher to use the data in anonymised form

Save & Continue to Next Page

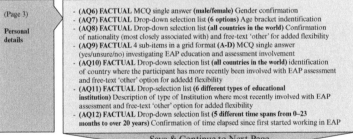

(Page 3) Personal details	- **(AQ6) FACTUAL** MCQ single answer **(male/female)** Gender confirmation - **(AQ7) FACTUAL** Drop-down selection list **(6 options)** Age bracket indentification - **(AQ8) FACTUAL** Drop-down selection list **(all countries in the world)** Confirmation of nationality (most closely associated with) and free-text 'other' for added flexibility - **(AQ9) FACTUAL** 4 sub-items in a grid format **(A-D)** MCQ single answer (yes/unsure/no) investigating EAP education and assessment involvement - **(AQ10) FACTUAL** Drop-down selection list **(all countries in the world)** identification of country where the participant has more recently been involved with EAP assessment and free-text 'other' option for addedd flexibility - **(AQ11) FACTUAL** Drop-selection list **(6 different types of educational institution)** Description of type of Institution where most recently involved with EAP assessment and free-text 'other' option for added flexibility - **(AQ12) FACTUAL** Drop-down selection list **(5 different time spans from 0–23 months to over 20 years)** Confirmation of time elapsed since first started working in EAP

Save & Continue to Next Page

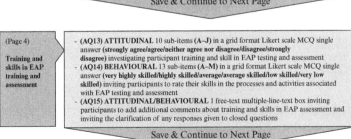

(Page 4) Training and skills in EAP training and assessment	- **(AQ13) ATTITUDINAL** 10 sub-items **(A–J)** in a grid format Likert scale MCQ single answer **(strongly agree/agree/neither agree nor disagree/disagree/strongly disagree)** investigating participant training and skill in EAP testing and assessment - **(AQ14) BEHAVIOURAL** 13 sub-items **(A–M)** in a grid format Likert scale MCQ single answer **(very highly skilled/highly skilled/average/average skilled/low skilled/very low skilled)** inviting participants to rate their skills in the processes and activities associated with EAP testing and assessment - **(AQ15) ATTITUDINAL/BEHAVIOURAL** 1 free-text multiple-line-text box inviting participants to add additional comments about training and skills in EAP assessment and inviting the clarification of any responses given to closed questions

Save & Continue to Next Page

Figure 2 (continued)

| (Page 5) Views on EAP testing and assessment design processes | - **(AQ16) ATTITUDINAL** 10 sub-items **(A–J)** in a grid format Likert scale MCQ single answer **(strongly agree/agree/neither agree nor disagree/disagree/strongly disagree)** inviting participants to identify views on the EAP test and assessment design process
- **(AQ17) BEHAVIOURAL** 8 sub-items **(A–H)** in a grid format, each with a drop-down selection list (9 options). Each of the 8 items represents a stage in the EAP test design process and participants are asked to identify their preferred sequence.
- **(AQ18) ATTITUDINAL/BEHAVIOURAL** 1 free-text multiple-line text box inviting participants to add additional comments about training and skills in EAP assessment and inviting the clarification of any responses given to closed questions |

Save & Continue to Next Page

| (Page 6) Views on validity and reliability in EAP testing and assessment | - **(AQ19) ATTITUDINAL** 10 sub-items **(A–J)** in a grid format Likert scale MCQ single answer **(strongly agree/agree/neither agree nor disagree/disagree/strongly disagree)** inviting participants to comment on their attitude towards situations concerning validity and reliability in EAP testing and assessment
- **(AQ20) BEHAVIOURAL** 8 sub-items in a grid format **(A–H)** MCQ single answer **(yes/unsure/no)** investigating participant views about actions which are likely to enhance validity
- **(AQ21) ATTITUDINAL/BEHAVIOURAL** 1 free-text multiple-line text box inviting participants to add additional comments about validity and reliability and inviting the clarification of any response given to closed questions |

Save & Continue to Next Page

| (Page 7) Views on analysis and interpretation of tests and assessment results | - **(AQ22) ATTITUDINAL** 10 sub-items **(A–J)** in a grid format Likert scale MCQ single answer **(strongly agree/agree/neither agree nor disagree/disagree/strongly disagree)** asking participants to comment on their attitudes and experience of situations concerning test and assessment analysis and interpretation
- **(AQ23) BEHAVIOURAL** 10 sub-items **(A–J)** in a grid format Likert scale MCQ single-answer **(strongly agree/agree/neither agree nor disagree/disagree/strongly disagree)** asking participants to rate their familiarity with methods of descriptive and inferential statistical analysis
- **(AQ24) ATTITUDINAL/BEHAVIOURAL** 1 free-text multiple-line text box inviting participants to add additional comments about analysis and interpretation of EAP tests and assessment results and inviting the clarification of any responses given to closed questions |

Save & Continue to Next Page

| (Page 8) Views on ethical considerations in EAP testing and assessment | - **(AQ25) ATTITUDINAL** 10 sub-items **(A–J)** in a grid format Likert scale MCQ single answer **(strongly agree/agree/neither agree nor disagree/diasgree/strongly disagree)** asking participants to comment on their attitudes towards a series of ethical dilemmas associated with EAP testing and assessment
- **(AQ26) BEHAVIOURAL** 8 sub-items **(a–h)** MCQ single answer **(yes/unsure/no)** investigating participant ethical stance and concern for their own situation and ethical responsibilities in EAP language testing and assessment.
- **(AQ27) ATTITUDINAL/BEHAVIOURAL** 1 free-text multiple-line text box inviting participants to add additional comments about analysis and interpretation of EAP tests and assessment results and inviting the clarification of any responses given to closed questions |

Save & Continue to Next Page

| (Page 9) Invitation to join a prize draw and to participate in interview stage | - **(AQ28) FACTUAL** 1 free-text single-line text box inviting participants to add their email address for inclusion in prize draw
- **(AQ29) FACTUAL** 1 free-text single-line text box inviting participants to add their email address and volunteer to participate in the interview stage |

Save & Continue to Next Page

| (Page 10) Thank you and confirmation of data submission | - Thank you message and confirmation of data submission
- Invitation to contact the researcher by email with any related queries
- Reminder of future contact for participants who opted into the interview stage |

Table 1 Assessment Literacy linked to items/sections within the research questionnaire

Key areas of EAP Assessment Literacy identified for exploration in this study	Coverage via questionnaire items/sections
Training, skills, strengths and weaknesses in EAP testing and assessment	AQ13, AQ14, AQ15
Approaches to EAP testing and assessment design	AQ16, AQ17, AQ18
Views on/experience of validity and reliability in EAP testing and assessment	AQ19, AQ20, AQ21
Practices involving analysis and interpretation of the results and scores of EAP tests and assessments	AQ22, AQ23, AQ24
Consideration of ethics in EAP testing and assessment	AQ25, AQ26, AQ27
Influence of research and other resources for the purpose of EAP testing and assessment on EAP teacher assessment practices	AQ13 (In particular, AQ13d)

Interviews were selected as the second research tool in order to collect more qualitative data regarding participants' views, feelings and experiences (Denscombe 2007:174). Interviews are also commonly used in conjunction with other research methods, such as questionnaires (Cohen, Manion and Morrison 2007:268) in order to follow up unexpected results or validate findings (Kerlinger and Lee 2000:693).

A series of questions was developed for the interviews which took into account the research questions for this project and the construct for Assessment Literacy. The set of interview items was then reviewed and condensed in order ensure that the interview encompassed only necessary items which were appropriate and distinctive from one another (Gillham 2000:21). Attention was paid to the ordering of questions so that respondents would feel comfortable with the content and tone from the start of the interview. Given the different range of experience amongst the research population, very technical terminology was also avoided, in recognition that not all interviewees would have knowledge of technical expressions associated with assessment (Dörnyei 2007:137).

Figure 3 provides an overview of the interview structure and objectives of each element and question item. Table 2 shows how areas of EAP teacher Assessment Literacy, demonstrated through practice and research are connected to items in the interview protocol.

Findings and the analysis process

The overall questionnaire respondent population amounted to 187 individuals. In order to focus on a population which could be considered adequately homogenous, certain decisions were made regarding which categories of respondent to include for further consideration. This represents part of the process of reducing variables in the dataset, so that key features can be identified. It also helps to demonstrate that the sample used is sufficiently similar to the identified target population (Dörnyei 2003:107–108).

Questionnaire respondents were attracted through sending an email request with an embedded link to a web-based questionnaire. The EAP-related distribution lists which were utilised for this purpose are as follows:

- the UK-based email-discussion list provided by BALEAP
- the USA-based online-discussion platform offered through the TESOL International Association
- the Australian-based email forum provided through the Association for Academic Language and Learning
- the internationally focused UK-based email-discussion list for practitioners in English for Specific Purposes, provided through the IATEFL ESP Special Interest Group.

After the filtration of the main data set, comprised of 187 respondents, a remaining total of 158 respondents was identified. This figure represents those respondents who had most recently been involved with EAP assessment either in universities or university partnership institutions, either in the UK or across the rest of the world.

Descriptive statistics associated with sets of individual items which took the form of Discrete Visual Analogue Scales (DVAS) were calculated. During analysis, this section revealed the respondent population's responses to individual survey items.

Following this stage, the findings and analysis focused on the clustered or composite results drawn from series of related Likert scales in the questionnaire. When completing Likert Scale items respondents specify a level of disagreement or agreement and as a result trends in feeling can be identified for related items which represent a particular construct. Questionnaire findings are of greater interest and significance when evaluated in terms of groupings of related questions, rather than individual items. This is due to the fact that '. . . multi-item scales maximize the stable component that items share and reduce the extraneous influences unique to the individual items' (Dörnyei 2003:34). Before the composite results were presented, a process of improving the validity and reliability of the data was explored through Factor Analysis and Cronbach's Alpha.

When considering the alpha levels which will be judged as acceptable in this study, it was determined that whilst lower levels are common on shorter scales which are usual in questionnaires which seek to measure many different areas, concern should be raised in situations where alpha falls below 0.6 (Dörnyei 2003:112).

Brown (2001:184) explains that, in the process of analysing a survey

Figure 3 Interview structure and item features

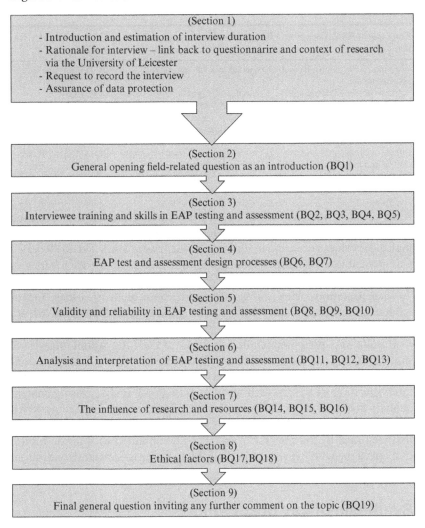

(Section 1)
- Introduction and estimation of interview duration
- Rationale for interview – link back to questionnarire and context of research
  via the University of Leicester
- Request to record the interview
- Assurance of data protection

(Section 2)
General opening field-related question as an introduction (BQ1)

(Section 3)
Interviewee training and skills in EAP testing and assessment (BQ2, BQ3, BQ4, BQ5)

(Section 4)
EAP test and assessment design processes (BQ6, BQ7)

(Section 5)
Validity and reliability in EAP testing and assessment (BQ8, BQ9, BQ10)

(Section 6)
Analysis and interpretation of EAP testing and assessment (BQ11, BQ12, BQ13)

(Section 7)
The influence of research and resources (BQ14, BQ15, BQ16)

(Section 8)
Ethical factors (BQ17,BQ18)

(Section 9)
Final general question inviting any further comment on the topic (BQ19)

instrument for validity, Factor Analysis can be used to explore the convergent and discriminate structures of subsections within survey instruments. With regard to results obtained via Factor Analysis, the researcher analysed the items in each distinct bank of questions which had been grouped with the intention of representing a series of different constructs. The process enabled a more scientific identification of which sub-items did actually group to form factors or constructs and which items did not group as the researcher expected.

Table 2 Key areas of EAP Assessment Literacy linked to items/sections within the interview protocol

Key areas of EAP Assessment Literacy identified for exploration in this study	Coverage via interview items/sections
Training, skills, strengths and weaknesses in EAP testing and assessment	BQ2, BQ3, BQ4, BQ5
Approaches to EAP testing and assessment design	BQ6, BQ7
Views on/experience of validity and reliability in EAP testing and assessment	BQ8, BQ9, BQ10
Practices involving analysis and interpretation of the results and scores of EAP tests and assessments	BQ11, BQ12, BQ13
Influence of research and other resources for the purpose of EAP testing and assessment on EAP teacher assessment practices	BQ14, BQ15, BQ16
Consideration of ethics in EAP testing and assessment	BQ17, BQ18

In order to identify which Likert scale items clustered into common factors or construct areas, and to identify those items returning sufficiently high eigenvalues according to the factors which were discerned, the Rotated Component Matrix output from SPSS was consulted for each series of items.

Open questions from the questionnaire were analysed using content analysis procedures, in line with models suggested by Gillham (2000:63–66) and Denscombe (2007:237).

Results were presented relating to the features of the overall interviewee sample population. Approximately 35 questionnaire respondents were contacted to be interviewed and 25 interviews were conducted. Results of the interview stage of the research were organised and analysed using content analysis tables to show the main clusters of factors or components which emerged from each respective interview question. Clusters of factors were first identified by the researcher and then corroborated with the assistance of a colleague with experience in the field, in order to substantiate or reject perceived observations.

Synthesis of key observations

This section will now synthesise the key observations which have been drawn from the analysis of research, in order to identify and group together interpretations which characterise the Assessment Literacy of participants in this study.

Observations relating to EAP teacher training, skills, strengths and weaknesses in EAP testing and assessment

With regard to practitioner levels of interest and confidence in EAP assessment, the results of the study appear to indicate considerably less than favourable levels in both areas, with data, collected from both composite Likert scales and individual items, suggesting relatively low levels. In addition, data drawn from the interview stage of the research shows clusters of comments from interviewees which refer to less-than-scientific mechanisms being used for test result interpretation.

The Likert scale items from the questionnaire, which collectively act as an overall skill self-evaluation tool, with relevance to Assessment Literacy in EAP, show that respondents position themselves predominantly as 'average skilled' in the key aspects of assessment in EAP which were listed.

Other skills such as use of statistics, defining test purposes and trialling and piloting tests, which were identified as areas of lower skill, may not be so easily developed through existing general training opportunities. A pattern of interviewee responses also described strengths in EAP testing and assessment but largely did not refer to analytical or interpretive stages of test development and usage. Consequently, there is a case for the provision of accessible in-service or pre-service training which makes such skills more easily available to practitioners.

With regard to the manner in which skills in EAP assessment have been developed, a series of sources from within the data sets suggest that skills relevant to EAP testing and assessment have predominantly been developed in the workplace due to a lack of related specialist training available.

A cluster of responses in the interview data shows that practitioners are aware of the need to undertake the task of EAP assessment to the best of their ability, given challenges which they face and the stakes in the balance. However, the results of a Likert scale and an additional individual item show that more than 50% of respondents did not actively acknowledge the high level of complexity associated with EAP testing and assessment.

A series of comments drawn from open questions in the questionnaire illustrate some of the views expressed by research participants associated with a lack of training in EAP assessment (Table 3).

Observations relating to the influence of research and other resources for the purpose of EAP testing and assessment on EAP teacher assessment practices

When data linked to practitioners' consultation of published research is considered, the interviews show a split response, with nearly half the interviewees claiming not to consult research actively. Eleven interviewee comments mentioned no reference to specific titles connected to EAP assessment. Results from the questionnaire also corroborated this. One conclusion which can arguably be drawn from these findings is the need for an intervention which assists in building practitioner skill in areas associated with EAP assessment in order that confidence can be built and key aspects of Assessment Literacy can be fostered. This could then serve as a means of providing EAP teachers

Table 3 Views relating to the absence of specialist or specific training, identified via item AQ15 Factor 1

1	Little to no specific training. General ELT experience + Delta was my entry requirement, and I wish I could have more training.
2	I have not had formal training in assessment and have sometimes felt this lack.
3	I have not attended any specialist training in EAP testing but have picked up some, including through reading. The headings in the questionnaire do not provide me with the best option. I consider I am above average in most of them, but not highly skilled, so I have put average.
4	It's hard to decide if I am skilled in something that I have learnt about 'on the job'. My experiences have shown me that it is incredibly difficult to write good tests and assessments. One has to be very certain of the objectives of the course being taught and then how to assess these objectives accurately and fairly.
5	For a number of years I was responsible for managing a high stakes test but I had no explicit training at the time, and most of the above skills were learned 'on the job'.
6	My MA Applied Linguistics did not focus on this area, and overall my skills have been developed through experience rather than formal training. Assessments I am involved in are related to institution-specific programmes. I therefore find it hard to evaluate my competence, hence the predominance of answers in the 'Average Skilled' column. I am aware of a lack of formal training, however it might be worth mentioning that the course design I am involved in, including assessments, have received good feedback from external examiners.
7	There is no provision in my job for any training in this area and it is much needed.
8	My skills have largely come from years of practice and from trial and error.
9	Very little specific formal training in EAP testing and assessment. Sometimes get the impression that it is not in the interests of my institution for staff to know too much about testing for operational reasons.
10	What training? There really isn't any training out there that is specific to EAP testing and assessment, especially if you think beyond large-scale external tests. For in-house assessments, we need to extrapolate from general testing literature which tends to focus too heavily on large-scale tests and not other types of assessment.

with the expanded Assessment Literacy (Taylor 2009) which they require, as language teaching professionals. Table 4 shows some samples of comments given by interviewees relating to their reference to existing assessment-related research.

Observations relating to approaches to EAP testing and assessment design

Analysis of the results also implies that a large proportion of EAP teachers engaged in assessment have a good understanding of what constitutes a principled approach for EAP test and assessment design (see Fulcher 2010:94). Likert scale results indicate respondents' understanding of test design as a collaborative venture requiring time and key stages in advance of item writing (Bachman and Palmer 1996:62, Fulcher and Davidson 2007:7).

Table 4 Examples of interview responses relating to use of research as identified via item BQ13

Factor number	Description of factors identified in interviews	Examples drawn from interviews (interviews coded using letters in brackets e.g. '(A)' denotes 'Interview A')		
1	Yes I'm influenced by research.	(L) Well, quite a lot really, I have a range of things on my shelf.	(P) Just at the moment a lot. Just because I'm in the middle of doing this literature review. You have asked me at the right time.	(W) Yeah, I mean more recent . . . that, I mean because that was a long time ago and things have got a bit rusty on things as you can probably tell.
2	No, not influenced much.	(D) Probably not a huge amount, to be very honest.	(H) Erm, I don't really think it's influenced.	(J) I think directly, not at all. It would be the honest answer.
3	BALEAP or IATEFL influence.	(G) I've been looking at the BALEAP teaching competencies and they also refer to assessment.	(W) But I like to read you know, when I get time, journal articles too, the testing SIG for IATEFL.	(X) I do keep an eye on what, for example the IATEFL organisation are looking at.
4	Reference to literature consulted.	(K) I've got a small number of books on testing and so on.	(S) All I know is that those ideas have come from the literature that I've read.	(Y) I think my main influences are really in terms of the kind of philosophical dimension of language testing really.

Free-text open responses in the questionnaire show that respondents see test design as a highly context-driven process based on the particular purposes for which the test is required. Responses to questions which ranked stages of test design and use in terms of priority, showed a pattern which was consistent with logical and principled sequencing of stages of test design. Nevertheless, despite practitioners' ability to recognise a principled approach, the findings from the interview stage showed that nearly half the interviewees were unable to describe an identifiable procedure or process which they may implement in their own EAP testing experience. Whilst it may be the case that interviewees were unable to define a process due to the need to vary the approach based on the context of testing or assessment (Calderhead and Shorrock 1997:194), the researcher raises the concern that the situation may also be attributable to a gap between theory and practice. A series of comments, drawn from the interview stage of data collection, have been included in Table 5, which relate to the EAP test design process:

Table 5 Examples of factors relating to the EAP test design process as identified in BQ6

Factor number	Description of factors identified in interviews	Examples drawn from interviews (interviews coded using letters in brackets e.g. '(A)' denotes 'Interview A')		
1	No identifiable procedure.	(C) I'm aware there isn't a process.	(M) I would like to be able to give you a clear set of steps but I feel it is a bit more of an organic process.	(F) (Set process?) Not at the moment. No.
2	Looking at what happened/ was done in previous years.	(B) Honestly looking at previous years, what we've already done is usually the baseline.	(I) I mean I suppose the conventional answer, is you'd look at what had come before.	(N) I'd look at previous models . . . Looking at what hasn't worked in the past.
3	Start by looking at students skills and needs.	(F) I'd start thinking about which sort of sub-skill area it was obviously and the level of the students in the class.	(S) So I would first of all make sure that I knew what those needs were. That I knew what they needed to accomplish and where they needed to go.	(Q) Yes, I suppose first of all starting with what needs to be tested, and I would usually do that on a skills basis.
4	Interviewee describes a set process or format.	(J) Usually two academic pieces of writing one of which would be a report or research-based paper, one of it would be an essay-based paper . . .	(T) In the situation I've done EAP before, there has been a set process and I've you know, used what was given and supplemented my own . . . just supplemented my own judgment and intuition.	(U) So I find the listening text first. And then try and find the reading text which are, which are thematically connected.
5	Assessment designed as part of or with reference to course design.	(K) I guess actually the assessment design is part of the course design.	(L) I'll draw up the specifications at first. Well, I need to know certain factors in which the test was meant to be used.	(W) I'm writing the outline and the assessment at the same time. And the task would be very linked to the outcomes.
6	Alignment with outcomes/ goals.	(O) Constructive alignment and so on. So, working out what I want the outcome to be and then making an assessment that would fit those outcomes.	(P) I suppose that the main principle will be to keep in mind their end goal and think about how close or far away people are from that and try to base assessment on appropriate steps towards the end goal.	(R) We had a sort of set formula where we were testing different things and it was to do with the outcomes of the courses.

Observations relating to views on/experience of validity and reliability in EAP testing and assessment

With reference to aspects of construct validity, the Likert scales show a varied pattern of opinion regarding the importance of domain specificity in EAP assessment (Carroll 1981:67, Kane 2012:41–42, Weir 1983). Although only 41.2% of respondents directly support the creation of assessments designed to represent specific domains of academic study, it is possible that this situation may reflect common dichotomies associated with English for Specific Academic Purposes (ESAP) and English for General Academic Purposes (EGAP) in the field. Despite this spread of views, 65% of respondents did report a need for different marking descriptors in different contexts of EAP such as for writing or speaking. This difference can potentially be attributable to the fact that contexts differ within subjects as well as across subject areas leading to a more immediate requirement to consider particular types of assessment tasks rather than the need to consider subject specialism.

In response to one particular Likert scale, it does also appear that the majority of teachers in the study recognise benefits in researching the features of different subject areas which students are studying. In addition, benefits are seen in working more closely with academic colleagues from different subject fields, with regard to the potential impact on enhancing validity of EAP testing and assessment. The benefits of working with other academic colleagues across the institution, in order to understand the features of academic subject areas, were also supported. Furthermore, the results also show that practitioners have a strong sense of responsibility to assist other colleagues in understanding test scores. Groups of comments from the interview stage also support the benefits to validity of collaborating with subject teachers across the institution (see Table 6). Collaboration for the purposes of moderation was also referred to in a group of seven comments to one particular questionnaire item. One concern is also acknowledged, where comments are also made regarding potential barriers to collaboration with colleagues within institutions.

Observations relating to practices involving analysis and interpretation of the results and scores of EAP tests and assessments

Further evidence of EAP teachers' observance of principles associated with Assessment Literacy can be identified in multiple references in the findings to outcomes-based approaches. This is evident in comments relating to the provision of feedback. It is then also supported with similar comments made in individual items in both the questionnaire and interview protocols.

Table 7 can also be used to show the ranking of respondents according to self-evaluations of 'High Skill' or 'Very High Skill' level in each of the skill areas represented in this set of items.

Table 6 Examples of interview responses relating to views on defining domain in EAP testing and assessment, identified via BQ10

Factor number	Description of factors identified in interviews	Examples drawn from interviews (interviews coded using letters in brackets e.g. '(A) denotes 'Interview A')		
1	Choose subjects related to course or general for EGAP.	(C) I think, we tend to just choose from 'serious' subjects which are related to academic studies in some way.	(G) I sort of focus on the context.	(P) Again, ideally it would be based on what people are going on to study so in a perfect world, you would be able to divide students according to if not subject, kind of faculty or area.
2	Journals, books.	(E) Looking at journals and books in the field of the study of the students.	(H) I would try to find you know, academic journals.	(U) Find something which is an academic text written, written within a law department or in a legal journal or something like that.
3	Newspapers.	(C) I think we tend to dumb down by choosing newspaper articles when we should be looking for suitable academic text.	(H) Newspaper articles or whatever that actually fit you for example.	(N) We used to use a lot of newspaper articles, something like this Telegraph one here.
4	Work with academics from the field.	(T) The best way, to be able to work with the professionals, although it isn't always the case that lawyers know the best about what is the best language to use.	(R) I think many universities have EAP and then you have the rest of the university and there has to be a bit more you know, more interaction.	(Q) Doing the sort of coordinating with the departments that they're going on to, finding out what is needed in those departments, and feeding that back into both your course design and your testing design.
5	Difficult to work with academics from the field.	(M) Well ideally, you know, in a perfect world, it would be nice to work with the subject teacher.	(Q) But that's in an ideal world; there's often difficulties over communication between EAP tutors or departments.	(V) If you can go up to the Law department and work out something with them then it's, it's very helpful for everybody if they are happy to do that, you know if you can sort of communicate with the department.

Table 7 Ranking of respondent skill areas in EAP assessment according to perceptions of high or very high skill

Item code	Respondent skill area in EAP assessment	Percentage of respondents claiming to be highly skilled or very highly skilled
AQ14k	Skills in giving feedback to students based on test scores	76
AQ14c	Skills in identifying what should be assessed	52.5
AQ14j	Skills in making instructional decisions based on test scores	48
AQ14l	Skills in helping other people who use EAP test results to understand them	46
AQ14e	Skills in writing test items/questions	45.5
AQ14m	Skills in identifying problems with tests or assessments	43
AQ14f	Skills in developing and using grading procedures	36.7
AQ14a	Skills in test and assessment design	32.2
AQ14i	Skills in drawing inferences from test and assessment scores	29.7
AQ14d	Skills in trialling/piloting tests	29.1
AQ14g	Skills in using descriptive statistics	17
AQ14b	Skills in defining test purpose	8.2
AQ14h	Skills in using inferential statistics	7.5

Likert scale items within the questionnaire revealed a clear indication that the majority of respondents do not consider themselves to be highly skilled or very highly skilled with regard to descriptive statistics or inferential statistics in the process of analysing tests and test scores. Whilst overall familiarity with descriptive statistics was higher than that of inferential statistics, those with experience of using either set of procedures was notably low. The lack of familiarity with these analytical tools suggests the need for a form of training that can demonstrate the powerful contribution which statistics can make, in a manner which is accessible to the non-statistically-minded EAP teacher.

Observations relating to practices involving the consideration of ethics in EAP testing and assessment

With regard to ethics, an important principle for Assessment Literacy, the results of the related Likert scale items, the free-text items from the questionnaire and the comments made by interviewees show that EAP teachers involved in assessment tend to adopt an ethical stance which favours the needs and best interests of test takers (see Table 8). This is paralleled by recommendations for good practice issued by champions of Assessment Literacy and critical language testing (McNamara and Roever 2006, Popham 2001, Shohamy 2001, Stiggins 1995). Nevertheless, when

Table 8 Statements of ethical position, identified via A27 Factor 1

1	This depends very much on University Policy . . . But some places are just so rigid in their enforcement of rules.
2	Teachers who write/correct EAP exams should be careful; if they are not students will eventually find out and start to mistrust the system and the teachers.
3	I feel that courses in EAP, ESP, etc. should play a supportive role and that small-group tuition/guidance based on real assignments, etc. will over time yield better results. Of course, the cost implications are such that this is unlikely to happen ever. It's easier to adopt a factory-like system with batches we process and 'rejects' that are left behind.
4	Bullying and unskilled assessors should be held to account given the gravity of final assessment particularly regarding borderline cases.
5	I have been involved recently in a project which assessed the performance of a group of international staff in a lecture context and this raised huge ethical issues.
6	Ethical considerations are of paramount importance in language testing. My own view is that we should establish a humane testing culture which is constructive and collaborative, rather than repressive. There is a school of thought (Shohamy, McNamara, etc.) which is looking more closely at the social impact of testing and the power of tests, and this strongly informs my practice. I think my own personal experiences and identity help me to see discrimination a bit more easily than is the case for some others, so I see my role as educative in this area.
7	I have written tests for our own EAP foundation course, also for our in-house IELTE equivalent for Chinese students who take our test in China, however, until very recently, none of the wider issues or in fact any knowledge about language testing was known about by me. I recently did my diploma so have a little more understanding now.
8	Pre-sessional course managers are essentially magicians whose job is to deliver a predetermined number of students to departments while using a smoke screen of procedures to give the satisfying illusion that students have been rigorously screened for their ability to cope linguistically with follow-on courses. The university cares about ethics only if there is a real danger of being used.

respondents were asked about the specific situations associated with their own practice through the Likert scale, only 41% felt able to declare that their employment and assessment practice was not associated with unethical practice. The researcher therefore recommends a more widespread campaign for EAP teacher-led awareness raising, related to ethics in EAP testing and assessment, undertaken by EAP teachers. The table below provides a series of open comments which relate to ethics in EAP assessment, as provided by questionnaire respondents.

Limitations

Despite the observations which have been described, which the researcher suggests can be generalised to the wider sector of EAP assessment, there are a number of limitations to this study which need to be considered.

The research tools used in this investigation represent the opinions of EAP teachers regarding their own Assessment Literacy rather than a more objective measure of Assessment Literacy undertaken through observation of assessment in practice. With regard to the questionnaire, the number of questionnaire respondents was restricted to practitioners with membership of professional bodies, which may have excluded less engaged practitioners. In addition, whilst the number of respondents was not small, a greater number of respondents may have influenced the nature of the data gathered. It should also be noted that responses to free-text items were smaller in volume as these items were marked as optional. As far as the interview stage is concerned, whilst the data collected was arguably rich, the number of interviews conducted was restricted to 25 and therefore more limited in scope than the questionnaire.

Recommendations

In order to summarise the recommendations made in this section, a series of five key action points has been identified as a means of drawing together the next steps which should follow on from this research.

Action Point 1: Provide a downloadable and transferable framework for in-service EAP Assessment Literacy training

A web-based transferable framework should be developed for the design and implementation of in-service training interventions by EAP departments or professional bodies such as BALEAP, TESOL or IATEFL which will assist in building practitioner skill in areas associated with EAP assessment. This resource could also draw attention to the key role played by in-service skill development through the complex yet necessary challenges of EAP assessment. Importantly the resource would allow departments to identify the EAP Assessment Literacy training needs which are specific to their staff. In this way such activity would take the form of a series of group-based self-help initiatives which could be implemented according to local needs and resources in different EAP departments. It is hoped that through this mechanism confidence and interest in EAP assessment can be built according to local requirements and simultaneously key aspects of Assessment Literacy can be fostered.

Action Point 2: Create an online annotated bibliography to foster research-led EAP Assessment Literacy

A medium for proactively introducing practitioners to published research is advocated. Ideally, this should be achieved by making EAP teachers aware of research which is relevant to EAP Assessment Literacy, in a manner which is perceived to be accessible. In this manner, knowledge embedded within these resources could be more easily absorbed and disseminated. This objective could be achieved through the provision of an online annotated bibliography which would allow EAP practitioners to identify key research materials relevant to EAP Assessment Literacy. A brief and straightforward summary of ways in which certain publications and research papers might be best applied to testing practice, would also be included.

Action Point 3: Promote collaborative research and learning opportunities in EAP assessment, both within institutions and across the sector

It is recommended that collaborative research and learning opportunities, linked to EAP Assessment Literacy, should be fostered, both within and beyond individual institutions. Such opportunities could include cross-institutional groups or pairings which can foster action research into EAP assessment. More structured and collective opportunities for research into EAP assessment and testing could also be instigated. Means could also be sought to promote and develop research opportunities and interactions between EAP practitioners and academic subject specialists within EAP practitioners' home institutions. This would assist in better operationalisation of relevant constructs in EAP tests and assessments and could enhance the validity of inferences drawn from test scores.

Action Point 4: Develop interpretive EAP Assessment Literacy skills through statistical analysis training, with the use of online video tutorials

Mechanisms to develop EAP teachers' interpretive Assessment Literacy skills should be sought through training in statistical analysis procedures. It is hoped that this will be beneficial for EAP teachers, who are not already skilled in this area and who are not naturally motivated to develop these skills. The intention is to achieve this aim through creating a series of video tutorials, provided online, showing how a software package, such as SPSS can be used to explore and analyse tests results. Whilst a number of books are already available which provide guidance on the use of statistics to analyse language tests, these are arguably still complex to follow. As a result, video tutorials could be utilised in order to demonstrate statistical procedures in a lighter manner which could be designed to appear less technical and more straightforward.

Action Point 5: Raise awareness about the key importance of ethicality as an aspect of EAP Assessment Literacy, through an online forum

An online forum could be created in order to raise awareness amongst EAP teachers and their institutions, regarding the dangers of unethical practice associated with EAP assessment. This could involve the more prominent publication of and adherence to a code of ethics, related to EAP Assessment, such as that published by EALTA (Erickson and Figueras 2010). EAP practitioners could also be encouraged to discuss ethical concerns more proactively through an online forum tool. Mechanisms could also be considered to educate colleagues across educational institutions beyond the confines of EAP departments, regarding the unreliability of standardised tests if their scores are interpreted inappropriately. This could involve briefing sessions, delivered by EAP specialists, for central admissions departments regarding the features and scope of standardised EAP tests and how results should be appropriately interpreted. This process might also draw attention to the dangers associated with the unprincipled use of estimated equivalences to scores from standardised tests, if these have been generated unscientifically.

Concluding comments

In order to determine how the conclusions from this study relate to the objectives and original drivers for this research project, it is crucial at this stage to consider both the research questions which steered the research and the hypothesis which the research sought to reject or prove.

The first research question for the study asked: 'To what extent do EAP teacher views on EAP testing and assessment practices reflect language testing research and practices which comprise Assessment Literacy?'

In this study a number of areas of good practice associated with Assessment Literacy in EAP, which can be linked to theory from research, have been identified in the practice of EAP teachers. The observations reached and the conclusions and recommendations identified also demonstrate that there also appear to be key areas where the assessment practices of EAP teachers can be improved or enhanced significantly with closer reference to theories emerging from language testing research and Assessment Literacy. The second research question asks: 'How can EAP Assessment Literacy be sustained or enhanced?'

Finally, in order to consider the hypothesis behind this research the null hypothesis (H_0) has been tested in order to determine if it can be rejected thus providing support for the original hypothesis. The null hypothesis is as follows:

> *EAP teachers who are involved in EAP testing and assessment do not have any identifiable development requirements with regard to their knowledge and ability to implement assessment good practice and recommendations stemming from research.*

Based on the conclusions cited in the section above, it is concluded that the null hypothesis can be rejected and that the original hypothesis has been supported.

It is the researcher's belief that the recommendations and actions which are advocated in this paper can be used to develop a set of tools for the realisation of practical initiatives for the enhancement of EAP Assessment Literacy. With this aim in mind, it is also the researcher's aim to create a series of internet-based resources, which will integrate contributions from the wider EAP practitioner community. It is hoped that such a resource will provide a user-friendly and accessible mechanism for the implementation of the recommendations which have been identified in this paper.

References

Alexander, O, Argent, S and Spencer, J (2008) *EAP Essentials: a Teacher's Guide to Principles and Practice*, Reading: Garnet.

ASKe (2012) *Assessment Standards Knowledge Exchange* 2013, available online: www.brookes.ac.uk/aske/

Bachman, L F (2000) Modern language testing at the turn of the century: assuring that what we count counts, *Language Testing* 17 (1), 1–42.

Bachman, L F (2004) *Statistical Analyses for Language Assessment*, Cambridge: Cambridge University Press.

Bachman, L F, and Kunnan, A J (2005) *Statistical Analyses for Language Assessment: Workbook and CD-ROM*, Cambridge: Cambridge University Press.

Bachman, L F, and Palmer, A S (1996) *Language Testing in Practice: Designing and Developing Useful Language Tests*, Oxford: Oxford University Press.

BALEAP (2008) *TEAP Working Party: The Competency Framework for Teachers of English for Academic Purposes 2011*, available online: www.baleap.org.uk

BALEAP (2012) *BALEAP Working Party on Testing: BALEAP Guidelines on English Language tests for university entry 2012*, available online: www.baleap.org.uk/projects/teap-working-party

Benesch, S (2001) *Critical English for Academic Purposes: Theory, Politics, and Practice*, Mahwah: Lawrence Erlbaum Associates.

Berry, R (2008) *Assessment for Learning*, Hong Kong/London: Hong Kong University Press.

Biggs, J B and Tang, C S-K (2011) *Teaching for Quality Learning at University: What the Student Does* (4th edition), Maidenhead: McGraw-Hill/Society for Research into Higher Education/Open University Press.

Blue, G M, Milton, J and Saville, J (2000) *Assessing English for Academic Purposes*, Oxford: Peter Lang.

Brown, J D (2001) *Using Surveys in Language Programs*, Cambridge: Cambridge University Press.

Bryman, A (2008) *Social Research Methods* (3rd edition), Oxford: Oxford University Press.

Calderhead, J and Shorrock, S B (1997) *Understanding Teacher Education*, London: Falmer.

Carroll, B J (1981) Specifications for an English Language Testing Service, in Alderson, J C and Hughes, A (Eds) *Issues in Language Testing*, Oxford: Pergamon Press, 66–110.

Chapelle, C A (1998) Construct definition and validity inquiry in SLA research, In Bachman, L F and Cohen, A D (Eds) *Interfaces Between Second Language Acquisition and Language Testing Research*, Cambridge: Cambridge University Press.

Cohen, L, Manion, L and Morrison, K (2007) *Research Methods in Education* (6th edition), London: Routledge.

Davidson, F and Lynch, B K (2002) *Testcraft: A Teacher's Guide to Writing and Using Language Test Specifications*, New Haven: Yale University Press.

Davies, A, Brown A, Elder, C, Hill, K, Lumley, T and McNamara, T (1999) *Dictionary of Language Testing*, Cambridge: Cambridge University Press.

Denscombe, M (2003a) *The Good Research Guide for Small-scale Social Research Projects* (2nd edition), Maidenhead: Open University Press.

Denscombe, M (2003b) *The Good Research Guide for Small-scale Social Research Projects* (3rd edition), Maidenhead: Open University Press.

Denscombe, M (2007) *The Good Research Guide: For Small-scale Social Research Projects*, Maidenhead: Open University Press.

Dörnyei, Z (2003) *Questionnaires in Second Language Research: Construction, Administration and Processing* (2nd edition), New York: Routledge.

Dörnyei, Z (2007) *Research Methods in Applied Linguistics: Quantitative, Qualitative and Mixed Methodologies*, Oxford: Oxford University Press.

Douglas, D (2000) *Assessing Languages for Specific Purposes*, Cambridge: Cambridge University Press.

Driscoll, A and Wood, S (2007) *Developing Outcomes-Based Assessment for Learner-centred Education: A Faculty Introduction*, Sterling: Stylus Publishing.

Duff, P (2002) Research approaches in applied linguistics, in Kaplan, R B (Ed) *The Oxford Handbook of Applied Linguistics*, Oxford: Oxford University Press, 13–23.

Erickson, G and Figueras, N (2010) *EALTA Guidelines for Good Practice in Language Testing and Assessment: Large Scale Dissemination Days*, available online: www.ealta.eu.org

Flowerdew, J and Peacock, M (2001) *Research Perspectives on English for Academic Purposes*, Cambridge: Cambridge University Press.

Fry, H, Ketteridge, S and Marshall, S (2003) *A Handbook for Teaching and Learning in Higher Education: Enhancing Academic Practice* (2nd edition), London: Kogan Page.

Fulcher, G (2006) Test architecture, *Foreign Language Education Research* 9(1), 1–22.

Fulcher, G (2010) *Practical Language Testing*, London: Hodder Education.

Fulcher, G (2012a) Assessment literacy for the language classroom, *Language Assessment Quarterly* 9 (1), 113–132.

Fulcher, G (2012b) *The Routledge Handbook of Language Testing*, Oxford: Routledge.

Fulcher, G and Davidson, F (2007) *Language Testing and Assessment: An Advanced Resource Book*, London: Routledge.

Fulcher, G and Davidson, F (2009) Test architecture, test retrofit, *Language Testing* 26 (1), 123–144.

Gillham, B (2000) *The Research Interview*, London: Continuum Publishing.

Hyland, K and Hamp-Lyons, L (2002) EAP: issues and directions, *Journal of English for Academic Purposes* 1 (1), 1–12.

Inbar-Lourie, O (2008) Constructing a language assessment knowledge base: A focus on language assessment courses, *Language Testing* 25 (3), 385–402.

Kane, M (2012) Articulating a validity argument, in Davidson, F and Fulcher, G (Eds) *The Routledge Handbook of Language Testing*, Oxford: Routledge, 34–47.

Kerlinger, F N and Lee, H B (2000) *Foundations of Behavioral Research* (4th edition), Fort Worth: Harcourt College Publishers.

Larson-Hall, J (2010) *A Guide to Doing Statistics in Second Language Research Using SPSS*, London: Routledge.

Lynch, B K (2001) Rethinking assessment from a critical perspective, *Language Testing* 18 (4), 351–372.

Malone, M E (2011) *Assessment literacy for language educators*, CAL Digest.

McNamara, T F (1996) *Measuring Second Language Performance*, London: Longman.

McNamara, T (2001) Language assessment as social practice: challenges for research, *Language Testing* 18 (4), 333–349.

McNamara, T and Roever, C (2006) *Language Testing: The Social Dimension*, Oxford: Blackwell.

Menter, I (2010) *Literature Review on Teacher Education in the 21st Century*, available online: www.scotland.gov.uk/Publications/2010/09/23094515/0

Messick, S (1989) Validity, in Linn, R L (Ed) *Educational Measurement* (3rd edition), New York: American Council on Education, 13–103.

Popham, W J (2001) *The Truth about Testing: An Educator's Call to Action*, Alexandria: Association for Supervision and Curriculum Development.

Popham, W J (2006) *Needed: A Dose of Assessment Literacy*, available online: www.ascd.org/publications/educational-leadership/mar06/vol63/num06/Needed@-A-Dose-of-Assessment-Literacy.aspx

Popham, W J (2009) Assessment literacy for teachers: faddish or fundamental? *Theory into Practice* 48, 4–11.

Schmitt, D (2012) *EAP Assessment in the UK*, paper presented at the BALEAP AGM 2012, London South Bank University, available online: www.baleap.org.uk/projects/teap-working-party

Shohamy, E (1998) Critical language testing and beyond, *Studies in Educational Evaluation* 24 (4), 331–345.

Shohamy, E (2001) *The Power of Tests: A Critical Perspective on the Uses of Language Tests*, Harlow: Longman.

Spolsky, B (1981) Some ethical questions about language testing, in Klein-Braley, C and Stevenson, D K (Eds) *Practice and Problems in Language Testing I*, Frankfurt am Main: Lang, 5–21.

Spolsky, B (2012) Language testing and language management, in Davidson, F and Fulcher, G (Eds) *The Routledge Handbook of Language Testing*, Oxford: Routledge, 495–503.

Stiggins, R J (1991) Assessment literacy, *The Phi Delta Kappan* 72 (7), 534.

Stiggins, R J (1995) Assessment literacy for the 21st century, *The Phi Delta Kappan* 77 (3), 238.

Tashakkori, A and Teddlie, C (2003) *Handbook of Mixed Methods in Social and Behavioral Research*, Thousand Oaks: Sage.

Taylor, L (2009) Developing assessment literacy, *Annual review of Applied Linguistics* 29, 21–36.

Weir, C J (1983) The Associated Examining Board's Test in English for Academic Purposes: an exercise in content validation, in Hughes, A and Porter, D (Eds) *Current Developments in Language Testing*, London: Academic Press, 147–153.

Woods, A, Fletcher, P and Hughes, A (1986) *Statistics in Language Studies*, Cambridge: Cambridge University Press.

17 Test fairness to prospective English teachers in Teacher Employment Examinations (TEEs): An investigation focusing on rater behaviour

Tomoyasu Akiyama
Bunkyo University, Japan

Abstract

This study examines the fairness of employment examinations taken by prospective English teachers in Japan, focusing on rater behaviour both quantitatively (Many-Facets Rasch Analysis, (MFRA) (Linacre 2005)) and qualitatively (the think-aloud method). In order to become an English teacher in a Japanese public school, a candidate must pass two tests: one knowledge based and the other performance based. This study focuses on the second test – the assessment of candidates' performance on the basis of a microteaching session (a demonstration of teaching skills).

In the language testing context, many previous studies (e.g. Eckes 2005, Lumley and McNamara 1995, Lynch and McNamara 1998) indicate that raters are one of the main elements impacting variation in score. However, there is little research into the processes involved in rating (Bejar 2012, Brown 1995, Chalhoub-Deville and Wigglesworth 2005, Taylor and Galaczi 2011). Thus, focusing on the rating process, this study examines the extent to which scores given to candidates by raters (employers) are fair to candidates (prospective English teachers), based on rating data (scores) across candidates.

To this end, 12 raters were asked to rate 30 candidates on six assessment criteria. Raters were required to give a reason for the specific rating assessment criteria they adopted (e.g. 'personality', 'instruction ability'); these criteria reflect the ones frequently used in actual tests. MFRA results show that approximately 25% of interactions between raters and candidates can be considered biased. The results of the think-aloud method reveal that despite the same assessment criteria having been provided to raters, different raters nevertheless rated candidates differently based on their core teaching values and ideal images of English teachers and English classes, aspects which were not included in the assessment criteria. To conclude, this paper discusses the concepts of fairness and values in the language testing field in the context of rater cognition research (Bejar 2012), based on implications drawn from this study.

Introduction

The purpose of this study

In order to become a teacher in a Japanese public school, a candidate has to take teacher employment examinations (TEEs). These are high-stakes tests, because the results have a direct impact on recruitment decisions and thus on the candidate's employability. Those who cannot pass a TEE cannot take it again until the following year which might change the course of their lives.

TEEs come in two types: *knowledge based* and *performance based*. In general, the former tests cover pedagogy; educational theory, such as educational law and student cognitive development; and liberal arts, while the latter includes individual interviews, group discussions, and a demonstration of teaching skills via *microteaching*. However, there is no information about the validity or reliability of either type (Watanabe 2008), and in fact, there has been little research into TEEs in general, or into the assessment of teaching skills via *microteaching*. This raises serious concerns about test fairness, especially given the high stakes for candidates. Focusing on rater behaviour, this paper investigates the fairness of the evaluation of the demonstration of teaching skills via microteaching in the TEE context.

Background information about TEEs

According to the Japanese Ministry of Education, Culture, Sports, Science and Technology (2014), 68 education school boards in the country develop and administer TEEs. Table 1 shows some general statistics about TEEs and their takers, including the number of candidates across school types and the average success rate.

Approximately 180,000 people took the 2013 TEEs (Japanese Ministry of Education, Culture, Sports, Science and Technology 2014). Of particular interest in this study are junior high school teachers, because it is mainly candidates for junior high schools who are required to demonstrate their teaching skills via microteaching. The success rate in junior high school is similar to that in senior high school and nearly half the success rate of elementary school teachers (23.2%).

Table 1 General statistics of 2013 TEEs (Japanese Ministry of Education, Culture, Sports, Science and Technology 2014)

School types	Candidates (N)	Candidates successful on both tests (N)	*Success rate (%)
Elementary school	58,703	13,626	23.2
Junior high school	62,998	8,383	13.3
Senior high school	37,812	4,912	12.9
Information about results for junior high school English teachers (Tokyo and Aomori prefectures)			
Tokyo	331	52	15.7
Aomori	83	4	4.8

* Success rate = The number of candidates who passed both tests divided by the number of candidates in each category.

Since local school boards predetermine the number of teachers who will be employed, success rates depend upon the needs of each local board of education. For example, the success rate for junior high school English teachers in Tokyo is 15.7%, which is larger than that nationwide average (13.3%), whereas the success rate in Aomori prefecture (4.8%) is much lower than the nationwide average. Please note that these prefectures were chosen for different reasons: Aomori had the lowest success rate in 2013, while Tokyo, the capital of Japan, was chosen as a kind of default case to show there are variations in success rates from local school board to local school board within a prefecture.

Microteaching (demonstration of teaching skills) test procedures

Microteaching was originally developed in 1963 (Cooper and Allen 1971). It is a tool for teacher training and refers to the teaching situation of a scaled-down lesson conducted for 5–10 minutes focusing on one or more teaching aspects (Gage 2008). A candidate's performance is usually videotaped for feedback and further analysis.

The goals of microteaching are to help candidates develop and refine their teaching skills and to give feedback to prospective teachers for their self-reflection and professional growth (Grossman 2005). A majority of the literature on microteaching states that it is an effective method of teacher training (e.g. Cochran-Smith and Fries 2008, Lakshmi 2009, Monk 2008).

A demonstration of teaching skills via microteaching is usually administered as part of the second test in TEEs. Although local school boards develop and administer their own tests with different formats, procedures, length, and number of raters, Figure 1 shows a typical microteaching test procedure.

There are three stages in microteaching testing: 1) preparation, 2) demonstration of teaching skills, and 3) assessment. At the preparation stage, a

Figure 1 A typical TEE microteaching test procedure

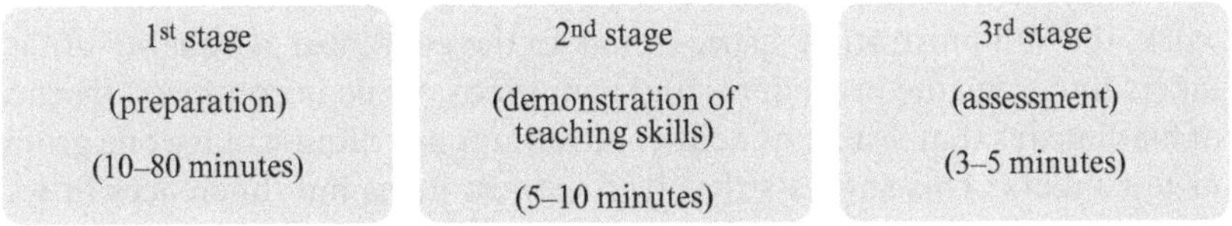

1st stage	2nd stage	3rd stage
(preparation)	(demonstration of teaching skills)	(assessment)
(10–80 minutes)	(5–10 minutes)	(3–5 minutes)

candidate or a cohort of candidates makes a teaching plan (e.g. for the introduction of a target grammar point). As can be seen in Figure 1, there is a wide range in terms of preparation time because each local school board sets a different amount of preparation time. Then, the candidates are required to demonstrate their teaching skills based on a teaching plan in front of assessors and sometimes their fellow candidates, who play the role of students but, in order to minimise variation, do not respond to the teacher. After finishing their demonstrations, raters (e.g. school board members, school principals, and in-service teachers) assess the candidates' performance based on assessment criteria. Example criteria might be instruction ability, personality, and teaching technique; more information about assessment criteria will be given later.

Problems with microteaching and scope of test fairness in this study

Problems with microteaching

Although microteaching has been viewed positively as a tool for teachers' training, there seem to be some problems with using microteaching to recruit prospective teachers. One issue is that the microteaching context is different from the real classroom context in that there are no actual students present (and thus no authentic response or feedback) (Borko, Whitcomb and Byrnes 2008, Grossman 2005). Monk (2008) observes that microteaching lacks reliability and validity as an assessment instrument, stating that it focuses on only a limited range of constructs (i.e. it suffers from *construct underrepresentation*; Messick 1989). Thus, although microteaching is an effective tool for teacher training, it seems that there are problems with its use in an assessment context. Since TEEs are high-stakes tests, it is necessary to investigate the extent to which the scores given to candidates are reliable and thus to which employment decisions based on them are fair.

Scope of test fairness in this study

As Xi (2010) points out, there is much discussion about how best to define *fairness* in an assessment context. For example, Kunnan (2004:37–40) proposed a test fairness framework, consisting of five factors: *validity*, *absence of bias*, *access*, *administration*, and *social consequences*. In his framework, the 'administration' aspect refers to the guarantee of equality of test takers under testing procedures and conditions, while in contrast, 'absence of bias' means that test items neither advantage nor disadvantage one group of test takers. This suggests that it is not test items but differences in test takers' ability that reside in the target groups. In order to investigate test fairness in the microteaching context, at least two main interactions need to be considered, namely, interactions between candidates and assessment criteria, and raters.

In relation to Kunnan's framework, Kane (2010:178) establishes two types of test fairness: *procedural fairness* and *substantive fairness*. Kane (2010:179) makes the distinction between these as follows: 'Procedural fairness is concerned with how we treat test takers, in particular with how consistently and fairly we treat them, and is therefore largely under our control. Substantive fairness is concerned with how the testing programme functions, and, in particular, with how well it functions for different groups'. (Procedural fairness is thus similar to Kunnan's concept of 'administration'.) Kane (2010) goes on to say that fairness should be considered as part of validity (that is, the extent to which we can have confidence in interpreting inferences made from data, in this case test scores).

In contrast to Kane's (2006, 2010) broad view of fairness, however, this study takes a narrow view of fairness, focusing on 'absence of bias' in the interactions between raters and test takers. This is because there is much research showing that the rater is a substantial source of error in language testing research (e.g. Eckes 2005, Lumley and McNamara 1995, Lynch and McNamara 1998, Schaefer 2008).

Figure 2 shows a chain of inferences based on McNamara and Roever (2005:26). If the chain of two adjacent assumptions is weak, the bridge of the two assumptions will be fragile, which will mean that inferences from the test scores are invalid. This chain of inferences has clear relevance for test result interpretations, as can be seen in the figure.

For example, the link between (1) and (2) seems weak in the microteaching test context because a microteaching test assesses so limited a view of teaching skills (i.e. only 5–10 minutes) that such a test may have difficulty in eliciting the candidate's teaching ability.

The relationship between (2) and (3) is also weak (again) in that scores drawn from microteaching may not represent typical teaching performance by the candidate. However, the assumption of procedural fairness in terms of Kane (2010) is warranted to some extent since the procedure is consistent and standardised established by each local board, as shown in Figure 1.

Although Figure 2 suggests that test fairness is relevant to every aspect of the testing process, this study investigates a technical aspect of test fairness

Figure 2   Chain of inferences (McNamara and Roever 2006:26)

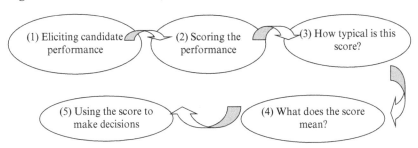

(in Kunnan's term, 'absence of bias'), focusing on scores given by raters of microteaching lessons, because rater error or discrepancy is one of the biggest confounding factors for valid test scores (e.g. Lumley 2002, Schaefer 2008).

Research questions, participants and assessment criteria

Research questions

Three research questions are set in this study to investigate test fairness, focusing on interactions between test takers and raters:

1. To what extent do raters assess candidates' performances reliably?
2. To what degree are interactions between raters and candidates affected by bias?
3. If bias occurs, what are possible reasons for rater biases?

The first question is investigated by considering the consistency of MFRA scoring patterns by rater. It is a prerequisite to research question 2, since this information is essential to investigate the extent to which raters assess candidates consistently. The second question investigates the extent to which interactions between raters and candidates are affected by bias. The third question examines possible reasons for rater bias using the think-aloud method.

Research participants

A total of 30 candidates (20 university students who were training to become English teachers and 10 in-service teachers) participated in this study. All participants were required to introduce one of the following six target grammar points in a microteaching lesson: 1) past regular verbs (*-ed, -d*), 2) *there are* _____, 3) *Do you* _____?, 4) *I want to* _____, 5) *be going to*, and 6) *Can you* _____? These were chosen because all are found in first- and second-year English textbooks and because some, such as 1), 3) and 6) have been used in actual TEEs. One of the six target grammar points was randomly assigned to each participant.

The test procedure was as follows: 1) a participant was assigned one of the six target grammar points and was asked to take 20 minutes to put together a teaching plan for the introduction of the assigned item. Then, the participants carried out their plans, demonstrating their teaching skills for approximately 5 minutes. All performances were videotaped for assessment.

Raters and assessment criteria

Twelve raters were invited to participate in this study. Six were junior high school teachers, each with more than two years of teaching experience; of the others, two were administrative teachers and four were officers at school boards (management educators) who had assessed candidates several times for TEEs. Please note that 'management educators' here refers to those who are in a position to supervise or give administrative guidance to teachers. All raters were required to rate 30 candidates individually, watching videotaped performances. Further, all raters were required to dictate specific observations for each assessment criterion into a digital voice recorder. These statements were analysed in order to investigate rating processes and possible reasons for bias in interactions between candidates and raters. All raters underwent rater training with the researcher for approximately 2 hours. The training included explanations of assessment criteria and the researcher rated the 1–2 candidates in collaboration with the raters being trained.

As mentioned above, six assessment criteria were chosen: 1) *lesson flow*, 2) *instruction ability*, 3) *delivery*, 4) *personality*, 5) *expertise*, and 6) *overall judgement* (see an example assessment sheet in Appendix A). The first five criteria have been frequently used in the TEEs (Japanese Ministry of Education, Culture, Sports, Science and Technology 2014), and the last, overall judgement, was intended to yield a holistic impression; it asked the rater to quantify the extent to which raters felt a candidate should be employed. All criteria were marked from 1 (poor) to 5 (excellent); thus the minimum total score for a candidate was 6 and the maximum, 30.

Results of quantitative and qualitative analyses

Quantitative analyses

Descriptive statistics (average scores, minimum and maximum scores, and largest differences)

Tables 2a and 2b exhibit descriptive statistics for raters' raw scores, indicating that raters' severity, as reflected by average score, varies. Average scores given by junior high school teachers (labelled J1–6) cluster around 21 points

Table 2a Descriptive statistics 1: Average and minimum/maximum scores

Rater name*	Average	Maximum scores (candidate no.)	Minimum scores (candidate no.)
J1	21.3	26 (No. 25)	17 (Nos. 15, 17, 26)
J2	21.9	30 (Nos. 4, 11)	18 (Nos. 15, 19, 20, 21, 23)
J3	21.2	28 (No. 11)	13 (No. 26)
J4	21.8	30 (Nos. 5, 11, 12, 13, 16)	9 (No. 17)
J5	17.5	24 (No. 16)	9 (No. 17)
J6	21.9	29 (Nos. 6, 10, 16)	16 (Nos. 26, 30)
M1	21.1	30 (No. 5)	13 (No. 20)
M2	15.3	22 (Nos. 2, 16, 23)	9 (Nos. 15, 17)
M3	18.6	28 (No. 24)	8 (No. 17)
M4	21.0	29 (Nos. 10, 22)	15 (Nos. 17, 19)
M5	20.8	28 (Nos. 10, 28)	14 (No. 15)
M6	17.8	27 (Nos. 10, 16)	11 (Nos. 9, 27)

* J = junior high school English teachers, M = management educators

with the exception of J5, whereas those given by management educators (M1–6) had a wider range from 15 to 21 points.

Focusing on maximum scores given by individual raters, for example, No. 11 was given the best score by J2, J3 and J4, while none of the M group identified this candidate as the best. One candidate (No. 10) was identified as the best by M4, M5 and M6, whereas in the J group only J6 gave this candidate the best score.

There was more agreement on minimum than on maximum scores. For example, No. 17 was assigned the lowest scores by J1, J4, J5, M2, M3 and M4, whereas No.15 was identified as the worst scoring candidate by J1, J2, M2 and M5.

A most surprising result was the discrepancy between the scores given by two raters (J2 and M2) to No. 23; J2 gave this candidate the minimum score (18 points) whereas M2 gave the maximum score (22 points). Although the difference between J2 and M2 was only 4 points, this still seems to have an impact on the employment decision, because candidates are employed on the basis of ranking of total scores. In other words, if J2 were to assess No. 23 in real life, there would be no chance of this candidate being employed whereas the same candidate would be highly likely to be employed on the basis of M2's rating.

Table 3 displays the five largest differences for candidates among raters in terms of total scores.

The largest difference (20 points) was assigned to No. 4 between J2 and M3, followed by J4 and M1 (No. 5, 18 points), by J6 and J4 (No. 6, 18 points), by J4 and M2 (No. 8, 18 points), and J4 and M6 (No. 11, 17 points). These results (Tables 2a, 2b and 3) suggest that employment decisions may be based on inconsistent rating. Thus, these results raise serious concerns about test

Table 2b Complete raters' raw scores

C*	Rater name												
	J1	J2	J3	J4	J5	J6	M1	M2	M3	M4	M5	M6	Mean
1	18	22	22	29	19	27	14	16	16	18	20	22	20.3
2	21	26	19	17	16	20	14	22	16	18	20	18	18.9
3	19	21	22	17	15	21	24	12	22	22	26	16	19.8
4	23	30	26	14	16	21	20	18	10	28	19	18	20.3
5	21	27	23	30	18	27	30	13	19	17	25	12	21.8
6	21	20	15	11	13	29	17	15	12	17	17	14	16.8
7	25	29	27	28	22	26	22	14	24	23	26	24	24.2
8	24	25	21	28	13	22	15	10	20	17	19	16	19.2
9	19	19	24	21	14	17	24	13	13	19	25	11	18.3
10	21	29	25	25	22	29	28	19	15	29	28	27	24.8
11	23	30	28	30	23	26	26	17	27	21	26	13	24.2
12	23	20	26	30	21	24	24	14	17	28	26	23	23.0
13	20	19	20	30	18	17	23	14	22	18	20	16	19.8
14	22	20	24	26	21	20	19	14	19	27	26	20	21.5
15	17	18	18	16	14	21	16	9	17	22	14	14	16.3
16	20	26	26	30	24	29	29	22	20	26	19	27	24.8
17	17	19	19	9	9	20	15	9	8	15	15	16	14.3
18	22	19	15	18	18	22	20	17	24	19	17	14	18.8
19	22	18	17	25	15	17	27	13	21	15	19	13	18.5
20	22	18	24	16	14	20	13	16	12	20	16	13	17.0
21	18	18	23	23	15	18	20	15	17	18	19	16	18.3
22	20	20	20	25	22	20	20	13	22	29	18	17	20.5
23	25	18	17	18	20	25	24	22	23	21	26	16	21.3
24	23	29	27	14	19	24	25	20	28	20	19	22	22.5
25	26	20	21	17	20	17	20	20	19	16	24	17	19.8
26	17	20	13	26	16	16	14	15	17	19	16	16	17.1
27	24	20	16	21	13	20	23	16	20	19	16	11	18.3
28	22	19	22	24	19	24	20	14	26	27	28	26	22.6
29	23	20	18	22	20	22	24	12	18	20	17	22	19.8
30	22	19	17	13	17	16	24	16	14	22	17	24	18.4
Mean	21.3	21.9	21.7	21.8	17.5	21.9	21.3	15.3	18.6	21.0	20.8	17.8	20.0

* C = candidate number

Table 3 Descriptive statistics 2: The five candidates who showed the largest differences among the raters

	20-points difference	18-points difference			17-points difference
Candidate	(C4)	(C5)	(C6)	(C8)	(C11)
J1	23	21	21	24	23
J2	30	27	20	25	30
J3	26	23	15	21	28
J4	14	30	11	28	30
J5	16	18	13	13	23
J6	21	27	29	22	26
M1	20	30	17	15	26
M2	18	13	15	10	17
M3	10	19	12	20	27
M4	28	17	17	17	21
M5	19	25	17	19	26
M6	18	12	14	16	13

fairness to candidates. The next question is concerned with the extent to which raters assessed candidates reliably and consistently.

Rater consistency (MFRA)

Figure 3 shows rater's (*in-*) consistency, as measured by the extent to which raters' rating patterns diverge from the rating patterns estimated by a Rasch model. If rating patterns are closer to those predicted by a Rasch model, the value of 'infit mean square' (IMS) will get closer to 1. The acceptable range of IMS is 0.75 to 1.3 (McNamara 1996). This means that if IMS is within the acceptable range, rating patterns will be similar to those of the Rasch model.

As can be seen, three raters (J4, J5 and M5) are outside of this range. The result for J4 (more than 1.8) is 'misfitting', indicating that J4's rating patterns are too varied to fit the Rasch model. This result therefore indicates inconsistent (random) rating patterns.

The results for J5 and M5, on the other hand (both less than 0.75), are 'overfitting', showing that their rating patterns are too predictable to fit the Rasch model. In other words, the rating patterns produced by J4 were more varied, and those by J5 and M5 are less varied than those predicted by the Rasch model. Importantly, McNamara (1996) states that overfit ratings do not have a destructive impact on overall data patterns when we interpret test scores. The results show that most of the raters rated candidates relatively consistently and appropriately for the Rasch model. The reliability index (0.97) shows that raters differed in terms of severity. Note that reliability in MFRA means the extent to which each rater can be differentiated from each other (Linacre 2005). Here, most of the raters were relatively consistent; however, each had their own characteristics in terms of severity, as also shown in Tables 2a, 2b and 3.

Figure 3 Consistency among 12 raters (infit mean square, IMS) (reliability 0.97)

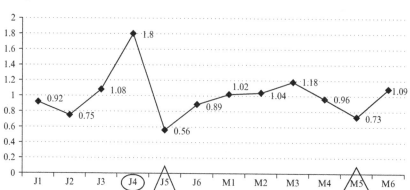

Bias analysis (MFRA)

The second research question (RQ2) was intended to identify the extent to which interactions between raters and candidates were affected by bias, analysing the extent to which a rater rated a candidate significantly more leniently or more harshly than the data patterns predicted by the Rasch model (Linacre 2005). MRFA identifies such patterns with t-statistics of either more than 2 or less than −2 standardised deviations. The former result means that the rater assesses a candidate more leniently than the Rasch model expected and the latter, more harshly.

Table 4 displays information about rater severity, the numbers of candidates for which each rater showed bias, and the candidates involved. In terms of rater severity, M2 was the harshest (1.4 logit) and J2 was the most lenient (−0.55). The difference between these raters was less than 2 logits. Among 360 interactions (30 candidates × 12 raters), there were 92 biased interactions, amounting to more than 25% of the total. Three raters (J4, M3 and M6) had more than 10 (out of 30) biased interactions apiece, for a bias rate of more than one-third.

Table 4 also shows that a relatively large number of the 30 candidates were rated in a biased way by some of the 12 raters in terms of t-statistics, that is, with results of either more than 2 or less than −2 standardised deviations. Three *circled* candidates (Nos. 4, 17, and 25) experienced bias from more than five raters, and three *squared* candidates (Nos. 24, 26, and 28) were rated more leniently or harshly than predicted under MFRA by four raters. These six candidates were thus taken as targets for a qualitative analysis of raters' utterances.

Of the six candidates mentioned above, two (Nos. 4 and 24) were chosen for further analysis because of the relatively large differences in t-statistics

Table 4 Summary of 92 biased interactions between some candidates and some raters (*n* = 360)

	J1	J2	J3	J4	J5	J6	M1	M2	M3	M4	M5	M6
Severity (logit)	−0.38	−0.55	−0.33	−0.5	0.71	0.63	−0.32	1.4	0.39	−0.29	−0.22	0.63
Numbers of biased interactions	4	6	7	14	3	6	9	8	11	8	5	11
Candidate experiencing bias $t > 2$	25, 26	2, 4, 24	4, 9, 17, 20	1, 5, 8, 13, 19, 26	17, 22	1, 6, 17	5, 9, 19, 30	2, 23, 25	11, 18, 19, 24, 28	4, 14, 15, 22	3, 9, 28	1, 10, 16, 17, 28, 29, 30
Candidate experiencing bias $t < -2$	10, 16	12, 23, 28	18, 23, 26	3, 4, 6, 17, 23, 24, 25, 30	8,	13, 25, 30	1, 2, 8, 20, 26	5, 7, 8, 12, 15	4, 9, 10, 12, 17, 20,	5, 11, 19, 25	16, 24	5, 9, 11, 27

among the 12 raters for these two candidates, as Figures 4 and 5 show (see Appendix B, which displays biased interactions between 30 candidates and 12 raters).

Figure 4 graphically represents the results for bias in interactions between candidate No. 4 and 12 raters.

For example, Figure 4 shows that the largest difference between M3 and M4 for No. 4 was more than 7 in terms of t-value. This means that M3 rated this candidate more harshly than MRFA expected at a statistically significant level, whereas M4 rated the candidate more leniently than expected at a statistically significant level. In other words, these two raters rated No. 4 in opposite directions.

Similarly, Figure 5 shows the results for bias in interactions between candidate No. 24 and 12 raters. The largest difference in terms of t-statistics occurred between M3 and J4; but this time, M3 rated the candidate more leniently than MRFA expected. It might be interesting to take a closer look at rater behaviour given findings like this. Taking into account the results of Table 4 and Figures 4 and 5, two candidates (Nos. 4 and 24) were chosen for qualitative analysis of the raters' utterances.

Figure 4 Biased interactions between candidate No. 4 and raters

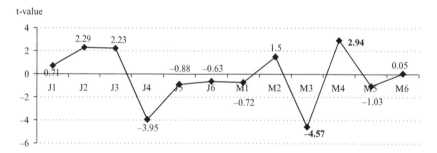

Figure 5 Biased interactions between candidate No. 24 and raters

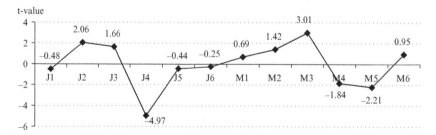

Qualitative analysis (think-aloud approach)

Although MRFA identified significant bias ($2 > t$ and $-2 < t$), in some interactions, it cannot identify explicit reasons why such unexpected rating behaviour occurs. In order to investigate this, the think-aloud method was employed. For this purpose, raters were required to give a reason for every rating for each assessment criterion.

Before analysing five raters' (J2, J3, J4, M3 and M4) comments on No. 4, it is worth describing No. 4's teaching performance. Note that although students were not in a classroom, she was teaching as if they were. This candidate was teaching can-questions ('Can you _____?'). First, she asked the question, 'Do you play table tennis?' Then, she said, 'I play table tennis, too' and 'I can play table tennis'. Then, she asked several students, 'Can you play table tennis?'

Of the five biased raters, the comments of three (J2, J3 and M4) who rated No. 4 more leniently than the Rasch model predicted and of two (J4 and M3) who rated No. 4 more harshly than expected were analysed separately.

As the statistical results at the bottom of Table 5 show, J2 rated No. 4 the most leniently, awarding 30 points (a full score) where the model expected 22.3 points.

J2 was impressed with No. 4's performance, stating that her class was well organised and her pronunciation was very good (see the underlined parts). Ultimately, J2 concluded that No. 4 was ready to teach English. However, J2 seemed to be unsatisfied with the fact that No. 4 gave explanations of the target grammar in Japanese although it seemed that her impressive teaching performance compensated for the provision of too many explanations in Japanese.

Table 5 Rater J2's comments on No. 4

Assessment criterion	Raw scores	Comments
Lesson flow	5	Her lesson flow was well organised and smooth.
Instruction	5	It appeared that she looked at students' reactions and responded to them very well.
Delivery	5	Her voice was clear. Her intonation and accent were very good.
Personality	5	She looked friendly to students and she had a passion for teaching English to her students.
Expertise	5	She used the blackboard and questions to students effectively. Although she gave them too much information about the target grammar in Japanese, her explanation was understandable.
Overall	5	It seemed that she was used to teaching. Well, she was a work-ready candidate.

t = 2.29; observed score, 30; expected score, 22.3

Table 6 shows J3's comments on No. 4. J3 gave this candidate 26 points, almost 5 more than the Rasch model expected.

J3 did not comment on each criterion; most of J3's comments were tips for better teaching performance. Like J2, J3 stated that No. 4's pronunciation was clear and beautiful. However, it is interesting that J3 did not make comments about No. 4's use of Japanese explanations of the target grammar, which was pointed out by J2. It seems that these raters interpreted the same criterion differently and paid attention to different aspects of the same criterion.

Table 7 shows M4's comments on No. 4. As the statistical values show, M4 gave this candidate almost 7 points more than expected.

Although the comments by M4 appeared positive, one striking difference among the raters was found in their assessment of 'lesson flow'. The definition of this criterion was 'a clear point and intention of this lesson and an image of the flow of the whole lesson smooth'. However, the comment made by M4 refers to the speed and clarity of the key sentence, whereas J2 commented on actual lesson flow and J3 did not make any comment on this category. Again,

Table 6 Rater J3's comments on No. 4

Assessment criterion	Raw scores	Comments
Lesson flow	3	If she had made a clear distinction between 'can' and
Instruction	5	'cannot', she would have got a higher score.
Delivery	4	I suggest that she should have used a game, which
Personality	5	could have interested her students more. She used the
Expertise	4	classroom effectively. Her pronunciation was clear
Overall	5	and beautiful.

t = 2.23; observed score, 26; expected score, 21.4

Table 7 Rater M4's comments on No. 4

Assessment criterion	Raw scores	Comments
Lesson flow	4	She was teaching the key sentence slowly and clearly.
Instruction	5	It seemed that she was very aware of her students' responses and checked their understanding.
Delivery	5	She talked to her students in a careful manner. It was very good. She used gestures and a loud voice.
Personality	5	She faced the students and talked to her students in a careful manner.
Expertise	5	She gave clear explanations to the students and she actually got the students to practise the key sentence.
Overall	4	She looked confident in [her] teaching skills.

t = 2.94; observed score, 28; expected score, 21.3

it appears that the raters paid attention to some criteria more carefully than others, in ways that varied across raters.

Table 8 shows J4's comments on No. 4. In contrast to the previous raters, J4 rated No. 4 more harshly than the Rasch model expected, by approximately 8 points. It is clear that all comments made by this rater on all criteria were negative, stating that the structure of No. 4's class was not smooth and that she gave a lot of explanations in Japanese. As also apparent, there was a striking difference between the result for the three previous raters and for this rater. Ultimately, J4 stated that it was not likely that this candidate would be employed. It seemed that this rater gave No. 4 a lower score mostly because of her long explanations in Japanese, which were a non-negotiable problem to this rater.

Table 9 shows comments made by M3 on No. 4, which are even more negative than those of J4.

This rater had a strongly negative attitude towards 'lesson flow' and Japanese explanations, stating that it was a fatal error that No. 4 provided two important grammar targets ('Do you ___?' and 'Can you___?') to her students at the same time, which in M3's opinion led to confusion and misinterpretation on the part of the students. In terms of blackboard use, M3 gave a negative comment on the 'lesson flow' criterion but a positive comment on the 'expertise' criterion. It seems that the negative impressions of lesson flow had a great impact, and as a whole were more impactful than the positive ones.

The different comments and rating of No. 4's microteaching by these five raters suggest that the assessment criteria, which are intended to represent the constructs, are interpreted and shaped by raters' interpretation of them and by their values (what they find important in the criteria).

Table 8 Rater J4's comments on No. 4

Assessment criterion	Raw scores	Comments
Lesson flow	2	On the whole, the structure of her class was not smooth.
Instruction	2	She used Japanese explanations a lot. The students got tired of her explanations.
Delivery	2	She seemed be aware of her students, but she was teaching while looking at the blackboard, not at her students.
Personality	3	Her Japanese explanations were long, which did not engage her students.
Expertise	3	She did not use the blackboard and pictures effectively.
Overall	2	There is only a slight chance that I would employ this candidate.

t = −3.95; observed score, 14; expected score, 22.1

Table 9 Rater M3's comments on No. 4

Assessment criterion	Raw scores	Comments
Lesson flow	1	She started with 'Do you ___?' in order to teach 'Can you ___?' This was not smooth and her students must have been confused. Also she used the blackboard right after this. She should have let her students practise 'Can you ___?'
Instruction	1	She used Japanese explanations a lot. This caused a lot of confusion.
Delivery	2	She was teaching while looking at the blackboard, not at her students.
Personality	2	Her explanations were not clear, which did not engage the students at all.
Expertise	2	She used the blackboard and asked questions to students effectively. It was impossible to teach by combining 'Do you ___?' with 'Can you___?' This was a fatal error.
Overall	2	Her score on this part is only 2 points because her explanations of the target grammar were not clear.

t = −4.57; observed score, 10; expected score, 18

Another example of this point is the comments on No. 24 made by four raters: J2 and M3, who assessed this candidate more leniently than the Rasch model expected, and J4 and M5, who assessed him more harshly. No. 24's task was to introduce 'There are ___'. To do so, he drew three pictures each representing a different number of stacked blocks and asked students how many blocks they could see. Thus, he tried to introduce the key sentence by means of a quiz.

Table 10 and 11 respectively show J2's and M3's comments on No. 24. These two raters have several similarities in terms of t-statistics, scores, and comments for this candidate. They both gave this candidate a higher score than the Rasch model expected, that is, they were lenient. Their comments were correspondingly positive: they noted that the candidate paid attention to his students and got them to pay attention to the key sentence. On the personality criterion, these raters made comments about No. 24's friendly attitude to his students. Therefore, overall, both raters thought that this candidate was likely to become a good English teacher.

Tables 12 and 13 show two raters' (J4's and M5's) comments on No. 24. In contrast to the results of the previous raters in Tables 9 and 10, J4 and M5 both rated this candidate more severely than the Rasch model expected. However, J4 was harsher than M5 in terms of both t-statistics and observed scores. J4 made negative comments on the introduction of the key sentence, stating that No. 24 should have introduced it more simply. In fact, J4 made similar comments on three criteria, lesson flow, personality and expertise, even though these comments seemed to be irrelevant to the last two criteria.

Table 10 Rater J2's comments on No. 24

Assessment criterion	Raw scores	Comments
Lesson flow	5	It seemed that he was aware of the structure of the class and he got his students to pay attention to the key sentence by using a game.
Instruction	5	He paid much attention to his students all the time. He provided much time for his students to answer his questions.
Delivery	4	His voice, eye contact and gestures were good. However, his pronunciation was not good.
Personality	5	His friendly attitude attracted his students. His questions reflected his passion for teaching.
Expertise	5	He prepared well for this class. Also he used the blackboard and picture cards effectively and appropriately.
Overall	5	I think that he can become a good English teacher if he teaches English in this way.

t = 2.15; observed score, 29; expected score, 24.5

Table 11 Rater M3's comments on No. 24

Assessment criterion	Raw scores	Comments
Lesson flow	4	Very good. However, he wrote the key sentence on the blackboard before he got his students to practise it.
Instruction	4	He paid attention to his students all the time. He gave them time to think what the key sentence was. However, he did not get his students to practise the key sentence, although they wanted to use it.
Delivery	5	His voice, eye contact and gestures were good.
Personality	5	His attitude could engage his students.
Expertise	5	His picture use during teaching performance was good.
Overall	5	His lesson still left something to be desired. But I guess that he could compensate for this later.

t = 3.01; observed score, 28; expected score, 21

These comments come from J4's idea of an ideal teaching approach, as evident in the comments, 'I have taught this key sentence ("There are ___') with prepositions'. J4 also made negative comments about No. 24's grammatical mistakes.

As can been seen, M5 did not make comments pertinent to each criterion, even though comments were provided that ostensibly related to each. M5 used only two criteria – lesson flow and expertise. Under lesson flow, he made a positive comment about No. 4's approach but also expressed concern about

Table 12 Rater J4's comments on No. 24

Assessment criterion	Raw scores	Comments
Lesson flow	1	The introduction of the key sentence was not good at all. His point was very unclear and it took a long time to introduce the key sentence. He should have done it more simply.
Instruction	3	Perhaps the game approach was interesting to students but it did not necessarily mean that the students were interested in the key sentence.
Delivery	3	He looked confident and had a dignified manner, but he made a lot of grammatical mistakes.
Personality	3	I can feel his passion for teaching, but his passion went into the wrong direction. He should have done it more simply.
Expertise	2	He introduced 'there are' without prepositions. I have taught 'there are' with prepositions. He should have done it more simply.
Overall	2	I can feel his passion for becoming a teacher, but he missed the point (the introduction of the target grammar).

$t = -3.01$; observed score, 14; expected score, 24.3

Table 13 Rater M5's comments on No. 24

Assessment criterion	Raw scores	Comments
Lesson flow	3	It was an interesting introduction of the key
Instruction	3	sentence, and increased students' motivation.
Delivery	4	However, the students paid more attention to 'how
Personality	3	many blocks there are' than to 'what today's key
Expertise	3	sentence is'.
Overall	3	Also his classroom English was inaccurate.

$t = -2.21$; observed score, 19; expected score, 23.3

No. 24's teaching performance, suggesting that No. 24's students' attention was distracted by the use of the game. Like J4, M5 observed that this candidate made grammatical errors.

These two raters made comments reflective of different teaching values. It seems that J4's comments were inspired by his ideal teaching style, whereas M5 expressed concern about students' failure to concentrate on the target sentence.

Discussion and conclusion

The purpose of this study was to investigate test fairness, focusing on how reliable raters were, the extent to which interactions between raters and candidates were biased, and the reasons causing this bias. Although there were a limited number of candidates and raters, it was found that:

- most raters rated the candidates consistently but rated them with different degrees of severity
- more than 25% of interactions between the raters and the candidates were biased, which suggests that we cannot exclude the possibility that a candidate's employment prospects may be limited due to rater bias
- the raters seemingly used assessment criteria differently, putting their own interpretations on the criteria; also, they introduced their own tacit assessment criteria, besides the provided assessment criteria, and
- biased interactions may have occurred when a candidate's teaching demonstration was not harmonious with a rater's ideal teaching scenario or core teaching values.

Raters differed in terms of severity but were relatively consistent in their overall rating patterns, except for three (J4, J5 and M5). This reflects previous research (e.g. Lumley and McNamara 1995) showing bias in approximately one quarter of interactions between raters and candidates. This means that it is not possible to eradicate the possibility of unfair rater impact on employment decisions based on unfair assessment of candidates by raters because raters do not necessarily interpret performance according to the intention of the assessment criteria. In order to maximise fairness for candidates at present, the analysis of rating is helpful, since it identifies rater behaviours and raters who perhaps should not be allowed to engage in this activity without further training.

In addition to random errors and rater fatigue, issues already pointed out by Taylor and Galaczi (2011), the raters in this study also rated candidates not only with different interpretation of and different levels of attention to aspects of assessment criteria but also according to different core teaching values and ideal images of English teachers or English classes possessed by the raters themselves, leading to both lenient and harsh ratings of the same candidates by different raters. As Bachman (1990) has pointed out, it is important to take into account both micro and macro-level values in assessment and evaluation of assessment: 'Language testing occurs in an educational and social setting, and the uses of language tests are determined largely by political needs that change over time and vary from one society to another. We must consider the value systems that inform test use – values of test developers, test takers, test users, the educational system, and society at large' (Bachman 1990:291).

This study shows that raters can have a direct impact on candidates' employment opportunities decisions and more specifically that their values had direct impact on fairness of assessment. Just as test constructs are not value free (McNamara and Roever 2006), nor are scores given by raters.

Implications for rater cognition research

One common finding about much research into rater performance is that it is affected by variance on the individual-rater levels such as unique tendencies on specific assessment criteria or overall leniency or harshness. As Taylor and Galaczi (2011) and McNamara (1996) point out, it is almost impossible to eradicate rater differences, and these authors question whether it is in fact necessary to diminish these differences. However, this does not mean that we should stop conducting rater cognition research, in particular in a high-stakes context like that considered in the present study, where rating may determine the course of lives and careers. Possible questions to be examined are how raters award test scores to candidates, and in particular what factors account for differences in rater severity or leniency and why rater biases occur.

Research into the processes undergone by raters conducting performance assessment has just begun and as this study shows, it is not clear yet how test scores are awarded to candidates in particular, in the rating process. Thus, research into rater cognition is urgently needed because better understanding of it could increase test fairness for test takers and also make a contribution to rater training and the development of empirically based assessment criteria.

In terms of rater cognition research, Bejar (2012) raises issues including the best approaches to collect and analyse data. Traditionally, rater cognition researchers have used either qualitative or quantitative approaches, not both. However, Bejar (2012) argues convincingly that qualitative and quantitative research complement each other's weaknesses in this context. As Bejar (2012) and Knoch (2011) point out, rater cognition research has multiple aspects, and rater interviews and questionnaires should be among the tools employed.

> When readers are involved in the scoring process, the opportunity exists for multiple factors to influence the scores they produce in ways that present a threat to the validity of scores . . . In that world, evidence from a special one-time study that supports score interpretation is not sufficient to support the score validity. In other words, validation should be seen as an ongoing process (Bejar 2012:7).

Despite this observation of Bejar's, however, the most intractable difficulty here is that we cannot directly observe the rating process. Lumley (2005:306) points out that 'lack of mention of a particular feature or features by a rater is *no* indication that the feature was not observed and noted. Raters explicitly make the point that far more passes through their minds than they can ever articulate' (emphasis in the original).

As Lumley (2005) points out, think-aloud methods are frequently used in rater cognition research, but they are not necessarily a valid way of revealing what raters actually think and how they actually go about assessing performance. In other words, when raters talk into a speech recorder, their utterances may imply or otherwise inadequately reflect their actual cognitive process. This is a challenging issue for rater cognition researchers.

One way of solving the problems in rater cognition research mentioned above is the use of 'wearable devices', examining eye movements and brain waves. This and possibly other approaches to addressing the issue mentioned may be only the first sojourn into deeper rater cognition research, which is a challenging and interesting area, facing many consequential questions.

Acknowledgements

This research was supported by a Japanese Ministry of Education, Culture, Sports, Science and Technology in Japan Grant-in-Aid for Scientific Research (C) (No. 22520580).

References

Bachman, L (1990) *Fundamental Consideration Language Testing*, Oxford: Oxford University Press.

Bejar, I (2012) Rater cognition: Implications for validity, *Educational Measurement: Issues and Practice* 31 (3), 2–9.

Borko, H, Whitcomb, J A and Byrnes, K (2008) Genres of research in teacher education, in Cochran-Smith, M, Feiman-Nemser, S and Mclntyre, D J (Eds) *Handbook of Research on Teacher Education: Enduring Questions in Changing Contexts* (3rd edition), New York: Routledge, 1,017–1,049.

Brown, A (1995) The effect of rater variables in the development of an occupation-specific language performance test, *Language Testing* 12 (1), 1–15.

Chalhoub-Deville, M and Wigglesworth, G (2005) Rater judgment and English language speaking proficiency, *World Englishes*, 24 (3), 383–391.

Cochran-Smith, M and Fries, K (2008) Research on teacher education, in Cochran-Smith, M, Feiman-Nemser, S and Mclntyre, D J (Eds) *Handbook of Research on Teacher Education: Enduring Questions in Changing Contexts* (3rd edition), New York: Routledge, 1,050–1,093.

Cooper, J M and Allen, D W (1971) *Microteaching: History and present status*, Washington: ERIC Clearinghouse on teacher education.

Eckes, T (2005) Examining rater effects in TestDaF writing and speaking performance assessments: A Many-Facet Rasch analysis, *Language Assessment Quarterly* 2 (3), 197–221.

Gage, N L (2008) Applying what we know, in Cochran-Smith, M, Feiman-Nemser, S and Mclntyre, D J (Eds) *Handbook of Research on Teacher Education: Enduring Questions in Changing Contexts* (3rd edition), New York: Routledge, 1,139–1,163.

Grossman, P (2005) Research on pedagogical approaches in teacher education, in Cochran-Smith, M and Zeichner, K M (Eds) *Studying Teacher Education:*

The Report of the AERA Panel on Research and Teacher Education, Mahwah: Lawrence Erlbaum, 425–476.

Kane, M (2006) Validity, in Linn, R L (Ed) *Educational Measurement* (4th edition), New York: American Council on Education, Macmillan Publishing, 17–64.

Kane, M (2010) Validity and fairness, *Language Testing* 27 (2), 177–182.

Knoch, U (2011) Investigating the effectiveness of individualized feedback to rating behavior – a longitudinal study, *Language Testing* 28 (2), 179–200.

Kunnan, A (2004) Test fairness, in Milanovic, M and Weir, C J (Eds) *European language testing in a global context*, Cambridge: Cambridge University Press, 27–48.

Lakshmi, M J (2009) *Microteaching and Prospective Teachers*, New Delhi: Discovery Publishing House.

Linacre, M (2005) *FACETS (Version 3.59)*, Chicago: MESA Press.

Lumley, T (2002) Assessment criteria in a large-scale writing test: What do they really mean to the raters? *Language Testing* 19 (3), 246–276.

Lumley, T (2005) *Assessing Second Language Writing: The Rater's Perspective*, Language Testing and Evaluation series volume 3, Frankfurt am Main: Peter Lang.

Lumley, T and McNamara, T (1995) Rater characteristics and rater bias: Implications of training, *Language Testing* 12 (1), 54–71.

Lynch, B and McNamara, T (1998) Using G-theory and Many-facet Rasch measurement in the development of performance assessments of the ESL speaking skills of immigrants, *Language Testing* 15 (2), 158–180.

McNamara, T (1996) *Measuring Second Language Performance*, London/New York: Longman.

McNamara, T and Roever, C (2006) *Language Testing: The Social Dimension*, Malden: Blackwell.

Messick, S (1989) Validity, in Linn, R L (Ed) *Educational Measurement* (3rd edition), New York: American Council on Education, 13–103.

Ministry of Education, Culture, Sports, Science and Technology (2014) *Heisei 25 nendo Koritugakkou Kyoinsaiyoushiken Jisshijoukounitsuite [Reports on the administrations of 2013 public school teacher employment examinations]* available online: www.mext.go.jp/a_menu/shotou/senkou/__icsFiles/afieldfile/2014/01/22/1343166_01.pdf

Monk, H D (2008) Notes from a pragmatist, in Cochran-Smith, M, Feiman-Nemser, S, and McIntyre, D J (Eds) *Handbook of research on teacher education: Enduring Questions in Changing Contexts* (3rd edition), New York: Routledge, 1,189–1,193.

Schaefer, E (2008) Rater bias patterns in an EFL writing, *Language Testing* 25 (4), 465–493.

Taylor, L and Galaczi, E D (2011) Scoring validity, in Taylor, L (Ed) *Examining Speaking: Research and Practice in Assessing Second Language Speaking*, Studies in Language Testing volume 30, Cambridge: UCLES/Cambridge University Press, 171–233.

Watanabe, Y (2008) *Development of a teacher certificate examination for non-native pre-service teachers of English*, paper presented at the AILA conference, Essen, 25 August 2008.

Xi, X (2010) How do we go about investigating test fairness? *Language Testing* 27 (2), 147–170.

Appendix A
Example of assessment criteria and assessment sheet

	Examples of description	1 = poor 5 = excellent				
1. Lesson flow	• Have a clear point and intention of this lesson • Have an image of the flow of the whole lesson	1	2	3	4	5
2. Instruction	• Making content comprehensible to students • Suitability of content and language for learners	1	2	3	4	5
3. Delivery	• Adequate eye contact • Vocally expressive • Appropriate movement and gestures	1	2	3	4	5
4. Personality	• Be full of enthusiasm • Be able to establish rapport with students	1	2	3	4	5
5. Expertise	• Adequate use of teaching materials • Understanding of grammatical accuracy/ knowledge	1	2	3	4	5
6. Overall	• Do you want to employ this candidate as an English teacher? (Holistic impression)	1	2	3	4	5

Appendix B Summary of 92 biased interactions between some candidates and some raters

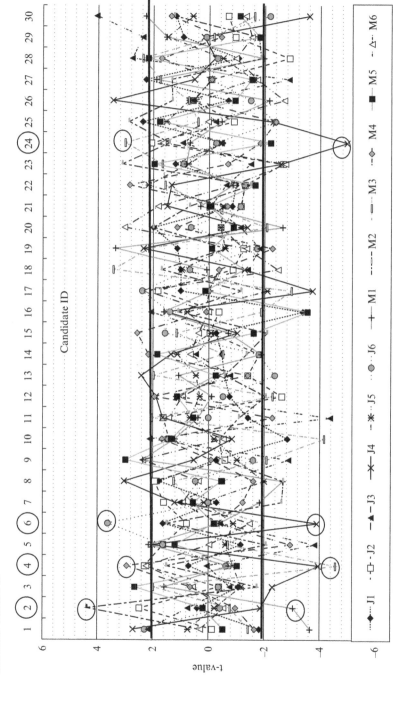

Section 4
Fairness, quality and validation

18 Ensuring test quality and fairness in the Asian EFL context: Challenges and opportunities for the GEPT in Taiwan

Jessica R W Wu
The Language Training & Testing Centre, Taiwan

Abstract

Although objective testing originated and was developed in ancient China (Spolsky 1995), today's English language assessment in China and other Confucian-heritage cultures in Asia, such as Taiwan, Japan, and Korea, has been heavily influenced by Western testing theories. Unlike generic international language tests that are intended to suit test takers around the world, the English language tests developed in the Asian EFL domain are tailored to the specific educational systems and the changing contexts of test use within those territories. Also, these locally produced tests are often high-stakes examinations conducted on a very large scale. This results in challenges of ensuring test fairness and quality, especially given the presence of various constraints such as tight schedules for development and operation, and limited resources. This paper looks at the issue of fairness and quality in Asia, taking a fuller accout of the social and cultural contexts of this region by using examples of the General English Proficiency Test (GEPT) practice in Taiwan. In addition, the paper discusses the continuing efforts of testing bodies in Asia to share information with one another about their attempts to ensure test quality and fairness. To conclude, the paper suggests that while language testers in both the West and the East face similar problems in language assessments and though they may adopt different methods to achieve their common goal, they have the same responsibility to achieve fairness and quality.

Introduction

This paper discusses test quality and fairness from an Asian perspective. Quality and fairness are the overriding concerns in all aspects of assessment;

in effect, this is the golden rule in international standards and codes of practice, such as the *Standards for Educational and Psychological Testing* (American Educational Research Association, American Psychological Association and National Council on Measurement in Education 1999), *ILTA Code of Ethics* (International Language Testing Association 2000), and *ALTE Principles of Good Practice* (Association of Language Testers in Europe 2001). No such professional standards for language testers have been specifically developed in Asia. However, the existing international professional standards are familiar to and commonly followed by major language testing bodies in Asia. Therefore, ensuring test quality and fairness is also a highly regarded topic in Asia, despite the fact that there are numerous challenges and difficulties to be overcome.

From the perspectives of culture and history, objective testing originated and was developed in ancient China (Spolsky 1995), and testing and assessment have been used for a range of purposes in Asia, including education and employment. In Asia today, English language tests are widely used, given that the continent is populated with the greatest number of learners of English in the world. Within the context of language testing in Asia, this paper focuses on how codes of practice can be used to ensure the quality of language tests and demonstrates this through a case study of the GEPT in Taiwan.

Unlike international language tests that are intended to suit test takers around the world, the English language tests developed in the Asian EFL domain are tailored to the specific educational systems and the changing contexts of test use within these territories. Also, these locally produced tests are often high-stakes examinations conducted on a very large scale. These factors contribute to the challenge of ensuring test fairness and quality.

The following is a brief introduction to four locally produced EFL tests (in chronological order):

- The EIKEN Test in Practical English Proficiency (EIKEN) was introduced in 1963 in Japan, and is conducted by the Eiken Foundation of Japan. The EIKEN tests are today taken by about 2.3 million candidates each year, most of whom are high school students. EIKEN certificates are recognised widely across educational levels in Japan. More details about EIKEN can be found at www.eiken.or.jp/eiken/en/

- The College English Test (CET) is a national EFL test in China. The purpose of the CET is to examine the English proficiency of undergraduate and postgraduate students in China. The CET is directly linked to the National College English Teaching Syllabuses. First administrated in 1987, the CET now serves a test population of 18 million people annually. More information about the CET can be found at www.cet.edu.cn/

- The GEPT (General English Proficiency Test) was introduced in Taiwan in 2000 for learners at all levels, with the aim of promoting life-long learning and encouraging the study of English. The GEPT is developed and administered by the Language Training and Testing Centre (LLTC). It has assessed 6 million Taiwanese learners since its first administration, serving a test population of 0.7 million annually. More details about the GEPT can be found at www.lttc.ntu.edu.tw/E_LTTC/E_GEPT.htm
- The NEAT (National English Assessment Test) is a test developed by the Korea Institute for Curriculum and Evaluation (KICE), aiming to enhance practical English conversation skills and writing ability among Koreans. It was launched in 2012. According to KICE, the NEAT test is expected to be administered throughout the country to allow about 50,000 test takers to take the test simultaneously. Further information about the NEAT can be found at kice.re.kr/en/contents.do?contentsNo=150&menuNo=406

One obvious commonality among these locally developed language tests is that they all have a stated objective of promoting a positive impact on English learning and education. This anticipated test consequence comes from the belief that a test developed within and for a specific education context is better positioned to incorporate the needs of learners, educators, and other stakeholders within that context. This by no means implies that a local test is better than an international test. However, as Weir (2013) suggests, global language tests taken by people around the world are unlikely to be particularly sensitive to the needs of people within a particular society. In contrast, local tests can more easily be tailored to the local educational system and the needs of learners within a country. Therefore, a locally produced test is believed to facilitate close interaction between its developers and stakeholders, including educators and learners, in promoting positive washback. Besides producing positive washback on teaching and learning, the other beneficial influences include increasing teachers' language testing and assessment (LTA) literacy, encouraging research in LTA, and promoting a better understanding of EFL learners' strengths and weaknesses (Wu 2012).

Challenges of ensuring test quality and fairness

It is widely accepted that it is test developers' responsibility to produce quality tests. According to Bachman and Palmer (2010:433), the primary responsibility of the test developer is achieving an appropriate balance among the four examination qualities, namely validity, reliability, impact and practicality (cited from the *ALTE Principles of Good Practice* (Association of Language Testers in Europe 2001). Also, as McNamara and Roever (2006) suggest, testing bodies should also develop guidelines and review principles to safeguard fairness during the test development process. The concept of fairness can be realised in various ways, e.g. equal opportunities, test security, special arrangements for test takers with disabilities, lack of bias, avoidance of construct-irrelevant variance, etc. (Association of Language Testers in Europe 2001). However, the four tests introduced above all face numerous challenges in ensuring test quality and fairness due to the large test-taking populations. In some cases, local contextual features are unique, which makes international standards and codes of practice inappropriate or too difficult to implement. For example, in the case of oral assessment in these four tests, it is considered too costly and impractical to use face-to-face interviews, involving direct interaction between the test takers and an interlocutor who would have had to be a trained native or highly proficient non-native speaker of English. Therefore, a semi-direct test format conducted in a digital language laboratory environment has been adopted in the GEPT speaking test, and the CET, EIKEN, and GEPT tests have also adopted a two-stage design which allows only the test takers who have passed the other components to take the speaking test. Nevertheless the validity of the speaking test format in these tests is questionable, which has led language testing researchers in these regions to conduct a number of empirical studies (e.g. Jin 2000, Weir and Wu 2006) to investigate various issues concerning the improvement of oral test development in an effort to strike a balance between controllability and spontaneity. Another example is the overuse of the multiple-choice (MC) format in the tests, which is a way to cope with the large scale of the tests and also a consequence of the 'psychometric-structuralist' approach to language testing adopted in Asia (Spolsky 1995). Although there are techniques for producing good multiple-choice items, more empirical research is required to provide evidence in support of the validity of this format.

The formidable number of test takers who take the tests every year and the limited resources that can be mobilised to employ enough qualified professionals (e.g. item writers, examiners and raters, statisticians) to work for the testing bodies in Asia are the main practical constraints which have prevented the testing bodies from adequately implementing their quality control procedures, particularly in the areas of pretesting (size and representativeness of the pretesting sample), marking (double-marking of constructed-response items, monitoring the marking process), and test equating. The inadequacies in the quality control procedures and safeguarding fairness were reported by Fan and Jin (2013). They conducted a survey of English language testing practice in China through empirically examining the testing practice of six EFL examination boards, operating at national, municipal, and university levels. The results indicated the testing practices of the six examination boards appeared to comply with good testing practices as prescribed in the international standards with regard to test purpose, specifications and test administration. However, the results identified much variation in the testing practice of the six examination boards in the areas of pretesting, marking, and test equating. The researchers concluded that the development of a set of professional standards for EFL testing in China, targeted at both test developers and stakeholders, is urgently needed.

Although the survey reported by Fan and Jin (2013) investigated testing practice only in China, the findings are likely generalisable to other Asian contexts. Therefore, it is clear that a set of professional standards suitable for EFL testing in Asia should be developed. In addition to the principles which are general and universal, context-specific principles should also be considered when developing professional standards for the Asian EFL context.

The GEPT as a case study

Despite the numerous challenges faced in ensuring test quality and fairness in the Asian EFL context, the developers of the above-mentioned four Asian-produced tests are aware of their responsibility for producing quality tests and have made tremendous efforts in addressing test quality and fairness in their practice. Using GEPT as an example this paper will discuss some GEPT validation cases to illustrate how test quality and fairness has been achieved in the Asian EFL domain.

Validation of the GEPT is considered an ongoing project by its test developer, Language Training and Testing Centre (LTTC). The application of the socio-cognitive validation framework (Weir 2005) is one approach that LTTC has used to investigate various aspects of GEPT validity. In the following sections, I will highlight a few of the studies which focus on construct validity (Cases One and Two) and criterion-related validity (Case Three).

Weir suggests that the *construct* should be considered as 'residing in the interactions between an underlying cognitive ability, a context of use, and a process of scoring' (Weir, Vidaković and Galaczi 2013:3). He further recommends that test developers in this century should be able to satisfy the increasing expectations of stakeholders (learners, employers, receiving institutions, professional bodies, etc.) concerning the comparability of the constructs measured by each test version in terms of cognitive, contextual, and scoring validity. Similarly, 'comparable validity' has been proposed by Xi (2010) in her discussion of fairness.

Case One – The GEPT speaking construct at the intermediate level

This is a multi-dimensional approach to investigating the construct of the GEPT speaking test at the intermediate level. A paper based on the study was published in *Language Testing* (Weir and Wu 2006).

Due to its large test population, the GEPT employs the semi-direct method in its speaking component at the first three levels. Each test administration consists of multiple test sessions, each requiring a different test paper. Therefore, it is essential to establish parallel-form reliability and to demonstrate the tests are comparable.

To establish parallel-form reliability in the speaking test, we compared the construct of three different test papers in terms of code complexity (lexical and syntactical difficulty), cognitive complexity (content familiarity), and communicative demand (time pressure). Data from different sources including task scores and interlanguage measures in the areas of accuracy, fluency, complexity, and lexical density were analysed. By means of both qualitative (expert judgements of task difficulty and language functions) and quantitative analyses (correlation, ANOVA, factor analysis, Multi-Faceted Rasch Measurement), the results support the claim that the test papers can be considered parallel. Similar methods and procedures are applied in achieving parallel-form reliability of the GEPT speaking tests.

Case Two – The GEPT Reading and Writing tests at the advanced level

The concept of 'validity by design' is evident in the GEPT. Unlike traditional reading comprehension tests that tend to focus only on careful reading, GEPT Advanced Reading assesses careful reading and expeditious reading, both of which are considered important constructs of reading comprehension at the advanced level (Khalifa and Weir 2009). As shown in Table 1, the GEPT Advanced Reading Test provides a simulation of reading tasks for academic purposes. Learners at this level are expected to understand a wide range of language functions and to extract complete meanings from different types of extended discourse. Weir (2013:7) commented positively, 'It is thus a positive development that the reading comprehension tests of the GEPT Advanced Level value both parts of the reading construct in equal measure'.

Another example of 'validity by design' is the GEPT Advanced Writing

Table 1 GEPT Advanced Reading and Writing test format and structure

Paper	Part	Task types	No of items	Time (mins)
Reading	1	Careful reading	20	50
	2	Skimming & scanning	20	20
Writing	1	Summarising main ideas from verbal input and expressing opinions (250 words)		60
	2	Summarising main ideas from non-verbal input and providing solutions (250 words)		45

Test, which requires candidates to summarise main ideas from both verbal and non-verbal inputs and express opinions. It provides a simulation of writing tasks for academic purposes, i.e. reading-to-write and writing for a specified purpose to a specific audience. Sample test tasks can be found at www.lttc.ntu.edu.tw/GEPT1/Advanced/writing/writing.htm

However, these two examples can only be considered *a priori* validation. We also need to demonstrate the test quality through *a posteriori* validation. Chan, Wu and Weir (2014), in a collaborative project between LTTC and the Centre for Research in English Language Learning and Assessment (CRELLA), University of Bedfordshire, investigated the context and cognitive validity of GEPT Advanced Writing Task 1. In a writing test context, context validity addresses the particular performance conditions under which the task is to be performed (e.g. purpose of the task, input to be processed, time available, length required, marking criteria as well as the linguistic demands inherent in the successful performance of the task, etc.) and, cognitive validity is what test takers will activate cognitively in response to the contextual parameters set out in the performance conditions. However, a more pertinent question for us to ask is whether or not all the requirements we placed on test takers when they perform in the writing test are similar to those they will meet in the non-test 'real-life' situations. In other words, we need to investigate the similarity between test takers' test performance and their actual performance in real-life tasks in terms of context and cognitive validity. Therefore, Chan, et al (2014) addressed two research questions:

1. What are the relationships between the contextual parameters set in the GEPT Advanced Writing Test and those set in the real-life academic writing tasks in a business school at a UK university?

2. What are the relationships between the cognitive processing activities elicited from the GEPT Advanced Writing Test and those elicited from real-life academic writing tasks in a UK university?

Both expert judgement and automated textual analysis such as VocabProfile (Cobb 2010) and Coh-Metrix (Graesser, McNamara, Louwerse and Cai 2004) were employed to examine the degree of correspondence between the overall task setting and input text features of the GEPT task and those of the target academic writing tasks in real-life university business courses in the UK. As for cognitive validity, this study examined the cognitive processes elicited by the GEPT task in comparison to the real-life academic writing tasks through a cognitive process questionnaire. The demonstration of a close similarity between the test and real-life conditions in the findings supports the context and cognitive validity of the GEPT Advanced Writing Task 1, an integrated reading-into-writing task. In addition, the results have important implications for university admissions officers and other GEPT score users when considering whether the test is a valid option for assessing English writing for academic purposes.

Case Three – GEPT–CEFR linking studies

Dr Michael Milanovic, the former Chief Executive of Cambridge English Language Assessment, advised language exam boards in Asia in his interview with the LTTC journal *The Way of Language* (Language Training and Testing Centre 2013:21) that: 'It is essential that any examination board follows clearly defined and public quality standards and aligns its tests to internationally-recognised frameworks, particularly the Common European Framework of Reference (CEFR, Council of Europe 2001), which is now used worldwide to explain levels of achievement in language learning.' In fact, Taiwan's Ministry of Education (MoE) has adopted the CEFR to serve as a common yardstick to help interpret learners' proficiency in English since 2005 and required that all tests be aligned to the CEFR. Therefore, to meet the MoE's requirement and to use the CEFR as an external criterion to validate the GEPT, LTTC has carried out a number of GEPT–CEFR linking studies, two of which are summarised below.

The first linking study (Wu and Wu 2010) largely followed the 'internal validation' procedure presented by *The Manual for Relating Language Examinations to the Common European Framework of Reference for Languages: Learning, Teaching, Assessment* (Council of Europe 2003). A total of 70 GEPT reading comprehension test questions that exemplify the test constructs of the different levels of the GEPT reading comprehension tests were judged by 15 EFL teaching professionals. The results show that the first four levels of the GEPT Reading tests, from elementary level to advanced level, correspond to the CEFR Levels A2 to C1 with a generally satisfactory rater agreement of .91. Another GEPT–CEFR mapping study was carried out using international standardised assessments (Wu 2011). In the study, in addition to the CEFR, *Cambridge English: Preliminary* and *Cambridge English: First* examinations served as external referents for a review of the similarities and differences between GEPT Reading tests targeting CEFR B1 and B2 levels in terms of test results, contextual parameters, and cognitive processing skills. Automated textual analysis tools such as VocabProfile and Coh-Metrix as well as expert judgement were used to help make a critical evaluation of the validity of the GEPT Reading tests. The findings support the construct validity of the GEPT in general and indicate that the GEPT Intermediate level and *Cambridge English: Preliminary* are equivalent, while the GEPT High-Intermediate level and *Cambridge English: First* are different not only in terms of test results but also contextual features and cognitive processing operations.

Increasing global outreach

Given that more and more university graduates have obtained their GEPT certificates before seeking overseas study opportunities, the LTTC began promoting the recognition of the GEPT internationally in 2010 in order to provide foreign universities with another reliable tool, in addition to international English examinations (e.g. *IELTS* and TOEFL) which they usually use, to assess Taiwanese applicants' English proficiency. By presenting the findings of GEPT validation research, GEPT score users, including foreign universities, can get a better understanding of the meaning of GEPT scores and test quality. As a result, more than 60 foreign universities have thus accepted GEPT scores for undergraduate/graduate admission, and the number of institutions is increasing.

Moreover, to further enhance the quality of the GEPT, in addition to in-house research, the LTTC established the GEPT Research Grants Program in 2010, annually funding a number of quality research projects undertaken by domestic and international scholars and external experts on the GEPT tests. The funded research projects have been carried out by international language test researchers in various countries, including the UK, USA, Australia, and Hong Kong and project reports are available on the GEPT website (www.gept.org.tw). The outcome of the programme has been fruitful, which not only benefits the GEPT's ongoing improvement, but also contributes to broader testing research. Through the GEPT research grants programme, we have seen how the insights of international language testing researchers can contribute to the improvement of a locally produced test.

Greater professional and social responsibilities

Test developers' responsibilities do not end with test development. The high-stakes nature of contemporary tests place ever greater professional and social responsibilities on test developers in Asia. Fairness concerns may arise not only at the test level, but also in the broader context of test use, which changes in response to the needs of test users and society. For example, the intended uses of CET and GEPT have changed from their initial aims (i.e. to improve English, promote positive washback on English instruction) to the subsequent, unintended uses such as selection for admission to domestic universities, college graduation, selection for admission to English-medium universities overseas, selection for employment, and even granting of residential permits (only CET in this case). Factors leading to changes in test uses include test users' lack of assessment literacy and the fiercely competitive culture in which opportunities are insufficient or unevenly distributed, making selection procedures necessary (Byczkiewicz 2004:203).

The problem of test overuse or misuse has resulted in an increase in malpractice (cheating, fake score reports), teachers teaching to the test (narrowing the teaching content to what is tested and replacing classroom teaching with test preparation), and students 'learning to the test' by focusing on what is tested and taking mock tests (of poor quality) produced by private publishers. All of these problems demonstrate that tests in Asia play a powerful role and they are 'embedded in political, social and educational, ideological and economic contexts' (Shohamy 2001:114). To ameliorate the changing or unintended consequences of test use, increasing teachers' language assessment literacy and educating stakeholders (decision makers, teachers, test takers, etc.) are possible approaches. However, these approaches would require test developers and test users to work together. In other words, both test developers and test users share a responsibility to strive for fairness, which is also an important component of the *ALTE Principles of Good Practice* (Association of Language Testers in Europe 2001).

Opportunities for joint efforts

The language tests developed in Asia are facing numerous challenges, with increased professionalism and measurement expertise among the test development teams and continued commitment to developing and administering quality tests. This is regardless of limited resources and often capricious educational policy contexts as commented by Professor Lyle Bachman at a symposium entitled *Challenges and Issues in Developing English Language Tests in the Asian EFL Context* in the 2013 Language Testing and Research Colloquium. However, I am confident that the challenges and difficulties can evolve into many opportunities for further development of EFL testing in Asia. One obvious opportunity is for Asian countries which are interested in developing their own locally produced tests to share knowledge and experience. The joint efforts of testing bodies in Asia can make a contribution to the overall improvement of English ability in these countries.

In fact, one platform for language testing bodies in Asia to exchange language testing research and practice, the Academic Forum on English Language Testing in Asia (AFELTA) has been established. The AFELTA was initiated by Prof Yang Huizong, the former chair of CET in China in 1998. It is now the 18th year since AFELTA first brought together organisations that are involved in language test development, administration, and research from the Asian region. AFELTA has been a key forum for facilitating the application of international standards in language testing research to local contexts in Asia. Currently, AFELTA has eight institutional members including the four testing bodies mentioned earlier, i.e. CET in China, EIKEN in Japan, LTTC-GEPT in Taiwan, and NEAT in Korea, and the remaining entities include the Hong Kong Exam and Evaluation Authority, the Singapore Examinations and Assessment Board, the College Entrance Examination Center in Taiwan, and Korea English Language Testing

Association. AFELTA is expanding and will likely welcome a testing body in Vietnam as its newest member soon.

For the future, it is predicted that AFELTA will continually grow not only in size, but also in the scope of projects on which its members co-operate. One recent example is that after Vietnam decided to develop a local English language test, Vietnam National University – University of Languages and International Studies invited the LTTC to train its faculty and staff members involved in the project. Other possible projects in need of collaboration in Asia include an empirical investigation of the testing practice of major test developers in relation to international standards and the development of a set of professional standards connected to the Asian context. The professional standards for EFL testing under development in China may be used as a starting point for language testers in Asia to facilitate further discussion and research in this area. In addition, ALTE's efforts in developing a code of practice and guaranteeing quality control can also provide us with a valuable point of reference.

Concluding remarks

In conclusion, while language testers in both the West and the East share similar concerns with quality control, and though they may adopt different methods to achieve their common goals, they have the same responsibility to achieve fairness and quality. I am confident that the challenges we face in ensuring fairness and quality in Asia will evolve into many opportunities for further discussion and collaboration to improve our work, not only among the testing bodies in Asia themselves, but more widely among the global community of language testing. To achieve this, language testers in Asia should actively participate in the development and revision of international standards and contribute their local knowledge to the development of language testing in the global context.

This paper presented the GEPT in Taiwan as an example to demonstrate how an EFL testing body in Asia ensures quality by complying with internationally recognised professional standards and employing a theoretical framework, and committing itself to sharing knowledge and expertise with the global language testing community.

References

American Educational Research Association, the American Psychological Association and the National Council on Measurement in Education (1999) *Standards for Educational and Psychological Testing*, Washington: American Educational Research Association.
Association of Language Testers in Europe (2001) *Principles of Good Practice for ALTE Examinations Revised Draft*, available online:

www.testdaf.de/fileadmin/Redakteur/PDF/TestDaF/ALTE/ALTE_good_practice.pdf

Bachman, L F and Palmer, A S (2010) *Language Assessment in Practice*, Oxford: Oxford University Press.

Byczkiewicz, V (2004) Filmic portrayals of cheating or fraud in examinations and competitions, *Language Assessment Quarterly* 1 (4), 195–204.

Chan, S H C, Wu, R Y F and Weir, C J (2014) *Examining the Context and Cognitive Validity of the GEPT Advanced Writing Task 1: A comparison with Real-Life Academic Writing* Tasks, RG-03, Taipei: The Language Training and Testing Centre.

Cobb, T (2010) *VocabProfile. The Compleat Lexical Tutor*, available online: www.lextutor.ca

Council of Europe (2001) *Common European Framework of Reference for Languages: Learning, Teaching, Assessment*, Cambridge: Cambridge University Press.

Council of Europe (2003) *The Manual for Relating Language Examinations to the Common European Framework of Reference for Languages: Learning, Teaching, Assessment (CEFR)*, Strasbourg: Council of Europe.

Fan, J and Jin, Y (2013) A survey of English language testing practice in China: the case of six examination boards, *Language Testing in Asia* 3 (7), available online: www.languagetestingasia.com/content/3/1/7

Graesser, A, McNamara, D S, Louwerse, M and Cai, Z (2004) Coh-Metrix: Analysis of Text on Cohesion and Language, *Behavioral Research Methods, Instruments, and Computers* 36, 193–202.

International Language Testing Association (ILTA) (2000) *Code of Ethics*, available online: www.iltaonline.com/index.php?option=com_content&task=view&id=57&Itemid=47

Jin, Y (2000) The washback effects of College English Test-Spoken English Test on teaching, *Foreign Language World* 118, 56–61.

Khalifa, H and Weir, C J (2009) *Examining Reading: Research and Practice in Assessing Second Language Reading*, Studies in Language Testing volume 29, Cambridge: UCLES/Cambridge University Press.

McNamara, T and Roever, C (2006) *Language Testing: The Social Dimension*, Oxford: Blackwell Publishing.

Shohamy, E (2001) *The Power of Tests: A Critical Perspective on the Uses of Language Tests*, London: Longman.

Spolsky, B (1995) *Measured Words*, Oxford: Oxford University Press.

The Language Training and Testing Centre (2013) Interview with Dr Michael Milanovic, *The Way of Language: Learning, Assessment, and Culture* 1, 20–21.

Weir, C J (2005) *Language Testing and Validation: An Evidence-Based Approach*, Basingstoke: Palgrave Macmillan.

Weir, C J (2013) Locally-produced language tests in Asia, *The Way of Language: Learning, Assessment, Culture* 1, 6–7.

Weir, C J and Wu, J R W (2006) Establishing test form and individual task comparability: A case study of a semi-direct speaking test, *Language Testing* 23 (2), 167–197.

Weir, C J, Vidaković, I and Galaczi, E D (2013) *Measured Constructs: A History of Cambridge English Language Examinations 1913–2012*, Studies in Language Testing volume 37, Cambridge: Cambridge University Press.

Wu, J (2012) GEPT and English language teaching and testing in Taiwan, *Language Assessment Quarterly* 9 (1), 11–25.

Wu, J R W and Wu, R Y F (2010) Relating the GEPT reading comprehension tests to the CEFR, in Martyniuk, W (Ed) *Aligning Tests with the CEFR: Reflections on Using the Council of Europe's Draft Manual*, Studies in Language Testing volume 33, Cambridge: UCLES/Cambridge University Press, 204–224.

Wu, R Y F (2011) *Establishing the Validity of the General English Proficiency Test Reading Component through a Critical Evaluation on Alignment with the Common European Framework of Reference*, unpublished PhD thesis, University of Bedfordshire.

Xi, X (2010) How do we go about investigating test fairness? *Language Testing* 27 (2), 147–170.

19 A TAP study of Thai test takers' processes of taking a Chinese vocabulary test

Xiangdong Gu

Yuwen Shen

Jian Xu

Chongqing University, the People's Republic of China

Abstract

HSK (Hanyu Shuiping Kaoshi in Pinyin, or Chinese Proficiency Test) is an internationally recognised Chinese proficiency test for speakers of other languages. The written test corresponds to six levels, from HSK-1 to HSK-6, which consists of listening, reading, and writing, excluding the speaking test (three levels: primary, intermediate and advanced). The vocabulary test component is an essential part of the reading section in the written test paper in HSK-6 as vocabulary is considered the building material of a language, and vocabulary plays an important role in Chinese learning. However, what the vocabulary test intends to measure is far from clear, and there is no related description in the HSK testing syllabus. Employing the Think-aloud Protocol (TAP) method, this study examined the test-taking processes of 12 Thai students taking the HSK-6 vocabulary test in terms of information sources and strategies. The result of the study showed that regarding information sources, information at clausal level was processed most frequently among the 12 subjects, followed by information at textual, sentential and extra-textual levels; regarding strategies, 12 strategies were identified, which could be classified into three categories: cognitive strategy, metacognitive strategy and test-wiseness strategy. The study may bear some implications on the teaching and learning of Chinese, as well as some theoretical and methodological references for future studies.

Rationale of the study

HSK (Hanyu Shuiping Kaoshi in Pinyin, or Chinese Proficiency Test) is a national standardised test designed and developed by the HSK Centre of Beijing Language and Culture University, China, to assess the Chinese language proficiency of non-native speakers (including foreigners, overseas Chinese and students from Chinese national minorities). It was first launched in 1990 and a new version called New HSK was introduced in November 2009 by the Office of Chinese Language Council International to promote the Chinese learning worldwide. Excluding the speaking test (three levels: primary, intermediate and advanced), there are six levels, from HSK-1 to HSK-6, in the writing test which consists of listening, reading, and writing. The number of words or phrases and characters which test takers are required to master progresses from HSK-1, the lowest, to HSK-6, the highest. As Hanban/Confucius Institute Headquarters (2009) claimed, these levels, from low to high, correspond on a one-to-one basis with the six levels of the Common European Framework of Reference for Languages (CEFR, Council of Europe 2001) (see Table 1).

Table 1 The correspondence between levels of HSK and CEFR (see www. hanban.edu.cn/tests/node_7486.htm)

New HSK	Vocabulary		
	Words and phrases	**Characters**	**CEFR**
HSK-6	5,000 or above	2,663	C2
HSK-5	2,500	1,685	C1
HSK-4	1,200	1,064	B2
HSK-3	600	617	B1
HSK-2	300	347	A2
HSK-1	150	174 or above	A1

The vocabulary test is the second part of the reading section in HSK-6, which is designed in a multiple-choice cloze format in which every item consists of at least two long sentences with 3–5 words deleted, and the test takers are required to choose the most appropriate one from the options.

Until now, few studies have investigated the HSK test and its vocabulary component. Moreover, what the vocabulary test intends to measure is far from clear, and there is no related description in the HSK testing syllabus. The New HSK-6, as the highest level, evaluates the teaching quality of Chinese language teaching institutions and provides feedback for Chinese teaching to higher level learners. Considering the key role of test takers among stakeholders, the present study, employing the Think-aloud Protocol (TAP) method, is conducted to explore how the test takers deal with the vocabulary test of the reading section in HSK-6.

Research questions

The present study intends to examine the processes test takers employ when taking the vocabulary test in the reading section in HSK-6 by addressing the following research questions:

Q1: What types of information sources do test takers use to answer vocabulary test items in the reading section in HSK-6? How do they use these information sources?
Q2: What types of strategies do test takers employ when taking the vocabulary test? How do they use these strategies?
Q3: Are there any differences between different proficiency groups in their use of information sources and strategies? If so, what are these differences?

Literature review

Vocabulary test

For this part, it conducts review from the following three aspects: vocabulary ability, approach of vocabulary testing and format of vocabulary testing.

As the vocabulary test component constitutes an essential part of the reading section in HSK-6 introduced earlier, concerning the purpose of the present study, it is necessary to understand vocabulary ability. Bachman (1990) concluded that the purpose of language testing is to allow us to make inferences about learners' language ability, which consists of two components. One is language knowledge and the other is strategic competence. Within the framework proposed by Bachman (1990) and Bachman and Palmer (1996), language knowledge can be classified into numerous aspects including vocabulary knowledge. Based on Bachman's (1990) general construct of language ability, Chapelle (1994) claimed that vocabulary ability includes: 1) the context of vocabulary use; 2) vocabulary knowledge and fundamental processes; and 3) metacognitive strategies for vocabulary use.

The traditional approach to vocabulary testing, namely the discrete-point approach, involves designing tests to assess whether learners have knowledge of particular structural elements of the language: word meanings, word forms, sentence patterns, sound contrasts and so on, which evokes a good deal of criticism (Read 2000). The criticism has led to the adoption of the communicative approach to the language testing. The communicative approach is based on tasks simulating communication activities that the learners are likely to be engaged in outside the classroom rather than just expounding on the specific meaning of some words. McNamara (1996) demonstrated that communicative tasks have become an indispensable element in contemporary test design.

The history of vocabulary assessment in the 20th century is closely associated with the development of objective testing. Among objective testing methods, the multiple-choice format is widely used in vocabulary assessment, both for native speakers and for second language learners. Previous research on vocabulary testing has mainly concentrated on vocabulary level, and the approach and format of vocabulary tests. However, the test takers' processes of taking a vocabulary test has been ignored (Haastrup 1987, 1991, Schouten-van 1989).

Simultaneous introspection

To examine what kind of information sources and strategies are elicited in the vocabulary test in the reading section of HSK-6, it is necessary to look into the test-taking processes of test takers. The research method adopted in the present study is the Think-aloud Protocol (TAP), also called simultaneous introspection. As Nunan (1992:115) defined it, 'Introspection is the process of observing and reflecting on one's thoughts, feelings, reasoning processes, and mental state with a view to determining the ways in which these processes and states determine our behaviour.'

Faerch and Kasper (1987) proposed three main introspective methods: simultaneous introspection, immediate introspection and delayed introspection. Simultaneous introspection refers to the procedure which involves the informants' verbalisation at the same time as they are working on the task. Therefore, it is also expressed in terms of thinking aloud, and the narrator's report is called the think-aloud protocol. The basic theoretical assumptions underlying the processing model for verbal reports are that a cognitive process can be seen as a sequence of states of heeded information or thoughts (Ericsson and Simon 1993). Against people's suspicions about the relevance, usefulness and acceptability of TAP, Ericcson and Simon (1980, 1983 cited from McDonough 2000) argued that such data is admissible, interesting and usable. Introspection has been applied to language testing research since the 1980s by numerous researchers (Cohen 1984, Cumming 1990, Yamashita 2003). Immediate retrospection requires the informants to verbalise their thoughts immediately after they have finished working on the task. During immediate retrospection, traces of the original cognition are still present in short-term memory. Delayed retrospection is a delayed consecutive introspective method. It can be exemplified by student diaries, documenting learners' experiences with L2 acquisition over some period of time, and group discussion about learners' emotionally relevant experiences with L2.

Information sources

Information sources are greatly used and studied mainly in the cloze test. As mentioned in the previous part, the vocabulary test in HSK-6 is a kind of non-standard short multiple-choice cloze. Bachman (1990) developed a classification framework for cloze item types according to the hierarchical context hypothesised as necessary to complete each item: 1) within clause; 2) across clause, within sentence; 3) across sentence, within text; and 4) extra-textual. The verbal protocols in this research were categorised according to a modified classification of Bachman's framework in order to see the amount of text information used to complete the vocabulary test items. The categorisation framework of the present protocols is: 1) clause level; 2) sentence level; 3) text level; and 4) extra-textual.

Strategies

There is no universally accepted theoretical basis for identifying and describing language learning strategies. Many researchers have classified language learning strategies (Ellis 1994, Oxford 1989, Rubin 1987). Among them, O'Malley and Chamot (1990) summarised 26 strategies which were placed under three broad categories: 1) meta-cognitive strategies; 2) cognitive strategies; 3) social affective strategies. The framework in terms of the strategy in the present study is mainly based on the research of O'Malley and Chamot (1990). Since there is no social affective strategy found in the present study, cognitive strategies and meta-cognitive strategies are mainly discussed in the present study.

Methodology

This study employs TAP to investigate the test-taking processes elicited by the HSK vocabulary test through the collection of simultaneous introspection protocols. As Gu and Shi (2012) pointed out, in collecting verbal protocols, the selection of participants matters: they should share a homogeneous educational and cultural background; they should be motivated to talk as required, and have little difficulty in expressing themselves; and participants should be clearly told the purpose of the study and what they should talk about. To ensure the reliability of the research, a pilot study was necessary.

Twelve postgraduates (four males and eight females) from Thailand majoring in Teaching Chinese to Speakers of Other Languages in Chongqing University participated in this study. Eight of them were in the second term of their first-year postgraduate study, and the other four were in the second term of their second-year postgraduate study. They had all learned Chinese for at least three years. Before they entered into the postgraduate stage, they all had passed the HSK test. The participants ranged in age from 24 to 28 years old. They were placed into three groups according to their HSK levels and scores as in Table 2: High group (n = 4), Medium group (n = 4), Low group (n = 4).

Table 2 The demographic information of participants

Participants identifier	Gender	Age	HSK level and score (300 is the top score for each level)
H1	M	27	HSK-6 (225)
H2	M	27	HSK-6 (218)
H3	F	28	HSK-6 (214)
H4	F	26	HSK-6 (206)
M1	M	25	HSK-6 (188)
M2	F	26	HSK-6 (192)
M3	F	24	HSK-5 (223)
M4	F	27	HSK-5 (221)
L1	M	25	HSK-5 (207)
L2	F	24	HSK-5 (183)
L3	F	26	HSK-4 (205)
L4	F	25	HSK-4 (211)

Testing material

The testing material was chosen from the April 2011 past paper of HSK-6. It contains five short passages testing vocabulary in the form of 10 multiple-choice (MC) questions. Each passage has three to five deleted words, which requires the test takers to choose the most appropriate answer among the four given options. Before using this test version, we had made sure that selected subjects in the present study had not sat this reading test before.

Here is a sample item from the HSK-6 vocabulary test:

> Directions: Choose the correct answer according to the context to make the sentence complete.
> 61. Compared with young people, the old tend to recall ____. They will no longer ____acquiring new knowledge but concentrate on their past experiences, and summarise their life-long ____.
> A. legend, test, deeds   B. the past, taste, time
> C. current situation, explore, career D. the past experience, try, years
> The correct answer is D

Procedure

The instructional phase

The subjects were informed orally of the objectives of the study. Subsequently, they were given written instructions on principles and procedures of performing a task with concurrent protocols. In the instructions, they were, for example, instructed to say everything they thought while taking this test. Verbalising their thoughts either in Chinese or Thai was allowed to ensure that the subjects could report their thoughts freely.

The pilot phase

To check the feasibility of the method, a pilot study was conducted, in which a Thai student, whose HSK-6 score is 186, was asked to verbalise what was going on in his mind when he was doing the vocabulary test of HSK-6. The whole process was recorded. Then the verbal protocol was transcribed and analysed and it was found to contain information that can be classified. Such a transcript was quite helpful in enhancing the reliability and validity of the TAP method.

The TAP phase

During this phase, the verbalisations of the subjects, including both protocols and pauses, were audio-recorded in a computer room. Sitting behind the subjects, the researchers made notes during the whole process for further analysis, and reminded them to keep talking by tapping the desk slightly if one fell silent for several seconds. No time limit was set.

The data transcription phase

During the transcription, the three principles of completeness, loyalty and reliability (Guo 2007) were adhered to. The subjects' verbal protocols were mainly in Chinese except when they inserted some Thai words/phrases. Since we transcribed the verbal reports of the test takers as faithfully as possible, some linguistic errors, repetitions and fillers etc. are found in the transcripts.

Data analysis

Rather than coding the protocols in linguistically 'small' clauses defined by the presence of one verb (e.g. Trabasso and Magliano 1996), the protocols are parsed into thought units. Each unit contained a more or less complete idea, irrespective of the number of verbs present (Whitney and Budd 1996). Each idea unit was examined in terms of information sources and strategies in order to answer the three research questions. The data was coded by two researchers independently and the inter-coder agreement was calculated as 81%. Moreover, two weeks later, one of the researchers coded a portion of the data again, and the intra-coder agreement was 88%, indicating that the coding of the verbal protocols is reliable.

Analytical framework

Based on the test takers' verbal protocols, the researchers put forward a framework theoretically driven by Bachman (1990) and O'Malley and Chamot (1990) and empirically by Gao and Gu (2008), Zheng and Gu (2009) and Gu and Shi (2012) for analysing the test takers' processes used when taking the vocabulary test in the reading section of HSK-6, which is illustrated in Figure 1:

Figure 1 The research framework for the present study

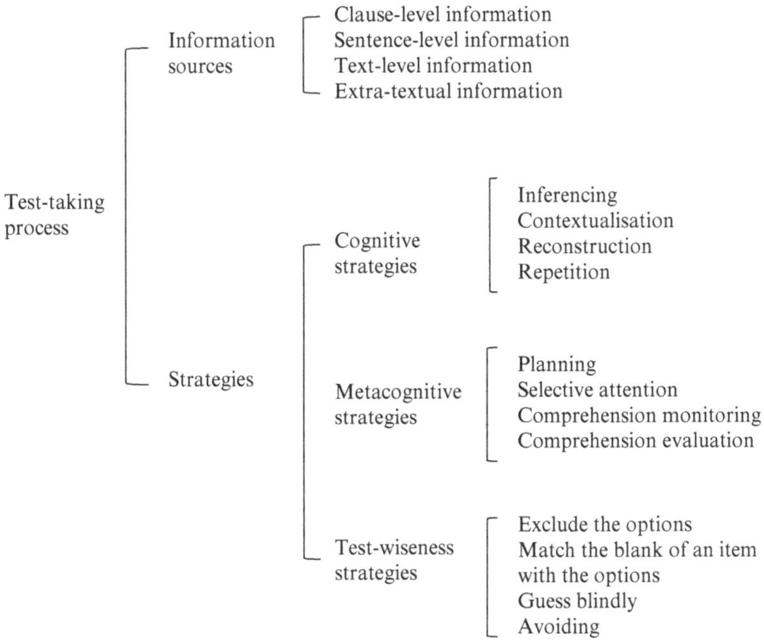

Findings and discussion

Information sources

All of the verbal protocols produced by test takers while answering the vocabulary test items were analysed in order to identify each information source or strategy used. The frequency and proportion of each information source was calculated and presented according to the level of the test takers' reading proficiency and the correct or incorrect responses to the items. We intended to reveal how these information sources work in the test takers' test-taking process. The results are shown in Table 3.

Table 3 Frequencies of information categories used by the three groups

Categories	Correct/incorrect response	High group	Medium group	Low group	Total
		F* (n)	F (n)	F (n)	F (n)
1) Clause	Correct	29	25	18	72
	Incorrect	7	9	10	26
2) Sentence	Correct	21	15	8	44
	Incorrect	4	6	6	16
3) Text	Correct	25	21	14	60
	Incorrect	3	5	6	14
4) Extra-textual	Correct	5	3	0	8
	Incorrect	2	1	1	4
Total	Correct	80	64	40	184
	Incorrect	16	21	23	60

* F = Frequency

The total number of information sources is greater than the expected number of 228 (12 test takers each with 19 blanks to fill in the test) with 244 information sources being identified. In light of this result, it seems reasonable to suggest that the test takers tend to use two or three information sources to answer one item. Table 3 shows that the number of information sources used by the high, medium and low groups was 96, 85 and 63, respectively. This indicates that the more proficient participants make use of more information sources than less proficient participants. Clause-level information was most frequently used by the three groups, followed by text-level information, sentence-level information and extra-textual information. In addition, the frequency of selecting the correct answer by employing an information source among the three groups was 33%, 26%, and 16%, respectively. This shows that the high group performed more successfully than the medium and low groups in all of the categories. This is probably due to the proficient test takers' better understanding of the items and higher level of reading ability, making it easier for them to combine more information sources and perform better in the vocabulary test.

Clause-level information

Clause-level information refers to the information provided by the clause in which an item appears. From Table 3, it can be seen that clause-level information was most frequently used by the three groups. In addition, clause-level information was used by the high group more frequently than both the medium group and the low group. This indicates that the more proficient test takers can identify the correct answer more easily and successfully with the help of clause-level information than less-proficient ones. The high group also used clause-level information in combination with sentence-level and text-level information in most cases, while the low group tended to use it as the single source of information. The texts in bold in the following examples could help readers focus on the testees' main test-taking processes quickly.

Example 1 (H1):
*Because when there are passengers in the car, **the driver has blahblah**. The driver has A. sign B. objective C. target D. focus. **Not clear yet and just go ahead.** Arriving at the crossroad, he hesitates to go left or right, hence awareness/attention/vitality/resolution is distracted. I think C is right. When passengers are in the car, the driver has a target and will focus on driving with caution against blahblah. However, when there are no passengers, he is impetuous. Arriving at the crossroad blahblah, his attention will be distracted.*

Example 2 (L3):
*When there are passengers, **the driver has a . . . target/objective**. The driver has an objective. Not suitable. **It should be that the driver has a target.***

Sentence-level information

Sentence-level information refers to the information provided by a larger context than the clause in which an item appears, but within the sentence. Among the four levels of information sources, sentence-level information is used less frequently than clause-level and text-level information. From Table 3, it can also be inferred that 84% of the sentence-level information can help the high group test takers reach the correct answer, while only 57.1% of sentence-level information can help the low group test takers get the right answer. This result is only obtained by analysing the testees' protocols. From their protocols, it seems that they only use this information source. A behavioural pattern frequently identified for the high group of test takers is that they tend to see the whole sentence as one unit and do not make decisions until they finish the whole sentence while the low group of test takers tend to look for the answers immediately once they meet the blank. The following two examples will be given to illustrate this behavioural pattern.

Example 3 (H3):
Tuangou is short for shopping in group. It refers to consumers known or unknown to combine/join/contact/merge together. I think the answer is 'combine together'. Then, to enhance buyers' bargaining ability with sellers. Only through combining customers together can enhance buyers' bargaining ability with the sellers. So I choose 'combine together'.

Example 4 (L1):
Tuangou is short for shopping in group. It refers to consumers known or unknown . . . together. Combine/join/contact/merge. Consumers known or unknown. . . together. **I think the answer is 'combine together', so I choose A.**

These two examples demonstrate that even though the high group have inferred the answer 'combine together', they used the whole sentence to confirm the answer. However, for the low group, once they encountered the blank, they immediately made their choice after getting some idea of the deleted word which may or may not have made sense in the context of the whole sentence.

Text-level information

Text-level information refers to the information provided by a context larger than the sentence in which an item appears. From Table 3, it can be seen that text-level information is the second most frequently used information source after clause-level source. Every item of the vocabulary test consists of 2–3 sentences with 3–5 words deleted, i.e. a short text. This kind of text generally has centralised information. When test takers cannot solve the problem from the obvious clause-level information, they tend to look for text-level clues. The following can provide an example of this.

Example 5 (H1):
Well, item 68, when is it the most dangerous for a taxi? for a taxi? The answer is when no passengers are in the car. Because when there are passengers, the driver has blahblah. The driver has A. sign B. target C. objective D. focus. I am not sure yet. He will blahblah. He will, cannot wait for, concentrate on. This . . . I think B is incorrect, on driving, blahblah, A. make concerted efforts, B. try every means, C. be cautious blahblah, D. make every endeavour to arrive at the destination as soon as possible. When there are no passengers, he is blahblah. He is confused/ blind/impetuous/irritable. D. He is irritable. D is wrong. Arriving at the crossroad, he hesitates to go left or right, awareness/attention/vitality/resolution is distracted. I think C is right. Because when passengers are present, the driver has a target and will focus on driving with caution against blahblah. However, when there are no passengers, he is impetuous. Arriving at the crossroad blahblah, his attention will be distracted.

Extra-textual information

Extra-textual information refers to information not provided by the text. The extra-textual information was not used very frequently by any of the three groups. When it was used, the test takers were able to find the correct answers in most cases. Further exploration of the protocols illustrates that the extra-textual information utilised by the test takers is mainly related to their background knowledge (see Example 6).

Example 6 (M3):
Companies and people like this are too blah to make great progress. ***According to my experience and knowledge****, stubbornness may not be good, and then they hardly make great progress. So D is correct.*

Strategy use

Strategies are deliberate, cognitive steps that the learners can take to assist in acquiring, storing, and retrieving information (Paris 1983, cited in Anderson 1991). This section aims to identify the strategies utilised by test takers in their process of taking the vocabulary test in the reading part of HSK-6, how these strategies are employed, and whether there are differences between test takers in their strategy use. Twelve strategies were identified by examining the concurrent verbal protocols of the test takers while they were taking the vocabulary test and these were further classified into three categories: cognitive strategies, metacognitive strategies, and test-wiseness strategies. The frequencies of each strategy category employed by the test takers in the three groups are illustrated in Figure 2.

Figure 2 Frequencies of the strategy categories used by the three groups

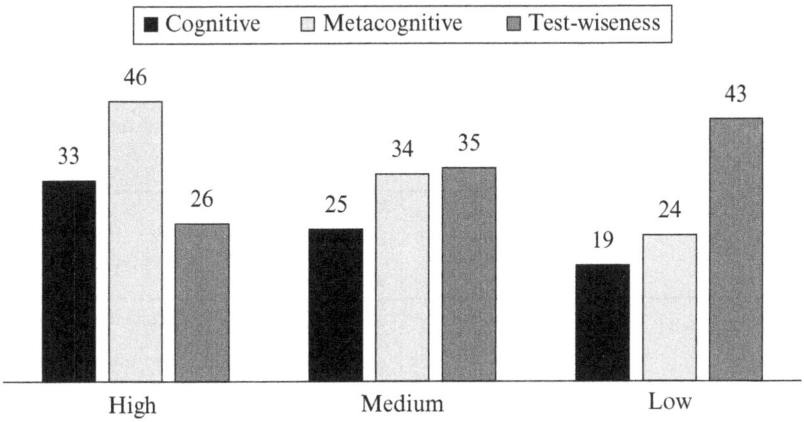

(Chi-square = 15.479, Sig. = 0.004)

In total, the number of strategies used by the high, medium and low group are 105, 94 and 86 respectively. It is clear that the high group report employing more strategies than the medium and low group. This result is similar to that of many previous studies such as Hopkins and Mackay's conclusion (1997).

It can be inferred from Figure 2 that the proficient test takers utilise cognitive and metacognitive strategies more frequently than less proficient ones.

The less proficient test takers employ test-wise strategies more frequently than proficient ones. This result offers supporting evidence for the conclusion that the less proficient test takers rely on test-wiseness strategies to solve the items more frequently, probably due to their limited understanding of the text or shortage of vocabulary.

Cognitive strategies

In terms of cognitive strategy use, test takers show a preference for inferring, contextualisation, reconstruction and repetition (see Table 4).

From Table 5, it can be seen that the high group employ cognitive strategies more frequently than the medium and low group. It seems reasonable to suggest that more proficient test takers are more able to access cognitive strategies than less proficient test takers because of language ability.

Table 4 Cognitive strategies employed

Strategy	Description	Protocol
Inferring	Infer or guess missing information or meaning of words or sentence	相对于年轻人来说, 老年人更乐于什么什么, 然后去看答案, A 传说, B 从前, C 现状, D往事, 这个呢, 我觉得先排除 A 和 C, 因为老年人更乐于回忆, 所以说, 更可能说是以前的事情嘛, **(The old are more inclined to recall things, so it's more about the past events)** 所以啊, 这个呢, 应该选 B 或者选 D, 从前或者往事。
Contextualisation	Relate new information to a wider familiar context	先有目标, 他会, 看B 的盲目, 看不到路, 也是看不到, 也不知道该怎么做, 后面也说了, **(Which has been stated in the following part)** 走到十字路口往往左转右转犹豫不定, 不知道该往哪走, 所以他的精力就被分散了。
Reconstruction	Recreate meaning using their own words according to their own understanding	然后我觉得焦点比目标好一些。这个意思就是说**(That is to say)**把乘客当成焦点。然后会聚精会神。然后没有乘客时, 精力会被分散。
Repetition	Repeat some words or sentences	是因为消费者联络, 联络**(combine, combine)**起来, 因为认识的或者不认识的得需要联络起来, 以求得最优的一种购物手段, 手段 **(means, means)**?

Table 5 Frequencies of cognitive strategy use

	Inferring	Contextualisation	Reconstruction	Repetition	Total
High	15	13	5	0	33
Medium	12	9	3	1	25
Low	8	6	2	3	19
Total	35	28	10	4	77

Metacognitive strategies

When reading, metacognitive strategies are self-monitoring and self-regulating activities, focusing on both the process and the product of reading. They include readers' awareness of whether or not they can comprehend what they are reading; their ability to judge the cognitive demands of a reading task; and their knowledge of when and how to employ a specific cognitive reading strategy according to text difficulty, situational constraints, and the reader's own cognitive abilities (Baker and Brown 1984, Gourgey 2001). Four metacognitive strategies were identified in the test takers' repertoire, including planning, selective attention, comprehension monitoring, and comprehension evaluation (see Table 6).

Based on Table 7, test takers in the high group use the planning strategy

Table 6 Metacognitive strategies employed

Strategy	Description	Protocol
Planning	Preview content in different forms; establish purpose for reading	相对于年轻人来说, 老年人更乐于回忆什么, 他们不再什么获得新的知识, 而是专注于昔日的经历, 为一生的什么做一个总结 (一个读题的过程, 明确目标) (A process of reading the text, in order to understand the requirements)。
Selective attention	Notice specific aspects of reading materials; reading selectively according to purpose	第**63**题, 我答 **B**, 是因为, 这些选项里我只知道万一的意思 (Of all the options I only know the meaning of in case), 把万一放进去, 万一制定了基本方针, 所以我就答 **B**。
Comprehension monitoring	Monitor understanding while reading	老年人更乐于回忆, 该是往事吧, 这个意思我不太懂它的意思, 先不做, 往后猜 (without choosing this blank and going on guessing the following ones)。
Comprehension evaluation	Check understanding for accuracy, completeness and acceptability	第 **63** 题, 我选择也是 **D**, 因为我觉得, 一旦制定了基本方针, 就一步都不打算妥协, 我觉得这样比较顺, 别的选择不太顺, 所以我选择 **D**。再看其他的空 (and then consider other blanks), 这样的公司及个人由于太固执, 很难有大的发展。固执就是不太好的吧, 就很难有大的发展。所以我确定D为正确答案 (So I choose D as the right answer)。

Table 7 Frequency of metacognitive strategy use

	Planning	Selective attention	Comprehension monitoring	Comprehension evaluation	Total
High	13	10	15	8	46
Medium	8	7	13	6	34
Low	5	3	12	4	24
Total	26	20	40	18	104

more frequently than the other groups. One possible explanation is that proficient readers are more inclined to answer the item only after they have possessed an overall understanding of the text. Instead, the less proficient readers tend to only focus on parts of the text. Most test takers thought that their task was to choose the appropriate answer to fill in the blanks, so they were only concerned with where the blank is and which vocabulary item fits the blank, and then pay attention to it. However, there is a considerable difference between the three groups in their use of the selective attention strategy. No great difference exists between the high and low groups in the use of the comprehension monitoring strategy. From the protocols, it can be seen that all three groups choose to figure out the familiar and easy blanks first. The protocols also show that the high group of test takers are more apt to apply the comprehension evaluation strategy than the medium and low group test takers. More often, the proficient readers will reflect on what item they have chosen and evaluate every blank by integrating the information from the overall text to assist them in deciding whether to make any changes. Instead, the less proficient readers just directly move to the next item after they have chosen an answer.

Test-wiseness strategies

Four remaining strategies (excluding the options, matching the blank of an item with the options, guessing blindly, and avoiding) are detected in protocols and labelled as test-wise strategies (see Table 8). Test-wiseness processing strategies are defined as a test takers' capacity to utilise the characteristics and formats of the test and/or test-taking situation to receive a high score (Crehan, Koehler and Slakter 1974).

According to Table 9, both the high group and low group employ the avoiding strategy. The results show that avoiding occurs more frequently in the protocols of test takers from the low group, which indicates that the less proficient readers are more inclined to deliberately avoid some words that are difficult or the ones that they are not familiar with and rely on the choices of other blanks. When using the strategy of matching the blank of an item with the options, the test takers often put the given options one by one in the blanks in order to see which is suitable in the context. Sometimes the test takers do not match the blanks with all of the options. Sometimes the test takers do not select an answer based on its correctness, but make decisions when they think the other options do not seem reasonable or are not understandable; this strategy is referred to as excluding the options. The high group tends to use this strategy more frequently than the medium and low groups. So far there is no consistent clear difference between the notions of inferring and guessing due to the similar cognitive processes of these two concepts.

Table 8 Test-wiseness strategies employed

Strategy	Description	Protocol
Avoiding	Do nothing about some blanks, relying on the choices of other blanks	**ABC**最后的词我不知道什么意思, 然后我再看, 做生意时总会有一些企业或个人只知道坚持自己的立场, 什么什么制定了基本方针, 就什么什么, 后面有就, 前面应该, 可能万一, 一旦, 一旦……就, 应该是一旦 … 就, 后面就不管了(The following blanks will not be considered.), 选 **D** 。
Excluding the options	Select an answer not because it is thought to be correct, but because the others do not seem reasonable or are not understandable	相对于年轻人来说, 老年人更乐于什么什么, 然后去看答案, **A** 传说, **B** 从前, **C** 现状, **D** 往事, 这个呢, 我觉得先排除 A和C (In my opinion, A and C could be firstly got rid of.), 因为老年人更乐于回忆 。
Matching the blank of an item with the options	Put the given options one by one in the blank in order to see whether it is suitable in the context	出租车在什么时候最危险？答案是没有乘客时。因为有乘客时, 司机有什么什么, 司机有 **A** 标志, **B** 目标, **C** 对象, **D** 焦点 (A. sign, B. destination, C. object, D. focus)。这个还不是很清楚, 他会怎么怎么, 他会, 迫不及待, 全神贯注, 我觉得 **B** 不对, 与驾驶, 什么什么, 齐心协力, **B** 想方设法, **C** 小心什么什么, **D** 千方百计 (B. try every means to, C. be cautious about blahblah, D. make every effort to) 。
Guessing blindly	Randomly choose from the given options without any particular consideration	这个 **63** 题, 答案的词我不太明白, 不知道它的意思, 然后看起来, 我觉得, 额, 它的答案就是 **C**, 这道题我就是猜的 (I worked out this question by mere guessing).

Table 9 Frequencies of the avoiding strategy

Strategy	Correct or Incorrect	High group	Medium group	Low group	Total
Avoiding	Correct	3	8	12	23
	Incorrect	2	6	9	17
Total		5	14	21	40

Conclusions

The present study investigated the test takers' processes of taking the HSK-6 vocabulary test. A framework for analysing the test-taking processes was proposed. Based on this framework, the test takers' protocols were further categorised and analysed.

The research findings demonstrate that test takers employ all four categories of information sources, i.e. clause-level, sentence-level, text-level and extra-textual information, among which clause-level information is the most frequently used, followed by text-level, sentence-level and extra-textual information. The test takers employ all three strategy categories, i.e. cognitive, metacognitive and test-wiseness strategies. Among the four cognitive strategies, inferring and contextualisation are much more frequently used than reconstruction and repetition. In terms of the four metacognitive strategies, comprehension monitoring is most frequently used, followed by planning, selective attention and comprehension evaluation. As far as the four test-wiseness strategies are concerned, avoiding is used more frequently than matching the blank of an item with the options, excluding the options, and guessing blindly. There exist some differences between different proficiency groups in their use of information sources and strategies. The higher the proficiency level of the group, the more information sources it uses, the more information from different levels it combines, the wider range of discourse it pays attention to and the more cognitive and metacognitive strategies it uses. Conversely, the lower the proficiency level of the group, the more test-wiseness strategies it uses.

Limitations and implications

There are several limitations that should be addressed in future research. Firstly, the present study included only five items of a vocabulary test and a small number of participants from a homogeneous cultural and linguistic background who may not be representative of the test-taking population as a whole. Future studies should include a greater variety of participants. And the number of items should also be increased. Thus, the generalisability of the research findings remain to be further tested.

However, the present study bears some implications for Chinese test design and reading instruction. Firstly, the text should be lengthened to provide more information and context for the test takers. Secondly, care should be taken to avoid activating test takers' extra-textual information and to avoid their use of test-wiseness strategies to obtain the correct answers. Lastly, more training and practice is needed for test takers to improve their appropriate use of information sources and strategies. Regarding language teaching, teachers should help the students recognise the importance of context and teach them how to solve the problems by making use of the context. In addition, Chinese teachers should not only teach the learners a certain amount of vocabulary, but also instruct them to learn better ways of learning Chinese vocabulary effectively by themselves, and cultivate learners' ability of inferencing word meanings and understanding the meaning of sentences according to word formation, the context and learners' experience and so on. From the methodological perspective, the study employs the introspection methodology to look into test-taking processes and provides useful data for the validity of the HSK-6 vocabulary test, which may offer insights for the application of this methodology in other components in the HSK in the future.

References

Anderson, N J (1991) Individual differences in strategy use in second language reading and testing, *Modern Language Journal* 75 (4), 460–472.

Bachman, L (1990) *Fundamental Considerations in Language Testing*, Oxford: Oxford University Press.

Bachman, L F and Palmer, A (1996) *Language Testing in Practice: Designing and Developing Useful Language Tests*, Oxford: Oxford University Press.

Baker, L and Brown, A L (1984) Metacognitive skills and reading, in Pearson, P D, Barr, R, Kamil, M and Mosenthal, P (Eds) *Handbook of Reading Research*, New York: Routledge, 353–394.

Chapelle, C A (1994) Are C-tests valid measures for L2 vocabulary research, *Second Language Research* 10, 157–187.

Cohen, A (1984) On taking language tests: what the students report, *Language Testing* 1, 70–81.

Council of Europe (2001) *Common European Framework of Reference for Languages: Learning, Teaching, Assessment*, Cambridge: Cambridge University Press.

Crehan, D K, Koehler, A and Slakter, J (1974) Longitudinal studies of test-wiseness, *Journal of Educational Measurement* 11 (2), 209–212.

Cumming, A (1990) Expertise in evaluating second language compositions, *Language Testing* 7, 31–51.

Ellis, R (1994) *The Study of Second Language Acquisition*, Oxford: Oxford University Press.

Ericsson, K A and Simon, H (1980) Verbal reports as data, *Psychological Review* 87 (3), 215–251.

Ericsson, K A and Simon, H (1993) *Protocol Analysis: Verbal Reports as Data*, Cambridge: MIT Press.

Faerch, C and Kasper, G (1987) *Introspection in Second Language Research*, Clevedon: Multilingual Matters.

Gao, X and Gu, X (2008) An introspective study on the test-taking process for banked cloze, *CELEA Journal* 31 (4), 3–16.

Gourgey, A F (2001) Metacognition in basic skills instruction, in Hartman, H (Ed) *Metacognition in Learning and Instruction*, Boston: Kluwer Academic Publishers, 17–32.

Gu, X and Shi, C (2012) A retrospective study on test-takers' cognitive and metacognitive processes in taking a compound dictation test, *Chinese Journal of Applied Linguistics* 35 (4), 400–420.

Guo, C (2007) *Think Aloud Protocols*, Beijing: Foreign Language Teaching and Research Press.

Haastrup, K (1987) Using thinking aloud and retrospection to uncover learners' lexical inferencing procedures, in Faerch, C and Kasper, G (Eds) *Introspection in Second Language Research*, Clevedon, UK: Multilingual Matters, 197–212.

Haastrup, K (1991) *Lexical Inferencing Procedures or Talking About Words*, Tubingen: Gunter Naar.

Hanban/Confucius Institute Headquarters (2009) *Chinese Proficiency Test Syllabus*, Beijing: The Commercial Press.

Hopkins, N M and Mackay, R (1997) Good and bad readers: A look at the high and low achievers in an ESP Canadian studies reading and writing course, *The Canadian Modern Language Review* 53 (3), 476–492.

McDonough, J (2000) *Research Methods for English Language Teachers*, Beijing: Foreign Language Teaching and Research Press.

McNamara, T F (1996) *Measuring Second Language Performance*, London: Longman.

Nunan, D (1992) *Research Methods in Language Learning*, London: Cambridge: Cambridge University Press.

O'Malley, J M and Chamot, A (1990) *Learning strategies in second language acquisition*, New York: Cambridge University Press.

Oxford, R (1989) Use of language learning strategies: a synthesis of studies with implications for teacher training, *System* 17, 235–247.

Read, J (2000) *Assessing Vocabulary*, London: Cambridge University Press.

Rubin, J (1987) Learning strategies: theoretical assumptions, research, history and typology, in Wenden, A and Rubin, J (Eds) *Learner Strategies in Language Learning*, Hemel Hempstead: Prentice-Hall, 15–29.

Schouten-van, P C (1989) Vocabulary learning through reading: which conditions should be met when presenting words in texts, in Nation, P and Carter, R (Eds) *Vocabulary Acquisition*, Amsterdam: Free University Press, 75–85.

Trabasso, T and Magliano, J (1996) Conscious understanding during comprehension, *Discourse Processes* 21 (3), 255–287.

Whitney, P and Budd, D (1996) Think-aloud protocols and the study of comprehension, *Discourse Processes* 21 (3), 341–351.

Yamashita, J (2003) Processes of taking a gap-filling test: Comparison of skilled and less skilled EFL readers, *Language Testing* 20 (3), 267–293.

Zheng, Y and Gu, X (2009) A study on the construct validity of long dialogue multiple-choice listening comprehension tests: Retrospection approach, *CELEA Journal* 32 (6), 15–26.

20 Exploring the Chinese proficiency test Hanyu Shuiping Kaoshi and its washback effects: The test takers' perspective

Shujiao Wang
McGill University, Montreal

Abstract

This study investigated how learner factors which include motivation, learning strategies and beliefs, related to the washback of a large-scale high-stakes Chinese language proficiency test, the Hanyu Shuiping Kaoshi (HSK). Using a mixed methods sequential explanatory approach, quantitative data was collected from Chinese as a second/foreign/heritage language (CSL) learner survey responses ($N = 60$) and qualitative data was elicited from eight interviews and the HSK-related documents. Findings revealed there were significant washback effects of the HSK on learning Chinese and that the HSK had positive impact on some learners but negative effects on others. Significant predictors for the change in learning strategies between regular and test-specific learning were nationality, language proficiency, HSK performance and motivation. Finally, although it is claimed that the validity and reliability of the HSK content are high, this study points to some aspects that could be improved, such as including more subjective question forms and emphasising the output (speaking and writing) measurements. This study has implications for HSK test developers, CSL teachers and CSL learners.

Introduction

High-stakes large-scale language tests have powerful washback effects on teaching and learning within different educational contexts (Andrews, Fullilove and Wong 2002, Cheng and Curtis 2004). There has been increasing interest in exploring the washback effects at micro level on classroom practice and activity (Turner 2009). However, compared to the considerable attention paid to washback effects on teaching, research on washback effects in terms of learning seems to be sparse (Shih 2007, Wall 2000, Watanabe

2004). Whether high-stakes tests have washback effects on learning process and learning beliefs has not been clearly examined previously.

In addition, much washback research has been done in the field of English as a Second/Foreign Language, but not on other languages. The rapid development of China's economy has boosted the popularity of Chinese language and culture globally. Hanyu Shuiping Kaoshi (HSK) (汉语水平考试) which translates literally to 'Chinese Proficiency Test', also known as the 'Chinese TOEFL', has become a widely accepted standardised test for Chinese as a second/foreign/heritage language (CSL) and it plays a vital role in certifying Chinese language proficiency for higher education and professional purposes. Despite the significance and the claimed high validity and reliability of this test (Chen 2009, Luo, Zhang, Xie and Huang 2011), very few empirical studies related to its validity have been conducted, in particular, with regard to its washback effect.

This study intends to investigate the impact of the HSK test on learner factors from the test takers' view. The *learner factors* in this study include motivation for learning, learning attitudes/beliefs, learning strategies and learning activities.

A brief overview of washback effects

Washback refers to the impact of a test on teaching and learning and it also refers to the extent to which the test influences language teachers and learners to do things 'they would not necessarily otherwise do because of the test' (Alderson and Wall 1993:117). Messick (1996) viewed washback as an 'instance of the consequential aspect of construct validity' (1996:242), which covers elements of test use, the impact of testing on test takers and educators, the interpretation of results by decision-makers, and any possible misuses, abuses, and unintentional effects of tests. Although different researchers prefer different terms, they all refer to facets of the same phenomenon: the influence of testing on teaching and learning. The washback of the HSK in this study is defined as the effects or influences of the test on CSL teaching and learning. In addition, since the intention of the current study is to explore test takers' perceptions and their learning methods/strategies under the influence of HSK, this research mainly examines the washback effects of the HSK on learning.

As the pioneers in the research on washback in language classrooms, Alderson and Wall (1993) provided the most thorough and comprehensive explanation of the term washback. They came up with 15 hypotheses regarding washback to illustrate tests' impacts on teachers and learners, teaching and learning, and attitudes concerning method and content of teaching and learning. Bailey (1996) further developed the hypotheses set out in Alderson and Wall (1993) by incorporating Hughes' (1993) ideas, leading to a model of washback which attempted to delineate the complicated mechanisms of it. In this model, unlike the 15 hypotheses that only show the linear relationships between tests and teaching or learning, it also demonstrates the interaction among components.

Although there is general agreement in the field of language assessment on the existence and importance of the washback phenomenon, there still is considerable variety in opinions about how washback functions (Bailey 1996). The way it is perceived depends on the theoretical standpoint researchers take as well as the educational context that they are associated with. A case in point is that no consensus can be reached in the language testing community as to whether washback effects are positive or negative, or both. Consistent with this view, Cheng and Curtis (2004) stated that the use of tests has been subject to criticism and pointing out positive or negative washback effects could be seen as a form of criticism.

The washback theoretical framework and models have sparked empirical research that has aimed to discover the effects of washback on language teaching and learning. It can be seen that most research findings showed that high-stakes tests had a significant impact on L2 teaching in that the tests altered teachers' methods (e.g. Alderson and Hamp-Lyons 1996, Cheng 1997, 2005). In addition, research has suggested that there are various factors mediating the process of washback. For example, Watanabe (2004) listed the following factors: 1) test factors (e.g. test methods, test content, skills tested, purpose of the test, and decisions that are made by the test results; 2) prestige factors (e.g. stakes of the test and status of the test within the entire educational system); 3) personal factors (e.g. teachers' educational backgrounds, their beliefs about the best methods of teaching and learning); 4) micro-context factors (e.g. the school setting in which the test preparation is being carried out); and 5) macro-context factors (e.g. social factors).

Whereas a majority of the research has investigated washback on teaching, few studies have examined the effects on learning, with the exception of the research conducted on the *International English Language Testing System (IELTS)*, General English Proficiency Test (GEPT) and Hong Kong Certificate of Education Examination (HKCEE). In Cheng (1997), the author examined the washback of the HKCEE on learning through a survey. Results indicated that the test was the most significant factor involved in motivating students to learn English, more so than future career plans. In her later study, Cheng (1998) found that although students changed their learning beliefs after the content of the test had been changed, they reported retaining their original learning processes, learning strategies and individual motivations to learn English.

As Watanabe (2004) stated, 'relatively well explored is the area of washback to the program, while less emphasis has been given to learners' (2004:22). Two notable exceptions and significant contributions were Green

(2007) and Shih (2007). Green's experimental study investigated whether dedicated test preparation classes gave learners an advantage in improving their *IELTS* writing test scores. The results show an improvement in test scores for learners in test-preparation or academic-oriented classes, but those in the former progressed no more than those in the latter. Although there was no explicit gain in scores of the test preparation group, it is worthwhile in bettering our understanding of how washback influences learning outcomes. Shih (2007) investigated the washback of the GEPT on English learning in Taiwan and found that existing theories did not fully explain the washback of this test on educational context, so a new tentative washback framework was proposed. This model includes extrinsic, intrinsic, and other factors that assist in the explanation of the complexity of the washback effects.

In addition, since most studies concerning washback effects on learning only employed qualitative research, or solely relied on questionnaires, I would argue that more in-depth information will emerge if diverse research methods are involved, such as mixed methods, which systematically combine both quantitative and qualitative data methodologies.

The *Scales* and the HSK

The *Chinese Language Proficiency Scales For Speakers of Other Languages* (Office of Chinese Language Council International 2009), abbreviated as *Scales*, serve as a reference standard for drawing up a syllabus of teaching Chinese for speakers of other languages, for compiling Chinese textbooks, and for assessing the language proficiency of CSL learners. It has drawn on the results of research on international language proficiency scales such as the Common European Framework of Reference for Languages (CEFR, Council of Europe 2001) and the Canadian Language Benchmarks (CLB, Center for Canadian Language Benchmarks 2012) (Office of Chinese Language Council International 2010). It provides a five-band all-round description of CSL learners' ability to use their knowledge and skills of the Chinese language for communication. From the general description of Chinese Language Proficiency (see Figure 1), it is clear that communicative ability is the core focus.

The HSK is a national standardised test designed to evaluate Chinese proficiency of non-native Chinese speakers (including foreigners, overseas Chinese and Chinese national minorities) based on the *Scales*. Development of the HSK began in 1984 and Hanban[1] (中国国家对外汉语教学领导小组办公室) is currently responsible for the HSK exams. The new HSK consists of a writing test and a speaking test, which are independent of each other. There are six levels of the writing test, namely the HSK Levels 1 to 6. There are three levels of the speaking test, namely the HSK Speaking Test, beginner, intermediate and advanced. The current test structure is presented in Table 2 on page 436.

Figure 1 Description of Chinese Language Proficiency (Office of Chinese Language Council International 2010:4)

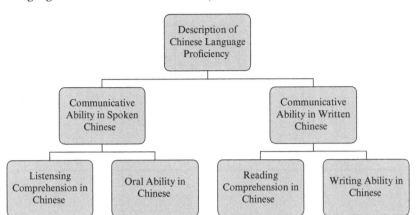

In 2010, Hanban stated that the HSK's six levels correspond on a one-to-one basis with the six levels of the CEFR. Accordingly, Table 1 shows the corresponding relationship between each level of the new HSK tests and the *Scales*. However, Hanban's estimated equivalent has been rejected by the German and the French association of Chinese language teachers, which argue that HSK Level 6 is equivalent to CEFR Level B2 or C1.

Table 1 Relationship among the new HSK tests and *Scales* and estimated equivalent CEFR levels (Office of Chinese Language Council International 2010:1)

New HSK (Written)	New HSK (Spoken)	Hanban estimate	German association estimate	French association estimate	Scales
HSK Level 6	Advanced	C2	B2	B2–C1	Band 5
HSK Level 5		C1	B1	B1	
HSK Level 4	Intermediate	B2	A2	A2	Band 4
HSK Level 3		B1	A1	A1–A2	Band 3
HSK Level 2	Beginner	A2	A1.1	A1.1	Band 2
HSK Level 1		A1	Below A1	Below A1	Band 1

Methods

This study is conducted in the framework of mixed methods sequential explanatory design, which implies collecting and analysing quantitative first. The output of the first phase is then used to inform the qualitative phase

Table 2 The new HSK test structure

Level	Words	Characters (cumulative/new)		Written test			Oral test	Description
		cumulative	new	Listening	Reading	Writing		
1	150	178	178	20 questions	20 questions	(Not tested)	17 min	Designed for learners who can understand and use some simple Chinese characters and sentences to communicate, and prepares them for continuing their Chinese studies.
2	300	349	171	35 questions	25 questions			Designed for learners who can use Chinese in a simple and direct manner, applying it in a basic fashion to their daily lives.
3	600	623	274	40 questions	30 questions	10 items	21 min	Designed for learners who can use Chinese to serve the demands of their personal lives, studies and work, and are capable of completing most of the communicative tasks they experience during their Chinese tour.
4	1,200	1074	451	45 questions	40 questions	15 items		Designed for learners who can discuss a relatively wide range of topics in Chinese and are capable of communicating with Chinese speakers at a high standard.
5	2,500	1710	636	45 questions	45 questions	10 items	24 min	Designed for learners who can read Chinese newspapers and magazines, watch Chinese films and are capable of writing and delivering a lengthy speech in Chinese.
6	5,000	2633	923	50 questions	50 questions	1 composition		Designed for learners who can easily understand any information communicated in Chinese and are capable of smoothly expressing themselves in written or oral form.

Source: en.wikipedia.org/wiki/Hanyu_Shuiping_Kaoshi

which follows to provide a holistic picture of a research problem (Creswell and Plano Clark 2011). As Greene (2007) noted, the primary purpose of a study conducted with a mixed methods research (MMR) focus is to better understand the complexity of the social phenomena being studied. The previous section has demonstrated that there are multiple facets of change and washback that can occur in a systemic environment as well as within an individual learning context. Thus, it shows that MMR is well suited to capture the complexity of the washback processes inherent in an educational context.

Research questions

This study aims to explore a global question: What are the washback effects of the HSK on CSL learner factors? There are three secondary questions:

1. What is the evidence of washback effects on the learner factors?
2. How does the HSK affect the way learners learn Chinese? In other words, what factors contribute to the change of learning strategies/practice used in regular Chinese learning[2] as opposed to HSK-specific learning[3]?
3. What are the views of the CSL learners towards the HSK and its impact?

Participants

In order to get a representative sample, the participants were chosen according to three parameters: 1) the type of CSL programme (e.g. university credit course, Confucius Institute course, weekend language school course, and HSK preparation course etc.) they have taken; 2) their Chinese language ability; and 3) geographical factors (e.g. nationalities). My previous experience as a CSL instructor in China and North America allowed me to have an insider's view which helped in my initial sample selection.

The population of the focus group (used in the pilot study) included four CSL learners, one HSK test developer and two experienced CSL teachers. In the quantitative data collection phase, 60 CSL learners (Female = 27, Male = 33) from 15 countries who had previously taken the HSK test volunteered to participate.

A sub-sample from the quantitative phase participated in the qualitative phase. The participants in the quantitative phase were given an opportunity to volunteer to participate in the qualitative phase. There were 21 questionnaire participants who indicated their willingness to be interviewed. Of these, I chose eight interviewees who were representative of the differences in gender (four females and four males), in age group (three aged 18–24, three aged 24–34, two aged 35+), and their self-reported Chinese competence (two low level, three intermediate level and three high level).

Instruments

The instruments pertinent to this paper are: HSK-related documents, structured questionnaires, and one-on-one interviews.

The HSK-related documents and reports issued by Hanban and the new HSK exam paper were reviewed by adopting qualitative content analysis. The purpose of it was to identify the characteristics of the HSK and to investigate what the HSK claims to measure (e.g. linguistic knowledge or language use ability), what is the test taker component, and whether or not the HSK construct and the underlying intentions represent the *Chinese Language Proficiency Scales For Speakers of Other Languages*.

An online questionnaire was developed by the author to explore the washback effects of the HSK on CSL learner factors. Its development was based on the learning strategy and learning belief theories, washback theories (e.g. the definition of washback proposed by Alderson and Wall (1993) and washback models. The questionnaire was piloted with my focus group and validated to meet statistical need of reliability. The questionnaire was structured in three parts and has 68 questions in total. Part1 asks for background information. Part 2 concerns participants' learning strategies used for regular learning and test-specific learning. Part 3 is related to participants' attitudes towards the HSK. Both Part 2 and 3 use 4-point Likert-scale items (e.g. Strongly disagree (1); Disagree (2); Agree (3) and Strongly agree (4)).

A semi-structured in-depth individual interview protocol was designed by the author and it was informed by findings from the students' questionnaire and HSK-related document review. Interviews were conducted in Chinese or English depending on the participants' preference. It served as a complementary tool to verify findings from the survey questionnaire (Phakiti 2003), and it helps contribute to a more comprehensive and nuanced understanding of the examined relationships.

Data analysis

A mixed methods sequential explanatory design was employed for this study. First of all, a quantitative analysis of survey data was undertaken, which provided the main data set, involved descriptive statistical analyses and inferential analyses. A series of t-tests was used to measure whether any washback effect exists. In addition, multiple regression analysis was conducted to explore which factors (gender, age, nationality, language proficiency, the course type, motivation, etc.) contribute to the washback effects. The computer program Statistical Package of the Social Sciences

(SPSS, 22.0) for Windows was used to perform descriptive statistics and inferential statistics. Secondly, a close examination and intensive content analysis of the pertinent documents were conducted. Moreover, the individual interviews were analysed by thematic analysis using the NVivo 9 trial version to identify categories relevant to the initial washback predictions and to provide deeper insights into the quantitative findings. Finally, the different types of data sources were cross-examined and joint displayed. The qualitative analyses findings helped to explain and expand the quantitative findings.

Presentation of results

Quantitative results

The questionnaire was used to measure the learners' learning strategies applied in regular learning and HSK test-specific learning in the four skills (speaking, listening, reading and writing). Under each skill, there are three sub-items questions/statements (two cognitive and one metacognitive item). The differences between the learners' learning practices (strategies and methods) used in the two learning types in the four learning skills were tested with a paired-sample t-test. Series comparisons were followed to find out where the differences are. An examination of the data results which is shown in Table 3 found statistically significant differences between 'regular learning' and 'HSK test-specific learning' in speaking (t (59) = −2.38, p = .020), listening (t (59) = −3.28, p = .002), reading (t (59) = −4.27, p < .001), writing (t (59) = −2.95, p = .005) and in total (t (59) = −3.32, p = .002). Therefore, overall, it indicates that there are washback effects of the HSK on learning.

Based on the previous research findings of factors mediating washback effects, nine language-learning variables were selected as potential predictors of washback effects of HSK from the test takers' perspective in the current

Table 3 Summary results for paired t tests of washback effects on learners' learning by skill

Variable	95% CI		Mean test-specific	Mean regular	df	t	p	Effect size
	Lower	Upper						
Speaking	−.38	−.03	2.29	2.48	59	−2.38	.020*	.27
Listening	−.44	−.11	2.31	2.58	59	−3.28	.002*	.38
Reading	−.55	−.19	2.07	2.44	59	−4.27	.000**	.56
Writing	−.31	−.01	2.61	2.78	59	−2.95	.005*	.22
Total	−.31	−.8	2.32	2.52	59	−3.32	.002*	.35

Note: df = differential, t = t-test statistic, p = significance value, p < .05 *; p < .001 **

study. These features are: gender, nationality, age, how long they have been learning Chinese, purpose of learning Chinese, purpose of taking HSK, type of courses taken, language proficiency, HSK performance and motivation.

In order to explore the significant factors contributing to the washback effects of the HSK, a multiple regression analysis was applied. Table 4 below reveals a significant model for the dependent variable, F (5, 54) =2.64, p = .014. It is found that nationality (β = .31, p = .05), language proficiency (β = 0.41, p = .05), HSK performance (β = .34, p = .01) and motivation (β = −.49, p = .002) were significant predictors. However, gender, age, the time of learning Chinese, purpose of learning Chinese and type of Chinese course were not significant predictors. Since motivation is the only factor (of the nine) with continuous data, it is found that the more motivated learner is more likely to change their learning practices or learning beliefs. The overall model fit was adjusted R^2 = .34. That is to say, these nine features contribute 34% to the independent variable, which is the washback effect.

The results of questions concerning the test takers' view about the nature and content of the HSK show that most of the participants agreed that the HSK test measures test takers' communicative competence and language abilities and that HSK score reports inform the test takers of their strengths and weaknesses. Meanwhile, 86.6% of the participants believed that the test pays too much attention to assessing test takers' linguistic knowledge (e.g. vocabulary, grammar rules and sentence structures), and that the test needs some improvement.

The results of questions related to the test takers' perspective on the HSK's influence on CSL learning and teaching show that the HSK test has potential washback effects. In the matter of learning, 70% of the

Table 4 Summary results for multiple regression model for the predictor variables

	B	SE	β	t	p
Gender	−.07	.12	−.07	−.53	.60
Nationality	.29	.15	.31	2.01	.05*
Age	.16	.11	.24	1.45	.15
How long they have learned Chinese	−.03	.09	−.05	−.29	.77
Purpose of learning Chinese	.06	.06	.14	1.08	.29
Purpose of taking HSK	−.09	.06	−.22	−1.75	.09
Type of Chinese course	.06	.05	−.18	−1.29	.20
Language proficiency	.18	.09	.30	1.98	.05*
HSK performance	.65	.24	.34	2.70	.01*
Motivation	−.21	.06	−.49	−3.34	.002*

Note: B = un-standardised beta coefficient, SE = standard error, β = standardised beta coefficient, t = t-test statistic, p = significance value, $p \leq .05*$

participants showed positive washback in reporting that the HSK test helps them adjust their learning strategies and leads to success in future Chinese learning. In contrast, more people believed that it encourages memorisation of vocabulary and grammar rules instead of use of language for communicative purposes. This can be seen as negative washback. Concerning teaching approaches, interviewees hold different opinions, for example, half of them thought the test would motivate teachers to improve their teaching methodology.

Qualitative data

The washback effects of the HSK

In general, according to the interviews, various degrees of washback (negative, positive and neutral) were found on learning among the participants. Most of the interviewees from Asian countries had spent much time and energy on preparing for the HSK, whereas Westerners spent less time preparing. Table 5 presents the general background of the participants.

When asked the question 'Did taking the HSK change your learning behaviors (both in the classroom and after-school contexts)?' one of the interviewees who studied the CSL course in a Chinese university described the differences of learning attitudes between Eastern and Western CSL learners, and provided an example of negative washback.

> S6: During my daily study/learning, I used to practice [more] speaking and writing, for example, talking with Chinese speaking student, writing diaries. [Because] the text content is to some extent different with what I put particular emphasis on, then while preparing for the HSK, my classmates, especially those from Korea and Japan, they learn Chinese by memorizing word lists and doing mock/practice exams. I followed their strategies and passed level 5 with a good score. After that, I forgot most of the vocabulary and lost the drive to learn Chinese.

Similarly, S2 holds similar views about the HSK, but from a different angle. Because of the test-driven culture in Korea and other East Asian countries, not only is most course content driven by exams, but also teachers' and students' attention is focused on the content that will be tested in the exams. S2 indicated that his experience of learning Chinese was greatly pressured by his Korean classmates, teachers and parents. Moreover, he expressed that it is hard to make connections between tasks and the university setting in China that they were preparing to enter.

S5, however, saw the effect of the HSK on learning in a more positive

Table 5 General information on the interview participants

	S1	S2	S3	S4	S5	S6	S7	S8
Gender	M	M	F	M	F	M	F	M
Countries	Canada	Korea	Korea	Japan	Canada	Canada	Korea	Italy
Age	25–34	18–24	25–34	34–45	45+	18–24	25–34	25–34
Years learning Chinese	4	3	2	2.5	<1	2.5	5	4
HSK level	Int.	Adv.	Int.	Int.	Ele.	Adv.	Adv.	Int.
Chinese course type	Confucius Institute	University CSL programme	HSK preparation course	Weekend language school	Self-learning	University CSL programme	University CSL programme	University CSL programme

Note: S = Student/Learner, Ele = Elementary, Int. = Intermediate, and Adv. = Advanced.

light. In contrast to the perceptions of other learners, S5 explained the impact of the HSK in a different way.

> S5: I have been learning Chinese for only half a year. I think it is a great experience taking the HSK. It is harder than what I thought before I took it. Because in the next level, there will be Chinese characters involved rather than just [Pinyin]. I will devote more energy to learning the characters. It is good for reading and writing. It motivates to enhance the proficiency in Chinese. You know your strengths and weaknesses, and then you strengthen that aspect. It is good for students.

This view showed that passing the HSK was not only a milestone in students' CSL learning, but also for some served as an impetus for their later studies.

What is the participant's view of the HSK?

Some interviewees believed that the HSK was valid and reliable, whereas others had neutral or negative perspectives on these issues. Participating students believed that the HSK was seen as a credible test in the public view. However, they still pointed out several issues and problems with the test. The following comments illustrate the participants' general opinion.

> S6: I think the most important thing in learning a language is the 'communicative' ability. The HSK doesn't even have a speaking task, and the majority of the test tasks are in the form of multiple choice (MC).
> Interviewer: HSK has a separate spoken test, didn't you know?
> S6: Really? I did not know that. I might have a try sometime later.

Questioning the validity of the HSK, S6 raised the issue of multiple-choice (MC) questions. In fact, a number of researchers (e.g. Alderson 2004, Hughes 2003, Shih 2007) have disapproved of MC questions in testing language skills. In addition, much evidence indicates that test takers can be coached in answering MC questions. The test scores therefore are not commensurate with language proficiency. There was a revision of the HSK in 2009. The new HSK has a speaking test, but only a few people are aware of this change.

> Interviewer: What did you think about the HSK, for example in terms of its content and the structure?
> S7: I hope the HSK can have different versions for different purposes. The current version could serve as a general-purpose test, and if people want to go to China to study, they could take the academic-purpose exams. . . . the HSK focuses on input but lack output. For example, there is no speaking part; also, the writing part is very easy and short.

In general, the participants thought that the test fairly and accurately reflected their proficiency levels. Of the eight participants, six felt that the test generally reflected their abilities, but the scores they received in the test were higher than their actual performance level. The other two learners experienced frustration about the mismatch of their usual class performance compared to their test performance (test performances are lower than in class), which fuelled their scepticism about the ability of the test to accurately reflect their language abilities. S8 suggested that a mismatch between ability level and test result could be attributed to nervousness and stress.

Participants perceived several advantages once they were HSK-certified, ranging from increased self-confidence to securing an edge over their competitors when applying for jobs. The first advantage a majority of participants could foresee was that the HSK certificate would be the badge of their Chinese proficiency. With respect to job opportunities, as S4 claimed, his company in Japan prefers to hire employees who know the Chinese language for potential internationalisation. Similarly, passing the HSK would also favour those students who applied for further studies in China. As S2 shared earlier in this section, the HSK certificate could facilitate people being admitted to undergraduate programmes in a Chinese university.

Discussion

After an analysis of all the data sets concerning the washback effects of the HSK on learning, I chose to discuss the most salient results that correspond to the global research question and the three secondary research questions.

The washback effects on learners

A significant finding from the survey is that there were washback effects of the HSK on learning behaviours. The HSK generates various degrees of washback on different individuals. In line with Alderson and Wall's (1993) observation that 'tests can be powerful determiners, both positive and negative' (1993:117), my results show that the HSK had a favourable impact on some learners but negative effects on others.

In terms of positive effects, taking the HSK benefits learners' motivation for learning Chinese and helps them understand their own learning needs. The qualitative data supports the quantitative findings as learners referred to the impact of the HSK to measure their strengths and weaknesses, justify their learning practices and motivate them to learn more. For some students, achieving a high score on the exam or passing the exam is a driving force for learning.

The high stakes of the HSK draws CSL learners' attention to their own learning. As Gardner (2012) clearly stated, 'assessment is our focus but learning is our goal' (2012:2). Although we are focused on assessment outcomes the main aim is to learn the language so assessment should support learning. Assessment for learning can help learners discern where they are and where they need to go in their learning. As S7 said, HSK could help learners to find out their language level and the strengths and weaknesses of their language abilities. It could be seen as a feedback tool for language learning. Being able to recognise one's current level and also being willing to take future steps is a clear sign that the learner's agency is activated, and a test is seen as part of the learning continuum.

Nevertheless, there are some negative effects of the HSK, such as encouraging memorisation of vocabulary and grammar rules instead of practising real-life language abilities. It forces the test takers to focus on test-taking strategies instead of content, thus leading students to forget vocabulary and grammar rules after the test. This, in turn, leads CSL teachers to focus on a structured teaching approach which neglects communicative competence, a significant goal of CSL. In addition, the lack of a mandatory spoken component makes the test less relevant to measuring students' communicative language skills. The inclusion of a compulsory speaking component in HSK could strengthen the development of communicative competence proficiency. Not only could it promote learners' interest in building up oral communicative abilities in and outside the classroom, but it can also help the learners apply the skill in real-life situations.

How does the HSK affect learning?

As discussed earlier, four significant predictors of the washback regression model are found: language proficiency, HSK performance, motivation and nationality. That is to say, these factors contribute to the change of learning strategies/practice used in regular Chinese learning as opposed to test-specific learning. For example, the washback effects on Asian CSL learners are more significant than Western CSL learners and Asian CSL learners are more like to learn to the test. The interview data also shows a great difference in learning beliefs and practices between Asian CSL learners and Western CSL learners.

As Little (2007) noted, the ability to take charge of one's own learning characterises learning autonomy. Independent or autonomous language learning has mainly been associated with Western and tertiary educational settings; it is sometimes perceived to be more problematic in an Asian context (Lamb 2004). While warning against stereotyping 'Asian learners', Littlewood (1999) suggested that socialisation practices in family and school inevitably influence learners' attitudes and responses to academic freedom, and therefore different types of learning autonomy may be suited to Asian educational contexts.

In order to investigate the deep reasons underlying the differences between East and West, here I highlight the characteristics of Asian students and the Asian test-driven context. The East Asian educational system is examination driven. One typical example is that almost all Korean participants in this research were aware of the overwhelming washback effects of the HSK. Under such an enormous impact, there is no denying that most CSL teachers would teach to the test and students would learn to the test. This may be attributed to the time-honoured Confucian tradition of the role played by testing in Asian countries. Confucius, who is acclaimed as the greatest thinker and educator in ancient China, has had an enduring impact on teaching and learning in East Asia for centuries. With this influence of Confucius and the Imperial Examination[4] (also called the Civil Service Examination), a test provides opportunities for individuals to climb the ladder of social status. Nowadays, exams play an equally important role in society. Test scores are viewed both as a marker of students' academic success, and as the premise to their future career. In other words, academic achievement leads to better job opportunities and higher social status.

The impact of the HSK

It should be noted that there was a debate among the test takers on the appropriateness of the HSK content. The first position holds that the HSK is well developed in the sense of being practical, scientific, valid and reliable. Compared to the previous version of the HSK, the reformed HSK, with its written part of the test, does require the use of language in real-life tasks. Besides, the difficulty level of the HSK, especially for the elementary levels, is not high, so learners' achievement can be recognised as accurate. The HSK can help boost learners' confidence in learning Chinese and benefits their long-term learning.

The second position, however, criticised the continuous focus on vocabulary and grammar, which indicates the HSK is outdated by comparing it to the other well-known language tests (e.g. *IELTS* and TOEFL). The vocabulary inventory provided in the Official Guide to the HSK test is seen as giving the wrong message to test takers. That is, as long as they have memorised the vocabulary list, they can pass the test. Meanwhile, critics state that there is an overwhelming reliance on MC and discrete-point tasks rather than performance-based question forms. As such, the test has exerted a considerable adverse influence on teaching and learning. As suggested by some learners, some alternative types of testing tasks such as translation, compound dictation, short-answer questions, and writing tasks should be added to the current format of the HSK. Such a modification could mitigate the negative washback of objective tasks of the test on CSL teaching and learning.

In addition, the participants questioned the absence of an oral HSK test. Apart from the mismatch between the *Scales* and the HSK, it is believed that the inclusion of the oral aspect of the language would result in more attention being focused on the practical use of the language by CSL learners and teachers. The chief goal for introducing the Oral HSK, according to the *Scales*, was to increase an emphasis on measuring the students' oral communicative competence. Based on the data described in the previous section, however, the passing rate of the Oral HSK is much lower than the Written HSK. This indicated that CSL students' spoken ability needed to be improved. Moreover, what is controversial is that the Oral HSK is optional and some students do not even know about this independent speaking test. From the perspective of institutions and job markets only the Written HSK is required. Consequently, the number of the Oral HSK test takers in this study was much lower than those who took the Written HSK and the passing rate of the Oral HSK was low as well. Thus test construction reform is needed.

Implications

This study points to implications for the HSK test developers, CSL teachers and CSL learners.

Implications for test developers

One implication of this study is that in future revisions of the test, HSK developers might give serious thought to whether positive washback might be enhanced by increasing the range of task types and other performance conditions; that is to further improve both its context and construct validity. Consideration needs to be given to making answers less predictable by varying the type and format of the tasks and by broadening the range of topics covered and the text types required in the tasks. This also should add relevance to the test because test stakeholders would be able to see the relationship between the testing activities and the potential language use in real life. Test relevance could also be improved by incorporating interactive testing methods and testing integrative skills that are used in daily communications. These changes could lead to more positive washback effects and a beneficial cycle among learning, teaching, and testing, with testing as a pivotal mediating role in the cycle.

Furthermore, as Huang and Li (2010) stated, the interpretation of scores on the HSK test needs to be more accessible, scientific and comprehensive. Score reports are one of the washback processes and provide direct feedback of the test takers' performance; they also serve as the medium for delivering the information to all the score users in the washback processes. Such feedback could help the learners and teachers discover their strengths and weaknesses and guide them in improving their learning or teaching methods.

Implications for students and teachers

As Shohamy (1993) pointed out, 'external tests are currently used to force students to study, teachers to teach, and principals to modify the curriculum' (1993:513). Although mastering vocabulary and grammar rules plays a major role in the HSK preparation, other aspects of language abilities cannot be ignored, particularly for the CSL learners who plan to pursue their higher education in China. The results of this study suggest that if CSL learners are to be adequately prepared for academic study in China, passing a specific level of the written HSK is not sufficient. Only by recognising the limitations of the HSK in this regard, will learners be able to make better informed choices about how to prepare themselves for university study. The HSK should not be the only element in this preparation.

According to the positive correlation between motivation and test outcomes, CSL teachers should create a supportive and dynamic learning environment by setting clear learning goals (e.g. set passing the HSK at the beginning of the class), fostering learner autonomy, increasing students' self-confidence, and maximising their free choice. In order to motivate themselves to enjoy the continual challenge of improving test results, learners should set clear short-term (e.g. pass a specific level of the HSK) and long-term (e.g. pass all the six levels of the HSK) learning goals, as well as maintain their positive attitudes and confidence.

In addition, due to the results of the strong impact of the job market and learning motivation, CSL teachers should encourage students to possess a global outlook, use critical thinking, and embrace multiple perspectives of languages, cultures, and identity. It is of pedagogical importance to draw lessons from the research findings concerning ESL/EFL teaching and make efforts to combine structural and communicative teaching approaches.

Implications for institutions

For institutions, it may no longer be sufficient to make gate-keeping decisions based on a simple formulaic approach relating to a level or band score of the HSK as happens in most institutions. Washback is a complicated phenomenon and no single policy can guarantee success without any side effects, especially when tests are adopted for high-stake purposes. The Oral HSK certificate should be required as one of the supplementary materials for decision-making. Interpretation of test scores by institutions should be made with full reference to the local context. The consideration of available support mechanisms in a particular institution, from CSL programmes to tutorial support, should be balanced against the demands of a particular course with regard to the academic-oriented learning. The institutions should understand that the international student experience would be enhanced if ongoing language support could be provided to help students become a part of the academic discourse community.

In conclusion, this study is unique in that it explored the relationships between CSL learners' factors and the HSK test using an MMR design. Both quantitative and qualitative data demonstrated the complexity of the washback processes that affect learning processes. The quantitative data makes generalisations about contributing factors, while the qualitative data offered more in-depth and detailed information about the learners' perceptions of the impact of the test. The analysis showed that it is important to make future improvements to the HSK that will emphasise positive washback and minimise negative washback. This study has enriched and expanded knowledge in washback theory development in second language assessment, and specifically contributes evidence to the validation of the HSK.

Acknowledgements

This study is partially based on my Master's thesis at McGill University, Canada. I greatly appreciated comments from my supervisor Dr Carolyn Turner. I would like to express my appreciation to all the contributing CSL learners who took the time to provide rich data.

Notes

1   Hanban is the colloquial abbreviation for the Chinese National Office for Teaching Chinese as a Foreign Language. It is a non-government and non-profit organisation affiliated with the Ministry of Education of the People's Republic of China. Hanban is most notable for the Confucius Institute programme, but it also sponsors the Chinese Bridge competition, which is a competition in Chinese proficiency for non-native speakers. The mission statement of Hanban: english.hanban.org/node_7880.htm
2   I define regular Chinese learning to include CSL courses, distance learning, or self-learning on a daily basis.
3   Test-specific learning reflects participants' learning largely on the basis of the test's impact and includes all the learning beliefs, strategies and processes that affect success on the HSK, such as learning test-taking strategies and practising simulated exam papers.
4   The Imperial Examination was a civil service examination system in Imperial China to select candidates for the state bureaucracy starting from as early as the Han dynasty. The examination system helped to shape China's intellectual, cultural, and political life.

References

Alderson, J C (2004) Foreword in Cheng, L Y Watanabe, Y and Curtis, A (Eds) *Washback in Language Testing: Research Contexts and Methods*, Mahwah: Lawrence Erlbaum Associates, ix–xii.

Alderson, J C and Hamp-Lyons, L (1996) *TOEFL preparation courses: a study of washback*, *Language Testing* 13, 280–297.

Alderson, J C and Wall, D (1993) Does washback exist? *Applied Linguistics* 14, 115–129.

Andrews, S, Fullilove, J and Wong, Y (2002) Targeting washback – a case-study, *System* 30, 207–223.

Bailey, K M (1996) Working for washback: A review of the washback concept in language testing, *Language Testing* 13, 257–279.

Center for Canadian Language Benchmarks (2012) *Canadian Language Benchmarks English as a Second Language for Adults*, Ottawa.

Chen, C (2009) The authenticity of the HSK and its washback effect, *Chinese Teaching News* 11, 46–48.

Cheng, L(1997) How does washback influence teaching? Implications for Hong Kong, *Language and Education* 11, 38–54.

Cheng, L (1998) Impact of a public English examination change on students' perceptions and attitudes toward their English learning, *Studies in Educational Evaluation* 24, 279–301.

Cheng, L (2005) *Changing Language Teaching Through Language Testing: A Washback Study*, Cambridge: Cambridge University Press.

Cheng, L and Curtis, A (2004) Washback or backwash: a review of the impact of testing on teaching and learning, in Cheng, L, Watanabe Y and Curtis, A (Eds) *Washback in Language Testing*, Mahwah: Lawrence Erlbaum Associates, 3–17.

Creswell, J W and Plano Clark, V L (2011) *Designing and Conducting Mixed Methods Research* (2nd edition), Thousand Oaks: Sage.

Gardner, J (2012) *Assessment and Learning*, London: Sage.

Green, A (2007) Washback to learning outcomes: A comparative study of IELTS preparation and university pre-sessional language courses, *Assessment in Education* 14, 75–97.

Greene, J C (2007) *Mixed Methods in Social Inquiry*, San Francisco: Jossey-Bass.

Hanyu Shuiping Kaoshi (2015) *Wikipedia*, available online: en.wikipedia.org/wiki/Hanyu_Shuiping_Kaoshi#Estimates_of_equivalent_CEFR_levels

Huang, C and Li, G (2010) Washback effect of HSK on teaching Chinese as a second language, *Chinese Examination* 11, 26–32.

Hughes, A (1993) *Backwash and TOEFL 2000*, unpublished manuscript, University of Reading.

Hughes, A (2003) *Testing for Language Teachers* (2nd edition), Cambridge: Cambridge University Press.

Lamb, M (2004) "It depends on the student themselves": Independent language learning at an Indonesian state school, *Language, Culture and Curriculum* 17, 229–245.

Little, D (2007) Language learner autonomy: Some fundamental considerations revisited, *Innovation in Language Learning and Teaching* 1, 14–29.

Littlewood, W (1999) Defining and developing autonomy in East Asian contexts, *Applied Linguistics* 20, 71–94.

Luo, M, Zhang, J, Xie, O and Huang, H (2011) Report on overseas enforcement of new Chinese Proficiency Test (New HSK), *China Examinations* 4, 17–21.

Messick, S (1996) Validity and washback in language testing, *Language Testing* 13, 241–256.

Office of Chinese Language Council International (2009) *Chinese Language Proficiency Scales For Speakers of Other Languages*, Beijing: Foreign Language Teaching and Research Press.

Office of Chinese Language Council International (2010) *Chinese Language Proficiency Test Levels 1 to 6*, Beijing: The Commercial Press.

Phakiti, A (2003) A closer look at the relationship of cognitive and metacognitive strategy use to EFL reading achievement test performance, *Language Testing* 20, 26–56.

Shih, C (2007) A new washback model of students' learning, *The Canadian Modern Language Review* 64, 135–162.

Shohamy, E (1993) *The Power of Tests: The Impact of Language Tests on Teaching and Learning*, Washington, DC: NFLC Occasional Papers.

Shohamy, E, Donitsa-Schmidt, S and Ferman, I (1996) Test impact revisited: Washback effect over time, *Language Testing* 13, 298–317.

Turner, C E (2009) Examining washback in second language education contexts: A high stakes provincial exam and the teacher factor in classroom practice in Quebec secondary schools, *International Journal of Pedagogies and Learning* 5, 103–123.

Wall, D (2000) The impact of high-stakes testing on teaching and learning: can this be predicted or controlled? *System* 28, 499–509.

Watanabe, Y (2004) Methodology in washback studies, in Cheng, L Watanabe, Y and Curtis, A (Eds) *Washback in Language Testing: Research Contexts and Methods*, Mahwah: Lawrence Erlbaum Associates, 19–36.

21 From monolingual to bilingual through testing: The OPENPAU Project (FFI2011-22442)

Jesús García Laborda
Mary Frances Litzler
Universidad de Alcalá

Abstract

Teachers in Spain have long criticised the effect of language testing in their classrooms. For example, García Laborda and Fernández Álvarez (2012) discuss the reactions of teachers from Navarre (northern Spain) and Madrid towards the country's current University Entrance Examination (*Prueba de Acceso a la Universidad*, henceforth, PAU), the most important high-stakes test in the country. The exam has no speaking or listening tasks, and the teachers feel that this format impedes development of oral skills. Although the potentially positive impact of including speaking and listening tasks (Alderson and Wall 1993, Hughes 1989) is one of the main reasons for changing the PAU, the delivery and rubrics of the components must first be designed (García Laborda and Martin-Monje 2013). The main goal of this paper is to address what has been done in the last year in relation to these issues. Some of the results of research carried out through the OPENPAU project in Spain, which emphasises the application of technology to individual and paired/group testing, are described here. The paper concludes that the use of low-cost technology for the test may have a very positive impact on the Spanish educational system. It also suggests that the integration of speaking tasks at the end of different educational cycles can also have a potentially positive washback effect (Wall 2000, Wall and Alderson 1993).

Introduction

As in many other countries around the world, people regard English highly in Spain for its value in commerce, media and work. Administrators, parents and students feel that one of the most important outcomes required by the end of secondary school is mastery of English (Breeze and Roothooft 2014).

The level of foreign language proficiency required changes from one educational region to another, but a general aim in Spain is for students to achieve the level of B2 on the Common European Framework of Reference (CEFR, Council of Europe 2001) upon completion of secondary school (Ashton, Salamoura and Diaz 2012).

Nevertheless, the results of international surveys show that, despite intense efforts made by the different national and regional educational administrations, Spanish students lag behind most other European countries in knowledge and use of English as a Foreign Language. For instance, according to the First European Survey on Language Competences (European Commission 2012), Spanish students begin to learn foreign languages at the age of 6, when they begin their compulsory education, but at the age of 15 as many as 32% of the students have only achieved a pre-A1 level in listening comprehension and 15% show this level in written expression (Figure 1).

This data may reflect the limited attention that listening skills receive in the classroom for students through the age of 15 (the end of compulsory secondary education in Spain) (García Laborda and Fernández Álvarez 2011). However, additional factors may also have a negative effect on the learning

Figure 1 Percentage of students achieving broad CEFR levels by skill and country/educational system (First target language)

Educational system	Language	Reading			Listening			Writing		
		Pre-A1	A	B	Pre-A1	A	B	Pre-A1	A	B
Bulgaria	English	23	43	34	23	37	40	15	52	32
Croatia	English	16	44	40	12	32	56	5	49	45
Estonia	English	7	33	60	10	27	63	3	37	60
Flemish Community of Belgium	French	12	63	24	17	62	20	19	59	22
France	English	28	59	13	41	46	14	24	61	16
French Community of Belgium	English	10	59	31	18	55	27	6	65	29
German Community of Belgium	French	10	52	38	11	49	40	8	51	41
Greece	English	15	40	45	19	35	46	7	41	53
Malta	English	4	17	79	3	11	86	0	17	83
Netherlands	English	4	36	60	3	21	77	0	39	60
Poland	English	27	49	24	27	45	28	19	59	23
Portugal	English	20	53	26	23	39	38	18	55	27
Slovenia	English	12	42	47	5	28	67	1	51	48
Spain	English	18	53	29	32	44	24	15	58	27
Sweden	English	1	18	81	1	9	91	0	24	75

Source: First European Survey on Language Competences (SurveyLang 2012:92)

of the language, such as the correlation between literacy in the L1 and L2 (Ganschow 1991), overuse of the first language in the classroom (Atkinson 1987), differences between the mother tongue and the foreign language (Chang 2009, Hutzler, Ziegler, Perry, Wimmer and Zorzi 2004), and others that make the learning of English harder for Romance language speakers than for other Europeans whose languages have a Germanic origin. While these issues may justify in part the fact that Spanish students find learning English problematic, the objective of the European Union for its citizens to speak at least two foreign languages by 2020 requires an urgent and robust solution.

Testing as a catalyst for change

There has been extensive debate over the impact of testing on the capacity to trigger learning (Green 2007, Nemati 2003, Perrone 2011, Spratt 2005) and on teachers' attitudes to teaching methodologies and materials (Cheng 1997, 1999, Turner 2006), both of which areas fall under the concept of 'washback' (Alderson and Wall 1993). García Laborda and Fernández Álvarez (2012) asked teachers when they felt their schools should begin specific instruction for speaking tasks if the PAU were to begin including them. The study revealed that some teachers thought that preparation should begin up to four years in advance. The research team was perplexed at this amount of time that would be devoted specifically to preparation for test tasks as opposed to opportunities for genuine learning.

If the test really were to have such a powerful influence, could the recent introduction of external English exams which include speaking tasks possibly trigger the introduction or reinforcement of speaking skills by most teachers and thus provide an indication of the effect of introducing a speaking component in PAU? External exams are currently being used in the relatively new state bilingual schools in the Madrid region (Dobson, Pérez Murillo and Johnstone 2010). The programme is especially strong at the primary level and consists of nine to 11 hours per week of instruction in content (typically maths and science) and language classes taught in the target language, which is often English. One of the most important activities to promote this programme is success on external language tests at the end of the sixth year. In general, schools prefer that their students take either Trinity or Cambridge English tests. Although the idea is motivating for students, it is even more so for parents, who are happy to see their children pass official tests. In fact, many parents seem to feel the level of an official exam is less important than the grade or mark obtained. In other words, a 'pass' on the *Cambridge English: Preliminary* (also known as *Preliminary English Test (PET)*), a test at the B1 level of the CEFR, is considered much the same as a 'pass' on the *Cambridge English: Key* (also known as *Key English Test (KET)*), at the A2 level, and a high mark in a lower proficiency level may even be viewed in a better light than a lower one on a more demanding test. Nevertheless, the bilingual programme is not without its problems, for instance, some students may not be able to adapt to a bilingual situation, especially in maths and science and may decide to change to regular non-bilingual programmes (Anghel, Cabrales and Carro 2012).

The Spanish Ministerio de Educación (2013, 2014) and other researchers (Spratt 2005) suggest that tests taken during the primary school period, especially external ones, may have a positive effect in developing positive washback. That is, they seem to impact classroom practice for the better, first by changing teachers' instructional practices and second by increasing motivation for achievement. However, more work is needed to determine how tests can potentially foster language acquisition at the secondary level. Possibilities for researching this level will increase as the bilingual programme is expanded in the coming years.

Towards an adequate testing procedure: The OPENPAU project work in progress

The OPENPAU project was funded by the Spanish Ministry of Education in 2010 (it has been administered by the Ministry of Science and Innovation from 2011). Its main goal is to obtain information on how to improve language results through the testing of 15 to 17-year-old students in post-secondary education in Spain and to suggest ways to improve the current situation. One of the most important parts is the design of a technology-delivered test.

In 2010, 22 researchers from 10 different universities in Spain and another from the US participating in the OPENPAU project were assigned different tasks, including a needs analysis, an analysis of the current situation in English classrooms, and a review of technology for exam delivery. A group of psychometricians also participated when required. The major outcomes of the needs analysis were detailed in an earlier paper (García Laborda and Martin-Monje 2013) and the findings of the second phase of work were presented at the ALTE conference in Paris. This section will address two main issues: the current situation in English classrooms in Spain and three proposals for delivery of the test.

The English language classroom in Spain today

In order to investigate the current situation in English classrooms in Spain, the following activities were undertaken. Forty native speakers of English working in the Madrid region as conversation assistants who were also studying towards a Master's degree in Bilingual Education or in International

Education were asked to report on their experience in schools. They reported their impressions as part of a teaching portfolio completed in partial fulfilment of the Master's degree programme. The two cohorts of 20 subjects each (one for each Master's programme) provided the following information for the Madrid area. Additional information on the rest of Spain was obtained from 27 co-ordinators of the University Entrance Exam who completed an online survey to point out problems detected in the exam. The results revealed by these different groups are summarised below.

Spain's foreign language classrooms have seen the arrival of an increasing number of native English speakers as conversation assistants, most of whom are assigned to the primary school level. In general, they lack language teaching skills and their previous experience is very limited, as the only educational requirement is to have a university degree. In addition, they often have limited knowledge of linguistics and language learning processes, and are only provided with an orientation of a few days' duration before starting at their schools. Interaction between conversation assistants and individual classes of students can be limited to 1 hour a week per group as some schools have only one conversation assistant for the entire school, which may have as many as 600 students. The target language speakers often support the teaching of Social and Earth Sciences and English language but they are not limited to doing so and sometimes they have to support teachers in subjects in which they have not specialised. Given the situation described in general here, there is often a gap between their preparation and their responsibilities, what they are expected to do and what they have been trained to do.

A second issue that was observed is that there is limited stimulation of actual language use through interaction due to discipline problems in the classroom. Many teachers must focus more attention on controlling their students' behaviour than on practising the language. Students have a tendency to talk amongst themselves and can even get up out of their seats during classroom explanations so many teachers find that they frequently need to call their groups to order. In addition, it is not unusual for teachers of other subjects to complain that there is 'too much noise in the school', so teachers tend to avoid extensive speaking activities in class. Student claims that their classes are taught in Spanish were also common, but the research team felt that this situation was becoming more unusual.

Related to this issue is the avoidance of pair and group exercises due to a lack of control of what goes on in the different groups around the classroom. With as many as 35 students in a classroom, it is impossible to monitor the different groups at all times. This kind of interaction is also avoided to assess speaking since most teachers would opt to do individual tests with their students, but their time is limited and they are unable to do so.

Another issue that has been seen is the discrepancy between what teachers assess and what students actually do in class. While classes do tend to be progressively communicative, teachers still often follow a textbook and workbook in their day-to-day lessons due to pressures to complete them from administrators and parents who have paid for them. Teachers in both private and public schools still often overuse grammar or discrete point tests. On many occasions, teachers were observed to use textbook tests despite incorporating more communicative activities in their classrooms.

Due to these factors students over-regulate their language production on tests as well as in real-life situations. In general, they feel uncomfortable and are unsure about their ability to apply correct grammar and vocabulary and to pronounce the language well in spoken interaction. They also demonstrate a high level of anxiety about external exams.

In terms of test performance and behaviour, a sub-study within this project revealed that the PAU co-ordinators observed in internal reports student difficulties in doing the PAU. When they write, students tend not to read the rubric properly, they interpret the wording of the questions literally, are unable to recognise the text type, cannot identify appropriate introductions or conclusions, and do not know how to organise their essays. The research team of this project also found in a mock-PAU speaking test, that the students tended to translate literally, did not parse what they were saying, and showed limited use of vocabulary to describe pictures. They also had difficulties in turn taking, showing interest, and expressing disagreement, etc. (i.e. communicative functions). At the same time, they did not listen actively to the examiner or their partner, and they lacked adequate content and form in their responses.

A Delphi study to improve language learning through testing

In order to improve this situation, a group of nine experts were asked to do a Delphi analysis to provide proposals to improve foreign language learning in Spain through testing. The Delphi Method is a systematic and interactive method in which a panel of experts answer a questionnaire in several rounds (generally between two and three) based on the other experts' responses and opinions on the same questionnaire. As a result, they must read the other participants' replies each time before answering the following time (Rowe and Wright 1999). In this case, the researchers suggested a list of questions, the nine experts responded individually and then their responses were sent to all the other experts. Afterwards, an online video conference was held. The original questions posed were as follows:

- How can tests benefit Spanish students' development of language skills?
- How can tests help students to improve their speaking/writing skills?
- What activities should the research group do to carry out the project?

The experts' individual comments and suggestions led to the following outcomes:

- compulsory speaking tests should be introduced (García Laborda and Fernández Álvarez 2012)
- specific in-class preparation and training for testing skills should be reduced as previous experience has shown highly negative washback involving considerable emphasis on grammar
- teacher training for speaking must be improved (Fernández Álvarez and García Laborda 2011, García Laborda 2013)
- a speaking construct and standards for performance required to achieve the ideal level should be defined (García Laborda 2010)
- consideration should be given to moving away from the current cognitivist paradigm in which students are asked to provide evidence of language knowledge rather than a capacity to communicate in the foreign language (Bejarano, Otero de Juan and García Laborda 2013, Canagarajah 2006)
- a social-constructivist/interactionist approach should be introduced and it should specifically emphasise interaction and mutual support between/among test takers
- the ICT tools to be used should be decided (García Laborda, Magal Royo, Litzler and Giménez López 2014).

The online meeting led to the following conclusions, which were later forwarded to the Ministry of Education. Specifically, the test construct, impact, delivery and testing sessions need to be revised. The test construct should include three speaking and two listening tasks in addition to the already existing exam format. The three speaking tasks represent what the experts considered the most important aspects of a student's use of a foreign language: dialogues about personal issues, presentations followed by questions, and organisation acts such as preparing for a meeting or exam, etc. The listening tasks should address monologue comprehension (i.e. a teacher's class presentation) and a social situation. These tasks are in line with Bygate (1999) and Weir (1993), who consider them informational and interactional functions.

It was also emphasised that there should be a continuous push towards speaking in class and the inclusion of speaking in tests starting in the primary level in order to increase their impact on learning. The tests should be required at the end of the second, fourth, sixth, tenth and twelfth years. Nevertheless, teaching for the tests should be avoided. In terms of delivery, the speaking tasks for the PAU should be done in pairs by two examiners. This could be done in person or online through the use of tablet PCs or netbooks. The speaking interviews should be limited to pair tests lasting a maximum of 15 minutes. If the delivery is done online, the productive time should be about 5 to 6 minutes per person.

A SWOT analysis for a speaking test for the PAU

A SWOT analysis of the potential inclusion of a speaking test as part of the PAU was also completed in this analysis phase of the project (see Table 1).

Table 1 presents the SWOT analysis drawn up by several participants in the Delphi analysis, three external experts and the research team. The strengths are related to the potential to meet the demands of both teachers and students to create and assess speaking skills in the PAU (and other tests) and the adequacy of the test construct for the purpose (face validity), washback (impact validity) and delivery. The weaknesses include a lack of teaching experience in teaching for a new test (as in the case of Saif 2006), which leads to a need for training and specific preparation in technology both for teachers and for students (Akinwamide 2012). The new test would have a positive effect on curriculum changes introduced as a result of a new educational law recently passed in Spain, and it would lead to new ways of teaching and learning for teachers and better learning and external certification of knowledge for students. These opportunities could potentially be jeopardised by problems in learning required for the test, abuse of teaching for the test, stakeholder difficulties in understanding the benefits of external and internal assessments (the culture of testing), student unwillingness to adapt to technology-delivered tests or to group tests, the overuse or excessive potential of tests to affect decisions (negative washback), and the difficulties intrinsic to the increasing importance of implementation of new skills in the process in foreign language learning.

Proposals for delivery

One of the most significant issues in planning the future University Entrance Examination is delivery (Figure 2). As mentioned above, one idea is to have

Table 1 SWOT analysis

Strengths:	Weaknesses:
1. Teachers' interest in improving their classes	1. Teaching resources
2. Students' motivation to improve	2. Teaching methods
3. Testing construct and FL learning	3. Teacher training
4. Ways of delivery	4. ICT issues
Opportunities:	**Threats:**
1. Policy-makers: Accountancy	1. Cultural perspective
2. Teachers' visions of language improvement	2. FL difficulties
3. Students' perceptions of the importance of English	3. Students' volition towards the new testing methods and delivery
	4. Overpowering tests (negative washback)

Figure 2 Delivery modes of PAU test

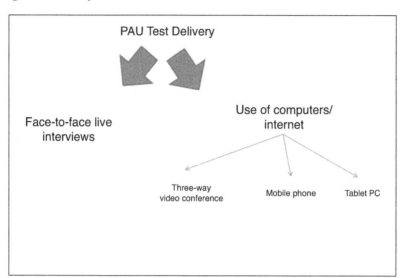

group interviews in face-to-face situations while another is to integrate computer and internet technologies in the test. While the latter suggestion relates to the use of tablet PCs and mobile phones, both possibilities could be done through the use of Voice-over-Internet-Protocol (VOIP) programs such as Skype, Tango or Viber.

While the first two of these computer applications, tablet PCs and mobile phones, are viewed by the research team to be more efficient in terms of practicality, and facilitate and trigger individual production, videoconferencing could be optimal if factors such as support, body language, language interaction and others are taken into account; all of these aspects of communication provide a more complete view of the speaker's communicative competence in oral situations. In terms of organisation, the first two applications are considered slightly better than the third but the research team also thinks that organisation of a VOIP video conference should not be problematic in high-stakes testing if Ministry secured lines are used. It is also recommended that students should be supervised by their own teachers or that other security methods – such as outside invigilators – should be set up to avoid potential cheating. The cost of delivery was another aspect also taken into consideration by the research team. Technological applications involve a design cost and mobile testing requires hardware, but VOIP technology is almost free even if a subscription rate for private channels is paid. For example, Skype allows videoconferencing from three or more computers for free, so two test takers and the examiner(s) would be able to see each other during the test session. In terms of internet security, mobile phones and tablets both require strong protection against any kind of attack, while in the case of VOIP many of the measures used to protect online platforms could be simplified because the test items are delivered in real time.

Conclusion

In conclusion, the research team members believe that testing can lead to improvement in language learning as reported for the Sri Lanka project in Wall (2006), who mentions improved teaching methodologies, development of the neglected skills of speaking and listening, a revision of the legal mechanisms to improve teaching quality, a revision of classroom practices, and so on. The researchers also feel that the use of mobile ICT technology can foster ongoing practice in and out of the classroom, as described in Towndrow and Wan (2012) and Chen, Chang and Wang (2008). At the same time, the methods suggested in the present paper can facilitate assessment of a large number of candidates by using paired interviews (or 3-person groupings) (Valk, Rashid and Elder 2010). In addition, the continuous practice of speaking needed to achieve a level potentially required to pass a test can lead to acquisition of the language (Muñoz and Álvarez 2010). As a consequence, teachers may change their practices and methods (Spratt 2005).

Future steps in the OPENPAU project include the design of new types of collaborative tasks for all four skills, in particular, co-operative writing, and the application of social networking to language testing. The project will finish by the end of 2015. The changes recommended by the research team may have political implications, such as better indicators and information for educational policy-makers and teachers and increased European labour integration, as suggested in Prapphal (2008). In conclusion, the introduction of language tests in general education, especially in post-compulsory education, can benefit the whole system and its different stakeholders, be they students, teachers or administrators. We feel, as the title of this paper indicates, that tests with communicative oral tasks delivered using new technologies will lead to a higher level of bilingualism throughout the country in the coming years. As oral tests are included throughout the different years of compulsory education, a greater emphasis will be placed on oral skills in the classroom. The end result will be better productive ability on the part of Spaniards compared to today.

Acknowledgements

The researchers would like to express their gratitude to the Ministry of Economy and Competitiveness (MINECO) for co-founding with ERDF under the 2008–2011 plan for supporting the development and implementation of the OPENPAU project (MINECO FFI2011-22442).

References

Akinwamide, T K (2012) Imperatives of information and communication technology (ICT) for second language learners and teachers, *English Language Teaching* 5 (1), 44–48.

Alderson, J C and Wall, D (1993) Does washback exist? *Applied Linguistics* 14 (2), 115–129.

Anghel, B, Cabrales, A and Carro, J M (2012) Evaluating a bilingual education program in Spain: the impact beyond foreign language learning, *Universidad Carlos Tercero Working Paper* 12–14, available online: he-archivo.uc3m.es/bitstream/handle/10016/14380/we1214.pdf?sequence=1

Ashton, K, Salamoura, A and Diaz, E (2012) The BEDA impact project: A preliminary investigation of a bilingual programme in Spain, *Research Notes* 50, 34–42.

Atkinson, D (1987) The mother tongue in the classroom: A neglected resource? *ELT Journal* 41 (4), 241–247.

Bejarano, L G, Otero de Juan, N and García Laborda, J (2013) Estructura, percepción, factores no-lingüísticos y cuestionamientos de entrevistas OPI en español: Una propuesta de aplicación a la Prueba General de Bachillerato, *Didáctica de la Lengua y Literatura* 25, 67–81.

Breeze, R and Roothooft, H (2014) Teacher perspectives on implementing *Cambridge English: Young Learners* exams in Spanish schools, *Research Notes* 57, 3–13.

Bygate, M (1999) Quality of language and purpose of task: Patterns of learners' language on two oral communication tasks, *Language Teaching Research* 3 (3), 185–214.

Canagarajah, S A (2006) TESOL at forty: What are the issues? *TESOL Quarterly: A Journal for Teachers of English to Speakers of Other Languages and of Standard English as a Second Dialect* 40 (1), 9–34.

Chang, F (2009) Learning to order words: A connectionist model of heavy NP shift and accessibility effects in Japanese and English, *Journal of Memory and Language* 61 (3), 374–397.

Chen, D G, Chang, K C and Wang, Y C (2008) Ubiquitous learning website: Scaffold learners by mobile devices with information-aware techniques, *Computers and Education* 50 (1), 77–90.

Cheng, L (1997) How does washback influence teaching? Implications for Hong Kong, *Language and Education* 11 (1), 38–54.

Cheng, L (1999) Changing assessment: Washback on teacher perceptions and actions, *Teaching and Teacher Education* 15 (3), 253–271.

Council of Europe (2001) *Common European Framework of Reference for Languages: Learning, Teaching, Assessment*, Cambridge: Cambridge University Press.

Dobson, A, Pérez Murillo, M D and Johnstone, R (2010) *Bilingual Education Project Spain. Evaluation Report*, Madrid: Ministerio de Educación.

European Commission (2012) *First European Survey on Language Competences*, available online: ec.europa.eu/languages/policy/strategic-framework/documents/language-survey-final-report_en.pdf

Fernández Álvarez, M and García Laborda, J (2011) Teachers' interest for a computer EFL University Entrance Examination, *British Journal of Educational Technology* 46 (6), E136–140.

Ganschow, L (1991) Identifying native language difficulties among foreign language learners in college: A 'foreign' language learning disability? *Journal of Learning Disabilities* 24 (9), 530–541.

García Laborda, J (2010) ¿Necesitan las universidades españolas una prueba de acceso informatizada? El caso de la definición del constructo y la previsión del efecto en la enseñanza para idiomas extranjeros, *Revista de orientación y Psicopedagogía* 21 (1), 71–80.

García Laborda, J (2013) Reacciones iniciales de los profesores a la preparación de la prueba informatizada de acceso a la universidad, *Lenguaje y Textos* 38, 133–140.

García Laborda, J and Fernández Álvarez, M (2011) Teachers' opinions towards the integration of oral tasks in the Spanish university examination, *International Journal of Language Studies (IJLS)* 5 (3), 1–12.

García Laborda, J and Fernández Álvarez, M (2012) Actitudes de los profesores de Bachillerato de Alcalá y Navarra ante la preparación y efecto de la PAU, *Revista de Educación* 357, 29–54.

García Laborda, J and Martin-Monje, E (2013) Item and test construct definition for the New Spanish High School Leaving Diploma: A proposal, *International Journal of English Studies*, 13 (2), 69–88.

García Laborda, J, Magal Royo, T, Litzler, M F and Giménez López, J L (2014) Mobile phones for a University Entrance Examination language test in Spain, *Educational Technology and Society* 17 (2), 17–30.

Green, A (2007) Washback to learning outcomes: A comparative study of IELTS preparation and university pre-sessional language courses, *Assessment in Education: Principles, Policy and Practice* 14 (1), 75–97.

Hughes A (1989) *Testing for Language Teachers*, Cambridge: Cambridge University Press.

Hutzler, F, Ziegler, J C, Perry, C, Wimmer, H and Zorzi, M (2004) Do current connectionist learning models account for reading development in different languages? *Cognition* 91 (3), 273–296.

Ministerio de Educación (2013) *Presentación explicativa del Proyecto de la LOMCE (17 March 2013)*, available online: www.mecd.gob.es/servicios-al-ciudadano-mecd/ca/dms/mecd/servicios-al-ciudadano-mecd/participacion-publica/lomce/20130517-aprobacion-proyecto-de-ley-nota.pdf

Ministerio de Educación (2014) Los exámenes externos de final de ciclo, *Boletín de Educación* 29, available online: www.fedea.net/docs/educaineeboletin29.pdf

Muñoz, A P and Álvarez, M E (2010) Washback of an oral assessment system in the EFL classroom, *Language Testing* 27 (1), 33–49.

Nemati, M (2003) The positive washback effect of introducing essay writing tests in EFL environments, *Indian Journal of Applied Linguistics* 29 (2), 49–62.

Perrone, M (2011) The effect of classroom-based assessment and language processing on the second language acquisition of EFL students, *Journal of Adult Education* 40 (1), 20–33.

Prapphal, K (2008) Issues and trends in language testing and assessment in Thailand, *Language Testing* 25 (1), 127–143.

Rowe, G and Wright, G (1999) The Delphi technique as a forecasting tool: issues and analysis, *International Journal of Forecasting* 15 (4), 353–375.

Saif, S (2006) Aiming for positive washback: A case study of international teaching assistants, *Language Testing* 23 (1), 1–34.

Spratt, M (2005) Washback and the classroom: The implications for teaching and learning of studies of washback from exams, *Language Teaching Research* 9 (1), 5–29.

SurveyLang (2012) *First European Survey on Language Competences*, available online: ec.europa.eu/languages/policy/strategic-framework/documents/language-survey-final-report_en.pdf, p.92 (last accessed 13 July 2015).

Towndrow, P A and Wan, F (2012) Professional learning during a one-to-one laptop innovation, *Journal of Technology and Teacher Education* 20 (3), 331–355.

Turner, C E (2006) Professionalism and high-stakes tests: Teachers' perspectives when dealing with educational change introduced through provincial exams, *TESL Canada Journal* 23 (2), 54–76.

Valk, J H, Rashid, A T and Elder, L (2010) Using mobile phones to improve educational outcomes: An analysis of evidence from Asia, *International Review of Research in Open and Distance Learning* 11 (1), 117–140.

Wall, D and Alderson, J C (1993) Examining washback: The Sri Lankan impact study, *Language Testing* 10 (1), 41–69.

Wall, D (2000) The impact of high-stakes testing on teaching and learning: can this be predicted or controlled? *System* 28 (4), 499–509.

Wall, D (2006) *The Impact of High-Stakes Examination on Classroom Teaching*, Cambridge: Cambridge University Press.

Weir, C J (1993) *Understanding and Developing Language Tests*, Hemel Hempstead: Prentice Hall.

22 Meeting standards in scoring speaking: Monitoring and improving the quality of examinations in Italian

Giuliana Grego Bolli
CVCL, Università per Stranieri di Perugia

Jane Lloyd
Cambridge English Language Assessment

Danilo Rini
CVCL, Università per Stranieri di Perugia

Abstract

This paper illustrates a specific project run by CVCL (Centro per la Valutazione e le Certificazioni Linguistiche) at the University for Foreigners in Perugia in order to identify and address inconsistencies in raters of high-stakes speaking assessments in Italian. It outlines the challenges of testing speaking and the importance of considering Quality Management processes to ensure tests are valid and fair. As a part of these processes, it discusses management, training and selection of raters, and how quantitative data analysis can be used to inform decision making for positive impact. The paper is also of interest both to language teachers and test providers who need an overview of how simple statistical procedures and practical data collection can be easily applied to their own contexts.

Introduction

Speaking is a fundamental component of overall language proficiency. Nevertheless, compared to the testing of other skills, many assessment organisations have only embarked upon standardised testing of speaking relatively recently. Despite an increased awareness of the value and importance of testing this skill, it is often omitted from national or large-scale tests because of cost, logistical issues, and the amount of training and standardisation required.

Specific theoretical models and descriptive frameworks with practical guidelines are necessary in order to design, develop and administer any valid language test. An added complication is the need for transparency. Examination boards and test providers are required to be accountable for their tests, especially in terms of the standards they refer to, the quality and validity claims they make and the kind of empirical evidence they provide in support of these claims. Assessment of speaking provides additional challenges in terms of the selection, management, training and monitoring of raters. There are further considerations such as the logistics of the exam day or speaking exam period, which may run over several days or weeks. There are issues of security, the time involved, and the cost, all of which are related to the often substantial number of candidates and raters involved. It is by no means straightforward to apply theory to practice, or to apply standards and guidelines to large-scale speaking assessment activities. There is no doubt that the assessment of spoken language ability is a complex and multifaceted endeavour. This paper provides an overview of the challenges of implementing speaking assessment, and the steps taken to ascertain the standardisation of the scoring process, in the context of a provider of Speaking tests of Italian, CVCL, of the Università per Stranieri di Perugia.

This paper is divided into three main parts: the first part presents a brief overview of the most common areas of concern that test providers face when developing speaking tests. The need to apply standards for validation purposes is also discussed. The second part describes the experience of the CVCL in applying the Quality Management System (QMS) produced by the Association of Language Testers in Europe (ALTE) in order to provide evidence of the correct application of standards and procedures to the scoring process of the Certificates of Italian (CELI) speaking tests. The third part reports the preliminary results of a monitoring study based on the data collected in the June 2013 session at the Italian Institute of Culture in Athens. Seventeen examiners and 99 performances were involved. The analysis of the data is particularly focused on assessors' consistency and severity, outlining the issues to be faced in terms of selection, training and management, and how quantitative data could usefully provide feedback for validation and decision-making purposes.

Aims

In recent times there has been a growing interest in a definition of the notion of standards in language testing (Grego Bolli 2014, Saville 2014, Taylor 2009) and how the notion of standards relates to the application of QMS (Grego Bolli 2014, Saville 2014) to language assessment. As Saville (2014:921) points out, a: 'QM approach can be incorporated into language assessment to monitor and improve practice with a view to meeting external standards, which in turn can be scrutinised through an audit or inspection.

The standards themselves may be based on a code of practice for language assessment'.

The aim of this paper is to support test providers, particularly in relation to the scoring phase, in order to help them guarantee the quality of their speaking tests. QMS can be a very useful tool for this, helping test developers to apply professional standards to their day-to-day practice.

Main areas of concern in assessing speaking

The focus of the first part of this paper is on the main areas of concern to test developers responsible for assessing speaking. We discuss issues related to assessing speaking, and how they are relevant to the validation process, looking in particular at the scoring system.

Recent work has been carried out by academic researchers in the field of language testing to investigate the different aspects of assessing speaking (see Fulcher 2003, Luoma 2004, O'Sullivan 2008, 2012, 2014, Taylor (Ed) 2011). The research highlights how crucial it is to have confidence in the quality of the information provided by test scores, in order to interpret and use these scores for decision-making purposes. Weir (2005) first adopted the phrase *scoring validity* within his socio-cognitive framework (Weir 2005, Shaw and Weir 2007, Khalifa and Weir 2009, Taylor (Ed) 2011) of test validation, where it closely and 'symbiotically' interacts with cognitive validity and context validity, and consequently with the other two dimensions in the framework: consequential validity and criterion-related validity.

One of the main strengths of Weir's validation approach is represented by its interest in the fundamental interaction between the five different types of validity evidence. O'Sullivan and Weir (2011:19–24) provide a clear description of the functions and implications of the socio-cognitive framework, focusing on the core elements of the system: the test taker, the test task and the scoring system. Accordingly, O'Sullivan (2012) proposed a very clear graphic representation (Figure 1) of what the important elements of a speaking test are and how they fit into the testing system.

Bearing in mind that any test in any domain is a balance between different stages and requirements, O'Sullivan (2012:245) explained the figure thus: 'a working idea of the theory behind the test (. . .) will help you to begin to piece together the various pieces of the assessment jigsaw'.

The scoring system

Developing the scoring system of a speaking test in order to provide evidence that we can depend on, necessitates considered and detailed decisions on how performances will be scored. Using Weir's socio-cognitive framework, Galaczi and Taylor (2011:171–233) provided an extensive analysis of *scoring*

Figure 1 Elements of a speaking test (O'Sullivan 2012:236)

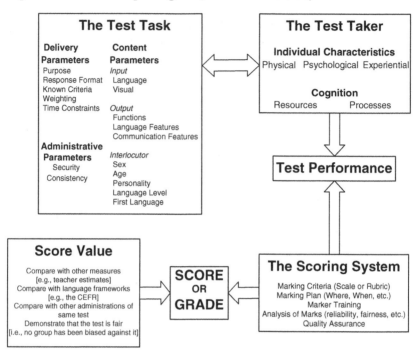

Figure 2 Aspects of scoring validity for Speaking (Galaczi and Taylor 2011:174)

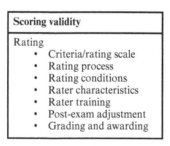

validity, listing and describing in great detail the seven parameters found in Figure 2, most of which intersect with the parameters in Figure 1.

To give an example, in order to define the rating criteria, we need to refer to the language features of the output in terms of grammar, vocabulary, pronunciation, functional competence, etc. Rater training is clearly a central issue in the system. In order to train raters we need to address several issues. These include establishing criteria and their related scales; how to take decisions when assessing the test takers' oral performance; the conditions and circumstances under which a rater takes decisions about the test taker's performance; and the variables that can affect rater decisions. All these parameters become part of the rater training and standardisation, which should in turn become part of the testing process overall.

Standards related to the scoring system

The sociocognitive framework developed by Weir (2005), and its subsequent application to speaking test production provided by O'Sullivan (2008, 2012) and Taylor (Ed) (2011) help identify the parameters that test providers need to consider and incorporate when developing their speaking tests and their scoring systems. Nevertheless test practitioners may not necessarily have the theoretical competence or experience to apply these parameters to their day-to-day practice (Grego Bolli 2014:180). Therefore it is not always straightforward for them to provide evidence that their procedures follow the standards which the testing community have adopted. This means that in those contexts where test practitioners have neither theoretical knowledge nor adequate experience in testing, the application of the sociocognitive framework and its applications to language skills does not necessarily provide a practical and directly applicable model of test validation (Kane 2006). As a practical alternative, test practitioners may consult and refer to a set of professional guidelines or standards that scientific communities and communities of practice agree upon. Three sets of such guidelines are summarised below.

The International Language Testing Association (ILTA) Guidelines

In response to the need for professional guidelines, ILTA established a task force to develop a set of shared standards soon after it was formed in the nineties. In 2000, ILTA published a code of ethics which provided guidelines for test developers in 2007.

A section of the ILTA Guidelines relates specifically to the scoring process. Speaking about the responsibilities of test designers and test writers, the Guidelines state that: 'Information guides on scoring (also known as grading or marking schemes) must be prepared for test tasks requiring hand scoring. These guides must be tried out to demonstrate that they permit reliable evaluation of the test takers' performance' (2007). Additionally, scoring procedures 'must be carefully followed and score processing routinely checked to make certain that no mistakes have been made' (2007). It is not specified which set of procedures should be followed, however.

The European Association for Language Testing and Assessment (EALTA) Guidelines

Working along similar lines, EALTA appointed a working group to produce the *EALTA Guidelines for Good Practice in Language Testing and Assessment* (2004). They are addressed to three different audiences, those involved in:

(a) training of teachers in testing and assessment

(b) classroom testing and assessment

(c) the development of tests in national or institutional testing units or centres.

Bearing in mind that all guidelines interact within the testing process, some of the EALTA ones are specifically related to the scoring process. They are not presented as statements, but in the form of checklists of questions. This implicitly stimulates reflection on the issues raised. Nevertheless how to answer, and which procedures to apply and follow, is left to test practitioners. A few examples related to quality control and test analysis are:

- 'Are markers trained for each test administration?
- Are benchmarked performances used in training?
- Is there routine double marking for subjectively marked tests?
- Is inter and intra-rater reliability calculated?
- Is the marking routinely monitored?
- What statistical analyses are used?'
  (EALTA 2014)

The Association of Language Testers in Europe (ALTE) Guidelines

The Association of Language Testers in Europe (ALTE), formally established in 1991, is a consortium of language test providers. Since its early beginnings, ALTE members have included many of the largest European institutions providing worldwide language certification. Consequently, the need for standardised test production processes was perceived as a fundamental one, in order for these institutions to be accountable and transparent. Because of this, one of the major commitments of ALTE was to support its members in applying standards of good practice.

The first ALTE *Code of Practice* was produced in 1994 and revised in 2001. The first version was focused on the process of developing and using language tests, including around 18 broad statements related to the different phases of the testing process; in any case, it was not designed to assist test practitioners in carrying out their day-to-day work of writing, administering, scoring, or providing valid results. The new version in 2001 was named *Principles of Good Practice* (ALTE 2001a), and four main test qualities were investigated: validity, reliability, impact and practicality. As Saville (2010:28) pointed out, the focus of the documents was 'on the role of various stakeholder groups in *striving for fairness*'. Neither the ALTE *Code of Practice*, nor the *Principles of Good Practice* were conceived to support test writers in carrying out their day-to-day work, or, as Saville (2010:25) specified: 'in agreeing as to what might be acceptable in terms of standards of quality in their work'. By consequence the members of the Association decided to agree on a set of 17 Minimum Standards derived from the previous documents, and on how they would be monitored through a quality management approach. These standards relate to five main areas in the test production phase: test construction, administration and logistics, marking and grading, test analysis and communication with stakeholders.

Within the ALTE Quality Management System, the monitoring of standards is now supplemented by external inspection or audit. Specific checklists developed to run the audit have greatly assisted ALTE members to better organise their day-to-day practice, also in relation to the scoring process. One of the five sections of the 17 Minimum Standards (MS) specifically relates to Marking and Grading. Neither the ILTA, nor the EALTA Guidelines, nor the ALTE Minimum Standards were designed to explain exactly which procedures are involved in the application of these guidelines to the day-to-day practice in language testing. A fundamental improvement in this direction was represented by the development of the ALTE *Quality Assurance Checklists* (ALTE 2001c). They explicitly define steps and procedures that are applicable both in the development of the testing process and its continuous process of improvement and monitoring.

These guidelines from different organisations provide advice for test developers of speaking tests. The guidelines recommend that mark schemes be piloted, and that raters are monitored in order to ascertain how accurately they are implementing the marking schemes. Issues of quality are highlighted, such as the importance of training, appropriate statistical analysis, and the role of external standards and frames of reference, for example in benchmarking and auditing processes. The second part of this paper discusses the scoring system for the CELI speaking tests, and how the ALTE *Quality Assurance Checklists for Marking, Grading and Results* have been used for the purposes of improvement, good practice and validation. It begins with an overview of the CELI speaking test format.

The CELI speaking test

The CELI 6-level examination suite for Italian was developed during the first half of the Nineties (Grego Bolli and Spiti 1993) and revised in 2004 (Grego Bolli and Spiti 2004).

CVCL is responsible for the production and administration of the CELI exams. The exams are aimed at a general adult population without any restrictions as regards mother tongue, country of origin, education or specific interests. Starting from 2005, the average number of candidates per year is around 12,000 and CVCL has adhered to the ALTE QMS, and has been audited three times since the launch of the tests in 2005. Bearing in mind that 'the main principle underlying the auditing system is that auditees build their own argument, explaining how and providing evidence that the 17 quality standards are met' (Grego Bolli 2014:189), it is fundamental to point out that for the auditee, this implies a systematic process of self-assessment, raising awareness of possible points of weakness in the system, and the actions to be taken for improvement and change.

Before describing which request for improvement was raised during the 2011 audit, and the actions taken, the following paragraphs will describe the CELI speaking test format, the CELI scoring system and how CVCL deals with rater training. Table 1 presents an overview of the test format, which is discussed briefly below.

The CELI speaking test format

The CELI speaking test is generally made up of three components or tasks, shown in Table 1. The task types most commonly used in designing speaking

Table 1 CELI speaking test format

Stage	Task format	Candidate output
1. Introduction	Interviewer asks candidate questions (CELI 1–3); Candidates introduce themselves briefly (CELI 4 and 5).	Responding to questions; expanding upon responses; asking questions; giving personal information; talking about the past, present, and future.
2. Individual long turn	Interviewer designates an individual task to the candidate based upon visual stimuli, calibrated to the exam level (CELI 1–5).	Sustaining a long turn; managing discourse; expressing ideas and opinions through comparing and contrasting; speculating.
3. Two-way collaborative task or discussion	Interviewer instructs candidates to engage with written stimuli. The interviewer interacts with the candidate in a role play (CELI 1–3).	Turn taking; initiating; responding; exchanging opinions; negotiating; agreeing and disagreeing; suggesting; justifying opinions; speculating.
	Interviewer leads a discussion with candidate after visual or written stimuli (CELI 4 and 5).	Initiating and responding; developing topics; exchanging and justifying opinions; agreeing and disagreeing.
4. Close	Interviewer thanks candidates and ends test.	Candidates express thanks and take their leave.

tests and the kind of decisions involved are described by O'Sullivan (2014) in a useful overview.

A feature of the CELI format is that the introduction is considered as an integral part of the exams for CELI 1 and 2, and as a consequence it also has to be assessed. Unlike some other language tests, this first part is not a 'warm up' stage for the candidate or the rater. The length of the CELI speaking test increases gradually from 10 minutes for CELI 1, to 20 minutes for CELI 5.

The CELI scoring system

Taking into consideration the coverage of CELI exams from CELI 1, an exam aligned with Level A2 of the Common European Framework of Reference for Languages (CEFR; Council of Europe 2001) up to CELI 5 (aligned with Level C2 of the CEFR), it is important to stress how scoring is considerably different in CELI 1 from CELI speaking tests at higher levels. Whereas CELI 1 is holistically assessed (with candidates scoring from 1 to 4, and 2.5 being the cut score), in all other CELI speaking tests the assessment is analytical: CVCL has identified four criteria which raters need to use in awarding scores. Different approaches to rating scales design are extensively described by Taylor and Galaczi (2011), Luoma (2004), Fulcher (1996:208–238), Fulcher (2003), Fulcher, Davidson and Kemp (2011:5–9). Taking into account that the rating scale development is an iterative, cyclical process, the approach adopted in the designing and development of the CELI rating scale was, in its early stages, mainly based on experts' judgement and construct definition. More recently, in the last decade, systematic analysis was introduced in order to collect data in terms of candidate performance, test scores and rater behaviour.

The four criteria the CELI scoring system refers to are: Vocabulary, Grammatical Accuracy, Pronunciation and Fluency, and Sociocultural Appropriacy. Each criterion has a score from 1 to 5, with the total cut score (given by the raw sum of the scores obtained in the 4 criteria) being 11. Nevertheless, the four criteria and the related scales would not be meaningful without a systematic reference both to the tasks and to the linguistic elements in Italian, which the criteria need to refer to at each level. The Italian Profile (*Profilo della lingua italiana*, Spinelli and Parizzi 2010), based on the CEFR approach and descriptors, was a key tool in making it possible to define the Italian language speaking constructs in terms of genres, functions, notions, grammar and vocabulary, and to identify criterial features at each level (from A1 to C2), provide examples and illustrate progression.

Tables 2 and 3 show the holistic scoring criteria for CELI 1 – A2 and the analytic scoring criteria for CELI 2. The following holistic scale for CELI 1 is focused mainly on the fulfilment of the task and differs slightly from the 1–5 point score used at other levels.

Table 2 A2 – CELI 1 scoring criteria

Points awarded	To a candidate who
4 points	Completes the assigned task in a simple but correct manner, manages to make their intentions understood and though with some effort, adapts well to prompts.
3 points	Completes the assigned task with some hesitation and imperfections; they are however clear in their exposition and respond to prompts, though slowly.
2.5 points	Completes the assigned task with some difficulty and with some lexical or morphological errors (the errors made are never such as to compromise communication). Always manages to make their intentions understood and responds to prompts though slowly and sometimes requiring repetition.
1 point	Manages to only partly complete the assigned task; requires further questions to better clarify what they mean to say; makes lexical or morphological errors which sometimes makes the communication inadequate or incomprehensible and expresses themselves with a lot of interference with the L1.

The training session

Although the tables provide criteria for the examiners, support is still needed when it comes to the interpretation of the scoring criteria and how to apply these. As already mentioned, the scoring of the CELI speaking component is decentralised and takes place in the examination centres. This requires a great deal of training by CVCL trainers, so that examiners can be confident they are using the criteria appropriately. The decision to decentralise the scoring was quite a difficult choice, made at the beginning of the 1990s, but was taken in order to disseminate a more systemic approach to language assessment in the context of Italian as a foreign language and also to contribute to a systematic training of teachers of Italian in the area of assessment. Being aware also of the impact on students' performance of raters' performance (McNamara 1996, O'Sullivan and Rignall 2007), rater training has been one of the main concerns of CVCL since the beginning of the CELI administration.

During training particular care is given to the interpretation of the descriptors of the CEFR and of the concepts underlying them. Three other fundamental tools are used: the *Profilo della Lingua Italiana* (Spinelli and Parizzi 2010), *Relating Language Examinations to the Common European Framework of Reference for Languages: Learning, Teaching, Assessment (CEFR)* (Council of Europe 2003), and the *Samples of oral production illustrating the levels of the CEFR for Italian* (Grego Bolli 2008), which provide a concrete representation of the CEFR language descriptors for speaking production and interaction. Once frames of reference have been presented and future examiners have familiarised themselves with the background of CELI examinations, training moves on to presenting CELI exams, first by

Table 3 B1 – CELI 2 scoring criteria

VOCABULARY (LEXICAL COMPETENCE)

Points awarded	To a candidate who expresses themselves using a dictionary:
5 points	Always fully appropriate for the situation.
4 points	Appropriate although sometimes requires prompting from the interlocutor.
3 points	Appropriate although limited (often repeats themselves and requires suggestions from the interlocutor).
2 points	So limited that at times it makes communication incomprehensible.
1 point	Very limited and at times inappropriate.

GRAMMATICAL ACCURACY (MORPHOLOGICAL AND SYNTACTIC COMPETENCE)

Points awarded	To a candidate who, in the context of oral interaction, expresses themselves:
5 points	In an essential yet correct way.
4 points	In an essential yet correct way, though you can notice difficulty in formulating their intentions and connecting statements appropriately.
3 points	Making errors which do not disturb the interlocutor neither for quantity nor severity.
2 points	Making lexical and/or morphological errors which disturb the interlocutor.
1 point	Making errors which compromise communication.

SOCIOCULTURAL COMPETENCE

Points awarded	To a candidate who expresses themselves:
5 points	In an appropriate way for the situation, understanding the prompts and adapting to them effortlessly, never limiting the exchange to a minimum.
4 points	In an appropriate way for the situation though with some hesitation.
3 points	In an appropriate way for the situation, even though the pauses require a sustained wait by the listener. Adapts slowly to the prompts.
2 points	In an inappropriate way for the situation or who requires numerous prompts in order to be able to complete the task.
1 point	In an inappropriate way for the situation and with such difficulty as to make the conversation unnatural.

PRONUNCIATION AND FLUENCY (PRONUNCIATION AND INTONATION)

Points awarded	To a candidate who expresses themselves:
5 points	With pronunciation which though noticeably denoting their linguistic origins, make themselves understood clearly. Intonation is always appropriate.
4 points	With pronunciation which markedly denotes their linguistic origins and which requires some correction. Intonation is always appropriate.
3 points	With difficulty both for pronunciation and intonation; but always comprehensible without effort.
2 points	With errors of pronunciation or intonation which in some cases make it incomprehensible.
1 point	With errors of pronunciation and intonation which hinder communication.

analysing the input given to candidates in order to elicit their speaking performances, and second, by showing videos of CELI exams, to be used both as a reference behaviour for the examiners, and as a reference approach for scoring the performances. Taylor and Galaczi (2011:188), Shaw and Weir (2007:146–147) properly highlighted the importance of using examples of student performance in order to concretely represent standards.

For standardisation purposes, during the training sessions, emphasis is placed on how to interpret the scale descriptors, and in guiding trainees to apply them appropriately when scoring performances. The training process ends with trainees rating video performances on the CELI, first individually, and then collectively, in order to share a common view of the score awarded. In addition, whenever possible CVCL integrates the assessment of recorded performances with that of live performances of future candidates of CELI exams, in a simulated session.

CVCL organises training twice a year in Perugia, before March and November exam sessions, and whenever needed by new examination centres, or by centres requiring refresher training for their examiners. To date, CVCL has trained over 3,000 examiners in over 400 centres around the world. During training sessions in Perugia a similar schedule (Table 4) is followed.

An updated version of the training programme is always available on the CVCL website (www.cvcl.it).

Needs for improvement

Since 2007, with the start of a regular pretesting process for CELI written exams, quantitative analyses of items has been carried out alongside qualitative analyses. As a result, CVCL became aware of the need to also obtain quantitative data for the scoring of the CELI speaking component, even though it was clear that the gathering of such data would be difficult. To this end, a seminar in Perugia was organised in 2012 with a CVCL consultant, where the grounds for the future monitoring were laid down. The actions for implementing monitoring of exams and rater performances were then

Table 4 Proportion of training hours during CELI training sessions

Training subject	Total hours
• **CEFR** • **Profilo della lingua italiana** • **Samples of oral production illustrating CEFR levels**	15
• **CELI exams** • **Tasks** • **Assessment (recording of a live exam)**	15

decided, such as choosing a suitable examination centre, identifying a standard rater, and covering a suitable number of performances.

A further stimulus for improvement came from the ALTE auditing process which CVCL underwent in 2011, where recommendations were made to CVCL about the need to undergo a systematic monitoring process to provide evidence supporting the consistency of the scoring system of the CELI speaking component. In particular, suggestions for improvement focused on Minimum Standard 11 (MS11), stating that ways to estimate the impact of consensus marking should be addressed and more data gathered for further analysis. As already outlined, the ALTE Quality Assurance Checklists were a very useful tool for supporting CVCL in order to describe the scoring procedures, how they respond to the ALTE Minimum Standards, providing evidence of the consistency of their application and raising awareness of the improvements needed. The Appendix reports a real example of how they work and were used during the last 2013 auditing, in relation to MS 11.

In 2012, similar procedures of data collection and analysis were set up for speaking, compared to the ones already established for scoring writing, and the first systematic series of monitoring was conducted in Athens. The results of the analysis, in terms of rater performances, have already been used for feedback and for training purposes.

Rating speaking during the live test sessions represents a challenge when it comes to data collection and analysis. The aim of the monitoring in Athens and of the subsequent analysis was to compare different raters' performance with each other and with the standard represented by a CVCL senior rater.

The ratings of the CVCL representative enable a comparison of performance of all raters with each other, and with the standard, and this is described and discussed in the following sections. The third part of this paper presents methodology, data collection, and results of the monitoring study in Athens.

Monitoring of CELI speaking tests: Methodology

Following the experts' suggestion and the remarks of the ALTE 2011 audit, alongside CVCL's own experience, in order to monitor the scores awarded by raters during the CELI speaking tests administration, it was decided to select one of the biggest CVCL examination centres, in terms of number of candidates. The centre selected was the Italian Institute of Culture (IIC) of Athens, which has administered around 14,000 exams at the time of writing, and has a pool of experienced raters who have all been previously involved in several CVCL projects. The raters involved, furthermore, have undergone a number of training sessions, and are appropriately prepared. Before the exam session, a full day was spent on refresher training, following a schedule similar to Table 4, putting more stress, though, on scoring issues, using both CELI videos and live exams which were locally organised.

The structure of the training session in Athens differed from general training for CELI exams because of the nature of the monitoring. As already outlined, the raters in Athens were generally very experienced, having taken part in several other exam sessions earlier. In addition they had been teachers of Italian in Athens for many years. Therefore more stress was put on assessment than on the examiner rubrics, which were assumed to be fully mastered by the examiners.

As regards the monitoring, it was decided not to interfere with the usual organisation of the exams, letting the centre organise them in their usual way, in terms of the schedule and of the pairing of raters. The monitoring took place throughout the oral test administration period: from 18 to 20 June 2013. Tests were then delivered and the performances assessed according to the mark schemes of CELI exams. The main differences were the presence of a third, silent rater from CVCL, considered as the standard, and the number of the scores awarded for each student's performance.

The local raters scored the performances first independently, and only after having decided their individual score and written it down, did they go on to reach an agreed assessment with the other rater. This meant that each performance had been scored four times: by the two examiners individually, by the standard rater, and by the examiners jointly after agreement. The aim was not only to monitor the final score awarded to the test taker, but also to check whether examiners behaved in a significantly different way when rating individually than when paired. In addition, the scores awarded to test takers in each single component were also recorded and analysed, so to have a clearer picture of the interpretation of the scoring criteria by the raters.

The analysis of the data

Data collection and analysis

The data was gathered according to the above described procedure, and therefore three sets of scores were analysed:

Table 5 Training session scheme in Athens, before monitoring

Training subject	Total number of hours
• **CEFR** • **Profilo della lingua italiana** • **Samples of oral production illustrating CEFR levels**	2
• **CELI speaking tests** • **Tasks** • **Assessment (recording of a live exam)**	5

1. The initial scores awarded by individual raters.
2. The initial scores given by the standard rater, Rater 1.
3. The final scores agreed on by rating pairs.

The total number of exams monitored was 99 (13 of which were CELI 1 with holistic scoring). All 99 candidates were awarded scores by the standard rater, Rater 1. The total number of raters was 18, and the number of pairs examining the candidates (based on different combinations of raters) was 14. Comparing the raters with a standard rater makes it possible to link all the raters in the data, thus overcoming the problem of raters rating only a small number of candidates. An analysis was run on the data, to compare raters for leniency and severity, as well as consistency, using Multi-Faceted Rasch Measurement (MFRM). This is a specific statistical model, which belongs to a class of models within Item Response Theory (Bond and Fox 2001).

Rater severity and leniency

The data was analysed twice. The scores given by the standard rater, Rater 1, were compared firstly to the scores awarded initially by individual raters, and secondly with the scores agreed on by rating pairs after discussion. The first analysis highlighted those raters who were either more lenient, or more severe, than the standard rater. This showed that four raters were more severe and four were more lenient, as can be seen in Figure 3.

Figure 3 Severity/leniency of individual raters

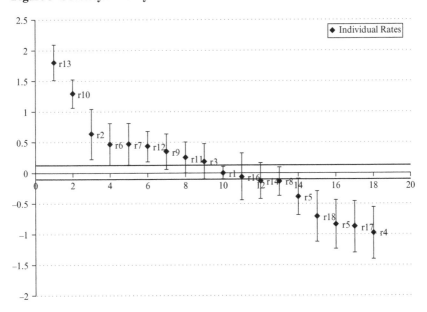

In the figure, individual raters are identified by letter r and a number, where **r1** signifies Rater 1, the standard rater. The raters are organised from most severe to most lenient, going from left to right. The vertical error bars either side of the raters is the envelope of error, representing measurement imprecision. This envelope of error does not imply rater error or misjudgement of any kind. Rater 1 rated all possible candidates, so we have more candidate scores from Rater 1 and therefore more evidence about their behaviour as a rater. Rater 1 consequently has a smaller envelope of error, compared to Rater 16, for example, who rated a smaller number of candidates, and provided less evidence of their behaviour as a rater. The thick lines either side of Rater 1 show their envelope of measurement error. If raters' envelopes of error overlap with that of Rater 1, it indicates that they are similar in severity or leniency to Rater 1. For example, Rater 9 overlaps but Rater 12 does not. Raters whose error bars overlap with each other are also similarly lenient or severe. So this graphical representation of the data also shows that, moving from left to right, the group of raters from Rater 2 to Rater 3 are equally severe, whereas Rater 13 is more severe than any other rater. On the far right hand side we can see a cluster of raters who are less severe than the standard rater because their error bars do not overlap.

The second analysis showed which pairs of raters were more lenient or severe than the standard rater.

Once again rating pairs are arranged in order of leniency and severity, in order to identify if there were groups of raters who were equally lenient or equally severe, in comparison to the standard rater. It showed that one pair was more severe, and six pairs were more lenient. In Figure 4 each diamond and set of error bars represents a pair of raters. Raters worked in different combinations so for example, r103 signifies Rater 8 and Rater 3, r114 signifies Rater 8 and Rater 5. The paired raters r103 were equal in severity to the standard rater, but the pair r114 were more lenient, as can be seen in Figure 4.

The analysis also highlighted which raters became more lenient or more severe as a result of discussion with their partner, or remained the same, because the individual raters and the paired raters could be compared by looking at both charts. In initial ratings for example, three raters (r3, r5 and r8) were all equal in severity or leniency to the standard rater, but after discussion the paired Raters 5 and 8 became more lenient. Generally the trend was for raters to become more lenient after discussion.

Rater consistency

Raters who do not fall within the upper and lower quality control limits should be monitored and it is generally the case that those with higher fit statistics are displaying inconsistencies in rating and as such are considered more problematic than those who are too consistent.

Figure 4 Severity/leniency of paired raters

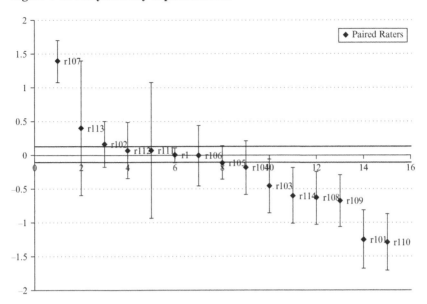

Pair	Raters	Pair	Raters
r107	r010+r013	r104	r009+r010
r113	r002+r013	r103	r003+r008
r102	r006+r007	r114	r005+r008
r112	r010+r003	r108	r014+r015
r111	r009+r014	r109	r008+r016
r106	r002+r003	r101	r004+r005
r105	r011+r012	r110	r017+r018

Bars above the line indicate less consistent raters, and bars below the line indicate more consistent raters. Bars which fall between 2.0 and −2.0 are acceptable. The two bars show less extreme and more extreme candidate performances. An extreme performance means the worst performing and best performing candidates; the other bar indicates candidate performances around the cut off, or borderline candidates who may be more difficult to judge. In Figure 5 raters 10 and 13 are too consistent: this indicates they may be awarding a narrow range of scores, or frequently award the same score. Conversely, rater 6 is too inconsistent.

The Intraclass Correlation Coefficient (ICC) is a measure of the reliability of measurements or ratings. In addition to the facets analysis, ICC correlations (which show the closeness of one rater to another) were provided for the raters, comparing them with the standard rater across the different criteria

Figure 5 Intra-rater consistency of individual raters

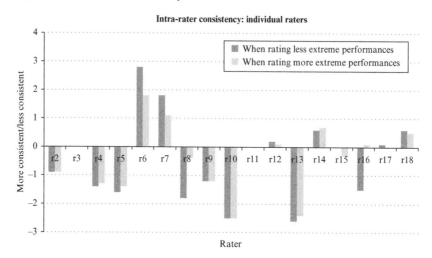

Intra-rater consistency: individual raters

for the speaking tests, so in essence looking at the level of agreement between raters. Overall no rater lacked agreement with Rater 1 across all rating scales. For some raters there was less agreement for certain criteria.

The analysis enabled identification of which raters had less agreement for certain criteria, and if they did, whether they were within an acceptable range for other criteria. The data showed, for example, that Criterion 1: Vocabulary (lexical competence) appeared to be the criterion which raters found most difficult to rate consistently. Since it was possible to investigate the consistency of these raters when applying other criteria, and they were within acceptable limits when assessing these, one conclusion coming out of the data was that this lack of agreement may have been a reflection of the design of the marking criteria for the lexical criteria, rather than rater performance.

Decisions and actions based on the analysis

It was recommended that the conclusions from the leniency/severity analysis should be taken together with those from the later information on self-consistency. A rater who is both too lenient or too severe and not very consistent should be dealt with before another rater who is only too severe, for example, as this might be an indicator of a careless evaluation of performances.

As a result of the analysis, a number of actions have been put into practice, and others planned as a follow-up. First of all, the centre and the raters have been informed about the results, in order to share opinions and comments. The actions to be taken were identified and, in observing how the consistency of raters could be generally considered satisfactory, we focused on the severity of those raters considerably out of the acceptable range. For instance, two raters emerged as being overly severe (r10 and r13), and they also worked in a pair (r107). While all other raters tended to become more lenient when agreeing scores with their counterparts, in the case of r10 and r13 this leniency effect seemed not to be working. Therefore it was recommended to the centre not to let raters work in the same fixed pairs, so that sharing opinions with more raters might lead to a shared understanding of the interpretation of scoring criteria and consequently of the score awarded. Even though this may not lead to a more effective internalisation of the criteria by raters, it can still lead to a more realistic scoring of test takers' performances.

A subsequent step will include new training on those aspects which were identified as being problematic (analyses showed that one of the criteria – Vocabulary (Lexical Competence) – could be one); a wider use of a tool such as the *Profilo della lingua italiana* (Spinelli and Parizzi 2010) might prove extremely useful in addressing this. Feedback from raters will be required to determine if their opinions overlap in any way with those of CVCL. After such action a clearer picture may emerge of which aspects are most problematic, not only on the quantitative, but also on the qualitative side. It will certainly be advisable, after the planned remedial action, to re-monitor the same group of raters, taking notes of all the possible changes in raters' behaviour. If results of this second monitoring are still a matter of concern, CVCL may ask the centre in question to improve their rater selection process. During this second monitoring, in order to have more reliable analyses and to learn from the experience, it would be advisable to have an additional standard rater and cross link results.

Conclusions

The testing process is typically a cyclical one implying a continuous search for improvement supported by systematic data analysis. This holds true for production, administration and scoring of speaking tests – all these processes can only become better over time if decisions are based on data and evidence. For example, one of the main aspects involved in providing evidence of the *scoring validity*, both in writing and speaking, is rater training.

The training of raters is a demanding endeavour in language testing and requires specific long-term investment but it is one of the main functions of a University Centre specialising in language assessment, as CVCL does. This can be particularly valuable in the context of Italian as a foreign or second language, where language teachers are not yet required to have any professional competence in language testing and assessment. The systematic training of raters supported by continuous monitoring through systematic analysis of the data can help to provide evidence of both the reliability of the scoring and the validity of the test's results.

QMS, alongside practical tools such as quality management checklists, can support test providers in increasing the awareness of the procedures adopted, of the evidence provided, of the strengths and weaknesses, and of the areas in need of improvement.

References

Association of Language Testers in Europe (1994) *Code of Practice*, available online: www.alte.org/attachments/files/code_practice_eng.pdf

Association of Language Testers in Europe (2001a) *Principles of Good Practice*, available online: www.alte.org/attachments/files/good_practice.pdf

Association of Language Testers in Europe (2001b) *Minimum Standards for Establishing Quality Profiles in ALTE Examinations*, available online: www. alte.org/attachments/files/minimum_standards.pdf

Association of Language Testers in Europe (ALTE) (2001c) *Quality Assurance Checklists*, available online: www.alte.org/resources/filter

Bond, T G and Fox, C M (2001) *Applying the Rasch Model*, Mahwah: Lawrence Erlbaum Associates.

Council of Europe (2001) *Common European Framework of Reference for Languages: Learning, Teaching, Assessment*, Cambridge: Cambridge University Press.

Council of Europe (2003) *Relating Language Examinations to the Common European Framework of Reference for Languages: Learning, Teaching, Assessment. Manual: Preliminary Pilot Version*, DGIV/EDU/LANG 2003, 5, Strasbourg: Language Policy Division.

European Association for Language Testing and Assessment (2004) *EALTA Guidelines for Good Practice in Language Testing and Assessment*, available online: www.ealta.eu.org/documents/archive/guidelines/English.pdf

Fulcher, G (1996) Does thick description lead to smart tests? A data-based approach to rating scale construction, *Language Testing* 13 (2), 208–238.

Fulcher, G (2003) *Testing Second Language Speaking*, Harlow: Longman/ Pearson Education Ltd.

Fulcher, G, Davidson, F and Kemp, J (2011) Effective rating scale development for speaking tests: performances decision trees, *Language Testing* 28 (1), 5–29.

Galaczi, E and Taylor, L (2011) *Scoring validity*, in Taylor, L (Ed) *Examining Speaking: Research and Practice in Assessing Second Language Speaking*, Studies in Language Testing volume 30, Cambridge: UCLES/Cambridge University Press, 171–233.

Grego Bolli, G (2008) *Esempi di Produzioni Orali a illustrazione per l'italiano dei livelli del Quadro comune europeo di riferimento per le lingue del Consiglio d'Europa*, Perugia: Guerra Edizioni.

Grego Bolli, G (2014) Using Quality Management Systems to improve test development and standards and to promote good practice: A case study of testing Italian as a foreign language, in Mansfield, G and Little, D (Eds) *Language Learning in Higher Education*, Berlin: De Gruyter, 179–206.

Grego Bolli, G and Spiti, M G (1993) *Verifica del grado di conoscenza dell'italiano in una prospettiva di certificazione*, Perugia: Guerra Edizioni.

Grego Bolli, G and Spiti, M G (2004) *La verifica delle competenze linguistiche. Misurare e valutare nella certificazione CELI*, Perugia: Guerra Edizioni.

International Language Testing Association (2007) *Guidelines for Practice*, available online: iltaonline.com/index.php?option=com_content&task=view& id=122&Itemid=133

Kane, M (2006) Validation, in Brennan, R L (Ed) *Educational Measurement* (4th edition), Westport: American Council on Education and Praeger Publishers: 17–64.

Khalifa, H and Weir, C J (2009) *Examining Reading: Research and Practice in Assessing Second Language Reading*, Studies in Language Testing volume 29, Cambridge: UCLES/Cambridge University Press.

Luoma, S (2004) *Assessing Speaking*, Cambridge: Cambridge University Press.

McNamara, T F (1996) *Measuring Second Language Performance*, London: Longman

O'Sullivan, B (2008) *Modelling Performance in Tests of Spoken Language*, Frankfurt: Peter Lang.

O'Sullivan, B (2012) Assessing speaking, in Coombe, C, Davidson, P, O'Sullivan, B and Stoynoff, S (Eds) *The Cambridge Guide to Second Language Assessment*, Cambridge: Cambridge University Press: 234–246.

O'Sullivan, B (2014) Assessing Speaking, in Kunnan, A J (Ed) *The Companion to Language Assessment*, Oxford: Wiley Blackwell, 156–171.

O'Sullivan, B and Rignall, M (2007) Assessing the value of bias analysis feedback to raters for IELTS Writing Module, in Taylor, L and Falvey, P (Eds) *IELTS Collected Papers: Research in Speaking and Writing Assessment*, Studies in Language Testing volume 19, Cambridge: UCLES/Cambridge University Press, 446–476.

O'Sullivan, B and Weir, C J (2011) Test development and validation, in O'Sullivan, B (Ed) *Language Testing: Theories and Practices*, Basingstoke: Palgrave Macmillan: 13–32.

Saville, N (2010) Auditing the quality profile: From code of practice to standards, *Research Notes* 39, 24–28.

Saville, N (2014) Using standards and guidelines, in Kunnan, A J (Ed) *The Companion to Language Assessment*, Oxford: Wiley Blackwell, 906–924.

Shaw, S D and Weir, C J (2007) *Examining Writing: Research and Practice in Assessing Second Language Writing*, Studies in Language Testing volume 26, Cambridge: UCLES/Cambridge University Press.

Spinelli, B and Parizzi, F (2010) *Profilo della Lingua Italiana*, Firenze: La Nuova Italia.

Taylor, L (2009) Setting language standards for teaching and assessment: a matter of principle, politics or prejudice? in Taylor, L and Weir, C J (Eds) *Language Testing Matters: Investigating the Wider Social and Educational Impact of Assessment – Proceedings of the ALTE Cambridge Conference, April 2008*, Studies in Language Testing volume 31, Cambridge: UCLES/ Cambridge University Press: 139–157.

Taylor, L (Ed) (2011) *Examining Speaking: Research and Practice in Assessing Second Language Speaking*, Studies in Language Testing volume 30, Cambridge: UCLES/Cambridge University Press.

Weir, C J (2005) *Language Testing and Validation: An Evidence-based Approach*, Basingstoke: Palgrave Macmillan.

Appendix: Sample ALTE Quality Assurance Checklist

1) Questions to be addressed in the argument and in the audit.	2) Description of the **auditee's argument and** documentation provided (Appendix 1).	Documents attached	3) Auditor comments and judgement: Is the evidence sufficient to meet the MS? If not, why not? Specify need for improvements and make suggestions for improvement.	4) Outcome
MS 11: Marking is sufficiently accurate and reliable for purpose and type of examination. See checklists: B6, D9, G1, G2				Satisfactory with RFI
1. How is the marking of productive skills carried out? Central or local marking?	Marking of written production is central. It is carried out at CVCL. Marking of oral production is local. It is carried out at the exam centre.			
a) If raters or examiners are used, how are they selected and trained?	See 1 a) for examiners of written production. Examiners for the oral component are either mother tongue Italian teachers with a meaningful experience in the field of language teaching or non-Italian mother tongue teachers with a university degree in Italian. Generally, they are all teachers of Italian, working in the exam centres. All examiners have to attend, at least once, examiner training which is held twice a year in Perugia or directly in the big exam centres.	Examiners training programme (March 2011)		

b) How is the accuracy of marking assured (e.g. rating criteria, rating procedures, handbooks, training, feedback)?	There are detailed rating criteria and analytical scales described in a handbook, instructions for raters and at the regular training sessions organised by CVCL.	*Grego Bolli, G – Spiti, MG (2004) La verifica delle competenze linguistiche. Misurare e valutare nella certificazione CELI. Perugia, Guerra Edizioni.*		
c) How is the reliability of marking assured (e.g. regulations, number of raters, quality check of rating, mode of arriving at final rating)?	Format for the oral component consists of one candidate and two examiners, one acts as an interlocutor and rater, the other as a rater. The final decision is made by both examiners after a discussion immediately after each candidate's performance.			
2. Why do you consider marking is appropriate considering the type and purpose of the exam?	Regular training, double rating for the oral component and the supervision by a staff member in large Centres, data from systematic inter- and intra-correlation analyses of the raters' performances of the written component (MS12) assure reliability to all the operation.	Report: rating data, November '10		

23 Assessment of spoken interactions in two conditions: Teacher-to-student versus student-to-student

Pascale Manoïlov

Claire Tardieu

Université Sorbonne Nouvelle

Abstract

According to the theory of the social mind and of sociocultural Second Language Acquisition (SLA) (Lantolf 2000, 2006, Leontiev 1981, Swain 2000, Wertsch 1985), every form of interaction is situated and strongly depends on the individualities involved, each one speaking from their own universe but also permanently adjusting to their partner's discourse. When it comes to the assessment issue, and more specifically spoken interaction assessment, both Cambridge English and the Centre International d'Etudes Pédagogique (CIEP) exams and certifications include the student-to-student and examiner–student conditions whereas the Goethe-Institut and the Cervantes Institute, which are also exam providers, prefer the teacher-to-student condition – the main argument for the latter being that the teacher's didactic/assessing positioning can better help the student to produce the best possible performance. The purpose of this research is to investigate which of the two conditions is preferable in terms of linguistic and pragmatic performance: teacher-to-learner or peer-to-peer.

Our hypotheses are the following:

1. Evidence of didactic/assessing positioning is not limited to language professionals but can be found in student-to-student interactions as well.
2. The teacher-to-learner condition is not necessarily more favourable to the student than the peer-to-peer one.

This research will deal with the results of a micro experiment completed in 2013 in connection with the Direction de l'Évaluation, de la Performance et de la Prospective (DEPP) at the French Ministry of Education in an assessment situation involving A1, A2 and B1 students and teachers/evaluators in order to compare the performances of the students doing the same task under two conditions: first with a peer and then a teacher.

Introduction

This paper deals with the results of an experiment in the field of language assessment. It focuses on spoken interaction, a skill that was introduced in the French curriculum for secondary schools not that long ago (2005) in response to the publication of the Common European Framework of Reference for Languages (CEFR, Council of Europe 2001). The question raised here is the condition in which students are to be assessed when speaking with others. Two options are available:

- Condition 1: student-to-student spoken interaction
- Condition 2: teacher-to-student spoken interaction.

In French schools and for French national exams such as the 'Baccalauréat', Condition 2 is mostly preferred since teachers are considered the experts who are there to lead or scaffold the student's speech. However, for teachers who have to assess their pupils in regular class situations, such a pattern is time-consuming and as a result they often opt for Condition 1. Both the Cambridge English and the Centre International d'Etudes Pédagogique (CIEP) exams and certifications include the student-to-student and examiner–student conditions whereas the Goethe-Institut and the Cervantes Institute prefer the teacher-to-student condition – the main argument for the latter being that the teacher's didactic/assessing positioning can better help the student to produce the best possible performance. This research takes its roots in the elaboration of the protocol for the French testing called Cycle des Evaluations Disciplinaires Réalisées sur Echantillons (CEDRE), organised by the Direction de l'Évaluation, de la Performance et de la Prospective (DEPP) at the French Ministry of Education. This CEDRE evaluation is performed every six years to assess the knowledge and skills of a large sample of French students. We will deal here with English which is one of the languages taught in secondary school. The participants we are interested in for this study are in their fourth year of secondary education and they are tested in five skills: oral and written comprehension and production as well as spoken interaction. For spoken interaction, the ministry has chosen Condition 2 to assess the students. However, this choice could be questionable since this is not the usual condition chosen by most teachers in normal class situations.

In order to investigate the appropriacy of using Condition 2 for spoken interaction, we organised an experiment to compare the two interactional patterns. Students were given a task to complete: they were provided with a touristic leaflet and had to decide with their partner (first a peer and then a teacher) how they would organise their weekend. The purpose of this research is to show which of the two conditions (teacher-to-learner or peer-to-peer) is preferable in terms of linguistic and pragmatic achievements.

Theoretical framework

According to the theory of the social mind and of sociocultural Second Language Acquisition (SLA) (Lantolf 2000, 2006, Leontiev 1981, Swain 2000, Wertsch 1985), every form of interaction is situated and strongly depends on the individualities (personality, character, age) involved, each one speaking from their own universe but also permanently adjusting to their partner's discourse. We believe that both content and form in interactions depend not only on individualities but also on the *social function* as it is perceived by oneself and by the others. Here we are relying on the notion of *social function* which is always a *social fiction* as Sartre puts it in *L'Être et le Néant* (1976) after observing a waiter at the Café de Flore. We also agree with Finkielkraut (1999) who stresses the different ways of behaving according to whether you are a waiter, a doctor or a teacher becoming 'second nature'. One may also refer to more recent studies on the topic:

> Social interaction is the very bedrock of social life. It is the primary medium through which cultures are transmitted, relationships are sustained, identities are affirmed, and social structures of all sorts are reproduced (Goodwin and Heritage 1990 in Heritage and Clayman 2010:7).

The specific issue of paired or group testing as opposed to conventional testing has already been tackled by a lot of researchers (see Weir, Vidaković and Galaczi 2013). Their work seems to confirm Skehan's (2001) assertion that such paired test tasks provide less asymmetrical situations (Brooks 2009, Gan, Davison and Hamp-Lyons 2008). It was found that paired oral tasks result in more equal speaking opportunities (Együd and Glover 2001, Galaczi 2008, Iwashita 1998, Kormos 1999, Lazaraton 2002, Taylor 2001), the use of a greater variety of speech functions (Galaczi and ffrench 2011), and greater task management skills. Other positive effects of paired oral interactions in a class situation can be noted in terms of exposure (Saville and Hargreaves 1999, Shohamy, Reves and Bejarano 1986), and readiness to speak (Folland and Robertson 1976).

In our experiment, the participants are involved in a difficult task because they have to take up roles that are close to real-life experience (Council of Europe 2001:121) – the students have to act as teenagers on a visit to an English-speaking country who want to organise their weekend. The teacher's role consists of becoming a host family member who will organise the weekend with the student. When engaged in task-based interaction, participants are expected to behave in a certain way and to produce a certain type of discourse as required by the specific assessment purposes (both in terms of linguistic and pragmatic criteria). They are indeed supposed to ignore the institutional context and their actual social role as students or teacher and feel free to express their likes/dislikes or even modify their true personality. We therefore assume that the interaction will depend on their greater or lesser readiness to fit the roles assigned by the task. In order to analyse the results according to the participants' positioning in the spoken interaction, we intend to transfer Clot's concept of 'clinical activity' (Clot and Faïta 2000). Although this framework was originally meant for any work situation, we believe that its methodological approach fits the study of the activity that takes place in the language class. This conceptual tool will enable us to measure the gap between the completion of the task as planned by the designer and the actual activity of the participants, i.e. what really happened.

Our first hypothesis is that the gap between the planned task (what is expected in terms of language and interactional patterns from the teacher) and reality (what learners actually produce) is narrower in Condition 1 (student-to-student) than in Condition 2 (teacher-to-student).

Our second hypothesis is that the wider gap in Condition 2 is due to the teacher's didactic positioning whose social role would overcome the one assigned by the task. In other words, the teacher who is supposed to play the role of a host family member would have difficulties in leaving aside the assessor's position.

Finally, our third hypothesis is that each condition will have an impact on the student's performance both in terms of pragmatic and linguistic behaviour.

The protocol

Our experiment was conducted in February 2014 in three different secondary schools in Paris suburbs. Twelve 14/15-year-old students (A2+/B1 levels) and their three teachers were video-recorded while performing a spoken interaction task in the two conditions. The task was a role-play which slightly differed according to who the students were interacting with. In both conditions, the participants were provided with a leaflet that displayed the pictures and the names of some famous tourist attractions either in London or in New York.

The protocol was as follows:

Step 1: Spoken interaction task to be performed in Condition 1 (student-to-student): the students were told they were both staying in a host family in a foreign city (London or New York). Their goal was to discuss and agree on the organisation of the following weekend.

Step 2: Spoken interaction task to be performed in Condition 2 (teacher-to-student): the students were told they were staying in a host family in a foreign city (London or New York, depending on which city had been chosen in Condition 1). The teacher was asked to play the role of the host family mother (all the teachers were female). The two participants had to discuss and agree on the organisation of the following weekend.

In both conditions, the instructions were to make suggestions, to react to suggestions and to reach an agreement on the organisation of the activities of the weekend. The conversations were due to last no less than 3 minutes and no more than 5 minutes.

The 18 spoken interactions were video recorded in a classroom according to the following order:

- student 1 with student 2
- student 1 with teacher
- student 2 with teacher.

Before the peer-to-peer interaction, it was made clear to the students that the video recordings would be used for two purposes: the first one for assessment by their teacher and the second one for research purposes. In Condition 1 (student to student), only the researcher stayed in the classroom (to monitor the video camera) and the teacher waited outside. The students were perfectly aware assessment was involved in both conditions.

After each dialogue with the teacher (Condition 2), the latter was asked to assess the student according to the grid design by the DEPP. In order to evaluate the students' performance in Condition 1, the same teacher watched the videos of the spoken interaction in the peer-to-peer situation. The same grid was used. The grid is divided into two parts: the first one deals with the pragmatic skills and the degree of achievement of the task (from 1 to 5 that is from the minimum to the maximum fulfilling of the task). The second part assesses the linguistic skills i.e. lexical variety, grammatical and phonological accuracy from A (the lowest) to E (the highest), the final grade being thus a combination of a number and a letter. The grid itself was elaborated by a group of language experts (in English, German and Spanish) relying on both the CEFR (Council of Europe 2001) and the French language curriculum.

At the end of the experiment, the students were asked to complete a questionnaire and were interviewed to ascertain their feelings regarding the experiment and their preference for one condition or the other. The questions were as follows:

1. Do you like English?
2. Did you like taking part in the experiment?

3. Who did you prefer performing the task with –your fellow student or your teacher? Which condition was most favourable to you?

The videos of the spoken interactions (amounting to 1 hour and 35 minutes) were transcribed on CLAN software (MacWhinney 2000) which allows for text and video alignment as well as for some automatic data processing. According to grounded theory (Strauss and Corbin 1990), our coding system was data driven and allowed for quantitative and qualitative analysis.

Analysis

When designing a task for students to develop their spoken interaction skills, the teacher always thinks ahead and has some specific expectations that would match his/her learning goals. The process is the same when designing a test because the assessor intends to check the knowledge and skills that were acquired by the learners. Some instructions are given to the participants so as to trigger the use of specific language functions. This is what is considered as the planned task and it usually reflects the assessor's goals.

Here are the instructions (in italics) given to the participants followed by the language functions that could be expected. We used the functions listed in the Threshold Level (Council of Europe 1990):

> *Where would you like to go? What would you like to see or do?*
> Enquiring about/Expressing wants, desires
> Enquiring about/Giving factual information
> *Make some suggestions*
> Suggesting a course of action
> *React to your friend's suggestions*
> Enquiring about/Expressing like–dislike
> Enquiring about/Expressing preference
> Agreeing /Disagreeing
> *At the end of the conversation, you should agree with your friend about your plans for next weekend.*

The aim of our analysis is to compare which functions were used by students and teachers to complete the task. Since one of our hypotheses is that the gap between the task and the activity is wider in Condition 2 than in Condition 1, we will study the patterns of interaction which emerge from each situation. This should allow for the analysis of the speakers' positioning.

Quantitative analysis

The close study of our data led us to investigate three aspects of the discourse that appeared to be relevant to measure the participants' positioning in the interaction:

1. The number of words uttered by each speaker would give us some information on who takes the floor in an exchange.
2. The use of subject pronouns ('I, you and we') to highlight who talks about whom. These pronouns are potentially a good indicator of the intersubjective positioning of the participants in the task.
3. The number of questions formulated by each participant. The goal of the task was to come to an agreement and therefore, it seems reasonable to think that requesting information or preferences would display a certain positioning in the conversation process.

In order to draw conclusions on comparable data, all the quantitative measures were made on the first 3 minutes 20 seconds of each dialogue since it was the length of the shortest conversation. Interestingly enough, the conversations among students were longer on average than the conversations in which a teacher was involved. The teachers were following a question/answer pattern which gave the conversation a quicker rhythm and did not really allow for pauses more frequently noticed in peer-to-peer conversations.

1. Who is the most talkative?

The students who took part in our experiment were at CEFR Level A2+/B1 (Council of Europe 2001). This means a difference in terms of fluency between the teacher and the learner with the former uttering more words per minute than the latter. This raises the question of who talks the most in a situation where the student is assessed by a teacher who is acting in the role-play. In Condition 2, are the teachers/assessors able to stick to their role (the role assigned by the language task in which they were meant to play one of the host family members) and does this role play enable the student to complete the task according to the task designer's expectations?

The following figures show the number of words uttered by each participant in Conditions 1 and 2.

In Condition 1, the dialogues between peers show an unbalanced number of uttered words with the more able students being more talkative than the less able ones. However this difference is not a major one and can be explained by the roles assumed by some students who were confronted by their less able peers and who needed to provide vocabulary, to reformulate or to scaffold their partner's speech. When in conversation with the teachers (Condition 2), the difference becomes wider for the less skilled speakers. These students explained that they did not feel confident and did not dare talk and uttered a minimum number of words because they feared the teacher's reaction to their

Figure 1 Number of words uttered by each participant in Condition 1

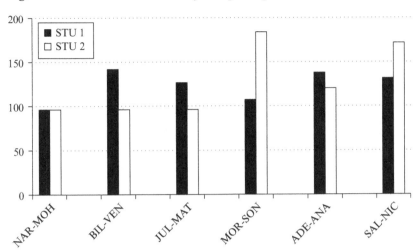

Figure 2 Number of words uttered by each participant in Condition 2

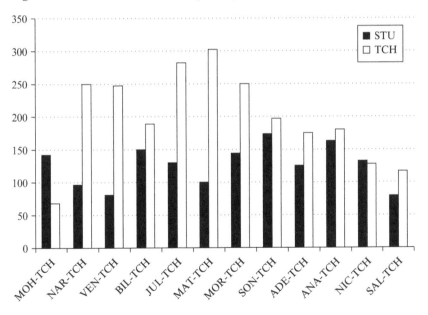

potential errors. As far as more competent learners are concerned, the number of words uttered by each speaker is usually better balanced. The proportions observed in Condition 1 were confirmed and amplified in Condition 2 with less able learners speaking even less with the teacher than with their peer.

There is one exception to this trend: one of the students (MOH) working in Condition 2 completely took the lead in the conversation which turned out to be more a monologue than a dialogue. He never looked at the teacher and was therefore unable to consider her reactions or nonverbal feedback. The teacher let the student speak without interrupting (and without really being able to interrupt) which resulted in an unbalanced exchange until the learner ran short of ideas. During the interview this pupil mentioned that he felt more comfortable with a peer than with the teacher. This position is confirmed by the dialogue in Condition 1, which is well balanced in terms of numbers of uttered words (NAR-MOH).

This data shows that even if the teachers tend to speak more than the students, this does not necessarily mean that the learners are disadvantaged. In other words, they do not speak less than with peers. It is only the difference between the two speakers that is bigger in Condition 2 but not the amount of learner speech. If we go back to the core of our subject – assessment – we may wonder how these unbalanced dialogues influence the teacher's perception when evaluating the students. Before examining the results of the assessment proper, we would like to focus on the reason why teachers tend to talk more than students. Does this mean that in Condition 2, the lead is on the teacher's side? More data might help us answer this question.

2. Who talks about whom?

One of the prominent characteristics that we discovered in the dialogues among the participants is the differential use of subject pronouns. These referential markers could potentially highlight how the participants position themselves in the dialogue and in the completion of the task.

Table 1 deals with the dialogues in Condition 1. We added the number of subject pronouns used by the 12 students in the course of their 6 spoken interactions. In Table 2, the number of conversations that we took into account doubled since each of the 12 students had a conversation with a teacher (Condition 2).

The difference in the number of pronouns used in Condition 1 (N = 159) and in Condition 2 (N = 432) is due to the number of dialogues that we analysed (six vs 12) therefore we shall only look at percentages. However, it is important to mention that there was also a difference in the structure and length of utterances produced in each condition. In Condition 1, what the students utter is often limited to incomplete sentences such as 'when?', 'on Monday', 'oh no Saturday', 'ah ok' whereas the conversations with the teachers are more elaborate. The latter would ask complete questions and require full answers. When the student did not provide a full answer, then the teacher usually reformulated it.

In Condition 1, the use of the pronoun 'I' (49%) shows that half the utterances are self-referential. Students talk about themselves, they express what they like or what they do not like, what they wish to do, their preference

Table 1 Total number of subject pronouns used by the participants in Condition 1

STU–STU		
I	YOU	WE
78	51	30
(49%)	(32%)	(19%)

Table 2 Total number of subject pronouns used by the participants in Condition 2

STU			TCH		
I	YOU	WE	I	YOU	WE
152	15	18	19	187	41
(36%)	(3%)	(4%)	(4%)	(43%)	(9%)

and finally their agreement or disagreement with their partner's suggestion. However, they also take into account their partner's point of view when they enquire about the other's desires, likes or preferences hence the use of 'you' (32%) as in 'Where do **you** want to go next weekend?'. The pronoun is also used because the speaker seeks information as in 'Do **you** know the MOMA?', therefore the interaction makes sense since the students collaborate in trying to know a thing or a fact (Council of Europe 1990). We can also notice that, to a lesser extent, students use 'we' in their dialogues. This demonstrates how the speakers engage in the task: the organisation of the weekend is meant to be a co-construction in which the role assigned by the fictional situation predominates. The participants were asked to come to an agreement therefore, having expressed their own point of view, they show that they reach an agreement in referring to the two of them as in 'and **we** will go shopping at Macy's because **we** have money and **we** want to spend money.' These 'we' are mostly found in the second part of the dialogues. As mentioned before, we only used the first 3 minutes and 20 seconds of each dialogue, therefore, for the longer ones, these pronouns do not appear in our analysis. Thus, it is likely that our figures underestimate the co-positioning of the participants since it appears that the '*I*' and '*you*' pronouns progressively change into 'we'. The dialogicality (Du Bois 2007) of their speech i.e. the interactional structure of the language reflects the *enaction of their personal and social relationships* with one another (Halliday and Matthiessen 2004).

In Condition 2, the use of the subject pronouns differs quite substantially. Whilst the students continue to predominantly use 'I' (36%), the teachers, who play the role of the host family member, only use it in 4% of all cases. Conversely, they mostly use 'you' (43%) in the conversations as opposed to students who only employ it in 3% of all sentences. This distribution reflects two important aspects of the type of relation that is built up between each pair. First, this shows that the conversation is clearly led by the teachers who tend to ask questions (the types and functions of these questions will be discussed later) to the students about their wants and desires, likes and dislikes or preferences but also on their knowledge of the possible places of interest to be explored. The whole range of questions that teachers generally use when addressing students and prompting them to develop their speech is displayed such as 'What would you like to visit?', 'When would you like to go?', 'Are you interested in art?', 'Where would you like to have lunch?'. Therefore, it is often the teachers who initiate the topics and suggest possible options. The students tend to respond to suggestions without almost ever offering or suggesting choices.

Second, the instructions given to the participants pointed out that they should enquire about the co-speakers' wants and desires but they also mentioned making and reacting to suggestions. The very small amount of 'I' pronouns used by the teachers and 'you' pronouns used by the students suggests that the dialogue serves as a task in which the pupils' speech is driven and supported by the adult. The interaction appears as highly unequal in terms of co-construction: the teachers talk about the students who in turn, only talk about themselves. If the latter seems to be able to stick to the role assigned by the task, the former tends to be caught up by their social role. Condition 2 favours an unequal positioning in the sense that the role-play is more difficult for the teachers who tend to play their actual social role rather than their fictional persona. The task involved a discussion on equal grounds (as far as the relationship between two teenagers could equal that of a student and a host-family parent) but the disproportion between the use of subject pronouns suggests an unbalanced relationship. This view is supported by the very low amount of 'we': 4% by the students and 9% by the teachers in Condition 2 as opposed to 19% in Condition 1. In Condition 2, the task is clearly not a 'team' construction as opposed to Condition 1 where the students tend to come to a co-constructed agreement based on shared points of view rather than a one-way spoken composition. This corroborates our hypothesis that the gap between the expectations raised by the task design and reality is wider in Condition 2 than in Condition 1.

3. Who asks questions and how many?

Another striking difference between the two conditions was the use of questions. The design of the task implied that the participants would enquire about their partners' likes or dislikes, wants and desires or preferences. Seeking information was also part of it. Therefore questions were expected in the participants' discourse but their number greatly differed from one condition to the other as shown in Tables 3 and 4.

Table 3 Number of questions asked by the participants in Condition 1

	STU 1	STU 2
BIL-VEN	9	10
MOH-NAR	9	7
JUL-MAT	2	3
SON-MOR	3	4
ADE-ANA	4	6
SAL-NIC	3	5

Table 4 Number of questions asked by the participants in Condition 2

	TCH	STU
TCH-VEN	32	2
TCH-BIL	20	5
TCH-MOH	4	0
TCH-NAR	28	3
TCH-JUL	17	1
TCH-MAT	22	1
TCH-MOR	14	2
TCH-SON	21	1
TCH-ADE	11	1
TCH-ANA	23	3
TCH-SAL	15	2
TCH-NIC	10	2

In Condition 1 (Table 3), the number of questions asked by the students is evenly shared and ranges from three to 10 over a period of 3 minutes 20 seconds. The participants share an equal status and no one seeks to take a leading role. However, in Condition 2 (Table 4), the pattern of the dialogue changed considerably with teachers asking between seven to 20 times more questions than students. The teachers were supposed to play a role in which they engaged in a discussion but the dialogue often took the form of an interview rather than a conversation. One pair (TCH-MOH), once again, appears to be an exception for the reason mentioned before. MOH decided to engage in a monologue and stated all his desires and wants for the organisation of the weekend. As the teacher was not able to speak much, she obviously did not ask many questions. For all the other dialogues, it seems that the teachers were willing to help the learners. The guidance offered by them was made in the form of questions as teachers would usually do. Therefore it appears that, once again, the dialogues in Condition 2 display an unbalanced structure in the exchange that accounts for and replicates the type of hierarchical relationship found in the classroom. As Goffman argued, 'the syntax of interaction

(. . .) is the place where face, self, and identity are expressed, and where they are also ratified or undermined by the conduct of others' (Heritage and Clayman 2010:9). The linguistic and pragmatic choices made by the teachers had thus an impact on the shaping of the participants' role and on their positioning in the interaction.

These conclusions, and more specifically the status of questions, require a more detailed qualitative analysis so as to understand the positioning of each participant in the interactions according to Conditions 1 and 2.

Qualitative analysis

As they completed the task, the participants came to express their communicative intentions through a certain number of language functions (LFs) that we classified. We used and adapted the typology of the Threshold Level, now B1 in the CEFR (Council of Europe 1990).

1 Imparting and seeking factual information
1.1 Identifying/defining
1.2 Correcting
1.3 Imparting/Enquiring about factual information

2 Expressing and finding out attitudes
2.1 Expressing agreement/disagreement with a statement
2.2.1 Stating whether one knows or does not know a thing or a fact
2.2.2 Enquiring whether one knows or does not know a thing or a fact
2.2.3 Asking for justification
2.3.1 Expressing ability/inability to do something + Expressing inability to SAY something
2.3.2 Enquiring about ability/inability to do something
2.4.1 Expressing wants/desires
2.4.2 Enquiring about wants/desires
2.5.1 Expressing preference
2.5.2 Enquiring about preference
2.6.1 Expressing like/dislike
2.6.2 Enquiring about like/dislike
2.7.1 Expressing lack of interest
2.8.1 Expressing approval

3 Deciding on courses of action
3.1 Suggesting a course of action
3.2 Agreeing to a suggestion
3.3 Advising someone to do something
3.4 Requesting assistance
3.5 Offering assistance

These LFs were not evenly used by the students or the teachers and the underlying purpose behind some of them also appeared to be different.

In Condition 1, the learners resorted to all the above LFs to complete the task. They did not often correct their partners but it was not a requirement. Therefore the actual spoken activity displayed by the students is in line with what was expected in planning the task.

Conversely, in Condition 2, not all LFs were found. In accordance with what was revealed by the use of subject pronouns, the teachers hardly ever expressed their own wants and desires, their preference or their likes and dislikes. They mostly enquired about what the students thought although the task implied sharing opinions on the subject to come to an agreement. In doing so, they positioned themselves not as co-organisers but as experts in charge of guiding a learner. As Jaffe puts it:

> [a] speaker positionality is built into the act of communication . . . **By taking up a position, individuals automatically invoke a constellation of associated social identities. In doing so, speakers project, assign, propose, constrain, define, or otherwise shape the subject positions of their interlocutors** . . . An utterance framed as a performance, for example, positions receivers as an audience; **a speaker who takes up an expert stance to give advice positions receivers as novices** (2009 (Ed):3–8; author's emphases).

This hierarchical position is also reinforced when teachers correct students even though the errors do not create a communication breakdown (Manoïlov 2010). It should be noted that the teachers were specifically required not to correct students because the completion of the task (a role play) did not require such discourse moves.

Example 1
```
30        ADE: uh I'd like to go to Times Square too.
31        TCH3: yes why?
32        ADE: uh because I was told there are big screens, large
          screens and uh with ad.
33        TCH3: ads yes, yes.
```

In line 33, the reformulation shows that the adult clearly goes back to her institutional role, that of a teacher, since this move does not add anything to the completion of the task.

This aspect is even more obvious in the meta-functions of the questions asked in the dialogues. On the one hand, they had a communicative purpose which was task oriented (Example 2) but in some cases they were clearly pedagogical (Example 3).

The following example is an extract from an interaction between two students who resort to questioning.

Example 2

60	SON:	and the MOMA when do we go?
61	MOR:	oh ok.
62	SON:	but when (.) do we go to the MOMA?
63	MOR:	uh the MOMA we can go on (.) uh six hour (.) pm.
64	SON:	we can go uh (.) uh after shopping.
65	MOR:	oh yes.
66	MOR:	err but it's uh it's [/] uh it's a momu(ment) it's a monument for, for what?
67	SON:	I don't know we should go and then we see.
68	MOR:	ah ok.
69	SON:	(.) because I don't know what is the MOMA so we can go there and see what it is.
70	MOR:	yes.

The two questions asked by SON (lines 60 and 62) are task oriented. In line 60, she is interested in the organisation of the weekend and asks her partner about the planned schedule (LF10). She has to repeat her question (line 62) because her partner did not understand it. When MOR asks a question (line 66) because she does not know what the MOMA is, she is genuinely enquiring for information (LF13). Seeking information has a communicative function. The whole extract shows that the two students are working towards the completion of the task. The process is a collaborative one, each participant being equally part of the co-construction.

However in Condition 2, some questions had a different intent when they were uttered by a teacher.

Example 3

38	TCH3:	what about Times Square?
39	TCH3:	what do you know about Times Square?
40	TCH3:	it's famous for, for?
41	ADE:	ben uh for large screens.

In line 38, the teacher's question could be understood as a suggestion but in line 39, she adds 'what do you know?'. Once again we could consider the question as an enquiry to find out information about Times Square but the third move (line 40) clearly displays the teacher's intention. She wants to find out whether the student knows about Times Square not because she is herself ignorant but because she wants to prompt the learner to display her knowledge. Therefore the question turns out to be a didactic one or what we call a 'quiz question'.

LF12 (Correcting) and LF13 (Imparting/Enquiring about factual information) were always task oriented when used by the students. However when used in Condition 2 by the teachers, LF12 and LF13 were sometimes task oriented and sometimes didactic questions.

LF 222 (Enquiring whether one knows or does not know a thing or a fact) and LF 223 (Asking for justification) were always used by the students with a communicative intent and always used by the teachers with a didactic intention. Therefore we can see that it was sometimes difficult for the teachers to play the role assigned by the task and to forget for a moment their teacher's status. This has an impact on the relationships in the interaction. When interviewed, some of the students mentioned that they were impressed and they did not always feel as confident as when they were talking with a peer. However, this feeling is not shared by all the students. Four of them (one third) declared that they preferred interacting with the teacher who was reassuring. They appreciated the fact that the expert was there to support them. We can then suppose that there is a correlation between the students' preferring Condition 2 and their own positioning more or less in line with the social role assigned by the task or the one assigned by the institution. In other words, Condition 2 is preferred by students who remain students no matter what.

We shall now turn to the results of the assessments to check if the previous findings had an impact on the teacher's appraisal of the students' performance.

Results of the assessments: What they tell us

As mentioned before, this experiment was meant to test the conditions in which students could be assessed on their spoken interaction skills. One of our goals was to seek whether one condition would be more favourable to the students than the other. The teachers were asked to evaluate them using the grid designed by the DEPP. The teachers first assessed the students' performance in Condition 2 immediately after their interaction with them. They were then asked to watch the video that had previously been recorded with two students completing the task and, they used the same grid to evaluate them in Condition 1. The grade is composed of two items, the figure concerns the pragmatic skills and the degree of achievement of the task (grade 1: minimum, to grade 4: maximum), and the letter concerns the linguistic skills (grade A: minimum, to grade E: maximum). In the grid, the range of grades for the linguistic skills is wider than the pragmatic skills because it was found that for practical purposes, it would help to have a more detailed description.

The hatched boxes represent the best grade obtained by each participant. In eight cases out of the 12, the students were given a better grade in Condition 1 than in Condition 2 (66%). The teachers were often pleasantly surprised by the way the students were able to engage in the conversation to complete the task in peer-to-peer interaction. They initiated a lot of interactions, they reacted to their partners' suggestions, they launched new topics, they asked about new information, and they organised the weekend in a very efficient manner so as to complete the task. Conversely, when in conversation

Table 5 Grades assigned by the teachers according to Condition 1 and Condition 2

		Condition 1 STU–STU	Condition 2 STU–TCH
TCH1	NAR	4C	3C
	MOH	4C	3C
	BIL	3D	4D
	VEN	4C	3C
TCH2	MAT	4D	3D
	JUL	4D	4E
	SON	4E	3D
	MOR	4D	3C
TCH3	ANA	3C	4D
	ADE	3C	4D
	SAL	4D	3C
	NIC	4D	3C

with the teachers, they were keener on answering suggestions or questions without initiating any new topics. They followed the teacher's guidelines thus positioning themselves as students and not really as partners in the task completion. This position, which was implicitly imposed by the social identities at stake in the interaction, certainly had an impact on the grading. If we look closely at the results, we can notice that it is almost always the pragmatic grade (i.e. the number) that is better in Condition 1 than in Condition 2. The linguistic one (i.e. the letter) remains the same in both conditions except for one student (JUL) who was deemed more skilled when in interaction with the teacher. This figure evaluated the ability to complete the task and the ability to interact in an efficient manner. It seems that the teacher considered that the communication between the students was more successful and productive when in Condition 1. The equal status enabled and led the students to be more active in the way they engaged in the conversation and in the task. The asymmetrical relationship in Condition 2 led to an unbalanced structured conversation where the teachers initiated topics through questions which the students answered. Their role was therefore more passive and this could explain the difference between the two grades. However, when in conversation with the teacher some students did better in terms of linguistic skills. This could be explained by the fact that students would concentrate more on the language forms when in interaction with the teacher because they know that teachers usually value this aspect of the language more.

Answering our hypotheses

Hypothesis 1: In the context of spoken interaction, the gap is bigger between the task planned and the activity observed in Condition 1 (TCH–STU) than in Condition 2 (STU–STU)

The qualitative analysis of the language functions displayed in the participants' speech shows that in Condition 1 there is little difference between what was expected and the actual activity. However, in Condition 2, the gap is bigger because the teachers did not fully adopt their imaginary roles. Their speech was often dedicated to guide the students and they were not involved in opinion sharing. We must point to the fact that the teachers' role was a difficult one that may have biased their production. The creation of roles that would be realistic implies that what the teachers and the students were expected to play was similar but not identical. This should be kept in mind.

Hypothesis 2: The main reason for this discrepancy lies in the positioning of the speakers, more or less in line with the social role imposed by the task or the social role imposed by the school context

Our analysis showed that the teachers tend to hold the floor when in conversation with the students, especially the less able ones. The former also oriented the conversation towards the learner in using the second person subject pronoun and in asking a tremendous number of questions. The unbalanced structure of the dialogue reflects the unequal status between students and teachers that the social fiction imposed by the task is unable to erase. The social function remains strongly significant.

Hypothesis 3: The positioning of the speakers has an influence on their performances

The results of the assessments show that eight students out of 12 were better evaluated by the teachers in Condition 1 than in Condition 2. When in interaction with the expert (i.e. the teacher) their status of learner was more obvious and they behaved in a different manner. The social positioning influenced the pragmatic behaviour of the participants which in turn had an impact on the grades. The teachers found the students more efficient when interacting with their peers than with them probably because, in Condition 2, the students took less initiative, asked fewer questions and were not actively involved.

Yet not all students behaved the same in Condition 2. In the interviews we conducted at the end of the experiment in order to ask the students which condition they preferred, their answers were in keeping with the attitudes displayed during the spoken interactions. Interestingly, the students can be placed on a continuum according to their greater or lesser dependency on the teacher as displayed in Table 6.

Table 6 The institutional–social continuum

Institutional posture	← →	Social posture
ANA	ADE BILL VEN MAR MOH MOR SON NAR MAT	JUL

One more proficient student (ANA) performs better with her teacher and clearly prefers this condition because she can draw the best from it. Another more proficient student (JUL) clearly states that scaffolding from the teacher is unfair and introduces a bias in the assessment. She is the most autonomous student. According to her the difference between her language skills and the teachers' in Condition 2 disadvantages students. Most students (nine out of 12) acknowledge the importance of scaffolding (provided by the teacher even in an assessment situation) although they prefer interacting with a peer and very often succeed better in this condition.

Conclusion

Our study suggests that Condition 1 seems more favourable to students than Condition 2 especially when they feel more comfortable with a peer than with a teacher.

When the task was chosen, the designers' intention was to erase or at least reduce the hierarchical relation that usually exists between a teacher and a student. While in the process of playing their assigned role the participants were meant to perform an ordinary conversation. However, it appeared that Condition 2 rather favoured institutional talk to the disadvantage of 66% of them (Heritage and Clayman 2010). Thus, it seems that the interactional roles are all the more reinforced by the institutional context which is a source of asymmetrical positioning even before any action is taken or any word is uttered by the participants. Our study shows that when engaged in dyads with students in an interactive assessment task, the teachers' position remains high. This is not only because of their mastery of the language but also because of their social function as teachers, which is deeply anchored in them within the institutional context. We also found that the places are collaboratively constructed in Condition 1 enabling the students to position themselves as equals in the conversation, whereas they seem to be imposed upon by the social context in Condition 2 where the teachers keep their dominant position. Although our experiment relies on a limited corpus and as such cannot prove to be generalisable, it tends to show that even with basic or independent language users (Levels A2–B1) the most favourable assessment condition for oral interaction is peer-to-peer. A larger-scale study is now planned to check these results and to take more precisely into account the proficiency levels of the participants. Indeed, it seems necessary to vary the level of each pair with more competent students interacting with less competent ones or pairs of students of equal competence. This study should have consequences not only for the way French teachers evaluate their students but also on the way they teach interactive skills both on a pragmatic and linguistic level.

References

Brooks, L (2009) Interactions in pairs in a test of oral proficiency: Co-constructing a better performance, *Language Testing* 26 (3), 341–366.

Clot, Y and Faïta, D (2000) Genres et styles en analyse du travail, *Concepts et Méthodes Travailler* 4, 7–42.

Council of Europe (1990) *Threshold 1990*, available online: www.coe.int/t/dg4/linguistic/Threshold-Level_CUP.pdf

Council of Europe (2001) *Common European Framework of Reference for Languages: Learning, Teaching, Assessment*, Cambridge: Cambridge University Press.

Du Bois, J W (2007) The stance triangles in Englebretson, R (Ed) *Stancetaking in Discourse: Subjectivity, Evaluation, Interaction*, Amsterdam: John Benjamins, 139–182.

Együd, G and Glover, P (2001) Oral testing in pairs – a secondary school perspective, *ELT Journal* 55 (1), 70–76.

Finkielkraut, A (1999) *L'Ingratitude. Conversation sur notre temps avec Antoine Robitaille*, Paris: Gallimard, Coll. Blanche.

Folland, D and Robertson, D (1976) Towards objectivity in group oral testing, *English Language Teaching Journal* 30, 156–167.

Galaczi, E (2008) Peer–peer interaction in a speaking test: The case of the First Certificate in English examination, *Language Assessment Quarterly* 5 (2), 89–119.

Galaczi, E and ffrench, A (2011) Context validity, in Taylor, L (Ed) *Examining Speaking: Research and Practice in Assessing Second Language Speaking*, Studies in Language Testing volume 30, Cambridge: UCLES/Cambridge University Press, 112–170.

Gan, Z, Davison, C and Hamp-Lyons, L (2008) Topic negotiation in peer group oral assessment situations: a conversation analytic approach, *Applied Linguistics* 30 (3), 26–29.

Goodwin, C and Heritage, J (1990) Conversation analysis, *Annual Review of Anthropology* 19, 283–307.

Halliday, M A K and Matthiessen, C M I M (2004) *An Introduction to Functional Grammar*, (3rd Edition), London: Hodder Arnold.

Heritage, J and Clayman, S (2010) *Talk in Action: Interactions, Identities, and Institutions*, Oxford: Wiley and Blackwell.

Iwashita, N (1998) The validity of the paired interview in oral performance assessment. Melbourne Papers, *Language Testing* 5 (2), 51–65.

Jaffe, A (Ed) (2009) *Stance: Sociolinguistic Perspectives*, Oxford Studies in Sociolinguistics, Oxford: Oxford University Press.

Kormos, J (1999) Monitoring and self-repair in L2, *Language Learning* 49, 303–342.

Lantolf, J (2000) *Socialcultural Theory and Second Language Learning*, Oxford: Oxford University Press.

Lantolf, J (2006) Sociocultural theory and L2: State of the Art, *Studies In Second Language Acquisition*, 28 (1), 67–109.

Lazaraton, A (2002) *A Qualitative Approach to the Validation of Oral Language Tests*, Cambridge: Cambridge University Press.

Leontiev, A (1981) *Psychology and the Language Learning Process*, Oxford: Pergamon.

MacWhinney, B (2000) *The CHILDES project: Tools for Analysing Talk*, Mahwah: Lawrence Erlbaum Associates.

Manoïlov, P (2010) *Study of errors, feedback and uptake on second language learners in an institutional setting*, unpublished MA thesis.

O'Sullivan, B, Weir, C and Saville, N (2002) Using observation checklists to validate speaking-test tasks, *Language Testing* 19 (1), 33–56.

Sartre, J-P (1976) *L'être et le néant*, Paris: Gallimard.

Saville, N and Hargreaves, P (1999) Assessing speaking in the revised FCE, *ELT Journal* 53 (1), 42–57.

Shohamy, E, Reves, T and Bejarano, Y (1986) Introducing a new comprehensive test of oral proficiency, *English Language Teaching Journal* 40, 212–220.

Skehan, P (2001) Tasks and language performance assessment, in Bygate, M, Skehan, S and Swain, M (Eds) *Researching Pedagogic Tasks: Second Language Learning, Teaching and Testing*, Harlow: Pearson Education, 167–85.

Strauss, A and Corbin, J (1990) *Basics of Qualitative Research: Grounded Theory Procedures and Techniques*, London: Sage.

Swain, M (2000) The output hypothesis and beyond: Mediating acquisition through collaborative dialogue, in Lantolf, J-P (Ed) *Sociocultural Theory and Second Language Learning*, Oxford: Oxford University Press, 97–114.

Taylor, L (2001) The paired speaking test format: Recent studies, *Research Notes* 6, 15–17.

Weir, C, Vidaković, I and Galaczi, E (2013) *Measured Constructs: A History of Cambridge English Examinations, 1913–2012*, Studies in Language Testing volume 37, Cambridge: UCLES/Cambridge University Press.

Wertsch, J V (1985) La médiation sémiotique de la vie mentale, in Bronckart, J-P and Schneuwly, B (Eds) *Vygotsky aujourd'hui*, Lonay: Delachaux et Niestlé, 39–47.

24 Comparing native and non-native raters of US Federal Government speaking tests

Rachel L Brooks
Federal Bureau of Investigation

Abstract

Previous language testing research has largely reported that although characteristics of raters may affect their evaluations of speaking performance (Reed and Cohen 2001), being a native speaker or non-native speaker rater does not significantly affect final ratings (Kim 2009). Some researchers conclude that performance and perception differences exist between native and non-native speakers (Barnwell 1989a, Eckes 2008, Galloway 1980, Kang 2008, Ludwig 1982, Reed and Cohen 2001), while others contend that there is little conclusive evidence to support end state differences (Fayer and Krasinski 1987, Ross 1979). The US Government requires speaking test raters to be both native and high-proficiency speakers of the test language due to the high-level language needed for its operational context (Federal Bureau of Investigation 2009). An exploration of how the native speaker construct is operationalised in research reveals a lack of common understanding of the term native speaker, referring both to an ideal speaker and a native acquirer of language.

This study, which focused on investigating the role of rater nativeness in speaking proficiency assessments, built on previous research by expanding the breadth of proficiency levels rated to include highly articulate examinees, regrouping the raters to represent three ideas of nativeness (native/non-native speakers, speaking proficiency and first language differences). Thirty Federal Bureau of Investigation (FBI) speaking testers, native and non-native speakers of English, rated 25 English Speaking Proficiency Tests. Using ANOVAs, the results indicated no significant difference between the native and non-native speaker groups. When raters were grouped by English proficiency level, lower proficiency raters gave significantly lower ratings, both in the final and in many linguistic category ratings, although with a small effect size.

The results suggested that rater training organisations should consider rater proficiency level rather than whether or not raters are native speakers. Additionally, the results supported the theory that non-native speakers can demonstrate language acquisition equivalent to native speakers, at least when evaluating spoken language. Finally, it was recommended that researchers and testing practitioners that use native speakers should clearly define and justify their use.

Introduction

Most language proficiency exams rely on human raters to evaluate speaking and writing. Despite efforts to minimise the subjectivity inherent in human rating, individual characteristics of the raters introduce error to test scores (Barnwell 1989a, Eckes 2008, Ludwig 1982, Reed and Cohen 2001). The validity of language test results is of great importance since many standardised language test scores are used to make high-stakes decisions (Messick 1996, Shohamy 2001), such as course placement, course or programme final evaluations, employment suitability, eligibility for incentive pay, or assignments abroad (Federal Bureau of Investigation 2009). Research to date has indicated that raters' scores are affected to some degree by such rater attributes as age, gender, occupation, international experience, personality, cultural background and opinion (Barnwell 1989a, Eckes 2008, Ludwig 1982, Reed and Cohen 2001). In addition to these, researchers in language testing have also focused on whether or not being a non-native speaker (NNS) rater introduces bias and affects the final test rating. Originally much of the research that has been conducted on native speaker (NS) versus NNS raters concluded that there were fundamental differences between how NS and NNSs perceived the examinees' language (Barnwell 1989b, Fayer and Krasinski 1987, Galloway 1980). These early studies based their conclusions on descriptive statistics. Since then, research has evolved to employ more rigorous statistical tests. Recent research suggests that whether or not a person is a NS does not significantly affect rater reliability or test score accuracy (Eckes 2008, Kim 2009, Zhang and Elder 2011), which challenges the idea that NSs are preferable raters to NNSs.

Comparing NS and NNS rater performances is complicated because it is more difficult to clearly define the variable in question, nativeness, than other rater characteristics, such as age, gender, or occupation, which may be easier to clearly categorise (Davies 2003). When scholars have addressed the NS in language testing research in the past, the NS was often undefined with the assumption that the reader understands what it means (Escudero and Sharwood-Smith 2001). Although the precise characteristics associated with being a NS in a study may be unclear, researchers still draw conclusions about what it means to be a NS or what NSs or NNSs can or cannot do. It is instead possible that differences that may appear between NSs and NNSs in studies may be attributable to the characteristics of the NS, such as language proficiency, rather than a person's nativeness.

Literature review

In a number of places in linguistics literature (Davies 2003, Maher 2001, Paikeday 1985), a NS is defined in two primary ways. A NS can refer either to the way a person learned the language (e.g. since youth and in an environment where the language was spoken) or to a level of language attainment (e.g. someone who reached a highly articulate level of language proficiency). When NSs are used as raters or evaluators, they are often selected because they meet the former definition (they acquired the language natively) and then are assumed to have the latter definition (they have a high level of language acquisition). However, the variation in what is meant to be a NS makes it difficult to compare results on NSs' rating abilities from study to study.

Although the native acquirer of a language may not be a completely inappropriate yardstick by which to measure a person's ability (Davies 2003, 2011), it is problematic because the average native acquirer of the language may not demonstrate a skill as high as the examinee. Also, the average native acquirer is not a homogenous concept (Hamilton, Lopes, McNamara and Sheridan 1993), leading to variation within a group that is assumed to be a unified concept. Still, Davies states that the idealised NS is needed as a model and a goal, although the average or typical NS (the native acquirer) is not useful as a measure. For many first and second language learners, the goal is the acquisition of an idealised standard language (Taylor 2006). So native-born speakers do not automatically acquire it, but have to become language learners themselves in order to reach certain levels of language proficiency (Brutt-Griffler 2002). Both the NS and NNSs have the same target language, the standard language (Davies 2011).

In the context of language testing, NS judges are often selected as participants because they acquired the language in a native setting (Abrahamsson and Hyltenstam 2009, Barnwell 1989a, Galloway 1980, Johnson and Lim 2009, Kang 2008, Kim 2009, Marinova-Todd 2003). They are then assumed to be high-level acquirers of the language and suitable arbiters of language correctness (Escudero and Sharwood-Smith 2001, Paikeday 1985). However, this relationship has never been explored and this assumption has not been justified.

Language testing has largely been interested in the comparison of NSs and NNSs as language evaluators. Previous research on the equivalence of native born and non-native born speaker raters has yielded mixed results (Reed and Cohen 2001). Early research comparing the ratings of native born and non-native born speakers has found differences between the rater groups

(Barnwell 1989a, Fayer and Krasinski 1987, Galloway 1980). However, research both during and following that time period did not always find significant differences between the groups' final ratings (Brown 1995, Hill 1996, Kim 2009, Ludwig 1982, Zhang and Elder 2011). According to Taylor (2002), the questions that are left unanswered regarding NSs and NNSs as raters involve: how the examiner's own language proficiency affects test delivery; how the relationship between the examiner and examinee's native languages affects test delivery; and whether or not NSs and NNSs' rating behaviours are comparable with each other.

Early research on differences between NSs and NNS raters examined teachers evaluating students' language to determine whether NNSs are well suited as teachers (Barnwell 1989a, Galloway 1980). Data collected is observational and usually descriptive, with emphasis on what NS and NNS teachers noticed or emphasised. In the mid-1990s, many published studies on NS and NNS differences begin to shift focus to research using trained raters. This shift is notable in Hill's (1996) examination of rater differences in an institutionalised language exam. Hill found the NS raters to be harsher in rating overall in this setting.

Shi (2001) takes a more in-depth look into written test evaluations by NSs and NNSs. Shi's research informs the issue of whether holistic scoring reflects analytical judgements, consequentially affecting the construct validity of the exam. In this case, there is no difference in the holistic, final ratings, yet differences appear in the analysis. Differences in how the raters arrived at the final rating may indicate that the raters are using different constructs for rating exams. Lazaraton (2008) reviews many of the studies that examine the use of NNSs as evaluators, concluding that there is no justification to exclude NNSs from becoming test raters and supporting the emerging trend to abandon the term 'NS' altogether.

Kim's (2009) research addresses the question of NS and NNS comparability in English speaking tests. Kim's analysis reveals that the raters are mostly internally consistent and the NS and NNS groups assign comparable scores, with only a couple of exceptions. However, Kim notes that the NS and NNS groups do not handle the rating samples equivalently. NSs are found to give more detailed and elaborate ratings, particularly in respect to pronunciation, grammar and accuracy. Kim (2009) conducts a subsequent study to further investigate differences in how NSs and NNSs rate. Kim finds that most of the variation in the scores is attributable to examinee ability rather than rater effect. Again, the rater groups show similar severity patterns, though NS raters contribute less variance to the overall score.

Zhang and Elder (2011) re-examine the comparability of NS and NNS ratings of oral language proficiency in the context of a high-stakes, institutionalised language exam. Like other recent research, Zhang and Elder do not find significant overall differences in the holistic ratings assigned by the two groups; however, the commentary provided to support those scores does deviate significantly in the frequency that some linguistic categories are mentioned. Overall, the NSs seem more communication focused and the NNSs seemed more form-focused.

Research questions and methodology

NSs continue to play an important role in language testing, but is the emphasis on whether or not a person is a NS really warranted? This study looks at differences in ratings on speaking tests from NS and NNS raters. The raters are grouped into three groups: NS vs NNSs, level of English proficiency and first language, leading to the three research questions:

1. Do NS and NNS raters assign comparable ratings on speaking tests?
2. Does speaking proficiency level affect a rater's ability to reliably evaluate speaking proficiency?
3. Does the first language learned affect a rater's ability to reliably evaluate speaking proficiency?

It is hypothesised that whether or not a person is a NS is less of a contributing factor to reliable speaking test rating than the characteristics that compose being a NS or NNS, such as speaking proficiency level or first language acquired. Positive results from research questions two and three would indicate that rater proficiency level or first language determines the reliability of ratings more than being a NS.

The NS and NNS raters come from the operational testing programme at the FBI. Thirty current, certified raters volunteered for the study from eight different first language backgrounds: English, Arabic, Farsi, French, German, Mandarin Chinese, Spanish and Vietnamese. The rater participants are all FBI Speaking Proficiency Test (SPT) raters and they normally rate tests in their native languages using the *Interagency Language Roundtable (ILR) Skill Level Descriptions for Speaking Proficiency*. The ILR Skill Level Descriptions, or ILR Scale, is one of a set of language assessment criteria used by all US Federal Government agencies to measure language ability in various skills. Ratings range from Level 0 to Level 5 with plus levels for each level, except 5. The *ILR Skill Level Descriptions for Speaking Proficiency* measure a holistic, functional ability to speak the language. The raters are all ILR Level 5 speakers of their native languages, meaning they are functionally equivalent to highly articulate well-educated NSs of the language (Interagency Language Roundtable 1985). Additionally, the rater participants all have an excellent level of English proficiency, with ILR speaking ratings of Level 2+ through 5. This range of proficiency is comparable to the ratings most NSs get. These raters evaluated recordings of 25 previously administered English SPTs, which follow an oral interview format.

The raters are instructed to conduct reviews of the tests, assigning ratings and completing the accompanying rater reports. The test sample represents the diverse population of English language examinees that the FBI encounters. Examinees ranged in English proficiency from mid to high-level speaking and were both NSs and NNSs of English. Each rater assigned ratings for the final, holistic ability of the examinee.

To address the first research question, the English testers compose the NS group (n=6) and the raters of other language tests compose the NNS group (n = 24). To address the second research question, the raters are further subdivided by language proficiency in English, the test language, resulting in four rater groups: Level 2+ (n = 6), Level 3/3+ (n = 14), Level 4/4+ (n = 4) and Level 5 (n = 6). To address the third research question, raters are not divided by their proficiencies in English, but strictly by first or native language background, forming eight language groups: English (n = 6), Arabic (n = 4), Farsi (n = 3), French (n = 3), German (n = 3), Mandarin (n = 4), Spanish (n = 4) and Vietnamese (n = 3). The comparisons of the final ratings given by three different rater groupings (NSs/NNSs, English proficiency and first language) address the first three research questions. All statistical tests are preceded by analyses of the descriptive and inter-rater reliability statistics. When final ratings are examined, Analyses of Variation (ANOVA) are used. All 25 English SPTs are analysed together at first and later they are divided into three groups by exam level (Level 2/2+, Level 3/3+ and Level 4/4+/5 exams).

Results

NS and NNS rater comparison

To answer the first research question (Do NS and NNS raters assign comparable ratings on speaking tests?), the raters were grouped into NS and NNS groups and the final ratings on the 25 FBI English SPTs were examined. The ratings assigned were holistic scores that reflected an examinee's sustained ability to complete functional tasks with the necessary quality.

The inter-rater reliability statistics of the NS and NNS rater groups were examined. For this study, the statistic would ideally be greater than 0.8, although at least 0.7 (Krippendorff 2004, Lombard, Snyder-Duch and Bracken 2003). An alpha value of 0.77 for the NS raters is considered acceptable for holistic ratings of proficiency, although not ideal (Krippendorff 2004, Lombard et al 2003). However, the NNS raters' alpha of 0.59 was below the 0.70 minimum acceptability threshold.

As shown in Table 1, there was virtually no descriptive difference between the mean ratings given by the NS raters and the NNS raters. The NS raters

Table 1 Final ratings: NS vs NNS raters

Rater native speaker group	Sample	Mean	SD	SE
		All exams		
Native speakers (n = 6)	150	3.45	0.79	0.06
Non-native speakers (n = 24)	600	3.44	0.90	0.04
Total (n = 30)	750	3.44	0.88	0.03
		Level 2/2+ exams		
Native speakers (n = 6)	36	2.62	0.45	0.08
Non-native speakers (n = 24)	144	2.54	0.53	0.04
Total (n = 30)	180	2.55	0.51	0.04
		Level 3/3+ exams		
Native speakers (n = 6)	84	3.41	0.46	0.05
Non-native speakers (n = 24)	336	3.47	0.69	0.04
Total (n = 30)	420	3.46	0.65	0.03
		Level 4/4+/5 exams		
Native speakers (n = 6)	30	4.56	0.51	0.09
Non-native speakers (n = 24)	120	4.44	0.62	0.06
Total (n = 30)	150	4.46	0.60	0.05

assigned a mean rating of 3.45 across all exams, with a standard error of 0.06; the NNS raters assigned a mean rating of 3.44, with a standard error of 0.04. Both groups had a median score of 3.6. The NNS raters had a slightly larger standard deviation from the mean (0.90) than the NS raters (0.79).

Considering that the main measures of central tendency, the mean and the medians, of the two rater groups were similar, it was no surprise that an ANOVA[1] of the NS and the NNS rater groups revealed no significant difference, $F(1, 749) = 0.02$, $p = 0.88$. A *post hoc* power analysis revealed that the power coefficient was 1.00, which means that if a significant result had existed, it should have been detected (Type β error). The final ratings given by the NS and NNS rater groups to all exams were not significantly different.

Since many of the NNS raters have not achieved the level of proficiency that they are rating (Level 2+ NNS raters rating Level 5 exams), it was hypothesised that the NNSs' capability to rate may vary across levels. As a result, it was important to look at the NS and NNS raters' evaluations on each of the ILR levels of exams: Level 2/2+ exams, Level 3/3+ exams and Level 4/4+/5 exams (Table 1).

On the ILR Level 2/2+ exams, the medians of both the NS and the NNS rater groups were the same: 2+. Likewise, there was very little difference between their mean ratings. The NS raters gave a mean score of 2.62, whereas the NNS raters assigned a mean score of 2.54 to the ILR Level 2/2+ exams. The standard deviation was slightly larger for the NNS raters, (0.53) than for the NS raters (0.45).

In the ILR Level 3/3+ exams, there was a median rating of 3+ from both groups of raters. The mean of the NS raters was 3.41; the mean of the NNS raters was only 0.06 higher at 3.47. The NS raters had a narrower standard deviation (0.46) than the NNS raters (0.69). Since plus level scores were converted to 0.6, this 0.23 difference reflects approximately one half of a plus level.

There was a similar pattern in the ILR Level 4/4+/5 exams as the ILR Level 2/2+ and 3/3+ exams. The NS and NNS rater groups shared a median of 4+. The mean NS rating was 4.56 and NNS rating is 4.44. The NS raters had a smaller standard deviation (0.51) than the NNS raters (0.62), indicating more uniformity within the NS rater group.

Although the measures of central tendency looked similar between the NS and NNS raters and among the three groups of varying levels of exams, an analysis of variance[1] (ANOVA) determined if any differences were significant. The value of p was greater than 0.05 for each exam level, indicating no exam levels where the rater's nativity made a significant difference in the final rating of the exams: Level 2/2+ exams $F(1, 178) = 0.81$, $p = 0.37$; Level 3/3+ exams $F(1, 418) = 0.53$, $p = 0.47$; Level 4/4+/5 exams $F(1, 148) = 0.98$, $p = 0.32$. A *post hoc* power analysis revealed that the power coefficient was 0.97 for the Level 2/2+ exams, 1.00 for the Level 3/3+ exams and 0.94 for the Level 4/4+/5 exams, which means that if a significant result had existed, it should have been detected (Type β error).

Overall, there was no evidence that NS and NNS raters assigned significantly different final ratings on speaking proficiency exams at ILR Level 2 through 5. These results provided the answer to the first research question: do NS and NNS raters assign comparable ratings on speaking tests? The data in the current study showed no statistically significant differences between the ratings of the NS and NNS rater groups. Even though there was not a significant difference between the means, a larger standard deviation appeared in the NNS rater group than in the NS rater group.

Rater English proficiency comparison

In this analysis, the study explored differences of the final ratings assigned by raters at different ILR Base Level ranges: Level 2 (2+ raters); Level 3 (3/3+ raters); Level 4 (4/4+ raters); and Level 5 (5 raters) to address the second research question: does speaking proficiency level affect a rater's ability to reliably evaluate speaking proficiency? The Level 5 raters were the NS raters, as there were not any NNS raters in the pool of qualified and available participants, although Level 5 NNSs exist. For the same reason, the Levels 2+ through 4+ raters were all NNS raters. The final ratings of raters with varying English speaking proficiencies were compared using descriptive statistics and ANOVAs[1].

The results of inter-rater reliability among the new grouping of raters according to English speaking proficiency were calculated. As before, the highest alpha value was found in the Level 5 (NS/English) raters at 0.77 (Krippendorff 2004, Lombard et al 2003). The other three English proficiency groups' inter-rater reliability statistics fell below the 0.70 acceptability threshold for proficiency testing. Interestingly, the Level 2 and Level 3 speaker group had the second-highest Krippendorf's alpha value (0.62), not the Level 4 group (0.58), whose English proficiency was closest to the Level 5 raters.

A review of the means of the four rater groups split by English speaking proficiency (shown in Table 2) revealed some differences among the final ratings. The ILR Level 5 speakers (previously known as the NS raters) assigned a mean rating of 3.45 across all exams, with a standard error of 0.06. The Level 4 range raters showed a similar final rating, with a mean of 3.46 and a standard error of 0.09. The Level 3 raters gave higher ratings, with a mean of 3.62 and a standard error of 0.05. The lowest mean rating was from the Level 2 rater group, who assigned a mean final rating of 3.24 and a standard error of 0.07. The lowest mean rating of the Level 2 group was also reflected in the medians of the groups. The Level 2 raters had a median final rating of 3, while the other groups had a median rating of 3+. As in the NS/NNS comparison, the Level 5 raters had a smaller standard deviation than the other groups in the comparison at 0.79. The Level 2 raters had a standard deviation of 0.89, the Level 3 raters had the largest standard deviation of 0.91 and the Level 4 raters' standard deviation was 0.85.

The NS/NNS rater group comparison revealed no statistical difference between the rater groups, but when the NNS raters were categorised by English speaking proficiency, significant differences between the groups were revealed. In this case, a one-way ANOVA[1] revealed a significant effect of raters' English speaking proficiency level on final ILR rating for the exams, $F(3, 746) = 3.71$, $p = 0.01$, partial $h^2 = 0.02$. A *post hoc* power analysis revealed that the power coefficient was 1.00, which meant if there had been a significant result, it would have been detected (Type β error).

The effect size (partial η^2) of 0.02 was very small[2], meaning that overall, the raters' English proficiency level accounted for very little of the differences in ratings among the rater proficiency level groups. Bonferroni *post hoc* tests showed significant differences between Level 2+ raters and Level 3/3+ raters ($p = 0.01$), with the Level 3 raters assigning ratings at an average of 0.28 higher than the Level 2 raters. No significant differences were found between the Level 5 raters and any of the other English proficiency level groups.

As before, the exams were divided into three categories (Level 2/2+, Level 3/3+ and Level 4/4+/5) to determine if the level of the exam affected whether or not there were any differences among the rater group divided by English proficiency. In the ILR Level 2/2+ exams, the Level 5 raters had the highest

Table 2 Final ratings: Rater English proficiency levels

Rater English speaking proficiency level	Sample	Mean	SD	SE
All exams (n = 25)				
Level 2 raters (n = 6)	150	3.24	0.89	0.07
Level 3 raters (n = 14)	350	3.52	0.91	0.05
Level 4 raters (n = 4)	100	3.46	0.85	0.09
Level 5 raters (n = 6)	150	3.45	0.79	0.06
Total (n = 30)	750	3.44	0.88	0.03
Level 2/2+ exams (n = 6)				
Level 2 raters (n = 6)	36	2.39	0.50	0.08
Level 3 raters (n = 14)	84	2.58	0.52	0.06
Level 4 raters (n = 4)	24	2.59	0.56	0.12
Level 5 raters (n = 6)	36	2.62	0.45	0.08
Total (n = 30)	180	2.55	0.51	0.04
Level 3/3+ exams (n = 14)				
Level 2 raters (n = 6)	84	3.22	0.65	0.07
Level 3 raters (n = 14)	196	3.57	0.71	0.05
Level 4 raters (n = 4)	56	3.51	0.62	0.08
Level 5 raters (n = 6)	84	3.41	0.46	0.05
Total (n = 30)	420	3.46	0.65	0.03
Level 4/4+/5 exams (n = 5)				
Level 2 raters (n = 6)	30	4.30	0.67	0.12
Level 3 raters (n = 14)	70	4.52	0.58	0.07
Level 4 raters (n = 4)	20	4.36	0.69	0.15
Level 5 raters (n = 6)	30	4.56	0.51	0.09
Total (n = 30)	150	4.46	0.60	0.05

mean score (2.62) and the Level 2 raters had the lowest mean score (2.39). There was not much difference between the mean ratings of the four groups, but the mean rating increased slightly as the English proficiency of the rater group increased. The Level 3 raters gave a mean rating of 2.58. The Level 4 raters gave a 2.59 overall. The median of all four rater groups was the same: 2+. The standard deviation varied by a small amount between the four rater proficiency groups. The Level 5 raters had the smallest standard deviation of 0.45 and the Level 4 speakers' standard deviation is 0.56.

In the ILR Level 3/3+ exams, the Level 2 group raters had a median rating of Level 3, lower than the other groups' medians of Level 3+. The Level 2 group also had the lowest mean (3.22). The mean of the Level 5 raters was 3.41, with the remaining two groups' means being higher than the Level 5 raters, with a mean rating of 3.51 from the Level 4 raters and 3.57 from the Level 3 raters. The Level 5 raters had the lowest standard deviation, 0.46 and the Level 3 raters had the highest at 0.71. This difference reflected approximately one half of a plus level.

There was a somewhat similar pattern in the ILR Level 4/4+/5 exams as the ILR Level 2/2+ and 3/3+ exams. The medians of all four rater groups were 4+. The Level 5 and Level 3 raters had similar mean ratings (4.56 and 4.52, respectively); whereas, the Level 2 and Level 4 raters had lower ratings (with mean ratings of 4.30 and 4.36, respectively). Table 2 also revealed the standard distribution of 0.51 for the Level 5 raters, still the smallest among the four rater groups. The Level 2, 3 and 4 groups had standard deviations of 0.67, 0.58 and 0.69 respectively.

Differences between the means did appear to be more substantive among the English proficiency level groups comparison than the NS/NNS group comparison. An ANOVA[1] determined if any group differences were significant at each of the three levels of exams. For the Level 2/2+ exams, the raters' proficiency level was not significantly related to their ratings: $F(3, 176) = 1.51, p = 0.21$, partial $\eta^2 = 0.03$. Similarly, for the Level 4/4+/5 exams, raters' proficiency level was not significantly related to their rating: $F(3, 146) = 1.41, p = 0.24$, partial $\eta^2 = 0.03$. In the Level 3/3+ exams, the English proficiency of the raters did affect the rating assigned: $F(3, 416) = 6.00, p = 0.00$, partial $h^2 = 0.04^2$. A *post hoc* power analysis revealed that the power coefficient was 0.90, which means if a significant result had existed, then it would have been detected (Type β error). The relatively low partial h^2 indicated that rater proficiency had very little effect on ratings. Bonferroni *post hoc* tests showed significant differences between Level 2 and Level 3 raters ($p = 0.00$), with the Level 2 raters giving final ratings of 0.35 lower than the Level 3 raters. Similarly, there was a nearly significant difference between the Level 2 and Level 4 raters ($p = 0.059$). Here the Level 2 raters were 0.29 lower than the Level 4 raters.

Overall, there was evidence that the English speaking proficiency of raters was related to the final ratings assigned for exams overall and in the Level 3/3+ range exams. These differences did not appear in the Level 2/2+ exams and the Level 4/4+/5 exams. The data showed some significant differences among the raters of varying English speaking proficiency levels. No significant differences emerged between the Level 5 raters (who were the NSs) and any of the other English proficiency level groups, the NNSs. These results should be interpreted with caution since the partial η^2 was small in both instances, meaning that it only contributed to a small part of rating variation. Consistently, the Level 5 speakers had a narrower standard deviation than any of the NNS groups (ILR Level 2 + −4+).

Rater native language comparison

Grouping NSs of various language backgrounds into a NNS raters group assumed that NNS are a homogeneous group, or at least they shared a unified trait (or lack of trait) of being not native. The results from the comparison of NS and NNS raters showed that there was no significant difference between the final ratings of the two groups, but do those results hold regardless of the native language of the rater? To investigate further the question of whether NS and NNS raters assigned equivalent ratings, NS raters' (English raters') performances were compared to each of the seven languages that were the NNS raters' native languages separately (Arabic, Farsi, French, German, Mandarin, Spanish and Vietnamese). This analysis addressed the third research question: does the first language learned affect a rater's ability to reliably evaluate speaking proficiency?

An examination of inter-rater reliability revealed that the English raters had the highest alpha statistic, 0.77. The other native language rater group that had an inter-rater reliability high enough to be consistent in their ratings was the German rater group, with an alpha of 0.74. All of the other six rater groups fell below the 0.7 minimum standard (Krippendorff 2004, Lombard et al 2003). The Mandarin, Farsi and Spanish raters had the lowest alpha statistics at 0.52.

Results from Table 3 show that the English raters' final rating was situated in the middle of the distribution of final ratings of the native language groups. The Arabic speaker raters (3.67) and the Vietnamese speaker raters (3.64) assigned the highest ratings. The Mandarin speaker raters (3.26) assigned the lowest ratings, with an average 0.41 below the Arabic raters or approximately a plus level. The standard deviations of the language groups varied from 0.73 (Spanish) and 0.79 (English) to 1.02 (Farsi and German).

An ANOVA revealed that the differences between the means of the rater language groups were significant: $F(7, 749) = 2.52$, $p = 0.01$, partial $\eta^2 = 0.02$. A *post hoc* power analysis determined the power coefficient to be 0.85, which meant if there had been a significant difference, as there was, it would have been detected (Type β error). The effect size (partial η^2) was small at 0.02^2. The small effect size meant that although the raters' native language did have an impact on their ratings of English, it accounted for very little of the difference among the native language groups. *Post hoc* t-tests revealed that 0.41 difference between the Mandarin and Arabic rater groups was significant ($p = 0.03$), with the Arabic raters giving higher ratings than the Mandarin raters.

Table 3 Final ratings for all exams: Rater native language

Rater native language	Sample	Mean	SD	SE
English (n = 6)	150	3.45	0.79	0.06
Arabic (n = 4)	100	3.67	0.82	0.08
Farsi (n = 3)	75	3.34	1.02	0.12
French (n = 3)	75	3.34	0.97	0.11
German (n = 3)	75	3.48	1.02	0.12
Mandarin (n = 4)	100	3.26	0.86	0.09
Spanish (n = 4)	100	3.36	0.73	0.07
Vietnamese (n = 3)	75	3.64	0.86	0.10
Total (n = 30)	750	3.44	0.88	0.03

Table 4 Final ratings for each proficiency level: Rater native language groups

Native language	N	Mean	SD	N	Mean	SD	N	Mean	SD
	Level 2/2+ exams (n = 6)			Level 3/3+ exams (n = 14)			Level 4/4+/5 exams (n = 5)		
English (n = 6)	36	2.62	0.45	84	3.41	0.46	30	4.56	0.51
Arabic (n = 4)	24	2.83	0.38	56	3.69	0.65	20	4.59	0.55
Farsi (n = 3)	18	2.51	0.77	42	3.25	0.82	15	4.59	0.49
French (n = 3)	18	2.26	0.51	42	3.42	0.68	15	4.43	0.71
German (n = 3)	18	2.29	0.34	42	3.54	0.76	15	4.73	0.43
Mandarin (n = 4)	24	2.44	0.38	56	3.31	0.73	20	4.11	0.71
Spanish (n = 4)	24	2.63	0.47	56	3.38	0.51	20	4.18	0.65
Vietnamese (n = 3)	18	2.69	0.60	42	3.71	0.61	15	4.59	0.54
Total (n = 30)	180	2.55	0.51	420	3.46	0.65	150	4.46	0.60

An analysis of the final ratings by exam level revealed whether or not differences between English and other language raters existed at Level 2/2+, Level 3/3+ and Level 4/4+/5 exams (Table 4). In the Level 2/2+ exams, the mean ratings ranged between 2.26 (French) and 2.83 (Arabic), for a spread of 0.57, approximately a plus level. The English raters' mean rating was 2.62, which was in the middle of the range and only 0.07 higher than the mean of the all raters together. The standard deviations ranged between 0.34 (German) and 0.77 (Farsi).

In the Level 3/3+ exams, the mean ratings ranged between 3.25 (Farsi) and 3.71 (Vietnamese), for a spread of 0.46, also about a plus level. The English raters' mean rating was 3.41, which was again in the middle of the range and this time 0.05 lower than the mean of the group. The standard deviations ranged between 0.46 (English) and 0.82 (Farsi). Although the English raters' standard deviation was practically the same in the Level 2 and Level 3 range exams, they went from having the fourth lowest (out of eight) standard deviation to the lowest standard deviation of the rater language groups.

In the Level 4/4+/5 exams, the mean ratings ranged between 4.11 (Mandarin) and 4.73 (German), for a spread of 0.62, the largest range of means found among the three exam groups. This difference represented a plus level rating on the ILR scale. The English raters' mean rating was 4.56, showing that the English scores were consistently in the middle of the range, on this occasion being 0.10 higher than the mean of the group. The standard deviations ranged between 0.43 (German) and 0.71 (French and Mandarin). As in the Level 3 range exams, the English raters had a low standard deviation (0.51), second lowest of the group. Particular rater language groups were either mostly consistently higher than the English group (Arabic, Mandarin, Spanish, Vietnamese) or lower than the English group (Farsi, French). Interestingly, the German raters varied from being stricter than the English group on the lower-rated exams, to more lenient on the higher-level exams.

The smallest standard deviations overall occurred in the lower level exams, indicating more consistency among language groups at that level.

Previously, the results of the ANOVA for all exams together indicated that the rater's native language made a significant difference in the rating that was produced, although the effect of that contribution was very small overall. ANOVAs of the different exam levels revealed significant differences[1]. In these cases, there was not only a strong power statistic, but also a larger effect size than for the ANOVA of all tests combined. The ANOVA of the ILR Level 2/2+ exams showed a significant difference among ratings of the native language groups: $F(7, 172)= 3.40, p = 0.00$, partial $\eta^2 = 0.12$[2]. This difference meant that in the ILR Level 2/2+ exams, the rater's native language made a significant difference in the final rating produced. Moreover, the partial η^2 of 0.12 showed that the raters' native language did account for a notable part of the variance. Bonferroni *post hoc* tests revealed that significant differences were found between Arabic raters and French raters, with the Arabic raters having a mean final rating of 0.58 above the French raters ($p = 0.01$). Additionally, the Arabic raters had a significant (= 0.01) final rating 0.54 higher than the German raters. It was important to note that none of the NNSs' first language groups' mean ratings differed significantly from the English group's mean rating.

Similar to the Level 2/2+ exams, the ANOVA of the ILR Level 3/3+ exams showed a significant difference among ratings of the native language groups: $F(7, 412) = 3.34, p = 0.00$, partial $\eta^2 = 0.05$[2]. However, the partial η^2 of 0.05 did not reveal a strong effect of rater language on ratings of Level 3/3+ exams. The Bonferroni *post hoc* tests revealed that the Arabic raters had a mean final rating significantly higher than that of the Farsi raters ($p = 0.02$). Additionally, the Vietnamese raters had a final rating significantly higher ($p = 0.03$) than the Farsi raters. The respective differences of 0.45 for the Arabic raters and 0.46 for the Vietnamese raters over the Farsi raters represented a difference on average of a plus level.

The ANOVA of the ILR Level 4/4+/5 exams showed a clear significant difference among ratings of the native language groups: $F(7, 142) = 2.67, p = 0.01$, partial $\eta^2 = 0.12$. The rater's native language made a significant difference in the final ratings given to high-level exams. The partial η^2 of 0.12[2] indicated a notable effect of rater language on ratings of high-level exams. Bonferroni *post hoc* tests indicated that there was a difference approaching significance ($p = 0.056$) between German raters and Mandarin raters, with the German raters having a mean final rating of 0.62 above the Mandarin raters.

Overall, an analysis of the NNS rater groups revealed that the NNS raters do not act homogenously, both over all the exams and when the exams were separated by level. In the distribution of ratings, the English (NS) raters did fall in the middle of the spectrum of language raters and never showed any significant differences with any of the other first language groups. Whether or not the rater's first language was closely related to English, such as German, or very different from English, such as Mandarin, there was not a significant difference between that language group and the English language group. There were, however, significant differences among the language groups themselves. The Arabic and Vietnamese raters had a tendency to give higher ratings at times and the Farsi and Mandarin gave lower ratings at times. The German raters gave low ratings to the lower level tests and higher ratings to the higher level tests. Trends did emerge among the language groups, but no trend involved the English raters.

Discussion and conclusions

The fundamental issue of this study is whether or not NSs and NNSs rate English speaking tests differently from each other. This study examines the NS/NNS issue in a new context: language testing within the US Federal Government. Language testing in this context offers better control over some rater variables and addresses a greater range of language proficiency levels by moving beyond the lower levels of language proficiency typically encountered in literature and into professional, advanced levels of language use. Additionally, this study explores the construct of a NS at a deeper level, by challenging the assumptions underlying that label and considering the implications for testers who have not earned or been given the NS label.

The first and overarching question is whether or not NS raters and NNS raters assigned significantly different holistic final ratings. There was no statistical difference between the ratings of NSs' and NNSs' final ratings of all 25 exams. When the ratings were grouped by exam level (Level 2/2+, Level 3/3+ and Level 4/4+/5), there were again no significant differences found between the NS and NNS rater groups at any of the exam levels. Therefore, the conclusion is that there is no fundamental difference in the English speaker rating abilities of NNs and NNSs.

While that may be the case, the unique characteristics of the raters may have minimised any differences. The participants are highly proficient, trained raters and most of them speak two or more languages well. Second, the process of rating according to a detailed set of criteria, such as the ILR Skill Level Descriptions, narrows raters' reasonable choices for ratings, which leads to increased rater uniformity. The inter-rater reliability statistics suggest that the NS raters rate more homogeneously than the NNS group. However, it is certainly not clear that the NS group should be considered homogeneous. Even though the NS group appears to be more consistent and homogenous in their ratings, it does not make the differences statistically significant.

The second research question addresses differences among raters grouped by English proficiency, derived from the idea that NSs have a high or even ideal level of speaking proficiency (Davies 2003). The raters were divided according to their English speaking proficiency ratings: Level 2/2+, Level 3/3+, Level 4/4+ and Level 5. Unlike the comparison in the NS/NNS dichotomy, the English-speaking proficiency of the raters does make a significant difference in the overall ratings, although these differences must be interpreted with caution. Across all exams, a significant difference is found between the ratings of the four English-speaking proficiency groups. However, the effect size is small. Significant difference was again found in the Level 3 range exams, again with a small effect size of 0.04. One of the reasons that more significant results are discovered in the Level 3 exams may be that there are more exams at that level (14) than all other levels combined (11).

Interestingly, no significant differences across ratings are found in the Level 2 exams or the Level 4–5 exams. The lack of significant difference in the Level 2 exams may be explained by the fact that all of the different rater groups had enough competence in English speaking proficiency to be able to accurately rate exams at this level. In the Level 4–5 exams, it is possible that there is a ceiling effect at the top of the scale, meaning that there are fewer possible choices among which the raters can select because the top of the scale prevents raters from rating too high. Actually, there are only a few plausible rating choices for a well-trained rater. Raters are trained to be able to identify the intended level of any question posed, so they can predict what the level of the test is.

The third research question addressed the rater's native, or first language, as a NS can be defined as a person who was born and raised in an environment in which that language was spoken (Davies 2003). Here, significant differences were discovered not only in the ratings of all tests combined, but also at each level of exam (Level 2, Level 3 and Levels 4–5). Although analysing the NS and NNS data by rater first language shows more instances of significant differences among ratings than analysing it by the English speaking proficiency of the raters, the *post hoc* tests show no clear pattern of which group may or may not be more biased, however thinking about the language families of the groups gives more insight into the results. The results show that there is much variation among the ratings of the different NNS rater groups. Since the pattern of distance between language families does not hold through the exam levels, a better explanation of differences among the NNS group may be the English proficiency of the raters.

This study has confirmed that a clear distinction between the ability of a NS and a NNS rater is not evident even when making distinctions between high-level proficiencies, defined as ILR Levels 3 through 5. The results support the theory that being a NNS does not preclude a person from being able to make distinctions between rating levels as accurately as NSs. Differences between the ratings given by NSs and NNSs on high-level exams can be overcome by extensive training and adhesion to detailed criteria.

Another issue that is raised through the course of this study is whether or not 'it takes one to know one'. In other words, does a rater need to be an ILR Level 5 in order to accurately rate at ILR Level 5 and below? The results show that it is possible to display a production competency at a lower level of proficiency and still accurately distinguish differences between levels higher than a rater's performance ability. NNS raters who have an ILR Level 3 and Level 4 proficiency in English were able to rate exams at all levels comparably to NS ILR Level 5 raters.

There are several possible explanations or mitigating factors that would affect the broad application of this study's conclusions. The holistic nature of the rating may have washed out differences in the rater groups. Differences may have also been lost because all of the participants have undergone equivalent rater training conducted largely in English. Thirdly, there is a considerable difference between the performance competence needed to score a particular level on the speaking proficiency test and the receptive competence that a person would need in order to rate the test (Chomsky 1965). The raters were also ILR Level 5 speakers and raters in another language, with a high level of linguistic and evaluative competence, which may have been transferred from their ability to evaluate in one language to their ability to evaluate English speaking tests.

Results of the current study show the impact of whether or not a rater is a NS on rater reliability and overall ratings, but also contribute to understanding of larger theoretical issues, such as the construct of the NS. Although some claim that the NS is only an abstract construct (Lantolf and Frawley 1985) or a myth (Davies 2003), the proposed research's expanded context over previous studies contributes to the debate on the existence of distinctive NS intuition (Davies 2003) and the NS construct, suggesting language proficiency as the appropriate primary criterion for determining qualified language arbiters (Paikeday 1985).

In conclusion, differences do not appear between traditionally defined NS and NNS groups even when including high-level examinees. Further investigation reveals that when the NNS group is subdivided by two underlying constructs of NS, language proficiency and first language, there are significant differences within that group. Consequentially, though some NNSs may be appropriately used as raters, Level 2+ English speakers should not be used. As a result, the construct of NS should be abandoned as a rater qualification unless properly justified and other more relevant rater qualifications, such as proficiency levels should be used. This shift in rater selection would work to avoid some of the negative social impacts of using the undefined NS as a measurement tool.

Notes

1. All assumptions for parametric tests were met prior to conducting the ANOVAs.
2. The effect size (partial η^2) for this data was interpreted as follows: 0.01–0.03 small; 0.04–0.09 medium; 0.10 and above large (Cohen 1973).

References

Abrahamsson, N and Hyltenstam, K (2009) Age of onset and nativelikeness in a second language: Listener perception versus linguistic scrutiny, *Language Learning* 59 (2), 249–306.

Barnwell, D (1989a) Proficiency and the native speaker, *Association of Departments of Foreign Languages (ADFL) Bulletin* 20 (2).

Barnwell, D (1989b) 'Naïve' native speakers and judgments of oral proficiency in Spanish, *Language Testing* 6 (2), 152–163.

Brown, A (1995) The effect of rater variables in the development of an occupation-specific language performance test, *Language Testing* 12 (1), 1–15.

Brutt-Griffler, J (2002) *World English: A Study of its Development*, Tonawanda: Multilingual Matters.

Chomsky, N (1965) *Aspects of the Theory of Syntax*, Cambridge: MIT Press.

Cohen, J (1973) Eta-squared and partial eta-squared in fixed factor anova designs, *Educational and Psychological Measurement* 33, 107–112.

Davies, A (2003) *The Native Speaker: Myth and Reality* (2nd edition), Clevedon: Multilingual Matters.

Davies, A (2011) Does language testing need the native speaker? *Language Assessment Quarterly* 8 (3), 291–308.

Eckes, T (2008) Rater types in writing performance assessments: A classification approach to rater variability, *Language Testing* 25 (2), 155–185.

Escudero, P and Sharwood Smith, M (2001) Reinventing the native speaker: or what you never wanted to know about the native speaker so never dared to ask, *EUROSLA Yearbook* 1 (1), 275–286.

Fayer, J M and Krasinski, E (1987) Native and nonnative judgments of intelligibility and irritation, *Language Learning* 37(3), 313–326.

Federal Bureau of Investigation (FBI), Language Testing and Assessment Unit (LTAU) (2009) *Speaking Proficiency Test Tester Manual*, unpublished manuscript.

Galloway, V B (1980) Perceptions of the communicative efforts of American students of Spanish, *The Modern Language Journal* 64 (4), 428–433.

Hamilton, J, Lopes, M, McNamara, T and Sheridan, E (1993) Rating scales and native speaker performance on a communicatively oriented EAP test, *Language Testing* 10 (3), 337–353.

Hill, K (1996) Who should be the judge? The use of non-native speakers as raters on a test of English as an international language, *Melbourne Papers in Language Testing* 5 (2), 29–50.

Interagency Language Roundtable (ILR) (1985) *Interagency Language Roundtable Skill Level Descriptions for Speaking*, available online: govtilr.org/Skills/ILRscale2.htm

Johnson, J S and Lim, G S (2009) The influence of rater language background on writing performance assessment, *Language Testing* 26 (4), 485–505.

Kang, O (2008) Ratings of L2 oral performance in English: Relative impact of rater characteristics and acoustic measures of accentedness, *Spaan Fellow Working Papers in Second or Foreign Language Assessment* 6, 181.

Kim, Y-H (2009) An investigation into native and non-native teachers' judgments of oral English performance: A mixed methods approach, *Language Testing* 26 (2), 187–217.

Krippendorff, K (2004) *Content Analysis: An Introduction to its Methodology*, Thousand Oaks: Sage.

Lantolf, J P and Frawley, W (1985) Oral-proficiency testing: A critical analysis, *The Modern Language Journal* 69 (4), 337–345.

Lazaraton, A (2008) Non-native speakers as language assessors: Recent research and implications for assessment practice, in Taylor, L and Weir, C J (Eds) *Multilingualism and Assessment: Achieving Transparency, Assuring Quality, Sustaining Diversity Proceedings of the ALTE Berlin Conference, May 2005*, Studies in Language Testing volume 27, Cambridge: UCLES/Cambridge University Press, 296–309.

Lombard, M, Snyder-Duch, J and Bracken, C C (2003) Practical resources for assessing and reporting intercoder reliability in content analysis research projects, available online: matthewlombard.com/reliability/

Ludwig, J (1982) Native-speaker judgments of second-language learners' efforts at communication: A review, *The Modern Language Journal* 66 (3), 274–283.

Maher, J C (2001) The unbearable lightness of being a native speaker, in Elder, C E, Brown, A, Grove, E, Hill, K, Iwashita, N, Lumley, T, McNamara, T and O'Laughlin, K (Eds) *Experimenting with Uncertainty: Studies in Honour of Alan Davies*, Studies in Language Testing volume 11, Cambridge: UCLES/Cambridge University Press, 292–303.

Marinova-Todd, S H (2003) *Comprehensive analysis of ultimate attainment in adult second language acquisition*, Doctoral dissertation, Harvard University, Boston.

Messick, S (1996) Validity and washback in language testing, *Language Testing* 13 (3), 241–256.

Paikeday, T M (1985) *The Native Speaker is Dead!: An Informal Discussion of a Linguistic Myth with Noam Chomsky and Other Linguists, Philosophers, Psychologists, and Lexicographers*, Toronto: Paikeday Pub.

Reed, D and Cohen, A (2001) Revisiting raters and ratings in oral language assessment, in Elder, C E, Brown, A, Grove, E, Hill, K, Iwashita, N, Lumley, T, McNamara, T and O'Laughlin, K (Eds) *Experimenting with Uncertainty: Studies in Honour of Alan Davies*, Studies in Language Testing volume 11, Cambridge: UCLES/Cambridge University Press, 82–96.

Ross, J R (1979) Where's English, In Fillmore, C J, Kempler, D J and Yang, W S-Y (Eds) *Individual Differences in Language Ability and Language Behavior*, New York: Academic Press, 127–166.

Shi, L (2001) Native- and nonnative-speaking EFL teachers' evaluation of Chinese students' English writing, *Language Testing* 18 (3), 303–325.

Shohamy, E G (2001) *The Power of Tests: A Critical Perspective on the Uses of Language Tests*, Harlow, England: Longman.

Taylor, L (2002) Assessing learners' English: but whose/which English(es)?', *Research Notes* 10, 18–20.

Taylor, L (2006) The changing landscape of English: implications for language assessment, *ELT Journal* 60 (1), 51–60.

Zhang, Y and Elder, C (2011) Judgments of oral proficiency by non-native and native English speaking teacher raters: competing or complementary constructs? *Language Testing* 28 (1), 31–50.

25 Investigating the use of text-to-speech assistive technology in the language testing of students with Specific Learning Difficulties (SpLDs)

Geraldine Ludbrook

Ca' Foscari University of Venice

Abstract

Language testers involved in assessing the language skills of Italian university students with Specific Learning Difficulties (SpLDs) in mandatory language tests are faced with the dilemma created between the need to ensure that such students have fair access to tests and the application of the accommodations made available under Italian educational legislation. In particular, the use of text-to-speech software in testing settings raises serious concerns regarding construct irrelevance and construct under-representation, especially in tests of reading comprehension.

The small case study reported on here sets out to investigate how Italian university students with SpLDs interact with a reading text using text-to-speech software. It specifically explores to what degree such students orient to a reading text on computer video monitor while using text-to-speech assistive technology. The study also examines whether text length, text format, and the language of the text (L1 or L2) influence the use of the software.

The findings of the study suggest that there is evidence that students with SpLDs read while using text-to-speech software, which, if confirmed by further investigation, may reduce the concern that their use may weaken test validity. The study also finds that students make varied use of the software to deal with different text lengths, formats and languages. This adds to evidence informing Italian universities of test item formats that are most accessible to students with such difficulties. Information from stimulated verbal recall and interviews also provides insights into the strategies students with SpLDs use to compensate for their individual learning difficulties.

Introduction

Increasing numbers of Italian students with Specific Learning Difficulties (SpLDs) are continuing their studies at university level in the wake of recent educational legislation that fully recognises these difficulties and provides accommodations to facilitate learning for these students. However, the availability under law of text-to-speech assistive technology in both classroom and testing settings has created concerns for language testing professionals who are committed to providing fair access to language tests for these students while ensuring the highest possible test validity. In this chapter I set out a small research project carried out at the University of Venice to explore issues of fairness and validity in first and foreign language testing of the reading skills of Italian university students with SpLDs, principally students with dyslexia.

I begin with a brief description of dyslexia and related learning difficulties, as they are relevant to this project, and some background information about the Italian legislation that has led to the dilemma for language testers. I then describe the case study and discuss our findings. Finally, I point to some future areas of research planned to further explore the use of text-to-speech technology by students with SpLDs to increase understanding of compensative strategies they employ and to gain insights into the cognitive validity of tests for students with such difficulties.

Dyslexia and Specific Learning Difficulties (SpLDs)

Dyslexia is a learning difficulty that primarily affects the skills involved in accurate and fluent wording, reading and spelling. This chapter does not aim to propose a detailed definition of dyslexia and related learning difficulties. However, it is useful to consider some basic features of the disorder for a better understanding of the complexities dyslexics face when processing language.

Dyslexia is neurobiological in origin and occurs across the range of intellectual abilities. In other words, it is not related to measured IQ. In typical readers, cognition and reading/spelling develop together, while in dyslexic readers they appear to develop differently (see Ferrer, Shaywitz, Holahan, Marchione and Shaywitz 2010, Gabrieli 2009).

Reading is a complex process that depends on adequate development of two component processes: word identification and language comprehension. Word identification involves lexical retrieval: visual recognition of an ordered series of letters as a familiar word and retrieval of the name and meaning of the word. Language comprehension involves integration of the meanings of words in ways that assist the understanding of sentences in spoken or written text so as to understand broader concepts and ideas. Thus, reading comprehension requires being able to identify the words contained in running text with enough accuracy and fluency to allow understanding of the meanings in the text within the limits of working memory (see Valencia (2010) and Vellutino, Fletcher, Snowling and Scanlon (2004) for more detailed descriptions of reading processes).

Characteristic features of dyslexia are deficiencies in reading sub-skills. These include difficulties in mapping phonemes to graphemes, which can lead to slow or inaccurate word identification, as well as problems with phonological awareness, verbal memory and verbal processing speed. Dyslexics have difficulties in retaining spoken information within their short-term memory systems, in accessing spoken information from long-term memory, and in reflecting on the units of sound within words (Kormos and Smith 2012, Shaywitz and Shaywitz 2003).

The frequency of dyslexia varies between languages. In fact, dyslexia is common in languages with deep orthography: writing systems with relatively irregular correspondence between sounds and letters. Dyslexia is less common in languages with more transparent orthographies: writing systems with more consistent mappings between sounds and letters. It is the orthographic irregularity of a language that may alter the degree of success in learning to read and that can affect the actual manifestation of dyslexic symptoms (Lindgren 2012).

Dyslexia is usually conceived as on a continuum ranging from mild to severe. It is not therefore a distinct category, with clear cut-off points, but is often a series of related linguistic difficulties, such as dysgraphia (difficulty organising letters, numbers and words on a line or page), dysorthographia (difficulty recognising, understanding, and reproducing written symbols) and dysnomia (difficulty retrieving words, names, or numbers from memory) (Payne and Turner 1999).

In addition, some common cognitive problems often related to dyslexia are dyscalculia (difficulty understanding simple number concepts and learning number facts and procedures), dyspraxia (difficulty with fine and/or gross motor co-ordination), short-term memory deficit, and attention deficit disorder (ADD), often associated with hyperactivity (ADHD). Dyslexics thus may have difficulties in retaining information in their working memory, which hampers reading and listening to longer written or spoken texts. At the same time a limited attention span adds fatigue to learning and requires repeated input of new knowledge. Difficulties with attention also lead to problems in managing time and personal organisation (Kormos and Smith 2012).

It is common to find considerable overlap among these linguistic and cognitive disorders; in fact comorbidity affects about 50% of dyslexics. Moreover, the disorders also manifest themselves in varying degrees of severity. (See Ferrer et al (2010) and Lyon, Reid, Shaywitz and Shaywitz (2003) for further information on defining dyslexia and related SpLDs.)

From this brief overview of potential language problems for dyslexics, it is clear that, in general, the process of second language acquisition brings with it an additional load for learners with dyslexia and related SpLDs. Deficiencies in the learner's native language system are transferred to a second language, and such learners have considerable difficulty in reading and using the second language (see Sparks and Ganschow 1991, Sparks, Ganschow and Patton 2008).

In addition to this generalised difficulty in acquiring a second language, the learning of English for Italian dyslexic students is additionally problematic if we take into consideration the contrast in orthographies between the two languages. English has a highly inconsistent match between the 26 graphemes and the 44 phonemes of its writing and sound systems. Indeed the British Dyslexia Association (www.bdadyslexia.org.uk/about-us.html) estimates that 10% of the British population are dyslexic, 4% severely so. This compares with the much lower numbers in languages with more transparent orthographies and a close matching between letters and sounds, like Italian (Associazione Trelle, Caritas Italiana and Fondazione Agnelli 2011, Lindgren 2012, Lindgren, De Renzi and Richman 1985, Vellutino et al 2004).

The Italian educational context

Although Italy has applied a policy of integration of disabled students in mainstream education since the 1970s, and students with SpLDs today represent about 4 to 5% of the Italian school population, specific legislation on SpLDs has been produced only in the last decade. Prior to this, legislation was limited to local regulations, regional laws and ministerial guidelines. Law 170/2010 recognised dyslexia, dysgraphia, dysorthographia and dyscalculia as SpLDs and sanctioned the right to education for students with official diagnoses of these difficulties.

In addition to the national guidelines to learning and assessment for students with dyslexia and SpLDs, further legislation has provided explicit reference to the teaching and testing of foreign languages (DM 12/07/2011: Legge Gelmini). As well as setting out principles for assessment, the law provides for the use of technological instruments in both classroom and testing settings. These include text-to-speech software to assist reading skills, and PC word processors with spelling and grammar checks, and online dictionaries to assist writing skills.

The 2011 law also refers explicitly to university students with SpLDs, and confirms their right to the same compensatory measures and exemptions provided in primary and secondary schools, which must also be applied to entrance tests and curricular examinations at university level. In addition, they also introduced a network of tutoring services in order to mediate with teachers and monitor the application of the law. See D'Este and Ludbrook

(2013) for further details regarding Italian legislation for students with SpLDs.

Text-to-speech assistive technology, often referred to as voice synthesis, speaks text on the computer screen using a generated voice, which is fairly natural sounding, produced by synthesised speech engines. In general, this software can read a variety of texts, such as webpages, Word documents, emails, and online books. The speed of the voice can be regulated, and the voice or accent can also be modified (male, female, British English, American English, etc.). Text-to-speech software was initially developed to allow people suffering from visual impairments to access written information. People with dyslexia and cognitive impairments also use it to assist them in carrying out daily life tasks. Such assistive software can also be programmed to highlight the words as they are spoken, a function that is particularly useful for dyslexic users as it helps focus attention and assist understanding of the content.

A dilemma for language testers

As a consequence of this greater legislative attention to special learning needs, students with SpLDs are attending Italian universities in ever-higher numbers. Italian universities now require mandatory certification of general English proficiency at CEFR B1 level on enrolment, and at CEFR B2 level before students complete their 3-year undergraduate studies. Students can present evidence of their English proficiency through possession of certification from an internationally recognised examination board. Otherwise, many universities have developed in-house computer-based tests that are used to replace external certification. Universities therefore now have to address the issue of delivering fair and valid tests of English language, while applying the national guidelines imposed by Italian law. As set out above, the guidelines include the use of technological assistive instruments such as text-to-speech software, and computerised spelling and grammar checks and online dictionaries, in tests and examinations.

A close analysis of these compensatory measures suggests that their use might create a serious threat to the validity of tests, i.e. the validity of the score interpretations, if used in the testing context. The assumption that students can be allowed to use the same technologies on tests that they are accustomed to using in the classroom, in particular text-to-speech software for a reading comprehension test, may alter the nature of the ability being tested. This would seem to be a case of one of Messick's two serious threats to validity in language tests – construct under-representation – in which important features of the construct are omitted from the test (Messick 1989). If the test claims to measure the test taker's ability to read a written text in the foreign language, text-to-speech software may measure instead the test taker's ability to understand spoken text, thus excluding reading skills. This leads to particular concern with regard to the validity of the sub-tests of reading comprehension.

Another essential aspect of test validity is fairness, and anything that weakens fairness compromises the validity of a test (Xi 2010). There are three generally accepted descriptions of test fairness: lack of bias, equitable treatment of all test takers in the testing process, and equity in access to learning the materials covered in a test. See Kunnan (2000) for a more detailed discussion of fairness in language testing.

Fairness with regard to test takers with disabilities is generally understood as providing access to a test applying appropriate accommodations. Accommodations are pre-approved alterations to the standard administration conditions designed to ensure accessibility to a test for test takers with disabilities. They do not alter the construct of the test being measured nor do they provide an unfair advantage for students with disabilities over students taking tests under standard conditions. Frequent forms of testing accommodations are flexibility in scheduling/timing; flexibility in the setting used for the administration of assessments; changes in the method of presentation; and changes in the method of response (see Khalifa and Weir 2009, Stretch and Osborne 2005).

Test fairness requires ensuring that irrelevant factors do not give rise to differences in test performance across subgroups and disabilities, i.e. that construct-irrelevant personal characteristics of test takers have no appreciable effect on test results or their interpretation (Xi 2010). Yet all test takers must be treated equally in the testing process.

International English language testing bodies generally allow test takers with SpLDs such accommodations as extra time and/or supervised breaks, use of a computer or a transcriber to write answers. These accommodations are devised to provide candidates with SpLDs fair access to the tests, compensating for slowness in reading and understanding questions, fatigue, and difficulties with handwriting.

However, test takers with SpLDs are not allowed to use spell-check, grammar-check or thesaurus functions, or text-to-speech software. The Cambridge English Language Assessment testing guidelines, for example, specify that 'there are important restrictions on the use of screen-reading software in Reading papers. Candidates will not be given permission to use screen-reading software or a human reader to read out the texts in a Reading paper . . . If a reader or screen-reading software is used to read out the texts in a Reading paper, the candidate will receive a certificate endorsement' (Cambridge English Guidance Notes: 9). These limitations are clearly in place to avoid both construct irrelevance and construct under-representation.

In the Italian context, language testers are faced with the dilemma of having to provide students with SpLDs fair access to mandatory English language tests by making available the compensatory measures permitted under

Italian law, including text-to-speech software, while nonetheless attempting to provide valid testing of these students' language proficiency. In the section that follows I will describe a small case study carried out with three students at the University of Venice designed to explore this apparent conflict between procedures deriving from Italian educational legislation and the issues of fairness and validity in language testing.

Case study design

Research questions

Two main research questions were drawn up to lead this study. The first research question was designed to investigate how Italian university students with SpLDs interact with a reading text using text-to-speech software (voice synthesis). In particular, we were interested in seeing whether students showed any evidence of reading while listening to the reading text. We drew on the work by Wagner (2007) who investigated the extent to which L2 listeners 'oriented' to non-verbal information while taking an L2 video listening test. Like Wagner, we used the term 'to orient to' according to Tomlin and Villa's (1994) definition, in which they use the term to refer to the directing of attention to a certain type or class of sensory information, while excluding other types or classes of information. In our study, the term 'orienting to' the video monitor meant the readers looked at and made eye contact with the monitor while the reading texts were being played.

The first research question was therefore formulated as: to what extent do Italian university students with SpLDs orient to a reading text on computer video monitor while using text-to-speech assistive technology?

In addition, we were interested to observe whether the type of reading text the students were engaging with influenced their use of text-to-speech software. In particular, we wanted to observe the influence of the length of the reading text, as people with SpLDs often suffer from visual stress. In other words, they may see blurred letters or unfocused words, moving or back-to-front words, and have difficulty tracking across the page. These symptoms can significantly affect reading ability, especially the fluency with which they are able to read long passages of text and their ability to comprehend text. They also find it hard to maintain focus when dealing with longer written and spoken texts. We therefore planned to present the students with both short and longer passages of reading texts to see whether this factor impacted on their use of voice synthesis.

The use of the multiple-choice format is extremely common in computer-based tests, including foreign language tests. However, it appears from the literature that students with dyslexia perform poorly on this kind of question format. Firstly, the eye movement required to shift focus up and down and from left to right can lead to inaccurate reading. Secondly, problems with short-term memory deficit can make it problematic for test takers to retain information (Professional Association of Teachers of Students with Specific Learning Difficulties 2006). We therefore planned to present the students with texts comprised of multiple-choice items.

There are few cross-linguistic studies that directly compare dyslexia in English and dyslexia in a different language. As mentioned above, reading problems associated with dyslexia differ in regular orthographies, such as Italian, compared to less regular orthographies, such as written English. In the second research question, we wanted to investigate whether we could perceive a different use of text-to-speech assistive technology in the students' L1 (Italian) and L2 (English).

The second research question was therefore formulated as: is the use of text-to-speech assistive technology by Italian university students with SpLDs influenced by the following variables:

(a) the type of reading text: short text, longer text, multiple-choice format

(b) the language of the reading text: L1 (Italian) or L2 (English)?

Participants

The University of Venice has been devising study programmes and delivering language tests to students with SpLDs for some years (D'Este and Ludbrook in press). We therefore had a small number of university students with these characteristics who were enrolled in undergraduate courses and had in addition reached a CEFR B1 level in English, or who were very close to reaching this level. Three of these students were invited to participate in the study. Each of the three students had diagnoses of dyslexia and related learning difficulties; however, analysis of the documentation did not reveal the severity of their individual disorders (see Table 1).

The students had different background use of text-to-speech technology. One had been encouraged to use voice synthesis for the last three years of

Table 1 Participants

	Student 1	Student 2	Student 3
Age	22	24	22
Diagnosis	Dyslexia, mild dysgraphia and dysorthography	Dyslexia and dysgraphia	Dyslexia and dyscalculia
University degree course	Architecture	History	Letters
Background use of text-to-speech software	University only	University only	Since 3rd year secondary school
Level of English proficiency	A1.2 certified, moving towards B1	B1 certified	B1 certified

secondary school; the other two had only been made aware of the possibility of using such technology once they had reached university.

Two of the students were enrolled in humanities degree courses, and the third was studying architecture. They were in the second or third year of their university studies with successful results. They were therefore all high-functioning dyslexics who had likely been taught or had developed personal strategies to compensate for their specific reading difficulties. We believed that they would provide important insights regarding their use of text-to-speech technology.

Reading texts

As mentioned above, the study was designed to observe how university students with SpLDs handled voice synthesis when reading different kinds of texts. The language of the reading text (L1 or L2), the text length and the type of text were all variables we wished to introduce into the study.

Three Italian-language reading texts were selected. The first was a reading passage of 255 words, containing both simple and complex sentence structures, on a general topic relating to Italian history. The second was a series of five non-contextualised multiple-choice items, each with a very short stem and three options, which involved completing simple factual items (53 words). The third was a short passage of 120 words with three multiple-choice comprehension items. They all had short stems and three short options that required inferencing abilities.

Five English-language reading texts were selected. Two were reading passages at an approximate CEFR A2 level of difficulty: short sentence length, simple sentence structure, simple concepts and familiar vocabulary. The first was 118 words in length and the second was 278 words in length. The A2 level was chosen because, although all three students had reached, or were about to reach, a B1 level of English proficiency, in this study we were interested in observing their natural use of voice synthesis without potentially placing too high a cognitive load on them and thus increasing anxiety.

The third English-language text was a series of five non-contextualised multiple-choice items, each with a very short stem and three options (80 words). The items involved completing short conversational exchanges.

The fourth and fifth texts were shorter reading passages (70–80 words in length), again at an approximate A2 level. The student had to choose the best title for the passage from a series of four one-sentence options. Unlike the previous multiple-choice questions, these items required the reader to process the text then identify explicit information, analyse, and interpret the passage. See the Appendix for the reading texts.

Procedure

The students participated in the study in separate sessions, and were all informed that the purpose of the study was to observe their habitual use of text-to-speech software when reading in both languages. The reading texts were delivered to the students in a Word file; the Italian texts were delivered first, followed by the English texts. The Alpha Reader voice synthesiser had been installed on a laptop and was adjusted to a speed each student felt comfortable with; a female voice using a British English accent was also selected. The students were invited to read the passages making a natural use of the software. They were also informed that, although they were to click on options in the multiple-choice items, their responses would not be recorded. No time limits were imposed.

While the students were reading, the computer webcam captured their eye movement and recorded any comments made. Two researchers also monitored the reading process and recorded their own observations.

After the reading phase, each student took part in a stimulated verbal recall interview in which they were asked to comment on the way they had used the software during this reading phase. They also discussed on the way they use assistive technology (text-to-speech software, audiobooks) in everyday reading and for university studies.

Results

The most important result that emerged from the analysis of the recorded eye movements of the three candidates was that they all appeared to be reading as they listened to the aural input through the text-to-speech software. Their eye movements (and in some cases their lip movements) clearly tracked the words across the page, following the text as they scrolled down from one line to the next and from one text to another.

The second interesting result was that in many cases the students did not actually use the software available, choosing instead to read the texts without any assistance. In the case of the Italian reading texts, Student 2 made no use of the software, whereas the other two participants used the software only for the reading passages. None of the participants used the software with the short multiple-choice items. Table 2 illustrates the use of text-to-speech software with the Italian texts.

All the participants made use of the software with the English language reading passages. However, there was a tendency not to use it with the multiple-choice items, whether short and de-contextualised or longer and linked to a reading text. Except for Student 2, who consistently read the multiple-choice items without assistance, Students 1 and 3 made some use of technological support. Table 3 illustrates the use of text-to-speech software with the English texts.

Table 2 Use of text-to-speech software with Italian texts

	Student 1	Student 2	Student 3
Text 1 **Reading passage** **(255 words)**	√	No	√
Text 2 **Multiple choice only: short factual**	No	No	No
Text 3 **Reading passage (120 words) with** **short inferencing multiple choice**	Reading passage: √ Multiple choice: No	No	Reading passage: √ Multiple choice: No

Table 3 Use of text-to-speech software with English texts

	Student 1	Student 2	Student 3
Text 1 **Reading passage** **(118 words)**	√	√	√
Text 2 **Reading passage** **(278 words)**	√	√	√
Text 3 **Multiple choice only:** **short conversational** **exchange**	Some	No	No
Text 4 **Reading passage (71** **words) with** **longer inferencing** **multiple choice**	Reading passage: √ Multiple choice: No	Reading passage: √ Multiple choice: No	Reading passage: √ Multiple choice: √
Text 5 **Reading passage (79** **words) with** **longer inferencing** **multiple choice**	Reading passage: √ Multiple choice: No	Reading passage: √ Multiple choice: No	Reading passage: √ Multiple choice: √

Stimulated verbal recall and interview

The second phase of the study involved each participant discussing the strategies they used while reading the various texts using stimulated verbal recall. This was done with each student individually immediately after completing the reading tasks. Their comments on their use of text-to-speech software demonstrated that the students had considerable awareness of how they compensate for their individual learning difficulties. Although the three participants had different comorbid difficulties and had diverse background experience with assistive technology (see Table 1), their comments had clear similarities.

All three students confirmed what had been recorded through observation and recording of eye movement in the first phase of the study: they generally all listen to and read a text first using text-to-speech software, and then they read the text again without it. They use text-to-speech software to gain a general understanding of longer reading texts especially when they encounter unfamiliar words.

The students all mentioned speed as an issue. They often choose not to use text-to-speech software with Italian reading passages or with short multiple-choice items as it is quicker for them to read these texts without assistance. However, the software allows them to accelerate their reading speed to complete timed tasks such as, for example, test tasks.

Interestingly, the students also individually pointed out differences in their use of assistive technology in different domains. All three use text-to-speech software or audio books when they read for pleasure. However, for study purposes they read without technology, preferring to interact directly on the reading text with coloured pens and visual markers, which helps them retain information more easily.

The interviews provided us with further insightful information about the students' background experience with learning in general, and with foreign language learning in particular. However, with immediate relevance to this study, their comments indicated that they appear to use text-to-speech software to compensate for the precise learning difficulties their disorders manifest – accurate word identification and fluent language comprehension – rather than to replace the reading process.

Discussion

Research question 1

To what extent do Italian university students with SpLDs orient to a reading text on computer video monitor while using text-to-speech assistive technology?

The participants in the study were free to use the text-to-speech software as they chose. If they had considered it more natural or more efficient to listen to the voice synthesis, ignoring the reading texts, they were able to do this. It was observed, however, that all three participants consistently oriented to the screen, choosing to read while they listened to the spoken input. They all also re-read the texts again without using the software. This pattern of reading while listening and then re-reading was confirmed by the comments recorded in the interview.

Research question 2

Is the use of text-to speech assistive technology by Italian university students with SpLDs influenced by the following variables:

(a) the type of reading text: short text, longer text, multiple-choice format

(b) the language of the reading text: L1 (Italian) or L2 (English)?

The length of reading text appears to influence the use of text-to-speech software. Short multiple-choice stems and options tended to be read without recourse to the software, as were longer, one-sentence options. However, assistance was needed in reading passages, regardless of the word length or language.

Multiple choice appeared to be the easiest format for the participants to read without any assistance. Only Student 3 used text-to-speech software to read the longer, one-sentence options; otherwise none of the participants used it to read multiple-choice items, regardless of the language.

As Tables 2 and 3 illustrate, the language of the text (L1 or L2) does seem to influence the use of text-to-speech software. Whereas some of the participants chose to read in Italian without assistance, all of them made use of the software to assist them with reading passages in English. Two of the participants also used the software to read multiple-choice items in English although they had read this format in Italian without assistance.

There are some possible limitations to the study. The participants were instructed to read the texts. This request may have influenced the way they oriented to the video, influencing their choice to read the texts instead of listen to them. Moreover, the availability of the software may have resulted in greater use of it than they might make in everyday situations.

Another limitation concerns the degree to which these finding can be generalised. The individual profiles of students with SpLDs present multiple disorders that occur comorbidly; they also manifest themselves in varying degrees of severity. It is therefore problematic making inferences from one individual to another as no individuals have the same linguistic and cognitive profile. Nevertheless, despite the fact that the three participants had differing comorbid disorders (see Table 1), they independently made similar use of the text-to-speech software.

Conclusions

The purpose of the present study was to examine how a sample group of Italian university students with SpLDs used assistive text-to-speech technology when interacting with reading texts delivered via computer. The sample group was a small one and heterogeneous only to a certain degree. However, the study does provide some insight into how these students used text-to-speech software to facilitate their reading. They all oriented to the monitor consistently and their eye and lip movements also revealed they were actually reading the texts. Their comments on the individual strategies each student had developed also confirmed that they use text-to-speech software to facilitate their reading and not to substitute it.

These findings provide some comfort to language testers involved in assessing the language skills of Italian university students with SpLDs in mandatory English language tests. There remains the dilemma created between the need to ensure that students have fair access to the test that will allow them to demonstrate their proficiency and the application of the accommodations provided for students with SpLDs under Italian educational legislation. However, the fact that there is evidence that the students read while using text-to-speech software reduces the concern for weakened test validity through construct irrelevance and construct under-representation.

Further research

The research project aims to continue investigating the use of text-to-speech technology by Italian university students with SpLDs. Despite the small number of participants, and the inherent variability in the nature and severity of their learning difficulties, the results of this exploratory case study appear to show some common trends in the use of text-to-speech software. Further replications will investigate the validity of the results.

The study also examined the influence of reading text type, length and format on the use of text-to-speech software by students with SpLDs. Interestingly, participants tended to engage with multiple-choice format items in both L1 and L2 without the assistance of the software. A large national research project is continuing the investigation of how Italian university students with SpLDs deal with different forms of multiple-choice items: binary true/false, and three, four or five options; contextualised and independent items. The results of this project will contribute to informing Italian universities of test item formats that are most accessible to students with SpLDs.

Further research is also planned to investigate the possible use of eye-tracking technology to investigate reading strategies employed by students with SpLDs during language tests to increase understanding of these students' reading behaviour. Eye tracking may also provide insights into the cognitive validity of English language tests for SpLDs (see Bax 2013). Little research on L2 learning of students with SpLDs has been carried out, and fails to provide an adequate basis for definitive conclusions about the mental processes elicited by language tests. Cognitive validity therefore remains an almost unexplored feature of the overall test validity (see O'Sullivan and Weir 2011). In addition, learning difficulties are not homogeneous, and similar disabilities may affect different people in different ways, making the identification of a possible standard mental process problematic. Nonetheless, investigation of cognitive validity may be decisive as the understanding of mental processes in the foreign language learning of students with SpLDs is potentially the basis for the identification of the test construct on which to design and build valid tests.

References

Associazione Trelle, Caritas Italiana and Fondazione Agnelli (2011) *Gli alunni con disabilità nella scuola italiana: bilancio e proposte*, Trento: Edizioni Erickson.

Bax, S (2013) The cognitive processing of candidates during reading tests: Evidence from eye-tracking, *Language Testing* 30 (4), 441–465.

Cambridge English (nd) *Guidance Notes for Special Requirements Reading and Use of English Tests*, available online: www.cambridgeenglish.org/images/170888-guidance-notes-for-special-requirements-reading-and-use-of-english-tests.pdf

D'Este, C and Ludbrook, G (2013) Fairness and validity in testing students with SpLDs: A case study from Italy, in Tsagari, D and Spanoudis, G (Eds) *Assessing L2 Students with Learning and Other Disabilities*, Newcastle upon Tyne: Cambridge Scholars Press, 169–188.

D'Este, C and Ludbrook, G (in press) Teaching and testing students with SpLDs: Experience from the Venice University Language Centre, in Williams, C (Ed) *Innovation in Methodology and Practice in Language Learning: Experiences and Proposals for University Language Centres*, Newcastle upon Tyne: Cambridge Scholars Press.

Ferrer, E, Shaywitz, B A, Holahan, J M, Marchione, K and Shaywitz, S E (2010) Uncoupling of reading and IQ over time: Empirical evidence for a definition of dyslexia, *Psychological Science* 21, 93–101.

Gabrieli, J D E (2009) Dyslexia: A new synergy between education and cognitive neuroscience, *Science* 325, 280–283.

Khalifa, H and Weir, C J (2009) *Examining Reading. Research and Practice in Assessing Second Language Reading*, Studies in Language Testing volume 29, Cambridge: UCLES/Cambridge University Press.

Kormos, J and Smith, A M (2012) *Teaching Languages to Students with Specific Learning Differences*, Bristol: Multilingual Matters.

Kunnan, A J (2000) *Fairness and Validation in Language Assessment*, Studies in Language Testing volume 9, Cambridge: UCLES/Cambridge University Press.

Lindgren, S D, De Renzi, E and Richman, L C (1985) Cross-national comparisons of developmental dyslexia in Italy and the United States, *Child Development* 56 (6), 1,404–1,417.

Lindgren, S-A (2012) Mild developmental dyslexia in university students: Diagnosis and performance features in L1, L2, and L3, *English Department Publications 6*, Turku: Åbo Akademi University, available online: www.doria.fi/bitstream/handle/10024/73898/lindgren_signe.pdf?sequence=2

Lyon, G, Reid, S, Shaywitz, S and Shaywitz, B A (2003) Defining dyslexia, comorbidity, teachers' knowledge of language and reading: A definition of dyslexia, *Annals of Dyslexia* 53 (1), 1–14.

Messick, S (1989) Validity, in Linn, R L (Ed) *Educational Measurement* (3rd edition), New York: Macmillan, 13–103.

O'Sullivan, B and Weir, C J (2011) Test Development and Validation, in O'Sullivan, B (Ed) *Language Testing: Theories and Practices*, Basingstoke, England: Palgrave Macmillan, 13–33.

Payne, T and Turner, E (1999) *Dyslexia: A Parents' and Teachers' Guide*, Bristol: Multilingual Matters.

Professional Association of Teachers of Students with Specific Learning Difficulties (2006) *Readability Project Final Report*, available online: bcs.org/upload/pdf/readabilityproject.pdf

Shaywitz, S and Shaywitz, B (2003) Dyslexia (specific reading disability), *Pediatrics in Review* 24 (5), 147–153.

Sparks, R L and Ganschow, L (1991) Foreign language learning difficulties: Affective or native language aptitude differences? *Modern Language Journal* 75, 3–16.

Sparks, R L, Ganschow, L and Patton, J (2008) L1 and L2 literacy, aptitude and affective variables as discriminators among high- and low-achieving L2 learners with special needs, in Kormos, J and Kontra, E H (Eds) *Language Learners with Special Needs: An International Perspective*, Clevedon: Multilingual Matters, 1–10.

Stretch, L-A S and Osborne, J W (2005) Extended time test accommodation: Directions for future research and practice, *Practical Assessment, Research & Evaluation* 10 (8), 1–8.

Tomlin, R and Villa, V (1994) Attention in cognitive science and second language acquisition, *Studies in Second Language Acquisition* 16 (2), 183–203.

Valencia, S (2010) Reader profiles and reading disabilities, in McGill-Franzen, A and Allington, R L (Eds) *Handbook of Reading Disability Research*, Routledge: Oxon, 25–35.

Vellutino, F R, Fletcher, J M, Snowling, M J and Scanlon, D M (2004) Specific reading disability (dyslexia): What have we learned in the past four decades? *Journal of Child Psychology and Psychiatry* 45 (1), 2–40.

Wagner, E (2007) Are they watching? Test-taker viewing behavior during an L2 video listening test, *Language Learning and Technology* 11 (1), 67–86.

Xi, X (2010) How do we go about investigating test fairness? *Language Testing* 27 (2), 147–170.

Appendix: Italian–language reading texts

Italian text 1

Quando si fa riferimento a qualcosa del Trentino-Alto Adige bisogna fare attenzione alla zona di cui si sta parlando. Spesso i media italiani parlano di "Trentino" con riferimento alla regione, anche se si tratta di avvenimenti accaduti in Alto Adige (per esempio: "...a Silandro, in Trentino ..., ...l'Adige nasce in Trentino..."), quelli tedeschi o slavi parlano di "Sudtirolo" per ciò che accade anche in Trentino, oppure usano entrambi.

In realtà sarebbe corretto e rispettoso della realtà regionale verificare a quale dei due territori ci si sta riferendo, evitando così errori. Per gli abitanti e ciò che è del Trentino si deve usare l'aggettivo o il sostantivo "trentino" (o "tridentino" se riferito alla storia o alla Chiesa, per esempio "il Concilio Tridentino"), per gli abitanti e ciò che è dell'Alto Adige si deve usare "altoatesino" (soprattutto se riferito ad abitanti di madrelingua italiana o al territorio, per esempio "il capoluogo altoatesino") o "sudtirolese" (soprattutto se riferito ad abitanti di madrelingua tedesca o alla cultura e storia locali, per esempio "la cucina sudtirolese"). Solo durante il fascismo per "tridentino" ci si riferiva agli abitanti e a ciò che si riferiva all'intera regione, da "Venezia Tridentina", il nome col quale veniva chiamato il Trentino-Alto Adige. Tuttavia l'inserimento della regione, ma soprattutto dell'Alto Adige, nell'area storico-geografica delle "Tre Venezie", non era altro che una mossa attuata dal fascismo per rendere la regione più unita e per rendere più "italiana" la provincia di Bolzano. Dopo la seconda guerra mondiale, la regione assunse il nome attuale quindi divenne "Trentino-Alto Adige/Südtirol" nel 1972.

Italian text 2

La capitale dell'Italia è:
a. Roma
b. Firenze
c. Venezia

La Sicilia è:
a. un'isola
b. un continente
c. una penisola

Le stagioni sono:
a. due
b. cinque
c. quattro

Gli spaghetti sono:
a. una bibita
b. un cibo
c. una verdura

Picasso fu:
a. un pittore
b. un inventore
c. uno stilista

Italian text 3

Quando ero giovane giocavo nella squadra di rugby della scuola. La cosa che mi piaceva di più è che potevo correre sul prato. Potevo giocare tutti i pomeriggi con i miei migliori amici, dopo che avevo finito di fare i compiti per la scuola. Ero molto piccolo ma a me non importava. Gli altri erano grandi e grossi, ma io ero il più veloce nella corsa. Ero tanto veloce che nessuno riusciva a raggiungermi. Durante le partite, i compagni mi gridavano spesso: Prendila tu! E quando prendevo la palla la lasciavo solo quando avevo fatto meta.

Sono passati alcuni anni, adesso sono cresciuto, mi sono allenato tanto e sono molto più forte. Un giorno spero di diventare un giocatore professionista.

Il testo parla di:
       a. un lavoro
       b. uno sport
       c. una partita

Chi parla è:
       a. un allenatore
       b. un giocatore professionista
       c. un ragazzo

Nel testo, quando i compagni gridano "PRENDILA!" si riferiscono:
       a. alla meta
       b. alla vittoria
       c. alla palla

English text 1

The story of speed skater Dan Jansen's Olympic career is a very special one. The world first saw Jansen at the 1984 Games in Sarajevo, when the young

Language Assessment for Multilingualism

American finished fourth in the 500-metre race. In 1988, in Calgary, he was the favourite to win the 500 and 1,000-metre races. Jansen's sister, Jane, suffered from leukaemia and died only minutes before one of these races. In their last conversation, he promised to win for her. But instead Jansen fell. Not just once, but in both races, and he left the Calgary Games empty-handed. Four years later, this time in Albertville, Jansen was again the favourite to win. But he didn't succeed, and again he left without a medal.

English text 2

Dear Margaret,
Hi! This is the best holiday I've ever had! Australia's so nice, the weather's incredibly hot and the people are really friendly. I knew it was a big country, but not this big! Adelaide and Melbourne look so near on the map, but when we got the train last week, the journey took ages. But it's nice to travel for pleasure, because at home I spend so much time on trains and on the motorway for my job, so I'm happy to just look out at the countryside and not have to think about anything. You know I love jogging, but not in this weather. I ran for about three minutes yesterday, but then I stopped and walked back home. Have you ever tried to run around in a sauna? Well, that's how it feels. It's the perfect place to sit on the beach all day, and that's what we're doing. It's so nice to switch my phone off and forget about work. The weather's nice for swimming, too, and you know how much I've always liked that. The food isn't bad. Restaurants? We've heard about some nice ones, but all our friends have barbecues in the garden in the evenings, and during the day we take sandwiches and fruit to the beach, so I don't know if we'll ever have a chance to eat out. We'll probably have lots of money when we come back, because at the moment we're not spending any! But I'm getting a bit fat, to be honest. When I get back I'll be straight back in the gym again, don't worry!
'Bye for now. I'll write again soon.
Love,
Diane

English text 3

. . .6 people in our car.
    a.   There is . . .
    b.   There are. . .
    c.   We are. . .

Hello, how are you?
    a.   Not bad.

     b. How do you do?

     c. I'm Turkish.

Hello, Peter.

     a. Pleased to watch you.

     b. Nice to see you.

     c. It's good for you to see me.

How's Luisa's sister?

     a. This is her.

     b. She's got red hair.

     c. She's fine.

Where's my pencil?

     a. There it is.

     b. Here it is.

     c. Here you are.

English text 4

A boy aged only seven left home while his parents were asleep in the living room . . . and in his pockets he had £50 in cash that he stole from his father's desk upstairs. Police found young Ricky Tomlinson at a bus stop five miles away twelve hours later. "I was bored and wanted to go and spend some money," said Ricky. "But I forgot that all the shops are shut on Sunday."

Choose the best title for this article.

a. Parents shocked as seven-year-old boy spends £50 a week on sports, food and public transport.

b. Firm silent about why seven-year-old boy is given £50 for twelve-hour working day.

c. Seven-year-old boy who ran away from home with £50 cash is found after twelve hours.

d. Seven-year-old child-runner takes home £50 cash for track win over big boys.

English text 5

As we were waiting for our luggage to appear, my boyfriend sat down and lit a cigarette. People were looking at him in a rather funny way, and in fact after a couple of minutes a voice came over the loudspeaker, saying that you had to go to particular areas if you wanted to smoke. He put it out straight away. I said to him: "Why don't you just wait until we've got our baggage and left the airport?"

a. Passengers are reminded that smoking is strictly prohibited aboard this plane.
b. Kindly refrain from smoking until you are well inside the terminal building.
c. WARNING: Do not leave any baggage unattended.
d. This is a public announcement: please remember that smoking is only permitted in the designated areas.

Notes on contributors

Tomoyasu Akiyama, who obtained his PhD from the University of Melbourne in 2004, is Professor in the department of English Language and Literature at Bunkyo University in Saitama, Japan. He has taught English in a wide range of contexts, in both private and public schools, and trained teachers. Also he has taught research methods, TESOL, and language testing for those who want to be an English teacher. His research interests include validity investigations of high school and university English tests and teacher employment examinations, and applications of Rasch measurement to performance tests. Currently, he is involved in rater cognition research in performance tests.

Vivien Berry currently works as Senior Researcher in the English Language Assessment Research Centre of the British Council in London. Prior to this, she worked at the University of Roehampton where she conducted a research project for the General Medical Council and for 15 years at the University of Hong Kong, where she taught courses in language testing and research methodology. Her book, *Personality Differences and Oral Test Performance*, was published by Peter Lang in 2007.

Giuliana Grego Bolli is Associate Professor of Glottology and Linguistics at Universita per Stranieri Perugia (USP), Italy. She is currently Director of CVCL (Centro per la Valutazione e le Certificazioni, Centre for Evaluation and Certification). Her research interests are in language testing and language teaching. Professor Bolli worked on the development of the CELI (Certificati di Lingua Italiana) Examinations Suite and has been collaborating with the Association of Language Testers in Europe (ALTE) since 1990. She is a member of the SurveyLang Programme Board in the project for the definition of the European Indicator of Language Competences. She was the Italian co-ordinator of the Reference Level Descriptions (RLD) project in Italian. She is the author or co-author of several publications on the CVCL's Certification activities and projects involving CVCL's collaboration with the Council of Europe with regard to possible applications of the CEFR, particularly in the field of language assessment.

Elaine Boyd has worked in assessment design and quality standards for 25 years for a range of international testing organisations. She has contributed to the development and validation of exams across a range of levels and domains and has published several exam coursebooks. She has also developed and delivered training in assessment literacy and test writing for teachers in Europe and India and has published articles in this field. She holds a PhD in spoken language and pragmatics from the University of Cardiff and is an Associate Tutor for the online MA in Applied Linguistics and TESOL at Leicester University. She is currently researching aspects of test construct and speaker identity from data in the Trinity Lancaster Corpus of Spoken Language. Her most recent publication is as the article 'Epistemic Stance in Spoken L2 English: The Effect of Task and Speaker Style' in *Applied Linguistics* (2015).

Rachel L Brooks serves as Program Manager of the Testing Standards Program in FBI's Language Testing and Assessment Unit, where she oversees the speaking tester program, quality control of FBI tests, research and validation projects, and training of testers. Dr Brooks' research and publications address testing in the US Federal Government, native speaker roles in speaking testing, and Forensic Linguistic methods to determine cheating. Dr Brooks co-chairs the Testing and Assessment Expert Group under the US Government Foreign Language Executive Committee. Dr Brooks received a PhD in Linguistics from Georgetown University.

David Donnarumma is Head of English for BPP University. He has been involved in the field of English language teaching for 15 years as a manager, academic, teacher educator, test developer and materials developer both online and in print. He is also an author of a communication skills textbook. He has presented at several international conferences and written in the areas of ELF communication and online learning. In his current role he is responsible for English language development and delivery at the university.

Sarah Ellis has an extensive background in teaching, teacher training and language testing, working with learners and teachers in both Italy and the UK. She is currently Head of Assessment Services, Southern Europe for Cambridge English Language Assessment, involved in co-ordinating impact studies and other research and validation projects in the region. Sarah has played a leading role in the implementation and management of the Cambridge English *Progetto Lingue 2000* Impact Study over the past four years.

Anne Gallagher is Associate Dean of Arts, Celtic Studies and Philosophy and Director of the Language Centre at the National University of Ireland, Maynooth, Ireland. The Language Centre develops and administers tests in Irish for adult learners. Over the past 30 years, Anne Gallagher's work has included language teaching, the development of language education policy, and research on multilingualism in Ireland. Widely published, Anne has also published research with the Council of Europe, and collaborated with Cambridge English Language Assessment. She is former chairperson of the Irish Association for Applied Linguistics (2004–2007) and Raidio na Gaeltachta (2010–2013), Ireland's national Irish language radio station. In November 2012 she was appointed Chairperson of the Board of Udaras na Gaeltachta, the Irish regional authority responsible for the economic, social and cultural development of the Irish-speaking regions.

Jesús García Laborda is an associate professor at Universidad de Alcalá (Madrid, Spain). Dr García Laborda has a PhD in English Philology and an EdD in Language Education. His current research covers many areas of computer implementations for language learning and testing along with English for Specific Purposes (ESP) and teacher training: (i) special applications of low stakes online testing, especially focused to the Spanish University Entrance Examination for concepts such as washback, test design, beliefs, emotions, etc. This also includes the study of interface and computer architecture in other languages and their evaluation and assessment; (ii) the development of socio constructivism approaches to computer assisted language learning, which applies ideas of Vygotsky to the development of speaking and listening skills in computer-based scenarios; (iii) it includes practical applications of mobile learning for commercial purposes to help to introduce a computer-based test in high stakes exams as DELE (Spanish) or the Spanish University Entrance Examination (English, French, German); (iv) the implications of implementing such test in teacher training along with more traditional approaches to teacher education and their development of both cognitive and computer skills.

Catarina Gaspar is Assistant Professor in the University of Lisbon, where she has taught since 2000. She holds a PhD in Latin Linguistics from the University of Lisbon. Her research interests include romance languages, disclosure policy and language policy. She is the author of articles and papers, and has presented in national and international conferences. Between 2009 and 2013, she worked as a researcher at the Center of Assessment of Portuguese as a Foreign Language (CAPLE). As part of her teaching or research, she teaches and she is co-ordinator of the Master in Portuguese as FL/L2 (Multilingualism and Language Policy, and Teaching, Learning and Assessment (FL/L2)) and also in the area of Intercultural Communication and Culture and Globalization.

Heinz-Peter Gerhardt is Vice President in Paulo Freire Kooperation, Oldenburg, Germany. He was Associate Professor and teacher in Germany (Johann Wolfgang Goethe Universität, Frankfurt am Main;

Fachhochschule des Bundes für Öffentliche Verwaltung, Brühl/Rheinland), in Brasil (Universidade Federal do Rio Grande de Norte, Natal) and in State University of New York (Albany/New York).

Maria José Grosso is Associate Professor in the University of Lisbon, and since 2012, Associate Professor in the University of Macau. She was formerly Director of the Center of Assessment of Portuguese as a Foreign Language (2009-2012). She holds a PhD in Applied Linguistics (2000) with the thesis 'The methodological discourse of teaching Portuguese in Macau to Chinese native speakers'. Her areas of study and teaching focus on applied linguistics to the teaching of Portuguese (FL/L2) and benchmarks in the areas connected to it, including teaching, learning and assessment (FL/L2), disclosure policy and language teaching and intercultural studies. In these areas she has developed governmental projects: *O Português para Falantes de Outras Línguas* A2 (2008) and B1 (2009) and *A Framework in Portuguese as a Foreign Language for Chinese Native Speakers: A Study of Macau and China Mainland* (2012), which is supported by in the University of Macau.

Xiangdong Gu is professor, PhD supervisor and Director of the Research Centre of Language, Cognition and Language Application in Chongqing University, China. She holds a PhD in Linguistics and Applied Linguistics from Shanghai Jiaotong University (China), and furthered her study and research at University of California, Los Angeles and the University of Cambridge as a visiting professor. She is an academic consultant of Cambridge English and an external reviewer of several academic journals and university presses in China. She has been teaching English for over 25 years from young learners to PhD candidates. She has published and presented widely on language assessment, EFL teaching and learning as well as teacher development. Her recent interests mainly focus on validation study and impact study of large-scale high-stakes national and international English tests in China.

Roger Hawkey's postgraduate qualifications, research and whole professional career have been in English language teaching and assessment. He has had British Council posts in East and West Africa as well as London, and done further ELT work in Thailand, Europe and Latin America. Since 1999, his consultancies have been mainly with Cambridge English Language Assessment. He is also a Visiting Professor at the Centre for Research in English Language Learning and Assessment (CRELLA) at the University of Bedfordshire. He has written four volumes in the *Studies in Language Testing* series, on: the *First Certificate in English* (*FCE*); the *Certificate in Advanced English* (*CAE*); the Certificate in English Language Skills (CELS) exams, and, with Mike Milanovic, on the history of Cambridge English exams in general. The focus of his recent research projects has been mainly on English exam impact, in particular in Italy.

Marita Härmälä works at the University of Jyväskylä in the Centre for Applied Language Studies. Her duties include compiling the tests for the National Certificate of Language Proficiency, as well as training raters and item writers. She also works as a sensor in the Finnish Matriculation Examination.

Paula Lee Kristmanson is an Associate Professor in the Faculty of Education at the University of New Brunswick in Fredericton, Canada, and a member of the research team at the Second Language Research Institute of Canada.

Neil Jones enjoyed a first career teaching English in countries including Poland and Japan, where he set up study programmes at university level. Having completed a PhD applying Item Response Theory to language testing, he joined Cambridge English to work on innovative developments including item-banking and computer-adaptive testing, and on the construction and use of multilingual proficiency frameworks, including the CEFR. He directed research for Asset Languages, developed for the UK government's national languages strategy, and more recently directed the first European Survey on Language Competences, co-ordinated by Cambridge English Language Assessment for the European Commission. His current interest in Learning Oriented Assessment relates back to his experience in English language teaching, and his conviction that the primary goal of assessment can and should be to provide a supportive and motivating framework for learning.

Trisevgeni Liontou holds a PhD in Linguistics from the Faculty of English Studies, National and Kapodistrian University of Athens. She holds a BA in English Language & Literature and an MA in Lexicography: Theory and Applications, both from the same faculty. She also holds a MSc in Information Technology in Education from Reading University, UK. She has worked as an expert item consultant for AvantAssessment, USA, a research assistant at the Research Centre for Language Teaching, Testing and Assessment (RCeL) and as a freelance item writer, oral examiner and script rater for various EFL examination boards. She has made presentations in national and international conferences and has published papers in the aforementioned fields. Her current research interests include theoretical and practical issues of EFL reading comprehension performance.

Mary Frances Litzler is a faculty member of Universidad de Alcala, she has worked on studies related to native English-speakers as language assistants collaborating with non-native teachers in classrooms in Madrid, and variations of learning logs for use in English classes for future translators. She has written for the *Journal of Language Teaching and Research*, and spoken at conferences such as the 5th World Conference on Educational Sciences in 2014.

Jane Lloyd holds a degree in Linguistics from York University, an MA in Linguistics and TESOL from Leicester University, and an MA in Language Testing from Lancaster University. Her current responsibilities involve working with three ALTE members on the statistical analysis of their tests and on improving quality assurance procedures. Before joining the ALTE Validation Unit, Jane worked in Japan, South-East Asia, Turkey and the Middle East as a teacher, trainer and manager in state schools and higher education. Her interests lie in change management, institutional culture and the validation of tests at national level, and research projects which involve national organisations, ministries or institutions involved in large-scale testing.

Geraldine Ludbrook is a researcher in English language and linguistics at the Ca' Foscari University of Venice where she teaches at undergraduate and postgraduate level. She is also involved in language teacher training, specifically in the field of Content and Language Integrated Learning (CLIL). Her research interests include English for Specific Purposes, Language Testing, and English as a Lingua Franca. She has recently been involved in several projects investigating the development of English language tests for specific purposes, including the assessment of the language of Italian CLIL teachers and the development of a language test for European university students within an ELF framework. She is currently involved in a national research project aimed at developing protocols for the delivery of fair and valid language tests to Italian university students with SpLDs.

Pascale Manoilov is a qualified teacher and a PhD student at Sorbonne Nouvelle under the supervision of Professor Aliyah Morgenstern. Her doctoral thesis focuses on a multimodal analysis of spoken interactions between students at Junior High school level. She works as a teacher trainer at Université de Cergy-Pontoise near Paris, in the department of Education. Her research unit is Prismes EA4398 and she is involved in the SITAF project.

Anthony Manning has been working in the field of international education for more than 20 years and has lived and worked in China, Japan, France, Germany and the UK. Anthony's academic specialisms are in the fields of English for Academic Purposes, language education and international pathways to university study. Anthony's current role is Dean for Internationalisation at the University of Kent, where he is responsible for the development, implementation and review of internationally-related activity across the institution. Prior to this he was Director of the Centre for English and World Languages. Before joining the University of Kent, Anthony worked at the University of Reading in the International Study and Language Institute. Anthony's publications include a range of textbooks on the topic of English for Academic Purposes (EAP), Academic Skills and ELT, published with Garnet, Cambridge University Press and Oxford University Press. Most recently, Anthony's research has led to the authoring of a book for EAP teachers, focusing on developing skills in EAP assessment. He is very keen to support teachers and departments in their continuing professional development linked to this important aspect area of educational measurement.

Paola Masillo has a master's degree in Linguistics and Intercultural Communication from the University for Foreigners of Siena. She is attending a PhD programme at the University for Foreigners of Siena. Her PhD research project is focusing on validity and reliability analyses on language tests developed in Italy for the obtaining of a long-term residence permit.

Eli Moe works at the Institute for Foreign Languages, University of Bergen and Uni Research Computing, Norway as a Language test Developer. She is a member of the Research Group for language testing and assessment at the University of Bergen.

Masashi Negishi is Professor of Applied Linguistics at Tokyo University of Foreign Studies (TUFS), Japan. He has participated in a number of research projects, including national education surveys and the development of English proficiency tests in Japan. He has also published several authorised English secondary school textbooks. His current interests focus on the application of the CEFR to English language teaching in Japan, and the analysis of criterial features across the CEFR levels. He is a member of the CEFR-J Project, and is at present a member of the Japanese Ministry of Education Committee on Foreign Language Education Policy.

Brian North worked for 37 years for Eurocentres, the Swiss-based foundation that teaches languages where they are spoken, an official NGO to the Council of Europe since 1968. The subject of his PhD was the development of the levels and descriptors for the Common European Framework of Reference (CEFR), of which he was co-author after co-ordinating the 1991 intergovernmental symposium that recommended it. He was also co-author of the prototype European Language Portfolio, of the manual for relating examinations to the CEFR, of Eaquals' Core Inventories for English and French, and of the European Profiling Grid for language teacher competences (EPG). He was Chair of Eaquals 2005-2010. His most recent publications are *The CEFR in Practice* (2014), volume 4 of the English Profile Studies series published jointly by Cambridge English Language Assessment and Cambridge University Press, and 'Putting the Common European Framework of Reference to good use' for issue 47 of *Language Teaching* (2014). Currently he is co-ordinating the project to extend the set of CEFR descriptors.

Barry O'Sullivan is Senior Advisor, English Language Assessment, to the British Council in London and worldwide. He is particularly interested in issues related to performance testing, test validation and test data management and analysis. His publications have appeared in a number of international journals and he has presented his work at international conferences around the world. His first book, *Issues in Business English Testing* was published by Cambridge University Press in the *Studies in Language Testing* series in 2006. His second, *Modelling Performance in Oral Language Testing*, was published by Peter Lang in 2008. He is currently working on two edited volumes which will appear in the coming year. In addition to his work in the area of language testing, Barry taught in Ireland, England, Peru and Japan before taking up his current post.

Enrica Piccardo is Associate Professor at OISE – University of Toronto and at the Université Grenoble-Alpes France. She has extensive experience in language teaching, teacher training and second/foreign language education research. A CEFR specialist, she has collaborated with European Institutions on international projects (the ECML in Graz –Austria – as project coordinator, and the Council of Europe as project member). Her monograph *From Communicative to Action-oriented: A Research Pathway* (2014) is available online: www.curriculum.org/storage/241/1408622981/TAGGED_ DOCUMENT_%28CSC605_Research_Guide_English%29_01.pdf. Her other research focuses on emotions and creativity in language education, assessment and its role in the curriculum, plurilingualism and teacher education. She has presented in many countries and published in different languages. Some recent articles include one in *TESOL Quarterly* (2013), a co-edited issue of *The Canadian Modern Language Review* (2015), and a book chapter entitled 'The impact of the CEFR on Canada's linguistic plurality: a space for heritage languages?' (2014) for Cambridge University Press.

Danilo Rini taught Italian as a foreign language both in Italy and abroad before joining the CVCL (Centro per la Valutazione e le Certificazioni Linguistiche) of the University for Foreigners of Perugia in 2005. There, he worked as a rater, examiner, and on the planning and development of the internal item banking system. He currently works on the development of a computer-based test, as a test developer and reviewer for CELI (Certificato di Lingua Italiana) exams, as an examiner and trainer for examiners, and co-operates with the ALTE Validation Unit for the quality assurance of CELI exams through statistical analyses.

Yuwen Shen has been working as an English editor in an editorial department of Journal of Human Settlements in West China, an academic journal undertaken by College of Architecture and Urban Planning, Chongqing University for more than 3 years. She has also participated in many projects related to the professional English in the field of architecture, urban planning and landscape architecture. The most recent publication she has ever participated is the translated book of *Urbanism: Imported or Exported?*

Maria Stathopoulou is a Research Fellow at the Research Centre for Language Teaching, Testing and Assessment (RceL), National and Kapodistrian University of Athens, an (Adjunct) Lecturer at the National Technical University of Athens, an (Adjuct) Lecturer at the Technological Educational Institute of Western Greece and a Tutor at Hellenic Open University. Since 2014, Maria has been a member of the ad-hoc working group concerning the CEFR. Her work, which primarily concerns translanguaging and multilingual practices in foreign language teaching and testing, has been presented in various national and international conferences around Europe. Her recent book, *Cross-Language Mediation in Foreign Language Teaching and Testing* (2015), has been published by the international publishing house Multilingual Matters (Bristol, Buffalo, Toronto).

Claire Tardieu is currently Professor of English Didactics at the University of Sorbonne Nouvelle Paris 3. She lectures on foreign language teaching and learning to undergraduates, postgraduates and teacher students. She is assistant director in the English Department, in charge of the Master of Education. Since 2002 she has worked for the French Ministry of Education as contributor to the Department of Evaluation, Prospective and Performance (DEPP). She took part in three European projects relating to evaluation and certification.She conducts her research with Prismes EA4398 at Sorbonne Nouvelle and is particularly interested in issues involving stance, standpoint and didactic positioning.

Yukio Tono is Professor of Corpus Linguistics at Tokyo University of Foreign Studies (TUFS), Japan. His current research interests include corpus applications in language syllabus and materials design, corpus-based analysis of learner language, second language (L2) vocabulary acquisition, and L2 lexicography. He is the author and editor of several books, including *Research on Dictionary Use* (2001), *Corpus-Based Language Studies* (2004) with Tony McEnery and Richard Xiao, *ACE CROWN English-Japanese Dictionary* (2009), *Developmental and Crosslinguistic Perspectives in Learner Corpus Research* (2012) and *Frequency Dictionary of Japanese* (forthcoming). He also directed a government-funded project for implementing a modified version of the Common European Framework of Reference (CEFR-J) into Japan.

Patricia Vella Briffa currently teaches at the University of Malta Junior College. She has taught English to learners at various stages of language learning for general, specific, examination and academic purposes. Her research interests include language teaching and assessment. Her involvement in the design and implementation of a speaking component forming part of the Advanced Level English examination was recognised by means of the British Council's 2014 Innovation in Assessment Prize.

Daniel Xerri teaches on the University of Malta's MA in TESOL and chairs the ELT Council. He is the joint co-ordinator of the IATEFL Research SIG. He holds postgraduate degrees in English and Applied Linguistics, and is currently completing a PhD in Education at the University of York. His main research interests are assessment and teacher education. His involvement in the design and implementation of a speaking component forming part of the Advanced Level English examination was recognised by means of the British Council's 2014 Innovation in Assessment Prize. Further details about his research and publications can be found here: www.danielxerri.com

Shujiao Wang is a PhD student in the Department of Integrated Studies in Education, at McGill University, Canada. She received her MA from McGill University, Canada in 2013 and received her MEd in Teaching Chinese to Speakers of Other Languages (CSOL) from Nanjing University, China, in 2008. She has been a Chinese language instructor for more than five years in Chinese and North American universities, during which time she has taught a variety of pre-university language courses, undergraduate courses and professional development courses. Her research interests focus on the impact of large-scale language testing on teaching and learning, the relationship between learning oriented assessment, instruction in language classrooms and teaching Chinese as a second language.

Jessica Wu is R&D Program Director, The Language Training & Testing Center (LTTC), Taipei, Taiwan. She holds a PhD in language testing. She supervises research and development of the GEPT, which targets English learners at all levels in Taiwan. She also serves as an adviser on the development of L1 tests in her country. She has published numerous articles and book chapters in the field of language testing. She is currently a member of the Editorial Board of LAQ and a member-at-large of ILTA.

Jian Xu is the PhD student of language assessment in the Faculty of Education, The Chinese University of Hong Kong. Previously he did the research on washback effect and got the master's degree in Chongqing University, China. His research interests include the impact of large-scale tests on instruction, and the validation studies on language assessment. He also has the rich teaching experience and taught the writing courses to undergraduates as the teaching assistant when studying in Chongqing University. He has written several articles related to language teaching and assessment. His most recent publication is *A Review on the Development and Research of FCE Test* (2014).

Beate Zeidler is senior validation officer at telc gGmbH, a not-for-profit supplier of language examinations in 11 languages owned by Deutscher Volkshochschulverband (DVV), the largest adult education association in Germany. She has been working full-time for DVV since 1991, after being an English teacher and doing freelance work for DVV. She has taught courses on language learning and testing at various educational institutions in Germany, has written items for Zertifikat Deutsch and other examinations, and has been involved in developing examinations such as, among others, the telc Deutsch B2, telc Deutsch C1 and Deutsch-Test für Zuwanderer (German for immigrants).

Presentations at the ALTE Conference in Paris, 2014

Katrin Ahlgren and Mark Rydell
Stockholm University, Sweden
Evaluation des capacités d'expression orale – le cas du suédois pour les immigrés adultes

Tomoyasu Akiyama
Bunkyo University, Japan
Examining Test Fairness: Focusing on Rater Behavior in the Case of Employing Prospective English Teachers

Ene Alas and Suliko Liiv
Tallinn University, Estonia
Working towards Fairness and Quality in Scoring Speaking Tests during National Examinations

Mohammad Alavi
University of Tehran, Iran
Examining Differential Item Functioning in a Rasch model, Logistic Regression, and Mantel-Haenszel

Susanne Altenberg
European Parliament, DG Interpretation and Conferences, Belgium
Wie testet man Dolmetscher für die Praxis – oder die hohe Kunst der Sprachbeherrschung?

Hatice Asvaroğlu
Girne American University, Cyprus
English as a Foreign Language Teachers' Intercultural Awareness and its Influence on Their Assessment Practices

Beverly Baker
McGill University, Canada
Determining the Language Assessment Literacy of Admissions Decision-Makers in Higher Education

Marie Beillet
Université de Mons, Belgium
Nouvelle épreuve du TEF-académique: évaluation de la fidélité inter-juge

Hichem Belhocine
CIEP, France
Effet du support de passation d'un test sur les résultats des candidats

Vivien Berry and Barry O'Sullivan
British Council, London, UK
Language standards for medical practice in the UK: issues of fairness and quality for all

Marion Blondel
Laboratoire SFL Paris 8, France
Elaboration d'un outil d'évaluation de la morphosyntaxe en LSF et ses enjeux linguistiques

Caroline Bogliotti
Université Paris Ouest Nanterre la Défense & Laboratoire, France
Elaboration d'un outil d'évaluation de la morphosyntaxe en LSF et ses enjeux linguistiques

Henrik Bøhn and Gro-Anita Myklevold
Østfold University College, Norway
Assessing spoken EFL in Norway: How native-speaker centered?

Inmaculada Borrego Ledesma and Jorge Sánchez-Iglesias
Universidad de Salamanca, Spain
Género textual e interculturalidad en la evaluación de la expression escrita: El parámetro de adecuación

Maria Brau and Ewa Zeoli
Federal Bureau of Investigation/Language Testing and Assessment Unit, USA
Assessing Competence in Intercultural Communication: The Interagency Language Roundtable Skill Level Descriptions

Lisbeth M. Brevik
University of Oslo, Norway
Mapping Tests: Comparing Upper Secondary Students' Reading Skills in L1 and L2

Rachel Brooks
Federal Bureau of Investigation/Language Testing and Assessment Unit, USA
Comparing Native and Non-native Raters of US Federal Government
Speaking Tests

Ines Busch-Lauer
Westsächsische, Zwickau, Germany
Assessing Language Skills in the English for Engineering Students'
Classroom

Gwendydd Caudwell
British Council, Dubai, United Arab Emirates
Exploring Judgements of Speaking Performance by Native and Non-native
Raters

Sathena Chan
Centre for Research in English Language Learning and Assessment, UK
The context validity of reading-into-writing test tasks

Jozef Colpaert, Ann Aerts and Margret Oberhofer
Universiteit Antwerpen, Belgium
Time for a new CEFR? Recommendations from the field

Emyr Davies and Anthony Green
CBAC-WJEC, United Kingdom
A less widely taught language in international perspective: linking tests of
Welsh to the CEFR

**Bart Deygers KU Leuven, Belgium, and Cecile Hamnes Carlsen, Vox,
Norway**
The B2 level and its applicability in university entrance tests

David Donnarumma
BPP University, UK
Communicating in a Lingua Franca – What's missing?

**Jamie Dunlea, British Council London, United Kingdom, and Karen Dunn,
Lancaster University, UK**
Investigating English learning outcomes in a multilingual learning context

Robert Edwards
Université de Sherbrooke, Canada
How good is good enough? Setting standards on a language test for pre-
service ESL teachers

Felix Etxeberria
University of the Basque Country, Spain
Assessing the Oral Competence in Basque of Native and Immigrant Pupils

Daniela Fasoglio, SLO, The Netherlands, and Claire Smulders, Graduate
School of Teaching, Leiden University, The Netherlands
Chinese A1 and A2 tests in Dutch secondary education

Ina Ferbežar
University of Ljubljana, Slovenia
"I swear by Apollo Physician ...": Language requirements for medical
doctors in Slovenia

Vincent Folny, CIEP, France, Chantal Surgot, Visuel-LSF, France, and
Delphine Petitjean, Visuel-LSF, France
Développement d'un examen standardisé en Langue des Signes
Française (LSF) destiné au public des entendants

Vincent Folny, CIEP, France, Chantal Surgot, Visuel-LSF, France, and
Delphine Petitjean, Visuel-LSF, France
Development of a standardised test in French sign language (Langue des
Signes Française) designed for people who can hear

Javier Fruns
Instituto Cervantes, Spain
Formación en línea de examinadores: el modelo DELE

Iwona Gajewska-Skrzypczak
Poznan University of Technology, Poland
Intercultural Communication at International Campus at Poznan
University of Technology

Anne Gallagher
National University of Ireland, Maynooth, Ireland
Multilingualism and the lingua franca: A role for assessment in redressing
the balance

Jesús García Laborda
Universidad de Alcalá, Spain
Improving quality output through Interactional Theory in the High School
Final Diploma

Jesús García Laborda
Universidad de Alcalá, Spain
From monolingual to bilingual through testing: Achievements of the
OPENPAU Project (FFI2011-22442)

Antonia García Rodríguez
Pace University, USA
Heritage Spanish speakers in the United States: how do we classify and
assess them?

Yuliyana Gencheva
Johannes Kepler University, Austria
Speaking of and in languages – towards more discerning assessment in the
international classroom

Sébastien Georges
CIEP, France
Contrôle de l'exposition des items utilisés dans des évaluations à grande
échelle

Sébastien Georges
CIEP, France
Items' exposure control used in large-scale assessments

Ardeshir Geranpayeh
Cambridge English Language Assessment, UK
Cheating trends in large-scale assessment

Bharti Girjasing
Adviser – International Affairs, City of Utrecht
Unlocking the gates of diversity through multilingualism

David Graddol
The English Company, United Kingdom
The changing status of English in the Pearl River Delta, China

Anthony Green, University of Bedfordshire, UK, and Colin Finnerty, Oxford
University Press, UK
How do we balance statistical evidence with expert judgement when aligning
tests to the CEFR?

Maria José Grosso, University of Macau, Macau/China and University of Lisbon, Portugal, and Catarine Gaspar, University of Lisbon, Portugal
Migrant associations get involved: A Portuguese experience on non-formal education and learning PLE

Katherine Groves, Istituto Statale Sordi di Roma, Italy, and Mathilde D De Geus, ADEL Summer School, The Netherlands
Academic English for Deaf Learners and the CEFR: Adapting the Self-Assessment Grid

Xiangdong Gu
Consultant to Cambridge English Language Assessment, Chongqing University, China
A TAP Study of Thai Test-takers' Processes of Taking a Chinese Vocabulary Test

Xiangdong Gu
Consultant to Cambridge English Language Assessment, Chongqing University, China
Voice from Test-takers: An Exploratory Study on Cambridge English: Business Certificate (BEC) within Chinese Context

Stefanie Haberzettl, Universitaet des Saarlandes, Germany, and Mirja Gruhn, Universitaet des Saarlandes, Germany
Language assessment for appropriate school placement – the case of German unaccompanied minor refugees

Kathrin Hahn
Goethe-Institut, Germany
BULATS: A tool for measuring and comparing progress in language learning?

Cecilie Hamnes Carlsen, Vox, Norway, and Eli Moe, University of Bergen, Norway
How valid is the CEFR as a construct for language tests?

Pierre-Antoine Harlaux
CIEP, France
Impact du type de support dans une épreuve d'expression écrite

Pierre-Antoine Harlaux
CIEP, France
Impact of the type of material in a written expression paper

Claudia Harsch
University of Warwick, UK
Intercultural Competencies for entering the global workplace – a possible approach to assessment and validation

Tobias Haug, University of Applied Sciences of Special Needs Education Zurich, Switzerland, and Bencie Woll, University College London, UK
Preliminary results on the test framework for an online sign language receptive skills test

Roger Hawkey, Consultant to Cambridge English Language Assessment, UK, and Sarah Ellis, Cambridge English Language Assessment, Italy
Impacts of international language assessments on multilingualism: evidence from iterative studies of Progetto Lingue 2000

Alexandre Holle, Chambre de Commerce et d'Industrie de Région Paris– Ile de France, France, and Dominique Casanova, Chambre de Commerce et d'Industrie de Région
Évaluer les compétences langagières propres à l'exercice d'un métier: le cas des infirmiers

Chia-Ling Hsu
Steering Committee for the Test Of Proficiency-Huayu, Taiwan
Evaluating Cut-off Scores for the Test of Chinese as a Foreign Language in Alignment with CEFR

Chihiro Inoue
Centre for Research in English Language Learning and Assessment, UK
Measuring Syntactic Complexity of Spoken Performance

Nedelina Ivanova
The Communication Centre for the Deaf and Hard of Hearing, Iceland
Assessing skills of school-aged deaf children with CI in Icelandic Sign Language

Neil Jones
Consultant to Cambridge English Language Assessment, UK
Learning Oriented Assessment and intercultural communication

Ana Jovanovic
University of Kragujevac, Serbia
Education for mobility or intercultural competence? Parents' attitudes toward foreign language learning

Laura Kanto and Ritva Takkinen
University of Jyväskylä, Finland
The process of adapting a BSL receptive skills test into Finnish Sign Language

Nahal Khabbazbashi and Hanan Khalifa
Cambridge English Language Assessment, UK
An investigation into the impact of a workplace English language programme in Egypt

Hanan Khalifa and Lynda Taylor
Cambridge English Language Assessment, UK
Assessing Students with Disabilities: Voices from the Stakeholder Community

Lid King
The Languages Company, United Kingdom
The Diverse Cosmopolis. Babel and the Multicultural City

Hella Klemmert
Federal Employment Agency, Germany
GER-bezogene berufliche Anforderungen an die Deutschkenntnisse bei Zweitsprachlern: Arbeiten aus der Bundesagentur für Arbeit

Winfried Koch, BDS Koch, Germany, and Kathrin Hahn, Goethe-Institut, Germany
BULATS: A tool for measuring and comparing progress in language learning?

Christian Krekeler
Konstanz University of Applied Sciences, Germany
Assessing language for specific purposes: The role of background knowledge

Gisella Langé
Ministry of Education, Italy
CLIL/Emile in Italy: a real driver for lifelong learning

Marianne Laurent
CIEP, France
Impact de la méthode de calcul du score sur les résultats des candidats

Marianne Laurent
CIEP, France
Impact of the score calculation method on the candidates' results

Bozena Lechowska
Universidad Industrial de Santander, Colombia
Pre-service language teachers and intercultural competence: a case study from Colombia

Trisevgeni Liontou
RCeL, Greece
Cultural Familiarity and Reading Comprehension Performance: The test-takers' perspective

Jane Lloyd, ALTE Validation Unit, UK, and Christina Gregor, Goethe-Institut, Germany
Exploring reliability in assessing language exam performance in the Goethe-Institut worldwide network of raters

Jane Lloyd, ALTE Validation Unit, UK, and Danilo Rini, CVCL, Italy
Meeting standards in assessing speaking: monitoring and improving the quality of examinations in Italian

Geraldine Ludbrook
Ca' Foscari University of Venice, Italy
Investigating the use of voice synthesis in the language testing of students with SpLDs

Denise Lussier
McGill University, Canada
Intercultural communicative competence in language education: the modelling of the Canadian conceptual framework

Lucia Luyten, KU Leuven, Belgium, and Petra Poelmans, Fontys University of Applied Sciences, The Netherlands, and Willemijn van den Berg, KU Leuven, Belgium
Task-based language testing – avoiding the pitfalls and strengthening the potential

Margaret Malone
Center for Applied Linguistics, USA
Assessment of heritage language learners: A pilot study of self-assessment and learner beliefs

Wolfgang Mann
City University London, UK
Introducing a new approach to assessment of deaf children's vocabulary
knowledge in signed languages

Anthony Manning
University of Kent, UK
Investigating aspects of Assessment Literacy for teachers of English for
Academic Purposes (EAP)

Gunter Maris
CITO, The Netherlands
An IRT-based extension of the Angoff and bookmark methods for standard
setting

Rita Marzoli
INVALSI, Italy
The interplay between bilingualism and reading abilities in predicting
reading literacy and attitudes towards reading

Paola Masillo
Università per Stranieri di Siena, Italy
Language assessment for migration and social integration: a case study

Stéphanie McGaw
University of Corsica, France
Language certification in French universities: an attempt to bridge the gap
between theory and practice

Bruno Mègre
University of Sorbonne Nouvelle, France
Quality initiative for assessing language skills and international mobility:
the case of French

Chariklia Michalakopoulou
2nd Junior High School, Greece
Teaching vocabulary in English as a tool for discovering linguistic and
cultural interrelationships among languages

**Eli Moe, University of Bergen, Norway, and José Pascoal, University of
Lisbon, Portugal**
The language of schooling and language requirements in mathematics and
history

Aleidine Moeller
University of Nebraska-Lincoln, USA
Language Assessment and Mixed Methods Research

Aleidine Moeller, Kristen Nugent and Sarah Osborn
University of Nebraska-Lincoln, USA
Assessing Intercultural Competence in the Language Classroom

Anika Müeller-Karabil, TestDaF Institute, Germany, and Claudia Pop,
TestDaf Institute, Germany
Fair assessment for impaired test-takers – problems and prospects

Masashi Negishi
Tokyo University of Foreign Studies, Japan
An update on the CEFR-J project and its impact on English language
education in Japan

Brian North
EAQUALS, Switzerland
Profiling Teacher Competences: the multilingual validation of the European
Profiling Grid (EPG)

Pei-Yu (Marian) Pan
National Taiwan Normal University, Taiwan
Investigating the Dimensionality of L2 Reading Comprehension
Competence of Taiwanese EFL Beginners

Cecilia Pani
Community of Sant'Egidio, Rome
The integration of migrants in the metropolitan area: the concrete actions of
the Community of Sant'Egidio in Rome

José Pascoal
University of Lisbon, Portugal
An impact study across Europe: the LAMI questionnaire

José Pascoal, University of Lisbon, Portugal, and Lorenzo Rocca, CVCL,
Università per stranieri di Perugia, Italy
Language competence for citizenship: a profile in intercultural
communication embracing general and language competences

Cristina Pérez-Guillot and Julia Zalbala-Delgado
Universitat Politècnica de València, Spain
Requisitos lingüísticos para alumnos de intercambio: salvando distancias entre expectativas y realidad

Enrica Piccardo
OISE-University of Toronto, Canada
Assessment as recognition: a Personal Language Portfolio (PLP) for valuing Canada's linguistic diversity

Sibylle Plassmann
telc GmbH, Germany
Assessment for the workplace: the new German test for doctors

Petra Poelmans
Fontys University of Applied Sciences, The Netherlands
Task-based language testing – avoiding the pitfalls and strengthening the potential

Laetitia Puissant-Schontz, Université Paris Ouest Nanterre la Défense & Laboratoire, France, Caroline Bogliotti, Université Paris Ouest Nanterre la Défense & Laboratoire, and Marion Blundel, Laboratoire SFL
Elaboration d'un outil d'évaluation de la morphosyntaxe en LSF et ses enjeux linguistiques

Gladys Quevedo-Camargo
University of Brasília, Brazil
Methodology Options in Washback Investigations

Daniel Reed, Heekyoung Kim and Susan Gass
Michigan State University, USA,
Establishing fair testing practices through an intercultural collaboration between Greek and American educational institutions

Monique Reichert
University of Luxembourg, Luxembourg
Do German speaking students take the same test as French speaking students?

Danilo Rini
CVCL, Italy
Meeting standards in assessing speaking: monitoring and improving the quality of examinations in Italian

**Angeliki Salamoura, Cambridge English Language Assessment, UK, and
Angela ffrench, Cambridge English Language Assessment, India**
An investigation into the use of standardised assessment for employability
purposes in India

Jorge Sánchez-Iglesias
Universidad de Salamanca, Spain
La evaluación de la producción escrita en situaciones multilingües por
movilidad: El rasero del nativo

Matteo Santipolo and Alberto Novello
University of Padua, Italy
Testing socio-pragmalinguistic competence for social integration

Liljana Skopinskaja and Suliko Liiv
Tallinn University, Estonia
Exploring Cultural Differences in Rating Oral Performance during the
National English Language Examination in Estonia

Carlos Soler Montes
Instituto Cervantes, Spain
Evaluación del español en contextos multiculturales: Datos sobre la
adquisición del nivel A1 en escuelas primarias de Norteamérica

Marina Solnyshkina and Elena Kharkova
Kazan Federal University, Russia
The first Language Assessment course in Kazan University (Russia):
Learning Outcomes

Maria Stathopoulou
University of Athens, Greece
Assessing Test-takers' Translanguaging Competence: The Case of theGreek
National Exams for Foreign Language Proficiency

Michaela Stoffers
Goethe-Institut, Germany
When Braille is not enough anymore: New technologies for assessing
candidates with special needs

Liliana Szczuka-Dorna and Iwona Gajewska-Skrzypczak
Poznan University of Technology, Poland
Intercultural Communication at International Campus at Poznan
University of Technology

Claire Tardieu and Pascale Manoilov
University of Sorbonne Nouvelle, France
Analyse des interactions orales professeur-élève et élève-élève en situation de
« speed meeting »

Julia Todorinova
Department for Language Teaching, Sofia University, Bulgaria
A Differential Item Functioning Study for Less Widely Taught Languages

Henna Tossavainen
University of Jyväskylä, Finland
Challenges of the test construct: Testing Samí as L2 in Finland

Rønnaug Katharina Totland, Margaret Farstad and Britt Greve
Vox, Norway
Developing tests adapted for the deaf – according to the CEFR

Geoff Tranter
MONDIALE-Testing, Switzerland
A Language Testing System Designed to Enhance Mobility for
Professionals in Technical Industries

John Tucker
British Council, Poland
Test specifications and item writer guidelines in a multilingual world: issues
and solutions

Paul Tucker
Avant Assessment, USA
Measuring Proficiency in Modern Standard Arabic among Native Speakers
of Arabic Dialects: Field Test Results

Piet Van Avermaet
University of Ghent, Belgium
Multilingualism in the context of globalization

Willemijn Van Den Berg
KU Leuven, Belgium
Task-based language testing – avoiding the pitfalls and strengthening the
potential

Koen Van Gorp, KU Leuven, Belgium, Lucia Luyten, KV Leuven, Belgium, and Sabine Steemans, University of Antwerp, Linguapolis – Institute for Language and Communication, Belgium
A concurrent validity study of two academic placement tests

Koen Van Gorp
KU Leuven, Belgium
A concurrent validity study of two academic placement tests

Jacqueline Van Houten
Kentucky Department of Education, USA
Innovation in the use of intercultural competency standards for state assessment data on student growth

Clara de Vega Santos, Universidad de Salamanca, Spain, and Laura Vela Almendros, Universidad de Wenzao, Taiwan
La evaluación lingüística como instrumento para motivar a los alumnos: el BULATS español en Taiwán

Laura Vela Almendros
Universidad de Wenzao, Taiwan
La evaluación lingüística como instrumento para motivar a los alumnos: el BULATS español en Taiwán

Patricia Vella Briffa
University of Malta, Malta
Teacher Involvement in High Stakes Assessment: Designing and Implementing an English Speaking Examination

Shujiao Wang
McGill University, Canada
Exploring the Chinese proficiency test, Hanyu Shuiping Kaoshi and its washback effects: The test-takers' perspective

Marine Willam
Université de Mons, Belgium
Analyse des feed-back proposés par les développeurs de contenus au sein de l'environnement électronique d'apprentissage «Franel»

Jessica RW Wu
The Language Training & Testing Center (LTTC), Taiwan
Ensuring Quality and Fairness in the Asian EFL context: Challenges and Opportunities

Rachel Yi-fen Wu
The Language Training and Testing Center, Taiwan
Establishing test form comparability: a case study of a Chinese-English
translation test

Daniel Xerri and Patricia Vella Briffa, University of Malta, Malta
Teacher Involvement in High Stakes Assessment: Designing and
Implementing an English Speaking Examination

Beate Zeidler
telc GmbH, Germany
Getting to know the Minimally Competent Person

Lightning Source UK Ltd.
Milton Keynes UK
UKOW06f1201210316

270572UK00002B/277/P